D1199108

Manual of Equipment and Design for the Foodservice Industry

Manual of Equipment and Design for the Foodservice Industry

Carl R. Scriven
James W. Stevens

VNR VAN NOSTRAND REINHOLD
New York

Library of Congress Catalog Card Number 88-27973
ISBN 0-442-28072-6

Printed in the United States of America

Van Nostrand Reinhold
115 Fifth Avenue
New York, New York 10003

Van Nostrand Reinhold International Company Limited
11 New Fetter Lane
London EC4P 4EE, England

Van Nostrand Reinhold
480 La Trobe Street
Melbourne, Victoria 3000, Australia

Nelson Canada
1120 Birchmount Road
Scarborough, Ontario M1K 5G4, Canada

16 15 14 13 12 11 10 9 8 7 6 5 4 3 2 1

Library of Congress Cataloging-in-Publication Data

Scriven, Carl.
Manual of equipment and design for the foodservice industry.
Includes index.
1. Food service—Equipment and supplies. 2. Food service management. I. Stevens, James W. II. Title.
TX912.S74 1989 641.5'7'028 88-27973
ISBN 0-442-28072-6

To our wives
JOYCE SCRIVEN
WINNIE STEVENS

NOTE

This *Manual* is a timely, informative, up-to-date working tool that will prove to be a valuable aid to operators, sales representatives, students, architects, consultants, and manufacturers. Each chapter contains current information that can save hours of research and provide innovative solutions for commercial feeding operations. Remember that the menu, the type of service, and the available space are the basis for the design of commercial kitchens.

Contents

Preface

The great technological explosion of the past few decades has advanced, increased, and improved the products of nearly every industry. Because the foodservice industry, with its many facets, is the largest single industry on earth, its progress has been phenomenal.

The natural fallout of this technological explosion has been widespread technical and scientific illiteracy. Individuals with high school educations have little, if any, opportunity to keep up with scientific advances. College students, too, must specialize in their chosen fields and cannot stay informed about technological developments.

Hundreds of industries manufacture thousands of products for the foodservice industry. Many of these products are new and revolutionary; many have numerous optional features. Just to keep track of what is currently available, one must have hundreds of catalogs and a computer-like memory.

This *Manual* was written to provide easy access to a wealth of information pertaining to foodservice equipment and design layout. With its many illustrations and practical, detailed text, the book covers the full range of available equipment. As an example, let us consider the fryer. A few years ago, selecting a fryer involved determining what size was required and whether it was to be powered by gas or electricity. Now, many considerations affect the purchase of a fryer, such as:

Power source—gas or electric
Automatic lifts
Oil or hot air style
Ventilation
Electronic timers
Built-in filter system
Automatic melt cycle
Split pot styles
Quick disconnects
Pressure or nonpressure design
Computer controls
Mobility
Automatic shutdown
Dump stations
Energy savers

The above example is from the authors' first book, *Food Equipment Facts,* which has served the industry since 1981 as a standard college text and handbook.

This *Manual* provides a needed link in the literature of foodservice equipment. All the books on the subject have made important contributions to the understanding of an industry that has grown several times over in recent years; but as the industry has become more complex, the ability to communicate the intricacies of foodservice equipment has not kept pace. This book attempts to remedy that situation.

Visually and with a minimum of text, this *Manual* shows architects, consultants, students, managers, equipment reps, sanitarians, and dietitians the full range of engineered equipment available in the late 1980s. It is meant to save time and money and avoid the improper selection of equipment. The authors trust that their efforts will be of great assistance, and they solicit their readers' input for future editions.

Use of the book begins when the conceptual planning phase commences for any new or proposed change in a commercial food operation. Many of the ideas presented here will lead the reader to a proper selection of foodservice equipment based on a true value analysis, not price.

Proper planning and purchasing will pay dividends. Readers who study their options and consider the selection opportunities page by page will be amazed at the many innovations that have made equipment selection an opportunity to utilize fully the benefits of an expanding technology.

Acknowledgments

The authors sincerely appreciate the cooperation received from the many manufacturers of foodservice and related equipment whose prompt responses to our request for additional information were a great aid in compiling this book. We gratefully acknowledge the assistance from our co-workers and the manufacturers reps who gave so freely of their time when and wherever it was needed.

Special thanks to:

DEBORAH A. STEVENS
MARIANNE C. STEVENS
JOAN STEFANACCI GILLESPIE, Secretary
Food Equipment Facts

ROBERT KOSKI
Designer
For the excellent detailed drawings.

Manual of Equipment and Design for the Foodservice Industry

1

Foodservice Equipment Planning

This chapter will guide the reader through the planning maze, from preplanning with a foodservice consultant or food equipment dealer on to preliminary drawings. Many useful tools are included, such as instructions for the reading of scale rules, equipment templates, and many forms used in the various planning stages and important plan notes. An accessibility guide shows ways to serve customers with disabilities. A complete foodservice equipment specification is presented. Philip Miller's ten steps for obtaining restaurant insurance are listed. The chapter concludes with a checklist of common errors in equipment purchases and a planning checklist of generally important items in foodservice operations.

FOODSERVICE EQUIPMENT CONTRACTS

WHAT IS A FOODSERVICE EQUIPMENT CONTRACT?

Whenever a public feeding operation is to be installed, using commercial foodservice equipment for storing, preparing, and serving food in hotels, restaurants, clubs, schools, hospitals, institutions, railroads, or ships, a qualified foodservice equipment consultant, dealer, or manufacturer should prepare the plans and specifications.

The following services are available from most foodservice equipment firms:

1. Survey analysis and physical layout planning to ascertain required facilities and the most efficient use of space.
2. Interior design to ensure an overall theme and harmonious blending of colors.
3. Mechanical planning to provide complete drawings and diagrams for required lighting, plumbing, equipment wiring, etc.
4. Specifications to coordinate construction plans with interior design plans.
5. Shipping, warehousing, and installation to meet critical time requirements. All furnishings and equipment shall carry full factory warranties.
6. Total planning to eliminate costly duplication of effort.

SEPARATE FOODSERVICE CONTRACTS

With a separate foodservice equipment contract, the owner maintains absolute control in selecting the contractor. The owner can negotiate a price with the foodservice equipment contractor of choice, or request competitive bids. The foodservice contract is preferred by owners who understand the complexities of the foodservice industry and who have learned, through experience, the value of working with one capable, experienced, and responsible foodservice equipment firm.

An architect or owner who prefers having complete responsibility for the project under one head should ask for direct bids on the foodservice equipment prior to the letting of the general contract. After selection of the successful bidder, the contract is turned over to the general contractor, who in turn receives a fee from the owner for coordinating and expediting the equipment contract. This will eliminate bid shopping. If the equipment is not provided for in a separate contract, it is advisable to have the work done by a qualified foodservice equipment contractor to get the best results.

WHO IS A QUALIFIED FOODSERVICE EQUIPMENT CONTRACTOR?

Any financially responsible foodservice dealer or equipment manufacturer who maintains an adequate foodservice planning department, installation department, and service department qualifies as a foodservice equipment contractor. By special training and long experience, the staff is familiar with all types of equipment, foodservice operations, and layouts. The dealer or manufacturer will cooperate with the owner, operator, and architect in the planning and installation.

Like other contractors, some foodservice contractors excel more than others in quality control, craftsmanship, service, and experience.

Qualified foodservice equipment contractors have much at stake because continued relationships with customers are vital to success. They serve as the link between manufacturers and operators. Because the dealers are in constant association with the foodservice industry and nationally known manufacturers, they are especially aware of industry changes and developments.

Also, because of the foodservice dealers' large and continuing volume with manufacturers, they are in a better position than general contractors to render good service and recourse when necessary.

WHAT AN ARCHITECT GAINS BY WORKING WITH A QUALIFIED FOODSERVICE EQUIPMENT CONTRACTOR

A qualified foodservice equipment contractor is the right arm of the project architect because the contractor has the ability to translate the owner's requirements into reality. The architect can consult directly with the planning and design departments of the equipment contractor to ensure the most efficient use of space and mechanical service. Because of his or her experience and constant association with the job, an equipment contractor can forestall serious errors in construction details and technical problems, protecting the architect from the conflicts that often develop between the original conception of the project and its final consummation. It is not the purpose of the foodservice equipment contractor to short-circuit the architect, whose advice and counsel are vital to a successful installation. Rather, the foodservice equipment contractor adds specially trained, qualified people to handle important work that means much to the ultimate success of the project.

WHAT THE OWNER GAINS BY WORKING WITH A QUALIFIED FOODSERVICE EQUIPMENT CONTRACTOR

A qualified foodservice equipment contractor works with the end user of equipment and influences the design and application of the equipment, thus assisting the owner-operator to maintain maximum efficiency of the operation while improving labor control and reducing food cost and maintenance.

When the owner takes separate bids from qualified foodservice contractors, he or she enters into a direct contractual relationship with the specialty contractor who performs the work, rather than dealing through a middleman (general contractor or broker). When so desired, the foodservice equipment could be included in the general contract after the taking of bids or negotiation with the foodservice equipment contractor.

The qualified foodservice equipment contractor will specify and deliver well-known, proven items of equipment, thus reducing the possibility of cheap substitutes that will not stand up and will increase costs. To ensure the quality of the installation, bid shopping must be discouraged.

The foodservice equipment contractor is better qualified to handle this equipment as a prime contractor than the electrician, plumber, or steamfitter, who is principally concerned with mechanical connections and has only a limited knowledge of equipment and its functions.

WHAT THE OPERATOR GAINS BY WORKING WITH A QUALIFIED FOODSERVICE EQUIPMENT CONTRACTOR

The person responsible for the foodservice operation has the opportunity to consult directly with the foodservice equipment contractor on functional details of all the equipment, including instructional information, start-up demonstrations, cleanability, and maintenance. The operator thus becomes closely associated with the foodservice equipment contractor, who talks the operator's language and knows his or her problems. This close relationship is particularly important at the time of equipment demonstrations and start-up. Also, in later years, when replacements and service are required, the foodservice equipment contractor will continue to represent the equipment manufacturers in the regular course of business.

THE ROLE OF THE CONSULTANT IN THE QUALIFIED FOODSERVICE EQUIPMENT CONTRACT

Although many foodservice equipment contractors maintain adequate and able planning and engineering staffs, they also recognize that there are many foodservice consultants who are dedicated to their profession and plan the complete installation without handling equipment or making direct sales. In many instances, the food equipment contractor will give estimates on plans and specifications prepared by the consultant in the hope of earning the contract. The equipment contractor will then cooperate with the consultant and architect to ensure a successful installation.

CONCLUSION

Too often, the general contractor will select a foodservice equipment subcontractor who lacks the experience, financial strength, or technical competency needed. Many times prices are bid-shopped after the bids are opened, a practice that frequently results in cheap substitutions, which later prove costly because of mechanical failure or short life. A separate foodservice equipment contract should lower costs for the owner and eliminate bid shopping, which, while intended to reduce costs, actually invites inferior equipment. With a separate contract, the responsibility for the quality of the equipment and its delivery, installation, and start-up is concentrated in one specialized contractor. No excuses or buck-passing can put the owner in the middle. The foodservice equipment contractor is responsible to one individual—the owner.

This responsibility, established by the separate contract for the foodservice equipment, will increase the coordination and efficiency of transactions between the labor unions involved and the owner, the architect, and the general contractor.

Given this responsibility, the foodservice equipment contractor can deal directly with all persons concerned, to ensure the quality of the installation.

SCHEDULING EQUIPMENT INSTALLATION

After a project has been bid or negotiations for the foodservice equipment have been completed, the critical path to successful installation and production generally follows these guidelines. The architect leads the team, and the foodservice designer or consultant prepares final plans locating all plumbing, electric, and ventilation requirements. The schedule included on the drawings will enable the architect's electrical, plumbing and heating, ventilation, and air conditioning engineers to prepare necessary drawings and specifications. The architectural staff, in the meantime, will have been preparing all of the structural detail plans, including excavation, landscaping, plumbing and electric roughing, building sectional details, elevations, and the many drawings required to make the job complete.

The foodservice equipment contractor must submit complete brochure books for all "buy-out" items, indicating any required optional components, points of connection for roughing requirements, and full dimensions.

Complete shop drawings must be submitted for all fabricated equipment. The supplier now becomes responsible for any subsequent drawings and submittals. Revised drawings may be required to conform to architectural details. Usually four or five weeks will be allowed for the kitchen equipment dealer to submit the necessary documents.

Once all submittals have received final approval, some fabricated items could take up to 14 weeks or more to be delivered. Some of the fabricated items may be too large to fit through standard doors, and must be brought into the area before outside walls are completed. This point must never be overlooked.

Once the general contractor completes work in the area, including mechanical and electric roughing, the equipment contractor will deliver the foodservice equipment, uncrate it, and set it in place. Large pieces may be set in place and field-welded. Internal electric and plumbing connections are made by the kitchen equipment contractor. The general contractor's tradespeople make the final connections.

The next step is to make a final checklist, reviewing all equipment in regard to compliance with all specifications and bidding documents. Any deviations are noted and must be corrected. It is important to note code violations and have them corrected.

A point that is often overlooked but should be included in the specifications is that the equipment must be demonstrated, and employees must be trained in its use. Training may be done by the food equipment contractor or the manufacturer's representative. Many manufacturers now provide videotapes, which are excellent reference sources for training later employees.

There are probably as many different ways to design a foodservice facility as there are foodservice installations. The preceding paragraphs generally describe the most common approaches, and the authors hope they will help prevent misunderstandings often encountered in the field.

AGREEMENTS WITH CONSULTANTS

The following sample agreement shows some key considerations involved in working with a consultant or food equipment dealer.

PLANNING NEW OPERATIONS

The discussion that follows is intended as a brainstorming guide for planning a new foodservice operation.

SAMPLE

Foodservice Equipment Agreement

The Stock Market Restaurant

GENERAL SCOPE OF CONSULTANT'S SERVICES
The scope of the services shall include complete foodservice equipment consulting services for the design of the work, and general foodservice consulting supervision of the performance and execution of the work by the contractor or contractors engaged by the owner.

CONSULTANT'S PARTICULAR SERVICES
The consultant's services shall include, but shall not be limited to, the following:

SCHEMATIC DESIGN PHASE

1. To discuss with owner and architect desired accomplishments of the project and to formulate a design program.
2. To prepare schematic design studies consisting of drawings and other documents illustrating the scale and relationship of project components for approval by the owner.
3. To submit a statement of probable cost.

DESIGN DEVELOPMENT PHASE

1. To prepare, for approval by the owner, the design development documents consisting of drawings and other documents to fix and describe the size and character of the project as to specific types of equipment, general mechanical and electrical utility requirements, and other essentials as may be appropriate.
2. To furnish a list of all items to be included in the foodservice equipment bid.
3. To submit to the owner a further statement of probable project construction costs.

CONTRACT DOCUMENTS PHASE

1. To furnish outline material to be included in the general contract specifications, designating the scope of the work of the various contractors in relation to the foodservice equipment phase of the project.
2. To prepare foodservice equipment specifications to be issued for bids by the consultant as a separate contract. If the architect desires the work to be issued as a separate contract, the general conditions, form of agreement, performance and payment bond, addenda, and other required materials will be made part of the documents.
3. To prepare foodservice equipment contract drawings, complete with equipment plans and index, utility connection requirements, elevations and details of fabricated equipment, and location of masonry bases and depressions.

A GUIDE FOR THE REVIEW OF FOOD-ESTABLISHMENT PLANS AND SPECIFICATIONS

Sanitary codes require the submission of properly prepared plans to local health officials for review and approval on all new construction, extensive remodeling, or conversion of existing structures before any work begins. The purpose for the review and approval of plans before the work begins is: (1) to ensure compliance with sanitary requirements; (2) to prevent misunderstanding by the operator as to what is required; and (3) to prevent errors that might later result in additional owner cost to the operator.

These three points should be impressed upon an operator when he or she first begins to think of entering the foodservice business or expanding present operations. Even the preliminary plans, which might be just a pencil sketch indicating the site where the building is to be constructed and the type of operation (short-order, full meal service, delicatessen, mobile food, etc.), should be thoroughly discussed before time and money are invested for architect's fees. The completed plans should be submitted to and given final approval by the health authorities prior to any start of construction.

The operator should be given all necessary information on his or her first contact with the health department as to operating permits or license fees, including building permits, if required, and the type of plans and specifications required for approval.

It should be remembered that specific recommendations about the amount of space for dry storage, refrigeration, food preparation, the number and sizes of pieces of equipment, or even the arrangement of facilities cannot be considered hard and fast rules. No two operations are exactly alike; so each proposal must be considered on its own merits, and all decisions must be based on the specific operation involved. Certain characteristics of the particular establishment should be considered in planning for space needs. The location, type of operation, frequency of deliveries, kinds of foods used (fresh, frozen, canned, etc.), and amount of processing to be done (meat cutting done at the establishment or pre-portioned cuts used) can cause considerable variation in the space requirements for production and storage. Health officials should try to determine some of this information before reviewing the plans with the operator.

To begin with, the owner should provide a scaled floor plan of the entire establishment that shows the layout of the rooms, including storage, and the proposed location of lights, plumbing, and all fixed equipment. In addition, the proposed location of kitchen equipment such as refrigerators, stoves, hoods, sinks, dishwashing machines, and slicers should be shown. Specifications for this equipment should also be provided so that a determination can be made as to the adequacy of the equipment to do the job, as well as its compliance with sanitation requirements, fire safety standards, and electricity and gas requirements.

The following sample form shows information typically required to obtain a license for food-establishment construction.

SAMPLE FORM

Specific Plan Requirements

PUBLIC EATING AND DRINKING PLACES
To be eligible for a license from the Bureau of Community Environmental Control, the applicant shall furnish the following information in the form of detailed plans and specifications.

OWNERSHIP

1. Name of the establishment
2. Type of business (proposed operation)
3. Name of owner(s)

SITE

1. See general plot requirements (see Figures 1–1 and 1–1a).

BUILDING

1. Complete floor plan of existing or proposed building showing location:
   a. Food preparation areas.
   b. Dressing or locker rooms.
   c. Toilet rooms.
   d. Refuse storage areas.
   e. Lighting and illumination fixtures.

(continued on p. 8)

(1) Zoning
- Current zoning of site ________
- Use permits needed ________
- Height restrictions ________
- Front line set back ________
- Side yard requirements ________
- Back yard requirements ________
- Restrictions on signs ________
- Parking requirements ________
- Other restrictions ________

(2) Area Characteristics
- Type of neighborhood ________
- Type of businesses ________
- Growth pattern ________
- Proposed construction ________
- Other available sites ________
- Zoning of adjacent sites ________

(3) Competition
- Number of food facilities in drawing area of site ________
- Number of seats ________
- Type of menu offered ________
- Method of service ________
- Check averages ________
- Number of cocktail lounges ________
- Quality of drinks ________
- Bar service available at tables ________
- Annual sales ________

(4) Physical characteristics
- Type of top soil ________
- Type of subsoil ________
- Depth of water table ________
- Presence of rocks ________
- Load-bearing capacity ________
- Direction of slopes ________
- Surface drainage ________
- Percolation test results ________
- Natural landscaping ________
- Other features ________

(5) Size and Shape (Including sketch)
- Length ________
- Width ________
- Total square feet ________
- Square footage needed for building ________
- Square footage needed for parking ________
- Space for other requirements ________

(6) Costs
- Cost per front foot ________
- Cost per square foot ________
- Total cost of site ________
- Cost of comparable sites nearby ________
- Costs for land improvements ________
- Real estate taxes ________
- Other taxes ________

(7) Utilities
- Location, cost, and size or capacity of:
  - Storm sewer ________
  - Sanitary sewer ________
  - Gas lines ________
  - Water lines ________
  - Electricity ________
  - Steam ________

(8) Streets
- Basic patterns ________
- Width or lanes ________
- Paved ________
- Curbs and gutters ________
- Sidewalks ________
- Lighting ________
- Public transportation ________
- Grades ________
- Hazards ________

(9) Positional Characteristics

Distance and driving time to:	Distance	Driving Time
Central business district	________	________
Industrial centers	________	________
Shopping centers	________	________
Residential areas	________	________
Recreational areas	________	________
Sporting events	________	________
Educational facilities	________	________
Special attractions	________	________
Other activity generators	________	________

(10) Traffic Information
- Distance to nearest intersection ________
- Traffic characteristics ________

Traffic counts:	Day	Time	Count
Site street	______	______	______
	______	______	______
	______	______	______
Adjacent streets	______	______	______
	______	______	______
	______	______	______

- Anticipated changes ________

(11) Visibility
- Distances of sight from:
  - Left ________
  - Right ________
  - Across ________
- Obstructions ________
- Location of signs ________

(12) Availability of local labor ________

(13) Services
- Quality of police protection ________
- Quality of fire protection ________
- Location of hydrant ________
- Availability of trash pick up ________
- Availability of garbage pick up ________
- Other services required ________

(14) General Recommendations
- Suitability ________________
- Desirability ________________
- Other recommendations ________________

Figure 1-1. Site analysis form. (Reprinted, by permission from Edward A. Kazarian, *Foodservice Facilities Planning,* Third Edition, © 1988 by Van Nostrand Reinhold)

PRELIMINARY SPECIFICATION SHEET

PREPARE Plan ☐ Study Plan Only ☐ Elevation ☐ Perspective ☐ Estimate ☐ Quotation ☐

TYPE OF JOB New ☐ Addition ☐ Alteration ☐ Other ______

OWNER'S NAME ______ HOME ADDRESS ______ Phone ______

NAME OF PLACE ______ Address ______ Phone ______

TYPE OF BUSINESS ______ REMARKS ______

______ BUDGET ______

Max. No. of Persons to be served ______ No. of service periods ______ Hours of operation ______ No. of employees ______

Seating cap. expected ______ No. of parties desired ______ Present seating cap. ______ Pres. No. of Parties ______

MENU TO BE FEATURED ______

ATMOSPHERE DESIRED ______

Materials and colors preferred ______

REMARKS ______

ENGINEERING DATA

COOKING FUEL DESIRED GAS ______ TYPE ______ B.T.U. ______

ELECTRIC VOLTAGE ______ PHASE ______ CYCLE ______ STEAM ______ lbs. pressure ______ H.P. ______

VENTILATING PROVISIONS FOR ______

AIR CONDITIONING PROVISIONS FOR ______

HEATING TYPE OF FUEL TO BE USED ______ HOT WATER SUPPLY- Temp. ______ Gal. per hr. ______

REFRIGERATION REQUIRED ______

REMARKS ______

STRUCTURAL DATA

CAN STRUCTURAL CHANGES BE MADE? ______

AUXILIARY SPACE Extent can be used ______

CAN CELLAR BE UTILIZED? ______

REMARKS ______

MEASUREMENTS

All measurements to be made from finished walls or allowance made for finish ______

Check point to point against overalls and diagonals ______ ARE CORNERS SQUARE ______ Wall thickness ______

CHECK AND LOCATE ALL OBSTRUCTIONS Radiators ☐ Pipes ☐ Columns ☐ Joists ☐ Flues ☐ Windows ☐ Skylights ☐ Doors ☐ Jogs ☐ Panel Boxes ☐ Meters ☐ Stairways ☐

TYPE OF FLOOR ______ CEILINGS- Type of ______ Height of ______

CHECK ENTRANCES- Size of opening ______ REMARKS ______

EQUIPMENT REQUIRED

FURNISHINGS
BOOTHS
BUS CARTS
CHAIRS
CIGAR CASE
CIGARETTE MACHINE
COFFEE WARMERS
COUNTERS
EMERGENCY LIGHTING
FLOOR MATS
HIGH CHAIRS
PASTRY CARTS
SERVICE STANDS
SETTEES
STOOLS
TABLES
TRAY STANDS
WATER STATIONS

BAR
BACK BAR
BAR
BOTTLE BOX
COCKTAIL UNITS
DISPLAY SECTION (S)
DRAUGHT STATION
FLOOR MATS
ICE CUBER
LIQUOR STORAGE
MIXER-BLENDER
PRECOOLER
REFRIGERATED CAB.
SERVICE STATION
SOFFIT
STOOLS
WORK BOARDS & SINK

STORAGE
BINS - PORT.
SCALE - PLATFORM - BEAM
STOREROOM SHELVING
TRUCKS
UPRIGHT FREEZER
WALK-IN COOLER - SIZE
WALK-IN FREEZER - SIZE

PREPARATION
BLOCK
CHOPPER
DISPOSAL
FOOD CUTTER
FLOOR MATS
MEAT SAW
MIXER
PEELER
PORTION SCALE
REFRIGERATOR
SINKS
SLICER
TABLES

COOKING
BROILER
CHARCOAL BROILER
CHEF'S TABLE
COMP'T. STEAMER
FLOOR MATS
FRYER
GRIDDLE
HOOD
KETTLE (STEAM)
MIXER
PAN RACK
POT & PAN STORAGE
POT RACK
RANGE
REFRIGERATOR
SINKS
WORK TABLE (S)

BAKING
BAKER'S TABLE
DOUGH DIVIDER
DOUGH RETARDER
DOUGH TROUGH
HOLD BOX
HOOD
MIXER
OVEN
PAN RACKS
PROOF BOX
PYRO STOVE
REFRIGERATOR
SCALE
WORK TABLE

SERVICE
BACK BAR
BAIN MARIE
CASHIER
COUNTER
FOOD CHECKER
FOOD WARMER
HEATED CARTS
HEAT LAMPS
LOWERATORS
PLATE SHELF
PLATE WARMER
REFRIGERATOR
ROLL WARMER
SINKS
SLICER
STEAM TABLE
TABLES
TRAY CARTS
TRAY STORAGE

PANTRY
COFFEE MAKER
COLD PAN
COLDPLATE REFR.
CREAM DISPENSER
DISHERWELL
DRINK MIXER
EGG BOILER
FROZEN DESSERTS CAB.
FUDGE WARMER
HOT PLATE
ICE BIN
ICE CREAM CABINET
ICE CUBER
ICED TEA
JUICE EXTRACTOR
LOWERATORS
MALT DISPENSER
MILK DISPENSER
MIXER
PASTRY CAB.
REFRIGERATOR
ROLL WARMER
SERVING COUNTER
SINKS & DRAINBOARDS
SLICER
TOASTER
URN STAND
WAFFLE BAKER
WASTE DISPOSAL
WORK TABLES

SCULLERY
BURNISHER
CLEAN DISH TABLE
CLEAN GLASS TABLE
DISH STORAGE
DISH TRUCKS
DISH WASHER
DISPOSAL
GLASS STORAGE
GLASS TRUCKS
GLASS WASHER
HOOD
HOT WATER BOOSTER
MOP SINK
O. H. SHELVES
O. H. SPRAY
POT SINK
POT STORAGE
POT WASHER
PRE-RINSE
RACK RETURN
SILVER DIP SINK
SOILED DISH TABLE
SOILED GLASS TABLE
TRAY RACK
TRAY REST
UNDER SHELVES
WASTE CANS

CUSTOMER FACILITIES
CARRY OUT FOODS
CASHIER
CHECK ROOMS
COAT RACKS
HAND DRYERS
MUSIC
TELEPHONE (S)
TELEVISION
TOILETS
WAITING LOUNGE
WINE DISPLAY

HELP FACILITIES
COT
HAND DRYERS
HAND SINKS
LOCKERS
TOILETS

EXISTING EQUIPMENT

Figure 1-1a.

f. All plumbing fixtures (including floor drains, traps, vents, hot and cold outlets, sinks, showers, tubs, urinals, vacuum breakers, back-flow prevention devices and air gaps).
g. Exhaust fans and vents.
h. Each piece of equipment listed on the plan. Distances from floors, walls, and adjacent equipment should be shown.
i. Equipment storage areas. (Utensil storage containers must be designed so that the utensils are protected from contamination, and so that the handle only can be grasped by the employees or customers.)

2. Supplemental information must be included on:
   a. Floor construction, including:
      1) Type of construction material.
      2) Location of floor drains.
      3) Information on the juncture between floor and walls.
   b. Walls and ceilings, including:
      1) Materials.
      2) Finish.
      3) Color.

This application must be signed by the owner or the proper officials of the corporation or legally constituted board or commission having charge of work. The signature of the designing engineer or other agent will be accepted if accompanied by a letter of authorization. Estimated cost of project $________.

This application must be accompanied by complete plans. All information required by form on the following pages and which is pertinent to the installation must be submitted. Information shown on plans need not be repeated on the form.

Plans must show relation of foodservice facilities to the building in which it is located, the various entrances, and the location of toilets.

The applicant is held responsible for reading material contained in part 14 of the New York State Sanitary Code and abiding by those rules and regulations when plan approval or operating permit is issued.

The applicant is responsible for obtaining all of the other required permits such as from the Alcoholic Beverage Commission Board, the local building departments, fire departments, zoning boards, Workmens' Compensation Boards, etc.

Construction work shall not begin until plans submitted to the Health Department are approved. *Food preparation, in any manner, shall not commence until a final inspection is made of the completed kitchen and a permit to operate is issued by the inspector.*

The applicant is to use the following checklist to review the submitted plans. This checklist will help to ensure that the plans are thoroughly conceived and that they will meet the requirements of the sanitary code. Some of the following items may not apply to your intended operation—indicate that on this sheet. If the item does apply but the question is unclear, call the Health Department or refer to the code book and the other handout material.

DO THE SUBMITTED PLANS INDICATE, LIST, OR SPECIFY:

(Check X)

__ The path outlined for processing of dishware and pots and pans from dirty to cleaned to storage areas.

__ The path indicated on plans for processing of food from preparation areas to cooking areas to waiter station.

__ Three bay sink for pot washing—indicate size of each bay ____________.

__ Adequate drain boards (one at each end of the three bay sink for dirty and cleaned utensils).

__ Adequate backsplash material behind three bay sink, lipped over and sealed to sink body.

__ Vegetable sink if needed (required indirect open waste)—size of bay ________.

__ Handwash sink in kitchen (in addition to ones in bathrooms).

__ Utility/mop sink or curbed floor facility with adequate backsplash.

__ If dishwashing machine used, model and supplier ______________.

__ Dishwasher installed with thermometers indicating wash and rinse temperatures, pressure gauge on the rinse line, vacuum breakers.

__ Indicate waiter station. Type of flooring at waiter station ______________.

__ Dipper well with open drain for ice cream service.

__ Adequate refrigeration capacity, all thermometers should have visibility from the outside of the unit.

List models of all units and cubic footage capacities of each.
___ (Are they on legs elevated 6 inches off the floor?)

_________ _________ _________

_________ _________ _________

___ All equipment, coolers, shelving units, 6 inches minimum off floor.
___ Cooking equipment (stoves, fryers, grills, broilers) spaced far enough apart to provide for easy cleaning between units.
___ All utility lines (cable, pipes) off the floor by a sufficient height to facilitiate easy floor cleaning.
___ Specify types of lighting with protective shielding:
In kitchen ____________________
At bar ____________________
In storage areas ____________________
___ Specify adequate dry storage space for foods, canned goods, single service items, paper goods.
___ Describe type of storage rack/shelving surfaces ____________.
___ Show hand sink.
___ Specify dish storage area.
___ Show area for just-delivered goods.
___ Show area for bookkeeping and office functions.
___ Specify dressing room or street clothing storage area.
___ Dressing room located away from food storage and food preparation areas.
___ Outside garbage storage shown on plans.
___ Indicate linen supply storage for clean storage _______ dirty storage _______.
___ Area shown for storage of toxic chemicals, soaps, cleaners, sprays, sternos.
___ Janitorial storage area shown for cleaning supplies, tools, buckets, hoses, mops.
___ Toilet facilities for employees and patrons indicated on plans.
___ Bathroom sinks: Hot water supplied _____ Cold water _______.
___ Are bathroom doors self-closing?
___ Vacuum breakers, check valve devices, back-flow preventors indicated—on freshwater lines, feeding machines, water-cooled ice machines, refrigerators, all chemical and soap dispensers, all hoses.
___ Indirect (open) drains installed for receptacles holding food or food dispensing machines and utensils, i.e., ice bins at the bar, vegetable sinks, cooler floor drains, dipper wells.
___ Indicate exhaust ventilation if needed:
Hood locations ____________________
Type of filters ____________________
Hood dimensions ____________________
CFM (cubic feet per minute) air capacity of exhaust fan ____________________

Vermin protection:
___ Rodent proofing of all potential entrance sites.
___ Roach proofing—use of boric acid between walls or on floors under equipment installed. *Health Department has more information on this subject.*
___ Outside doors self-closing to prevent fly entrances.
___ All outer openings screened for insects and heavy gauge—for rodents 17 gauge, $\frac{1}{4}$-inch mesh for mice.

Indicate materials used for:
Ceilings ____________________
Walls in kitchen ____________________
Walls behind cooking areas ____________
Walls behind dishwashing areas ________
Walls in storage area ______________
Flooring in kitchen ______________
Flooring in walk-in cooler ____________
Flooring in bathroom ______________
Water supply source ______________

Hot water supply:	Regular tank	booster for dishwasher
Storage capacity in gallons	________	________
Heating capacity, Btu/hr	________	________
Temperature setting, *T*°F	________	________

Waste disposal:
Liquid wastes via sewer pipes: Public _____ Private _____
Food waste discarded in: Grinder _____ Garbage cans with lids _____
Trash and garbage removal: Public _____ Private _____
Type of trash receptacles ____________________
_____ Will oleomargarine be served?
_____ Will ice cream products be produced?
_____ Sample menu submitted.
_____ Is a salad bar or other self-service facility planned?
_____ Is a catering or food delivery service planned?

Number of anticipated employees ________
Planned seating capacity ________
CONSTRUCTION: Anticipated start ________
Completion ________

APPLICATION FOR PERMIT TO OPERATE A FOODSERVICE ESTABLISHMENT

Please print or type—Type of Application: Original/Renewal

1. Name of establishment ________
2. Location of establishment (town/city) ________
3. Name of permit holder ________
4. Address of permit holder ________
5. Telephone number of establishment ________
   Telephone number of permit holder ________
6. Name of property owner ________
7. Property owner's address ________
8. Operating hours ________
9. Seating capacity ____ Estimated number of patrons/day
10. If mobile food operation, vehicle license number ________
11. Sales tax number ________

COFFEE SHOP APPLICATION

The application that follows is an example of information needed for a small coffee shop permit in many states.

Figure 1–2 shows a plot plan for the coffee shop operation.

Seating capacity: 36
Estimated number of meals per day: 200
Number of employees: 5
Menu:
Breakfast: juices, coffee, milk, eggs, bacon, toast, pastry, ham, cereal.
Lunch: hot and cold sandwiches, limited hot dinners, coffee, milk, soft drinks, ice cream, fruit pies.
Dinner: limited selection of hot meals, coffee, milk, soft drinks, ice cream, fruit pies, cakes.
Method of food service: Regular meals will be served on multiuse tableware, while carryouts and short orders will be served on single-service articles.
Method of garbage disposal: Garbage inside will be kept in plastic bags in covered metal garbage cans. The outside garbage will be kept in a covered metal dumpster, which will be serviced twice a week by the XYZ Company.
Method of insect and rodent control: The BCD Pest Control Company has been contracted to service this establishment twice a month and on request. The kitchen windows will be screened. All other windows will not open. All outside doors will be self-closing.

LEGEND
1. HERMAN'S COFFEE BAR
2. SIDEWALK-CONCRETE
3. PARKING LOT-BLACKTOP
4. DUMPSTER
5. PUBLIC WATER SUPPLY
6 PUBLIC SEWERAGE SYSTEM

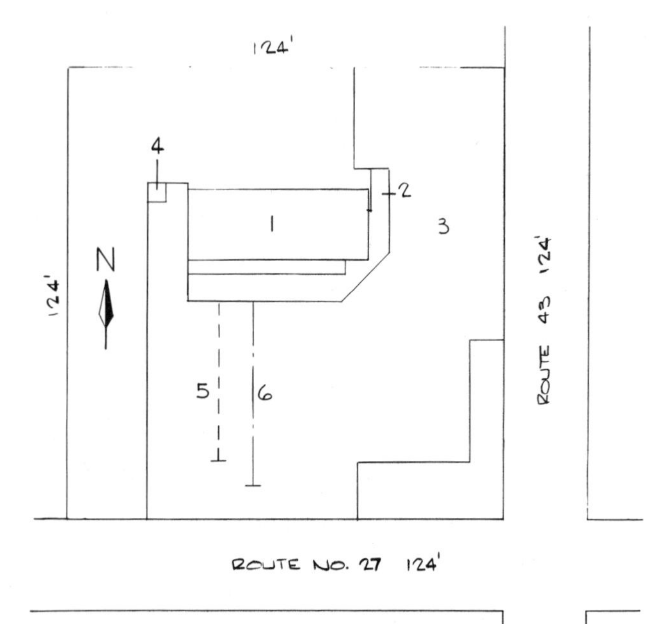

ROUTE NO. 27 124'

PLOT PLAN
SCALE: 1"=50'

Figure 1–2. Plot pan.

ACCESSIBILITY GUIDE FOR FOODSERVICE PATRONS

After learning many of the general requirements for commercial food operations, a prospective operator should become familiar with the planning process for handicapped persons that is used under federal guidelines adopted by most states.

In many areas, state and local codes control exactly what accessibility codes a restaurant must meet when building or remodeling; so operators must check the laws in their own areas. Here are some examples of features that will make traffic by customers with disabilities easier and more convenient:

1. Reserved parking spaces wide enough—12 feet by 16 feet—to give users of wheelchairs access to their cars.
2. Curb ramps 40 inches wide with a slope no greater than 1 inch in 12.
3. Walkways 48 inches wide to allow wheelchair users to pass others.
4. Doors that are easy to operate with a clear opening of at least 32 inches; thresholds at door rising no greater than $\frac{1}{2}$ inch.
5. Aisle space allowing clear pathways (48 inches wide) to tables; ramps for multilevel dining areas.
6. Telephones with coin slots 54 inches from floor if approach is from a side reach; otherwise, 48 inches. Also, volume control handset equipment on the telephone for persons with hearing impairments.
7. Toilet room accommodation:

- Entrance door clearance of 32 inches.
- Top of toilet seat 17 inches to 19 inches from floor.
- Grab bars on both sides of toilet stall extending a minimum of 42 inches and mounted $1\frac{1}{2}$ inches from wall.
- Lavatories with faucets that are easily operable, such as lever type.
- Accessories (towel dispensers and mirrors) hung 48 to 54 inches from floor.
- Floor surfaces that are smooth and hard or a tightly woven, slip-resistant carpet.

For more information on how to improve services on an ongoing basis for patrons with disabilities, one may contact the Human Resources Department of the National Restaurant Association, 311 First Street, NW, Washington, D.C. 20001.

THE SCALE RULE AND HOW TO READ IT

We are all used to taking a yardstick or tape measure to determine the size of equipment or rooms in a building; but when we must draw a whole building, it must be proportionately scaled down to a size that will fit on paper. The scale most commonly used to show small components is $\frac{1}{4}'' = 1'\text{-}0''$ or more. (See Figure 1-3.)

Scale rules generally come 6 inches long, flat, and beveled on two or four sides; or they are triangular in shape with six edges, each having two different scales.

The most used scale rule is 6 inches long, flat and beveled on four sides. It can easily be carried in one's pocket, and the four sides provide eight different scales: $\frac{1}{8}$, $\frac{1}{4}$, $\frac{1}{2}$, and 1, as well as $\frac{3}{8}$, $\frac{3}{4}$, $1\frac{1}{2}$, and 3 inches per foot.

All drawings will show the scale to which they are drawn. When reviewing drawings, first find the scale. It is usually shown in the title box.

Now let us assume that you have a plan drawn to the $\frac{1}{4}'' = 1'\text{-}0''$ scale, and you wish to measure the width of an item on the drawing that is $10'\text{-}6''$ long, not dimensioned. Referring to Figure 1-3, find the quarter-inch scale on your rule. Note that the 1-foot marks begin at 0 (zero) and read from right to left on the longer lines. Ignore the smaller numbers going the other way, that is, the eighth-inch scale. Now place your scale on the item to be measured with the zero

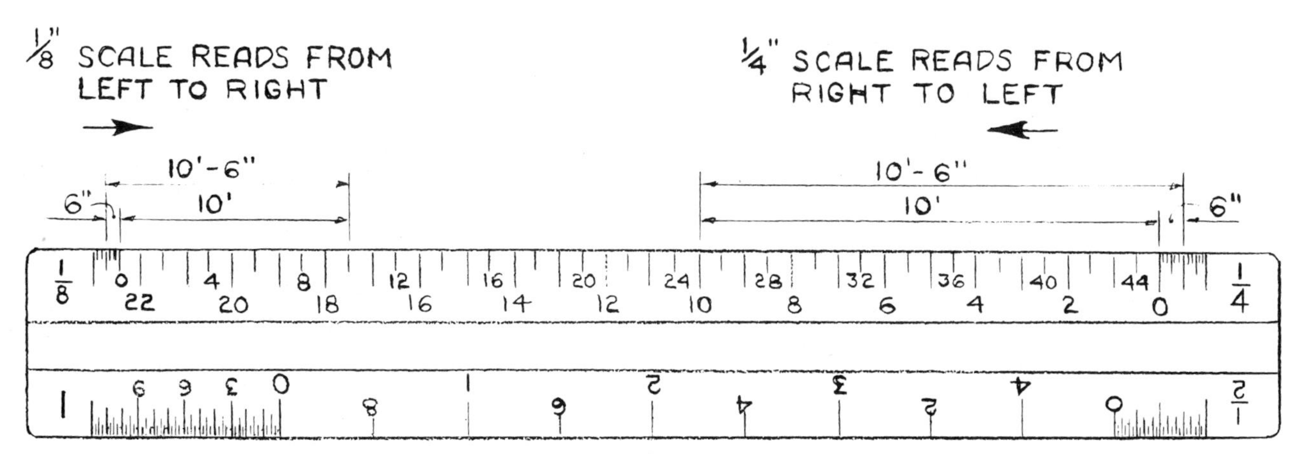

Figure 1-3. Scale rule.

aligned with the right end of the item to be measured. You will note that the other end extends beyond the 10-foot mark. Now slide the rule to the left until the 10-foot mark aligns with the item to be measured. Glancing back to the zero, we see that the item is 10 feet plus 6 inches by counting the small divisions reading from zero toward the end of the scale rule. Thus, the procedure is simple: Pick the scale you want; ignore the numbers going the other way, and read the even feet marks running toward the opposite end and starting at zero; then determine the inches, going from zero to the end you are using.

DESIRABLE FEATURES PLAN

The plan shown in Figure 1–4 is not intended to be the perfect plan for any restaurant. It was prepared as a resource for anyone intended to design or build a restaurant. (Figures 1–5 through 1–18 will also be useful in planning restaurant layouts and are to be consulted as needed.)

The entrance shown would be suitable where parking areas are located on both sides of the building. The desirable feature is the double doors, which minimize heat and air conditioning losses.

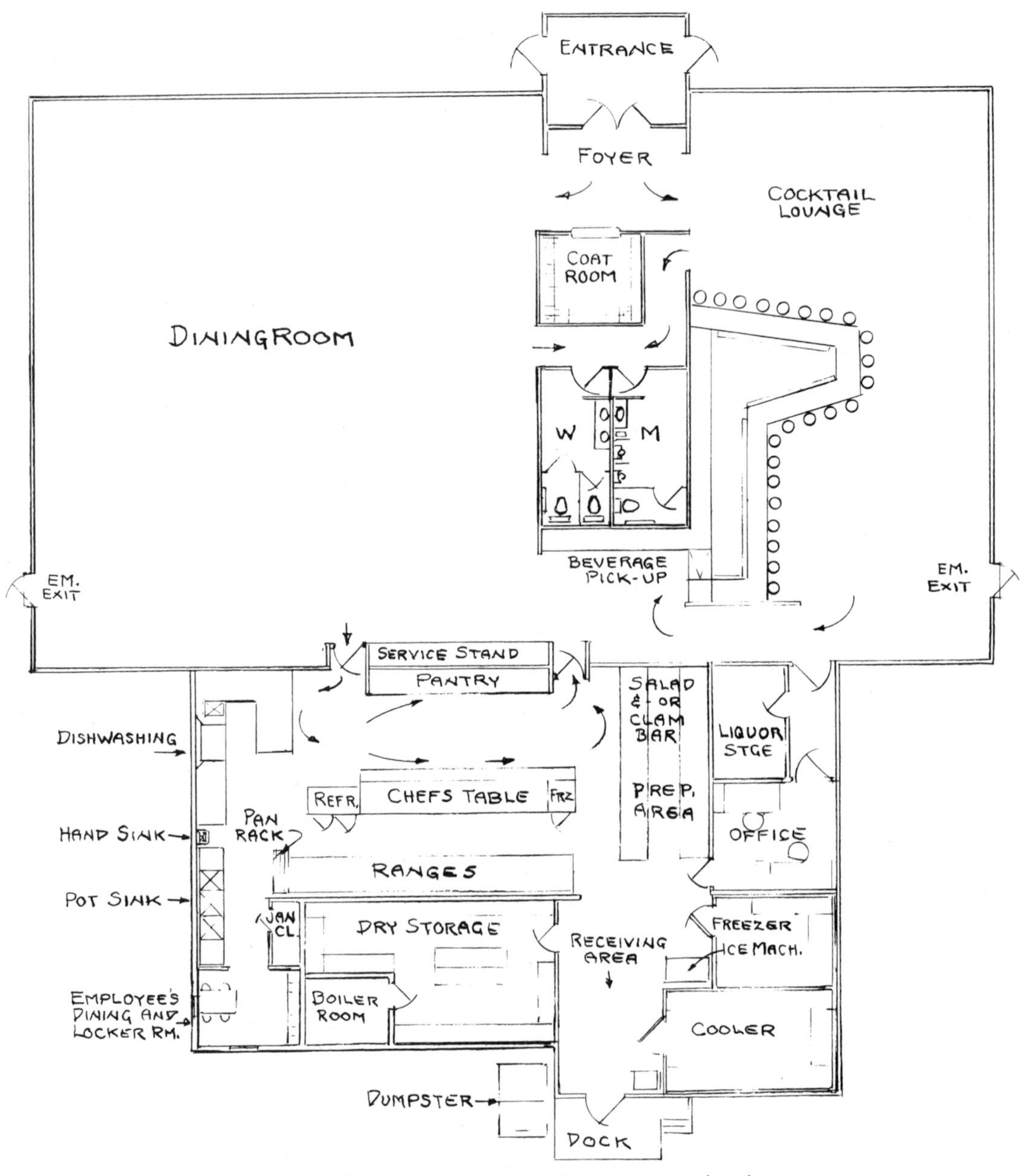

Figure 1-4. Desirable features in restaurant planning.

The foyer provides direct access to the coat room and to either the dining room or the cocktail lounge. Dining customers usually do not wish to pass through the cocktail lounge to reach their table.

The hallway behind the coat room provides direct access to the restrooms from both the dining and the lounge areas.

Placing the restrooms, the bar, and the beverage pickup station back to back, as shown, will help keep plumbing costs down. The bar shown is one of the authors' favorite designs: its "U"-shaped extension into the lounge area provides friendly corners that give most of the customers an opportunity to look at other people instead of staring at the wall. The configuration also provides a maximum of seats with a minimum of expensive backbar. The beverage pickup area, located behind the backbar wall with easy access from either the dining room or the cocktail lounge, provides a quiet, private place for service that does not take up valuable seating space at the bar. It has the added advantage of providing servers their own beverage makeup area, thereby saving the bartender a great deal of work. This subject is illustrated in detail in the bar design section (see Chapter 10).

The kitchen traffic pattern shown in Figure 1–4 is a classic arrangement of equipment for efficiency. Soiled dishes are promptly disposed of on the soiled dish table. The serving person may then proceed directly to the chef's table for main course items, or to the pantry area, or to the salad and clam bar counter, and then exit the kitchen with no cross-traffic. Many variations and refinements of this design are shown in later chapters.

The dishwashing equipment, hand sink, and pot sink, located as shown, enable one employee to handle the complete dishwashing operation. Clean pots and pans are placed directly on the pan rack with easy access for the chef.

The employees' dining room and locker space are a desirable feature, to which toilet facilities may be added.

The boiler room, which might also house the power panels, is shown primarily to remind foodservice equipment designers that such a room may be required.

The area designated as the salad or clam bar, along with the preparation area, can have infinite variations. The location shown is desirable.

The liquor storage room is readily accessible from the bar and is secure. This room could house the soda system and an additional ice machine.

The office has both a private entrance and one opening into the kitchen. Windows with curtains or blinds on the kitchen side would permit both privacy and surveillance.

The walk-in cooler, freezer, and ice machine, arranged as shown, allow condensate waste lines from the walk-ins and the drain lines from the ice machine to flow into a single floor drain. All of these items require indirect waste disposal.

Both the refrigerated and the dry storage rooms are located adjacent to the receiving area. The receiving area is open to view from both the kitchen and the office, an arrangement that discourages pilferage.

The dock area elevation and design will depend on architectural conditions at the site. Desirable features for docks are illustrated in Chapter 2.

To scale, the dining room shown would seat approximately 200 people. As a single room it should have tastefully designed room dividers that will not interfere with efficient service, but will provide the patrons with intimate dining areas.

People opening a restaurant hope business will be so good that they will have to expand the facility. With this "Desirable Features Plan," any of the three components could be enlarged without disrupting the traffic pattern. The cocktail lounge could expand forward or to the right, the dining room forward or to the left, and the kitchen to either side or to the rear.

GENERAL NOTES

The following example of general notes can be used as a guide to help the bidder understand the intent of a bid or a request for quotation. This formula is very popular in the remodeling of existing food facilities.

1. This project is the remodeling of the existing snack bar in the Rathskeller and existing pizza shop located in the corridor of the basement level of McNeil Hall. The existing office shall be relocated to create a new sub shop in conjunction with a new pizza shop, both using a common beverage counter. The snack bar shall be made larger and additional equipment added for better service.
2. The general contractor shall be responsible for all engineering and engineering drawings for plumbing, electrical, heating, and cooling systems, either by a professional engineer or his subcontractors or by someone who is familiar with the present systems in the building.
3. Remove walls shown by broken line on drawing number one. Construct new walls as shown. The new walls shall be of 2″ × 4″ metal studs, covered on both sides with ⅝ F. C. (type X) gypsum board. All joints shall be taped, spackled, and sanded smooth, ready to receive paint or wall covering. All walls behind equipment shall be of ceramic tile for cleanliness.
4. All new doors to be installed shall be of solid core type (birch). These doors shall have two coats of clear finish (urethane).
5. The entrance to the sub/pizza shops shall be of the same details as the entrance to the bookstore with the exception of more glass for visibility into the shops. On drawing number one, elevation "C," the frame of the glass window wall to the left of the entrance shall be of the same wood material as the entrance.
6. Concerning the snack bar, the work platforms shall be extended as shown. The dessert cases shall be cut away from the table and relocated as shown. All cut joints shall be finished smooth and polished. A new front serving counter shall be fabricated. A roll-down grille shall be installed for security when the snack bar is not in operation.
7. All new floors in work areas shall be quarry tile, in the snack bar and in the pizza and sub shops.
8. The existing electric panel in the new sub shop shall be enclosed to form a column (unless the cost of relocating this panel falls within the budget).
9. All new stainless steel counters, custom-fabricated or stock item, shall be austenitic 18-8, type 302 and shall be USS, Armco, Enduro, or approved equal. Sheets shall be nonmagnetic, free from buckles, warps, and surface imperfections, and shall have a number 4 mill finish.
10. Exposed galvanized iron, cast iron, and iron pipe shall be given one (1) coat of duco or hammerloid.
11. Grind and polish welds level to match adjoining surfaces and finish on two sides where exposed. Wherever sheared edges occur, they shall be free of buckles, burrs, warps, and surface imperfections after welding. Joints shall be welded, ground and polished smooth. Spot-weld or butt joints are not permitted.
12. All workmanship shall be of highest quality throughout and shall be in accordance with the best standard practice of the foodservice equipment industry for this type of equipment.
13. The general contractor or his subcontractors shall obtain and pay for all permits concerning their part of the work.
14. All trades shall work in harmony so as not to create any delays in the progress of the project.
15. The premises shall be kept reasonably clean during construction. All rubbish caused by construction shall be removed from the premises and dumped by the contractors.

Note: This plan is an instrument of service only, prepared for the convenience of other contractors. The facility will not be held responsible for any discrepancies that may develop between dimensions shown and actual finished dimensions. This plan is based on the architect's plan submitted to us for the preparation of kitchen and/or cafeteria layouts in areas allocated, and of necessity was prepared for use prior to the erection of walls, from which actual field dimensions given on this plan cover the exact location of fittings on the piece of equipment as nearly as can be held in manufacture. Allowance must be made for valves, traps, J. boxes, outlets, working clearances, etc. Although each point of service is given and located, it is naturally assumed that certain inlets, outlets, etc. will be multiplexed, depending on sequence of units, thus minimizing holes in floor. Follow local and state plumbing and electric codes to plot roughing.

SOLICITING BIDS

The form that follows may be used for soliciting bids for one or a few pieces of new or replacement equipment.

Enclosed you will find the specifications and design for a new kitchen that our company is building. Bids for the equipment in this facility are currently being solicited. The following considerations should be covered in your bid:

1. Vendors will be selected on the basis of the total price of the foodservice indicated in the accompanying specifications.
2. The successful bidder will provide all plumbing and electrical layouts for the equipment provided and will cooperate with our architect doing this process.
3. Shop drawings and detailed specifications will be provided for all foodservice equipment.
4. The successful bidder will furnish supervision for assembling and setting equipment in place ready for plumbing and electrical connections to be done by other tradesmen.
5. The successful bidder will instruct employees on the use and care of the foodservice equipment. All equipment will carry a standard factory warranty.
6. Your organization will stipulate shipping arrangements in the bid.
7. No orders are to be placed without prior approval or purchase order.
8. All equipment and installation are to meet foodservice industry sanitation standards.
9. It is requested that bids be returned to our office by (bid due date).

SAMPLE REQUEST FOR PRICING

Dear Sir/Madam:

We are currently in the process of requesting bids for a commercial grade microwave oven, approximately 650 watts. Specifications are attached.

When submitting your bid request, please follow the outline listed below:

1. Quote must be on company letterhead paper.
2. Terms of purchase.
3. Delivery terms and time.
4. Warranty period.
5. Sales representative and company name, address, and phone number.
6. Shipping cost.

This microwave will be used occasionally by our employees for the purpose of heating food purchased from vending machines.

If you have any questions concerning this request, please feel free to contact my office at (123) 456-7890 Ext. 000 between 8:00 a.m. and 4:00 p.m. Monday through Friday. In order for your bid to be considered, it must be received on or before (bid due date).

Sincerely,

TYPICAL PLAN INFORMATION

The following forms, schedules, and notes are typical of trade communications found on foodservice equipment plans.

It is an excellent idea to have the following plan information printed on all foodservice equipment drawings:

- This plan is as accurate as can be determined at this date; unless otherwise noted, all dimensions are from finished walls, floors, and columns.
- Locations shown are for the actual *connections* on the equipment.
- Allowance *must* be made for traps, valves, switches, and other connection requirements. It is not within the authority of this company to dictate where roughing should originate or run.
- No roughing should be attempted unless the contractor performing the work is in possession of a complete set of final shop drawings and a brochure for every item of equipment shown, and thoroughly understands each.
- Unless otherwise specified, all roughing shown under equipment should not extend more than 3″ above finished floor.
- We will not be held responsible for any discrepancies between dimensions shown and actual finished dimensions.

The following example of general plan information reflects some ideas from the above list:

> All dimensions shown are from finished walls, floors, ceilings and/or from centerline of columns and are to be verified on the job by all fabricators, contractors, and others utilizing these plans in connection with this job.
>
> Indicated plumbing, electrical, and mechanical information and outlets have been located as accurately as possible and are intended to suit requirements of fixtures and equipment to be supplied. The facility is not responsible for the engineering thereof, or for any plumbing, electrical, or mechanical fittings, work, and/or connections unless otherwise specifically provided for in the plans and specifications.
>
> The facility will not accept responsibility for work done by other contractors or changes made necessary by local building codes, ordinances, structural conditions, or substitutions or changes in equipment shown on these plans.
>
> Connections shown in schedule are for one unit. To determine total requirements, multiply by number in quantity column.

TYPICAL FOOD SERVICE ESTABLISHMENT PLANS

Construction Materials

Room	*Floor and Base*	*Walls*	*Ceiling*
Kitchen and receiving area	Quarry tile	5 ft. quarry tile Painted sheetrock	Smooth acoustic on sheetrock Suspended acoustic
Service area	Quarry tile	Painted sheetrock	Suspended acoustic
Dining area	Quarry tile	Painted sheetrock	Suspended acoustic
Restrooms	Quarry tile	Ceramic tile	Suspended acoustic
Storage area	Quarry tile	Painted sheetrock	Suspended acoustic

Ventilation Schedule

- Restroom: mechanical ventilation to outside.
- Kitchen: screened windows.
- Grill, fryer, stove: filtered hood, mechanical ventilation to outside.

Plumbing Schedule

- Hot and cold potable water provided to food preparation, dishwashing, and handwashing areas.
- Anti-siphon mechanisms on water lines in toilet tanks.
- Vacuum breaker on water line to dishwashing machine.
- Sewage lines from restroom sinks, toilets, urinals.

PLUMBING NOTES

1. All rough-in and connections shown are relative to fixture and equipment work scope. See architect's plans for additional plumbing requirements.
2. Plumbing plan is intended to show rough-in locations, connection positions, and load requirements for final rough-in.
3. Outlets to stub out of walls 4″ at height indicated from finished floor, not curb, to centerline of outlet. Outlets to stub up a maximum of 2″ above finished floor or finished curb. All floor openings are to be sealed watertight by means of sleeves or otherwise 1″ above finished floor or flush with curbs.
4. General water pressure in kitchen shall not exceed 50 lbs. pressure, for dishwasher or glasswasher to be 25 lbs. maximum.

Plumber to furnish and install pressure-reducing valves as required.

5. All floor sinks to be set flush with finished floor or finished curb. Fully or partially exposed floor sinks to be complete with top grate. Type as indicated in the event local codes require floor sinks to be set above or below finished floors or curbs. Plumbing contractor shall promptly advise architect and designer.
6. Plumbing contractor to provide service and connect all water lines, gas lines, waste lines, etc., for fixture and equipment items, provide and install all valves, stops, traps, and pressure regulators necessary to connect lines, gate valves on all water and gas lines, and shock-stops (wade W-5 or equal) on glass fillers, unless otherwise noted.
7. Water provided to coffee urns or coffee brewers shall not feed from water softeners, unless so specified.
8. Plumbing contractor to verify height of dishwasher and potwasher waste connections and make proper provision for trap, and set in or under floor if necessary.
9. Plumbing contractor shall provide and run all required indirect drain lines from refrigerated units, ice machines, ice bins, bain maries, steam tables, disher wells, etc., to floor sinks. Plumbing contractor to install and connect faucets.
10. Drain tubing from walk-in cooler and freezer evaporators shall be provided under refrigeration work scope.
11. Kitchen equipment division shall provide water chillers and ice plates with interconnecting lines to ice plates or koroseal stainless steel braid between unit and faucet. Plumbing division to provide cold water service, stops, and make final connection.
12. Plumbing contractor shall provide all required refrigeration equipment, water, and waste services, including back-flow prevention assembly and piping to remote machines.
13. Kitchen equipment shall provide steam tables and bain maries with a bypass control assembly.
14. Steam system pressure for foodservice equipment shall be 25 psi maximum; for equipment requiring lower operating pressure, kitchen equipment division shall provide reducers.
15. If necessary, grease interceptors are to be sized, located, and provided by plumbing contractor according to all state and local codes.
16. Plumber to make all water connections as required between water wash control panels and exhaust hoods. Also, any and all field water and drain connections inside hoods.
17. Compliance with all local and national codes to be the responsibility of the local plumbing contractor.

GUIDELINES FOR PLUMBING IN FOODSERVICE ESTABLISHMENTS

1. New installations are to be constructed in accordance with local code.
2. Installations undergoing major renovation are to be constructed in accordance with local code.
3. Fixtures that can be readily modified are to be refitted in accordance with local code.
4. Fixtures that cannot be readily modified and in which back-flow of sewage would result in readily observable signs (such as sewage on floors) may be permitted to continue in service under an appropriate waiver issued by the proper agency. Such waiver is to be for a definite period of time and is to require that the piece of equipment be replaced or that the equipment or establishment be renovated to comply during the term of the waiver.
5. Any fixture permitting the back-flow of sewage without causing said back-flow to be readily observable (such as flooding on a floor that is in regular use) is to be modified to conform to the Sanitary Code or removed from service and the premises.

Waste Connections

Fixtures and equipment used for storage, preparation or processing of food, drink, kitchenware, tableware, or utensils (except for open dishwashing or culinary sinks) are not to be directly connected to a sewer connection and may be used for washing food under direct flow from a tap; however, these sinks are not to be used for thawing, soaking, or storing food. Sinks for thawing, cooking, or storing food are to have indirect connections.

Fixtures and equipment requiring indirect drains are:

Refrigerators	Coffee urns
Potato peelers	Steam tables
Ice-making machines	Hot or cold food storage devices
Ice storage bins	Dishwashing machines
Vegetable-washing sinks	Cooking kettles
Meat-washing sinks	Walk-in coolers
Refrigerator coils	

Fixtures that do not require indirect drains are:

Toilets and urinals	Pot-washing sinks
Handwashing sinks	Bar sinks
Garbage grinders	Dishwashing sinks
Slop sinks	Floor drains

Confirm all drain requirements with local codes.

PLUMBING INSTALLATION IN FOODSERVICE ESTABLISHMENTS

Installation of Indirect Waste Piping

- *Method 1:* Locate an air break in the waste line 2 feet from the waste outlet of the fixture and on the inlet side of the trap. Waste lines from all equipment requiring indirect drains are to be installed to prevent back-flow from drains and sewers and from other fixtures.
- *Method 2:* Install an individual drain line for each fixture to a water-supplied sink or floor drain, approved for such use. Such lines shall terminate at least one inch above the food rim of the sink or drain. A water-supplied sink or floor drain is to have a properly protected water supply that is readily available to flush the sink or floor drain. Indirect drains may not discharge into any sink or fixture used for food preparation, or dish, kitchenware, or utensil washing, or food storage.
- *Method 3:* Commercial dishwashing machines are to be indirectly connected, except when the dishwasher is located within 5 feet of a trapped floor drain; then the waste may be connected directly to the inlet side of a properly vented floor drain trap.
- *Method 4:* In existing installations, a "telltale device" is to be an open-ended pipe connected to the fixture wasteline, upstream of the trap, which terminates below the lowest elevation of water in the fixture. This pipe is not to be smaller than the drainline from the fixture, and is installed so that no part of it exceeds the elevation of its open end. This "telltale device" is to be used only as a last resort and is in no case to be permitted on a new installation, or when new equipment is installed.

HEALTH AND SAFETY NOTES

1. *Health Requirements*
   A. Garbage inside will be kept in plastic-bag-lined, covered cans. Owner shall contract with a private sanitation company for four pickups per week or more if required.
   B. Owner shall contract with a pest control company to completely service this establishment twice monthly and on request.
2. *Hood Requirements*
   A. Walls behind and at side of each cooking area shall have an approved-type fireproof and washable surface applied over type "X" sheet rock.
   B. Hood shall be equipped with an approved-type fire protection system. Hood shall be filtered and equipped with approved-type grease container. Hood shall conform to N.F.P.A. 96 manual.
3. *Kitchen Finishes*
   A. Floors and base shall be quarry tile with an abrasive finish.
   B. Walls shall be paneled over gypsum board with "Masonite" brand "flame test" washable paneling.
   C. Ceiling shall be "Armstrong" "Geramagard" nonfissured washable hood ceiling system with two-hour rating.
   D. Freezer floors and walls shall be "easy clean" type.

ELECTRICAL NOTES

- Run all outlet boxes in horizontal plane.
- Vapor-proof and heat-resistant fixture is provided with exhaust hood. Electrical contractor is to provide, mount switches, and make final hookup to junction box in equipment.

- Light and final hookup for walk-in refrigerators and freezers are to be provided by electrical contractor.
- All electrical stub-ups must be waterproof.

Electrical Schedule for Circuit Breaker Panel Box "A"

Griddle	12.0 kw	208/3
Hot food well	1.2 kw	208/3
Broilers	4.6 kw (ea)	208/3 (ea)
Compressor	1/3 HP	208/3
Display lights and DCO	1500 W	115/1
Bun warmer	.45	115/1

Electrical Schedule for Circuit Breaker Panel Box "B"

Fryers	12.0 kw (ea)	208/3 (ea)
Dump station warmer	680 W	115/1
Hot dog warmer	1110 W	115/1
two (2)-compartment hot food well	1.9 kW	208/3
Coffee Urn	15.0 kW	208/3
Display lights and DCO	1500 W	115/1

COMPUTER-AIDED DESIGN AND DRAFTING FOR THE FOODSERVICE INDUSTRY

CAD can dramatically increase your design productivity and precision. The system brings cost-effective and easy to use Computer-Aided Design to the Food Service Industry.

CAD uses a computer to store and reproduce your drawings. Designing with CAD is similar to normal manual methods . . . it is just much quicker, more efficient and more precise; especially when modifying. CAD can generate drawings at any point in the design/drafting process.

CAD comes complete with a Library of Food Equipment Designs. The Library contains standardized drawings in plan, side & elevation views, including connections, specifications and a comprehensive equipment Index. By simply using the Library, an entire facility lay-out can be created! (You insert parts from the Library into your plan . . . you tell the computer, where you want it to go, and IT does the work.)

Today's most advanced computer technology has been integrated into one outstanding design package. Depending on your specific needs, options to the basic system are available.

The FEDA (Food Equipment Distributors Association), NAFEM (National Association of Food Equipment Manufacturers) and F.C.S.I. (Food Consultants Society International), have all cooperated to bring standard industry guidelines to users of CAD. Over 40 Manufacturers are users of this Software and their products to facilitate drawings.

COMPUTER ASSISTED

FOOD EQUIPMENT DESIGN

WITH
EQUIPMENT LIBRARY

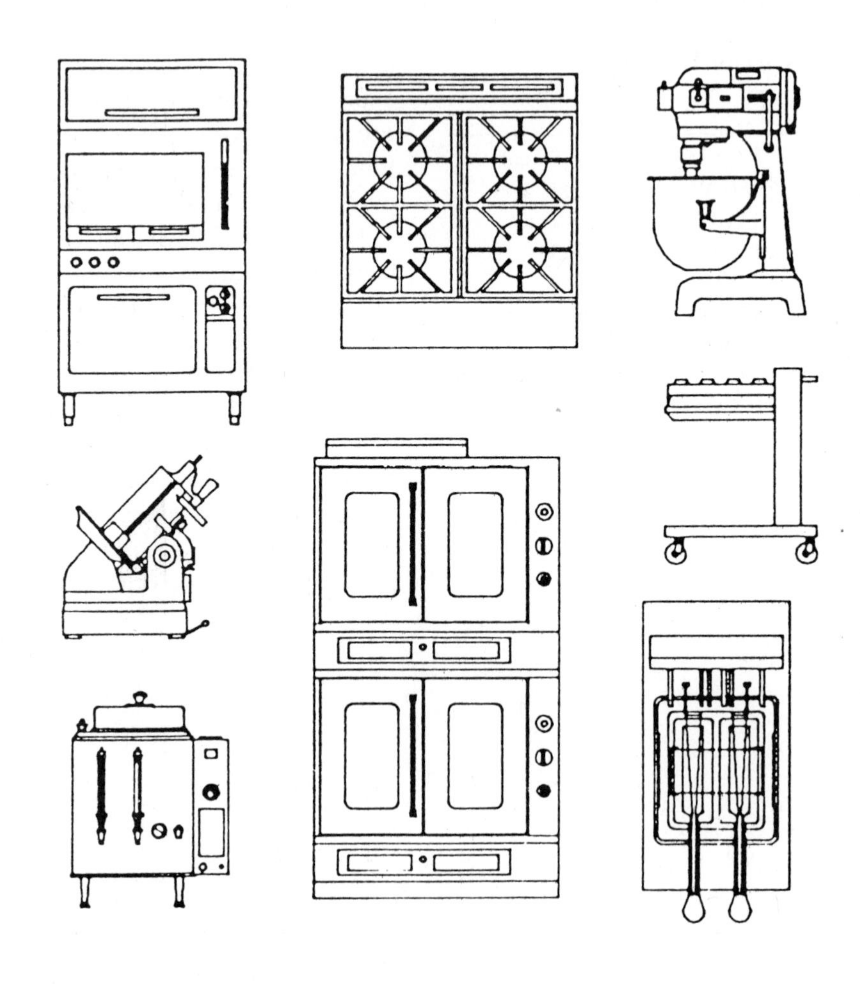

THE FED-CAD SYSTEM IN ACTION

The following drawings show the development of a typical beverage counter. The pictures labeled step 1 through 6 represent what is seen on the computer screen and include the time required to complete each step.

Step one shows the insertion of the wall lines as supplied on architectural drawings. There are several ways of doing this, including one method that involves calibrating and tracing the existing drawing into the computer.

STEP 1

OUTLINE OF YOUR CLIENT'S SERVING AREA :

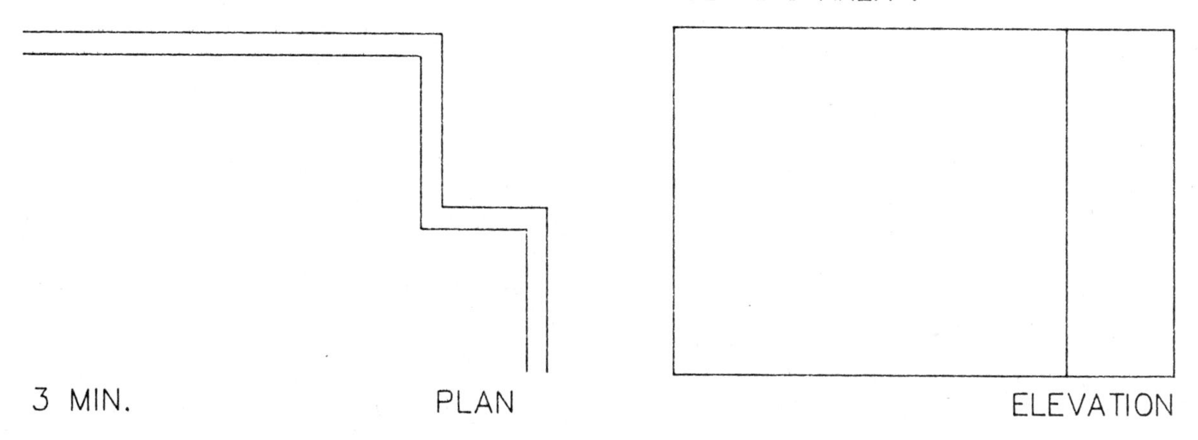

In the second step a standard counter is inserted from the Library. The item was found in the Index, the file name typed in, and the part was electronically copied into the drawing. Once inserted, the counter could easily be changed with modifications such as increasing or decreasing the length, changing the door pulls, etc.

In steps three and four, additional beverage equipment drawings are inserted from the library, and in step five, a computer commmand is used to put the milk dispenser on the left and the coffee urn on the right. Working by hand, this type of revision would be messy and time consuming.

MANUFACTURER:	SAMPLE INDEX		PG 1
MODEL NO.	DESCRIPTION	DSK/FILE	
CUSTOM	BEVERAGE COUNTER ENCLOSED WITH HINGED DOORS WITH 6" BACKSPLASH & 6" TILE BASE 108"L X 44"W X 34"H	-9- BEVCNTRE BEVCNTRP	
FE-75	CECILWARE COFFEE URN 21.5"L X 17.5"W X 28.5"H	-9- CWCQ1E CWCQ1P CWCQ1S	
5000	KENCO DRINK DISPENSER 14"L X 18"W X 22"H	-8- KEDV500E KEDV500P KEDV500S	
LD40	LERN ICE DISPENSER 17.5"L X 21.5"W X 28"H	-8- LEIM40E LEIM40P LEIM40S	
EC	LILY CUP DISPENSER ELEVATOR TYPE 6.5"DIA X 30"H	-8- LIDIECE LIDIECP LIDIECS	
N-10-S	NORRIS MILK DISPENSER 25.5"L X 18"W X 40.5"H	-8- NSDMN10E NSDMN10P NSDMN10S	
CCA-ST	SERVOLIFT CUP AND GLASS DISPENSER 21"L X 29"W X 36"H	-8- SVDP12E SVDP12P SVDP12S	

(This demonstration page is different than the actual index which is organized alphabetically by manufacturer and model number.)

STEP 2

INSERTION OF THE BEVERAGE COUNTER :

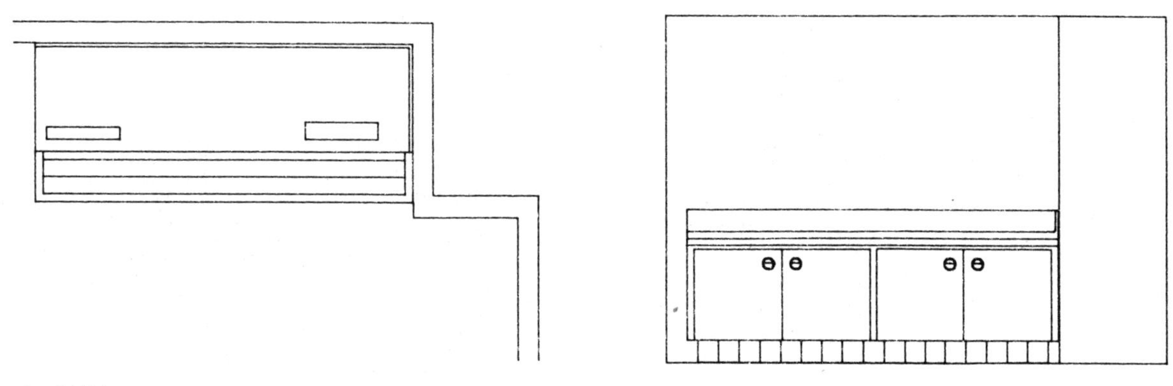

1 MIN.

STEP 3

INSERTION OF THE COFFEE URN AND MILK DISPENSER :

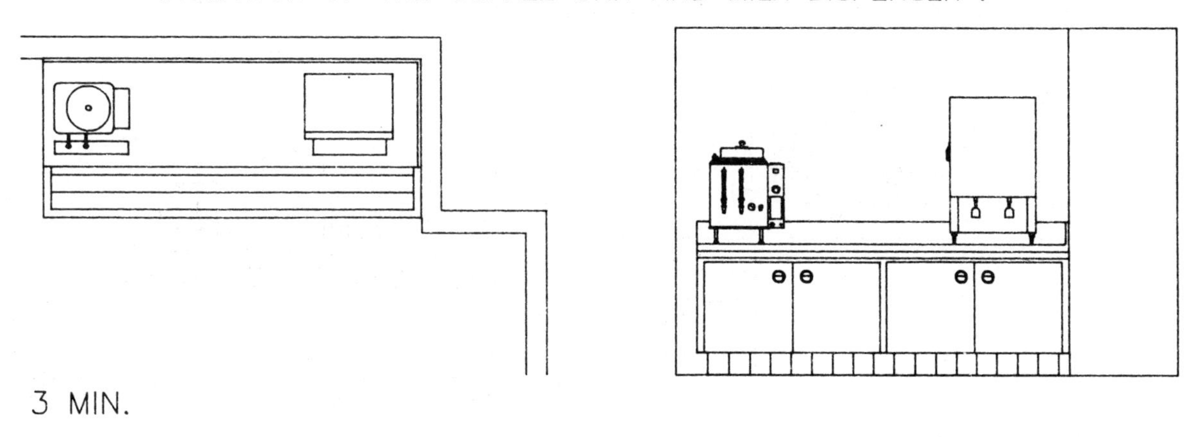

3 MIN.

STEP 4

INSERTION OF THE CUP DISPENSERS :

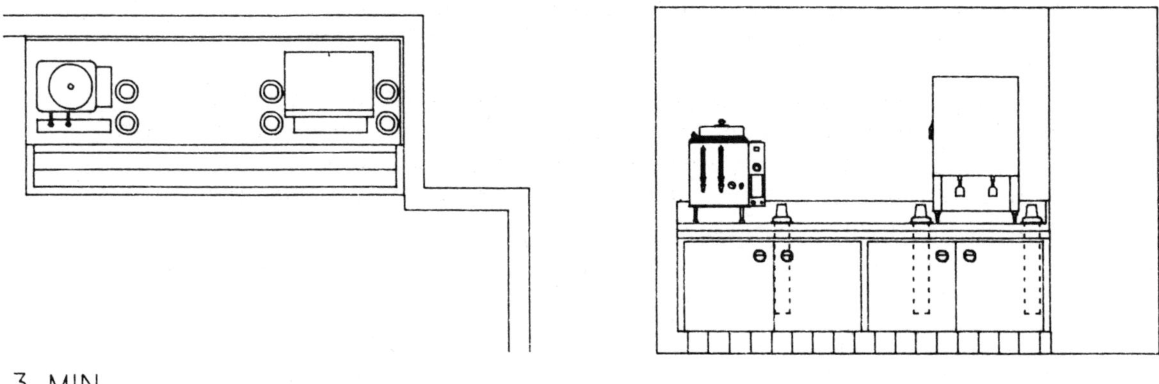

3 MIN.

STEP 5

THE CLIENT WOULD LIKE THE COFFEE URN AND THE MILK DISPENSER REVERSED :

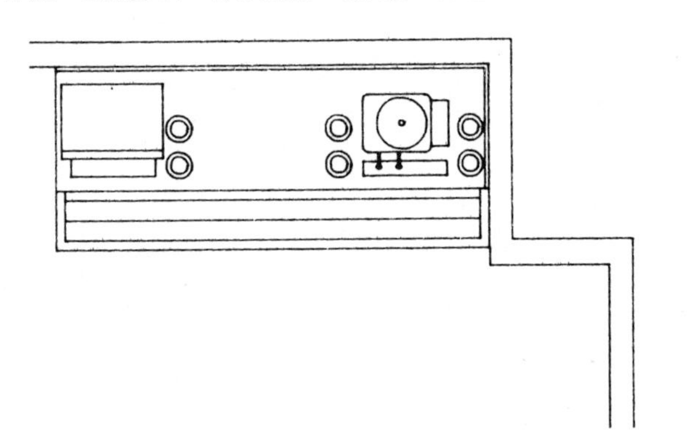

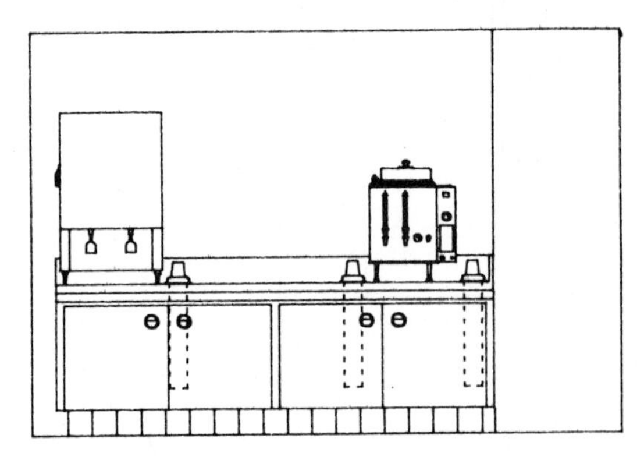

1 MIN.

STEP 6

FINALLY THE INSERTION OF THE ICE, MILK, CUP AND GLASS DISPENSERS :

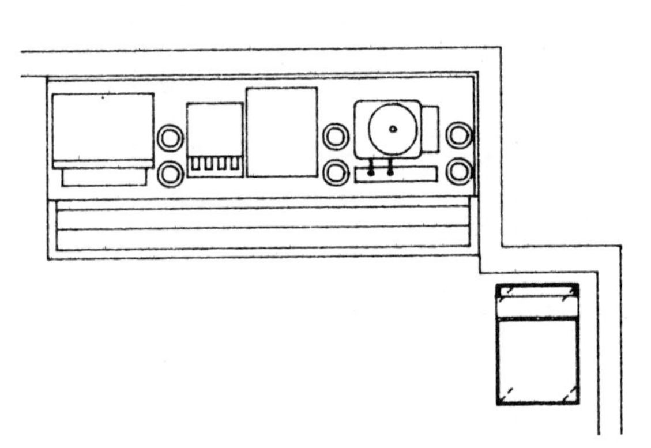

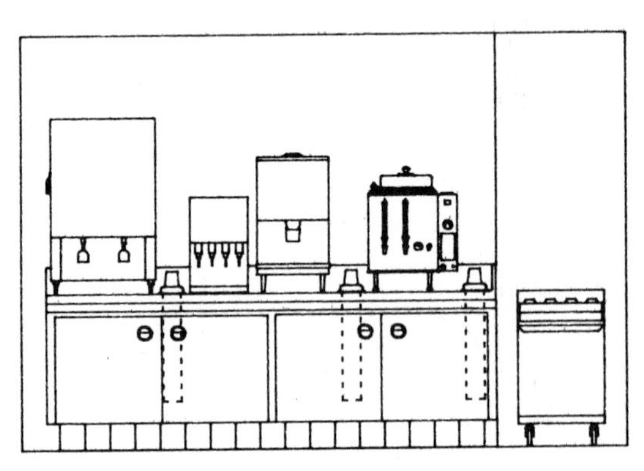

3 MIN.

Step six shows how you could quickly and accurately put "ten feet of equipment into a nine foot space" if you really had to.

The next two pages show typical (though somewhat reduced) drawings the system can produce. Since a layer (over–lay) scheme is used, the actual plan view is drawn only once, but plotted with different layers selected so as to create the presentation drawing, roughing drawing, etc.

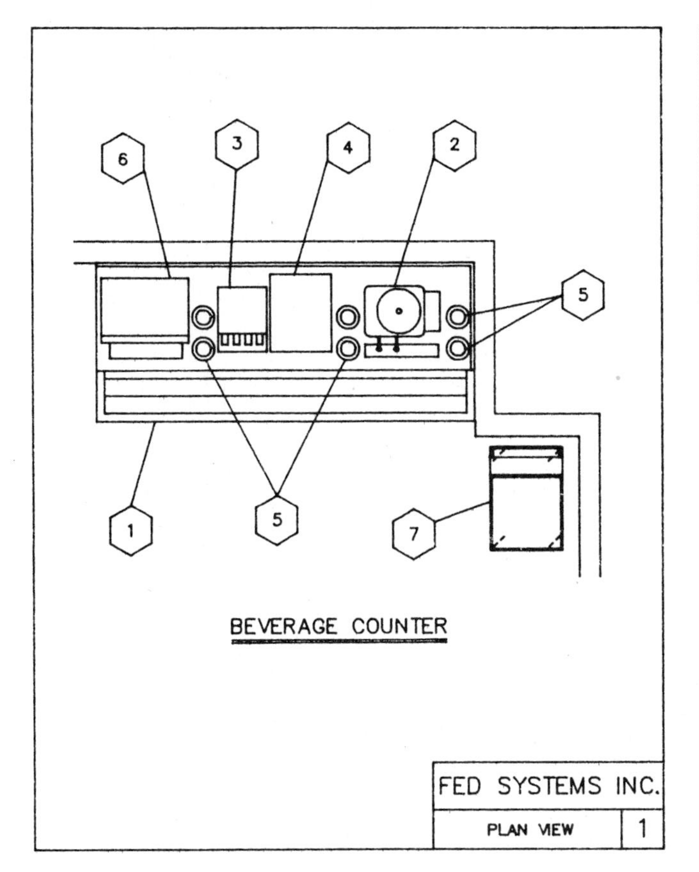
6
3
4
2
5
1
5
7
BEVERAGE COUNTER
FED SYSTEMS INC.
PLAN VIEW
1

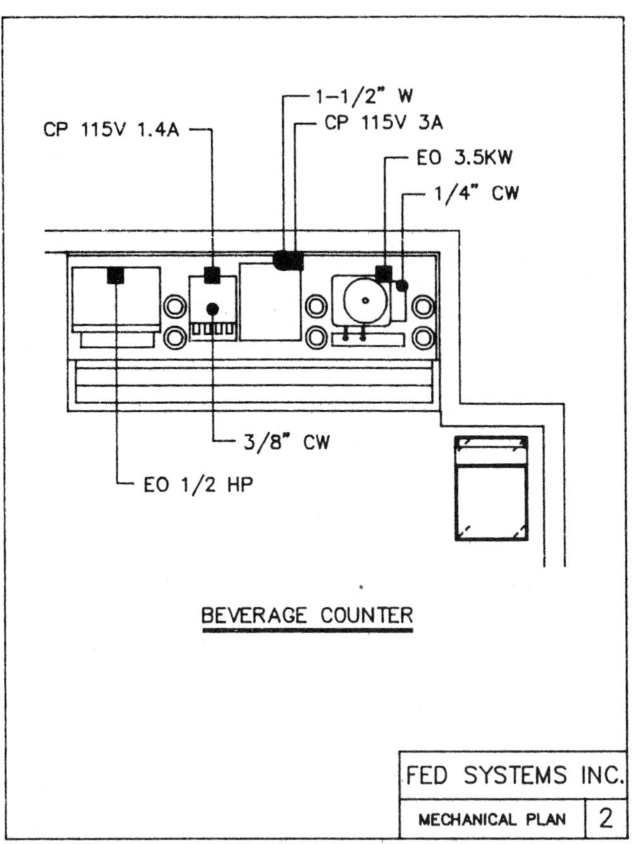
1-1/2" W
CP 115V 1.4A
CP 115V 3A
EO 3.5KW
1/4" CW
3/8" CW
EO 1/2 HP
BEVERAGE COUNTER
FED SYSTEMS INC.
MECHANICAL PLAN
2

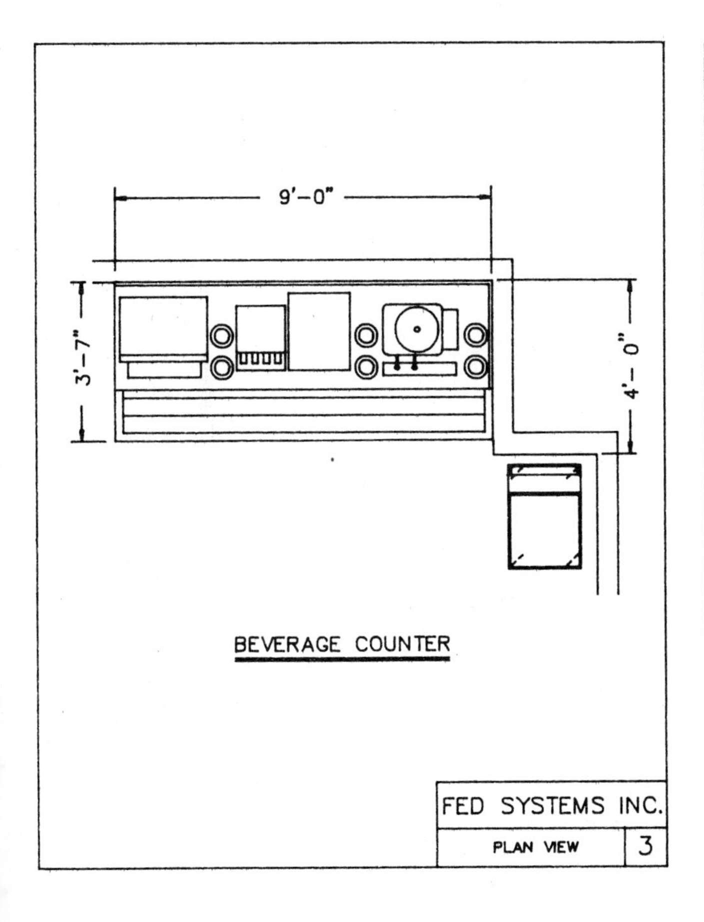
9'-0"
3'-7"
4'- 0"
BEVERAGE COUNTER
FED SYSTEMS INC.
PLAN VIEW
3

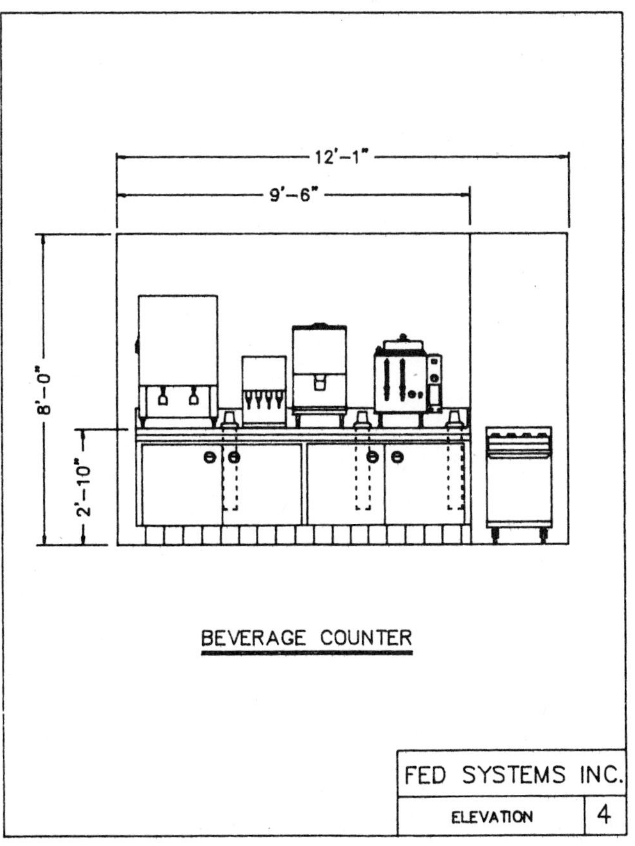
12'-1"
9'-6"
8'-0"
2'-10"
BEVERAGE COUNTER
FED SYSTEMS INC.
ELEVATION
4

SCHEDULE OF EQUIPMENT & CONNECTIONS

ITEM NO.	QTY	DESCRIPTION	H	C	W	IW	G	S	R	HP	KW	EL	EO	DR	VOLTS	PH	REMARKS
1	1	BEVERAGE COUNTER				1"											CURB1,CURB2
2	1	COFFEE URN		1/4"		1"					3.5		1				3.5 KW CURB 1 & 2
3	1	BEVERAGE DISPENSER		3/8"						1/2	1.4A				115		1/4 CARBONATER
4	1	ICE DISPENSER		3/8"	1/2"					1/3	3A				115		1/3 HP CURB 1 & 2
5	6	CUP DISPENSER															
6	1	MILK DISPENSER				1"				1/2			1				1/2 HP CURB 1 & 2
7	1	CUP & GLASS DISPENSER															
8																	
9																	
10																	

FED SYSTEMS INC.

SCHEDULE OF EQUIPMENT 5

The schedule of equipment is completed in a few minutes of typing instead of hours spent hand lettering.

FOODSERVICE EQUIPMENT SPECIFICATION

The following specification for foodservice equipment is an excellent example of a well-written document that will ensure a good job.

PART 1—GENERAL

1.01 *Related Documents*

A. This section constitutes a separate prime contract.

B. The general conditions of Division 1 including supplementary conditions and general requirements apply to the work specified in this section.

1.02 *Related Work Specified Not Included by Foodservice Equipment Contractor*

A. Plumbing: Refer to division including:

1. Rough-in.
2. Piping for supply and waste lines.
3. Traps, grease traps, line strainers, tail pieces, valves, stops, shutoffs, and miscellaneous fittings required for complete installation.
4. Final connection.

B. Ventilation: Refer to division including:

1. Final utility connections.

C. Electrical: Refer to division including:

1. Rough-in.
2. Conduit, wiring, line and disconnect switches, safety cutoffs and fittings, control panels, fuses, boxes and fittings required for complete installation.
3. Final connections, including mounting and wiring of starters and switches furnished as part of the foodservice equipment (unless otherwise indicated on the drawing).

1.03 *Work Included in This Section*

A. Furnish point of connections and install all foodservice equipment herein, including that which is reasonably inferred, with all related items necessary to complete work shown on contract drawings and/or required by these specifications.

B. Electric Work:

1. Interwiring of foodservice equipment between components within equipment, such as heating elements, switches, thermostats, motors, etc., complete with junction box or disconnect switch as is applicable, ready for final connection.
2. Voltages shall be as indicated on contract drawings. Any difference in electrical characteristics at job site from those shown on contract documents must be submitted to architect for consideration prior to ordering equipment.

C. Plumbing Work:

1. Furnish all equipment with faucets and sink waste assemblies, as specified in this section.

1.04 *Quality Assurance*

A. It is required that all custom-fabricated equipment such as tables, sinks, countertops, etc., be manufactured by a foodservice equipment fabricator who has the plant, personnel and engineering required. Such manufacturer shall be subject to approval of architect. All work in above category shall be manufactured by one manufacturer, and shall be of uniform design and finish.

B. Manufacturer of this equipment must be able to show that he is now and for the past five years has been engaged in manufacture or distribution of equipment, as required under this contract.

C. Manufacturer of this equipment herein specified shall be a recognized distributor for items of equipment specified herein that are of other manufacture than his own.

D. Only manufacturers who can meet the foregoing qualifications will be acceptable.

1.05 *Submittals*

A. Submit shop drawings as required by general conditions.

B. Shop drawings and bound brochures covering manufactured or "buy-out" items covering all work and equipment included in this contract shall be submitted to owner as soon as possible after award of contract. After approval, foodservice contractor shall furnish to architect sets of shop drawings and brochures, corrected as required by virtue of review comments, for distribution to various interested trades on project. All costs of reproductions and submission shall be part of contract.

C. Provide fully dimensioned rough-in plans at ¼" scale, showing all required mechanical, electrical, ventilation, water, waste, and refrigeration services for equipment and rough-in location for same. Rough-in locations shown shall make allowances for required traps, switches, etc., thereby not requiring interpretation or adjustment on the part of other contractors. Drawings shall indicate dimensions for floor depressions, wall openings, etc., for equipment.

D. Foodservice equipment contractor shall visit site to verify all rough-in and sleeve locations prior to installation of finished floors, and shall cooperate with other contractors involved in proper location of same.

E. Fully dimensioned and detailed shop drawings of custom-fabricated equipment items shall be submitted, drawn at ¾" and ½" scale for plans, elevations, and sections, respectively. Drawings shall show all details of construction, installation, and relation to adjoining and related work where cutting or close fitting is required. Drawings shall show all reinforcements, anchorage, and other work required for complete installation of all fixtures.

F. Do not begin fabrication of custom-manufactured equipment until approvals of shop drawings have been received, and until field measurements have been taken by foodservice equipment contractor, where such measurements are necessary to assure proper conformance with intent of contract drawings and specifications.

G. Make field measurements, giving due consideration to any architectural, mechanical, or structural discrepancies that may occur during construction of building. No extra compensation will be allowed for any difference between actual measurements secured at job site and dimensions shown on drawings. Field measurements shall be submitted to architect for consideration before proceeding with fabrication of equipment.

H. Submit illustrated brochures for manufactured or "buy-out" equipment items, complete with illustrations, specifications, line drawings, rough-in requirements, and list of accessories or other specified additional requirements. Brochures shall be bound and shall include data on all equipment that is to be provided, arranged in numerical sequence that conforms to item numbers of specifications. Omission of data does not reduce obligation to provide items as specified.

1.06 *Substitutions—Standards*

A. Proposals shall be based on brands, materials, and forms of construction specified unless products of other manufacturers that conform to requirements of plan and specifications are approved in writing by owner as equal to that specified.

B. Any equipment offered for approval as "equal" to equipment specified must conform to space limitations of layout. Cost of any deviation from kind or location of mechanical service provided in layout due to furnishing of an approved equal will be the responsibility of foodservice contractor, at no extra cost to owner.

C. If no equals are approved in writing by owner, the brands and materials specified must be furnished, and no other substitution will be permitted subsequent to award of contract except by specific change order issued by owner.

1.07 *Drawings*

A. Drawings that constitute part of contract documents indicate general arrangement of piping and location of equipment. Should it be necessary to deviate from arrangement indicated in order to meet structural conditions, make such deviations without expense to owner.

B. Specifications and drawings are reasonably exact, but their extreme accuracy is not guaranteed. Drawings and specifications are for assistance and guidance of contractor, and exact locations, distances, and levels shall be governed by the building.

1.08 *Manufacturer's Directions*

A. Follow manufacturer's directions in all cases where manufacturers of articles used in this contract furnish directions or prints covering points not shown on drawings or specifications.

1.09 *Industry Standards*

A. Electrically operated and/or heated equipment, fabricated or otherwise, shall conform to latest standards of National Electric Manufacturers Association and of Underwriters Laboratories, Inc., and shall bear the U.L. label.

B. Items of foodservice equipment furnished shall conform to standards of National Sanitation Foundation, Ann Arbor, Michigan, and shall bear the N.S.F. seal.

C. Foodservice equipment shall be installed in accordance with N.S.F. standards.

D. Work and materials shall be in compliance with requirements of applicable codes, ordinances, and regulations, including but not limited to those of the National Fire Protection Association, State Fire Marshal, State Board of Health, Local Health Codes, etc.

E. Rulings and interpretations of enforcing agencies shall be considered part of regulations.

PART 2—PRODUCT

2.01 *Manufactured Equipment*

A. Except as may be specified otherwise under individual item specifications in "Equipment Schedule," all items of standard manufactured equipment furnished shall be complete in accord with manufacturer's standard specifications for specific unit or model called for, including finishes, components, attachments, appurtenances, etc., except as follows:

B. Substitutions for manufactured equipment specified will be accorded consideration under terms set forth in "Substitutions—Standards."

2.02 *Fabricated Equipment*

A. Work shall be done in an approved workmanlike manner, to complete satisfaction of owner.

B. Stainless steel shall be U.S. standard gauges as

called for, 18-8, Type 304, not over .012% maximum carbon, No. 4 finish.

C. Galvanized iron shall be Armco or equal. Framework of galvanized iron shall be welded construction, having welds smooth, and where galvanizing has been burned off, touched up with high-grade aluminum bronze.

D. Legs and crossrails shall be continuously welded, unless otherwise noted, and ground smooth.

E. Bottom of legs at floor shall be fitted with sanitary stainless steel bullet-type foot, with no less than ½″ adjustment.

F. Legs shall be fastened to equipment as follows:
   1. To sinks by means of closed gussets. Gussets shall be stainless steel, reinforced with bushing, having set screws for securing legs.
   2. To tables and drainboards with closed gussets which shall be welded to galvanized hat sections or channels, 14 gauge or heavier, exposed hat sections having closed ends. Bracing shall be underside of tops.

G. Closed gussets shall be 3″ minimum diameter at top, welded to frame members or to sink bottom.

H. Sinks, unless otherwise specified, shall be furnished with lever-type waste outlets, without connected overflows: Fisher Brass Foundry Model 250A; Klein Hardware Model 416-A; or approved equal. Where exposed, furnish wastes chromium-plated.

I. Rolls shall be 1½″ diameter, except as detailed to the contrary, with corners bullnosed, ground, and polished.

J. Seams and joints shall be shop-welded. Welds to be ground and polished to match original finish. Materials 18 gauge or heavier shall be welded.

K. Metal tops shall be one-piece welded construction, unless specified otherwise, reinforced on underside with galvanized hat sections or channels welded in place. Crossbrace to be not more than 30″ on centers.

L. Drawers to be 18 gauge stainless steel channel-type housing and drawer cradle, both housing and cradle being reinforced and welded at corners, housing being secured to underside of tabletop, and both housing and cradle being sized for and fitted with 20″ × 20″ × 5″-deep stainless steel drawer insert having coved corners. Drawer insert shall be easily removable from cradle without tools or having to remove entire drawer.

M. Drawer fronts and doors: Except where single-pan construction is indicated, provide double-pan type, not less than ⅝″ thick, with seams on inside face. Deaden sound by inserting mineral wool insulation (Cetotex) between pans.

N. Hardware shall be solid materials and except where unexposed or specified to the contrary, of cast brass, chrome-plated. Identify all hardware with manufacturer's name and number so that broken or worn parts may be ordered and replaced.

O. Fabricate sink compartments with ¾″ coved vertical and horizontal corners. Multiple-compartment partitions to be double thickness, continuously welded where sheets join at top. Front of multiple-compartment sinks to be continuous on exterior. Bottoms shall be creased to drain.

P. Ends of fixtures, splashbacks, shelves, etc., shall be finished flush to walls or adjoining fixtures.

Q. Dishtables, drainboards, splashbacks, and turn-up edges shall have radius bends in all horizontal and vertical corners, coved at intersections.

R. Rounded and coved corners or radius bends shall be ½″ radius or longer.

S. Undersides of tops to be coated with heavy-bodied resinous material compound for permanent, non-flaking adhesion to metal, ⅛″ thick, applied after reinforcing members have been installed, drying without dirt-catching crevices.

T. Shelves are to be turned up 2″ on the back edge. Turn other edges down 1½″ to form open channels. Reinforce shelf units to support 40 lbs. per square foot loading, plus 100% impact loading.

U. Casework at fabricator's option, unless otherwise indicated. Provide either box-type framing or open-channel-type (complying with N.S.F. requirements in either case).

V. Enclosures: Except as otherwise indicated, provide each unit of casework (base, wall overhead, and free-standing) with a complete-enclosure metal cabinet, including fronts, backs, tops, bottoms, and sides.

W. Metal components, unless specified or noted otherwise, to be the following gauges:

Tabletops	14 gauge	Stainless steel
Wall shelves	16 gauge	Stainless steel
Undershelves	16 gauge	Stainless steel
Drawer fronts (single pan)	16 gauge	Stainless steel
Enclosed cabinet bases	18 gauge	Stainless steel
Sinks and drainboards	14 gauge	Stainless steel
Exhaust hoods	18 gauge	Stainless steel
Legs (1⅝″ dia.)	16 gauge	Stainless steel
Cross bracing (1″ dia.)	16 gauge	Stainless steel
Doors (outer pan)	18 gauge	Stainless steel
Doors (inner pan)	20 gauge	Stainless steel

2.03 *Heating Equipment*

A. Wherever heating equipment or thermostat control for such equipment is specified, it shall be complete, and of the materials, size, and rating specified within equipment items or details. All such equipment shall be designed and installed to be easily cleaned or to be easily removed for cleaning.

B. Electrical appliances or heating element circuits of 120 volts shall not exceed 1650 watts, unless specifically shown to the contrary.

2.04 *Switches and Controls*

A. All internal wiring for fabricated equipment items, including all electrical devices, wiring, controls, switches, etc., built into or forming an integral part of these items shall be furnished and installed by foodservice equipment contractor in his factory or building site with all items complete to junction box for final connection to building lines by electrical contractor.

B. Provide standard 3-prong plugs to fit "U" slot grounding-type receptacles, for all equipment items powered by plugging into 110–120 volts,, single-phase AC.

2.05 *Connection Terminals*

A. All equipment shall be complete with connection terminals as standardized by equipment manufacture, except where specified otherwise.

2.06 *Locks*

A. Fit all doors for reach-in refrigerated compartments with locking-type latches.

2.07 *Laminate Plastic*

A. Wherever laminate plastic materials are specified, veneer all materials using urea base cement, waterproof, and heatproof. Rubber base adhesives are not acceptable. Apply materials directly over close-grained plywood face exposed surfaces and edges with $\frac{1}{16}$" material, and corresponding back faces with $\frac{1}{32}$" reject material. Place top sheet on and over finished edge.

PART 3—EXECUTION

3.01 *General*

A. Work under this contract and covered under this section of specification includes but is not limited to:

1. Cutting of holes and/or ferrules on equipment for piping, drains, electrical outlets, conduits, etc., as required to coordinate installation of kitchen and foodservice equipment work of the other contractors on project.
2. Field checking of building and rough-in requirements, and submission of brochures and shop drawings, all as required herein before under "submittals."
3. Repair of all damage to premises as result of this installation, and removal of all debris left by those engaged in this installation.
4. Having all foodservice equipment fixtures completely cleaned and ready for operation when building is turned over to owner.

3.02 *Installation Procedures*

A. Foodservice equipment contractor shall make arrangements for receiving his custom-fabricated and "buy-out" equipment and shall make delivery into building as requisitioned by his installation superintendent. He shall not consign any of his equipment to owner or to any other contractor unless he has written acceptance from them and has made satisfactory arrangements for the payment of all freight and handling charges.

B. Foodservice equipment contractor shall deliver all of his custom-fabricated and "buy-out" equipment temporarily in its final location, permitting trades to make necessary arrangements for connection of service lines.

C. This contractor shall coordinate his work and cooperate with other trades working at site toward the orderly progress of the project.

D. Owner or owner's agent shall have access at all times to plant or shop in which custom-fabricated equipment is being manufactured, from time contract is let until equipment is shipped, in order that progress of work can be checked, as well as any technical problems that may arise in coordination of equipment with building. Any approval given at this point of manufacture shall be tentative, subject to final inspection and test after complete installation.

E. Foodservice equipment contractor shall assist owner, and/or owner's agent, in making any desired tests during or prior to final inspection of equipment; he shall remove immediately any work or equipment rejected by owner, and/or owner's agent, replacing same with work conforming with contract requirements.

F. This contractor shall keep premises free from accumulation of his waste material and rubbish, and at completion of his work shall remove his rubbish and implements, leaving areas of his work room clean.

G. This contractor shall provide and maintain coverings or other approved protection for finished surfaces and other parts of his equipment subject to damage during and after erection. After removal of protective coverings, all field joints shall be ground and polished, and entire work shall be thoroughly cleaned and polished.

3.03 *Trimming and Sealing Equipment*

A. Seal completely spaces between all units to walls, ceilings, floors, and adjoining (not portable) units with enclosed bodies against entrance of food particles or vermin by means of trim strips, welding, soldering, or commercial joint material best suited to nature of equipment and adjoining surface material.

B. Close ends of all hollow sections.

C. Equipment butting against walls, ceilings, floor surfaces, and corners to fit tightly against same; backsplashes or risers that fit against wall to be neatly scribed and sealed to wall with Dow Corning 732 RTV or General Electric clear silicone sealant, wiping excess out of joint to fillet radius. Where required to prevent shifting of equipment and breaking wall seal, anchor item to floor or wall.

3.04 *Testing and Demonstration of Equipment*

A. After complete installation, all items of equipment furnished under this contract shall be thoroughly tested to ensure proper and safe operation.

B. Foodservice equipment contractor shall arrange to have all manufactured, mechanically operated equipment furnished under this contract demonstrated by manufacturers' representatives. These representatives to instruct owner's designated personnel in use, care, and maintainance of all items of equipment after same are in working order. Demonstration and instruction shall be held on dates designated by owner.

C. Foodservice equipment contractor shall provide a competent service representative to be present when installation is put into operation.

3.05 *Equipment Handling and Storage*

A. Deliver equipment to site, properly crated and protected, and store in safe place. Protect from damage until time for installation.

3.06 *Guarantee*

A. Equipment furnished under this contract shall be guaranteed for a period of one year from the date of final acceptance thereof against defective materials, designs, and workmanship. Upon receipt of notice of failure, any part or parts shall be replaced promptly, at the expense of foodservice equipment contractor. Until replacement equipment is installed, owner shall have full use of defective equipment. Warranty shall include labor, all parts, and driving time to and from job site.

B. This guarantee shall include installation, start-up, and one year free service for all self-contained refrigeration equipment furnished under this contract, with evidence of manufacturer's one-year guarantee on entire cabinet, and additional four-year warranty on sealed compressor motor assembly (optional).

3.07 *Operating and Maintenance Manuals*

A. After completion of installation, foodservice equipment contractor shall present to owner three sets of all operating and maintenance manuals, covering all mechanically operated equipment furnished under this contract, each set being bound in looseleaf binder having durable cover.

B. Include in each binder a list of names, addresses, and telephone numbers of servicing agencies authorized to make necessary repairs and/or adjustments of equipment furnished under this contract.

10 STEPS TO ENSURE RESTAURANTS GET INSURANCE

By Philip Miller

Many entrepreneurs opening a restaurant for the first time should have some idea how insurers decide whether to offer coverage or not—and how much coverage will cost.

Here are 10 ways to improve your chances of getting broader coverage and better rates.

• *Document your experience as a restaurateur.* Most companies don't insure restaurateurs who are novices. They like to see a minimum of three years' experience. They also look for a history of ownership by the current owner. If he or she has been in the restaurant business for a number of years, it reassures the insurance company that the restaurant will be around for a while.

• *Be sure all cooking facilities are covered under a hood-and-duct cleaning contract,* since the ducts leading to the external exhaust are very susceptible to grease fires. They can be especially hard to fight and control.

• *Make certain you have installed proper burglary equipment.* Your liquor stock, slicing, and cooking machines, blenders, and, if you own one of the better restaurants, the silver or silverplate you use, are all tempting targets for thieves.

• During the construction of your restaurant, *take care that the building has proper access and egress.* If you want your operation to accommodate 200 people, they will need more than one way to get out, since fire is always a possibility.

• *Install emergency lighting* to help people escape in case of a conflagration or any other emergency.

• *Set up a sprinkler system.* It may be costly, but it's well worth the expense, in terms of your own protection and that of the property.

• *Make sure your fire-extinguishing equipment is more than adequate* for doing the job. Some states, including New York, require installation of a system to protect cooking facilities. The extent of the system you need will, of course, vary according to the size of your kitchen and the quantity of equipment you have.

• If you will be dealing in cash more than in credit cards—or if you plan to open a fast-food operation, which is cash only—*use a drop safe.* The device is bolted or cemented into the ground and helps to reduce holdups because it cannot be blown up and because two keys are required for opening it. Your manager has only one. Your armored car service keeps the other key.

Such a precaution is especially critical because cashiers and patrons could be hurt or killed during a holdup, a factor that insurance companies evaluate much more closely than the money loss when they determine your exposure to risk.

• *Eliminate any "trip and fall" hazards* as quickly as possible. That may mean getting rid of low lighting, which may be aesthetically pleasing but can make steps too dangerous. Of course, the advice also applies to loose wires and other obstructions.

The aisles should be clear. Overcongestion creates a number of problems for the waiters walking around with hot food or breakable items as well as for the customers.

• *Provide in-step illumination* on any steps of the premises.

• *Insist on proper maintenance.* If your restaurant is carpeted, take care of any rips or tears immediately. Otherwise, a customer can twist her heel, fracture her hip, and sue you for damages.

COMMON ERRORS IN PURCHASE OF FOODSERVICE EQUIPMENT

CHECKLIST

- Faucets—responsibility of what contractor?
- Disconnects—gas or electric needed?
- Floor drains—have we allowed for drains?
- Hand sinks—has Health Department approved locations?
- Drains for beverage machines—shown on plan?
- Foot pedals for hand sinks—or will regular faucets be used?
- Inner plumbing connections—whose responsibility?
- Exposed piping chrome—is chrome or standard pipe specified?
- Ventilator connections—what contract is responsible?
- Voltage—has power been verified?
- Total amps—adequate?
- Phase—one or three or both?
- Cords, plugs, and receptacles—to be installed by whom?
- Options—have we verified all options for equipment needed?
- Field checks—will contractor verify all conditions?
- Door openings—are they adequate?
- Heights and ceiling height—known for hood clearance and other equipment?

FOODSERVICE REGULATIONS COMMONLY OVERLOOKED

Dishwashing Facilities—Alternatives

1. A commercial dishwasher with a final rinse of at least 180°F.
2. A three (3)-compartment sink of adequate size *with drainboards* (minimum requirement, including the cleaning of pots and pans).
3. A three (3)-compartment sink with drainboards for bar glasses.
4. Any other facilities with specific approval of the Health Department.

Food Holding and Storage Facilities

1. Adequate facilities for storing potentially hazardous foods at 45°F or below.
2. Adequate facilities for holding potentially hazardous foods either at 45°F or below or at 140°F or above while being displayed for service or pending service.

Handwashing Facilities

1. Conveniently located within or adjacent to food preparation areas as well as restrooms.
2. Equipped with hot and cold potable running water, hand cleanser, and approved hand-drying devices.

Restroom Facilities

1. Walls must be of a light color, smooth, nonabsorbent, and washable.
2. Public restrooms are required when the seating capacity is 20 or more.
3. The number of toilet facilities required is directly proportional to the seating capacity.
4. Ventilation to the exterior is done mechanically or by screened windows.
5. Doors are self-closing.

Floor Finish Material

1. Floors in all food preparation, food storage, and utensil-washing areas, behind bars, in walk-in refrigerators, in dressing or locker rooms, in handwashing areas, and in toilet rooms are to be constructed of smooth, durable, nonabsorbent, and easily cleanable materials such as ceramic tile, quarry tile, durable grades of linoleum, etc.
2. The junctures between floors and walls in the above areas are to be covered.
3. Carpeting is allowed only in lounges and dining areas.

Water Supply and Sewage Disposal

1. Private water supplies and sewage disposal systems must be specifically acceptable to the Health Department and are primary considerations in the issuance of foodservice permits.

Plumbing

1. The water lines supplying equipment such as dishwashing machines and toilet facilities must be equipped with vacuum breakers.

PLANNING CHECKLIST

The following list of general items is very important to both new and older foodservice operations. A quick review of the list may reveal omissions in the planning process.

- Local code approvals
    - Building
    - Health
    - Fire
- Phone booths
- Vending machines
- Fly–rodent protection
- Manager's office
- Soiled linen area
- Delivery areas
- Emergency lighting
- Illuminated signs
- Coatroom area
- Lockers
- Janitor closets
- Smoking areas
- Security systems
- Disabled provisions
- Alarm system
- Water softener

ACKNOWLEDGMENTS

Material in the sections on "Foodservice Equipment Contracts" and "Agreements with Consultants" has been reprinted courtesy of Ideal Food Service Equipment. Material included under "A Guide for the Review of Food-Establishment Plans and Specifications" is from the Food Service Division of the New York State Department of Health, and is based on federal guidelines. Philip J. Miller of Kornreich Insurance Services is the author of "10 Steps to Ensure Restaurants Get Insurance."

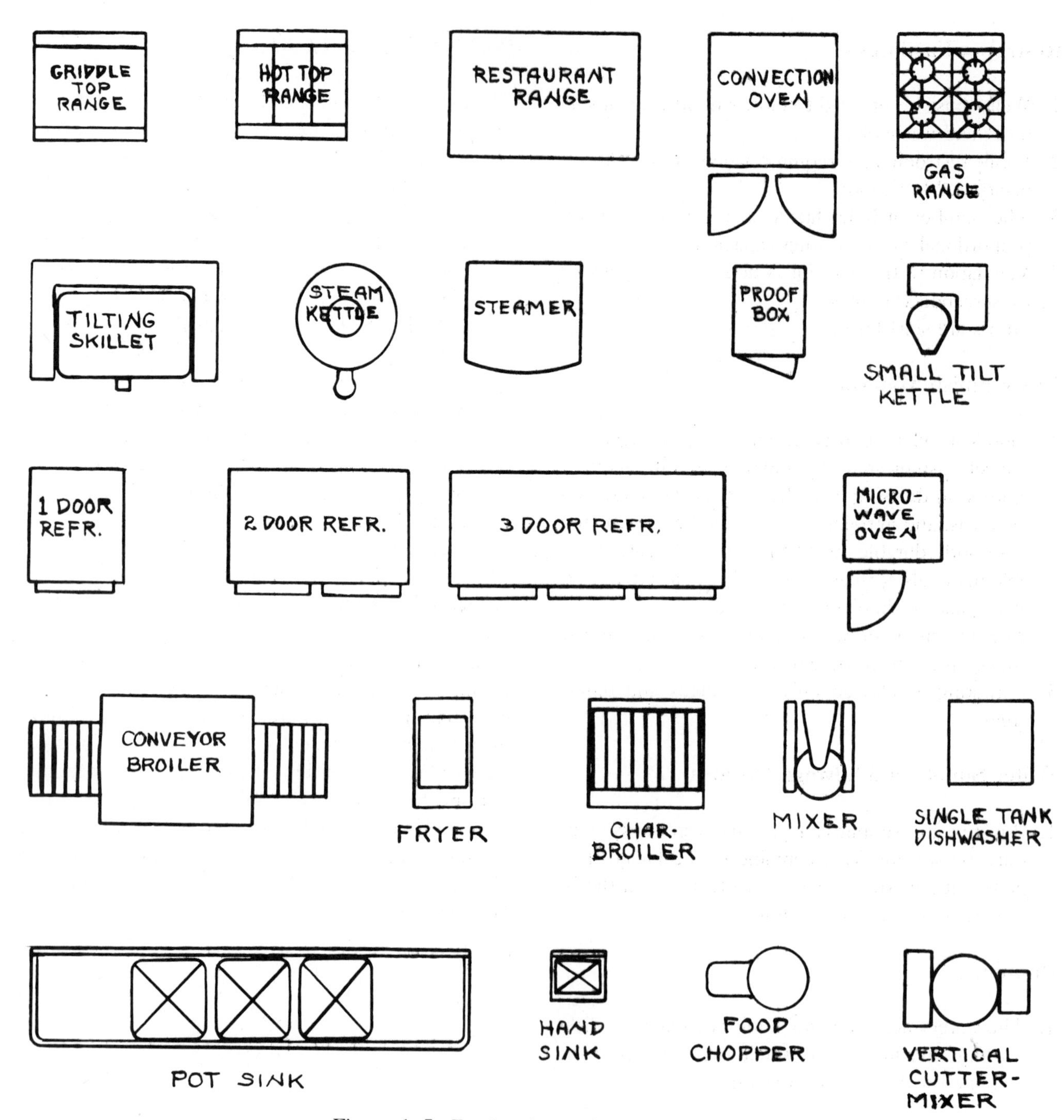

Figure 1-5. Foodservice equipment templates.

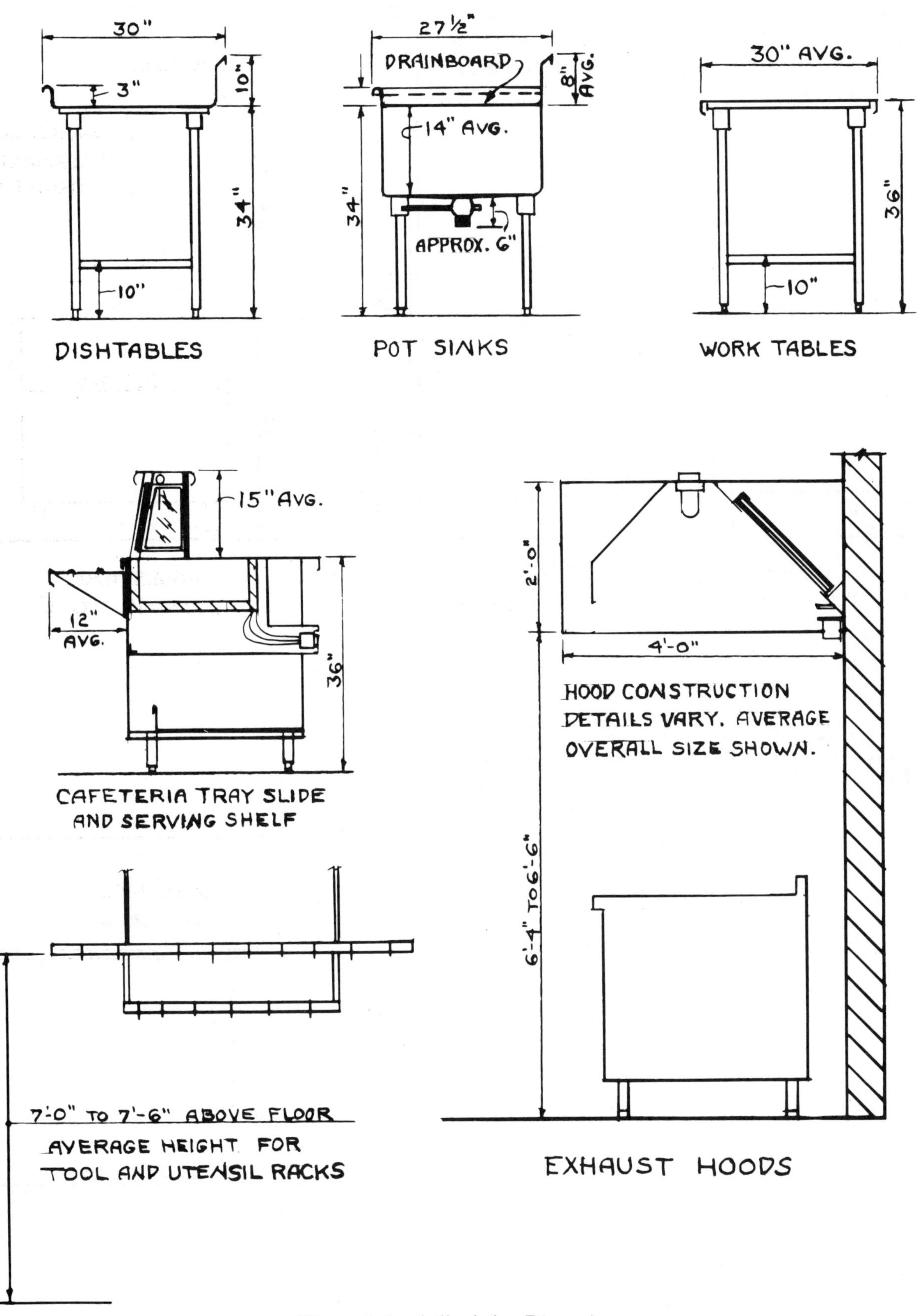

Figure 1-6a, 1-6b, 1-6c. Dimensions.

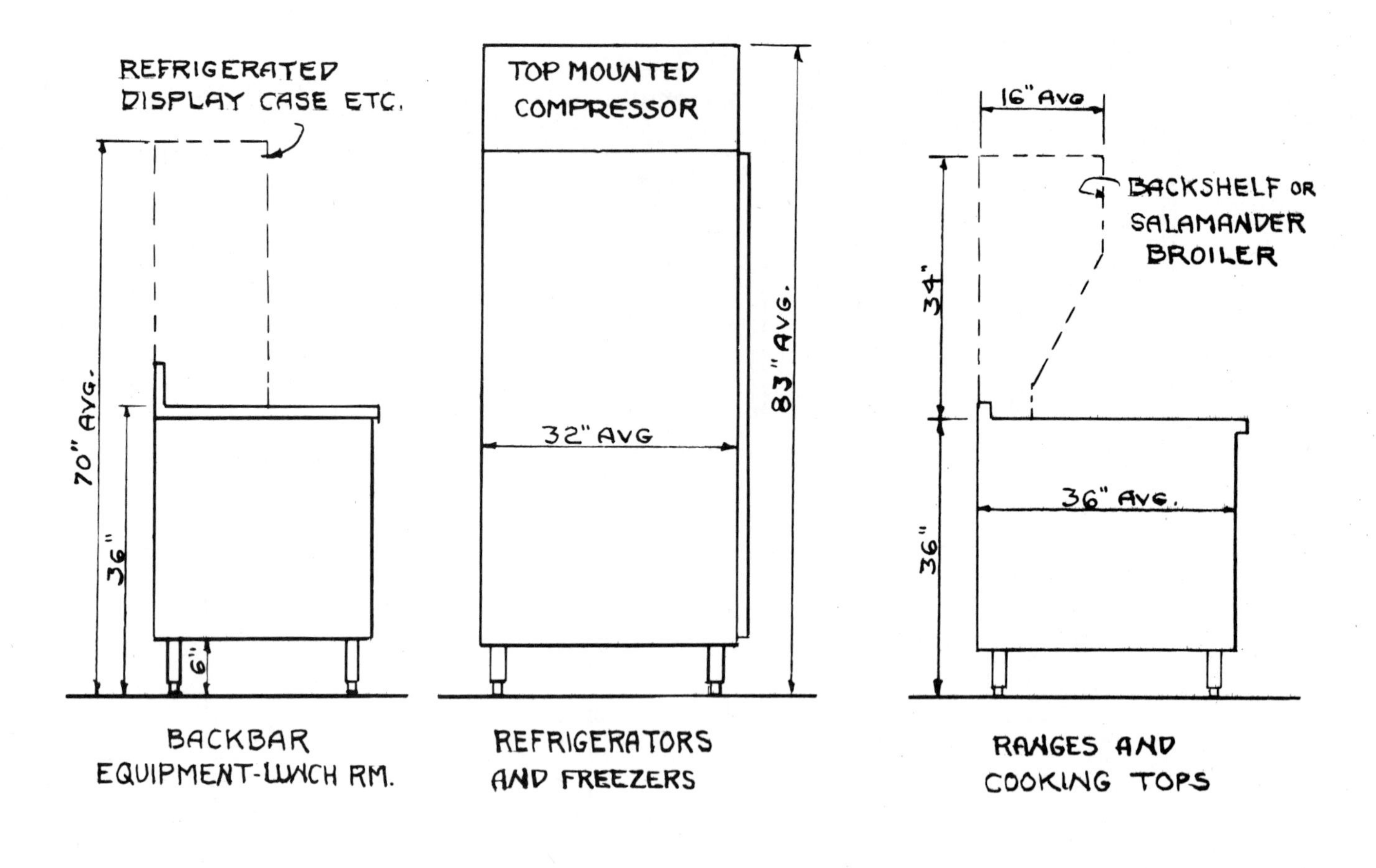

REFRIGERATED DISPLAY CASE ETC.
70" AVG.
36"
6"
BACKBAR EQUIPMENT-LUNCH RM.
TOP MOUNTED COMPRESSOR
32" AVG
83" AVG.
REFRIGERATORS AND FREEZERS
16" AVG
BACKSHELF OR SALAMANDER BROILER
34"
36" AVG.
36"
RANGES AND COOKING TOPS

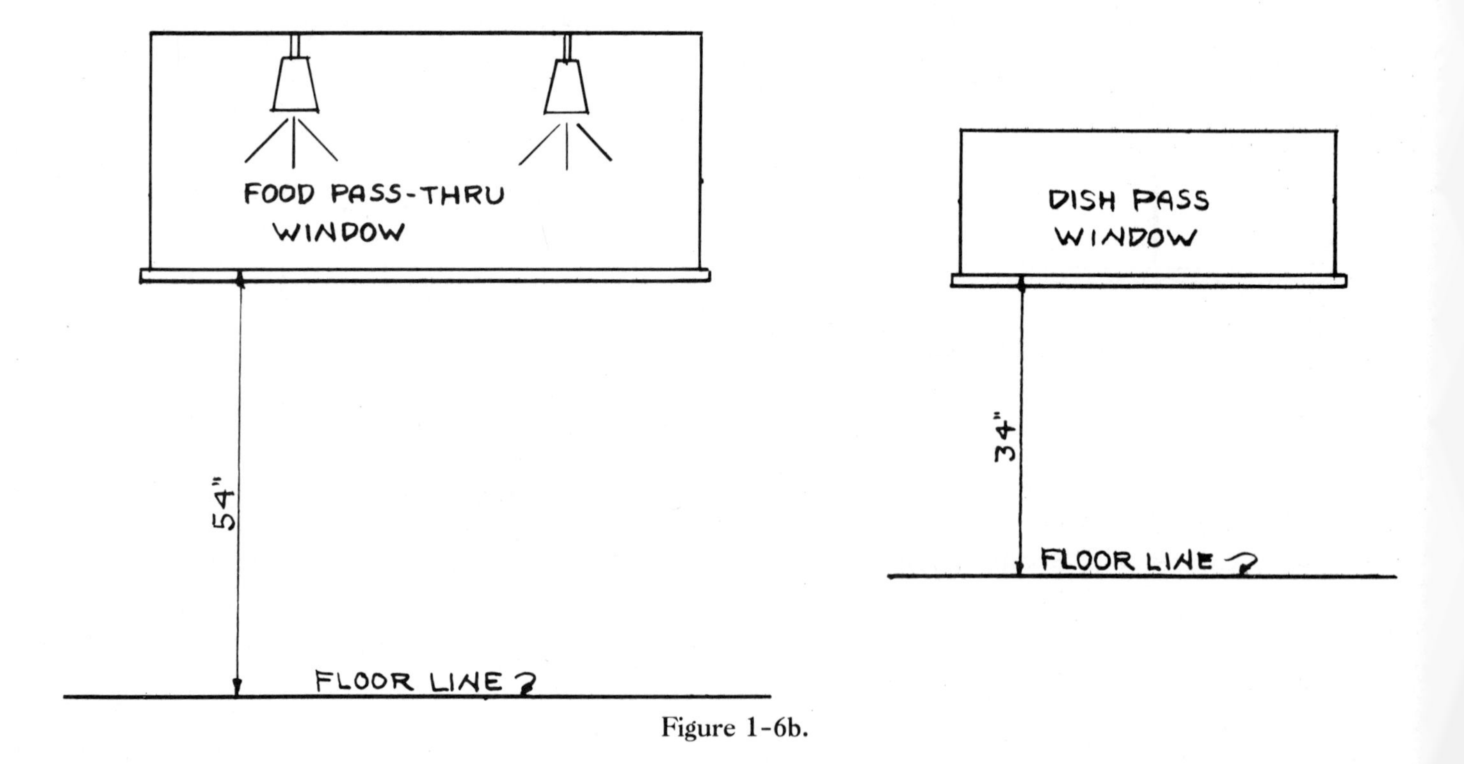

FOOD PASS-THRU WINDOW
54"
FLOOR LINE
DISH PASS WINDOW
34"
FLOOR LINE

Figure 1-6b.

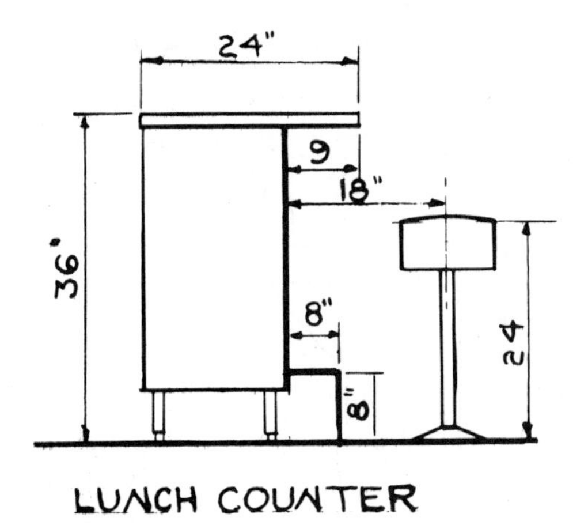

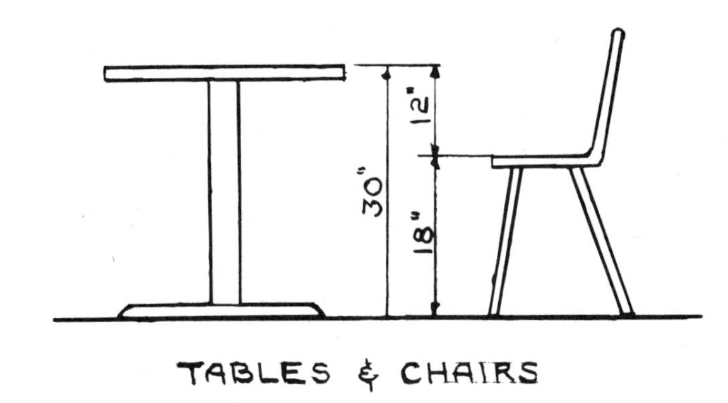

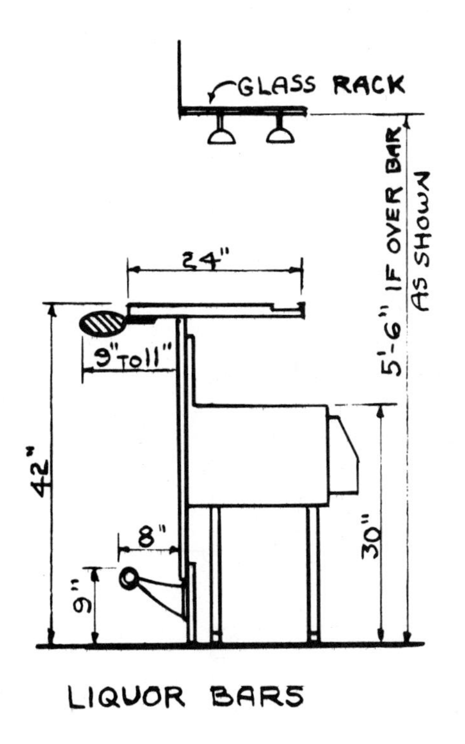

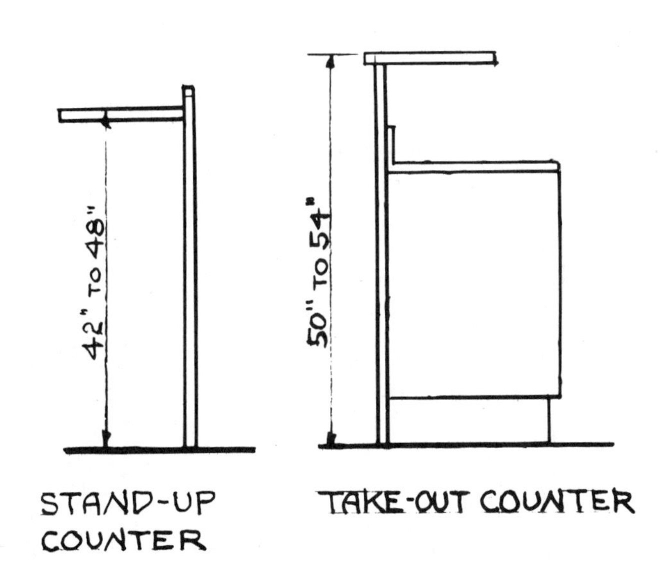

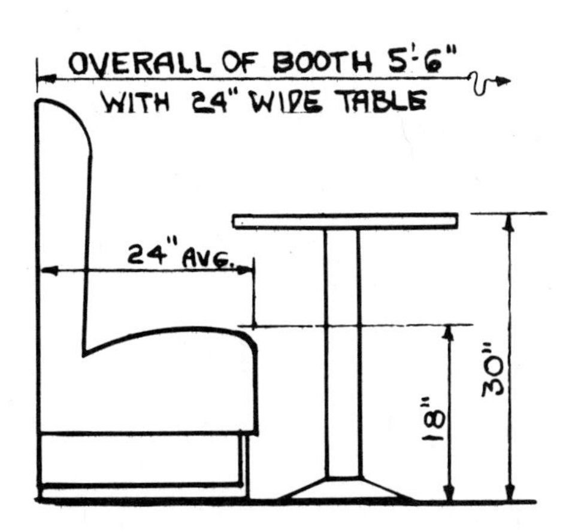

AVERAGE SPACE ALLOCATON IN DINING ROOMS IS FROM 10 TO 15 SQ. FT. PER PERSON.
10□' PER PERSON WOULD BE TIGHT BANQUET SEATING.
12□' PER PERSON IS AVERAGE.
15□' PER PERSON TENDS TO LUXURIOUS.

Figure 1-6c.

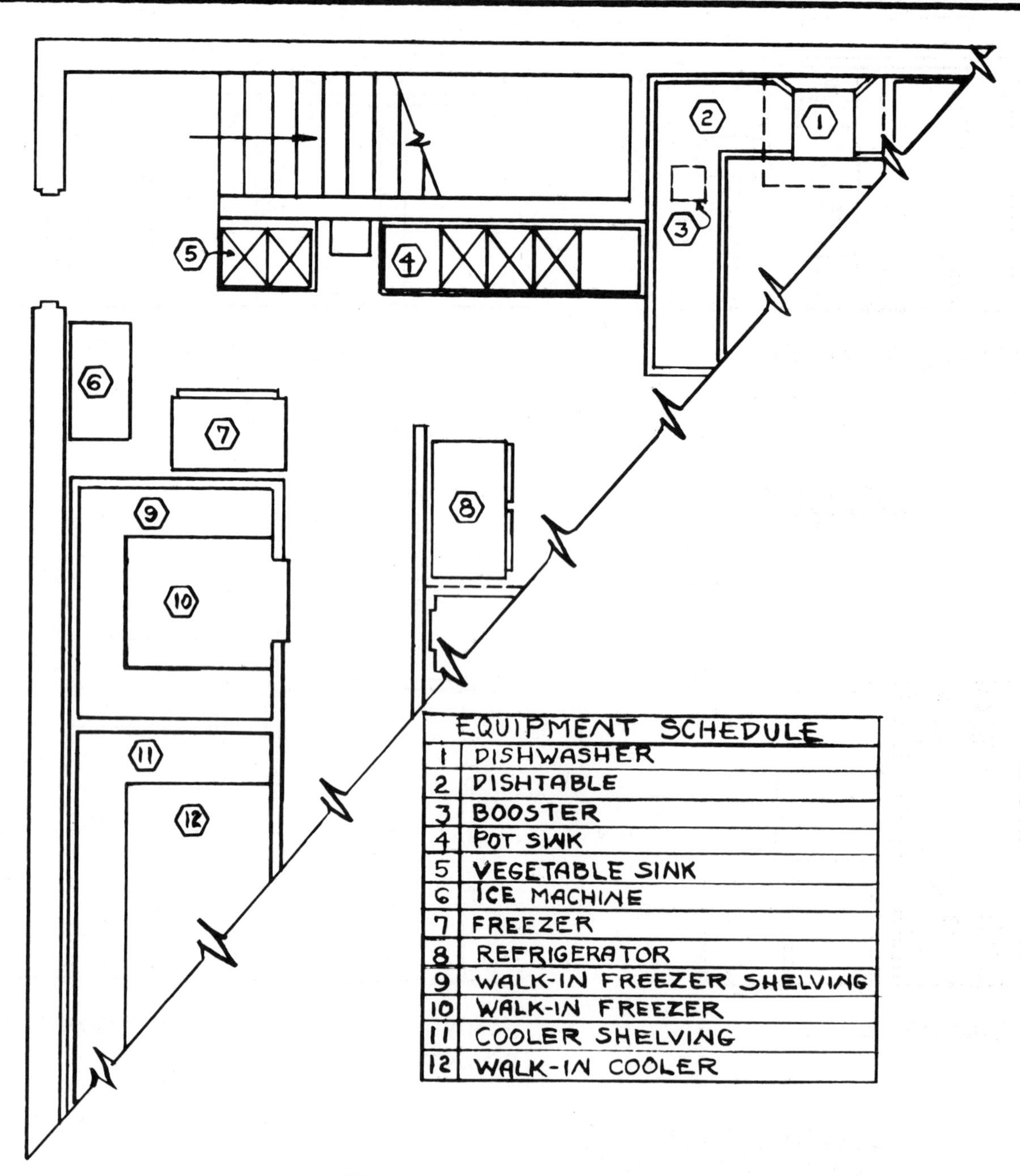

EQUIPMENT SCHEDULE
1 DISHWASHER
2 DISHTABLE
3 BOOSTER
4 POT SINK
5 VEGETABLE SINK
6 ICE MACHINE
7 FREEZER
8 REFRIGERATOR
9 WALK-IN FREEZER SHELVING
10 WALK-IN FREEZER
11 COOLER SHELVING
12 WALK-IN COOLER

Figure 1-7. Equipment layout.

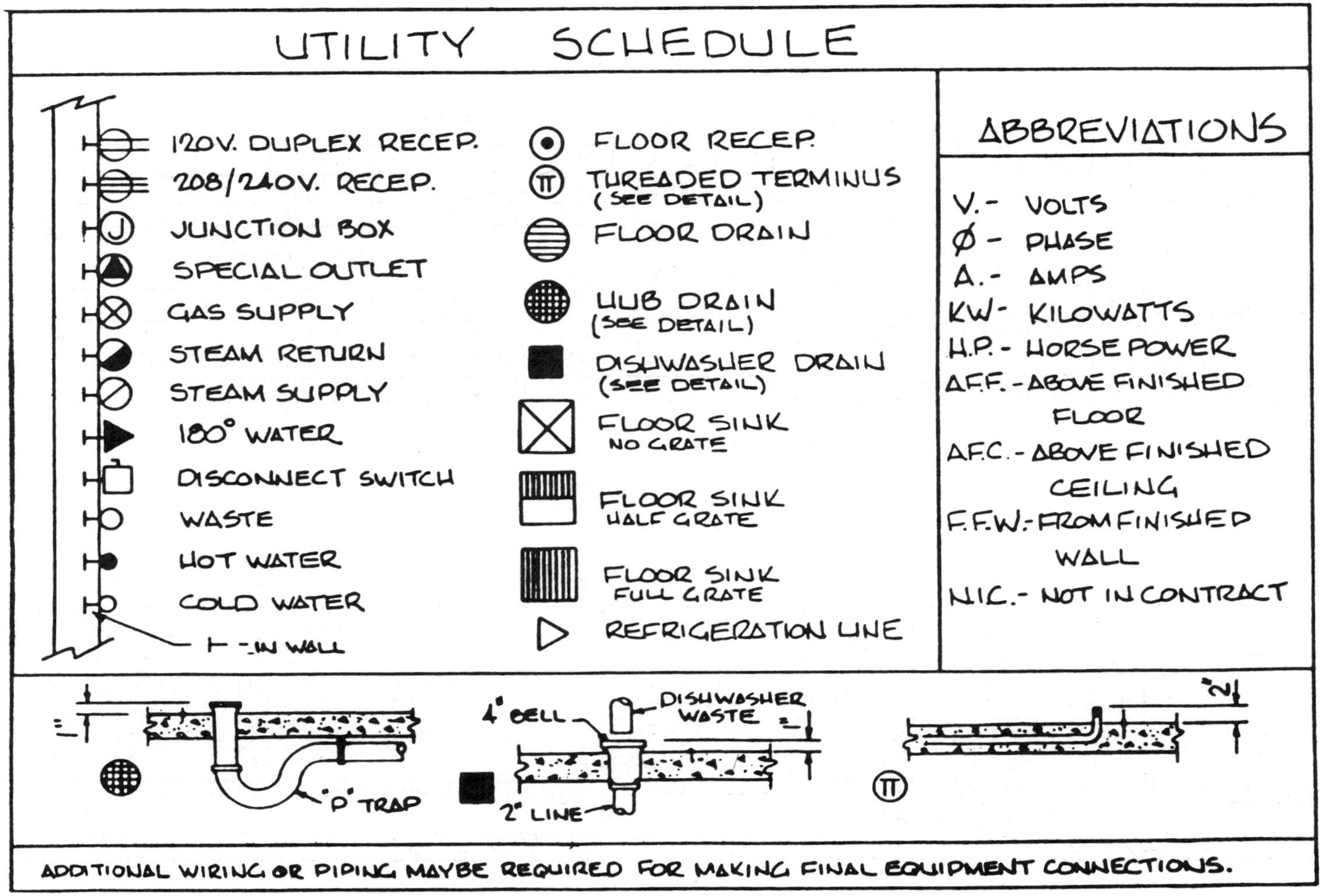

UTILITY SCHEDULE

120V. DUPLEX RECEP.
208/240V. RECEP.
JUNCTION BOX
SPECIAL OUTLET
GAS SUPPLY
STEAM RETURN
STEAM SUPPLY
180° WATER
DISCONNECT SWITCH
WASTE
HOT WATER
COLD WATER
⊢ - IN WALL

FLOOR RECEP.
THREADED TERMINUS (SEE DETAIL)
FLOOR DRAIN
HUB DRAIN (SEE DETAIL)
DISHWASHER DRAIN (SEE DETAIL)
FLOOR SINK NO GRATE
FLOOR SINK HALF GRATE
FLOOR SINK FULL GRATE
REFRIGERATION LINE

ABBREVIATIONS

V. - VOLTS
Ø - PHASE
A. - AMPS
KW - KILOWATTS
H.P. - HORSE POWER
A.F.F. - ABOVE FINISHED FLOOR
A.F.C. - ABOVE FINISHED CEILING
F.F.W. - FROM FINISHED WALL
N.I.C. - NOT IN CONTRACT

1"
"P" TRAP
4" BELL
DISHWASHER WASTE
1"
2" LINE
2"

ADDITIONAL WIRING OR PIPING MAYBE REQUIRED FOR MAKING FINAL EQUIPMENT CONNECTIONS.

Figure 1-8. Typical utility schedule used on foodservice plans.

GENERAL							ELECTRICAL		
ITEM NO.	MODEL NO.	EQUIPMENT IDENTIFICATION	MANUFACTURED BY	DIMENSIONS IN INCHES					
				WIDTH	DEPTH	HEIGHT	VOLTS	PHASE	AMPS
1	B20	MIXER	BLAKESLEE	18 1/8	22	30 3/4	120	1	8.2
2	H339-128-3	HOLDING CABINET	CRES COR	17 5/8	25 3/16	36 3/4	120	1	10
3	MIRACLEAN	48" GRIDDLE	KEATING	48 3/16	38	17	208/240	3	
4	COS-1015	COMBI-OVEN/STEAMER	RATIONAL	40	40	33	208	3	52
5	6514	COFFEE MACHINE	SILEX	8 3/4	14	18	120	1	14.1
6	DFG-101-3	CONVECTION OVEN	BLODGETT	38 1/8	38 7/8	57	120	1	9

ELECTRICAL CONTINUED												PLUMBING					APPROVALS			
ITEM NO.	PHASE LEG AMPS			KW OR KVA	HP	No. OF POLES	BRKR. REQD.	No. OF WIRES	CORD LGTH.	NEMA STD.		H.W	C.W.	WASTE	GAS	B.T.U.	U.L.	NSF		A.G.A.
	L-1	L-2	L-3							CORD	PLUG							STD.	SEAL	
1				.9	1/2	1	A	3	6'0"	5-15	5-15						*	3,4,8	325	
2				1.2		1	A	3	6'0"	5-15	5-15						*	2,4,7	180	
3	28-36	18-24	28-36	14.4		3	50	3		10-50	10-50						*	4	387	
4	52	52	52	18		3	60	3					3/4"	1"			*	2	314	
5				1.7		1	A	3	5'-3"	5-15	5-15		1/4"				*	4	163	
6					1/3	1	A	3	6'0"	5-15	5-15				3/4	55,000	*	2	278	*

Figure 1-8a. Typical mechanical job schedule.

ELECTRIC SYMBOLS AND NOTES STANDARDS*

GENERAL

- Conduit stub flush couple with curb
- Flex tubing feeder (36" minimum exposed)
- Waterproof conduit stub
- Junction box, waterproof with final connection to equipment (36" min. seal tight flex.)
- Junction box at ceiling
- Junction box at wall
- Junction box above floor
- Junction box with final connection to equipment (36" minimum exposed)
- Junction box installed in equipment
- Single convenience outlet (wattage as shown)
- Duplex convenience outlet (wattage as shown)
- Single convenience outlet w/switch
- Duplex convenience outlet (installed in equipment)
- Single purpose power outlet, 1 phase
- Single purpose power outlet, 1 phase (installed in equipment)
- Single purpose power outlet, 3 phase
- Single purpose power outlet, 3 phase (installed in equipment)
- Floor outlet, flush or pedestal
- Floor junction box
- Recessed convenience outlet, single (wattage as shown)
- 120V Motor
- 208–240 V 1 phase motor
- 208–240 V 3 phase motor
- Clock outlet
- Ground connection
- Buzzer
- Infrared warmer
- Heat lamp
- Incandescent light (number when scheduled)
- Pull box (installed in equipment)

*Reprinted from "NEWS AND VIEWS," Food Equipment Distributors Association, January, 1977.

Figure 1-9. Electrical symbols. (Courtesy National Sanitation Foundation)

SWITCHES

S	Switch
S_3	3-way switch
S_4	4-way switch
S_P	Switch with neon pilot
S_{VP}	Vaporproof switch
S_D	Automatic door switch
S_{2WP}	Double pole waterproof switch
(P)	Pull switch
	Push button switch

LIGHTING

	Incandescent strip (number when scheduled)
	Fluorescent fixture (number when scheduled)
	Fluorescent strip light (number when scheduled)
	Wall washer light (number when scheduled)
---	Neon tubing
	Exit light
T	Transformer
	Lighting panel
	Power panel

REFRIGERATION

(T)	Thermostat
	High temperature alarm relay w/red light and bell
	Safety alarm bell w/red light
	Vaporproof light — 100 watts
	Evaporator (blower coil) w/fan
S_L	Liquid line solenoid
===	Conduit run for refrigerant, Co, gas and carbonation lines
	Pull box

Figure 1-9. (*continued*)

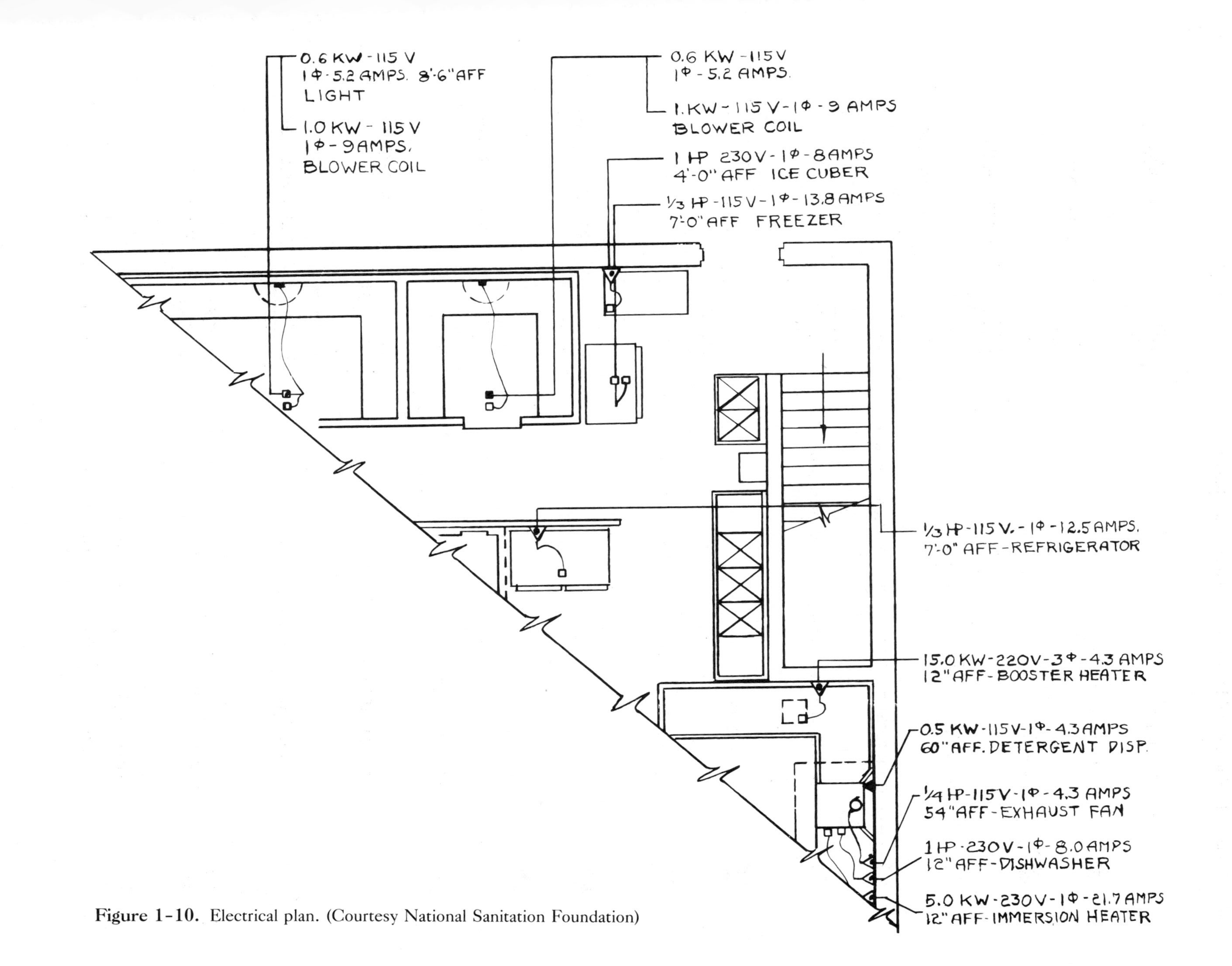

Figure 1-10. Electrical plan. (Courtesy National Sanitation Foundation)

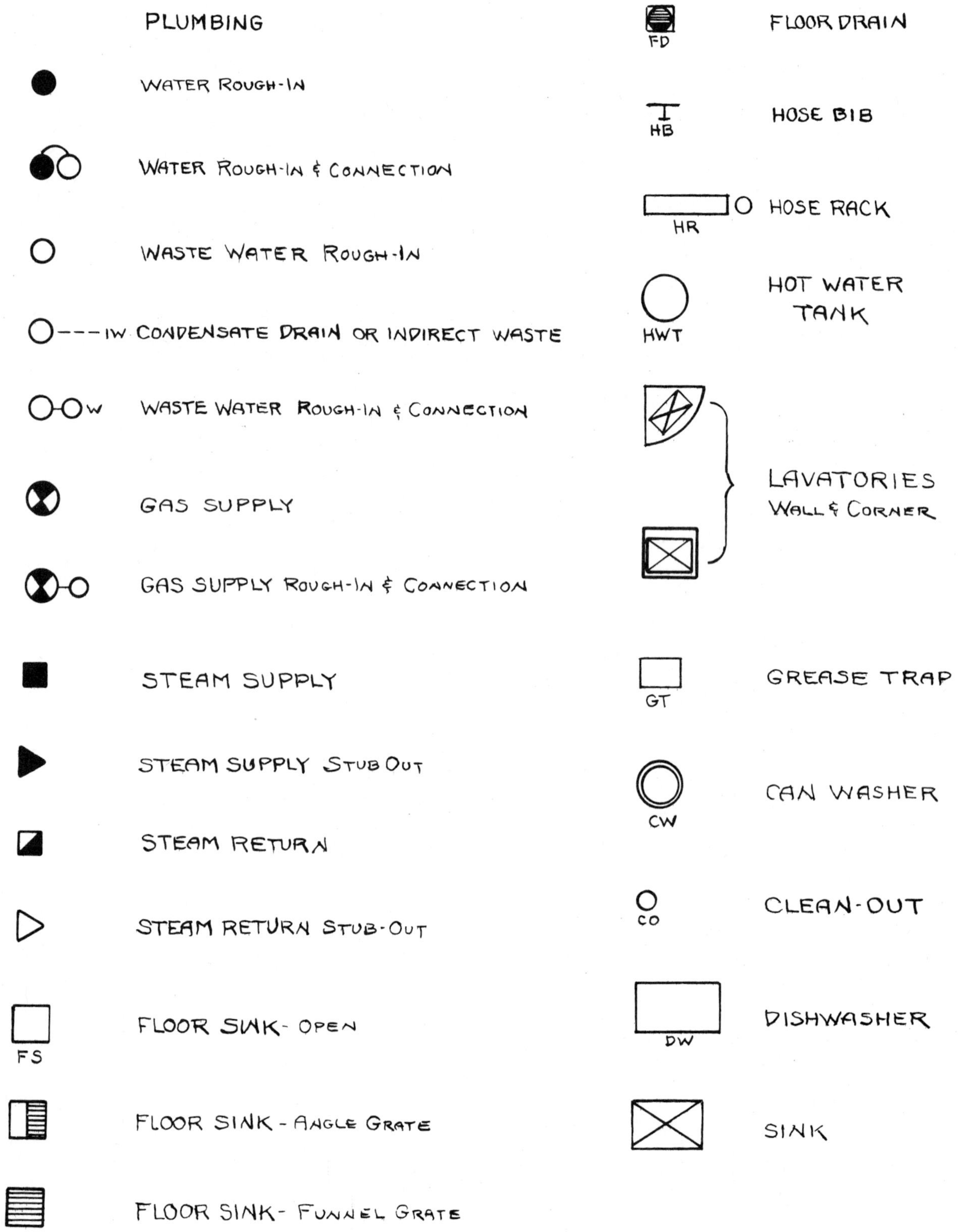

PLUMBING

	WATER ROUGH-IN	FD	FLOOR DRAIN
	WATER ROUGH-IN & CONNECTION	HB	HOSE BIB
	WASTE WATER ROUGH-IN	HR	HOSE RACK
---IW	CONDENSATE DRAIN OR INDIRECT WASTE	HWT	HOT WATER TANK
W	WASTE WATER ROUGH-IN & CONNECTION		LAVATORIES WALL & CORNER
	GAS SUPPLY		
	GAS SUPPLY ROUGH-IN & CONNECTION		
	STEAM SUPPLY	GT	GREASE TRAP
	STEAM SUPPLY STUB OUT	CW	CAN WASHER
	STEAM RETURN		
	STEAM RETURN STUB-OUT	CO	CLEAN-OUT
FS	FLOOR SINK-OPEN	DW	DISHWASHER
	FLOOR SINK-ANGLE GRATE		SINK
	FLOOR SINK-FUNNEL GRATE		

Figure 1-11. Plumbing symbols. (Courtesy National Sanitation Foundation)

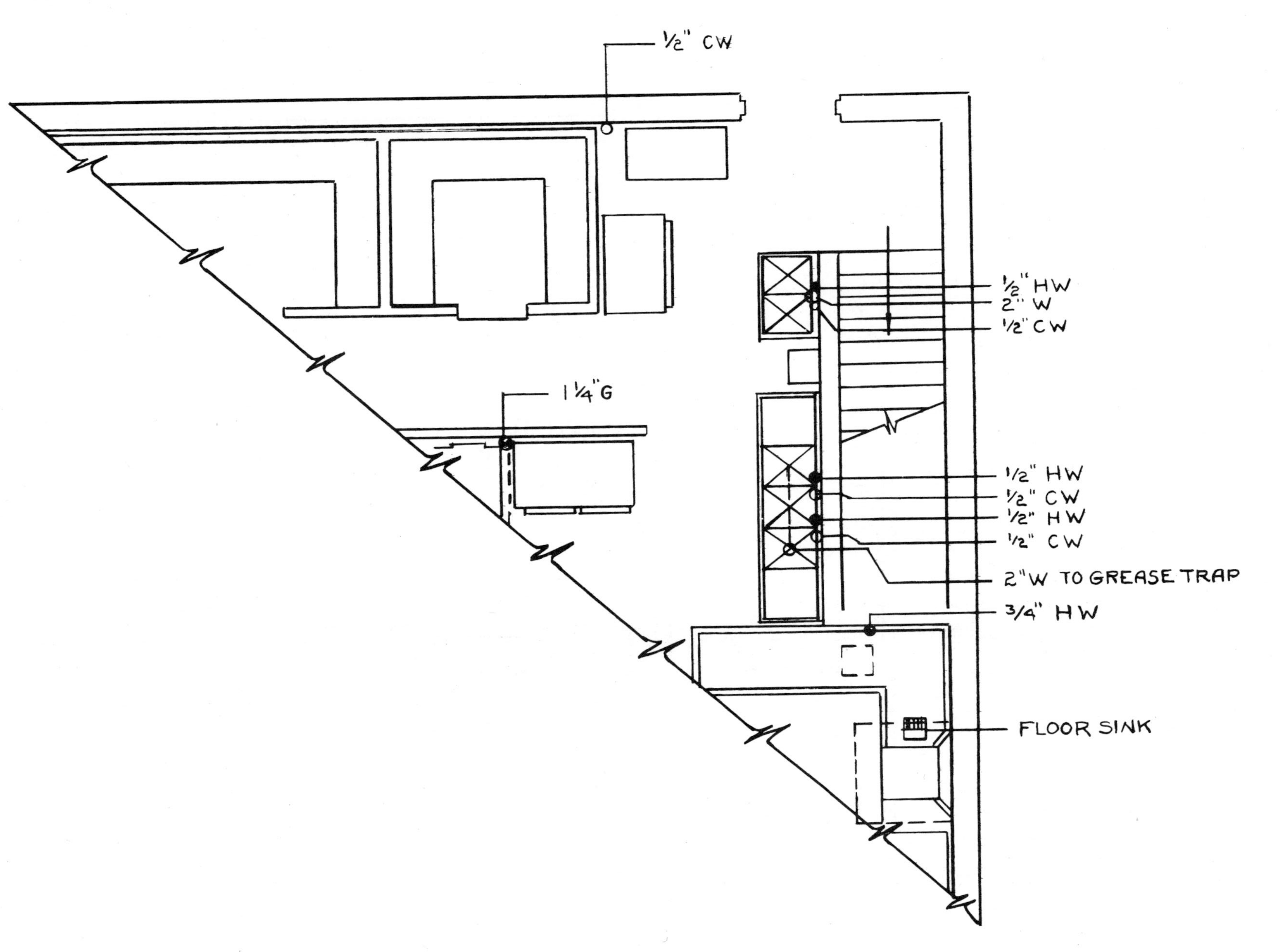

Figure 1-12. Plumbing plan (Courtesy National Sanitation Foundation)

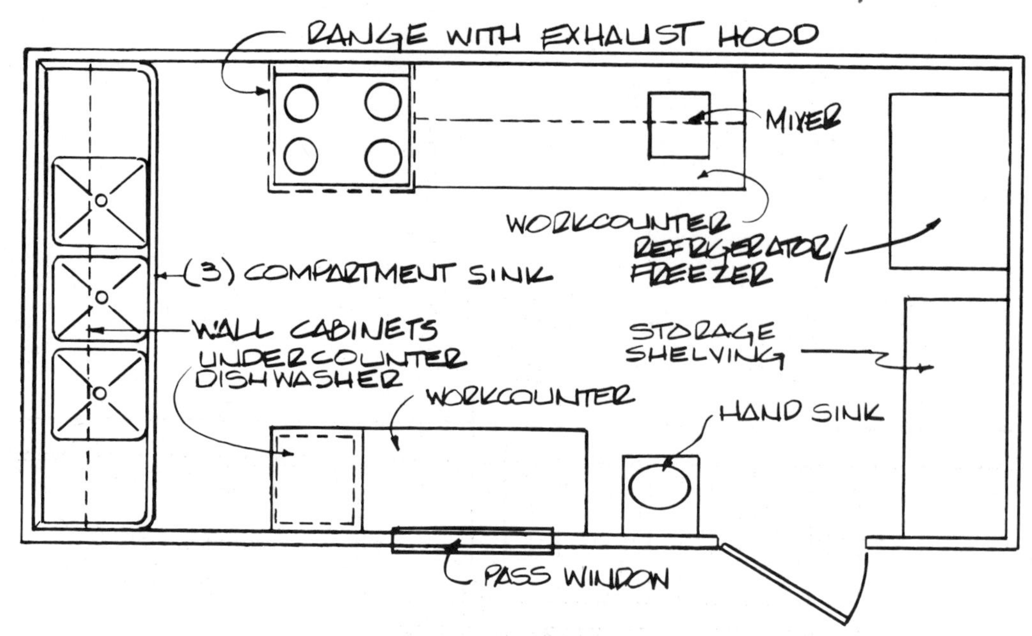

Figure 1-13. Small, specialized kitchen.

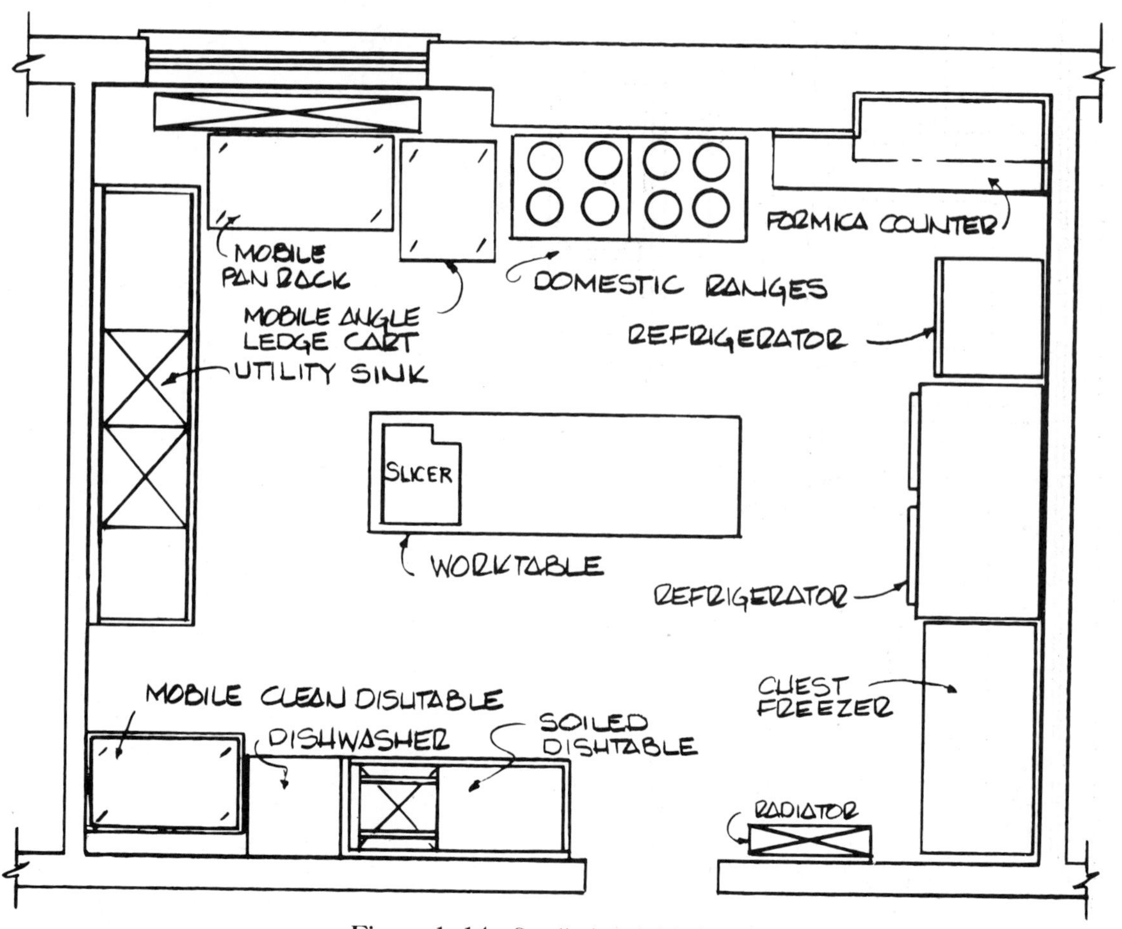

Figure 1-14. Small church kitchen.

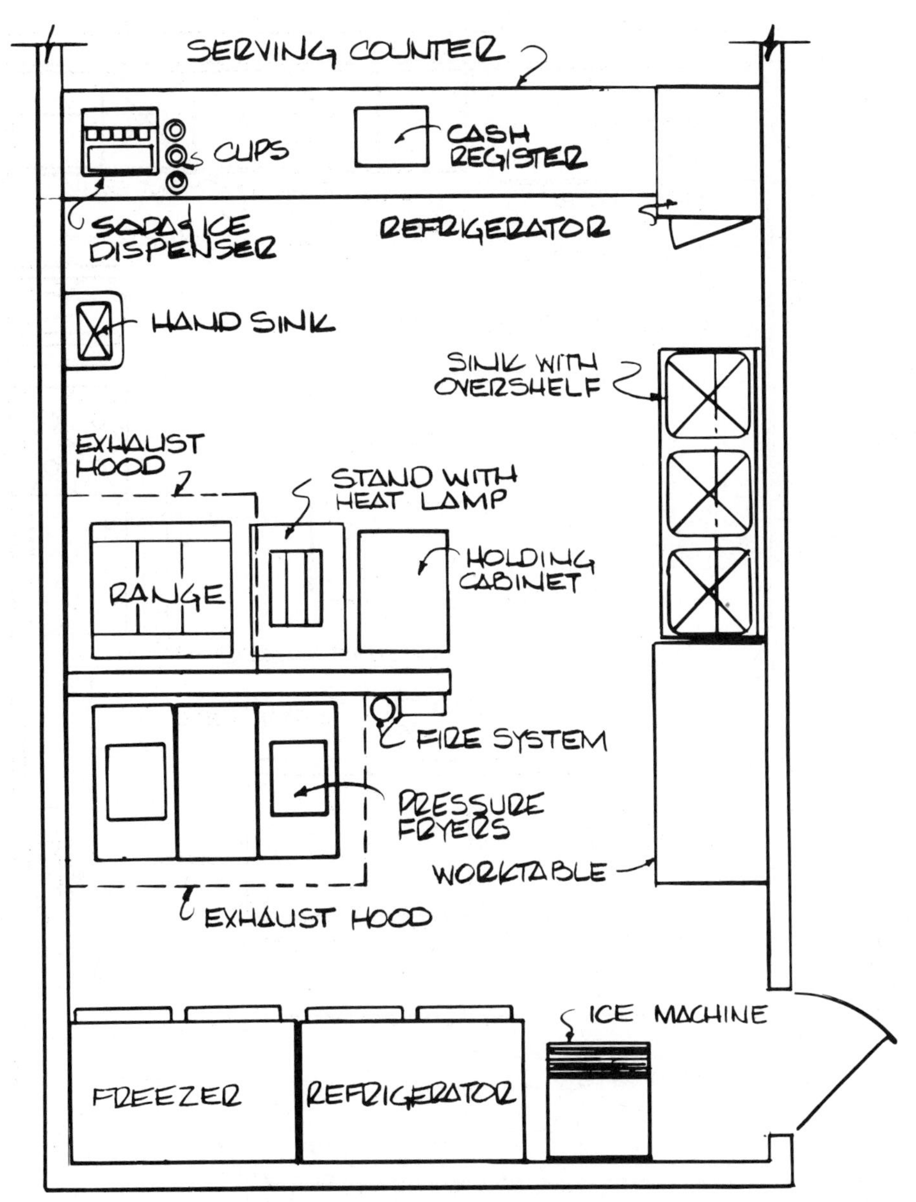

Figure 1-15. Sample fast food layout.

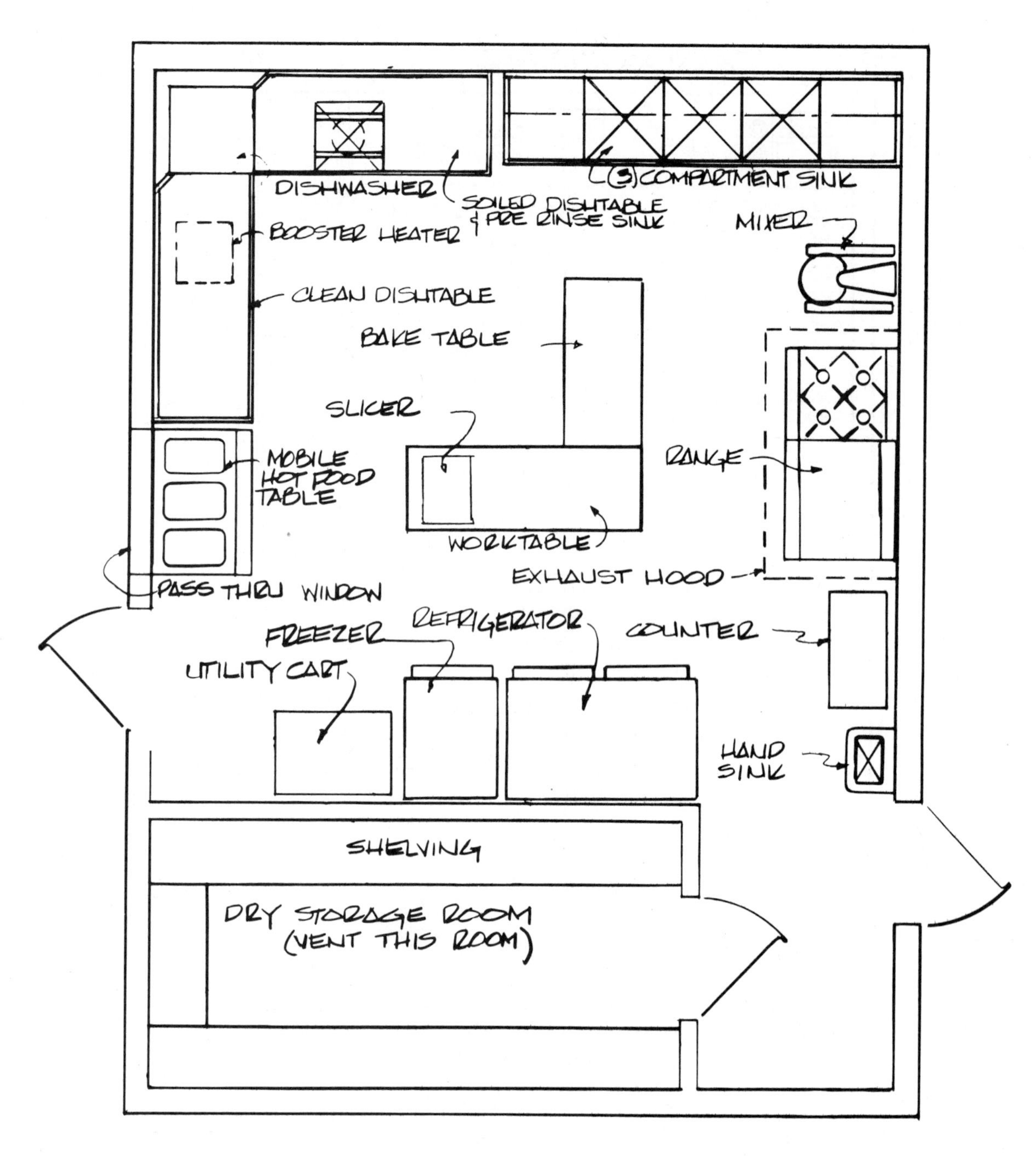

Figure 1-16. Compact kitchen.

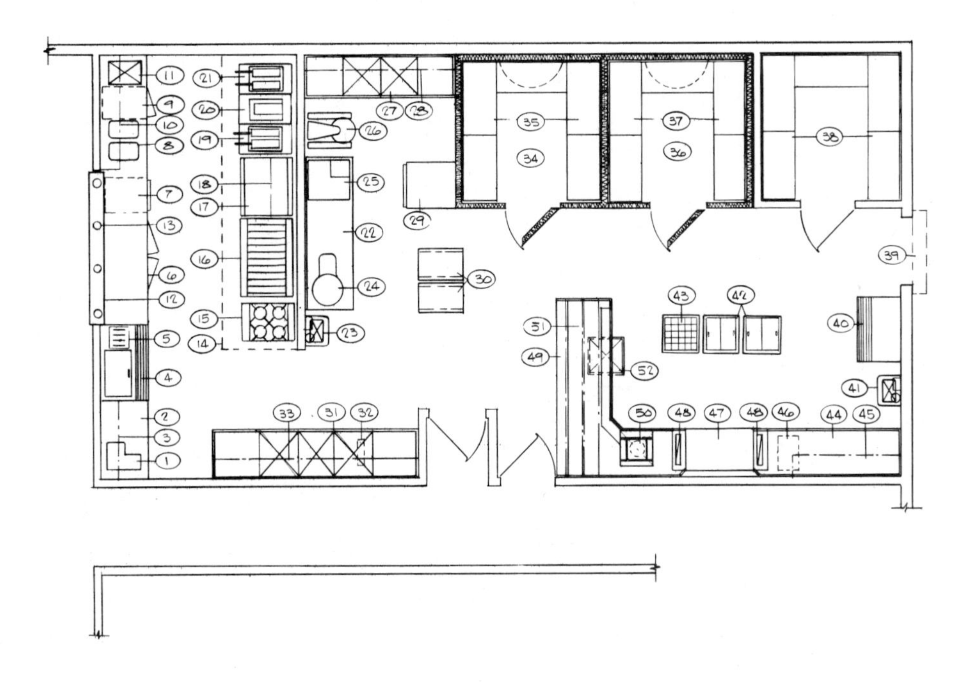

EQUIPMENT LIST

ITEM	DESCRIPTION
1	SLICER
2	WORKCOUNTER
3	WALLSHELF
4	SANDWICH UNIT
5	TOASTER
6	REFRIGERATED BASE
7	ROLL WARMER
8	(2) HOT FOOD UNITS
9	UNDERCOUNTER FREEZER
10	NEW SHELF
11	COUNTER W/SINK
12	PASS THRU SHELF
13	HEAT LAMPS
14	EXHAUST HOOD W/FIRE SYSTEM
15	(2) BURNER RANGE
16	CHAR BROILER
17	GRIDDLE TOP RANGE
18	CHEESE MELTER
19	FRYER
20	FRYER FILTER W/HEAT LAMP
21	FRYER
22	WORKTABLE
23	HAND SINK
24	FOOD CUTTER
25	SLICER
26	MIXER
27	VEGETABLE PREP SINK
28	OVERSHELF
29	REFRIGERATOR
30	PAN RACKS
31	POT & PAN SINK
32	SINK HEATER
33	OVERSHELF
34	WALK IN COOLER
35	WALK IN COOLER SHELVING
36	WALK IN FREEZER
37	WALK IN FREEZER SHELVING
38	STORAGE ROOM SHELVING
39	AIR CURTAIN FAN
40	ICE MACHINE
41	HAND SINK
42	DISHCARTS
43	RACK DOLLY
44	CLEAN DISHTABLE
45	OVERSHELF
46	BOOSTER HEATER
47	DISHWASHER
48	DISHWASHER PANT LLG DUCTS
49	SOILED DISHTABLE
50	DISPENSER
51	RACKSHELF
52	SOAK SINK

Figure 1-17. Family style restaurant.

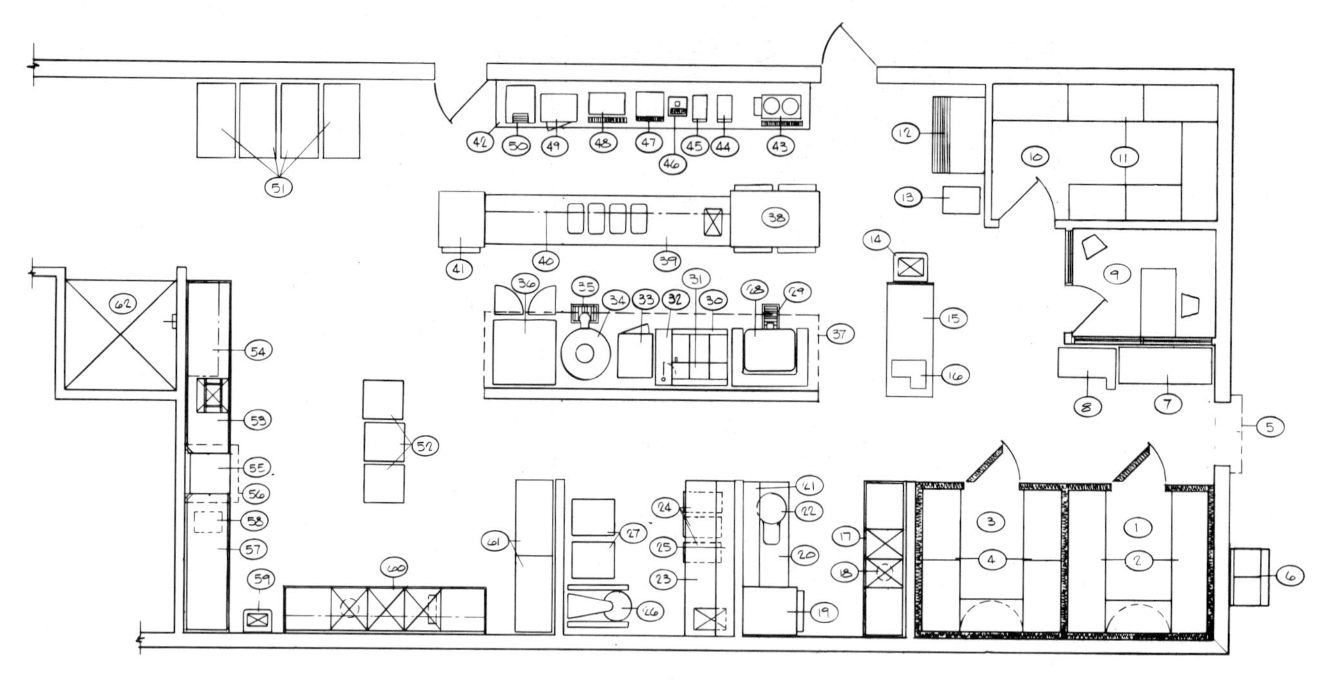

EQUIPMENT LIST

ITEM	DESCRIPTION
1	WALK IN FREEZER
2	WALK IN FREEZER SHELVING
3	WALK IN COOLER
4	WALK IN COOLER SHELVING
5	AIR CURTAIN FAN
6	WALK IN COOLER/FREEZER COMPRESSORS
7	RECEIVING TABLE
8	SCALE
9	OFFICE
10	STORAGE ROOM
11	STORAGE ROOM SHELVING
12	ICE MACHINE
13	ICE CART
14	HAND SINK–TABLE MOUNTED
15	WORKTABLE
16	SLICER
17	VEGETABLE PREP SINK
18	DISPOSER
19	REFRIGERATOR
20	WORKTABLE
21	OVERSHELF
22	FOOD CUTTER
23	BAKE TABLE W/SINK
24	INGREDIENT BINS
25	OVERSHELF
26	MIXER
27	PROOF CABINETS
28	BRAISING PAN
29	FLOOR GRATE
30	HOT TOP RANGE W/OVEN
31	SALAMANDER BROILER
32	SPACER W/POT FILLER
33	STEAMER
34	40-GAL. KETTLE
35	FLOOR GRATE
36	CONVECTION OVEN
37	EXHAUST HOOD W/FIRE SYSTEM
38	PASS THRU REFRIGERATOR
39	HOT FOOD COUNTER W/SINK
40	OVERSHELF
41	FREEZER
42	BEVERAGE COUNTER
43	COFFEE URN
44	HOT CHOCOLATE DISPENSER
45	ICED TEA DISPENSER
46	WATER DISPENSER
47	JUICE DISPENSER
48	MILK DISPENSER
49	MICROWAVE OVEN
50	TOASTER
51	TRANSPORT CARTS
52	DISH CARTS
53	SOILED DISHTABLE
54	RACKSHELF
55	DISHWASHER
56	EXHAUST HOOD
57	CLEAN DISHTABLE
58	BOOSTER HEATER
59	HAND SINK
60	POT & PAN SINK W/DISPOSER SINK HEATER & OVERSHELF
61	CLEAN POT STORAGE SHELVING
62	CART WASH

Figure 1-18. Complete layout plan.

2

Receiving and Storage

In the drawings and text of this chapter the reader will find many desirable features of receiving areas along with shelf planning guides and construction details. Many unique specialized racks are shown, and many good ideas are presented for utilizing available areas for maximum storage. Refrigeration, the subject of Chapter 3, is discussed briefly here.

DRY FOOD STORAGE AREA

The dry food storage area should be convenient to the kitchen and delivery entrance with adequate precautions for security. (Dock and receiving area features are shown in Figures 2–1 through 2–3.)

Space and equipment should be provided for the orderly storage and protection of all foods. The shelf or pallet width plus 3 feet of aisle space is adequate.

Space requirements will vary with the number of meals served, the purchasing practices, and the frequency of deliveries. An allowance of one-third to one-half a square foot of floor space for each meal served per day is based on normal conditions and a two-week supply of staples, exclusive of space for nonfood storage.

The ventilation must be adequate to remove all offensive odors or fumes and to prevent condensation on walls or equipment.

A room temperature below 70°F should be maintained in the dry food storage area.

Equipment should include shelving, floor racks, or portable platforms.

Allow at least 1-inch clearance from walls and 6 inches from floor for air circulation and ease of cleaning; a minimum of 30 inches of aisle space for access to shelves is desirable, or 42 inches if portable platforms or platform trucks are to be used.

The first shelf should be at least 10 inches from the floor. Each shelf should be at least 10 inches wide, with 18 inches between shelves.

Locking devices, a security sash, and entrances to storage areas should be carefully planned.

Storage space is needed for cleaning supplies, disposables, and paper goods. This area should be separated from food storage to keep foods from absorbing chemical odors. It should be located adjacent to kitchen, dishwashing, and maintenance areas.

Windows are not recommended unless required by state and local regulations. Where windows are required, they should be equipped with a security-type sash, security screen, or security bars and located to avoid interference with shelving. To protect foods from direct sunlight, windows should be frosted.

Lighting and wiring should meet the National Electrical Code requirements (American Standard) together with local requirements. In order to provide adequate lighting for the storage area, illumination levels of approximately 15 foot candles are desirable; this is normally achieved by about 2 watts per square foot of

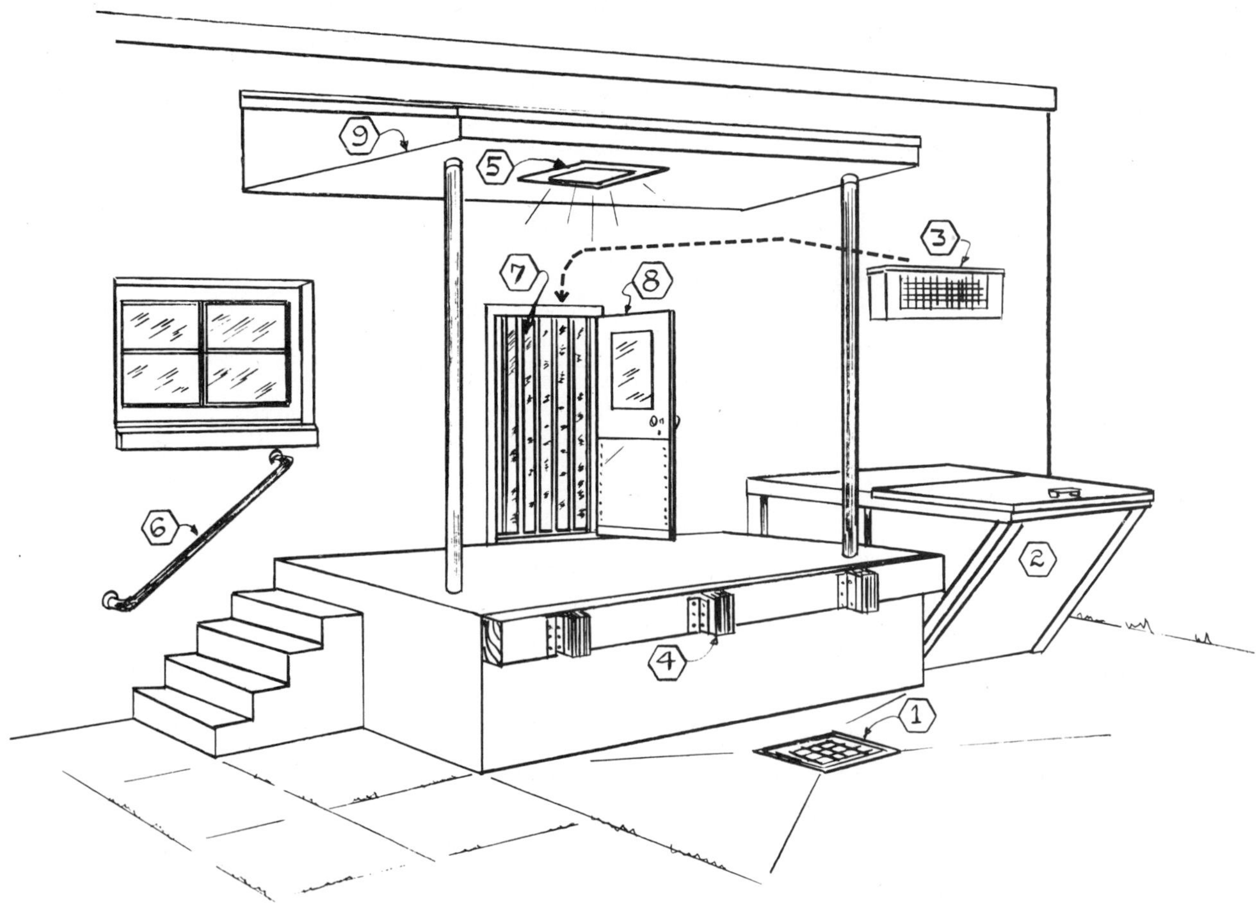

Figure 2-1. Desirable dock area features: (1) drain for hose down; (2) adequate dumpster–compactor area; (3) fly-chasing machine; (4) bumper docks; (5) good lighting; (6) hand rail; (7) air strips; (8) wide stainless-steel-lined door with window; (9) overhang. Physical layout and budget constraints usually do not allow for the ideal design, but many large institutions share common receiving areas, and some of these features could be incorporated into other areas as well.

floor area. For best distribution of light, the fixtures should be centered over each aisle.

Wherever foods are stored, a reliable easy-to-read thermometer is essential, to ensure that proper temperatures are maintained to prevent spoilage and deterioration. Wall thermometers are suitable for the dry food storage area, mounted in the vicinity of doors where there is little danger of breakage from bumping, and at about eye level for easy reading. Thermometers should not be mounted on a door, near a light bulb, or in a recessed pocket. Some of the characteristics of a good wall thermometer are: overall length of approximately 12 inches; mounting holes at top and bottom; a temperature range of −20°F to +120°F, in 2° increments; a red, liquid-filled or mercury-filled, magnifying glass tube for easy reading; a rust-resistant scale; full protection of the thermometer bulb and tube by side flanges on the frame, to avoid breakage.

Good ventilation in the dry food storage area is essential for the proper storage of any type of food. Ventilation helps retard the growth of various types of bacteria and molds, prevents mustiness and rusting of metal containers, and minimizes caking of ground or powdered foods, by helping to control the temperature and humidity. A temperature between 50°F and 70°F is recommended for the dry food storage area. However, during some months it may be possible to maintain temperatures between 40°F and 45°F, which is a desirable range for many foods normally kept in the dry food storage area.

In cooler climates, the recommended temperatures usually can be held by proper insulation and by natural

Figure 2-2. Desirable receiving area features: (1) receiving scales; (2) bread racks; (3) hand trucks; (4) drum dollies; (5) platform trucks; (6) time clock; (7) water fountain; (8) hand sink; (9) towel dispenser; (10) receiving table; (11) calendar; (12) small scale. After dock receipt and before food storage (either dry or refrigerated) there is a receiving or checking-in area, an often neglected but very important part of total planning and design. The key equipment shown here is worth considering in any size operation, as proper receiving procedures have a direct bearing on quality and financial control of purchases.

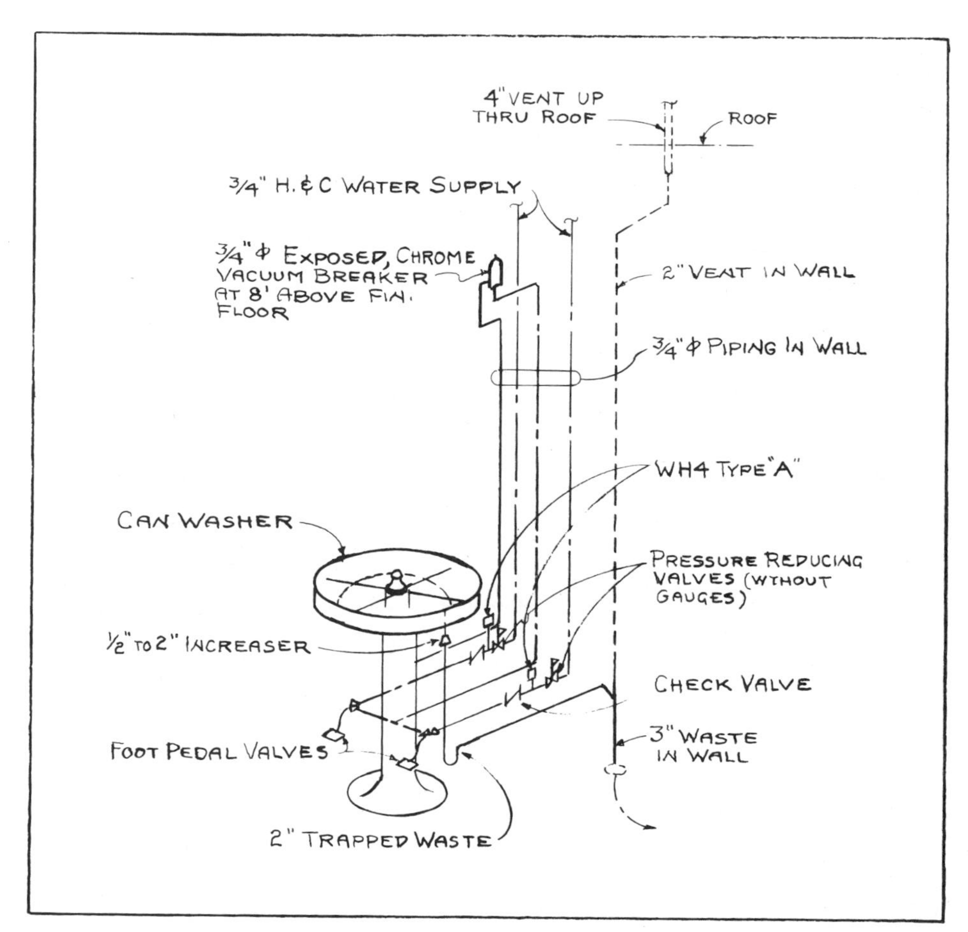

Figure 2-3. Adjacent area. Can-washing and truck-cleaning areas adjacent to a dock are common to institutional facilities. This figure shows a can sanitizer. The proper location and installation of these facilities is critical in health-related food operations.

and/or mechanical ventilation. Natural ventilation is obtained by proper construction of the storeroom to permit the entrance of fresh cool air through louvers at the floor level and the escape of warm air through louvers at the ceiling or roof level.

In hot, humid climates, where the recommended temperatures of 50°F to 70°F cannot be maintained by natural or mechanical ventilation, and/or humidities are consistently high (over 80%), it may be necessary to install air conditioning.

Mechanical or forced-air ventilation with intake and/or exhaust fans keeps fresh air circulating.

Generally, four air changes per hour will be adequate. During the winter months, it may be necessary to use heating equipment to keep certain foods from freezing.

The storeroom should be free of uninsulated steam and water pipes, water heaters, transformers, refrigeration condensing units, steam generators, and other heat-producing equipment.

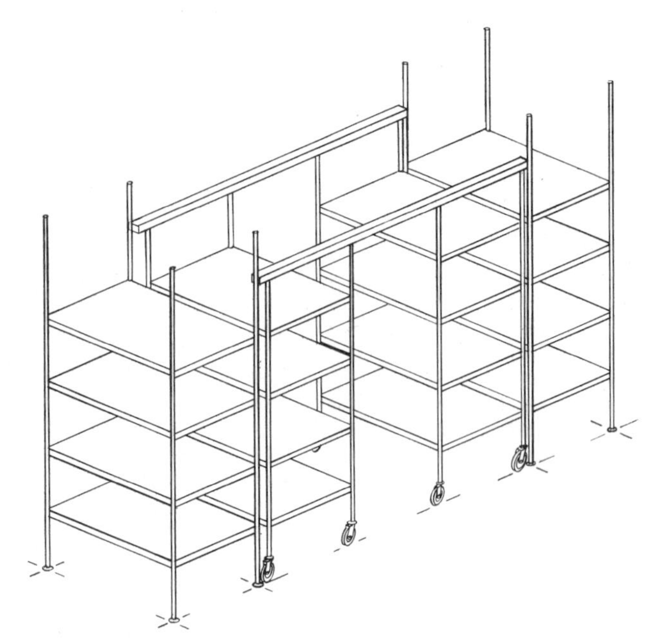

Figure 2-4. Track shelving, top-mounted. To capture valuable space, consider top- or bottom-mounted track shelving. The sample drawings in this figure show how to utilize available storage areas to the maximum. (Courtesy Inter Metro)

IMPROVING STORAGE

It is a good idea occasionally to look at the overall kitchen operation to see how it might be improved.

One problem area may be food storage and handling because facilities for these functions usually tend to "grow like Topsy." An easy solution is to use a modular storage system.

ARE YOU MOBILIZED?

Kitchen planners increasingly are using mobile shelving to move food and utensils to and from preparation locations. (See Figures 2-4 and 2-5.) This allows cleaner, more open work areas. Supplies can be wheeled into place easily when needed, and then quickly put in the most efficient position. Mobile shelving can be any number of shelves high, be sized up to 5′-6″ long and 27 inches wide, and have rubber bumpers and back or end ledges for extra protection.

IS YOUR REFRIGERATOR STRAINING?

Unfortunately, the refrigerators may not be able to provide the extra storage required when the volume of a kitchen increases. Often the solution is to make more efficient use of space with scientifically sized shelving, taking advantage of adjustable and modular arrangements. Figure 2-6 shows typical shelving layouts for walk-in-refrigerators.

"HIDDEN" STORAGE FROM SPACING!

Considering the many different heights of bottles, cans, and packages, it is easy to see how they can literally "rob" an operation of storage room. However, by maximizing the use of vertical space, it is possible to add previously unnoticed capacity.

If same-size items are kept together on shelves of adjustable height, only the exact amount of height needed will be used, thus increasing the overall vertical storage capacity.

Food cans and packages are heavy; so care should be taken to use adjustable shelving of sturdy-enough construction to keep the shelves from wobbling or bending.

LOOK DOWN FOR SPACE!

Using wide base counters with narrower overhead shelves in a storage system provides an extra surface that becomes a very handy work counter as well as a place to keep larger cartons and bulky goods neat.

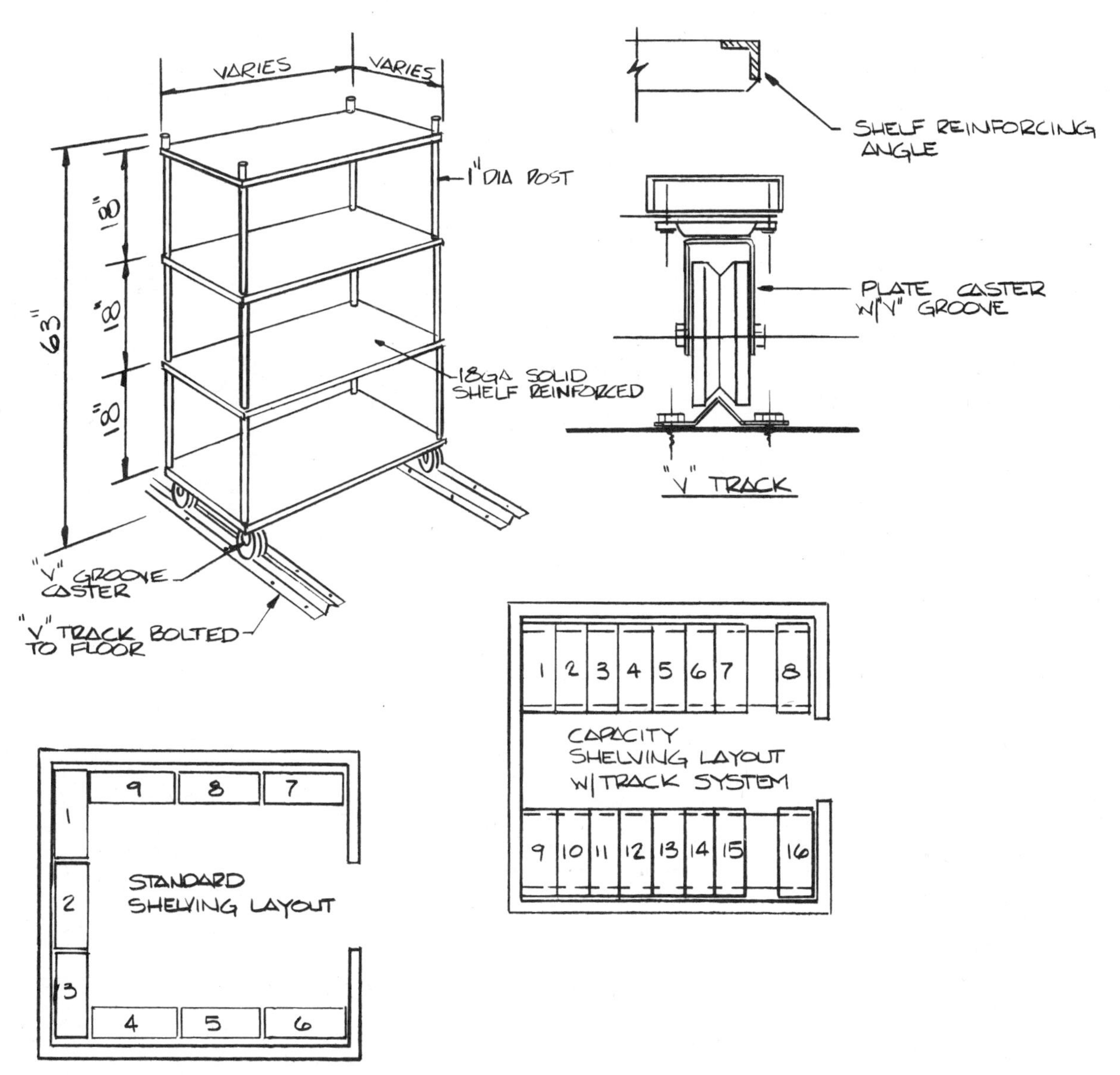

Figure 2-5. Track shelving, bottom-mounted. The latest innovation in shelving is the track style. This figure illustrates a layout that increases storage capacity by approximately one-third for the same floor area. Increased storage space continues to be critical for many food operations, and track shelving now provides a viable alternative. (Courtesy Inter Metro)

HOW TO FIGURE SHELF SIZES

It is possible to plan much of one's shelving requirements in advance because modular units have been scientifically designed to store common items without overhang or waste "air."

These sizes are typical:

- No. 10 cans, four deep: 20″ wide shelf
- No. 10 cans, two deep: 14″ wide shelf
- Dish and glass racks, 20″ × 24″: 20″ wide shelf
- Gallon jugs, two deep: 14″ wide shelf
- Cafeteria pans, 18″ × 26″ size: 20″ wide shelf
- Cafeteria pans, 12″ × 20″ size: 20″ wide shelf
- No. 2 cans, six deep: 20″ wide shelf

ESTIMATING DRY STORAGE REQUIREMENTS

Rule of thumb is one-half square foot of floor space for each meal served daily, or approximately a 15′ × 8′ room for 150 seats. The temperature should be 40°F to 70°F, never to exceed 80°F.

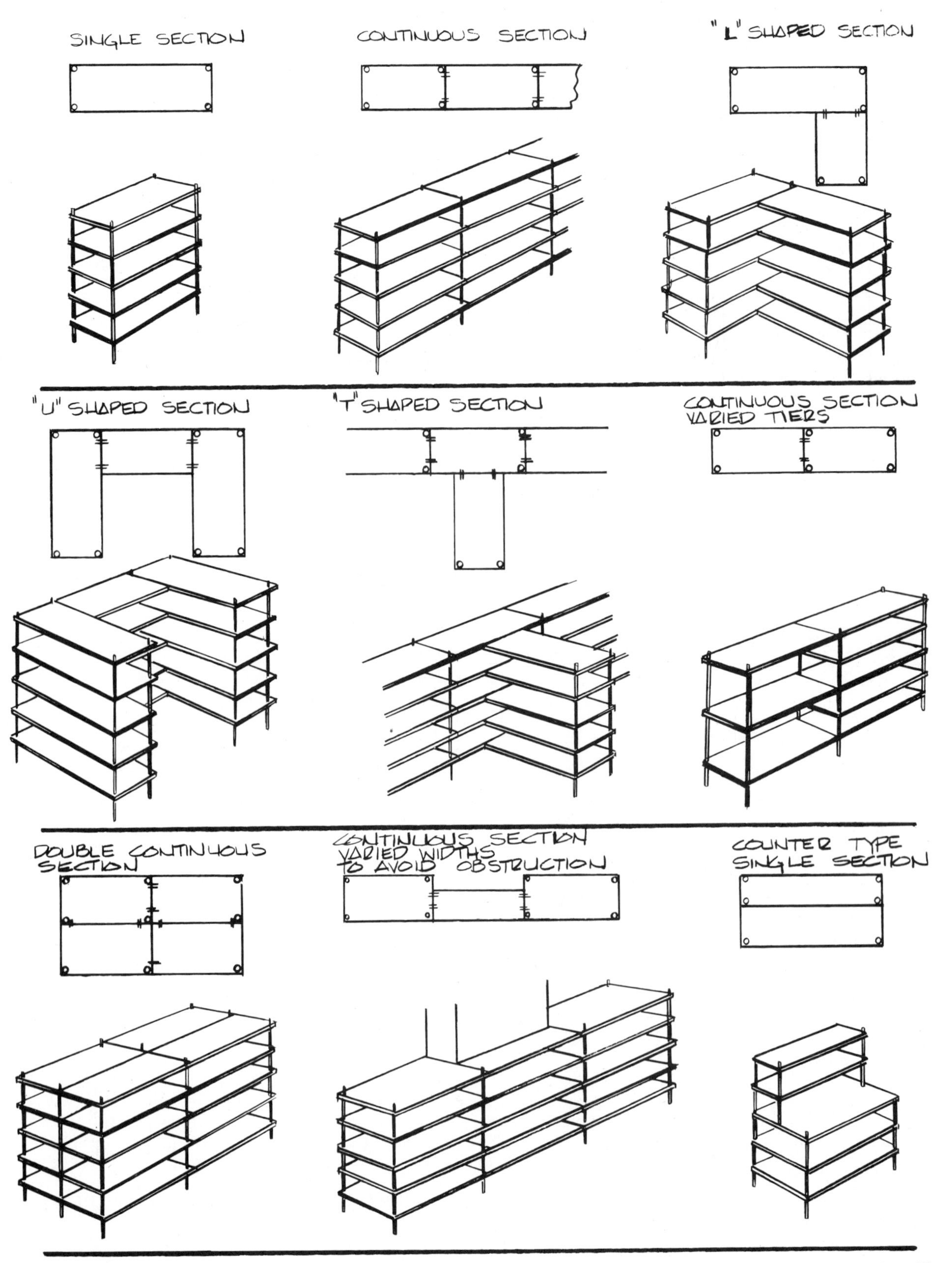

Figure 2-6. Stationary shelf arrangements. Shelving can be obtained in various lengths, widths, and construction. Types available include zinc and chrome wire, aluminum, galvanized steel, stainless steel, and plastic. Shelves can be solid, ribbed, or louvered, in the materials listed. (Courtesy Market Forge)

ESTIMATING REFRIGERATED
FOOD STORAGE SPACE

1. Consider local eating habits and preferences.
2. Calculate weight of food needed per heaviest day, (approximately 2 lbs. per meal per person) and multiply it times the number of days' supply that you plan to store (probably five days, depending on your purchasing and receiving schedules). You can approximate an average of 45 lbs. of food for each cubic foot of storage space. The pounds of food that can be stored per lineal foot of shelving is shown in the chart below for different width shelves and also for complete five-tier-high shelf units.

	Width of Shelves					
	12″	14″	18″	20″	24″	27″
Lbs. food stored per lineal foot of shelving	45	52	67	79	90	102
Lbs. food stored per lineal foot of shelving 5 tiers high	225	260	335	395	450	510

Note how important it is to use every available inch of shelf width and length. Every inch of space wasted means the loss of storage for several pounds of food.

Dividing the Refrigerated Area

- In general, storage space requirements are as follows: meat and poultry, 35%; fruits and vegetables, 30%; dairy products, 20%; and frozen foods, 15%.
- It is not considered economical to build walk-in boxes less than 8′ × 10′ in size.
- Foods other than the above group that may require separate boxes are fish, bakery products, beverages, and ice cream.

Storage Temperatures

Recommended storage temperatures for refrigerated food are: frozen foods, −20°F to 0°F; ice cream, 5°F to 10°F; fish and shellfish, 23°F to 30°F; meat and poultry, 33°F to 38°F; dairy products, 38°F to 46°F; fruits and vegetables, 44°F to 50°F.

Use All Available Storage Space

One should choose storage shelving that can be custom-fit to walk-in boxes to eliminate space, using the full width of the box and allowing a minimum of 36 inches for aisle space and door width. Doors should be high enough, and the floor of box should be level with the corridor, so that mobile shelving can pass through.

Plan Ahead

One should choose shelving that individual shelves can be removed from or added to at any time to allow complete flexibility. It is important to plan enough refrigerated storage. Most food service operators wish they had more walk-in refrigerated food storage space. Shelving is a minor part of the entire cost of the refrigerator. Every inch of space gained increases the capacity and value of the walk-in box. The increased capacity allows the operator to buy plentiful foods at the lowest prices.

Rules For Safe Storage

- Air must freely circulate around the food.
- Hang meats away from wall on adjustable meat racks with removable hooks.
- Keep newer purchases in back.
- Cover cooked or other open foods.
- Use cooked foods and leftovers and discard waste food promptly.
- Consider the use of mobile shelving that may be easily removed for the complete cleaning of the walk-in box.
- Use storage shelving approved by the National Sanitation Foundation.
- Above all, keep the refrigerated areas spotlessly clean.

SOURCE MATERIAL

The preceding material on dry food storage and improving storage was obtained from:

- U.S. Department of Agriculture, Agricultural Marketing Service.
- U.S. Department of Health and Human Services, Public Health Service.

DRY STORAGE AREAS—EQUIPMENT

The purchasing cycle and frequency of deliveries will determine the actual space requirements for storage of both dry and refrigerated products. The composite drawings of Figure 2–6 show many features available in shelving and allied storage equipment. Also available are new styles of storage such as the can rack and specialized trucks.

Many users of shelving have purchased too quickly, to realize later they could have had better utilization and greater flexibility of choice.

Some available shelving styles are:

- Open wire
- Wire coated
- Solid flat
- Solid louvered
- Solid embossed
- Various widths

Some available finishes are:

- Stainless steel
- Zinc
- Zinc with plastic coat
- Chrome
- Coated steel

Specific shelving finishes are used for dry and refrigerated areas. One should check local codes and suppliers for the best value.

Figures 2–7 through 2–15 show many possible storage systems available from standard shelving and storage components.

RECEIVING AND STORAGE CHECKLIST

In selecting receiving and storage equipment, one may consider:

- Scales
- Trucks
- Shelving styles
- Shelving sizes
- Receiving tables
- Dunnage racks
- Bread racks
- Syrup tank trucks
- Can dollies
- Wall shelving
- Meat racks
- Pallets
- Door curtains
- Air doors
- Dumpsters
- Compactors
- Can washers

APPROXIMATE SHIPPING WEIGHTS-SELECTED EQUIPMENT

Receiving Scale Platform 175#

Wire Shelving 72″ High—4 Shelves Various Sizes

18″ Wire	72″ Long	120#
21″ Wire	60″ Long	102#
24″ Wire	60″ Long	108#
24″ Wire	72″ Long	132#

Dunnage Rack 24 × 48 24#

#10 Can Dispenser Rack 200 Can Capacity 200#

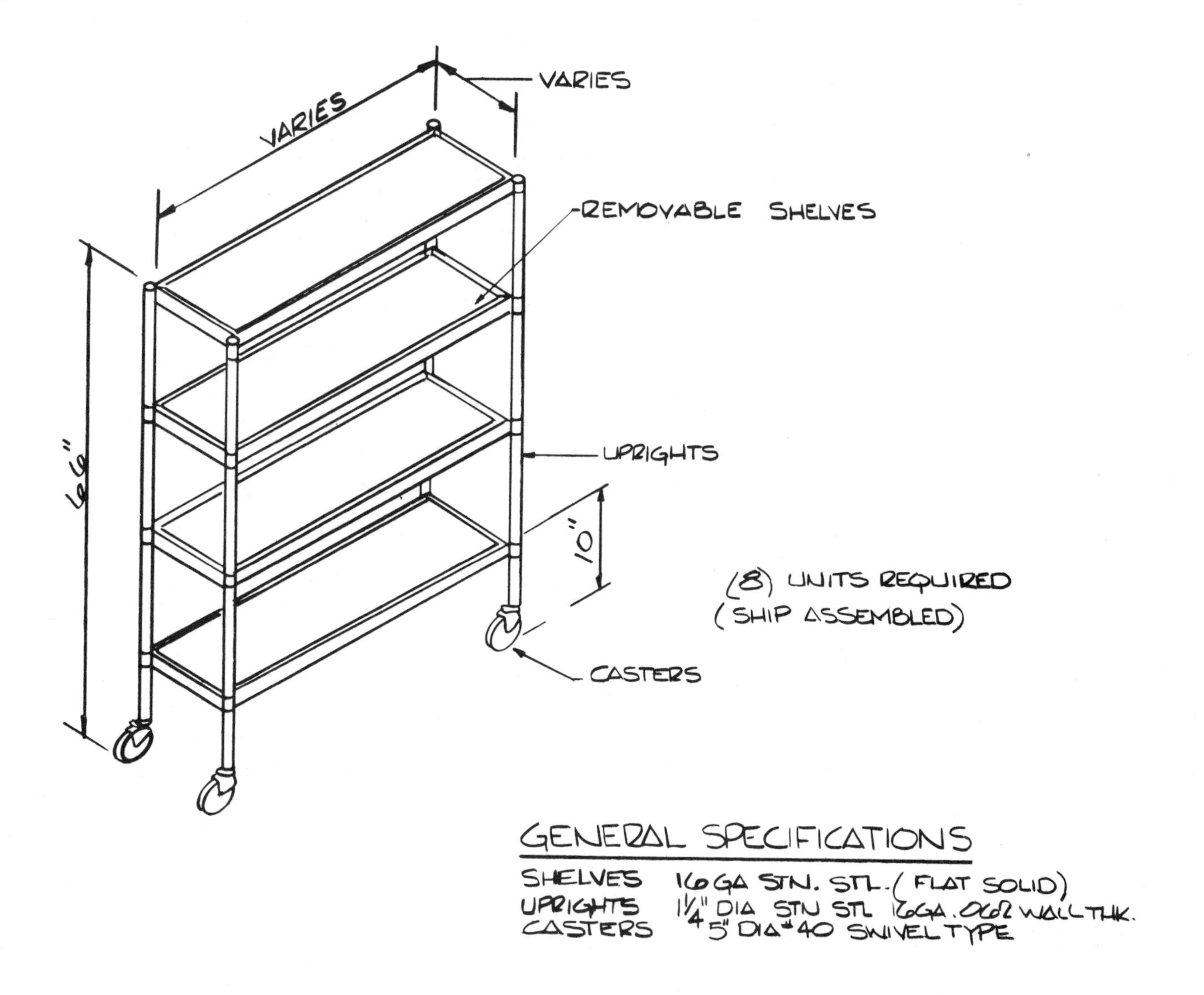

SHELVING UNITS - SCHEDULE				
QTY	"L"	"W"	"H"	REMARKS
1	48"	18"	66"	(4) SHELVES HIGH
2	60"	18"	66"	" " "
2	48"	24"	66"	" " "
1	60"	24"	66"	" " "
2	36"	18"	66"	(4) SHELVES HIGH

Figure 2-7. Mobile shelving unit. This figure details a good specification for a shelving unit. Use of isometric drawings will always prevent misunderstanding and make communication easier.

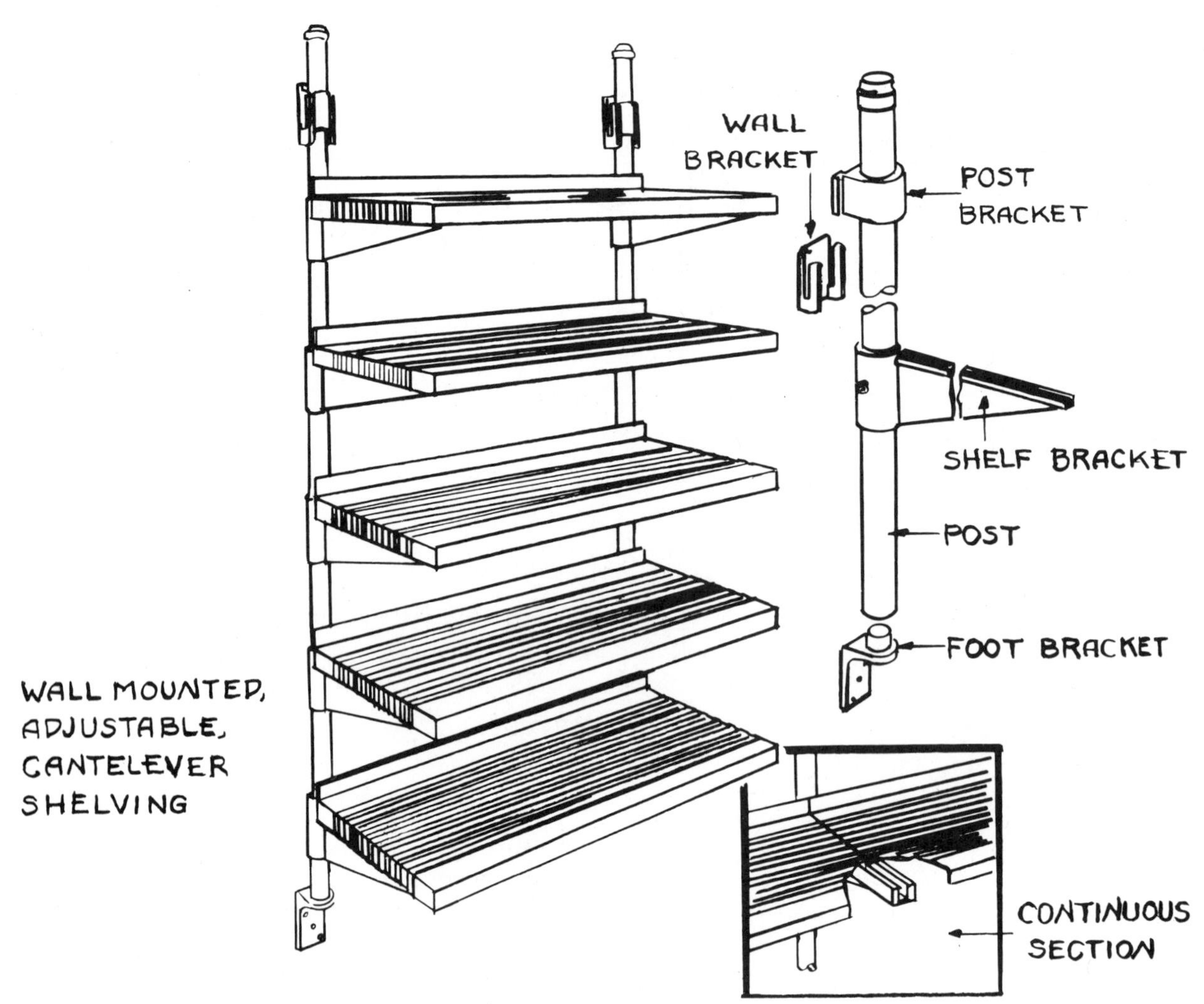

Figure 2-8. Cantilever shelving—details of wall-mounted shelving. Ease of cleaning is the greatest advantage of this style; it is very good for walk-in coolers.

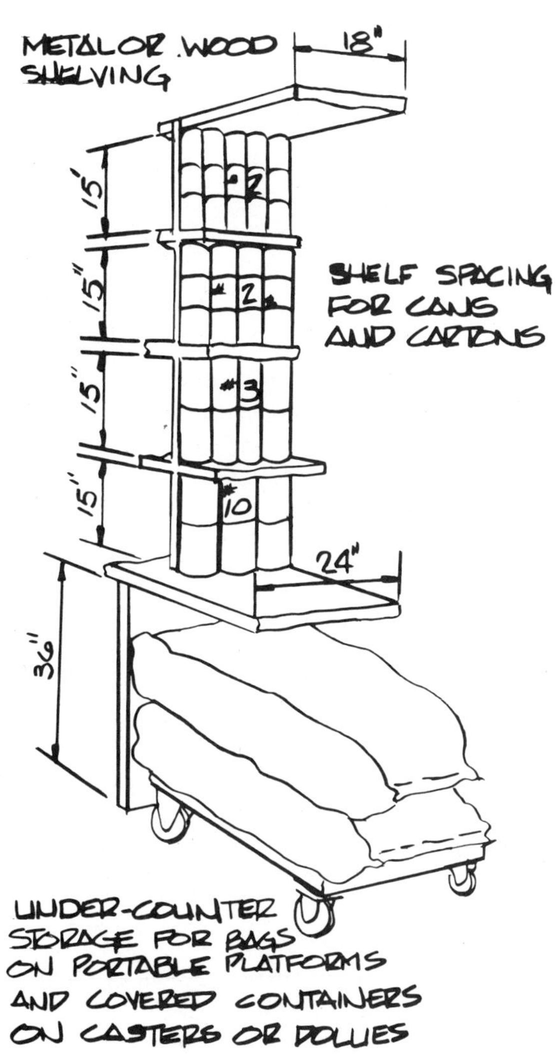

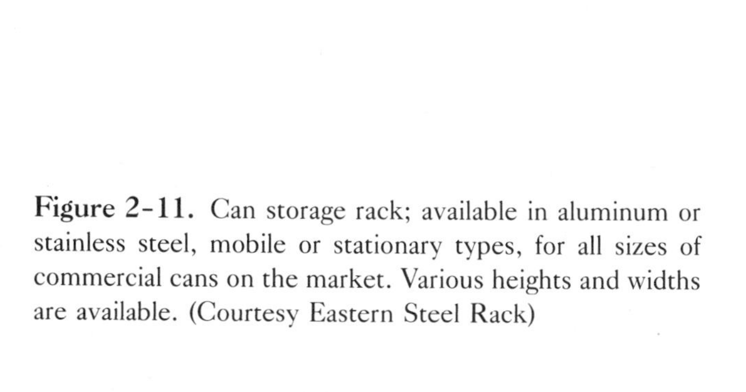

Figure 2-9. Shelving planning guide, showing space taken by #2, #3, and #10 cans.

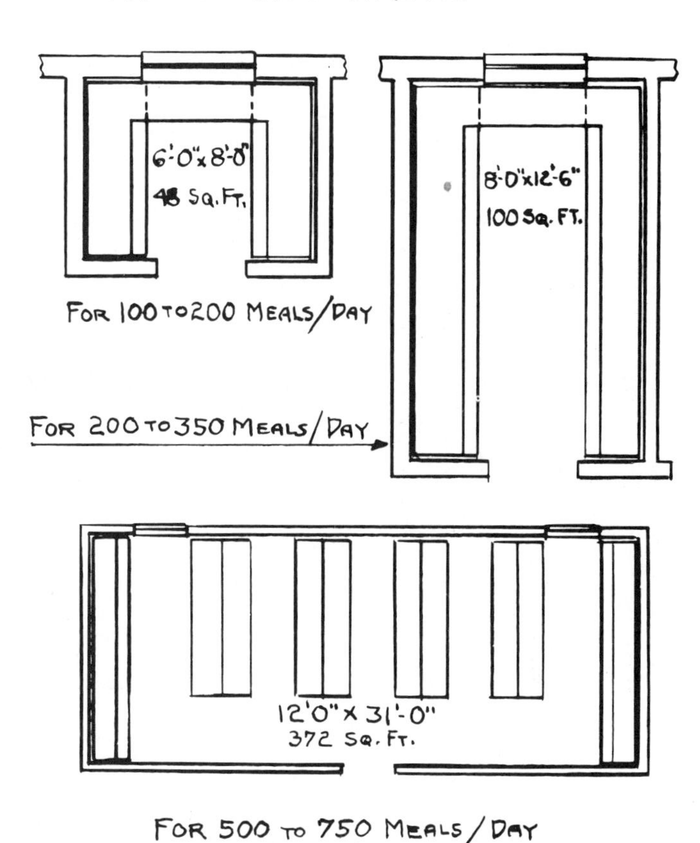

Figure 2-10. Suggested sizes for dry storage areas. Plan views of dry areas, enabling the reader to see approximate shelving in areas of 48, 100, and 372 square feet.

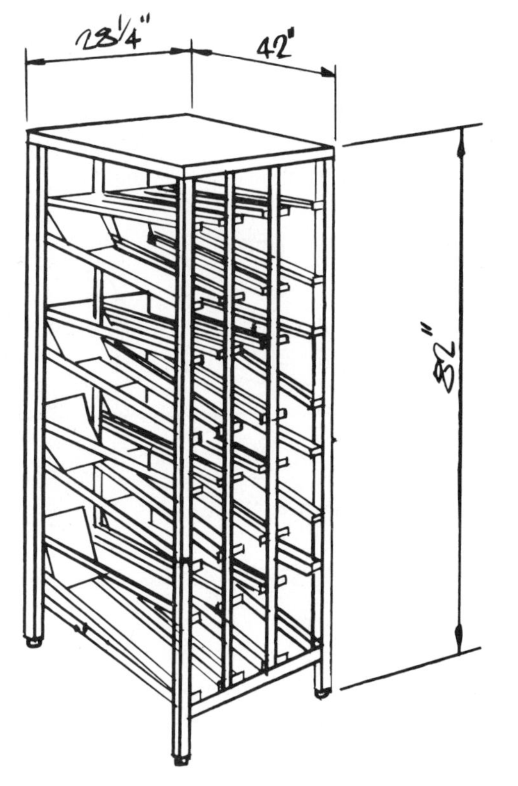

Figure 2-11. Can storage rack; available in aluminum or stainless steel, mobile or stationary types, for all sizes of commercial cans on the market. Various heights and widths are available. (Courtesy Eastern Steel Rack)

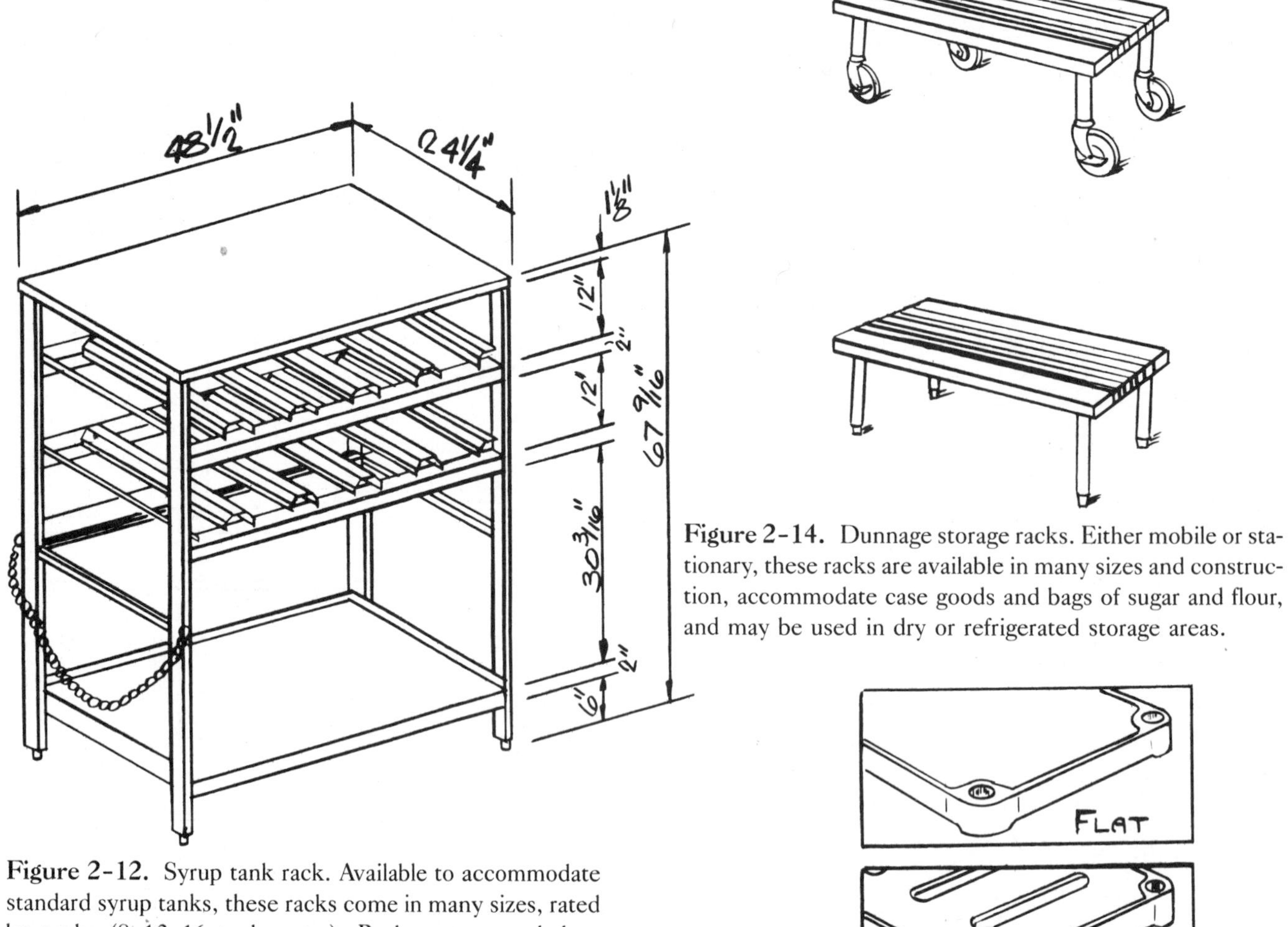

Figure 2-14. Dunnage storage racks. Either mobile or stationary, these racks are available in many sizes and construction, accommodate case goods and bags of sugar and flour, and may be used in dry or refrigerated storage areas.

Figure 2-12. Syrup tank rack. Available to accommodate standard syrup tanks, these racks come in many sizes, rated by tanks (8–12–16 tanks, ets.). Backup storage shelves make inventory an easy chore. (Courtesy Eastern Steel Rack)

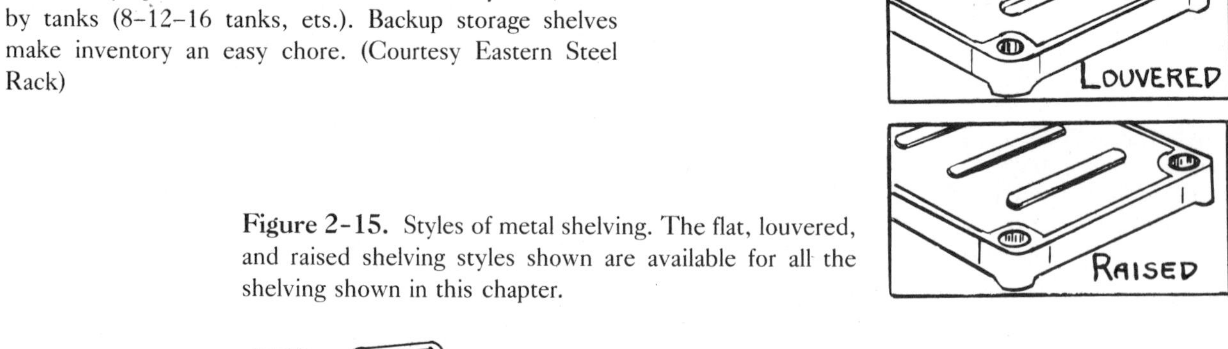

Figure 2-15. Styles of metal shelving. The flat, louvered, and raised shelving styles shown are available for all the shelving shown in this chapter.

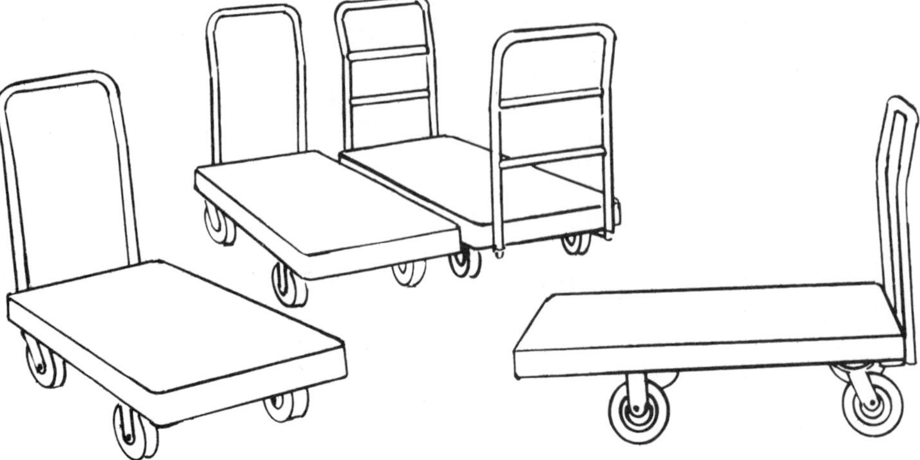

Figure 2-13. Various styles of platform trucks; available in aluminum, steel, plastic, and stainless steel, various wheel sizes, and all rates, by total capacity.

3

Refrigeration

This chapter is a thorough and practical guide to refrigerated storage systems. Descriptions and illustrations are presented of walk-in refrigeration, with its many options, and reach-in refrigeration, with changeable interiors. Typical plan notes, desirable equipment features, and drawings of specialty refrigerators are included to facilitate planning. Detailed specifications for reach-in refrigerators and walk-in models conclude the chapter.

In the following pages we examine "back of the house" refrigeration such as walk-ins and kitchen refrigerators and freezers. The information given will aid prospective buyers and students in selecting, by size, refrigeration requirements matched to menu items and frequency of deliveries.

The options and variations available for refrigerators, freezers, and walk-in units are numerous. It will pay to study them carefully. Initial costs may have a rapid payback in energy savings and improved service.

A word of warning regarding freezers: they are not blast freezing units, and overloading them with unfrozen products will cause problems.

WALK-IN COOLER/FREEZER COMPONENTS

Nearly all modular walk-ins have the same general construction and assembly methods as well as the same optional variations. (See Figure 3–1.) The individual panels that make up the units are usually 4 inches thick, with the main differences being in the height and width of the panels and corner pieces. Some manufacturers use modules of even 1′-0″ divisions; when assembled, their coolers could measure 8′-0″ × 12′-0″. Other manufacturers' units of comparable size might measure 7′-8″ × 11′-6″, 7′-9″ × 11′-7″, and so on. It is important to consider these variations when planning shelving for walk-ins. Standard heights of common walk-ins average 7′-6″, 8′-6″, and 10′-6″. Modular paneling and interior support systems are available for constructing huge two-story refrigerated warehouses, but these systems require a considerable amount of engineering and will not be discussed in this book.

Many standard options are available for walk-in refrigeration units. (See Figures 3–2 through 3–4.) They are listed below; and their careful consideration, supplemented by study of the illustrations that follow, will aid prospective buyers in selecting the units that they need.

WALK-IN REFRIGERATOR OPTIONS

Planning for refrigerated storage areas resembles the planning for dry storage areas. One must plan rows of shelving along with the aisle space required, keeping in mind that simply adding 2 or 3 feet of additional width to a walk-in box may accomplish nothing more than adding extra cost to the unit.

1. WEATHER CAP OUTDOOR USE
2. INTERIOR LIGHT SWITCH
3. POWER FAILURE INDICATOR
4. THERMOMETER
5. INTERIOR LIGHT SWITCH
6. FLOOR TREADS
7. KNOCKOUT FOR DRAIN OUTLET
8. FLOOR DRAIN
9. EXTERIOR DOOR RAMP
10. INTERIOR DOOR RAMP
11. WINDOW PORT
12. AIR CURTAIN
13. DOOR CLOSURE
14. VENT PORT

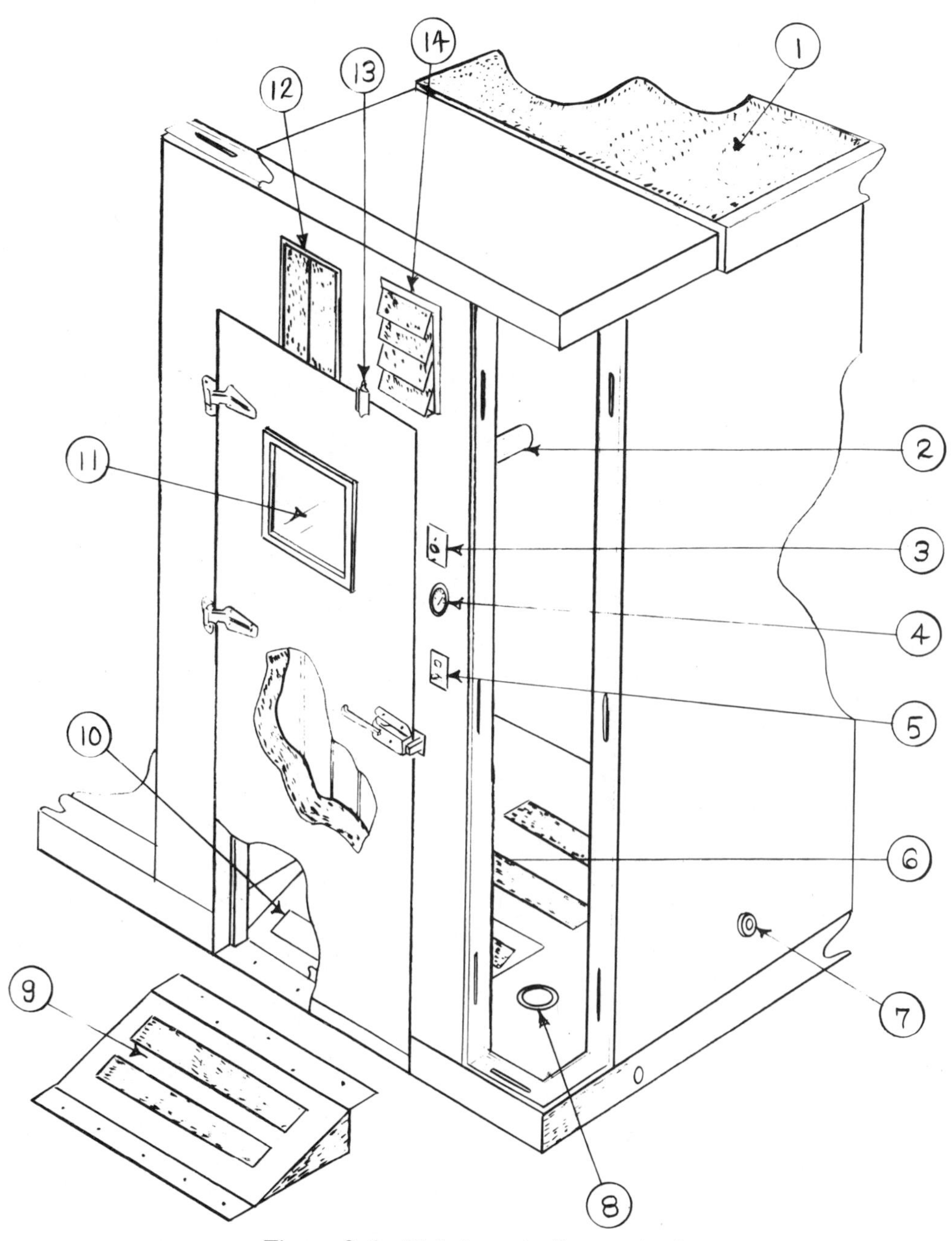

Figure 3-1. Walk-in cooler/freezer detail.

Fully coved "T" panels.
A complete break in metal continuity eliminates frost conduction between compartments. No need for extra breaker strips and heater wires which can increase operation costs.

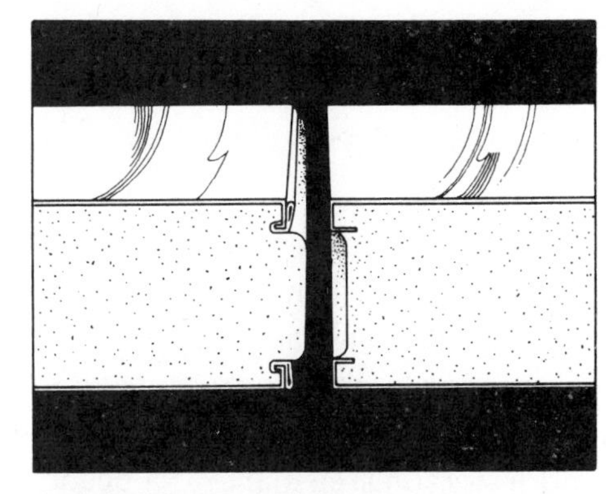

Gasketed tongue and groove.
Tongue sides of all panels are provided with double PVC gaskets foamed-in-place to eliminate costly, time-consuming caulking between panels, and to assure a tight secure fit. No butt joints are used.

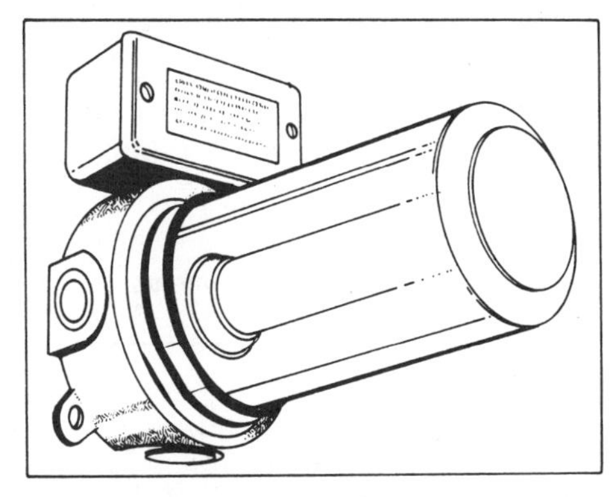

1. Vapor-proof interior light.
Shatter-proof incandescent light mounted on the interior side adjacent to door opening is prewired to exterior switch with pilot light.

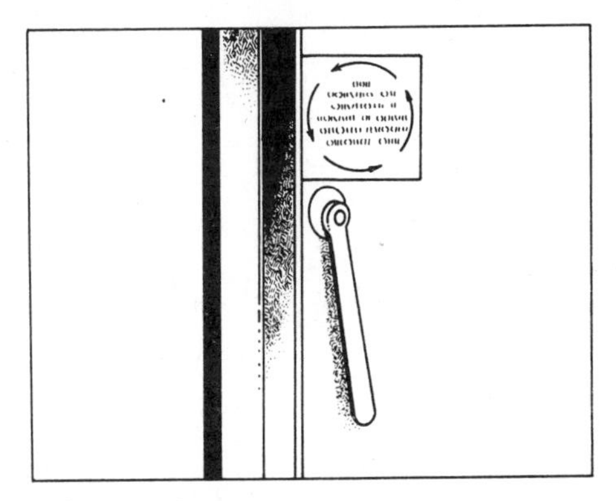

5. Safety release.
Prevents entrapment within walk-ins when locked from outside. A simple quarter turn releases handle. Release instructions mounted on panel next to handle.

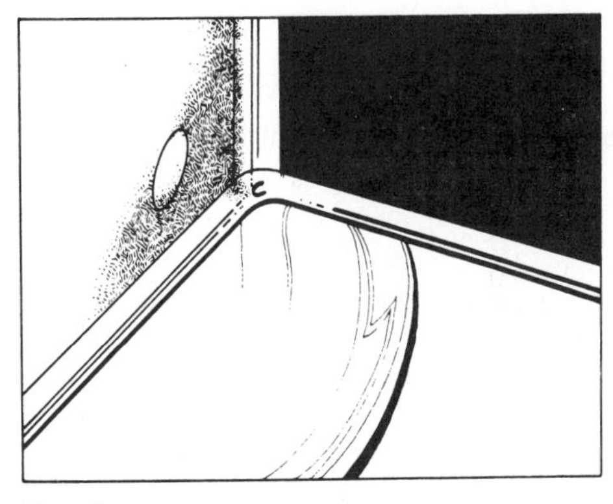

Coved corners.
Floor and ceiling joints of FS models are ¾" radius coved for easier cleaning, and greater sanitation. Only floor joints of NS models are coved as standard. Non-coved floors are also available on NS models.

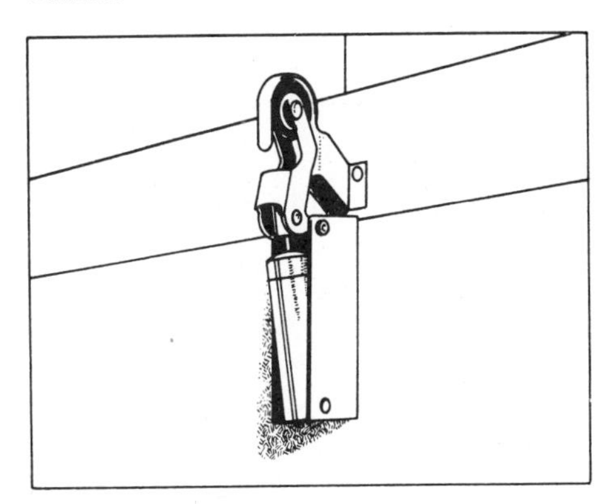

3. Posi-seal door closure.
Introduced by Vollrath and standard on all walk-in doors, the posi-seal closure catches the door, cushions the closing movement with proper venting, shuts the door noiselessly and keeps it firmly closed. Precision-designed for long-lasting dependability. Closure cylinder is filled with a special oil, highly insensitive to temperature fluctuations. Spring loaded plunger incorporates check valve for easy opening, positive closing.

Figure 3-2. Construction features of a well-designed walk-in. (Courtesy Vollrath Refrigeration)

Some factors to consider when selecting the proper walk-in include storage area needed, space available, shelving requirements, and type of business. For example, an establishment preparing a wide variety of foods obviously requires more storage area than those serving a simple menu. Similarly, food service operations in isolated areas need greater storage capacity than those receiving frequent delivery. In addition to their own knowledge and experience, walk-in users can follow this guideline in determining the storage area needed: ½ cubic foot of storage space per person per meal. For example, 400 cubic feet capacity would be needed to serve 800 meals per day. (These are net capacities and do not include space for aisles and for air circulation.)
Also consider the use of partitioned rooms, or a separate walk-in cooler and freezer. Many kitchens find it advantageous to store produce, bakery, dairy products, etc., separately.

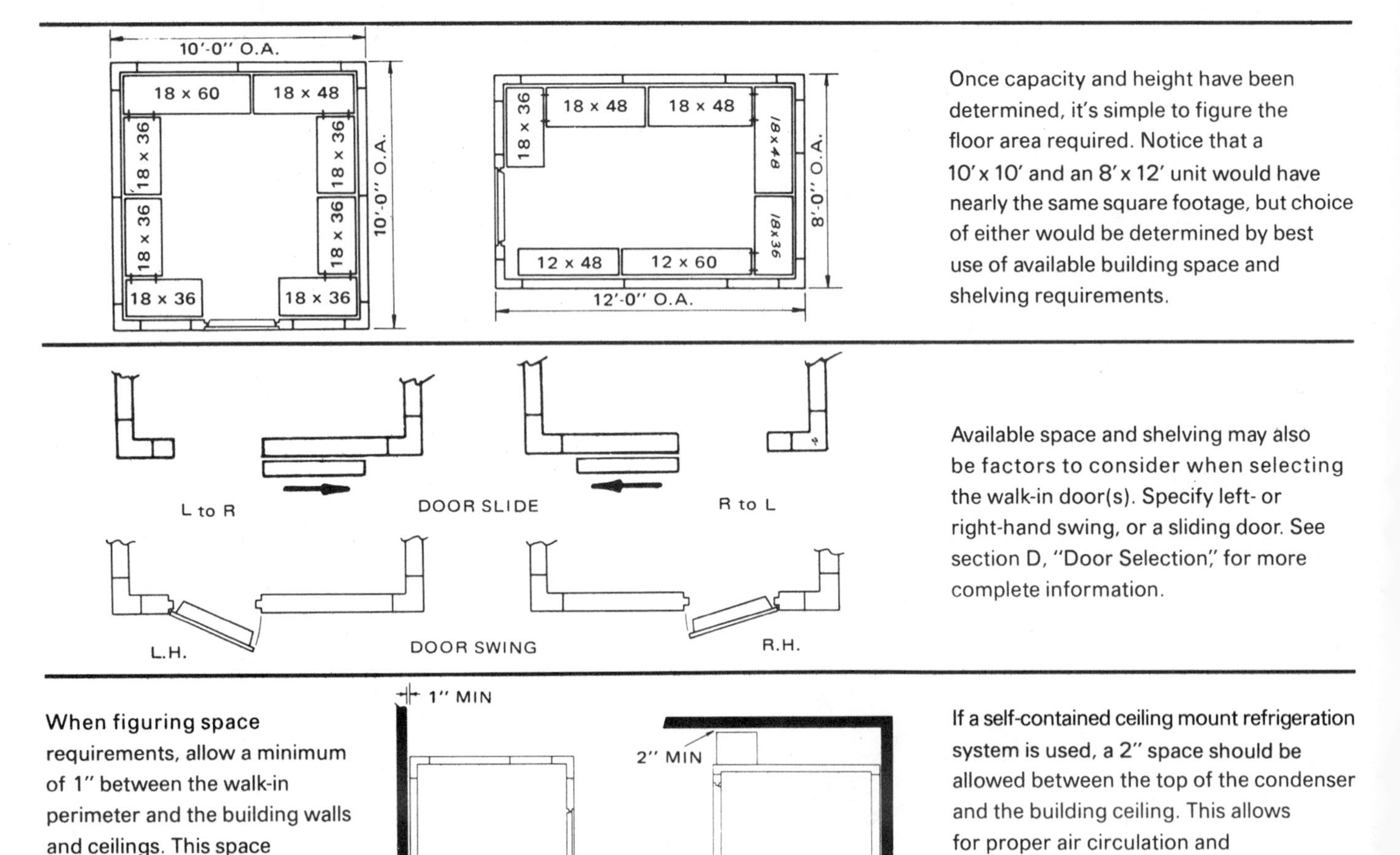

Once capacity and height have been determined, it's simple to figure the floor area required. Notice that a 10' x 10' and an 8' x 12' unit would have nearly the same square footage, but choice of either would be determined by best use of available building space and shelving requirements.

Available space and shelving may also be factors to consider when selecting the walk-in door(s). Specify left- or right-hand swing, or a sliding door. See section D, "Door Selection", for more complete information.

When figuring space requirements, allow a minimum of 1" between the walk-in perimeter and the building walls and ceilings. This space allows for deviations in building construction and provides an air space to improve efficiency of walk-in operation.

If a self-contained ceiling mount refrigeration system is used, a 2" space should be allowed between the top of the condenser and the building ceiling. This allows for proper air circulation and easier maintenance.
Selection of finish, type of doors, floors and refrigeration units are covered in other sections of this manual.

In the interest of continued product improvement, we reserve the right to change specifications without notice.

Figure 3-3. Selection of size and layout for walk-in coolers. Many good ideas are shown for the proper selection of walk-in refrigeration. (Courtesy Vollrath Refrigeration)

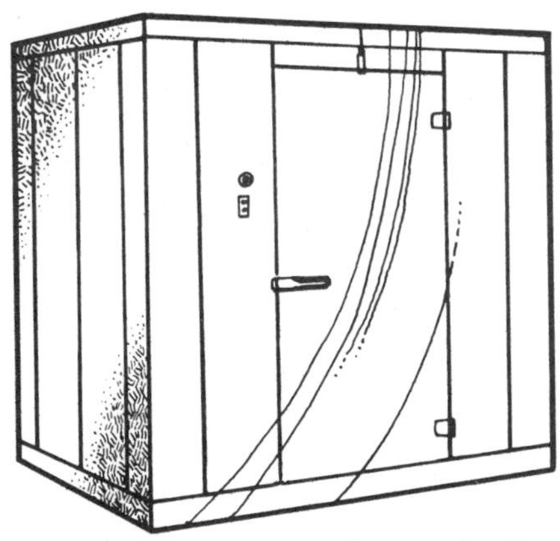

A. Walk-in cooler or freezer detail.

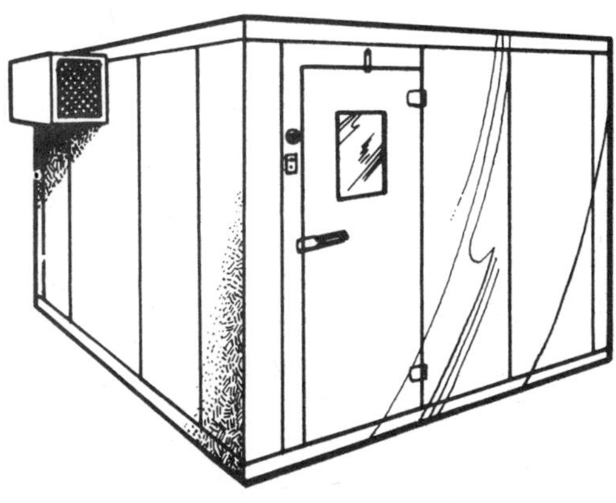

B. Walk-in cooler or freezer with side mount compressor window in door.

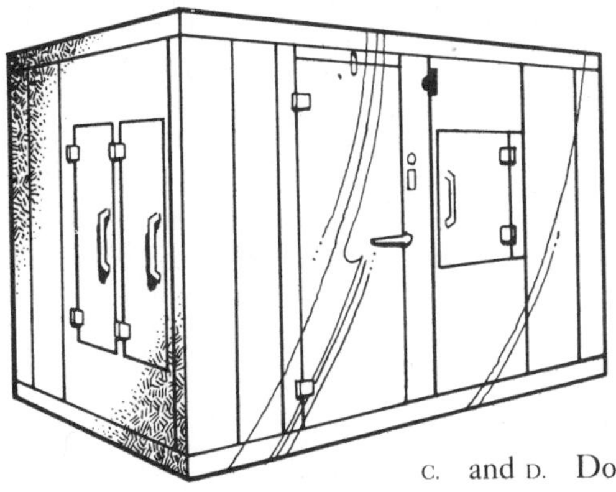

C. and D. Door variations walk-in cooler/freezers.

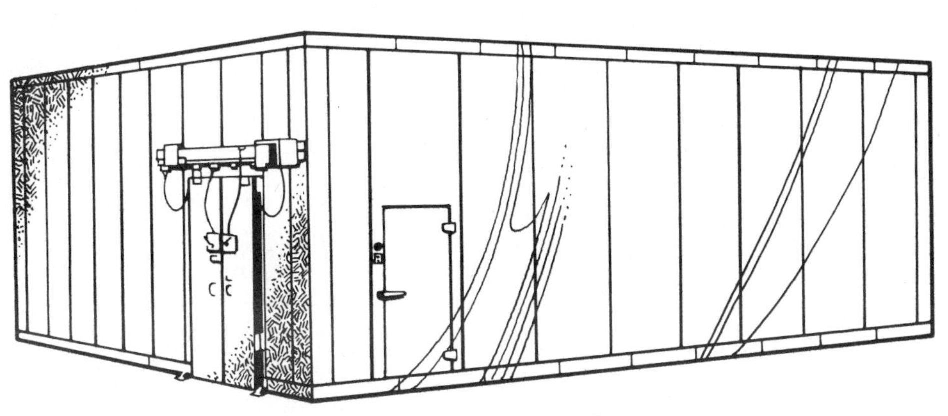

E. Outside storage—cooler or freezer.

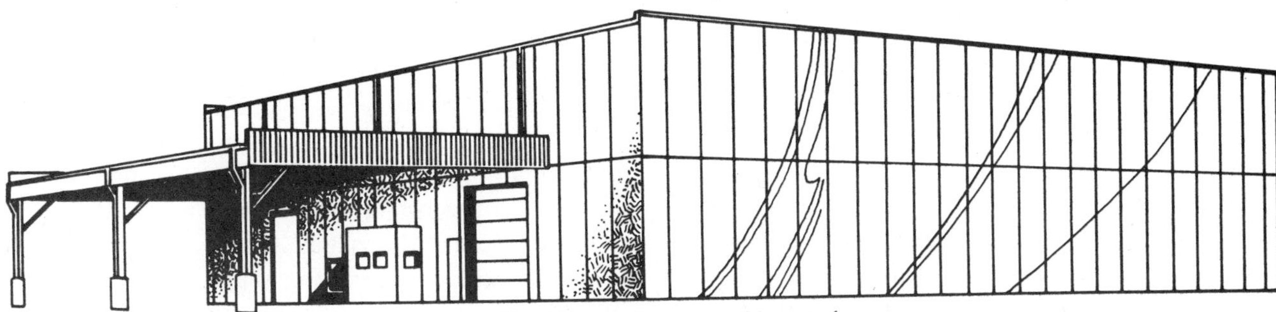

F. Outside warehouse—refrigerated.

Figure 3-4. Walk-in cooler composites. (Courtesy Vollrath Refrigeration)

A number of options may be considered:

1. Walk-ins are available for either indoor or outdoor installations. Outdoor units require weather caps for the roof, and rain hoods are available for the doors. The compressors may be self-contained and winterized if required. Allowance must be made for the condensate drain line from the blower coils.
2. Indoor units are available in various finishes and with decorator-color panels.
3. Walk-in coolers may be erected directly on an existing concrete or tile floor by using screeds available for this purpose, thereby eliminating the step-up at the door. This is possible only where the floor is on the ground and should not be attempted with freezers.
4. It is possible to recess the walk-in floor so that it is level with the outside floor, or to carry a tile floor into the walk-in units. All manufacturers have detailed drawings of suggested designs to aid the contractor.
5. Where the walk-in floor is to set on an existing floor, interior floor panels with built-in ramps are available for either floor. Skid-proof treads are recommended.
6. Reinforced floors of diamond tread aluminum and other materials are available, which vary by manufacturer. One should check with a supplier for types available.
7. Pressure relief vents are available, and are strongly recommended, especially in large freezer units. Warm air will fill the walk-in as the cold air runs out during stocking-up periods. Then when the door is closed, the air contracts as it cools, building up a partial vacuum inside and making it very difficult to open the door. (The authors remember well a college installation where the chef used a crowbar to yank open the freezer door and collapsed the roof of the unit!)
8. Thermometers, usually built into door panels, are available, and are required by health departments in some areas.
9. Audio and visual alarm systems are available for both coolers and freezers.
10. Door options: Standard door panels—which usually contain the thermometer, the vapor-proof light and switch, and the door heater cables—are available with 24-, 30-, and 34-inch-wide doors hinged to right or left. Self-closing hinges are available, as are door pulls with cylinder locks or padlock holes. Inside safety releases are standard. Foot treadle openers may be ordered. Glass view ports with triple-thick glass, heated for freezers, may be installed. Kick plates and bumper strips may be attached. Track ports above the door opening are available where overhead trolley systems are used.

    - Reach-in doors, either one above the other or one door on the top, are available in glass or solid, hinged on either side or sliding.
    - Full-height glass display doors, with built-in adjustable shelving, vertical fluorescent lighting, and heater cables to prevent condensation, are available, either hinged or sliding. These units may be installed adjacent to each other for the full length of the cooler or freezer.
    - Sliding doors, either manual or powered, are available in various widths for use where hinged doors are impractical, or where forklift trucks are used. They may be right or left sliding or bi-parting.

11. Various options are available for the refrigeration systems. They may be self-contained with the compressor mounted on top of the unit, or saddle-mounted with the condensing unit and the blower coils hung over a wall panel; or they may be self-contained remote systems, which have pre-charged snap-on refrigerant lines, allowing the compressor to be located in any convenient spot within approximately 20 feet.
12. Plastic air curtains hung at door openings can cut down running time of the compressor and save money. (An air curtain is shown in Figure 3–1.) (*Note:* the above options for walk-in units may not all be available from any single manufacturer.)

A few final reminders: One must not forget about the condensate drain lines from the blower coils. This can be a real headache on a union job. These lines must be trapped, and then run to an indirect waste. A heater tape is required in the freezer, and floor drains are not permissible inside walk-in boxes. Also, one must be sure that the voltage, phase, and horsepower are compatible with the power supply. Last, but by no means least, the purchaser must thoroughly understand the equipment warranty.

DEFINITIONS

Btu (*British thermal unit*): amount of heat required to raise the temperature of 1 pound of water 1°F, starting at 39°F.

Btu heat loss/gain: To determine the btu heat loss/gain per 1000 square feet of wall/roof area, multiply the "U" factor by 1000 and then multiply the result by the difference between the inside and outside temperatures.

"K" factor: determined only by laboratory test, the amount of heat in Btu's that will penetrate 1 square foot of a homogeneous material, 1 inch thick, in 1 hour, due to heat pressure of 1°F difference in temperature between the two sides of the material. The "K" factor is always measured for 1 inch of thickness.

"C" factor: the same as "K" factor except for thickness—the amount of heat that will penetrate materials of any thickness under the same conditions of time and temperature, determined by dividing the thickness of the material into the "K" factor. For example, K-13 insulation has a "K" Factor of .126563, 1 inch thick. To determine the "C" factor for 2 inches thick, dividing .126563 by 2 gives a "C" factor of .063282.

"R" factor: A quantity indicative of the heat resistance (i.e., the less a material allows heat to penetrate it, the greater its resistance, or "R" factor), equal to one divided by the "K" factor. To find the "R" factor for another thickness of material, first find the "R" Factor for 1 inch thick and then multiply the result by the thickness of the material.

"U" factor: a quantity equal to one divided by the sum of all "R" factors. The "U" value is defined as the heat transmitted per square foot per degree of temperature difference between inside and outside air.

Perm: water vapor transmitted in grains in 1 hour through 1 square foot of material. Perm ratings may be classified as: 0.1 to 0.3, excellent; 0.3 to 0.5, good; 0.5 to 0.8, poor—acceptable only in dry occupancy with low humidity; 1 and above not considered a vapor barrier.

Therm: unit of heat equivalent to 1,000,000 Btu, used in the measurement of fuel costs. Figure natural gas at 75% conversion efficiency.

Flame spread: a measure of the flammability of a material. Asbestos is considered to have a 0 flame spread, and untreated dry red oak a 100 flame spread. All other construction materials tested by the same method will have a flame spread of 0 to 100.

DEFROSTING EVAPORATORS*

In a commercial refrigeration system some method of defrosting ice buildup on the evaporator coil must be used. This frost buildup is caused by moisture from the air first condensing on the coil surface, then subsequently freezing. As the frost grows thicker it reduces the cooling efficiency of the evaporator.

In walk-in cooler applications (box temperatures above 33°F) air defrosting is usually adequate as a means to clear the coil of any frost. In an air defrost system while the condensing unit is running, the temperature of the coil is low causing frost to accumulate on it. When the compressor terminates, the coil warms up to above 32°F and the frost melts. In some cooler applications a defrost timer may be necessary to force the refrigeration system into several scheduled defrost periods per day. This will help to ensure a clear and efficient coil.

For freezer applications (box temperatures below 32°F) where air defrosting is not feasible, the evaporator coil will need outside heat of some kind for defrost. Electric heat is the most popular method for defrosting low temperature coils. This method provides resistance heating elements mounted on or installed inside the evaporator coil, as well as, under the drain pan. A timer stops the refrigeration unit, closes the liquid line, then pumps the refrigerant from the coil. When the frost is gone a thermostat terminates the heaters and fans, and returns power to the condensing unit.

Another low temperature system defrosts evaporators by means of hot gas. In this system hot refrigerant discharge gas is pumped from the compressor directly into the evaporator coil. The hot compressed vapor goes through the evaporator defrosting the coil and then returns to the compressor. Hot gas defrost systems usually clear the evaporator quickly and efficiently.

*Mr. David Comiskey, W. A. Brown Mfg.

TYPICAL PLAN NOTES: WALK-IN REFRIGERATORS AND FREEZER

1. Installation and interwiring of lights in ceilings of walk-in boxes shall be provided by the electrical contractor. Lights to be provided by the kitchen equipment contractor.
2. Electrician to field-wire thermostats to solenoid valves in the walk-in boxes.
3. Temperature alarms provided by the kitchen equipment contractor to be installed by the electrical contractor.
4. Indirect wastes at the walk-in blower coils furnished and installed by the plumbing contractor.
5. Kitchen equipment contractor to furnish and install all the necessary refrigeration lines from the compressors to the evaporators in the walk-in boxes.
6. All walk-in box compressors to be air-cooled type. See architectural drawings for location.
7. Freezer: Electrician to interwire thermostat to solenoid valves in the field. In addition, electrician to interwire time clock at the compressor to junction box located at the evaporator.

DESIRABLE EQUIPMENT FEATURES

WALK-IN REFRIGERATION SYSTEM

- Separate refrigeration systems are required for walk-in refrigerator and freezer compartments.
- Refrigerator compartment 36°F to 40°F with a 10°F temperature differential between refrigerator (coil temperature) and walk-in compartment temperature, or 36°F to 40°F while operating at ambient temperature of 90°F. Compressor to operate for no more than 70% of the time under no-load conditions (i.e., empty walk-in).
- Freezer compartment maximum storage temperature 0°F while operating at ambient temperature of 90°F. Compressor to operate for no more than 80% of the time under no-load conditions (i.e., empty walk-in).
- Dual pressure controls (high and low pressure cut-off) for 36°F to 40°F compartment. An automatic, low ambient control unit also is required for installations having a remote refrigeration system where compressor is subject to ambient temperatures below freezing.
- Dual pressure controls (high and low pressure cut-offs) for −10°F to 0°F compartment. A time clock for electric defrost of evaporator. An automatic, low ambient control unit also is required for those installations having a remote refrigeration system where compressor is subject to ambient temperatures below freezing.
- Thermostatic expansion valve.
- Liquid line strainer and dryer and moisture-indicating sight glass.
- Automatic audiovisual safety alarm system.
- Underwriters Laboratories (U.L.) seal of approval.

WALK-IN COMPARTMENTS

- For an efficient operation, the floor of the walk-in refrigerator should be level with the adjacent flooring.
- The following installation is recommended for concrete slabs. Other types of installations may be prone to point loading and moisture in floor panels.
- The system for locking panels should ensure an airtight durable seal, which the manufacturer will guarantee for a minimum of five years under normal usage. If gasket material is required as a seal, it should be of an approved type.
- The first preference for insulation is a foamed-in-place or froth-type urethane.
- Insulated floor screeds should be used where prefabricated walk-in units are installed on concrete slab floors.
- Where factory-fabricated floors are used, there should be a minimum floor loading of 300 lbs. sq. ft.
- There should be replaceable anti-sweat heaters around each walk-in unit door and frame.
- The main door to each compartment should be 34 to 36 inches wide with an optional insulated glass view port.
- There should be a positive safety latch with lock and cam-lift hinges.
- There should be a flush, exterior-mounted thermometer 2½"-diameter for each compartment.
- There should be an interior-mounted, vapor-proof incandescent light per each 100 square feet of space.
- Equipment should have National Sanitation Foundation (N.S.F.) seal of approval and Underwriters Laboratories (U.L.) seal of approval.

Figures 3–5 through 3–17 may be consulted for help in planning the features of a refrigeration system. Figures 3–18 through 3–24 provide a good representation of styles of specialized units. Many options are available: choice of finish (lamination or stainless steel); wheels; pan combinations; tops made of marble, wood, plastic, or stainless steel; compressors, either remote or self-contained; drain eliminators; automatic defrosters; light emitting diode thermometers; interior rack glides for pans; and others.

DETAILED SPECIFICATIONS: REFRIGERATORS

ITEM 1 ROLL-IN, QUICK CHILL, THREE-SECTION REFRIGERATOR

The refrigerator shall be a three-section, three-door model. Dimensions shall not exceed 101¼″ long, 37¼″ deep over the hardware, and 86½″ high. The quick chill refrigeration system shall be capable of cooling a 600-lb. load, properly loaded allowing air circulation, from 160°F to 45°F in less than seven hours. A minimum 3 HP air-cooled remote condensing unit for 208/60/3 operation complete with all necessary valves, controls, refrigerant, etc. shall be provided by this contractor for installation by others next to the refrigerator. Both the compressor and refrigerator shall be equipped with quick disconnects. Mating disconnects shall also be provided for use by agency personnel when installing their tubing between the compressor and the refrigerator. Provide stainless steel interior floor. Exterior color to be agency choice from manufacturer's standard selection. *See Note.

ITEM 2 ROLL-IN, THREE-SECTION REFRIGERATOR

The refrigerator shall be a three-section, three-door model. Dimensions shall not exceed 101¼″ long, 37¼″ deep over the hardware, and 86½″ high. The refrigerator shall be designed for normal roll-in refrigerator use and shall have a self-contained top-mounted condensing unit, minimum ¾ HP 230/60/1 operation. The refrigeration system shall be complete with an automatic condensate drain evaporator. The refrigerator shall be similar and equal to Hobart model #HEV-3 with stainless steel insulated interior floor. Exterior color to be agency choice from manufacturer's standard selection. *See Note.

ITEM 3 ROLL-IN, TWO SECTION REFRIGERATOR

Shall be the same as item 2 except it shall be a two-section, two-door model. The self-contained condensing unit shall be a minimum ½ HP 115/60/1. The refrigerator shall be similar and equal to Hobart model #HEV-2. *See Note.

ITEM 4 REACH-IN REFRIGERATOR

The refrigerator shall be self-contained type with a top-mounted minimum ¼ HP 115/60/1 condensing unit. Shall be a single-section unit having a net storage capacity of approximately 23 cubic feet. The cabinet shall be provided with two half-height doors hinged on the right side facing the cabinet. The top half of the refrigerator shall be equipped with 13 pair of adjustable wide angle stainless steel pan slides spaced 2″ O.C. to hold one 18″ × 26″ or two 14″ × 18″pans. The bottom half of the refrigerator shall be provided with three stainless steel pull-put shelves. The refrigerator shall not exceed 31¼″ left to right, 84″ high including 5″ heavy-duty casters and the top-mounted unit, 34½″ deep over the doors. The refrigerator shall be of stainless steel construction inside and out for all exposed surfaces. Shall be similar and equal to Victory Model #RS-1D-S3-HP.

*NOTE: all roll-in-refrigerators shall be designed for operation with Crescor racks model #207-UA-12C or equal.

DETAILED SPECIFICATIONS: WALK-IN MODELS

PURPOSE: It is the intent of this specification to describe one walk-in freezer; one walk-in cooler; and one refrigeration system.

GENERAL: The walk-in freezer and cooler are to be contractor-installed outdoors on slabs provided by the agency. Installation of equipment provided under this contract shall include: delivery, uncrating, assembly, connection to utilities, and start-up of the system to ensure it is operating properly. Rooms shall be properly sealed to prevent water from seeping under the floors. The contractor shall be responsible for cleaning up the area after installation.

Items furnished shall be in accordance with the following specifications and the attached drawing.

ITEM #1—WALK-IN FREEZER

DIMENSIONS: Exterior dimensions shall be not less than 17′-4″ or more than 18′-0″ left to right; not less than 11′-6″ or more than 12′-0″ front to back; not less than 9′-6″ or more than 10′-0″ high.

MATERIALS: All panels shall be tongue and groove construction using foamed-in-place polyurethane insulation not less than 4″ or more than 5″ thick. Panels shall be metal-clad inside and out. Exterior finish shall be minimum 22 gauge galvanized steel. Exterior walls shall be painted white. Interior ceiling shall be 22 gauge galvanized steel; interior floor shall be minimum 14 gauge galvanized steel; and the interior walls shall be #3 finish, 20 gauge, type 302 or 304 stainless steel. Interior surfaces shall be unpainted. A cap roof of minimum .050″-thick aluminum shall be installed over the freezer. An asphalt felt barrier shall be installed between the walk-in and the roof cap. The interior floor shall be designed to withstand a load of 700 lbs. per square foot. No wood shall be used in the construction of the room.

DOOR: The door shall be located as near the left end of one long wall as possible and shall be hinged on the right side facing the room from the outside. The door shall have a clearance of 60″ left to right and 84″ high. Heaters shall be installed behind the door jambs and around the door perimeter. The door shall be clad the same as the interior and exterior walls. A minimum 35″-high kick plate shall be installed on both exterior and interior of the door.

HARDWARE: The door shall be equipped with a minimum of three heavy-duty strap hinges and a safety latch designed to receive a padlock.

REFRIGERATION SYSTEM: The system shall consist of a wall-hung, minimum 3 HP 208/60/3 air-cooled condensing unit with matching electric defrost blower coil. The system shall be mounted on the center of the back wall of the room. The refrigeration system shall maintain an interior temperature below −10°F in 100°F ambient conditions without operation more than 18 hours out of a 24-hour period. The system shall be designed for outdoor installation with all necessary valves, controls, timers, vibration eliminators, insulation, crankcase heater, weather enclosure, dryer, etc.; the system shall be wired to an agency-supplied disconnect box located approximately 60 feet away inside an adjoining building; the agency will supply conduit through which the wiring shall be installed; the condensate drain line shall be heated to prevent freezing.

ACCESSORY ITEMS: The room shall include all features normally supplied by the manufacturer as well as the following: coved corners built to N.S.F. requirements where the walls join the floor panels; a floor drain with trap (the agency will provide a heated drain in the slab located as required); interior vapor-proof light with outside weather cap over the door openings; 3″-diameter dial thermometer located on the front wall near the door; and an adjustable high-temperature alarm having an audible and visual alarm loud enough to be heard 500 feet away. The alarm shall be adjustable, with set point anywhere between approximately −20°F and +10°F.

ITEM #2—WALK-IN COOLER

The walk-in cooler shall be installed by the contractor on a slab provided by the agency. The cooler shall be installed without an insulated floor.

DIMENSIONS: Exterior dimensions shall be not less than 19′3″ or more than 20′0″ left to right; not less than 11′7″ or more than 12′0″ front to back; height shall be not less than 10′0″ or more than 10′6″.

MATERIALS: All panels shall be tongue and groove construction using foamed-in-place polyurethane insulation not less than 4″ or more than 5″ thick. Panels shall be metal-clad inside and out. Panels shall be minimum 22 gauge galvanized steel inside and out. Exterior walls painted white, interior unpainted. Where called for in the proposal, bidders shall indicate the additional cost for type 302 or 302 #3 finish 20 gauge stainless steel interior walls instead of galvanized steel. A cap roof of minimum .050″-thick aluminum shall be installed over the cooler with an asphalt felt barrier between the cap and the cooler roof. No wood shall be used in the construction of the room.

DOOR AND HARDWARE: Same construction and location as specified for the freezer, item #1, except a track port shall be provided above the door for use with the agency's meat rail system.

REFRIGERATION SYSTEM: The system shall consist of a wall-hung, minimum 1½ HP 208/60/3 air-cooled condensing unit with matching electric defrost blower coil. The system shall be mounted on the center of the right end wall of the room. The refrigeration system shall maintain an interior temperature between 30°F and 35°F in 100°F ambient conditions without operating more than 18 hours out of a 24-hour period. The system shall be designed for outdoor installation with all necessary valves, controls, timers, vibration eliminators, insulation, crankcase heater, weather enclosure, drier, etc.; the system shall be wired to an agency-supplied disconnect box, located approximately 60 feet from the unit inside an adjoining building.

ACCESSORY ITEMS: The room shall include all features normally supplied by the manufacturer, as well as the following: coved interior moulding around the bottom interior wall; interior vapor-proof light with outside weather-proof switch and pilot light; pressure relief port protected from the weather; weather cap over the door opening; 3″-diameter dial thermometer located on the front wall next to the door; and an audible and visual high-temperature alarm loud enough to be heard 500 feet away. The alarm should be adjustable, with set point anywhere between 30°F and 50°F.

ITEM #3—REFRIGERATION SYSTEM

A new refrigeration system shall be provided and installed to convert an existing walk-in cooler to a walk-in freezer. The room is 9′ × 10′ × 9′-6″ high.

CONDENSING UNIT: Shall be a remote low-temperature type, water-cooled, 208/60/3 minimum 2 HP capacity. The unit shall be installed in the kitchen basement area.

BLOWER UNIT: Shall be electric defrost type mounted inside the existing walk-in. It shall be matched in capacity to the condensing unit. The system shall maintain a room temperature of −10°F or lower in an ambient temperature of 100°F without operation more than 18 hours out of a 24-hour period.

ACCESSORY ITEMS: The system and installation shall include all necessary valves, controls, lines, vibration eliminator, dryer, timer, condensate drain line heater, etc. to provide a complete operating system. The following accessory items shall also be provided and installed. A 3″-diameter dial thermometer shall be provided and installed next to the door. An audible and visual high-temperature alarm shall be provided and installed. The audible signal shall be heard 200 feet from the room. A heated pressure relief port shall be installed. The contractor shall remove the old condensing unit and blower coil and move them to a storage area designated by the agency. Agency will retain these units.

The above specifications were prepared by a State Agency for an existing prison and show some unusual requirements which are possible.

REFRIGERATION CHECKLIST

Considerations may involve: See checklist.

- Walk-in coolers
- Walk-in freezers
- Air curtains
- Reach-in refrigeration
- Interior selections—refrigerators
- Pizza makeup tables—check the options
- Taco station
- Low boy refrigeration
- Remote compressors—precharged or to be piped
- Over- and under-refrigeration styles available

APPROXIMATE SHIPPING WEIGHTS—SELECTED EQUIPMENT

Walk in Cooler/Freezer Galvalume Construction *without* Compressors, with Floor:

8″ × 10′	1400#
8 × 14″	1800#
12 × 16′	2660#

Compressors

1/2 HP	160#
3/4 HP	210#
1 HP	280#
1 1/2 HP	440#
2 HP	540#
3 HP	580#

All following Units include Compressors

1 Door Upright Refrigerator	350#
2 Door Upright Refrigerator	550#
3 Door Upright Refrigerator	770#
1 Door Sandwich Unit	180#
2 Door Sandwich Unit	253#
3 Door Sandwich Unit	370#
1 Door Pizza Prep Table	229#
2 Door Pizza Prep Table	427#
3 Door Pizza Prep Table	545#
Deli Case 50″	450#
74″	660#
98″	880#
Taco make up Table 84″	550#

PLANNING SHEET—WALK IN COOLERS AND FREEZERS

Salespeople should analyze the job site from the viewpoint of the installer and the possible problems that the installer may encounter. Doing so will assure that the job quote will be sufficient to assure proper installation with the greatest efficiency and to the satisfaction of the customer.

Customer: ______________________ Sales Manager: ______________________

Person in charge at the job site: ______________ Telephone: ______________________

Floor:

On what type of floor is the unit being built? ______________________

What is the condition of this floor: ______________________

Ceiling:

What is the ceiling height above the standard units? ______________________

Will the ceiling of the larger units be suspended? ______________________

From what type of structure will it be suspended? ______________________

In what direction are the beams, joints, or purloins in relation to the unit? ______________________

What is the distance of the suspension? ______________________

What is the interval between points of suspension? ______________________

Access:

What access is there to the work area? ______________________

What is the size of the work area? ______________________

Is there ample space to carry panels into the installation area? ______________________

Refrigeration:

What is the distance from the compressor to the evaporator? ______________________

Where is the location of the drains? ______________________

Is there ample space or ventilation for air cooled compressors? ______________________

Additional Considerations:

Around the unit are there any obstructions: Pipes, electrical curbs, etc.? ______________________

Special equipment that will be required ______________________

What power is available? ______________________

Location: ______________ Voltage: ______________ Phase: ______________

Is the work area heated? ______________________

Is other work being done at the job site? __________ How will this other work affect the delivery and installation of the job? ______________________

What days and times can the work be delivered and installed? ______________________

Are there Union conflicts at the job site? ______ Are any anticipated? ______________________

If so, what is the nature? ______________________

Is the reverse side of this check list being used for additional information, comments or instructions?

Figure 3-5. Planning sheet—walk-in coolers and freezers.

Directions to the job site: ____
____
____
____
____

Sketch:
Sketch the cooler/freezer in the space provided. Draw or outline the most prominent features or fundamental facts. Show the placement of the doors and how they are hinged. Clearly label the dimensions of the unit—it's length, width, and height; and the dimensions of any partitions or special features.

Indicate on the sketch anything that will affect the placement of the unit (any obstructions), the refrigeration or the operation of the doors. Include: existing walls, columns, pilasters, beams, pipes, drains, fixtures and so forth. Please be clear with your instructions.

Job: ______________________ Sales Manager: ______________________
Unit Size: Length ________ Width ________ Height ________
Type: ____Cooler ____Freezer ____Combination ____Display ____Portable
____Other ____

Courtesy of: ONE ENERGY, INC.

Use for Pencil Sketch

Figure 3-5. (*continued*)

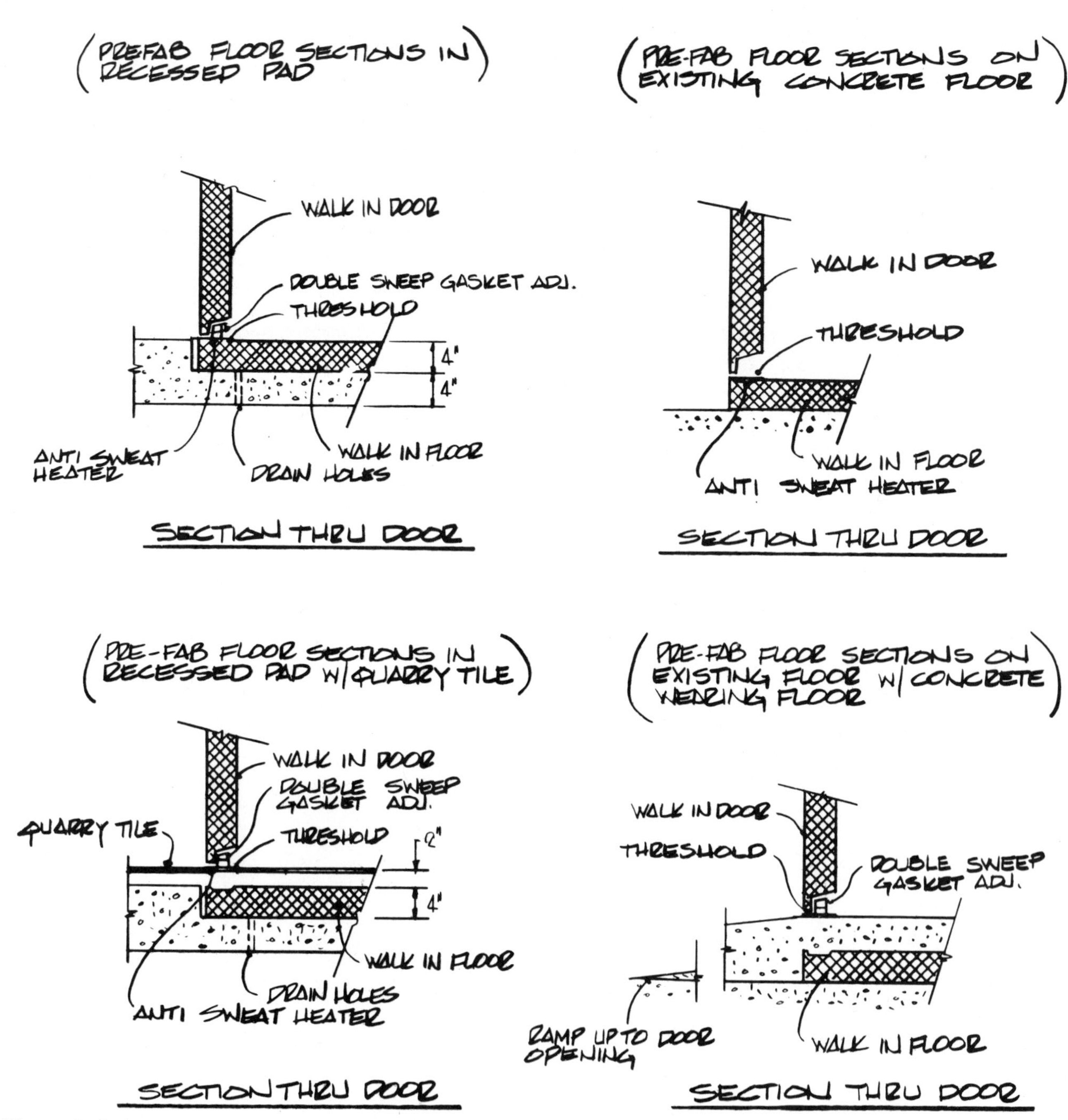

Figure 3-6. Typical indoor cooler installations; pre-fab floor sections installed in pads and on existing floors. Many other styles are available. Working drawings showing this detail are necessary for job coordination. (Courtesy Vollrath Refrigeration)

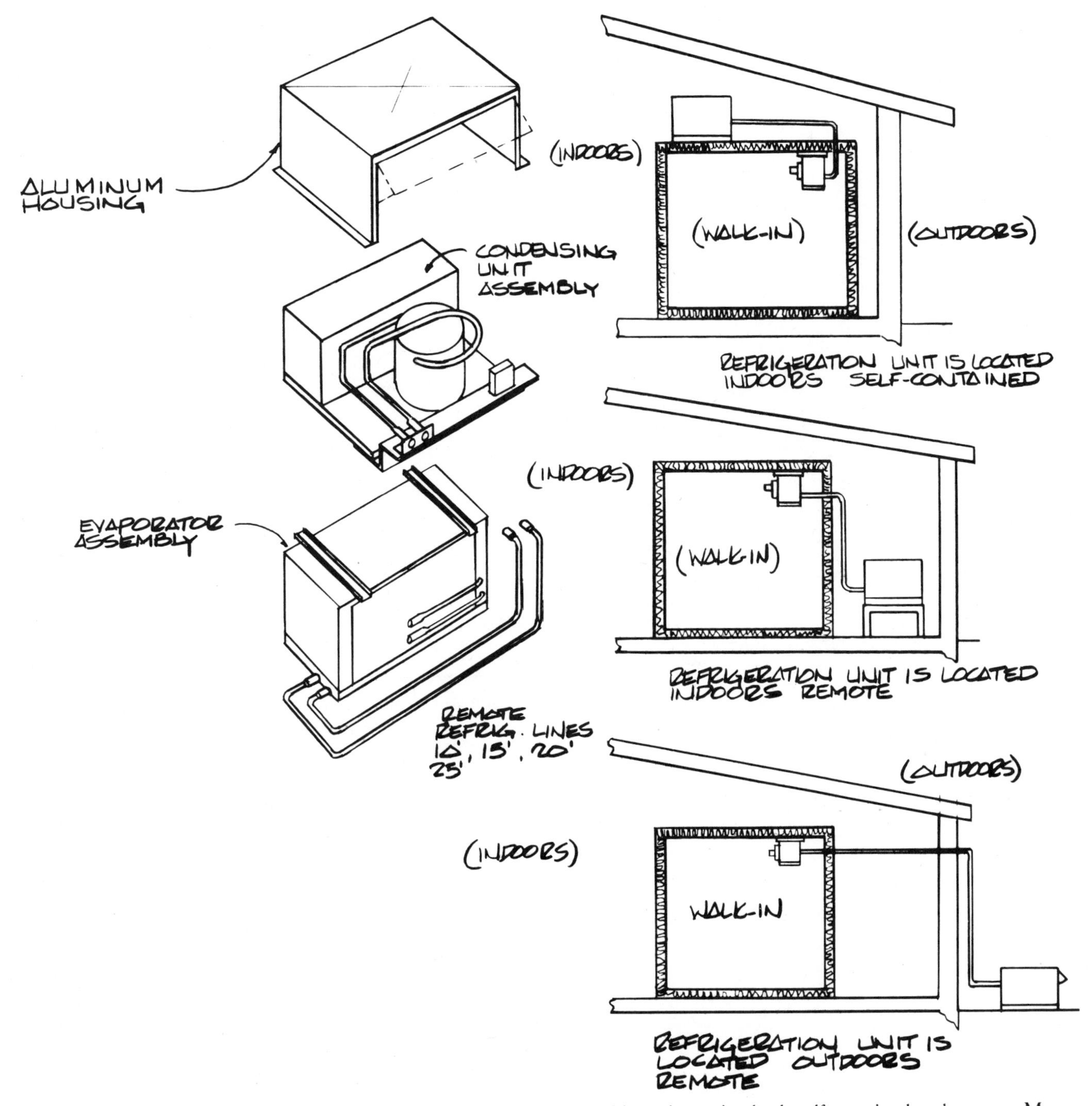

Figure 3-7. Compressor variations. Some typical applications of refrigeration units, both self-contained and remote. Many other variations are available. (Courtesy Vollrath Refrigeration)

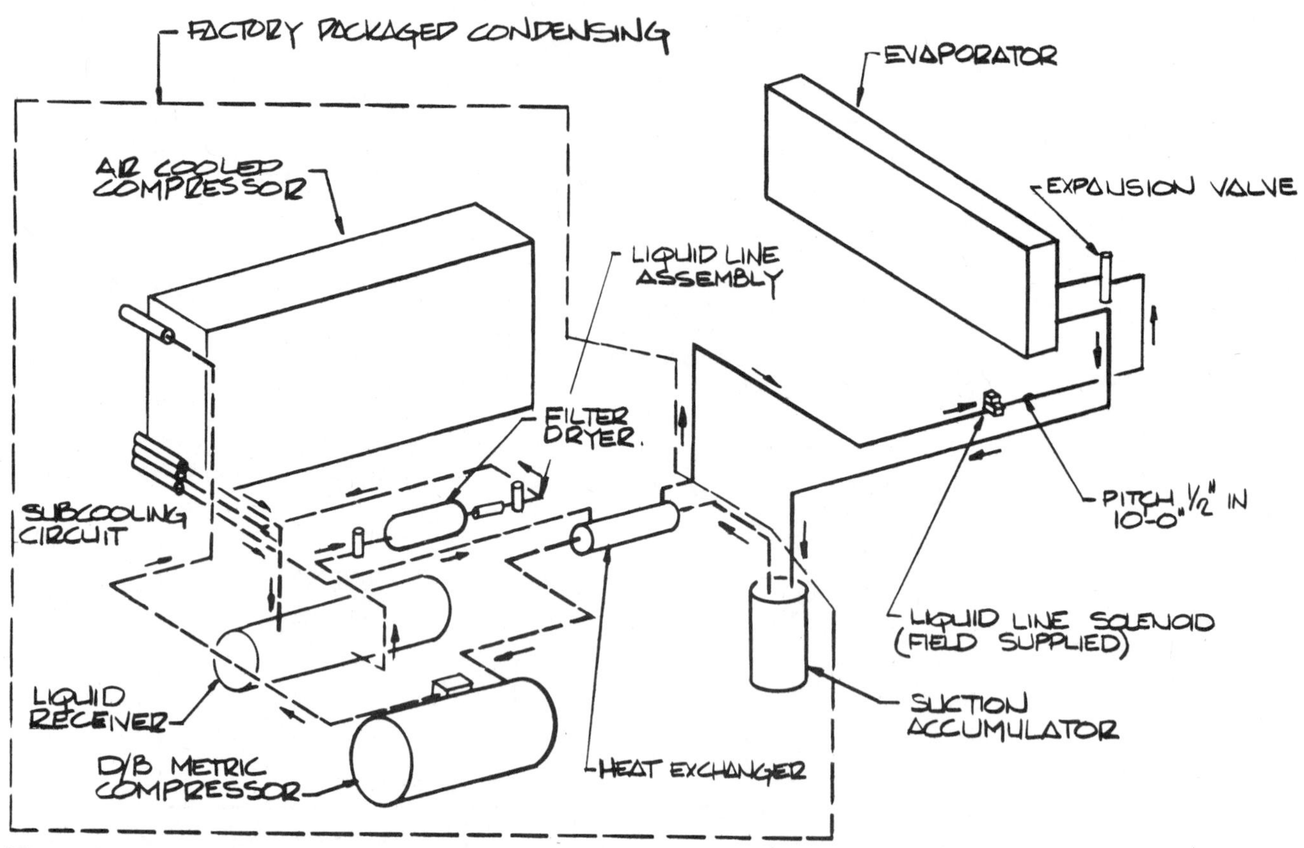

Figure 3-8. Sample refrigeration schematic. In many elborate combination walk-in refrigerators and freezers, it is advantageous to use remote refrigeration components, the result being extensive piping. This illustration shows the complexities of such a system. (Courtesy Vollrath Refrigeration)

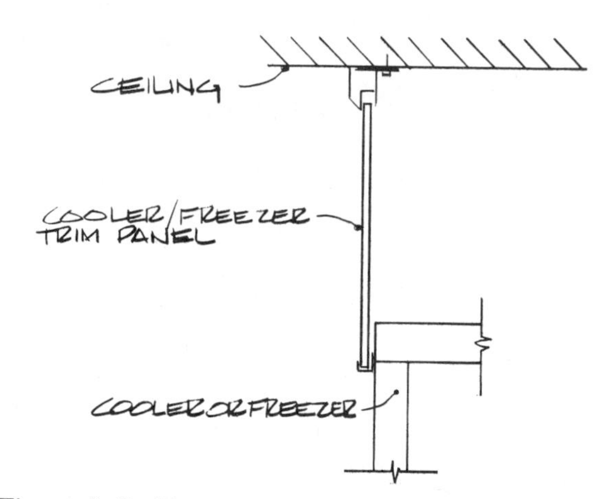

Figure 3-9. Trim panel detail—walk-in cooler/freezer.

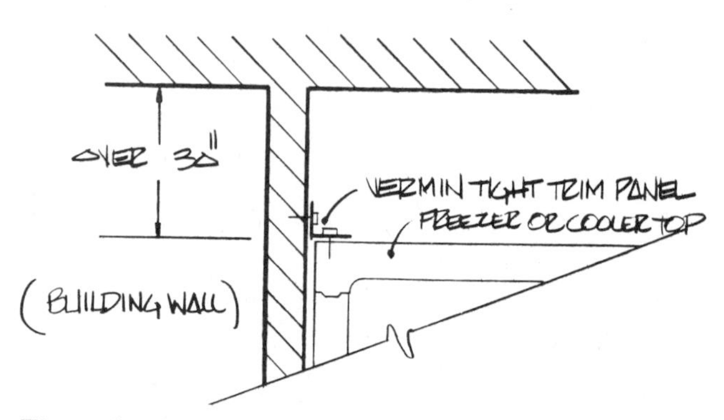

Figure 3-10. Acceptable method of closing walk-in cooler or freezer top to adjacent wall.

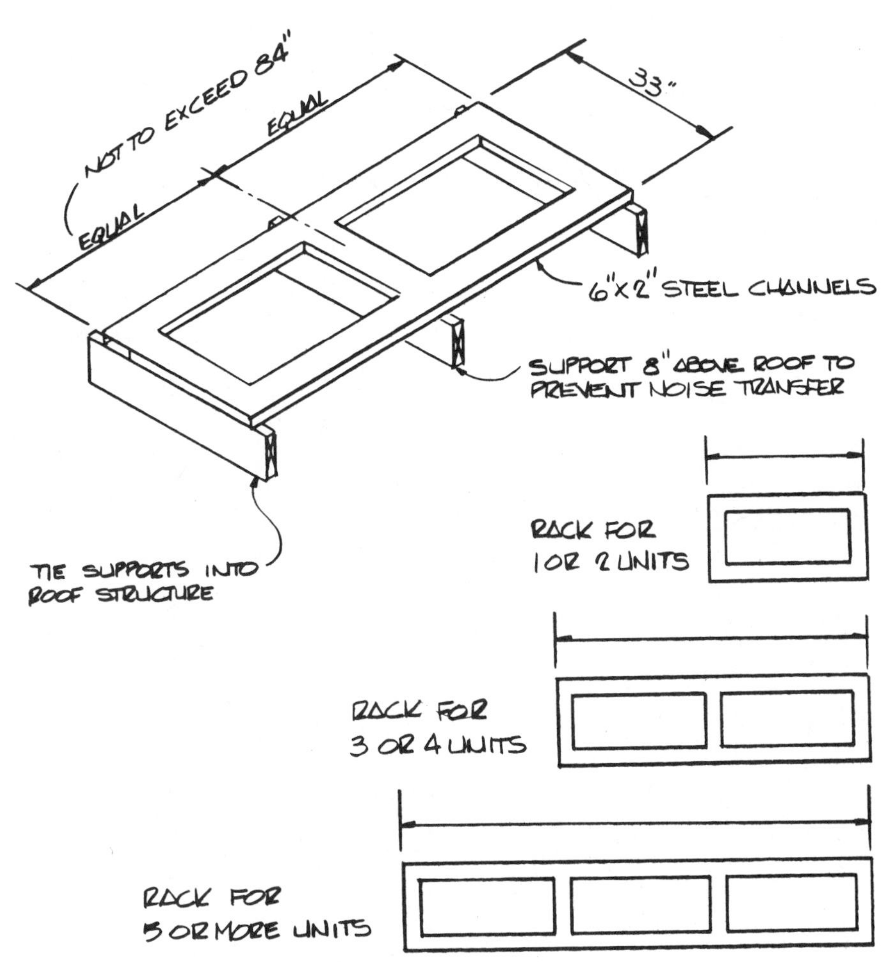

Figure 3-11. Condensing unit racks.

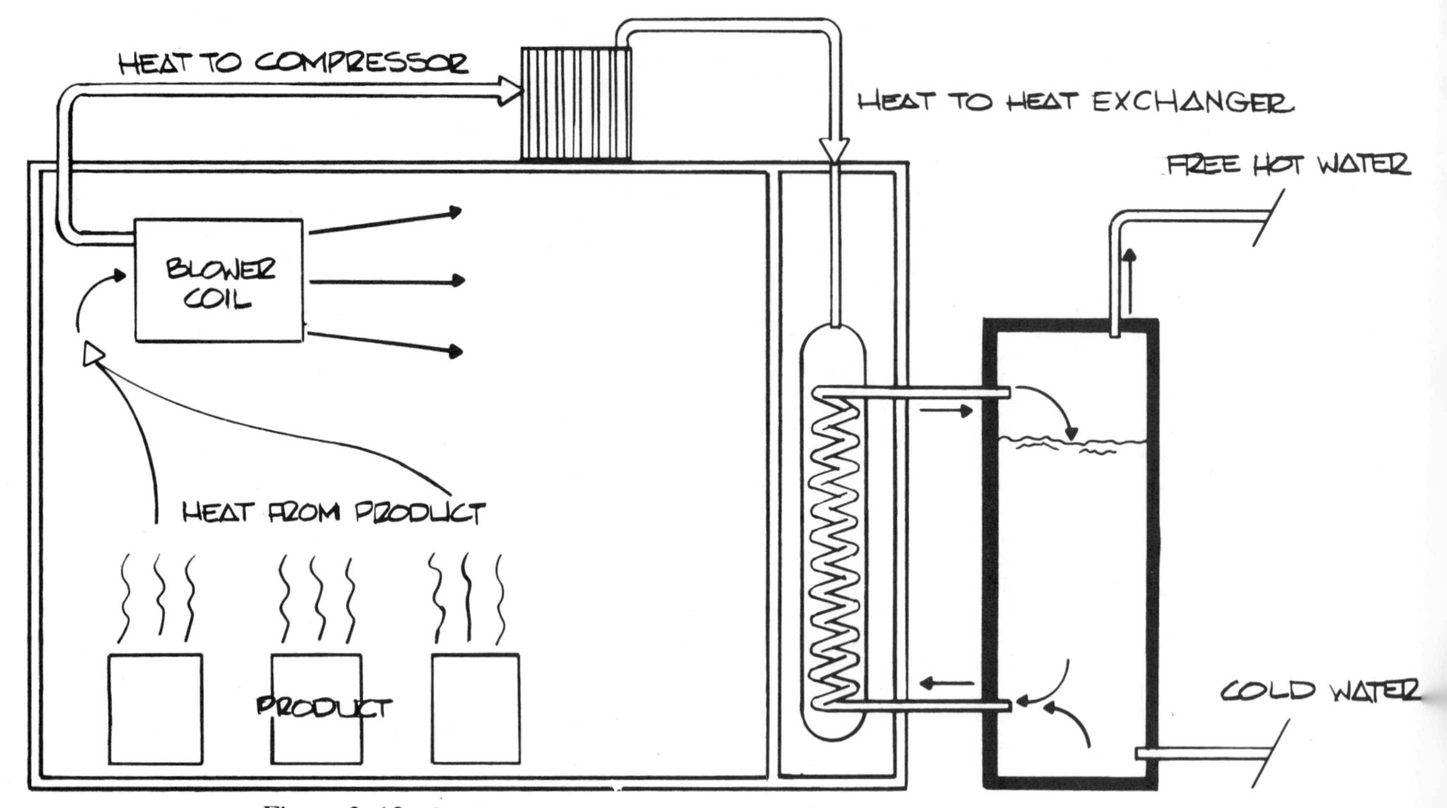

Figure 3-12. Cooling system with water-cooled condenser showing a heat exchanger.

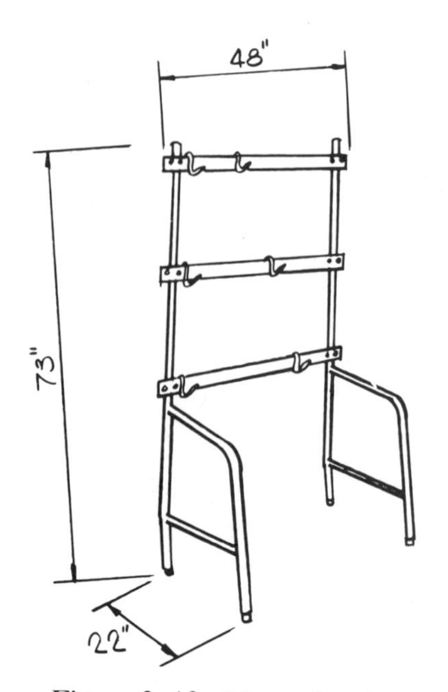

Figure 3-13. Meat rail rack.

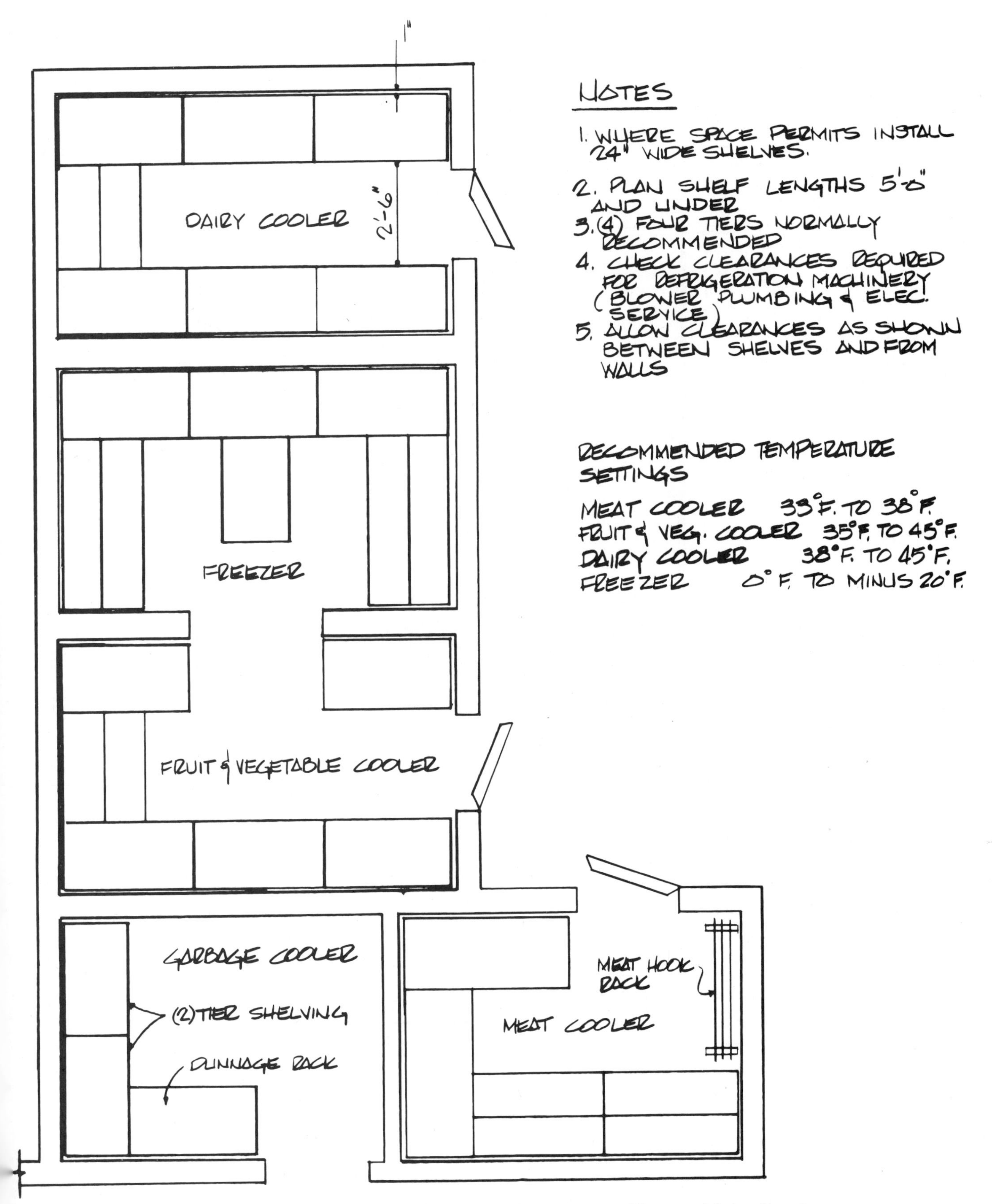

Figure 3-14. Typical shelving layout for walk-in refrigerators (Courtesy Market Forge)

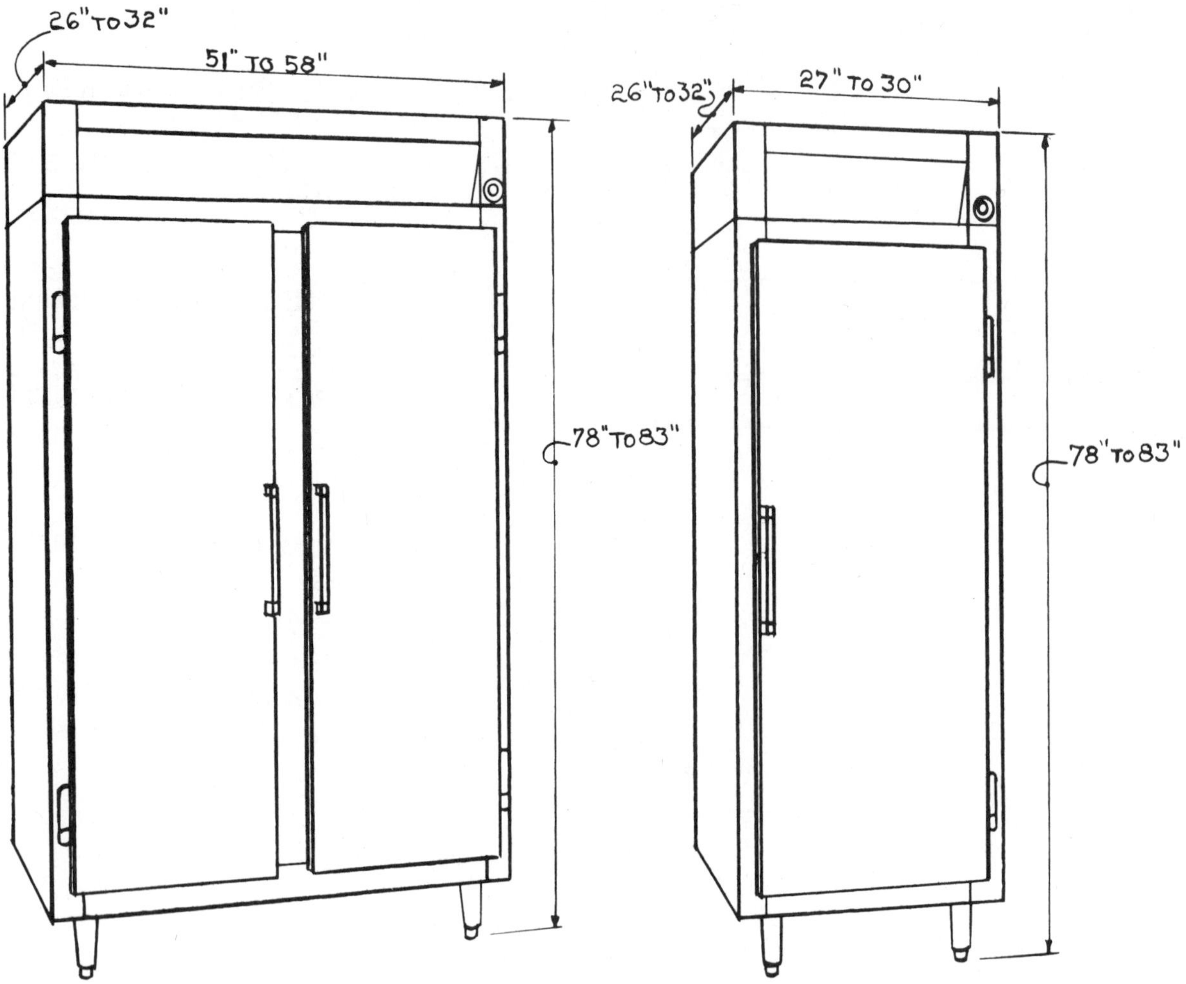

Figure 3-15. Exterior details of commercial reach-in refrigerators or freezers.

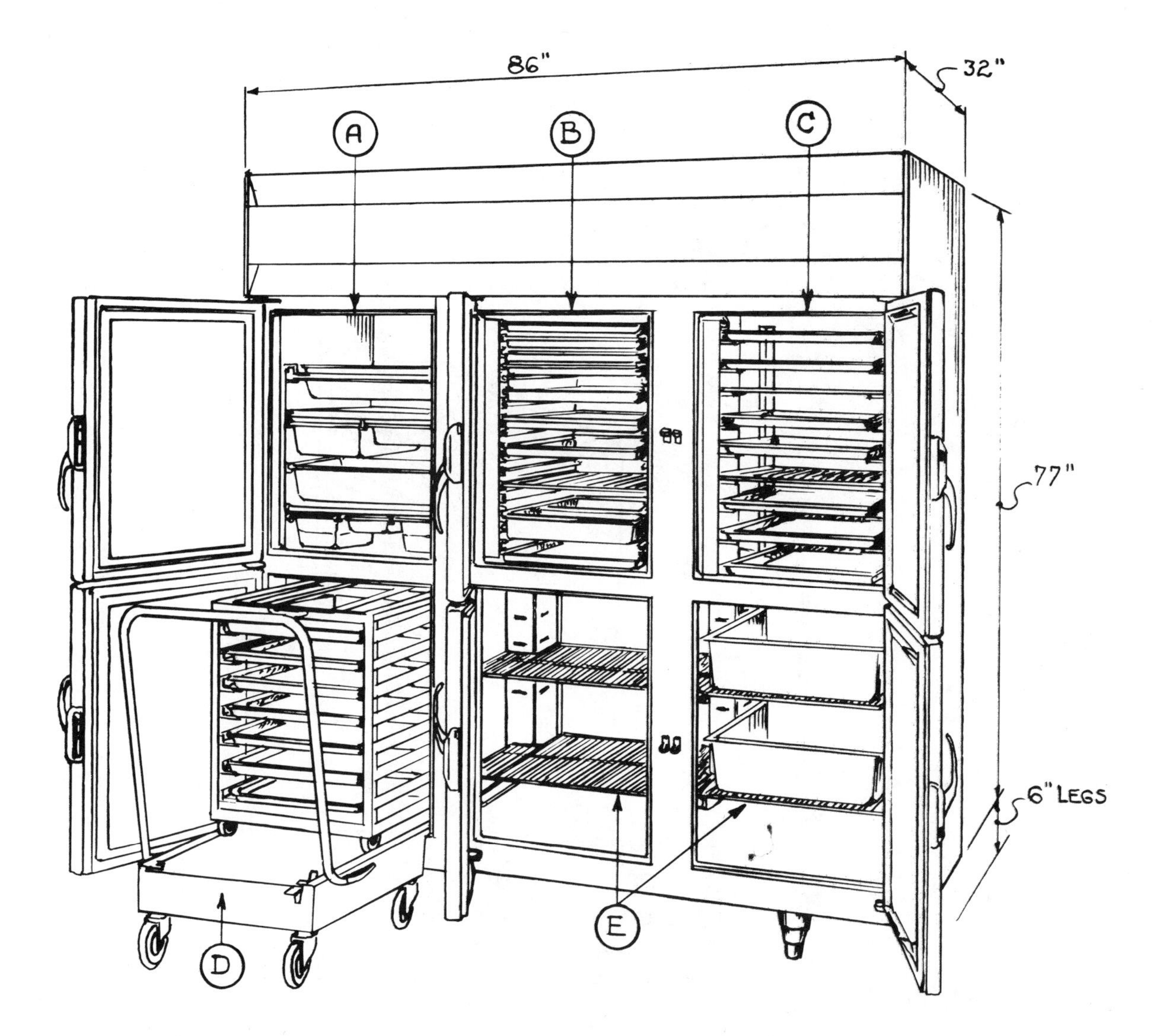

A. PAN GLIDES FOR 12 X 20 AND FRACTIONAL FOOD SERVICE PANS
B. PAN GLIDES FOR 18 X 26 FOOD SERVICE PANS
C. UNIVERSAL PAN GLIDES FITS MOST STANDARD PANS
D. TRANSPORT TRUCK MODULE 18 X 26 PANS
E. STANDARD WIRE SHELVING

Figure 3-16. Interior features of commercial reach-in refrigerators.

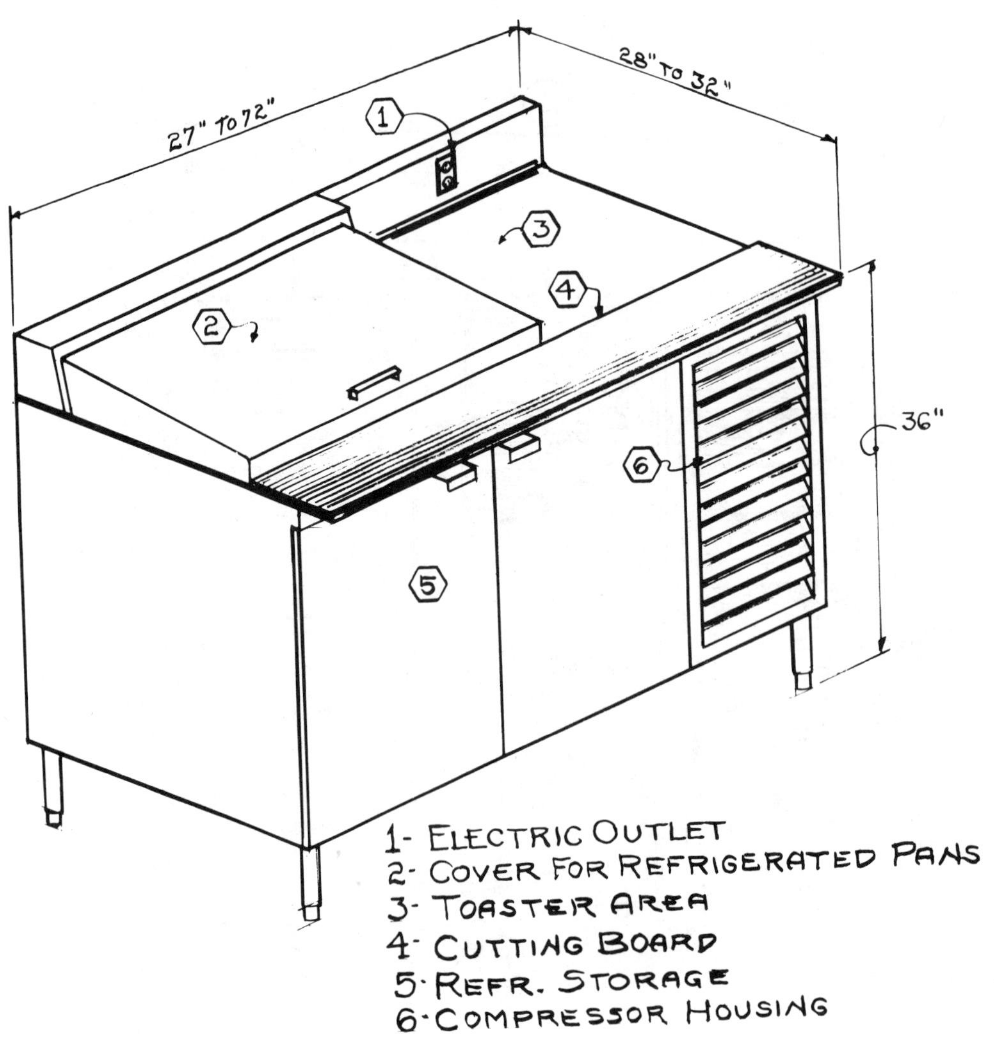

Figure 3-17. Typical sandwich unit.

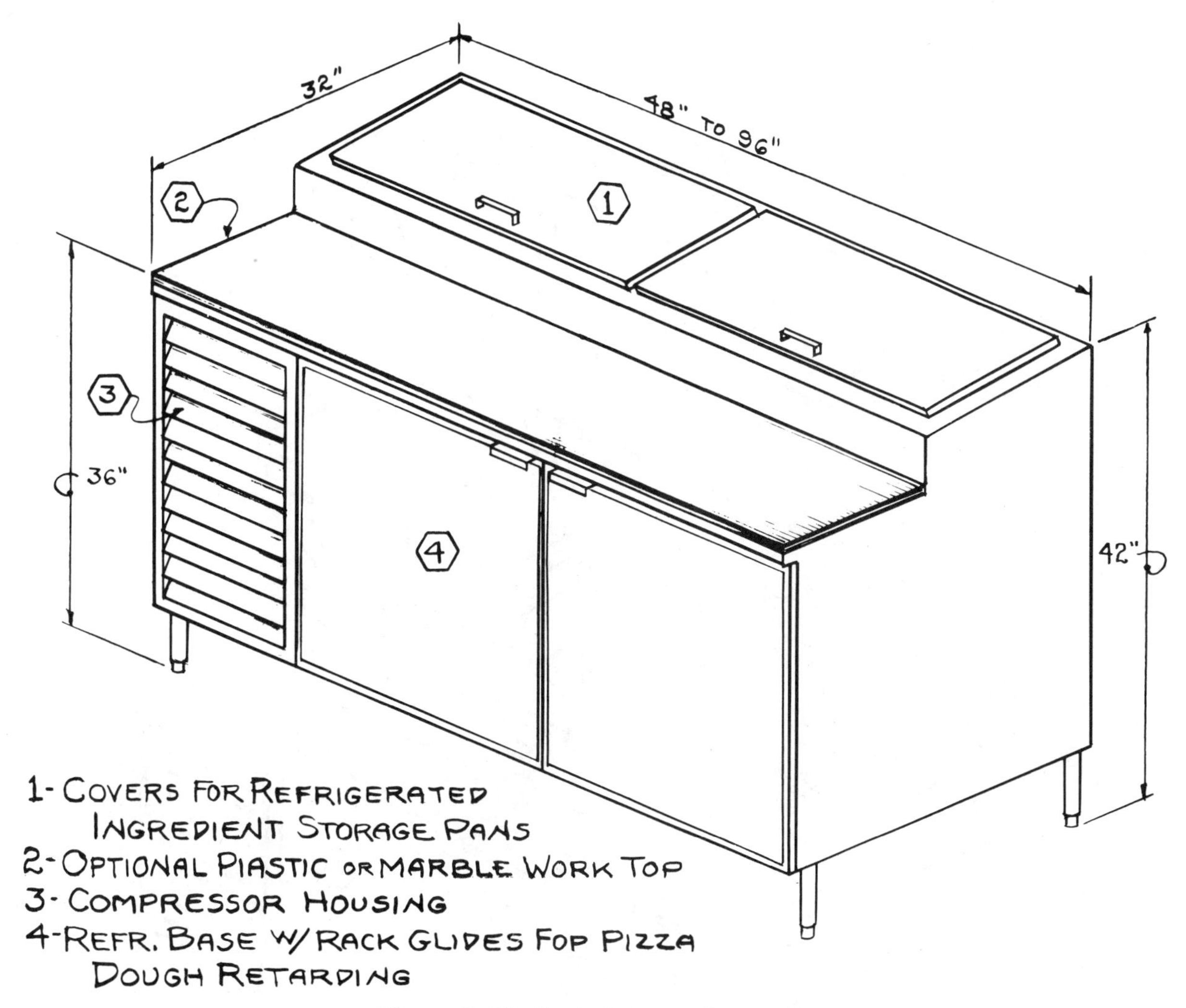

Figure 3-18. Typical pizza makeup table.

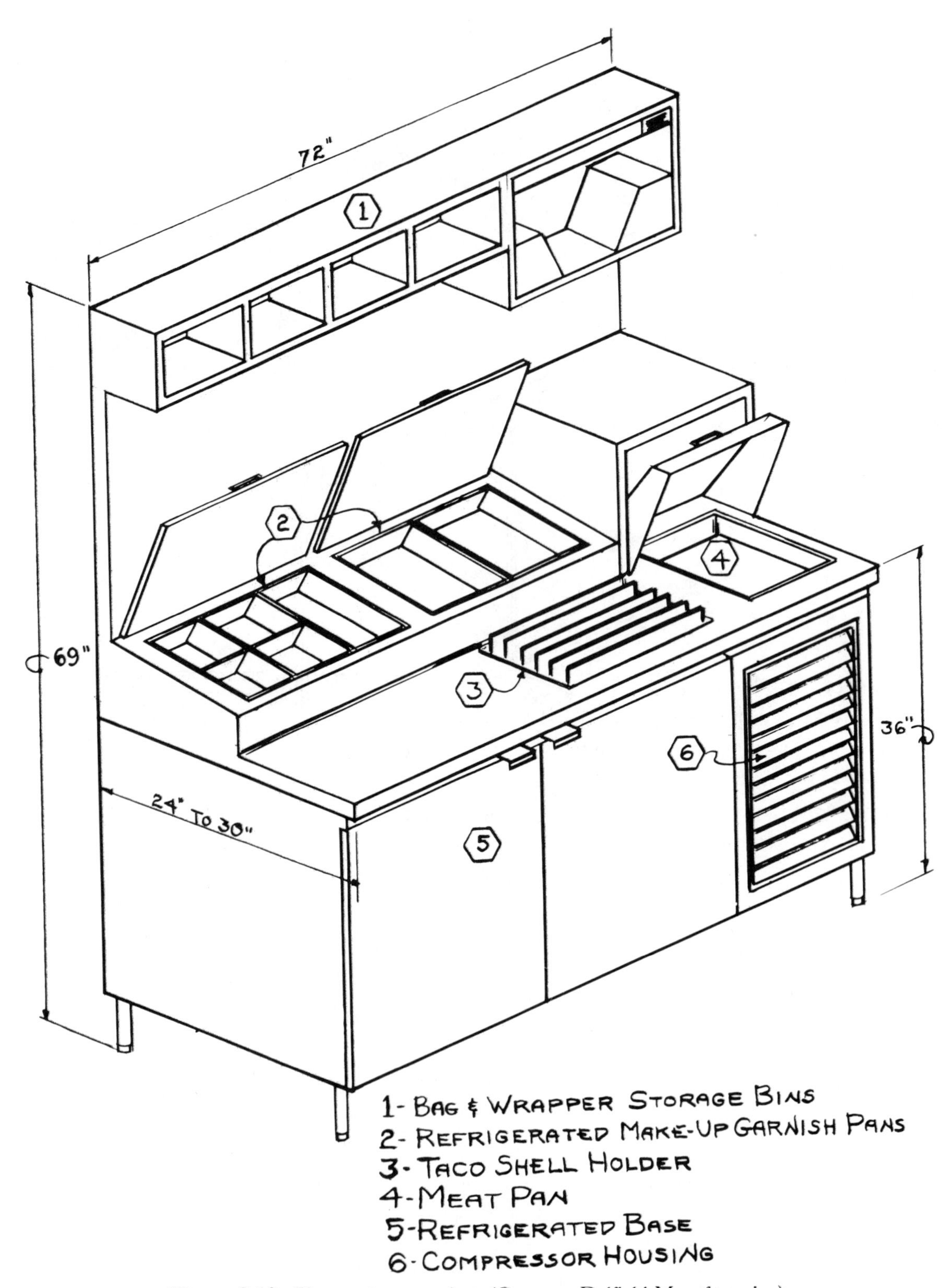

Figure 3-19. Taco makeup station. (Courtesy Delfield Manufacturing)

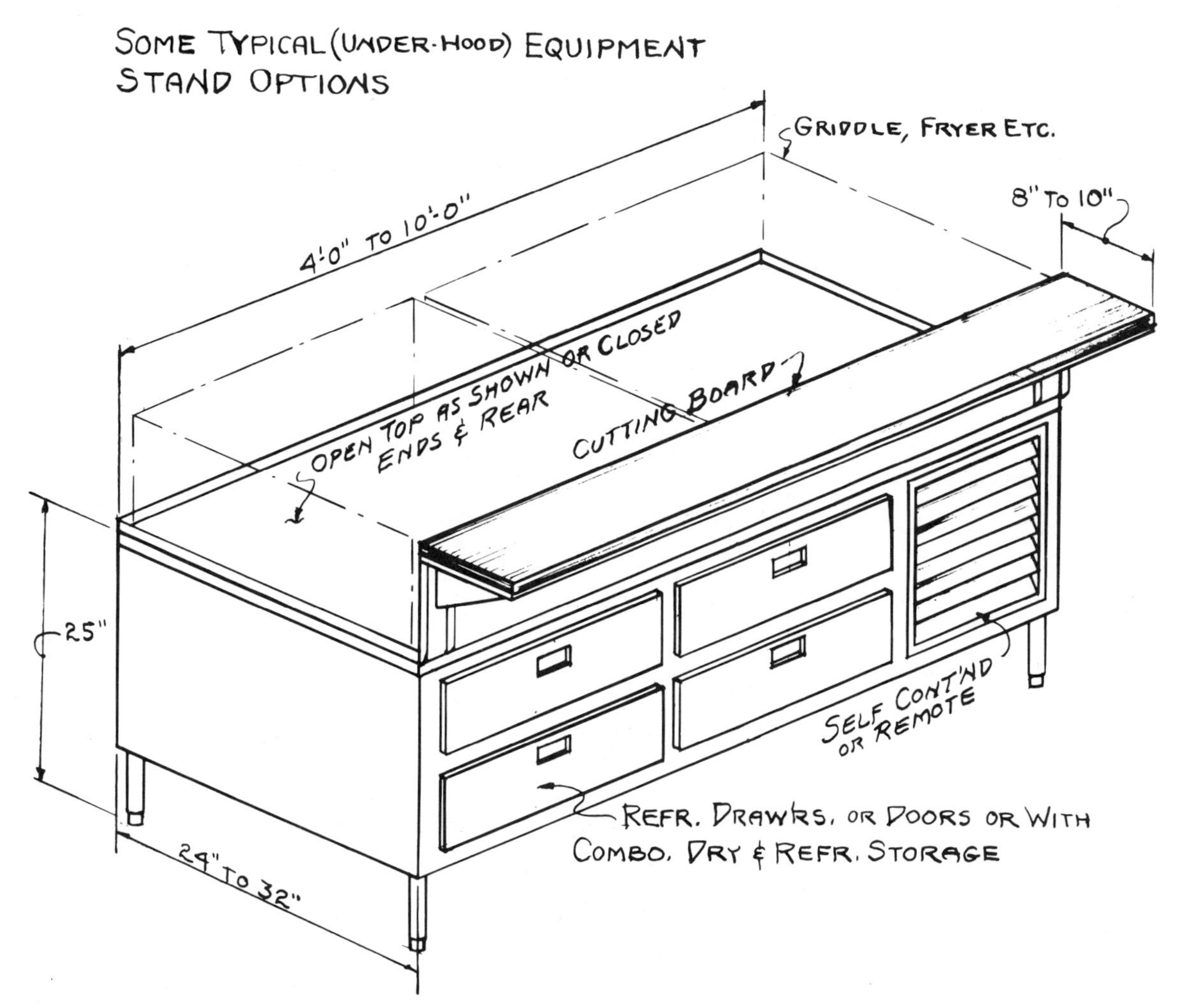

Figure 3-20. Refrigerated equipment stand.

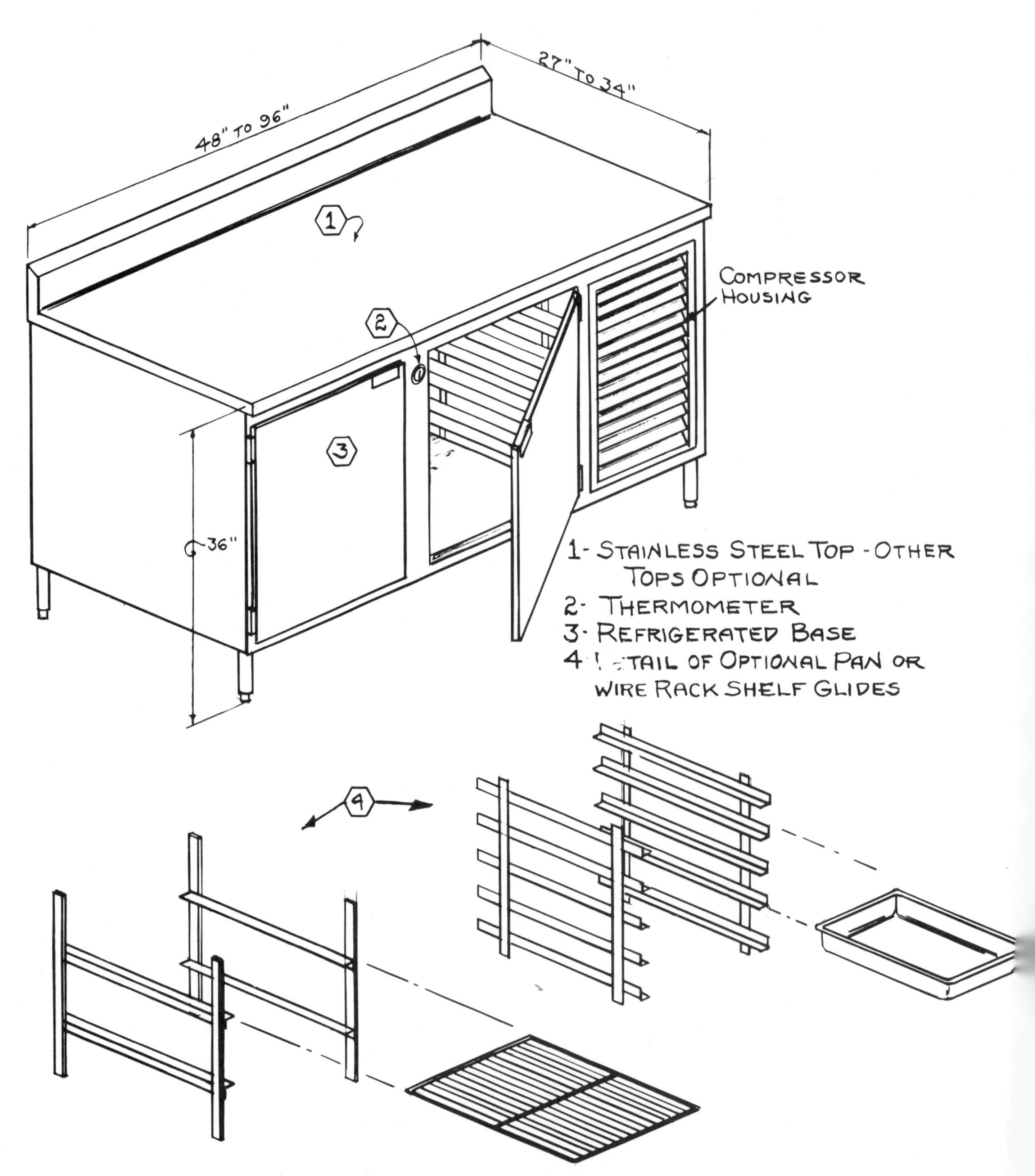

Figure 3-21. Refrigerated base worktable.

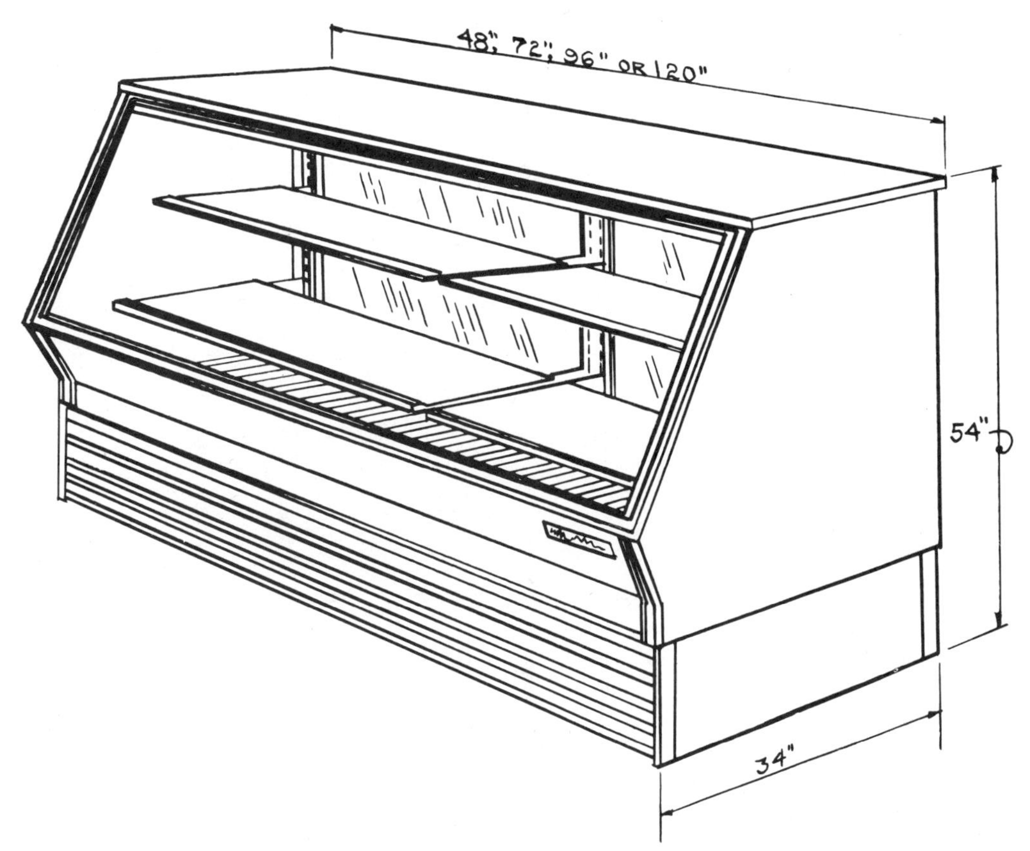

Figure 3-22. Delicatessen cooler.

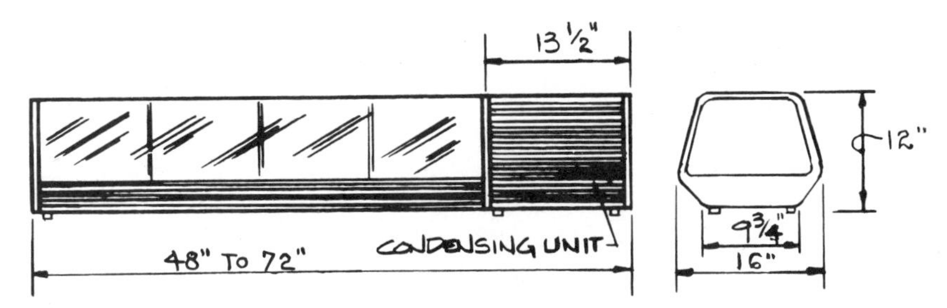

Figure 3-23. Sushi refrigerator display case.

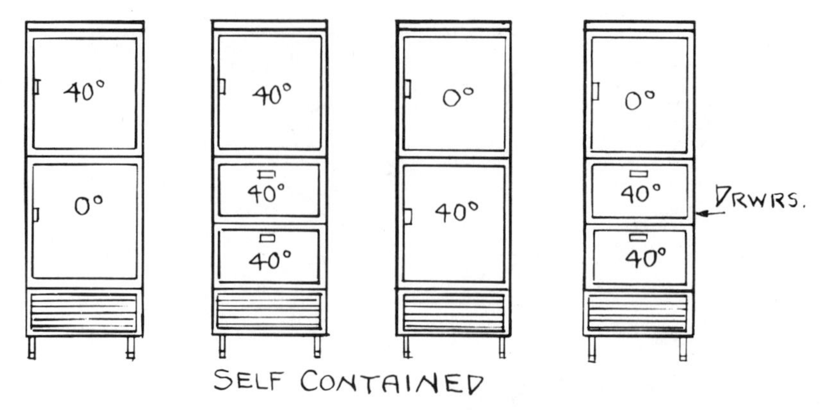

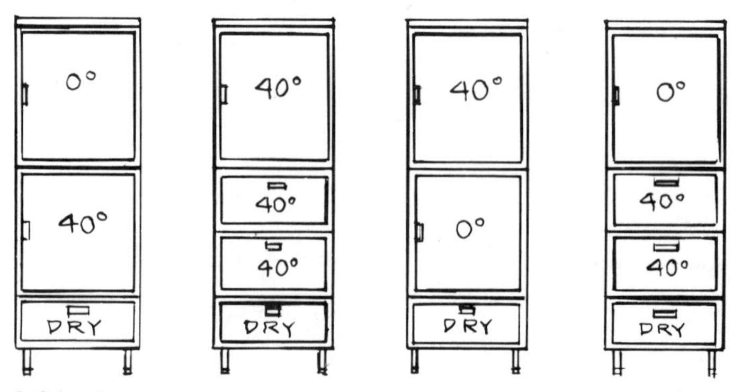

Figure 3-24. Over and under refrigerator/freezer units. (Courtesy Delfield Manufacturing)

4

Preparation Equipment

This chapter takes the operator beyond the normal machinery of food preparation and into a world of construction and detail that, properly studied, will provide the best possible tools for the food processing department.

Most of the isometric drawings are self-explanatory; and, in combination, the details will produce work stations. Users can study the array of equipment illustrated, and select the best options for their particular needs. Figure 4–1 shows a basic preparation area.

Some often forgotten considerations in prep areas are worth reviewing.

1. Would wheels be advantageous on tables?
2. Have planners allowed for electrical outlets in walls or backsplash of equipment?
3. Are tool drawers removable and easily cleaned?
4. Is there room for cutting boards under the table for storage?
5. Is there need for a lazy Susan or pole for small whips, ladles, etc.?
6. Has the proper pot rack been selected? Can employees reach the utensils?
7. Are the gauge and finish correct for the job?

It is a good idea to ask the supplier for elevation drawings, as shown in Figures 4–2 and 4–3, to alleviate any misunderstandings about content or construction of this equipment.

Details of tables, cabinet bases, backsplash design, cutting boards, kickplates, shelves, drawers, leg support, tray locks, garnish pans, stainless steel tops, pot racks, sinks, and so on, are shown in the illustrations (Figures 4–4 through 4–32).

Figures 4–28 through 4–31 present good examples of problem solvers that are available but not generally known:

- False bottom for sink (Figure 4–28): Often sinks are too deep for shorter people to work at them comfortably. This simple drop-in platform can be fabricated in any width or height.
- Mobile floor sink (Figure 4–29): This unit has many uses; it can serve as a soak sink for silverware, as a bridge to the regular drain for kettles, and as a drainer for meats and produce.
- Food cutter table (Figure 4–30): This table is ideal for food cutters of all makes and sizes. It functions as a total prep area, allowing the operator water and a pan area, and the entire unit can be cleaned at the point of service.
- Glass filler sink (Figure 4–31): This special sink is the perfect fill area for water for large parties and banquets, and also doubles as a soak or defrost area.

The food preparation machinery listed at the end of this chapter has a certain reasonable life span. The reader will be better-prepared for selecting individual items of equipment after becoming familiar with the good construction that is available in stainless steel,

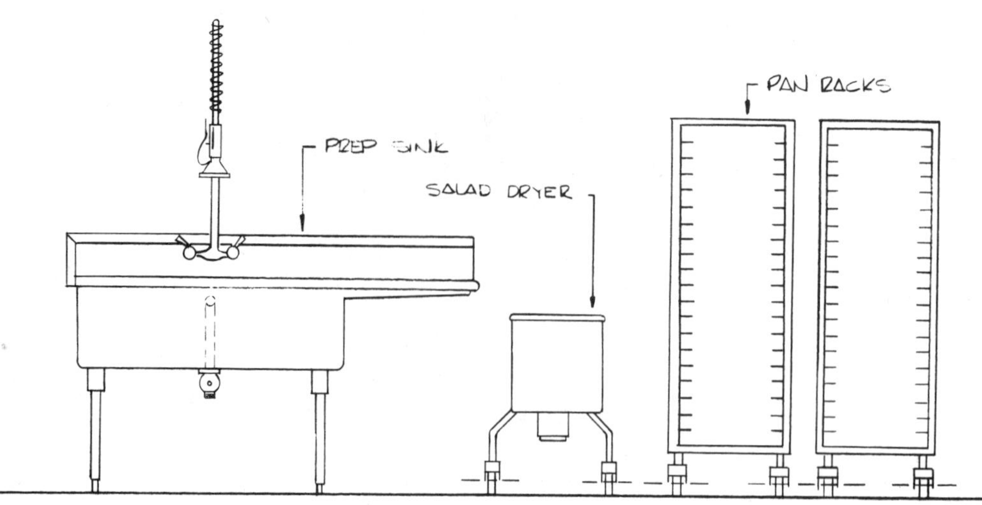

Figure 4-1. Basic preparation area. Note that 18″ × 26″ pan trucks are available at the sink area to move washed foods, either to walk-ins for refrigeration (e.g., salads) or for vegetable steaming. Hotel pans measuring 12″ × 20″ also may be trucked in pan racks with universal slides.

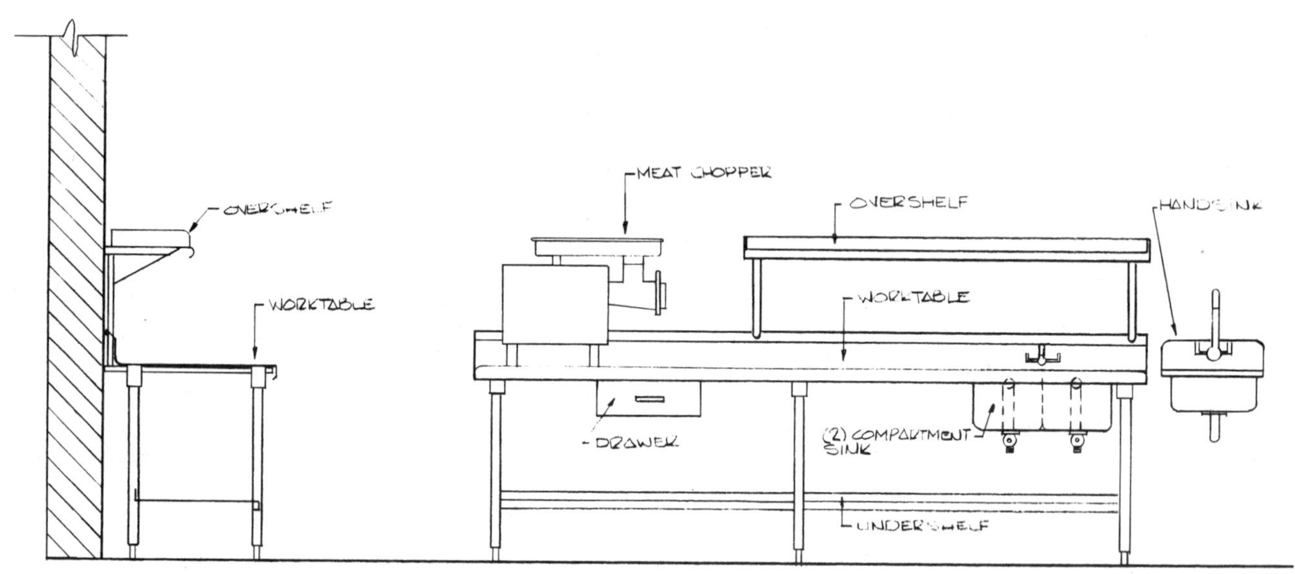

Figure 4-2. Preparation area. This area has incorporated the necessary hand sink, full undershelf storage, a valuable tool drawer, and an overshelf.

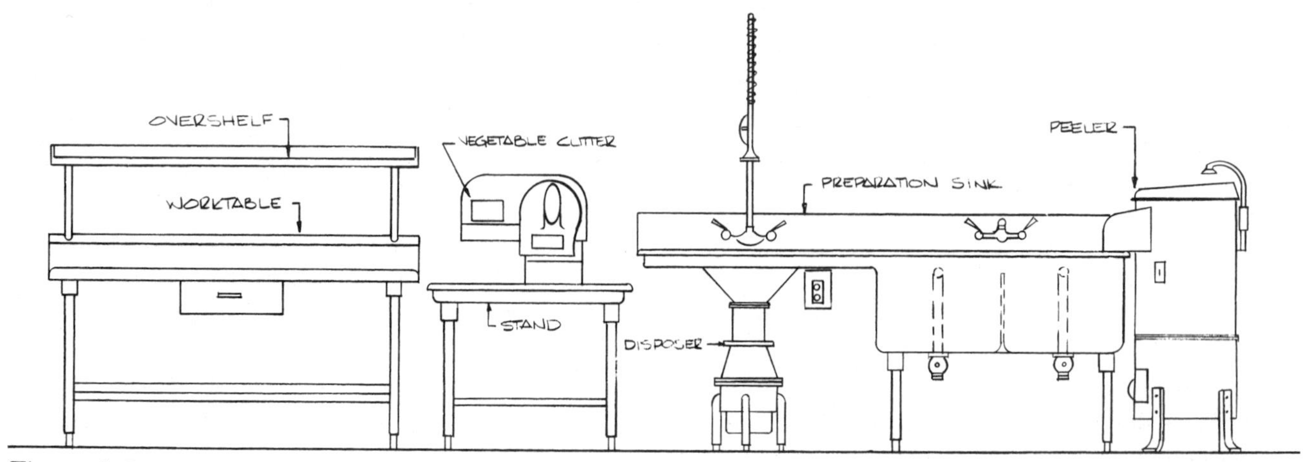

Figure 4-3. Preparation area. A more detailed preparation area as shown could include a garbage disposal and room for mobile preparation equipment such as choppers, food cutters, and other specialized prep equipment between sinks and tables.

worktables, sinks, and prep areas, which the text and illustrations of this chapter describe.

STAINLESS STEEL

The specifications for foodservice equipment included in Chapter 1 serve to highlight the key information and terms used in the good construction of custom stainless steel work.

Too often in the foodservice industry, after equipment arrives, the actual user wishes the purchaser had added options to ensure efficiency. It is impossible to overstate the importance of researching one's options thoroughly.

The stainless steel edge styles shown in Figure 4–5 represent standards used in the foodservice industry. Many of these edges are shown in this chapter and throughout the book.

STAINLESS STEEL SHEET

Gauge	Decimal	Product Use
16	.075	Tabletops, sinks, overshelves, undershelves, underbracing
16	.059	Undershelves, brackets
18	.048	Body panels, partitions, access panels, portable bins, sliding doors, interior shelving, drawer bodies, canopies
20	.035	Refrigerator liners, interior drawer and door panels

STAINLESS STEEL AND GALVANIZED STEEL TUBING

Size	Gauge	Decimal	Product Use
1″ O.D.	18	.051	Tubular tray slides (S/S only)
1¼″ O.D.	16	.063	Connecting rails, tubular undershelves
1⅝″ O.D.	16	.063	Legs, supports for overshelf, and pot racks
2″ O.D.	18	.051	Gussets and leg holders, traffic rails

WORKTABLES AND COUNTERTOPS

DESIRABLE FEATURES OF WORKTABLES

- Dimensions: Tables should be 4 to 8 feet in length, 30 inches wide (24 to 48 inches wide commonly available), 34 inches high.
- Materials: Worktable tops should be 14-gauge 18-8 stainless steel with 1½-inch rolled edge; adjustable, tubular legs can be galvanized steel.
- Mobile tables should have 5-inch locking swivel wheel casters.
- Undershelf and utensil drawer(s) should have recessed handles, or open-front table can be used to accommodate mobile storage bins, mobile drawer units, racks, etc. Undershelf should be full length for storage of sheet pans, hot foodservice pans, etc.
- Construction should meet National Sanitation Foundation (N.S.F.) standards. If tables are fabricated locally, particular attention should be given to exposed edges, table legs, and feet.
- Optional features: Shelf over table is available for condiments, overhead utensil racks, curbing, sinks, etc.
- Check with local health department officials to find out whether worktables with laminated plastic, maple, or solid plastic tops are acceptable.

PREPARATION EQUIPMENT CHECKLIST

Preparation equipment may include:

- Blenders
- Burger-forming machines
- Breading machines
- Crepe maker
- Doughnut-sugaring machine
- Mobile cookie dropper
- Cutter mixers
- Salad driers
- Pan racks
- Croissant rollers
- Pie dough rollers
- Pizza rollers
- Pie formers
- Choppers
- Marinators
- Dough dividers
- Mixers
- French fry cutters
- Pasta makers
- Peelers
- Disposers
- Ice cream makers
- Ingredient bins
- Dough rounders
- Doughnut glazers
- Worktables
- Sinks
- Pot racks
- Mobile pan racks
- Food processors
- Saws
- Slicers
- Sheeters
- Rollers

Important considerations are:

- Having water and drains nearby.
- Matching equipment to the menu.
- Ease of cleaning.
- Keeping instruction and repair manuals handy.

APPROXIMATE SHIPPING WEIGHT SELECTED EQUIPMENT

Work Tables 16 Gauge Stainless Steel

24 × 36	68#
24 × 48	79#
24 × 60	93#
30 × 45	96#
30 × 60	111#
30 × 72	127#
30 × 96	235#

Sinks 16 Gauge—3 Compartment with Drain Boards

24″ × 72″	100#
24″ × 94″	125#
30″ × 120″	175#

Meat Chopper	#12 Hub	1/2 HP	135#
	#32 Hub	3 HP	300#

Meat Saw	20 QT	192#
Mixer	30 QT	450#
Mixer	60 QT	700#
Mixer	80 QT	850#

Commercial Slicer 12″ Knife	116#
Pizza Dough Roller-Counter	295#
Buffalo Food Cutter 1-HP	204#
Vertical Cutter Mixer 30 QT	340#
Vertical Cutter Mixer 45 QT	365#
Potatoe Peeler 30 LBS. W/Base	212#

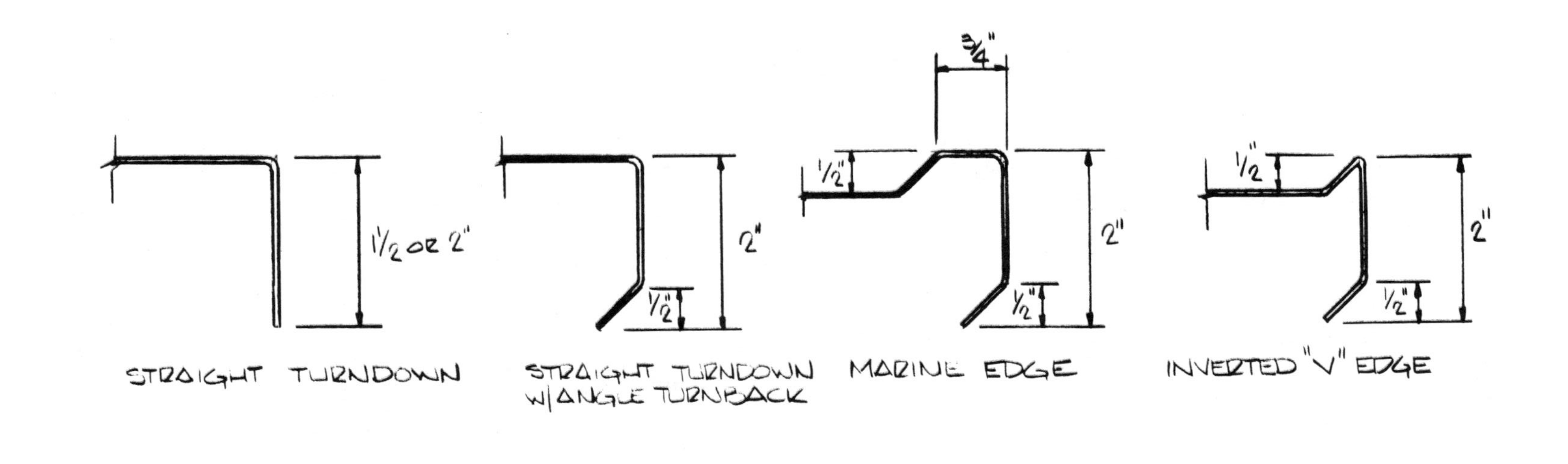

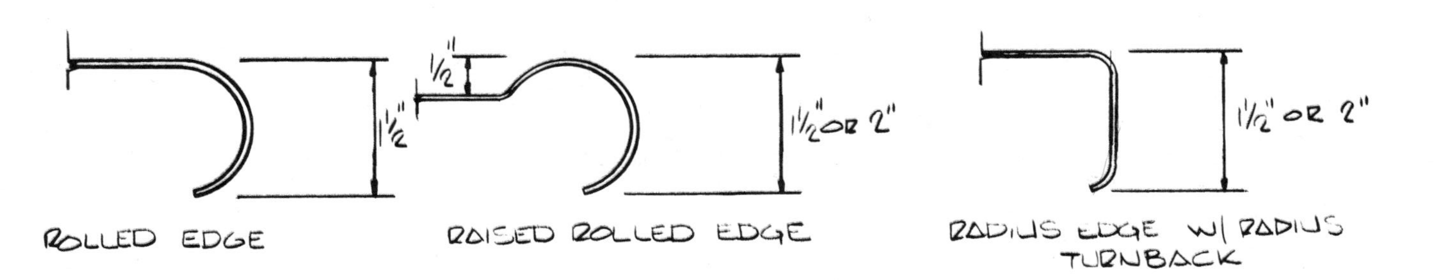

Figure 4-4. Table edges. Stainless-steel-constructed tables, backsplash, and sink edge styles vary according to manufacturer and need; so a buyer of stainless steel equipment should be specific about needs. For example, a marine edge as shown would hold liquids within the table body, as opposed to standard construction. Also, a backsplash with a wide return to the wall would allow for plumbing or electrical connections, whereas a short return might not accommodate utilities.

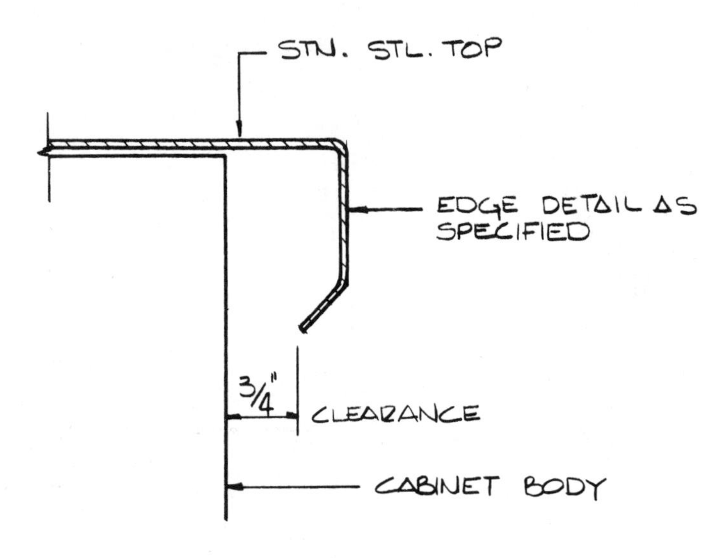

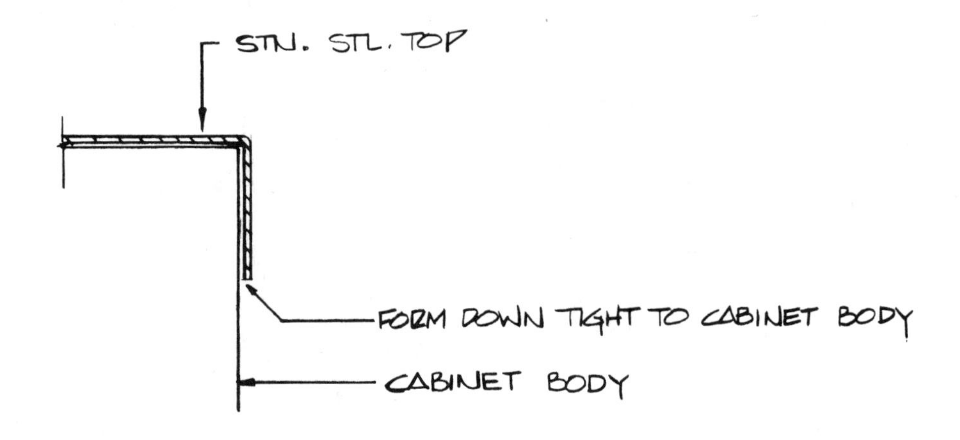

Figure 4-5. Stainless steel details: two types of stainless steel turndown for cabinet bases, and bull nosed corner for a work-table. The location and actual use of the cabinet will determine the turndown style. A bull nosed table corner is of much greater value than a sharp intersection.

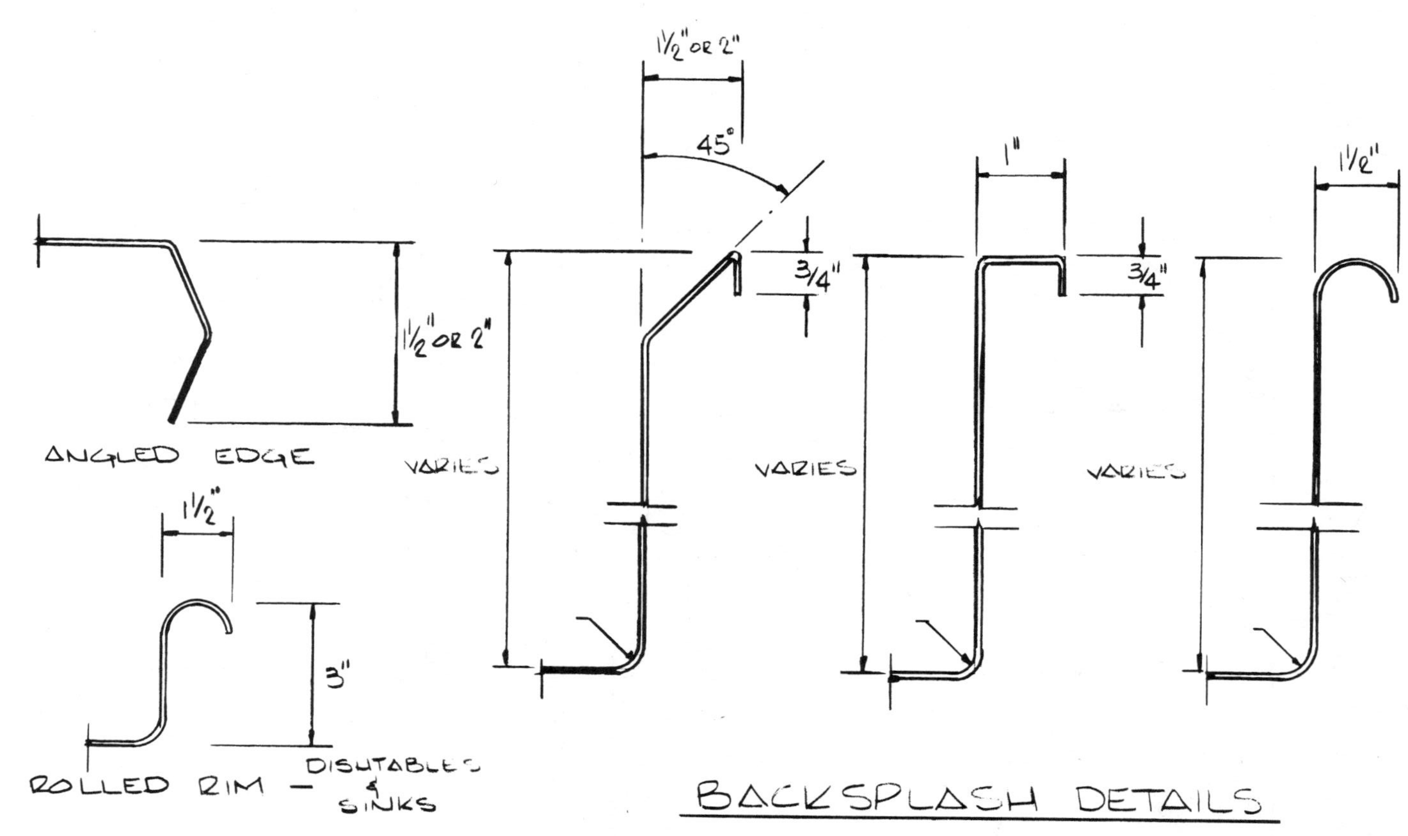

Figure 4-6a, b, c. Examples of the detail available in good construction for backsplash use on tables and counters. This type of backsplash fills many needs in health-related facilities and where the purchaser seeks long-term product value.

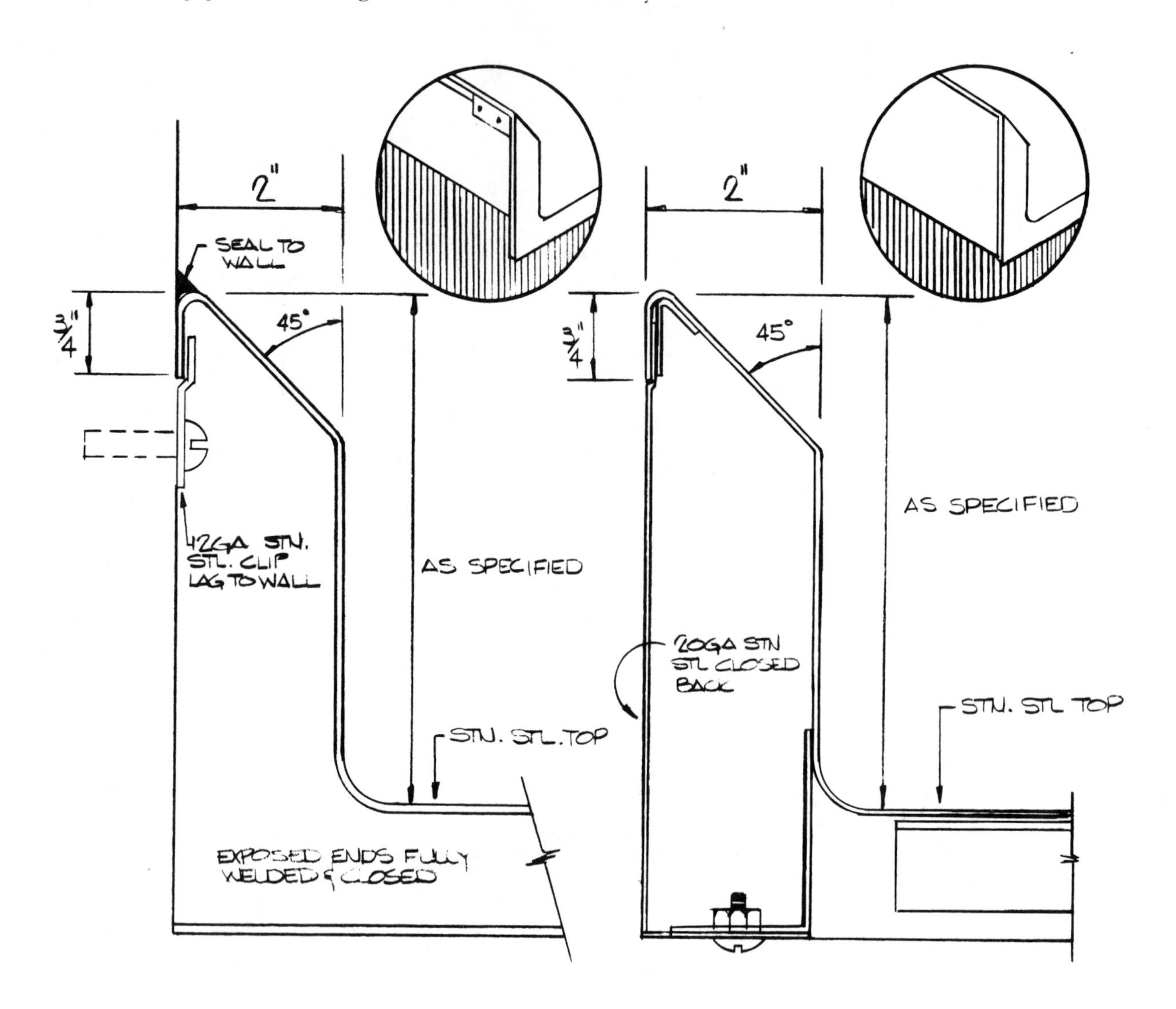
2"
SEAL TO WALL
3/4"
45°
12GA STN. STL. CLIP LAG TO WALL
AS SPECIFIED
STN. STL. TOP
EXPOSED ENDS FULLY WELDED & CLOSED
2"
3/4"
45°
AS SPECIFIED
20GA STN STL CLOSED BACK
STN. STL TOP
BACKSPLASH DETAILS FOR WALL & FREE STANDING UNITS

Figure 4-6b.

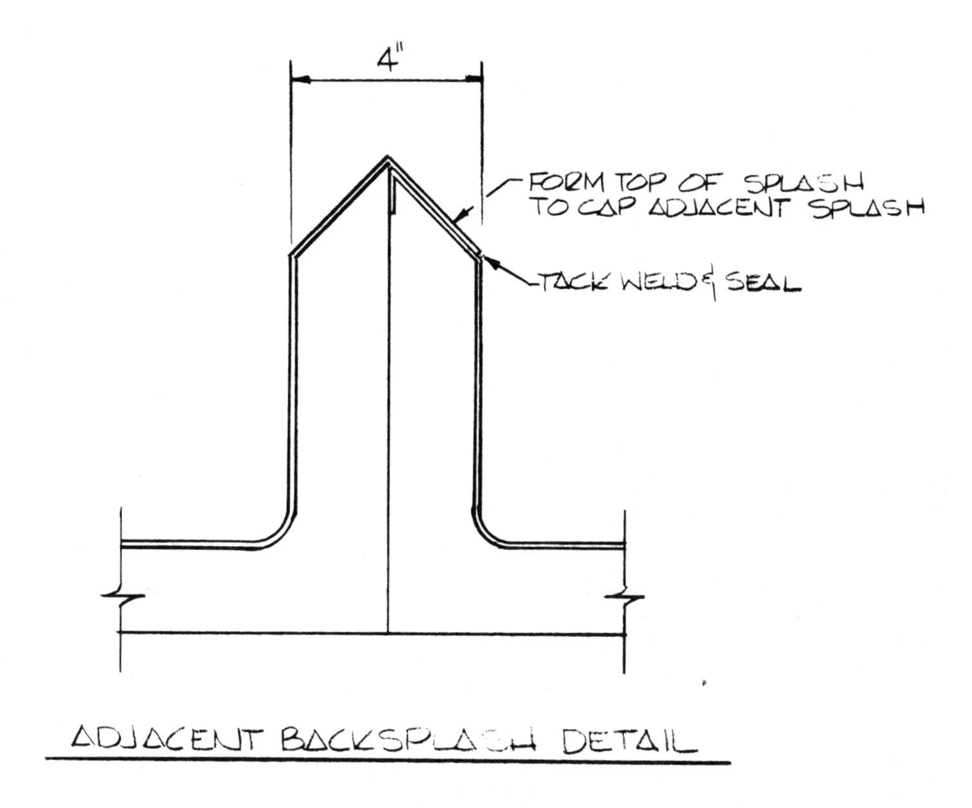

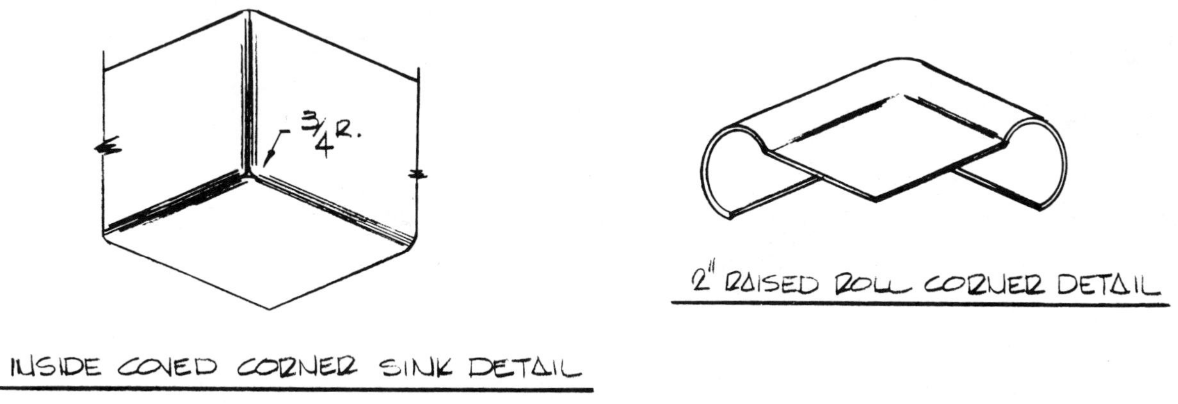

Figure 4-6c. Stainless steel top details. When adjacent work areas are to remain in a fixed area, two backsplashes may be attached as shown. This eliminates a hard-to-clear crevice area and makes housekeeping easier. Also shown is a nationally approved interior corner for a sink. Another style is square-cornered. A raised roll corner is also available for worktables and counters.

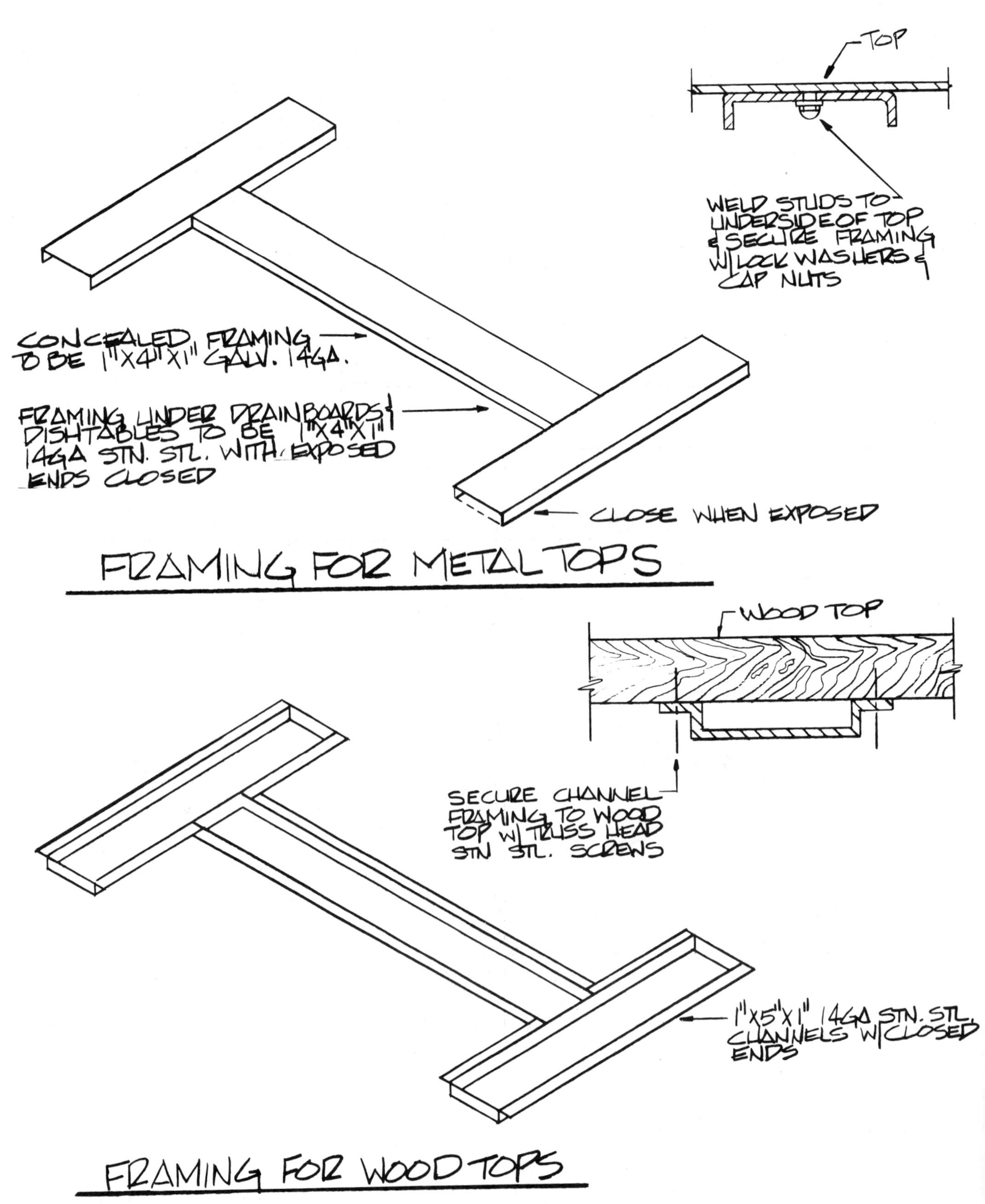

Figure 4-7. Table framing (table underframing). A drawing of this type will clarify the underside construction of either wood or stainless steel tables. A buyer wishing to change or vary a purchase can use this guide to assist in that communication.

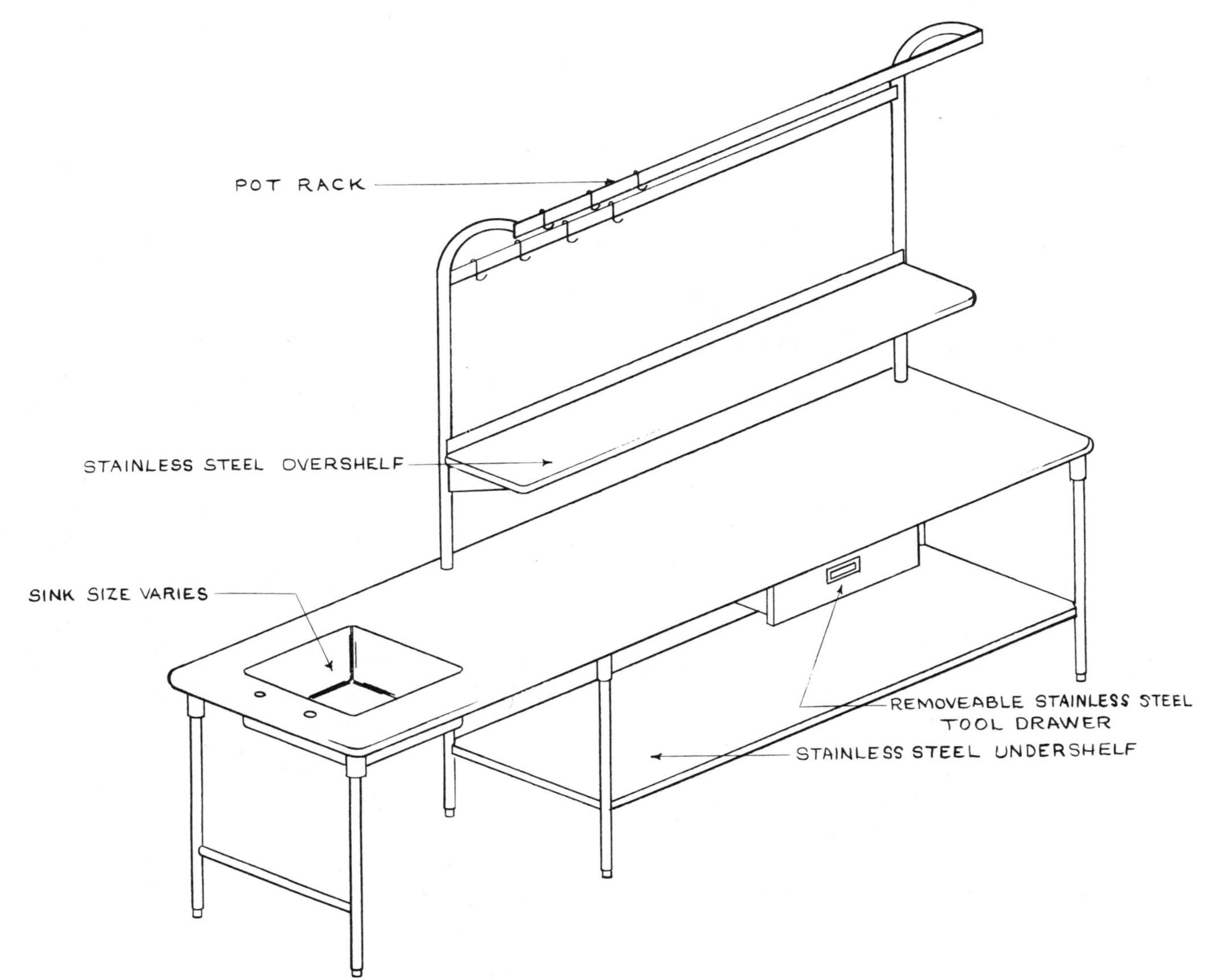

Figure 4-8. Worktable accessories. The valuable stainless steel tool drawer incorporates the best construction features, even a portable cutting board docking station under the drawer. Note that tool drawers are available, in various sizes, in plastic, galvanized steel, and stainless steel. One must select carefully—not all drawers are completely removable. Many do not have roller bearings, and many come in smaller sizes without handles. The buyer must read the specification sheet closely.

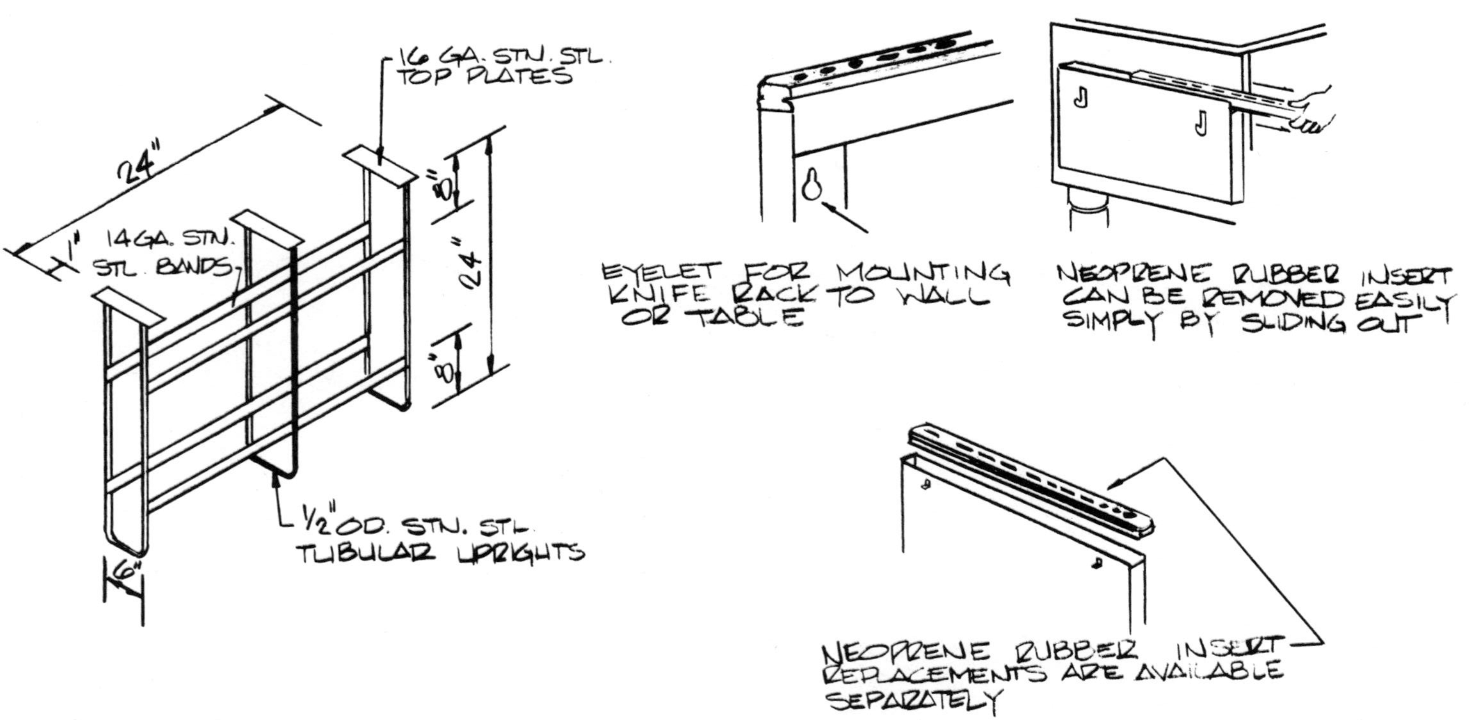

Figure 4-9. Worktable cutting board detail. The tray–cutting board holder may be mounted under a standard worktable. Also shown is a health-department-approved style for an easily removed knife holder attached to a worktable or wall.

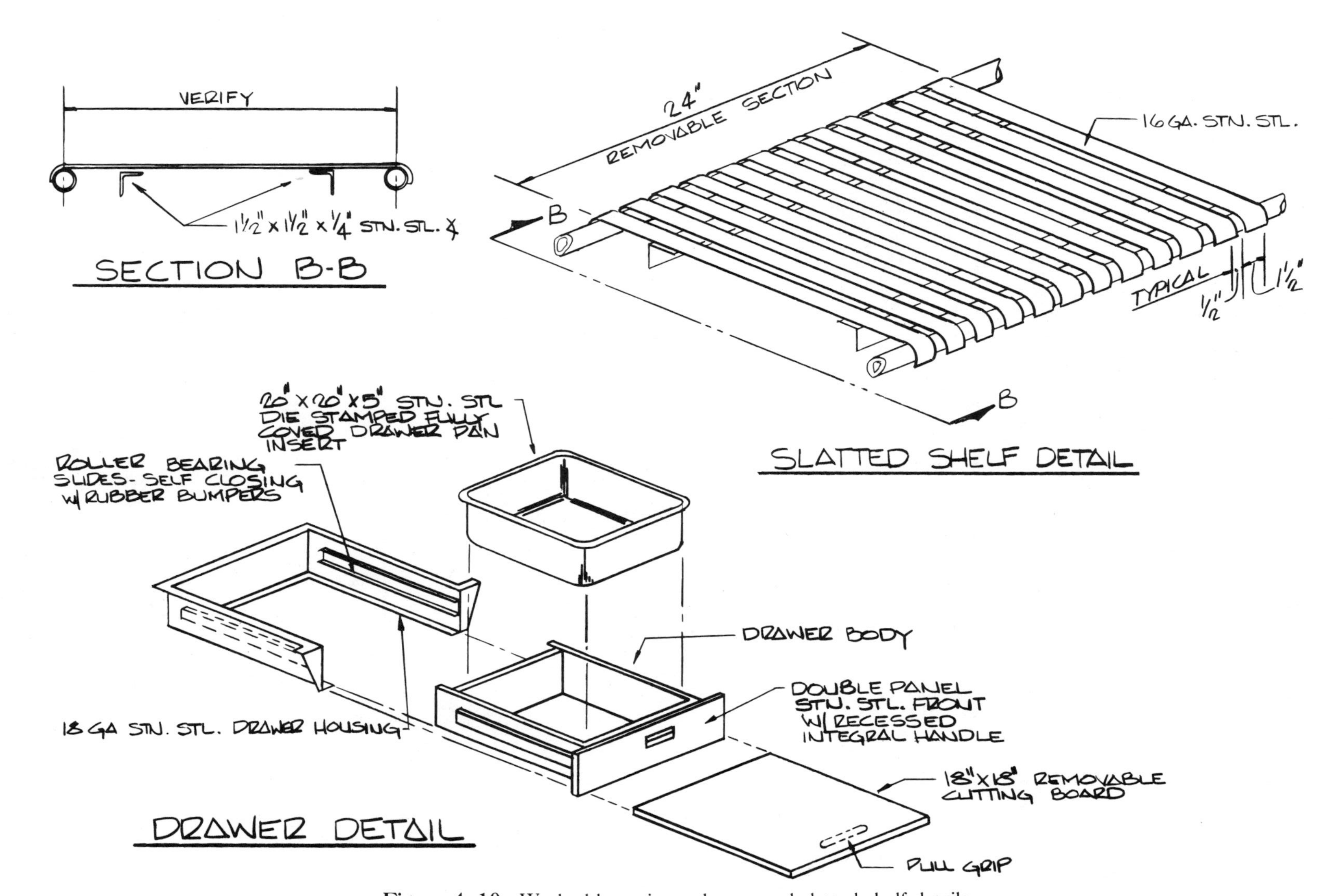

Figure 4-10. Worktable options: drawer and slatted shelf details.

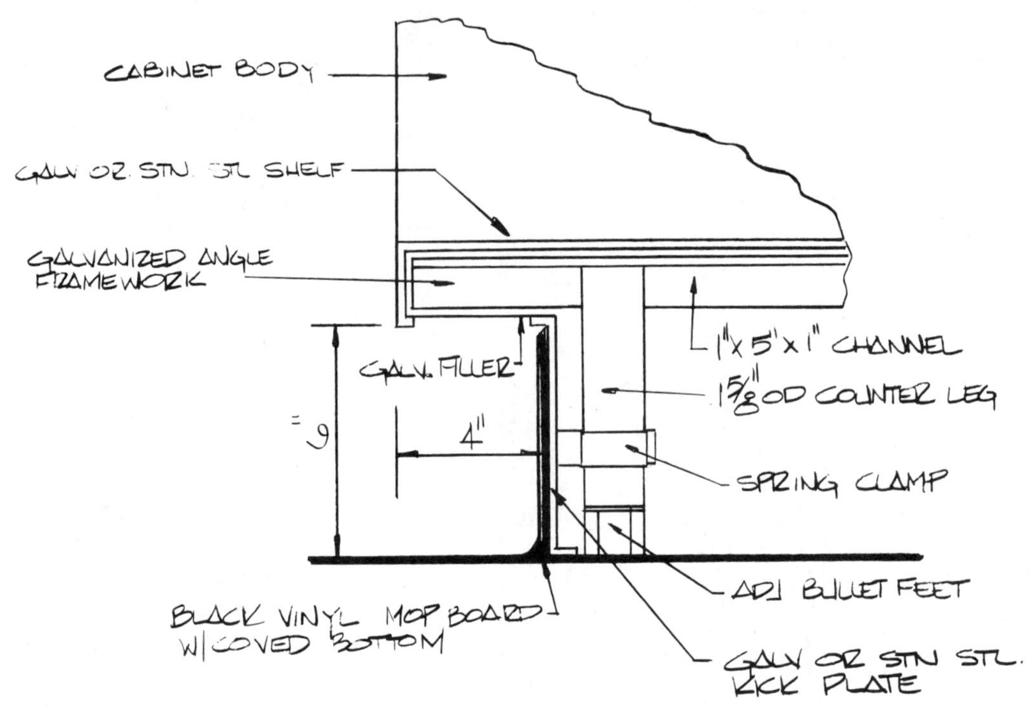

Figure 4-11. Kickplate detail; for consideration when cabinets are built-in, as in a pantry area or perhaps a church kitchen–storage work area.

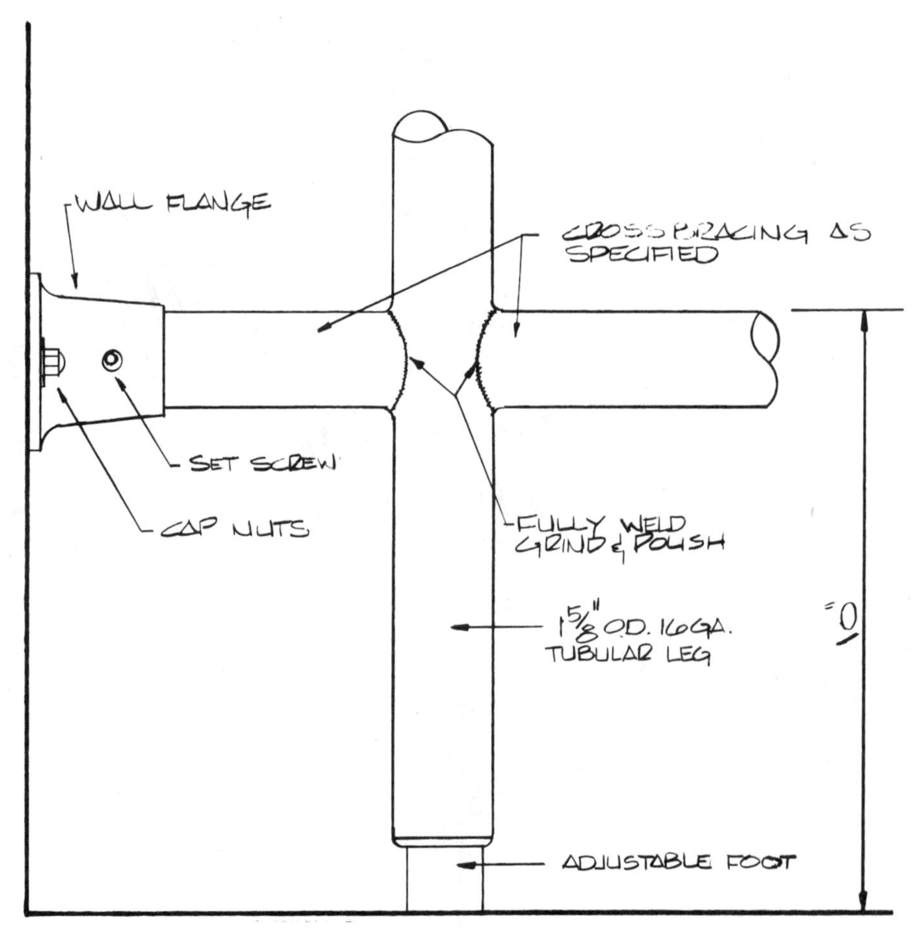

Figure 4-12. Leg support. When extra strength is needed to hold work areas in place, a wall support is an available option.

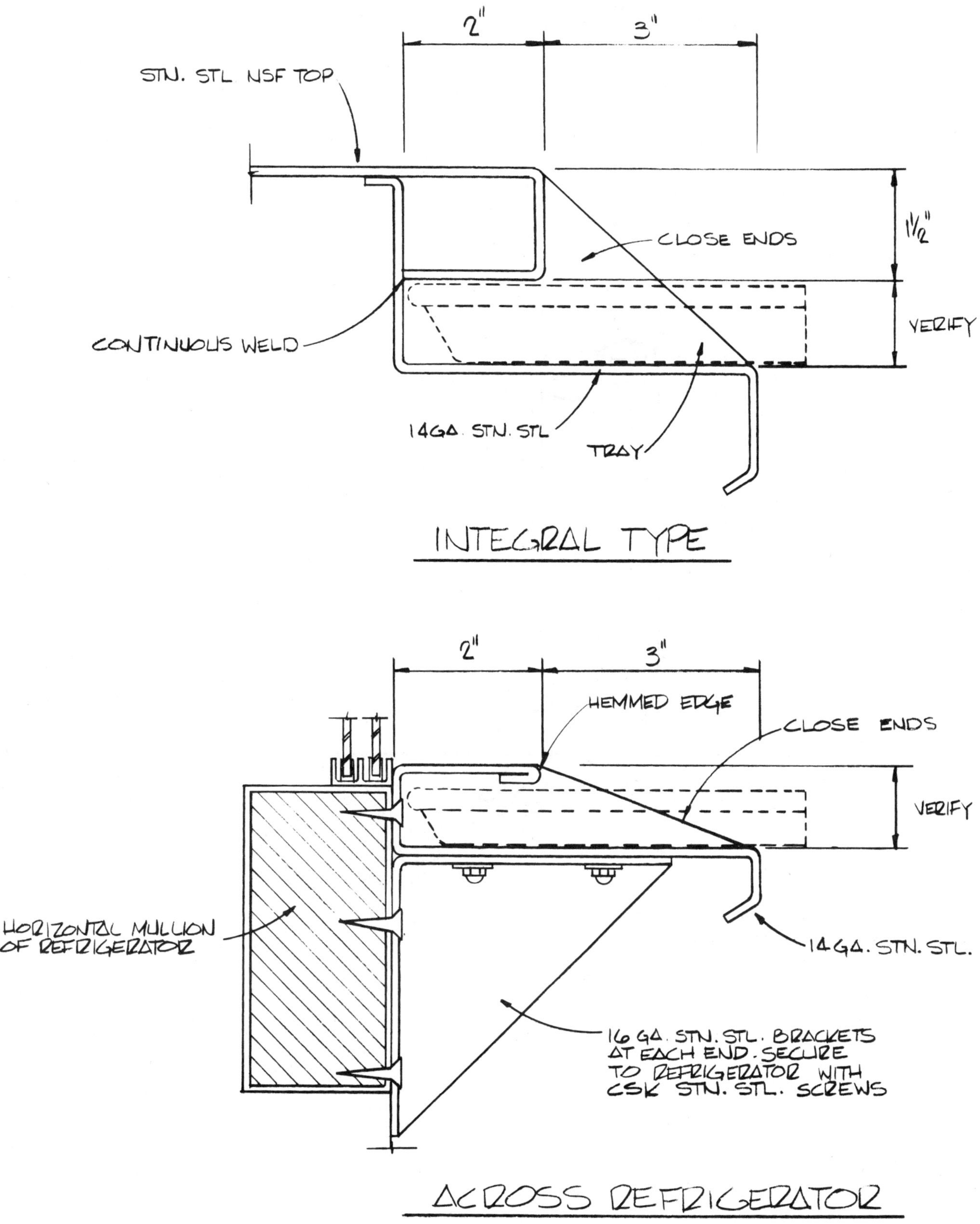

Figure 4-13. Tray lock details. The tray lock is a sleeper used by foodservice consultants. In many installations, this device is designed to hold 18″ × 26″ pans for loading or unloading of pickup tables; or it is used on refrigeration units such as the lower section of an upright refrigerator that has half doors. It enables the user to have free hands during loading.

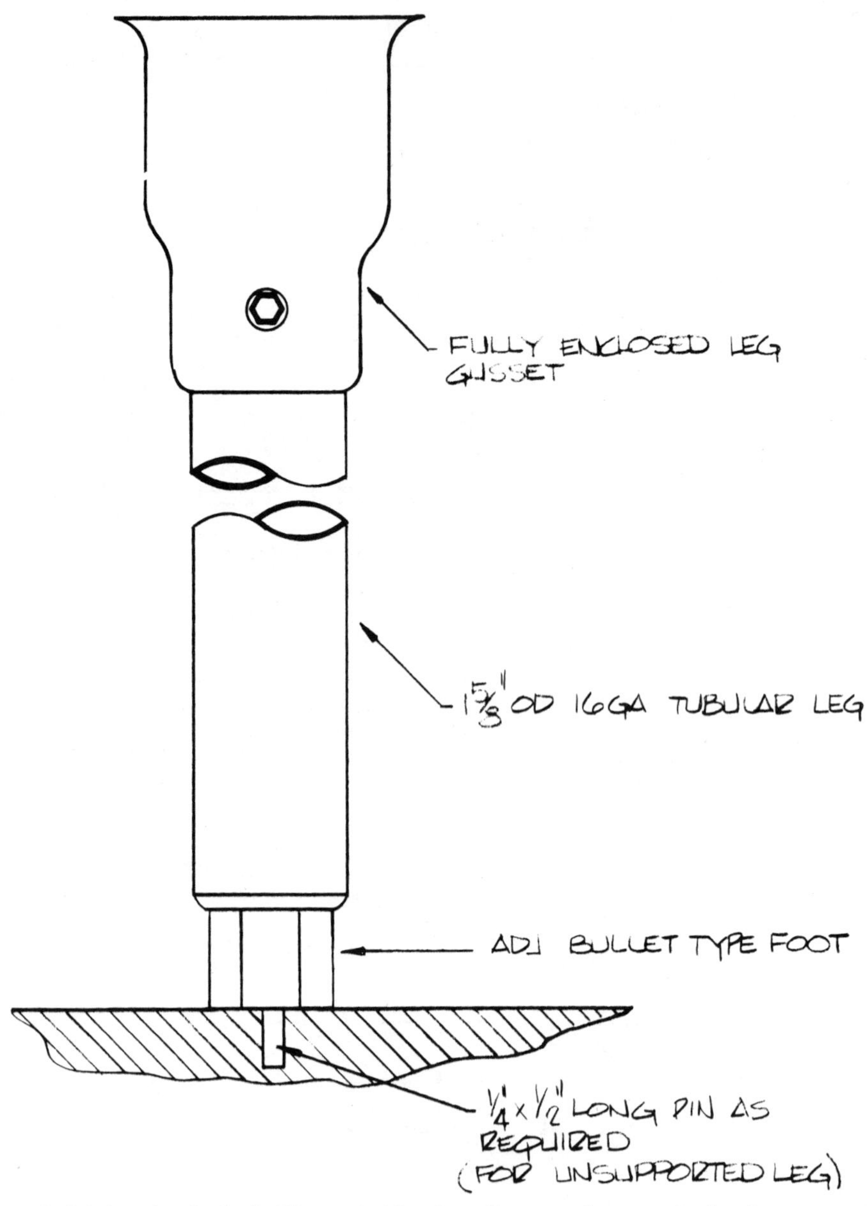

Figure 4-14. Table and sink leg detail. As in Figure 4-12, when firm attachment of a leg for any working table or sink is desired, this construction is available.

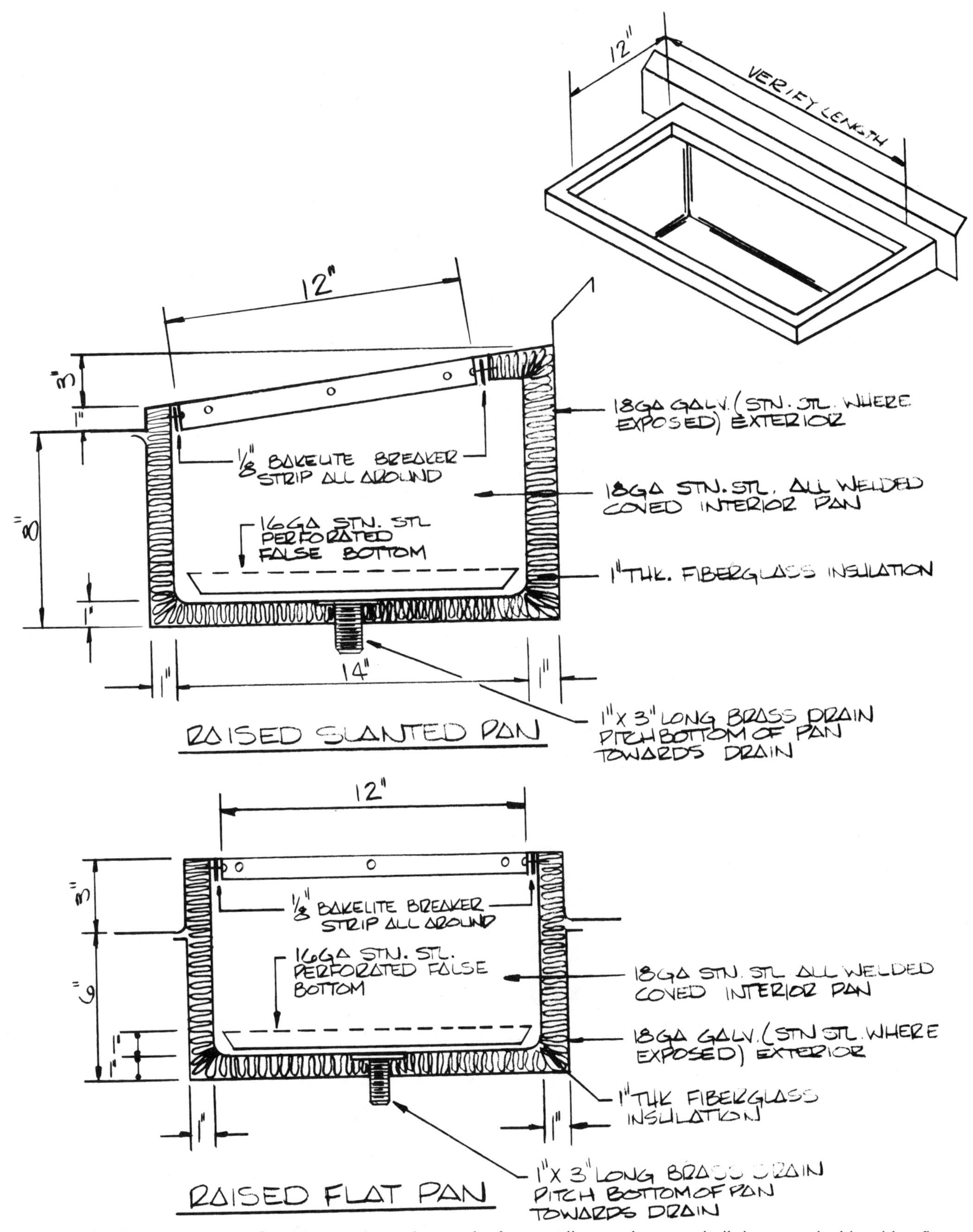

Figure 4-15. Garnish pans. Garnish pans, ice style, may be free-standing, as shown, or built into a worktable, either flat or raised. Normally made to accommodate hotel pans of all sizes, they are valuable in any cold station of a pantry or waitress area.

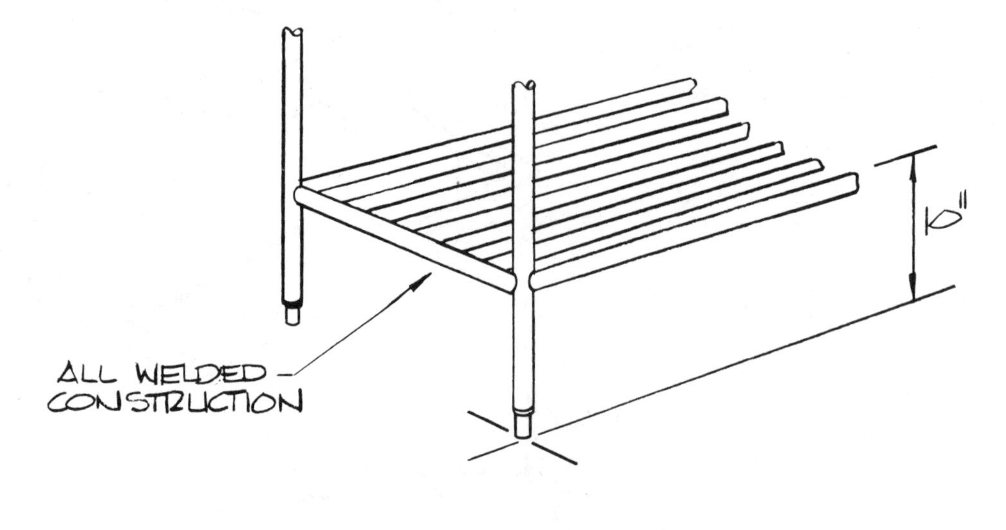

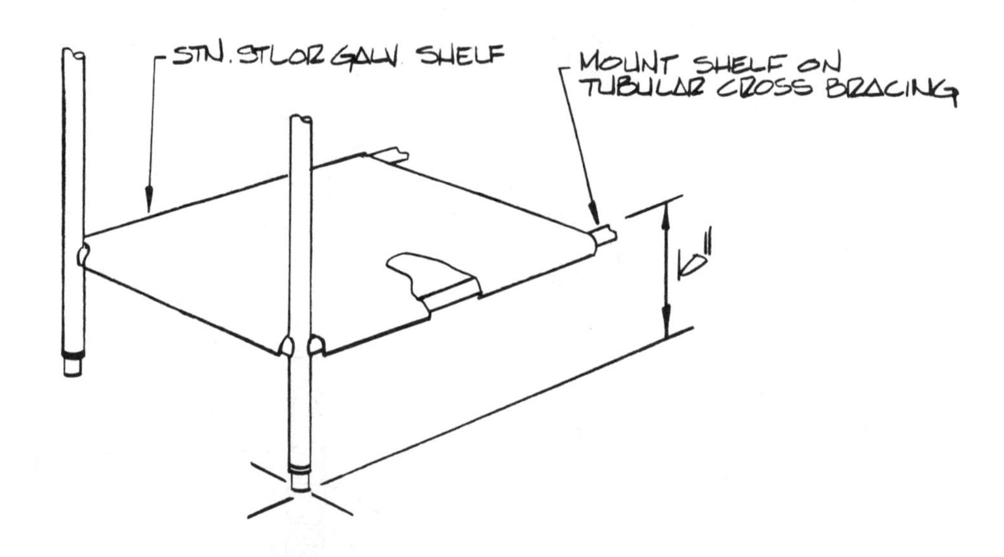

Figure 4-16. Undershelves. The tubular undershelf is stainless steel, of fixed or welded construction. The solid removable-style shelf is available in either stainless or galvanized steel.

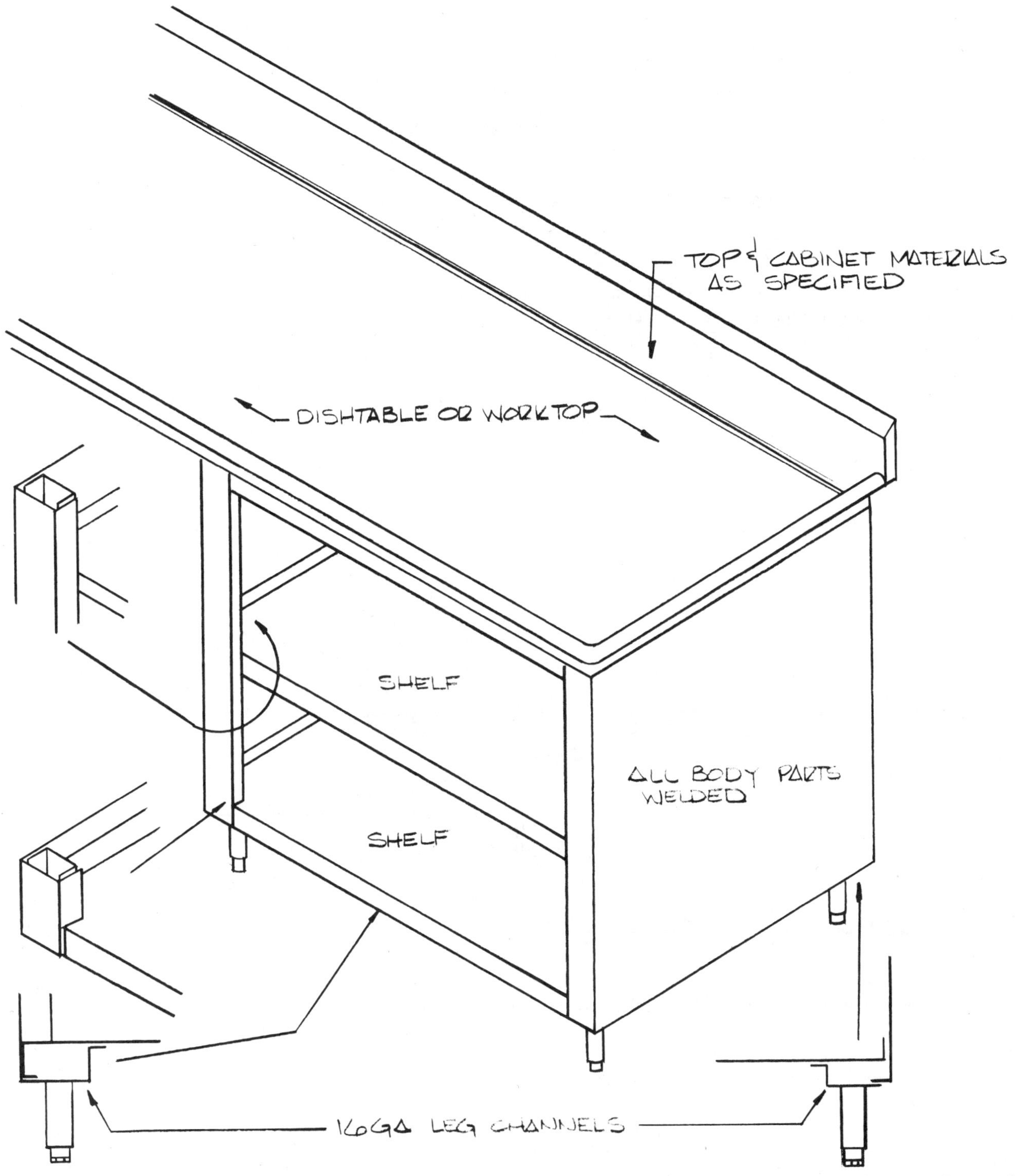

Figure 4-17. Enclosed table. When a counter or table is to be enclosed, the construction is critical. Many details must be considered: backsplash style; edge style; channel support; removable shelf; shelf clearance; finish of top, ends, and interior; leg construction; and feet detail.

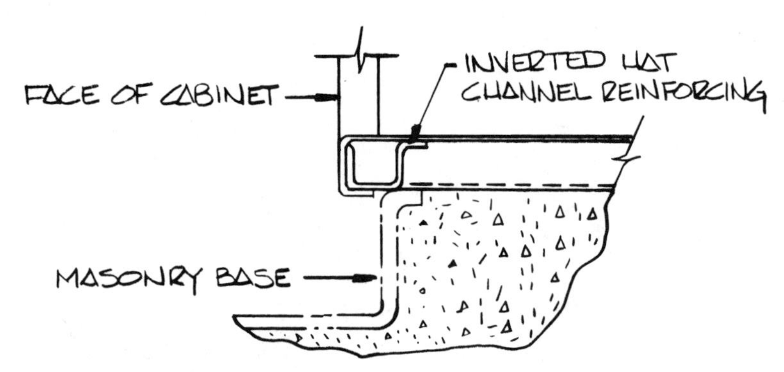

Figure 4-18. Cabinet bases. Many styles of construction are available for legless cabinet bases on a raised bottom such as masonry; the illustration shows a popular sanitation-approved style.

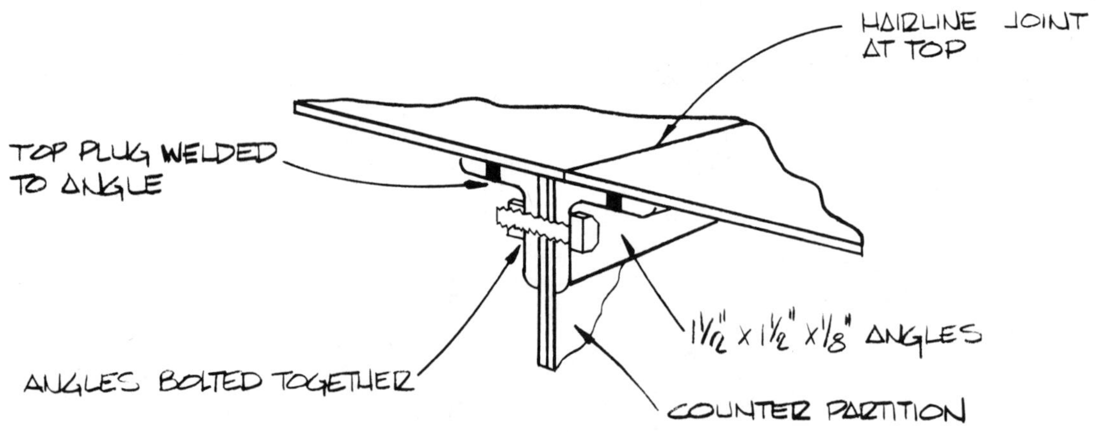

Figure 4-19. Shown is a field joint bringing two pieces of equipment together tightly. Other construction methods, such as field welding, grinding, and polishing, also are used for cabinet bases.

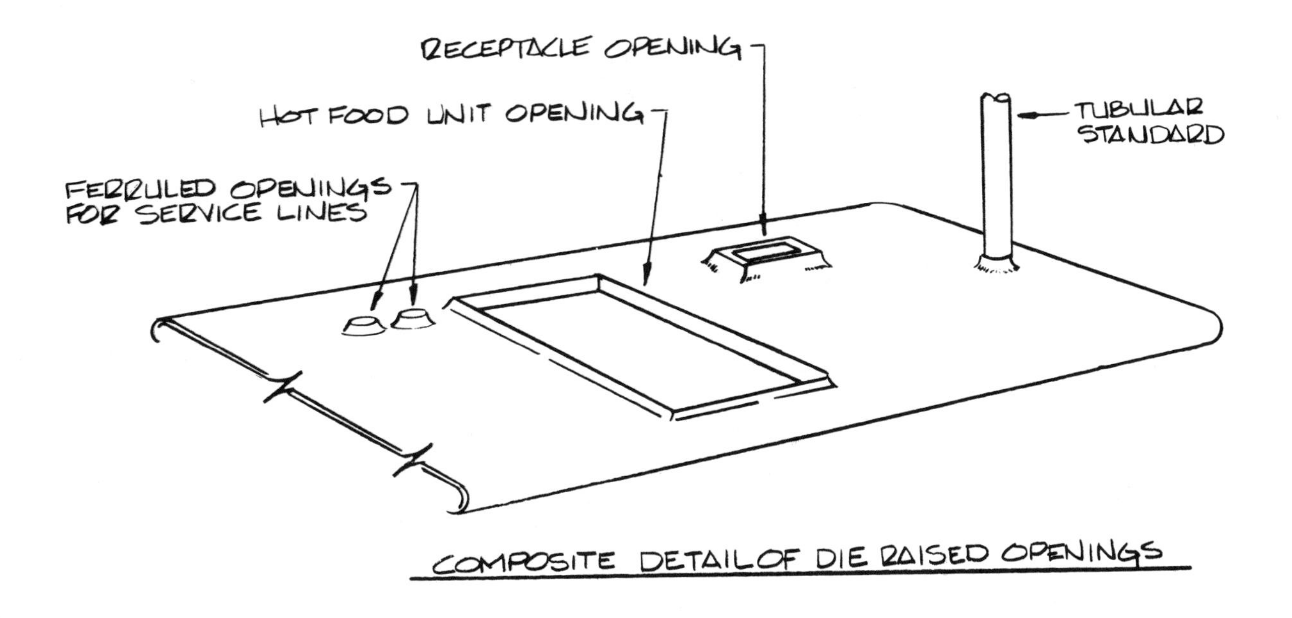

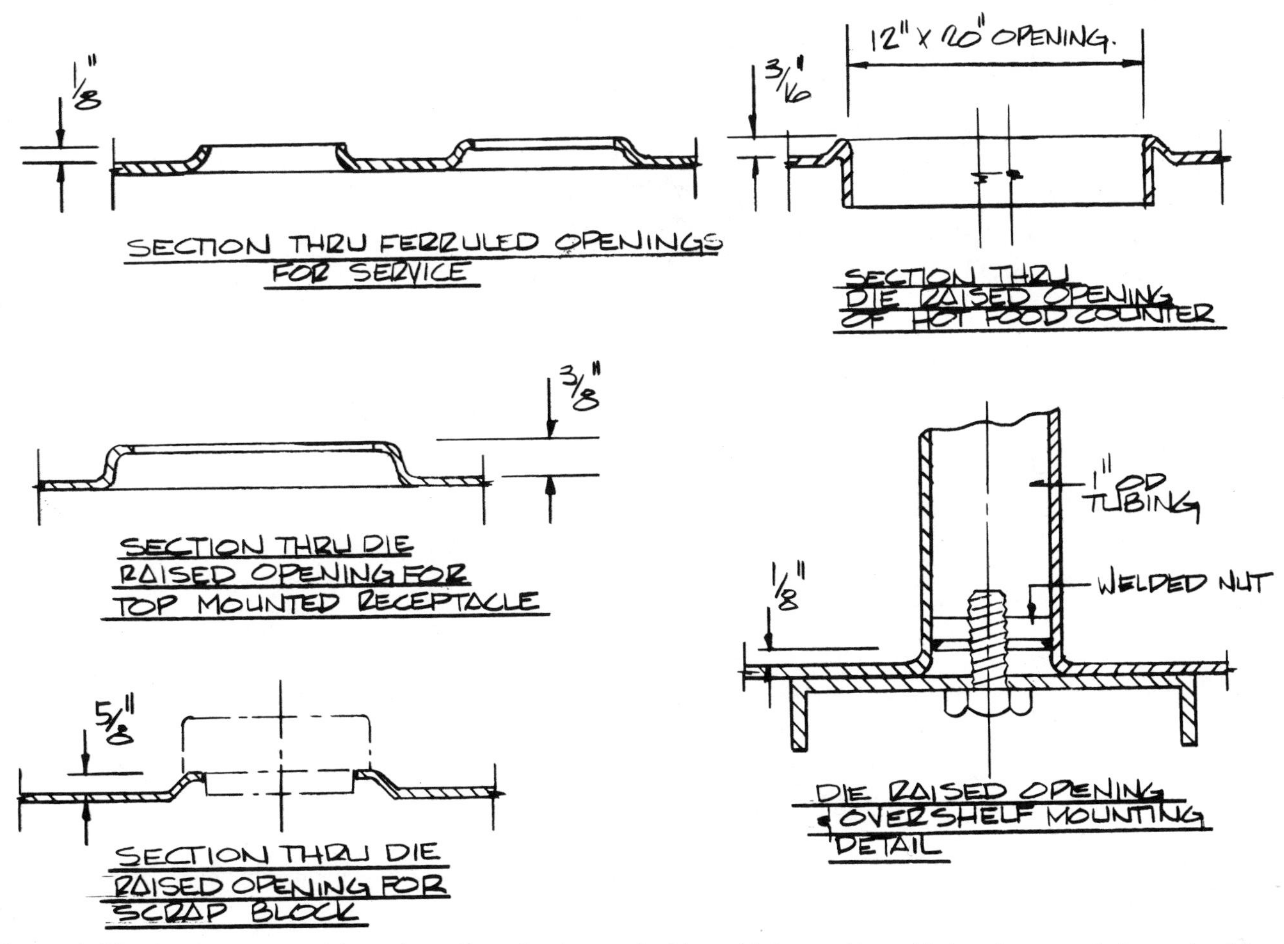

Figure 4-20. Stainless steel table options. For adapting worktables with hot and/or cold drop-ins, overshelves, plumbing, or electrical fixtures, this detail will help to clarify the actual cutouts and details. *Note:* These openings are raised many times. This may be substituted with regular, flat cutouts. Also note the section through opening drawings.

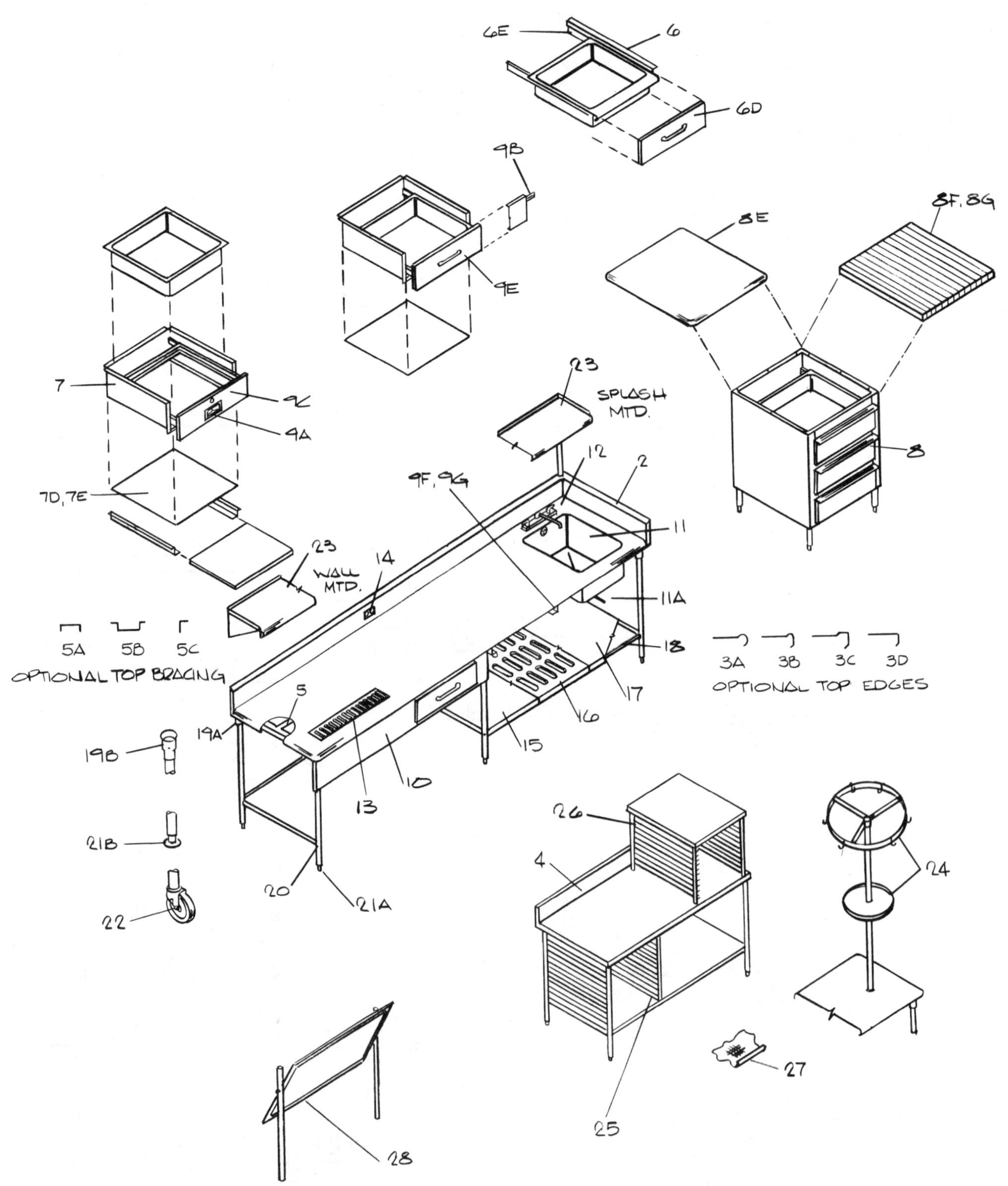

Figure 4-21. Typical worktable. This typical preparation area composite shows most popular options available for worktables.

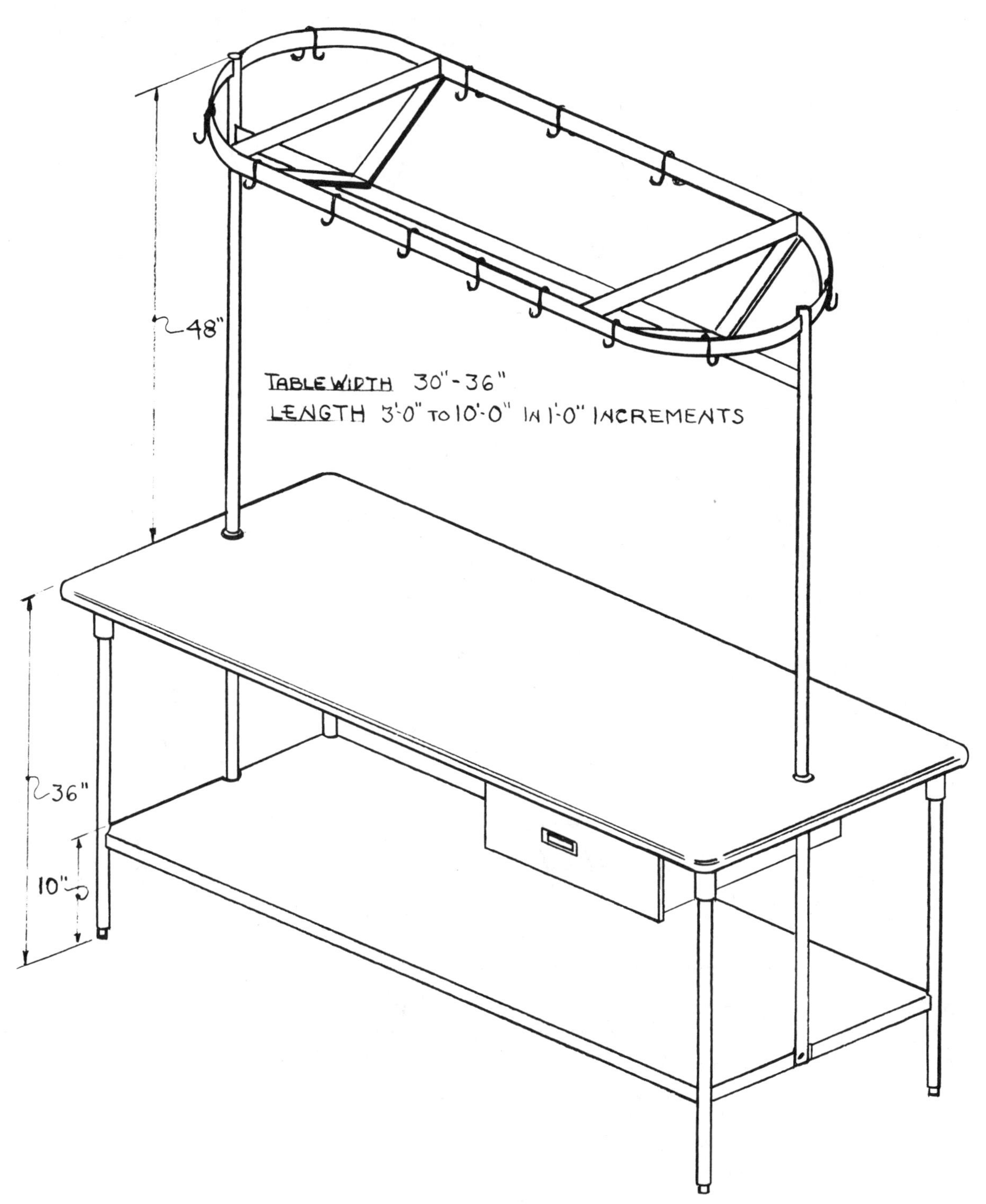

Figure 4-22. Table-style pot rack. One particular style is shown; other options are available, based on construction, style of hooks, overall height, and how the rack is attached to the table. If not properly attached many styles will sway.

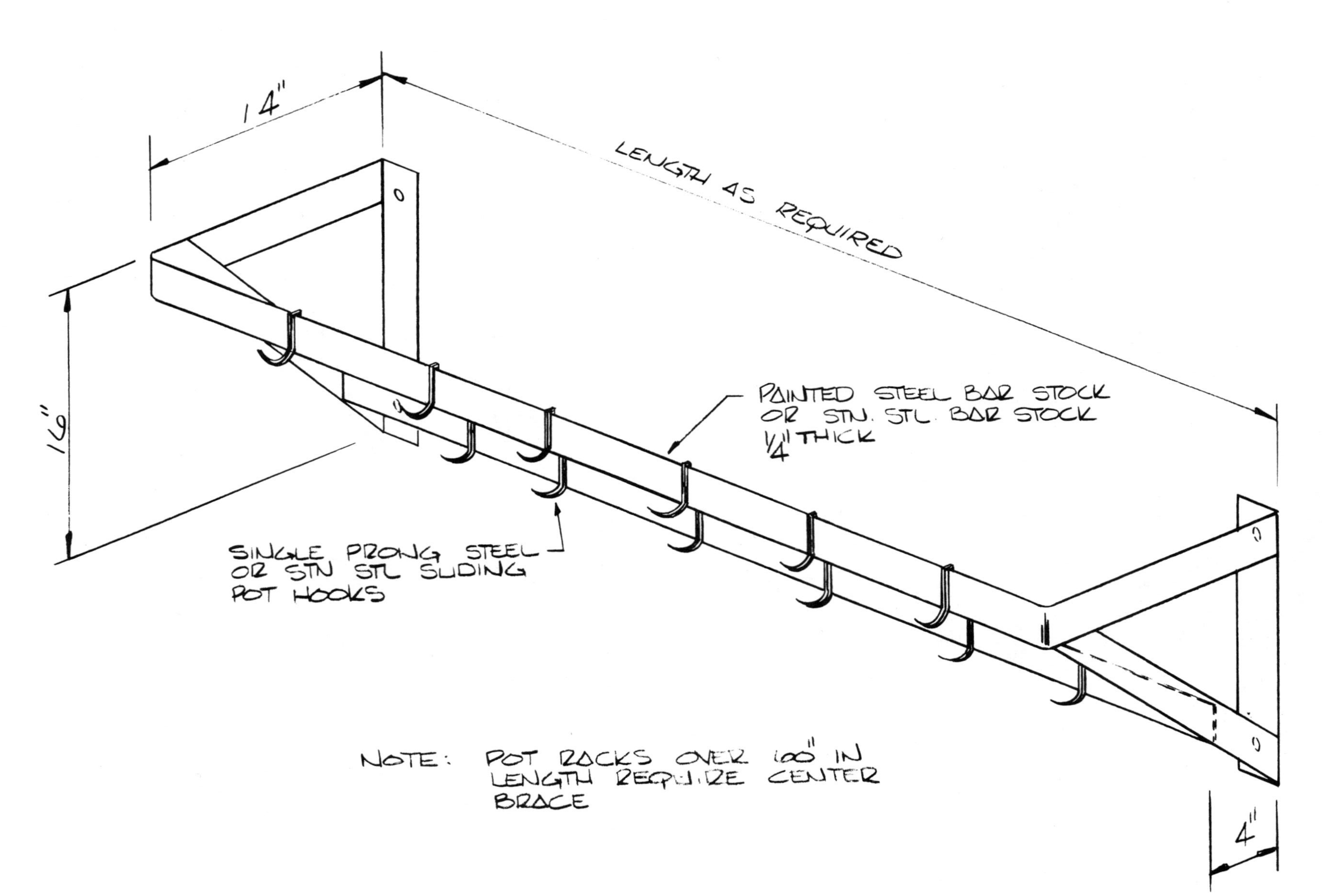

Figure 4-23. Wall pot rack. The rack shown is well-constructed with a well-braced double bar.

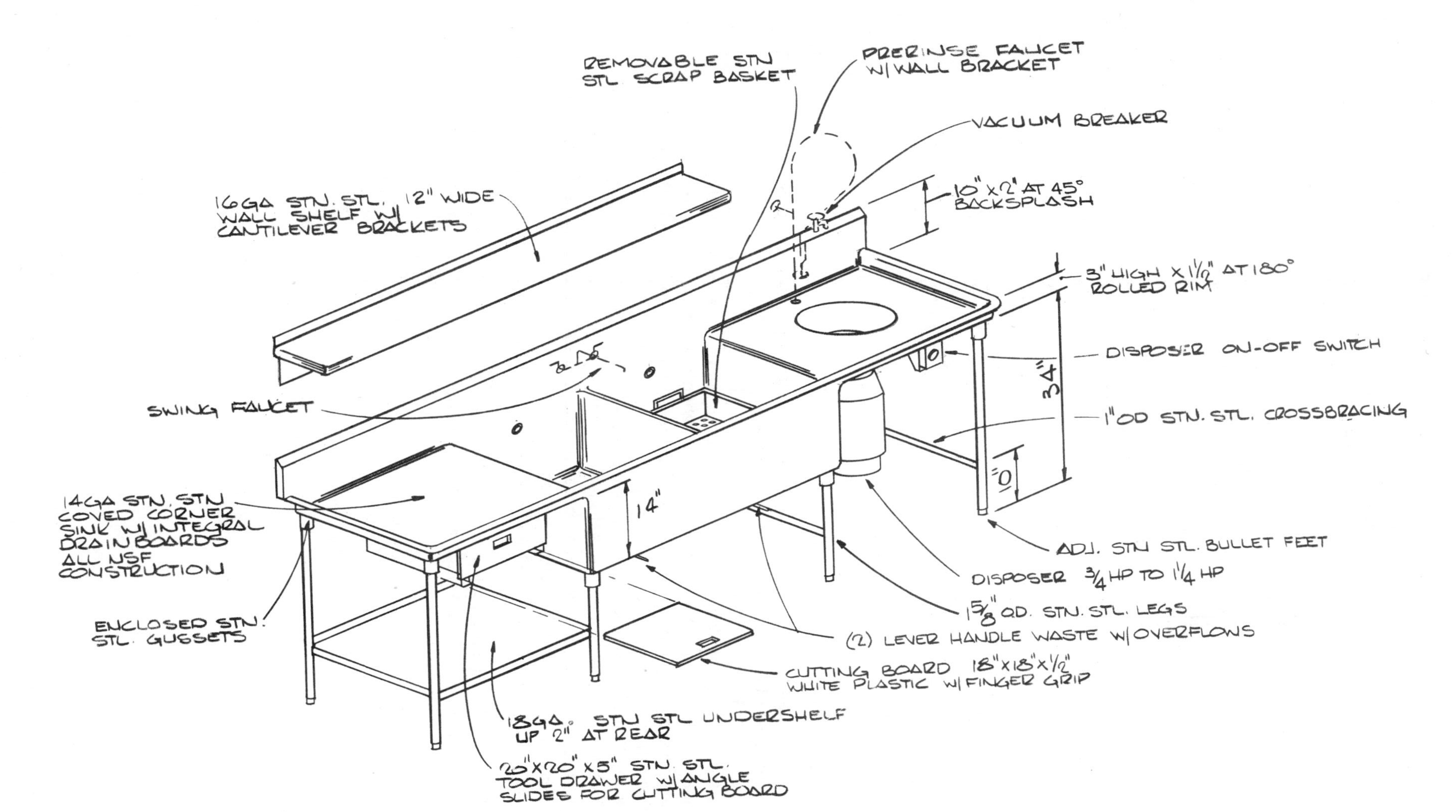

Figure 4-24. Preparation sink details. This productive prep area sink combines many previously illustrated features, such as tool drawers, cutting boards, and undershelving. This sink accessory composite shows all of the popular options. Buyers who take the time to satisfy their needs can make a productive piece yield more value for any given area of a commercial kitchen.

SINK AND DISHTABLE OPTIONS

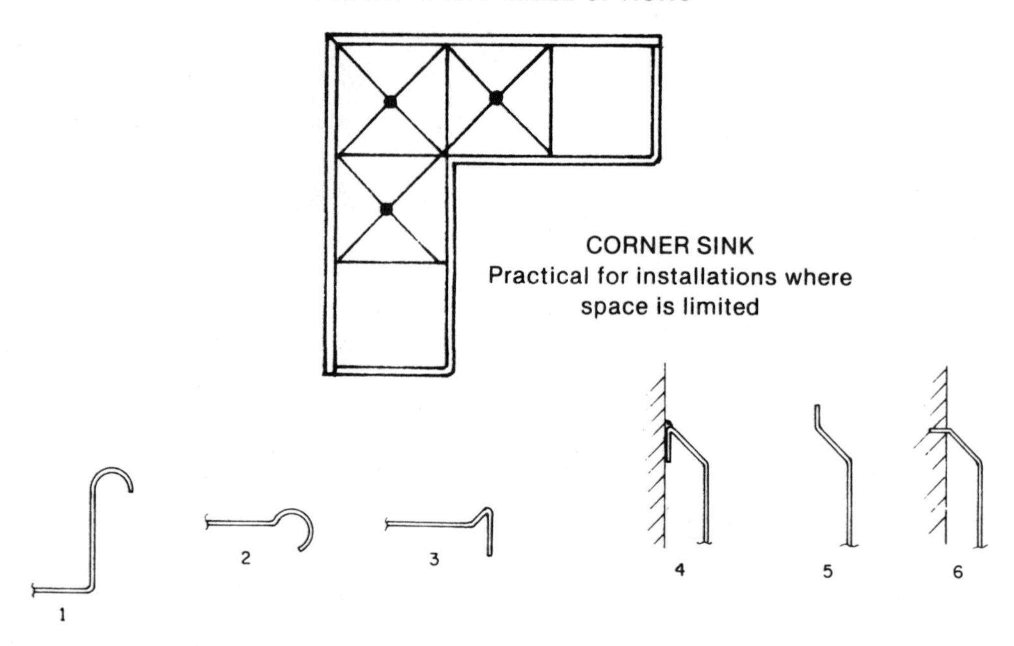

1—Standard Rolled Edge - usually ¾" in diameter x 3" high - normally used for ends and work side of dishtables and sink drainboards

2—Raised Rolled Edge

3—Inverted "V" Edge - either fig. 2 or 3 are used for work tables where water spillage is heavy or frequent wash-down is required. When applied to the clean dish table of a single tank machine these edges provide an auxiliary work table during periods when dishes are not being washed

4—Sink or Dishtable Backsplash - turned back 2" on 45° then down approx. ¾". Sinks and dishtables should be installed at least 3" off from walls. Where necessary the units may sometimes be mounted against the wall and sealed with silicone caulking as shown. Other approved methods are available.

5—Backsplash turned back 2" on 45° and then up. Detail used by some manufacturers.

6—Backsplash kerfed into wall. For high quality installations against masonry or tile walls such as in hospitals, etc. Requires considerable coordination of construction and installation.

Figure 4-25. Sink and table options. (Reprinted, by permission, from Carl Scriven and James Stevens, *Food Equipment Facts*, © 1988 by Van Nostrand Reinhold)

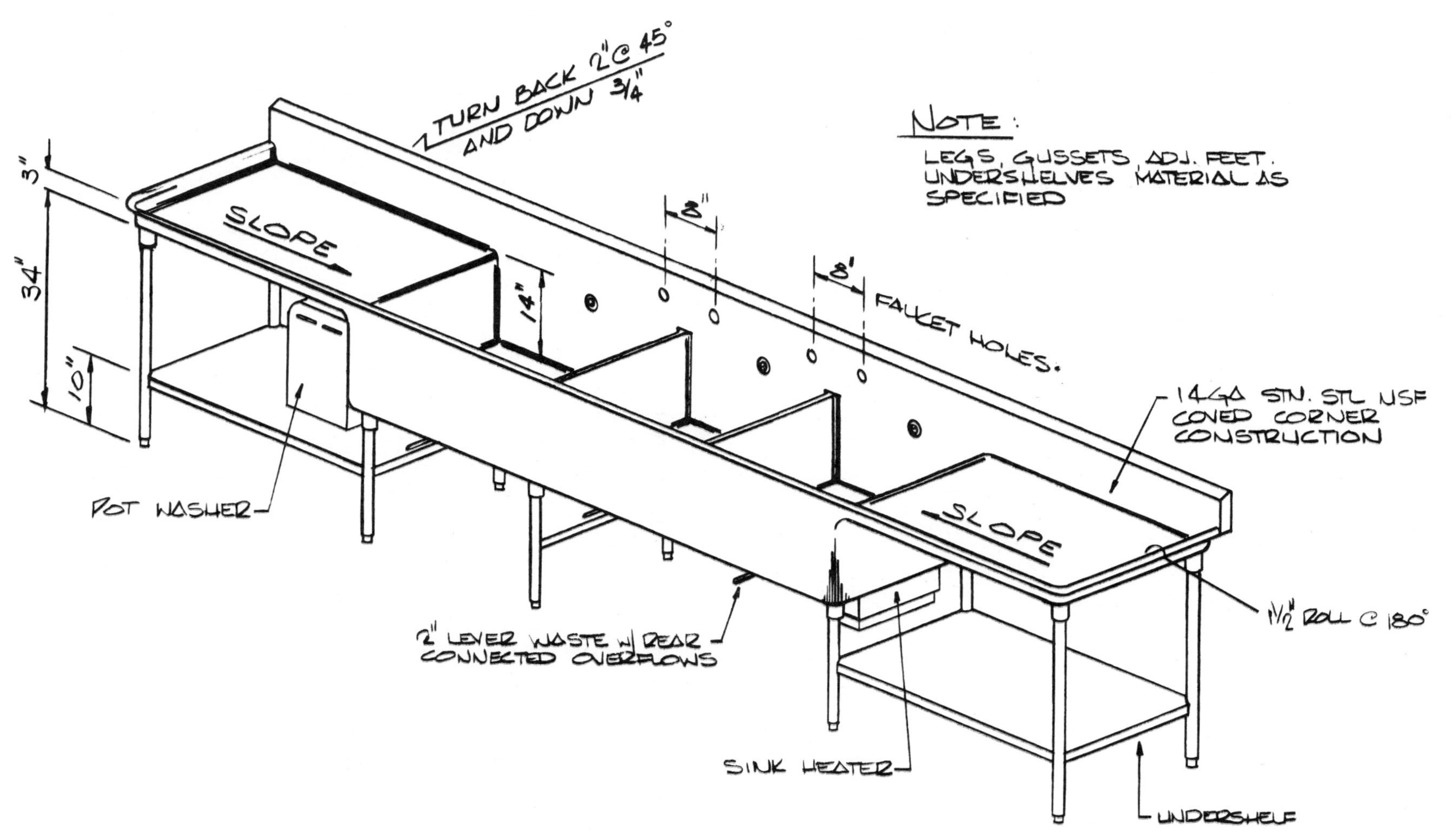

Figure 4-26. Pot sink. This pot sink composite can be used to build this part of the sanitation area. *Note:* One must verify both inside compartment sizes and overall dimensions, making sure faucets and drains are included by the equipment contractor. Note the availability of electric pot washers and sink sanitizers 180 as shown, very desirable aids to this area.

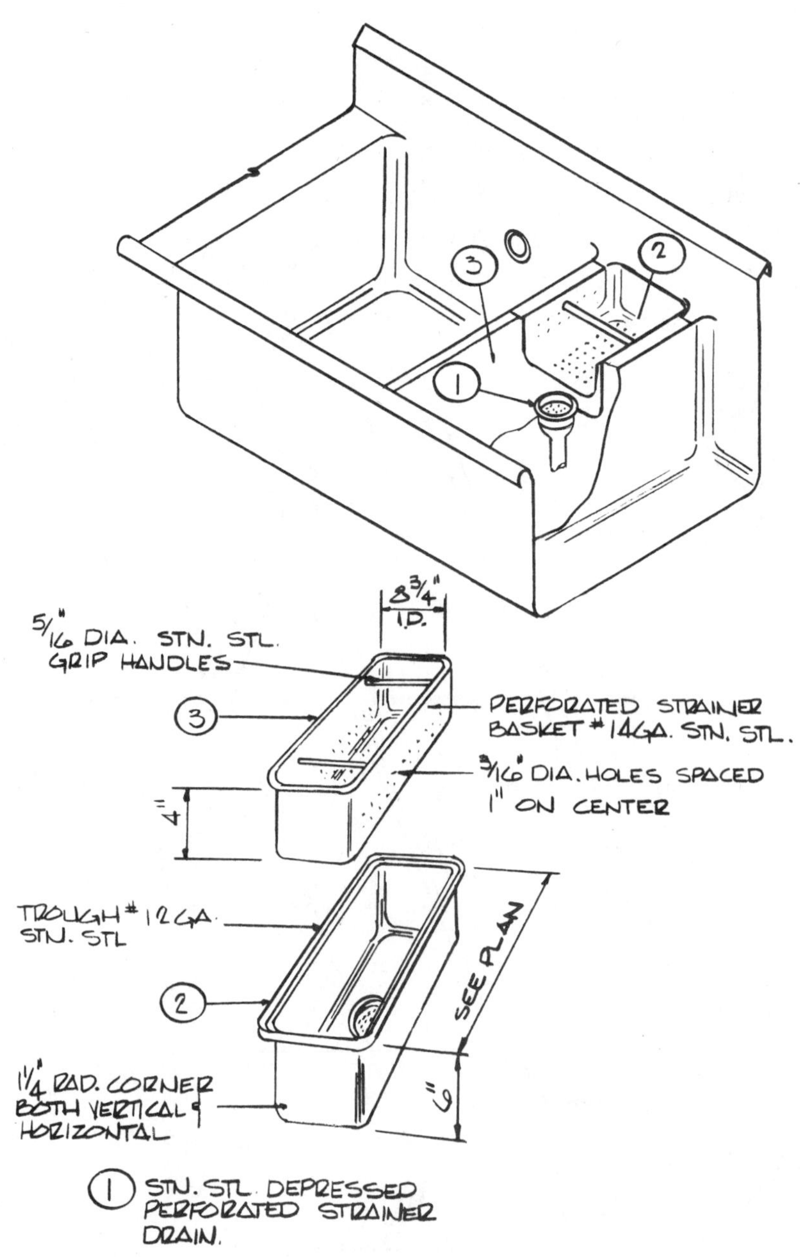

Figure 4-27. Sink options (sanitizing area). This section can be built into the pot sink, affording the kitcher worker an opportunity to scrape heavy residue into a perforated basket. This helps to eliminate clogged drains.

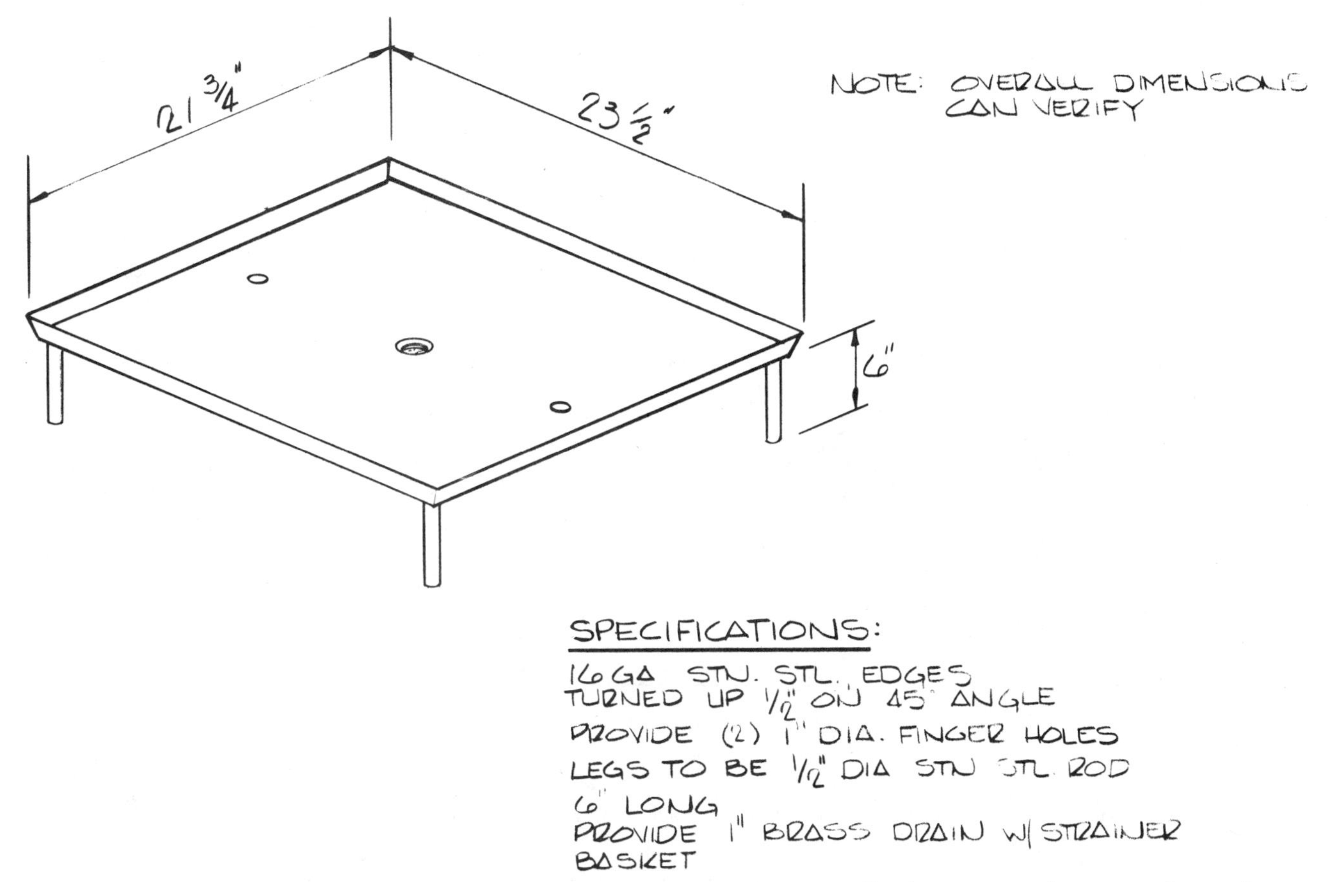

Figure 4-28. Sink bottoms. False bottom platform raises the work area, allowing many workers an easier reach.

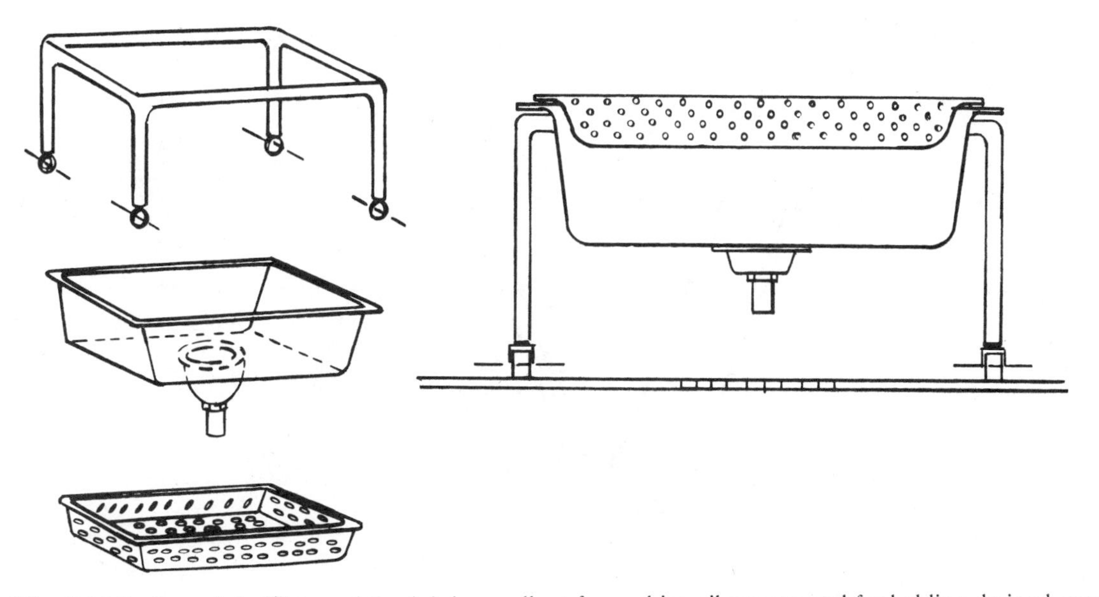

Figure 4-29. Mobile floor sink. This mobile sink is excellent for soaking silverware and for holding drained water from a steam equipment cooker until it can reach the nearest available drain.

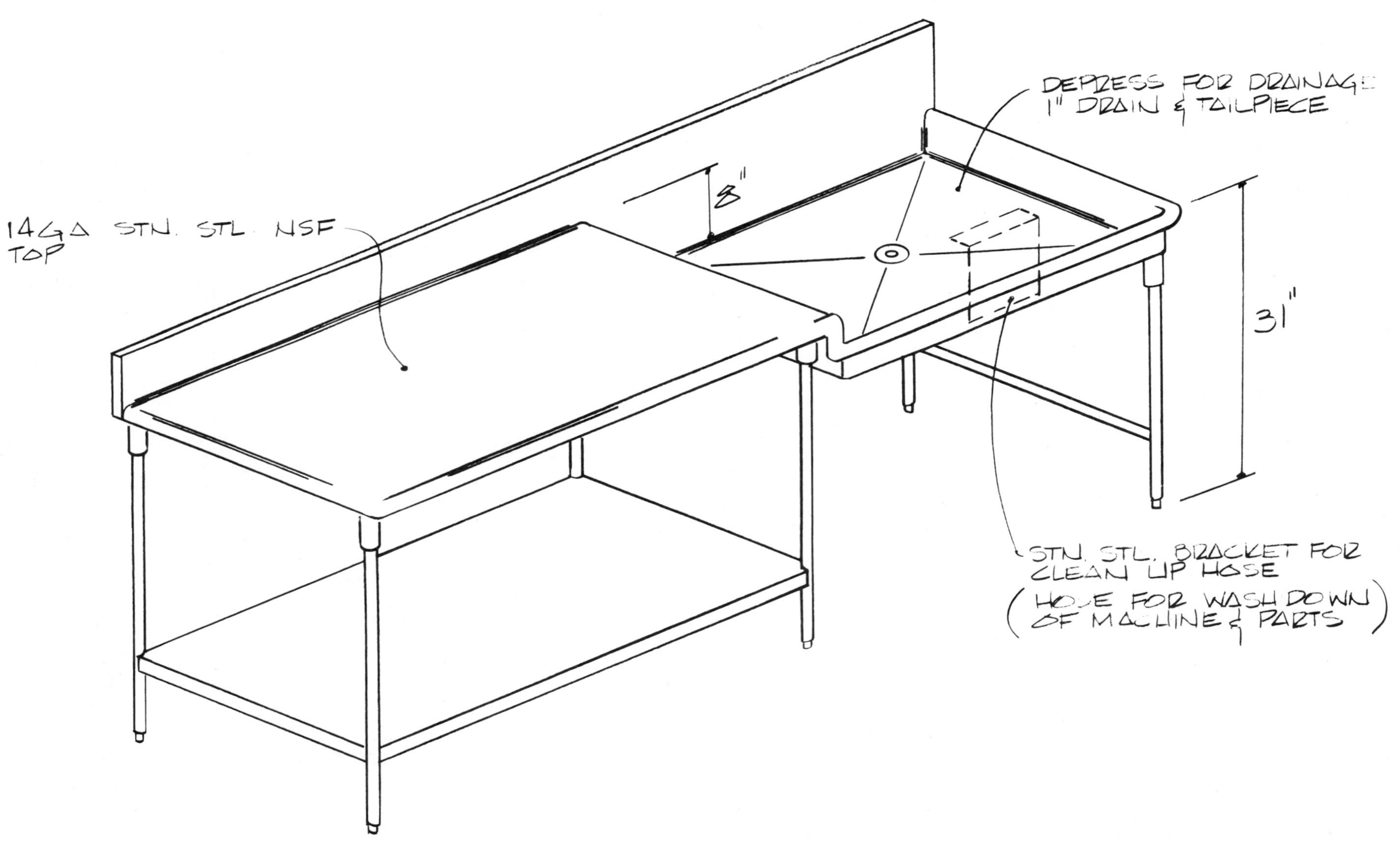

Figure 4-30. Food cutter table. Used to facilitate cleaning and wash-down of most popular food preparation machines, this table is valuable in high-volume installations.

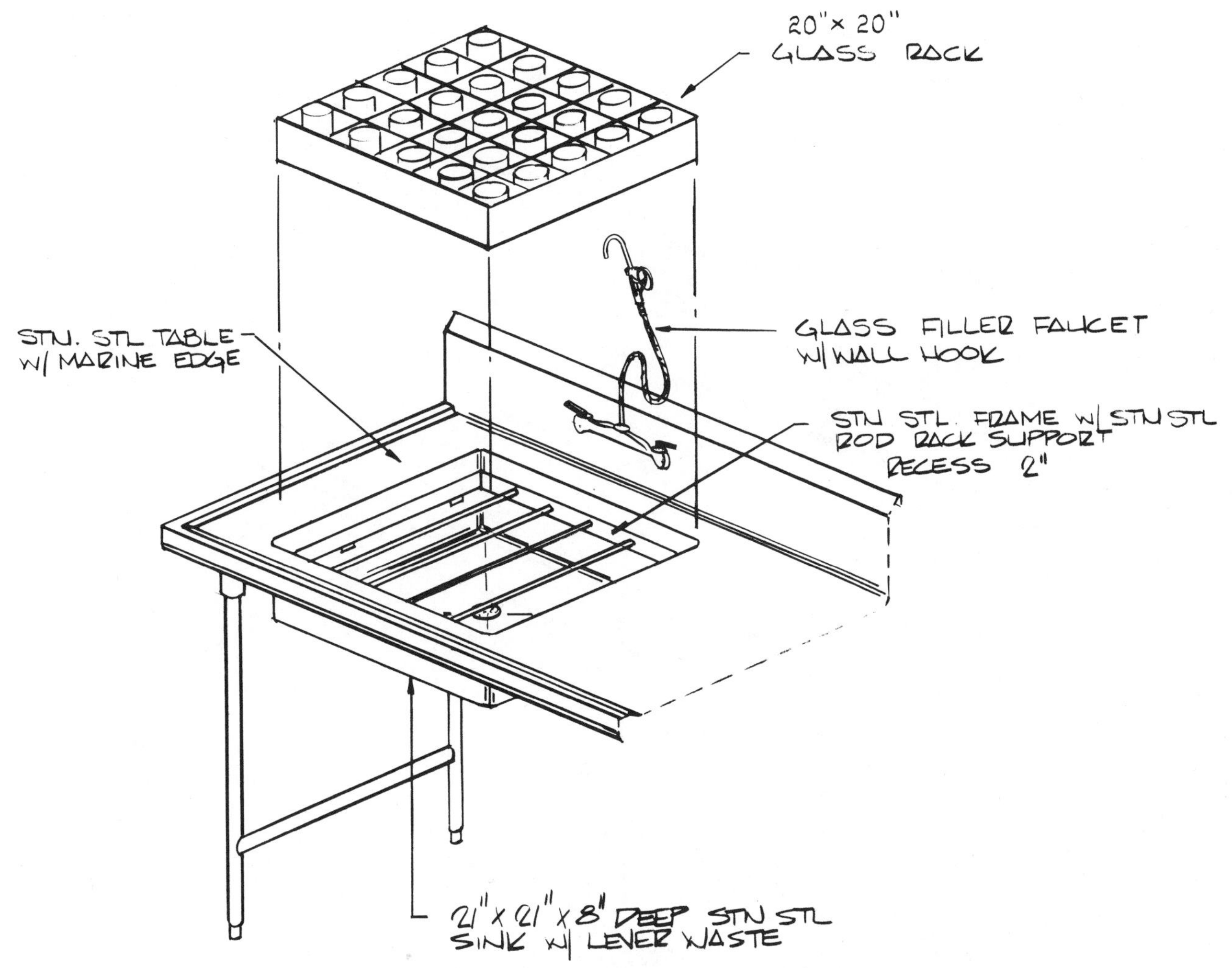

Figure 4-31. Glass filler. Using standard 20″ × 20″ glass racks, this unique fill area for water solves a problem for high-volume banquet or commercial feeding operations.

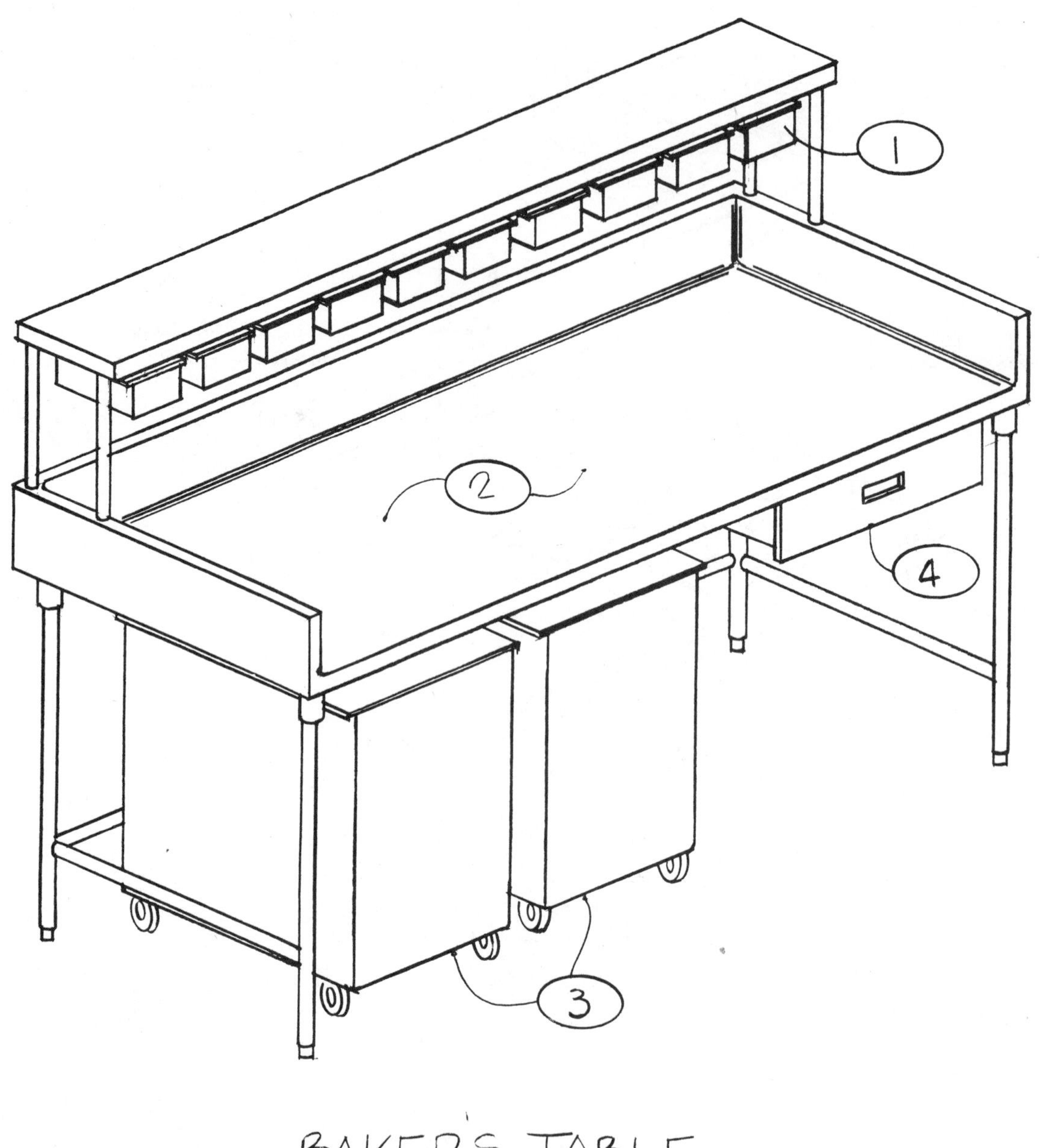

Figure 4-32. Baker's table. Options to consider are: size of the riser splash on both back and ends; top construction of stainless steel, wood, or composition plastic; style of ingredient bins, either fixed or mobile as shown; construction of bins; and details of tool drawers.

5

Cooking Equipment

Dozens of manufacturers produce hundreds of food equipment cooking products. A variety of these pieces of equipment are shown in this chapter (Figures 5–1 through 5–13). The well-worn phrase "Menu-match your equipment selection" still holds true. From counter equipment to drive-in rack ovens, the menu dictates selection.

The chapter addresses three of the most important recent advances in cooking systems: cook chill systems, conveyor cooking, and maximum-use combination cookers and ovens. Unique cooking aids also are discussed.

Table 5–1 shows equipment and service requirements for preparation of 50 to 750 meals.

COOK CHILL SYSTEMS

Many foodservice directors, faced with the pressures of rising food, energy, and labor costs, are exploring the concept of centralized food production. Currently, there are several different approaches to centralization, many of which rely on a cook-and-freeze method of producing for inventory, such as individually frozen, preplated meals. This section discusses alternatives to cook-and-freeze methods.

CAPKOLD SYSTEM

One system, in particular, relies on a cook and rapid chill approach that has proved successful in the school foodservice environment. In addition to economies of scale and planning and control benefits, the CapKold System (jointly developed by Groen and Cryovac) provides the benefits of extended refrigerated storage without the cellular breakdown or energy requirements associated with freezing.

Before we look at its application in the Portland, Oregon, public school system, a brief description of this system is in order:

1. CapKold incorporates centralized purchasing, storage, and preparation of all ingredients and seasonings necessary for production of the bulk of main menu entrees and side dishes.
2. All pumpable items are prepared in large batches in special cooker/mixers (100–250 gallons). An inclined agitator does all the mixing and maintains even distribution of solids throughout the batch.

   Prepackaged meats and many prepared items are slow-cooked overnight in one or more cook tanks. Slow coolking in circulating hot water reduces meat shrinkage by as much as 25%. Cooking in sealed casings enhances meat flavor and tenderizes inexpensive cuts of meat.
3. Measured amounts of kettle-cooked items are pumped into special casings, sealed, and labeled. A single operator uses a pump/filter equipped with a positive displacement pump that can handle items such as beef stew without damaging delicate solids. All cooked items are pumped at pasteurization tem-

Table 5-1. Selecting Equipment for Banquet Kitchen

Meals	Convection Oven	Kettle	Convection Steamer	Tilting Fry Pan	* Coffee	** Ice	No. of Servers
50	½	1-20 g.	1 Dbl.	1-30 g.	Twin 3	200#	2
100	½	1-20 g.	1 Dbl.	1-30 g.	Twin 3	200#	2
150	1	1-20 g.	1 Dbl.	1-30 g.	Twin 3	200#	2
200	1	1-20 g.	1 Dbl.	1-30 g.	Twin 3	200#	2
250	1	1-30 g.	2 Dbl.	1-30-35 g.	Twin 3	400#	2
300	1	1-30 g.	2 Dbl.	1-30-35 g.	Twin 6	400#	3
350	1	1-40 g.	2 Dbl.	1-40 g.	Twin 6	400#	3
400	2	1-40 g.	2 Dbl.	1-40 g.	Twin 6	400#	3
450	2	1-60 g.	2 Dbl.	1-40 g.	Twin 6	600#	6
500	2	1-60 g.	2 Dbl.	1-40 g.	Twin 10	600#	6
600	2	1-60 g.	2 Dbl.	1-40 & 1-20	Twin 10	600#	6
750	3	2-40 g.	2 Dbl.	1-40 & 1-20	Twin 10	1000#	8

*Average of 20 cups per gallon—1½ cup per meal.

**If there are meeting rooms, add 3 lb. ice per seat.

NOTE: Heated carts are relatively simple to size since most manufacturers advertise them by dish capacity. One thing to keep in mind is that it is better to provide as many different size charts as possible since functions will occur with different amounts of people up to the banquet room capacity.

peratures directly into casings, with no human or utensil contact.

4. Filled casings are immediately loaded into a tumbling chilled water cooling bath. Depending on product viscosity and casing size, product temperatures are reduced to 40°F in 20 to 60 minutes.
5. After chilling to 40°F, casings are loaded into standard walk-in refrigerators with temperatures maintained at 32°F to 36°F. Because of the aseptic preparation and packaging methods used and very rapid chilling, most products have a refrigerated shelf life of 30 to 45 days, thus saving the energy costs of freezing and then thawing frozen items.
6. As needed by the menu cycle requirements, casings are pulled from storage and distributed to remote locations for rethermalization. Refrigerated trucks or insulated holding boxes are required. Steam-jacketed kettles, steamers, ovens, or ranges can be used to reheat items.

The cost of food quality benefits of this system can be illustrated by the experience of the Portland public school system. Prior to 1980, the school system had operated 76 separate kitchens for an elementary school lunch and breakfast program that served more than 30,000 meals daily. The move to a centralized kitchen started when the school system closed several kitchens and transferred their production to nearby "cluster facilities."

Seeing that a slight move toward centralization reduced costs, school system administrators retained a consulting firm to evaluate whether additional centralization would be further cost-effective. From that study came the initial recommendation for the move to a CapKold-equipped central commissary.

Since the move to a centralized food preparation, storage, and distribution concept, the Portland public schools' foodservice department has experienced significant cost and food quality benefits throughout the foodservice operation. With centralized purchasing and storage, Portland reports that savings from reductions in food supply and inventory have amounted to more than $100,000 per year. And because bulk deliveries are made to only one location, drop-off charges have been eliminated and shipping costs substantially reduced.

As impressive as the benefits gained from centralized purchasing are, the greatest savings arise in food preparation. Because satellite kitchens simply reheat most foods that are prepared in the central commissary, it is unnecessary to have supervisory managers at every school. Through attrition, the school system was able to eliminate 68 kitchen managers at the school level. Even with the addition of a lead assistant position at each satellite kitchen, the labor cost saving has amounted to approximately $500,000 per year. The school system currently averages about 35 meals per man-hour from its satellite kitchens—double the pre-CapKold average.

Control benefits also are realized at the central commissary. All ingredients are premeasured and proportioned before entering the cooking area. Not only does this step consolidate the task of production, but it also provides for tight ingredient control and error-free recipes. Food waste can be precisely determined and easily controlled.

Consolidating food production also contributes to a higher systemwide level of food quality. Because personnel at satellite kitchens are not required to execute complex recipe instructions, product quality has become more consistent. Because foods are quick-chilled rather than frozen, there is no cellular breakdown of products due to the freezing process. Also, the rethermalization done at satellite kitchens allows the products to retain the smells and aromas of just-cooked foods for appetite appeal. Although the Portland school system has experienced significant enrollment decline (more than 10% since 1980), participation rates in the school lunch program have increased.

This system's advantages of labor, energy, and raw material savings, combined with inherent planning and control benefits, have enabled it to benefit colleges and universities, health care and government institutions, and restaurant chains. As the Portland public school system example demonstrates, however, this system is especially suited to the foodservice challenges of a multiunit school system. According to Robert Honson, Portland's foodservice director, "The CapKold System has far exceeded our original expectations. I believe anyone considering a move to the central commissary concept must consider CapKold."

ACKNOWLEDGMENTS

The section on the CapKold System was reprinted courtesy of Groen Manufacturing. The Grilstone! material was used courtesy of Grilstone International.

SOUS-VIDE COOKING

Sous vide is French for "under vacuum." A sous-vide system is used on a small, individual scale for restaurant and catering-style serving. In essence, it is a mini cook chill system.

Food products are prepared, cooked, and placed in plastic pouch-style packs. The pouch is then vacuum-drawn and sealed for future serving, and is quick-chilled and stored for 21 to 30 days at 32°F to 37°F. The product may be dropped in boiling water or steamed for reconstitution as needed.

Among the advantages of sous-vide cooking are: precise portion control, varied menu, ease of serving, reduction in equipment, and flavor retention.

In the future, it is likely that a great variety of ethnic take-out foods will be served in this manner. For example, an early favorite was duck breasts in wine sauce, served with a mound of buttered noodles. Many applications are anticipated for this method.

CONVEYOR COOKING

Conveyor ovens are available in both gas and electric designs. Menu items that lend themselves to conveyor cooking include pizza and bakery items such as rolls, croissants, biscuits, cakes, and cookies. Also, entree items such as tacos, boneless chicken breasts, and fish items are excellent candidates for conveyor cooking. Broiling conveyors can be used for such items as meats, poultry, and fish.

This section describes one style of conveyor oven, which will give the reader insight into the basics of this type of cooking technology.

Generally, conveyor ovens will bake, reheat, and finish food two to four times faster than conventional ovens. These ovens operate at lower temperatures than regular ovens, preheat in half the time, and, when turned down, recover to cooking temperature much faster.

Cooking and baking technologies historically have been extremely ineffective in penetrating the cold boundary that surrounds a food product. The air flow technology involved in the air impingement process substantially increases baking efficiency by effectively "sweeping away" the cold air boundary layer. The result is an incremental, significantly improved, heat transfer from the heat source to the food.

AIR IMPINGEMENT TECHNOLOGY BASICS

The air impingement process involves high-velocity, focused, heated air. Air jets direct columns of heated air perpendicularly to the food surface as the food travels horizontally through the oven on a wire mesh conveyor. Zoning the air jet configurations independently, both horizontally and vertically, provides enhanced cooking control.

Progressive degrees of surface heating produce the following results:

- As heating occurs, surface moisture begins to evaporate.
- Internal cooking takes place at the same time, while energy is being absorbed by the food.
- Further heating causes the surface to dry, while steam begins to pass through the surface of the food from the middle of the product.
- As the surface temperature increases, crisping occurs.
- Continued heating causes browning in increasing degrees.
- Exposure to yet higher temperatures causes a seared effect.

PROGRESSIVE CHARACTERISTICS

Benefits of air impingement baking are:

- Programmed, conveyorized baking occurs, in a first in–first out process.
- Fresh product is available faster than by conventional methods, on demand.
- It is possible to zone the air impingement baking process, matching the food product mix profile and heat-absorbing characteristics to the air impingement process heat transfer and baking effects.

Zones are opened, closed, or tempered in prescribed spatial arrangements to properly balance the energy going into the food products according to a particular product's heat acceptance capabilities. The result is an optimal heat transfer match to a food's specific "cooking profile."

COMBINATION COOKERS AND OVENS: THE NEW BREED

A new breed of specialized cooking ovens and steamers arrived in the mid-1980s to fill several specialized equipment needs. New menu items that required versatility, as well as competition and changing eating habits, culminated in some important advances in combination cookers. Some examples are:

1. A new pressure/convection steamer that allows each compartment to operate independently. This breakthrough will permit more fresh foods to appear on the menu, yet still allow bulk cooking with speed and quality to take place. A versatile addition to steam cooking, these combo units are available in counter or full size and may be stacked.
2. A convection combo steamer and oven that can do the following:

    - Roast and bake like a convection oven, steam like a pressureless steamer, and combo-cook with dry or steam heat.
    - Cook and hold overnight.
    - Proof dough.

3. A convection and steam model that offers a four-function cooking mode:

    - Hot air.
    - High steam temperature.
    - Normal steam temperature.
    - Hot air with moisture added.

Combo convection/steam ovens are available in counter or full size.

Many family-style restaurants and fast-food outlets have zeroed in on the breakfast business. New menu items such as croissants, biscuits, muffins, and rolls have stimulated development of a new generation of point-of-service ovens:

1. Electric or gas counter convection ovens with steam injection for browning and crusting.
2. Electric counter proofing devices.

These pieces can be stacked to provide a production center.

Another new counter cooker, known as the menu maker, requires no water connections, uses very little electric power, weighs only 150 pounds, and is quite versatile. Units can be stacked three high and require no hood. The menu maker can make 300 half-cup portions of rice in 48 minutes and may be used to boil, steam, poach, and braise a variety of menu items.

Traditional cooking equipment, such as ranges, broilers, fryers, steam equipment, and a host of smaller devices, continues to be improved, with new solid state controls, better insulation, and more energy-efficient, more serviceable designs. Buyers should consult food equipment representatives for assistance in selecting from this broad array of equipment.

UNIQUE COOKING AIDS

Many useful cooking devices that are available from foodservice equipment manufacturers receive too little attention. However, the unique aids described in this section all deserve particular notice. Special cooking problems sometimes have simple solutions; the devices described below all filled such special needs. Additional information on these cooking aids can be obtained from foodservice equipment representatives.

THE BURG'R TEND'R

This unique steamer, which picks up its heat source from any existing electric or gas burner, is known in the Connecticut area as the "New England cheeseburger chest." Its fame spreading by word of mouth in recent years, the Burg'r Tend'r has been shipped around the world, and cooks now report using the chest for muffins, poached eggs, hot dogs, rolls, and more. The steamed cheese it prepares also is delicious on pies, tuna, and vegetables. A self-contained electric model will be available soon. No ventilation is necessary.

RIB CHEF

A unique Plexiglas, single-portion primary cooker for prime ribs, this device uses the defrost cycle of a microwave. In four to five minutes, this cooking tool will prepare an eight- to ten-ounce portion of prime rib to perfection. Shrinkage averages only 5%. It is great for late arrivals, or for upgrading any menu. Because the unit is transparent, the cook can see the cooking rib and judge its doneness.

ADD-A-BROILER-GRIDDLE

Use of an Add-A-Broiler-Griddle is the space-saving way to convert existing gas range tops into broilers and griddles. Its installation is accomplished in minutes. The broiler option adds charbroiled flavor to steaks, chops and burgers, and brand meats. The griddle option permits griddle cooking with a quick preheat time and efficient heat removal through the rear flue. With this device, there is no need to spend extra equipment dollars for separate broiler and griddle conversion units; the Add-A-Broiler-Griddle is a double-duty broiler and griddle converter.

THE SIZZLE PRESS

The Sizzle Press is a portable top-of-the-grill tool that is similar in appearance to a steak weight. Grilled items can be cooked in less than half the usual time with this press. The Sizzle Press sears the top side of burgers, steaks, and sausage, sealing in moisture; and the stored energy in the press is designed to prevent the temperature of the product from dropping below the searing point during the entire cooking operation.

THE TENDER PRESS

One of the greatest advantages of the Tender Press is that it allows one to cook frozen meats, *without* defrosting, faster than one can cook them after thawing. It reduces handling, staging, and shrinkage, as well as improving the shelf life of the meat. One puts frozen meat on the grill, places the press on the meat, and applies a little pressure to obtain a sear. Residual heat in the device's pins and bottom plate will defrost the top side while the grill begins to cook the bottom. The pins will not completely penetrate hard frozen meat; but after the meat is turned, the pins will go through the meat and touch the grill, so that the meat cooks by internal heat. The total cooking time is at least 50% faster than without the press. For example, a quarter-pound hamburger will cook in approximately 55 seconds on each side.

BASTE N BROIL

The Baste N Broil broils the top of steaks, burgers, chops, bacon, ham, and so on, with stored conduction heat. Placed on top of cooking meats, it also speeds up the broiling and grilling of underfired broilers and griddles, and holds meat tightly against cooking surfaces. The Baste N Broil is especially useful in preventing curling of steaks, bacon, chops, and so on; and it saves energy in two ways: (1) by holding meats tightly to the cooking surface, and (2) by cooking top surfaces by conduction and convection plus steam from condensed vapors in its self-basting inverted grooves. The Baste N Broil has a built-in thermometer that indicates the degree of doneness of foods being basted and broiled, and enables control over the temperature of the device by showing when to place it on a grid or broiler for reheating.

GRILSTONE!

The Grilstone! system is based on the ancient art of cooking on a natural stone with unique characteristics. The system comes from Europe, is F.D.A.-approved, and has been submitted to the National Sanitation Foundation for testing.

The Grilstone! concept involves the restaurant patron in the food preparation experience. It combines the basic principles of grill and fondue cooking, using no fats or oils. The cooking time and pace of the meal are controlled by the patron.

The restaurant customer chooses from a varied list of menu items. The foods (raw product) are plated on prewarmed plates in the kitchen, and are presented to the customer. The patron in turn cooks the food on his or her own Grilstone! cookware.

The Grilstone! can work anywhere. The concept is so flexible that it can be implemented in any type of restaurant operation. The plates and heavy-duty oven used in this system are described below.

GRILSTONE!

The Grilstone! material is characterized as follows:

- Natural, nonporous stone.
- Attractive gray/white marble appearance.
- High-density material that absorbs a substantial amount of heat and releases it slowly. This characteristic allows for a cooking time of 30 to 45 minutes. In addition, the slow release of heat prevents the food from burning.
- Physical and chemical properties deemed noninjurious to health.
- Self-cleaning at specific temperatures.
- High resistance to breakage and thermal shock.
- Can be rinsed in water even when hot.

GRILSTONE! PLATES

Four types of plates are available:

1. Ceramic dish with built-in vegetable and sauce compartments.
2. Round wood base.
3. Oval wood base with three individual sauce cups.
4. Square wood base.

Wooden sets are available in light or dark wood, and ceramic sets in a glossy black or brown. All sets come complete with a stainless steel insert. Optional ceramic sauce holders are available for use with round and square wood sets.

GRILSTONE! OVEN

A heavy duty oven was designed for use with this cookware. Its characteristics are:

- Compact size: 26″ W × 28″ D × 29″ H.
- Capacity: 80 stones (double-deck); 40 stones (single-deck).
- High temperature range: 650–675°F.
- Voltage: 208/1/60 or 230/1/60, 5900 watts (double-deck); 2950 watts (single-deck).
- Countertop installation.
- Optional stand for oven.

GRILSTONE! LIFTERS

- Large stainless steel lifter to load and unload oven.
- Small stainless steel lifters to use in dishwashing operation.

COOKING EQUIPMENT CHECKLIST

Before selecting equipment, one must ask: will it fit, is it stackable, is an exhaust hood required, is a floor drain or floor sink required, is gas or electric preferred and can it be mounted on casters?

The following types of equipment are available:

- Broilers
- Char broilers
- Fryers
- Fryer filters
- Computer timers
- Grills
- Griddles
- Convection ovens
- Bakers' ovens
- Roast ovens
- Microwave ovens
- Smoker ovens

- Ranges
- Steam cookers
- Steam kettles
- Combination cookers (steam and convection)
- Tilting skillets
- Radiant ovens
- Cheese melters
- Egg cookers
- Hot dog rollers, steamers, conveyors, rotisserie
- Conveyor cookers
- Rotisserie broilers

The buyer should remember to:

- Save instruction and repair manuals.
- Ask for list of all options for all equipment at all times.
- Determine whether the equipment requires more power than is available.
- Verify the utility connections.

APPROXIMATE SHIPPING WEIGHT; SELECTED EQUIPMENT

--- Broiler Floor Model, With Oven	825#
--- Broiler, Salamander	175#
--- Char Broiler, Floor Model 36″	445#
--- Fryer Counter, 28 Pound	70#
--- Fryer Floor Model, 40 Pound	260#
--- Grill Gas, 28 × 36 Top	347#
--- Grill Electric, 20 × 36″ Top	160#
--- Convection One Single, Full Size	480#
--- Convection One Double Full Size	960#
--- Heavy Duty 36″ Electric Range, With Oven	500#
--- Restaurant Series Range 60″ 2 Oven	800#
--- Pizza Oven 1 Deck 78″ Gas	975#
--- Pizza Oven 2 Deck 78″ Gas	1,810#
--- Bake Oven 1- 8″ High Deck, Electric 78″	1,490#
--- Bake Oven 2- 8″ High Deck, Electric 78″	2,690#
--- Tilt Skillet, Floor Model 30 Gallon	370#
--- Combi Cooker – 18 × 26 Pans Floor Model	600#
--- Conveyor Cooker Gas --	
Size 78″ Single Section	1,091#
Size 78″ Double Section	1,935#
--- 2 Compartment Pressureless Steamer on 24″ Generator Base	725#
--- Kettle, Floor Model 20 Gallon	500#
--- Kettle, Floor Model 30 Gallon	550#
--- Gas Fryer 40 Pd Fat Capacity	595#
--- Counter Steamer, Convection	175#

CAPKOLD

Central
Commissary
Systems

What is CapKold?

- *Centralized bulk purchase*
- *Centralized preparation*
- *Large batch kettle cooking*
- *Cook Tank preparation of meats*
- *Filling/Packaging*
- *Rapid product cooling*
- *Long-term refrigerated storage*
- *Reheating at remote locations*

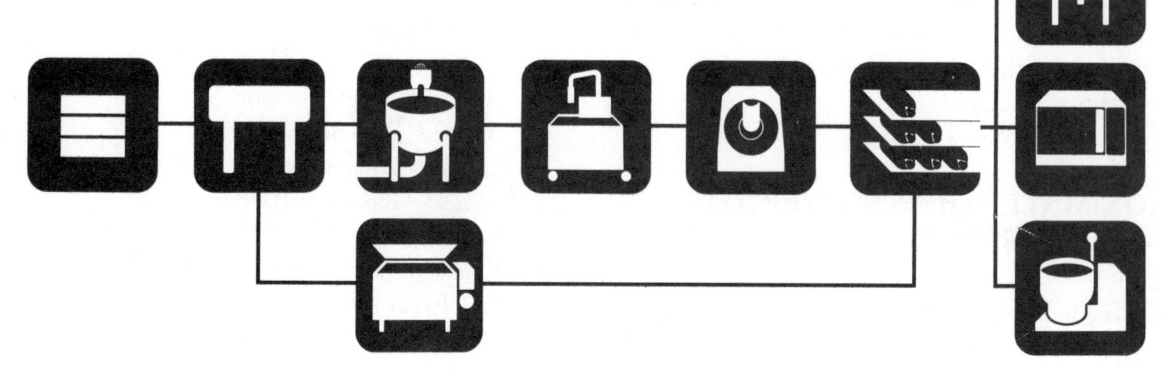

The CapKold System............ Savings At Each Step Of The Process!

Bulk Purchase
Preparation
Kettle Cooking
Filling Casings
Casing Cooler (40°F)
Refrigerated Storage (28°-32°F)
Cook Tank Slow Cooking
Re-Heat

Figure 5-1. Cook chill food preparation. (Courtesy Groen Manufacturing)

LEGEND

A. WATER SPRINKLER PIPE & VALVE
B. BACKSPLASH EXTENSION AND GUTTER WITH FIELD JOINT AND DUAL SWING POT FILL FAUCET
C. 24" LONG MATCHING BACKSPLASH AND DUAL SWING POT FILL FAUCET
D. FIELD JOINT FOR (2) WOKRANGES
E. WOKRANGE CHAMBER REDUCER
F. STAINLESS STEEL WELDED SPICE SHELF
G. STAINLESS STEEL DRIP TRAY

Figure 5-2. Chinese ranges. Chinese range options shown on a composite drawing will assist the purchasers's selection. *Note:* Plumbing and gas connections are quite detailed. One must be sure that coordination with utility trades and approvals for ventilation are investigated before purchasing. (Courtesy Sterling Metalware)

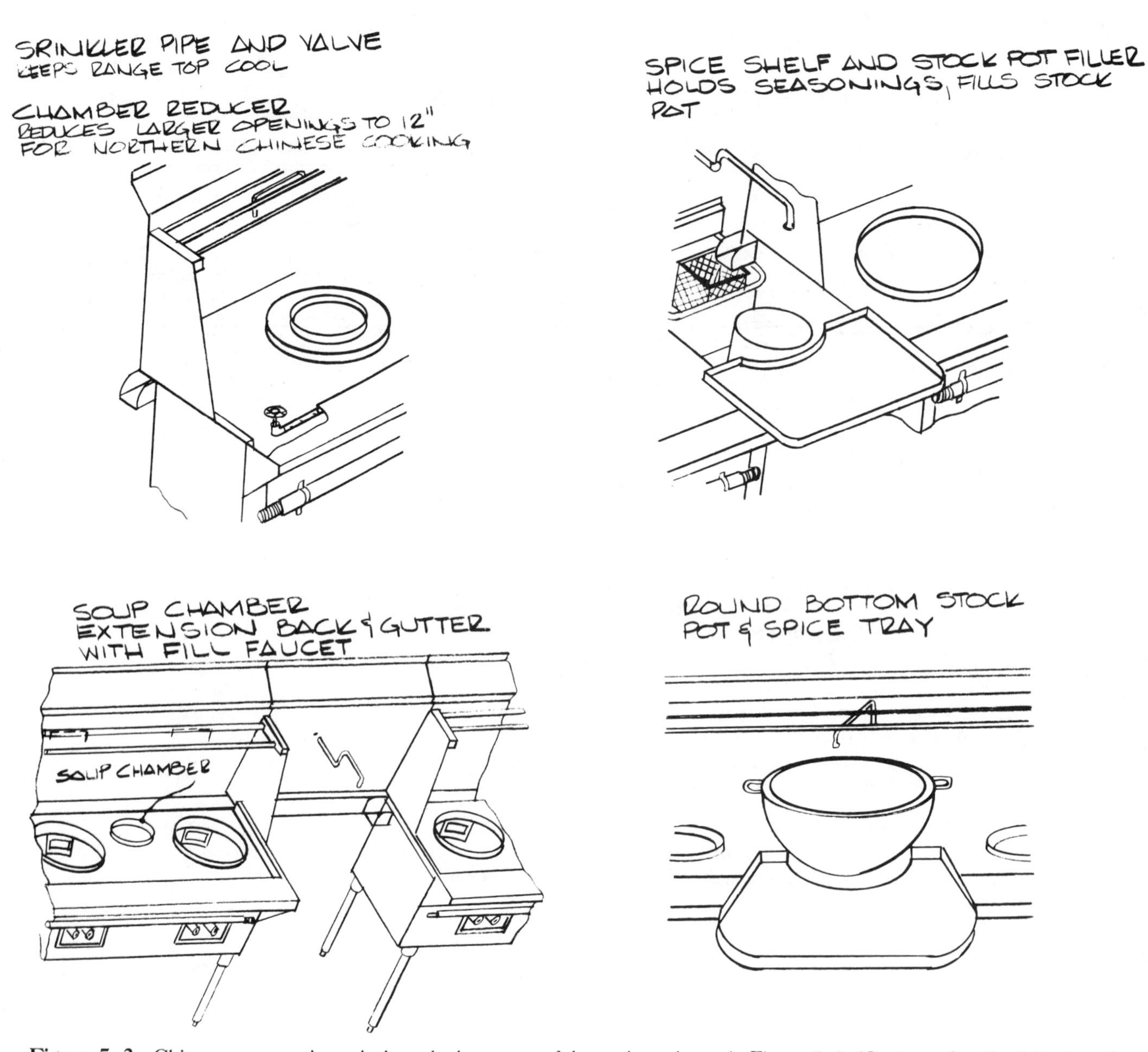

Figure 5-3. Chinese range options. A closer look at some of the options shown in Figure 5-2. (Courtesy Sterling Metalware)

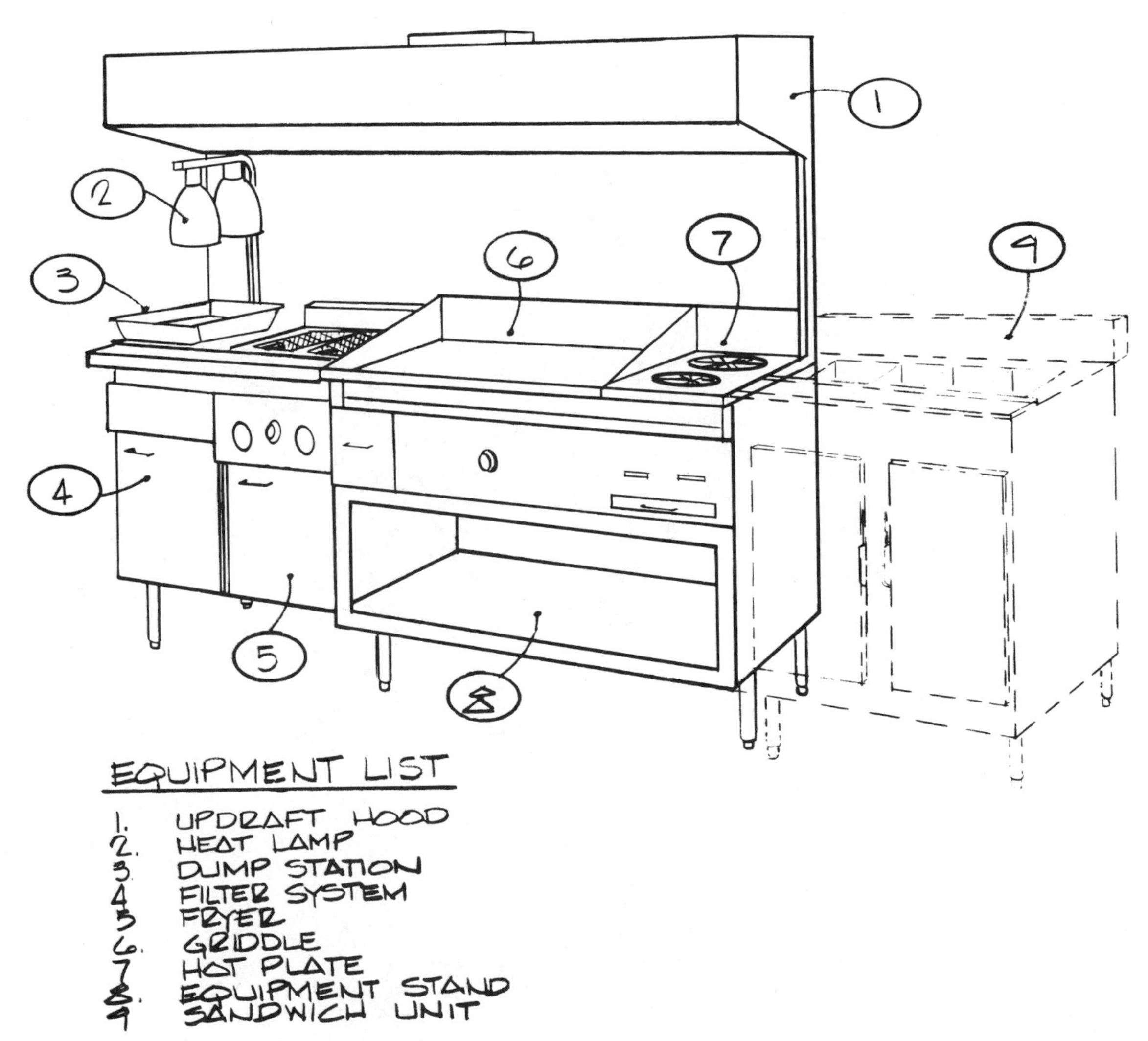

Figure 5-4. Short-order cook station. This type of cooking arrangement is found in many limited-menu family-style restaurants and snack bars. Note that the ventilator is known as a back shelf style; other ventilators also are shown in this chapter. This equipment also is available in a drop-in design for counter and in a grill-stand style. (Courtesy Keating Manufacturing)

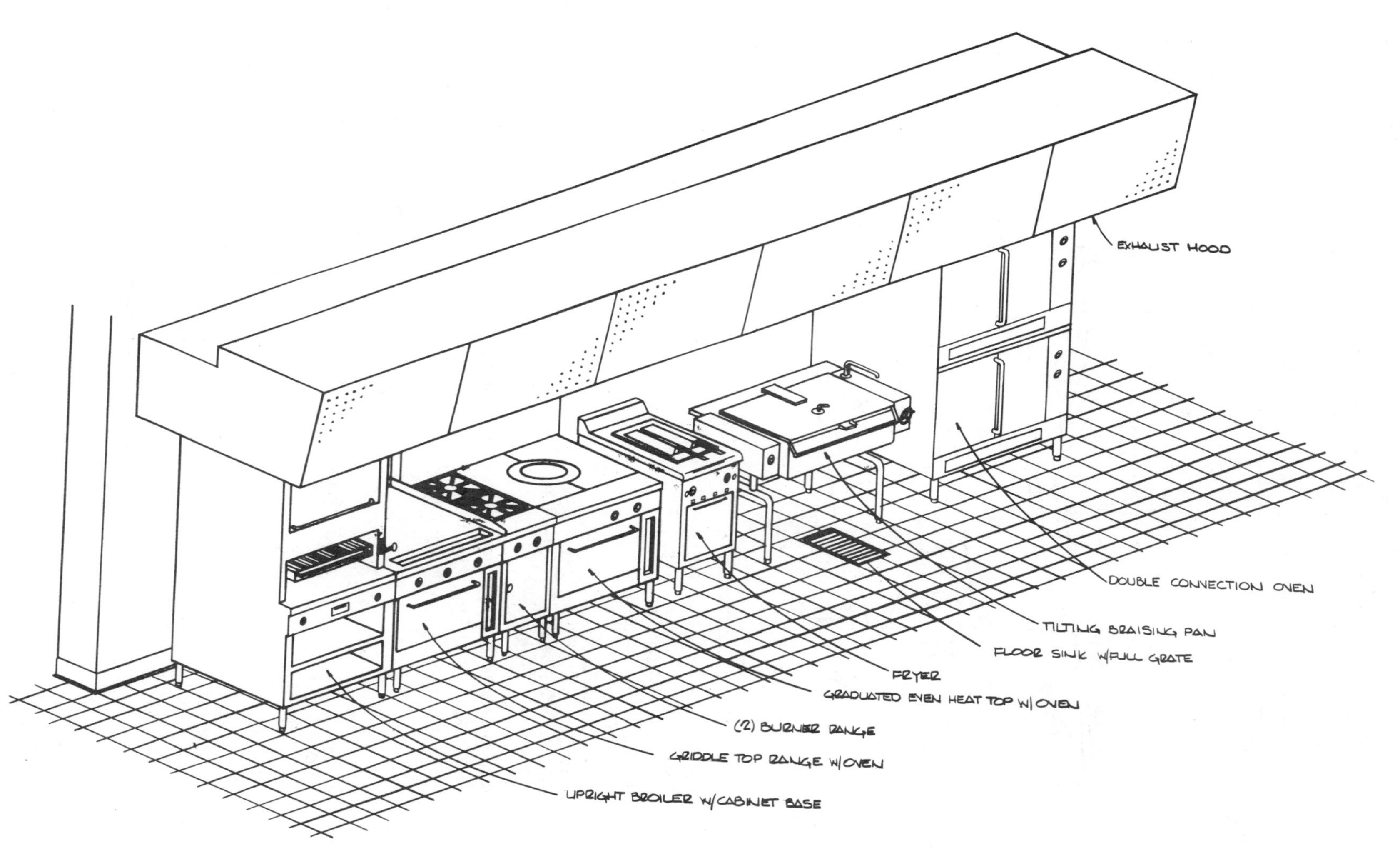

Figure 5-5. Typical heavy duty cooking lineup.

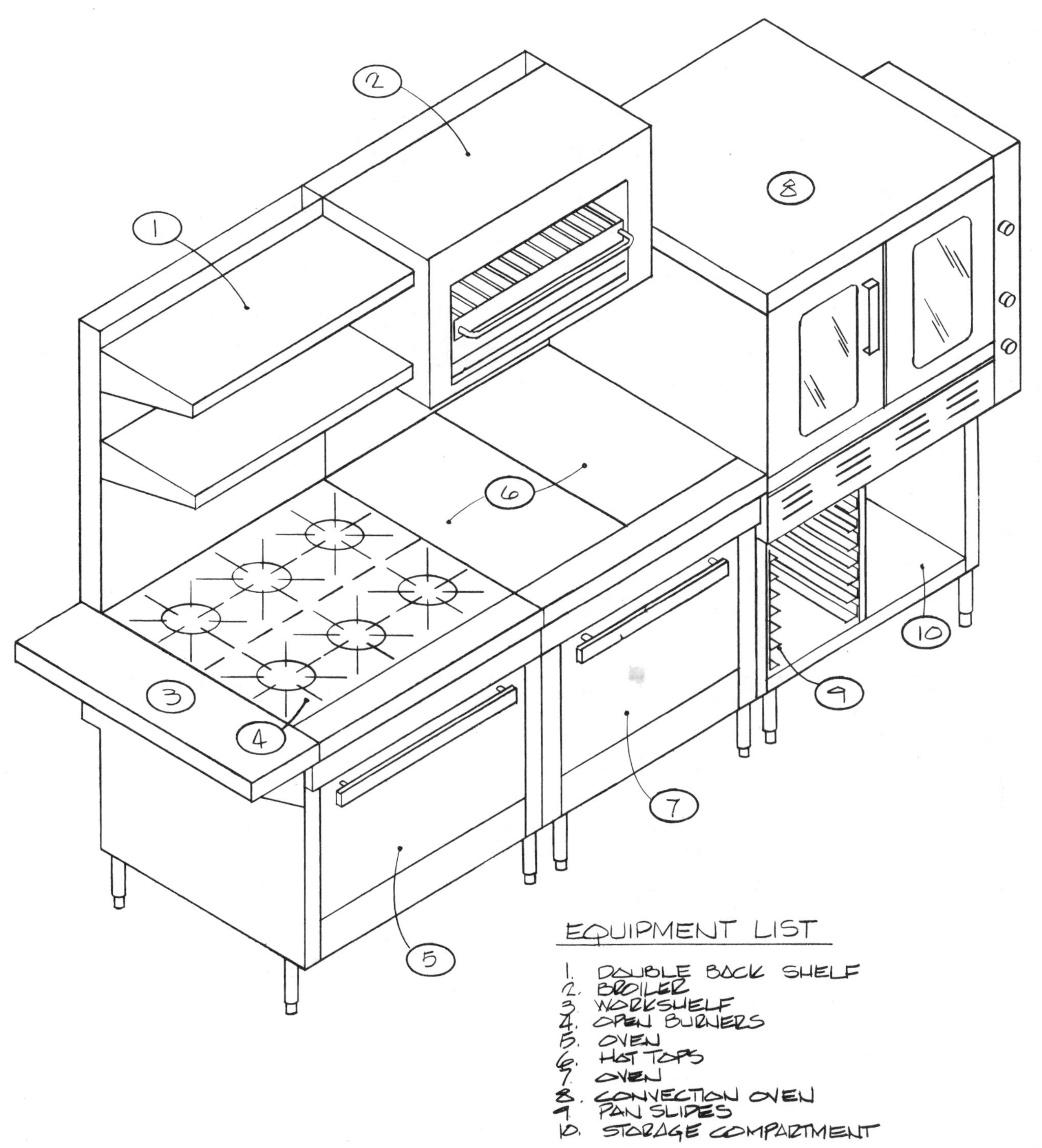

Figure 5-6. Heavy duty cooking equipment. Both gas and electric types are available, their options varying with the manufacturer. Options shown here include landing ledge to left of burners, double back shelf, broiler, and pan storage for cooling or holding under convection. Menu matching may lead to selection of various options, such as: a char broiler; a warmer area under the char-grid area; either a tilt grid or fixed flat grid; a mobile stand; a quick disconnect for ease of cleaning; splash guards; a work shelf; a broiler (with or without an oven); forced air; infrared, ceramic, or electric heat; a fryer (taking into account a filter needed, automatic cleaning, solid state controls, basket styles available, and production figures); and convection ovens (considering such options as steam capability, roast and hold, two-speed fan, solid or glass door, pan capacity, and two-stage power level).

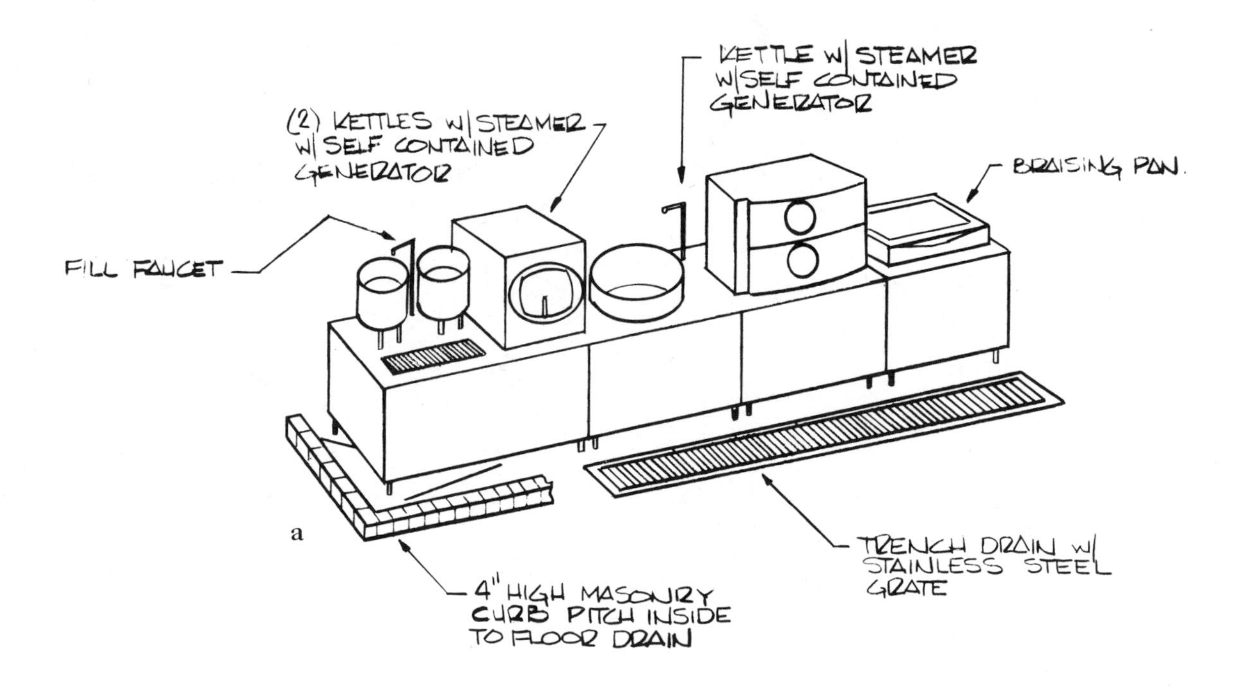

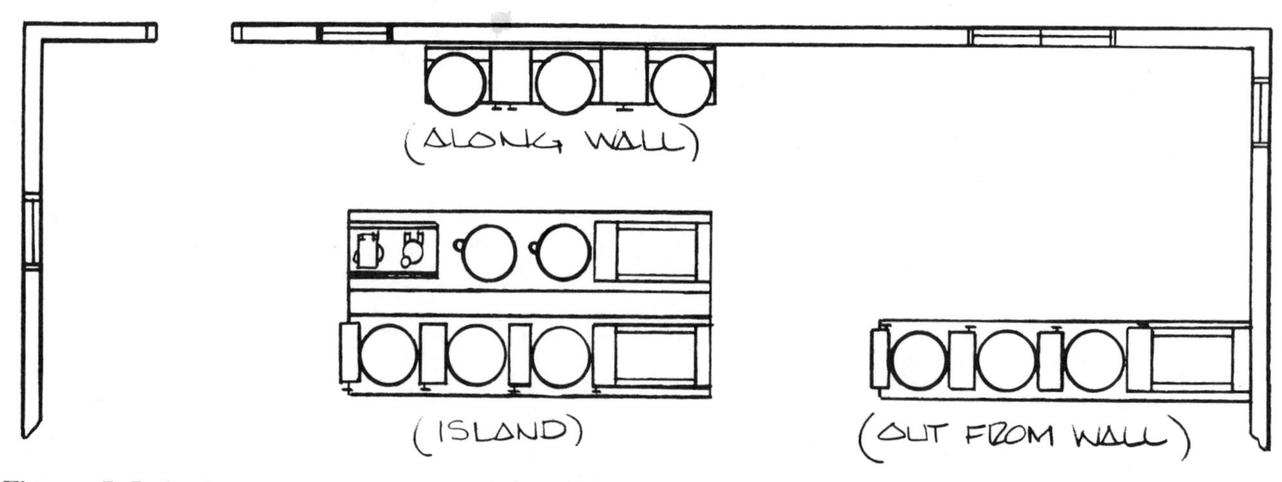

Figures 5-7a,b. Steam cooking equipment. Available in gas, electric, and direct steam designs, this equipment can be installed along the wall, in an island, or out from the wall. Besides the draining detail shown here, the buyer must select from various sizes, based on meals served daily. A consultant or food equipment dealer will assist the buyer with the generator sizing and ventilation requirements. Options include pan holders, strainers, power assists, and many more specialized features. (Courtesy Market Forge)

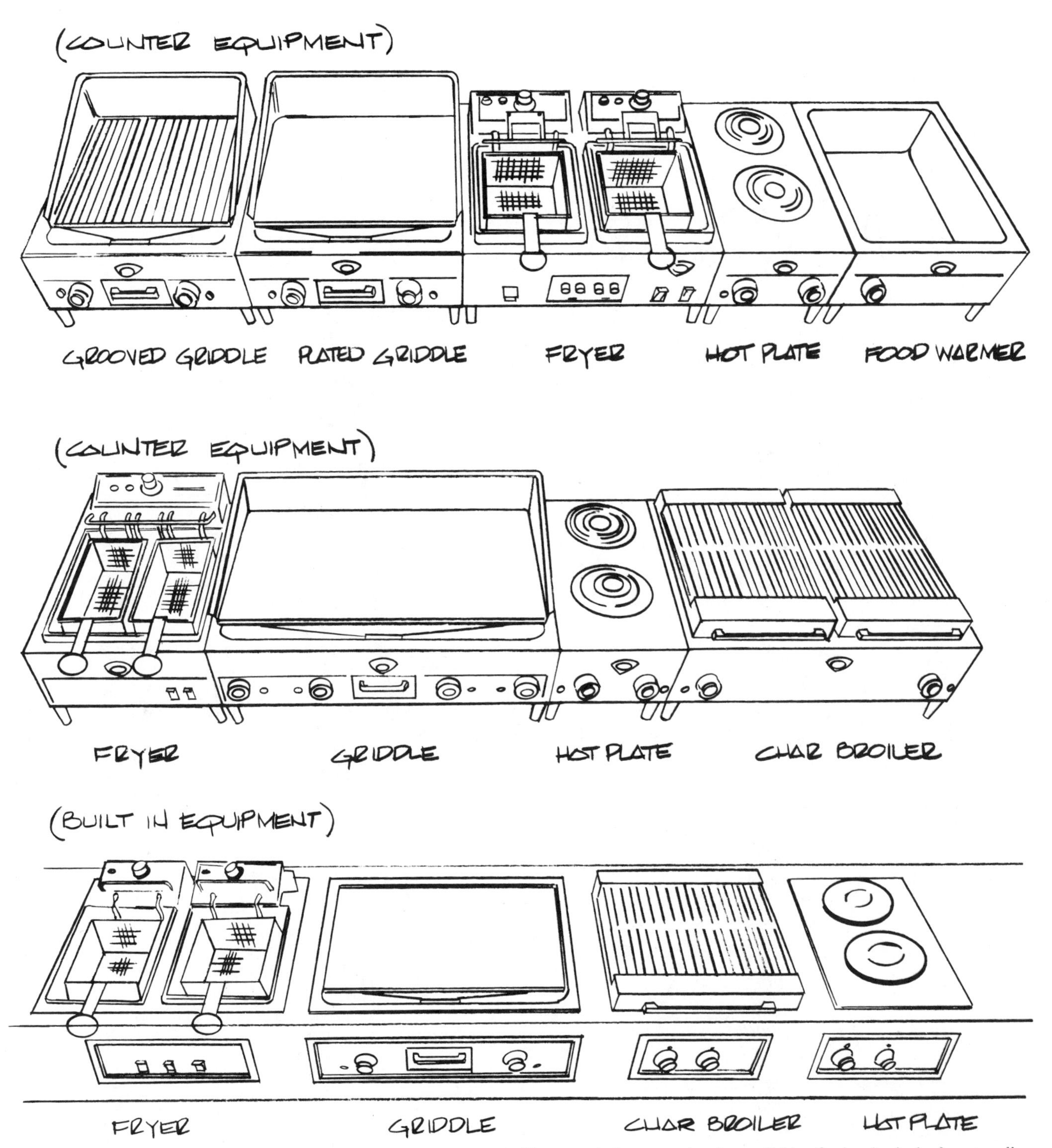

Figure 5-8. Counter cooking equipment. Electric type is illustrated, but gas also is available. Styles include freestanding with legs, built-in, and many other designs. Ventilation for these cooking devices is shown elsewhere. (Courtesy Wells Manufacturing)

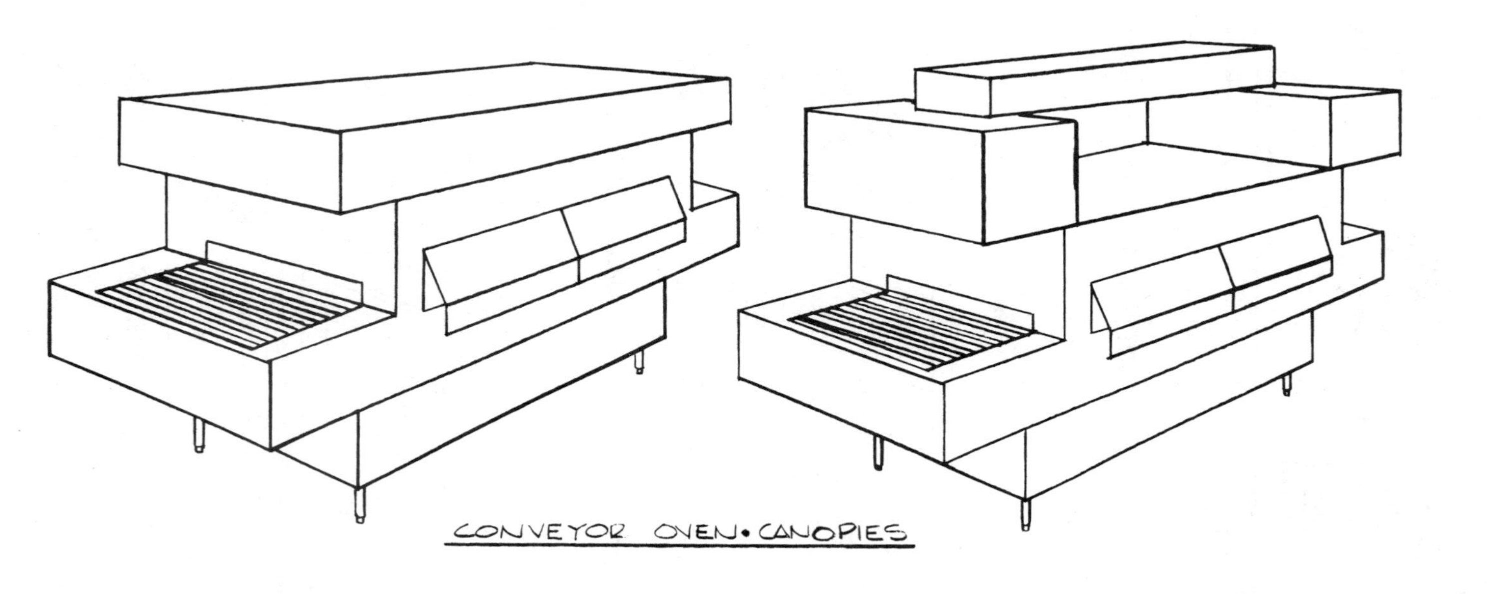

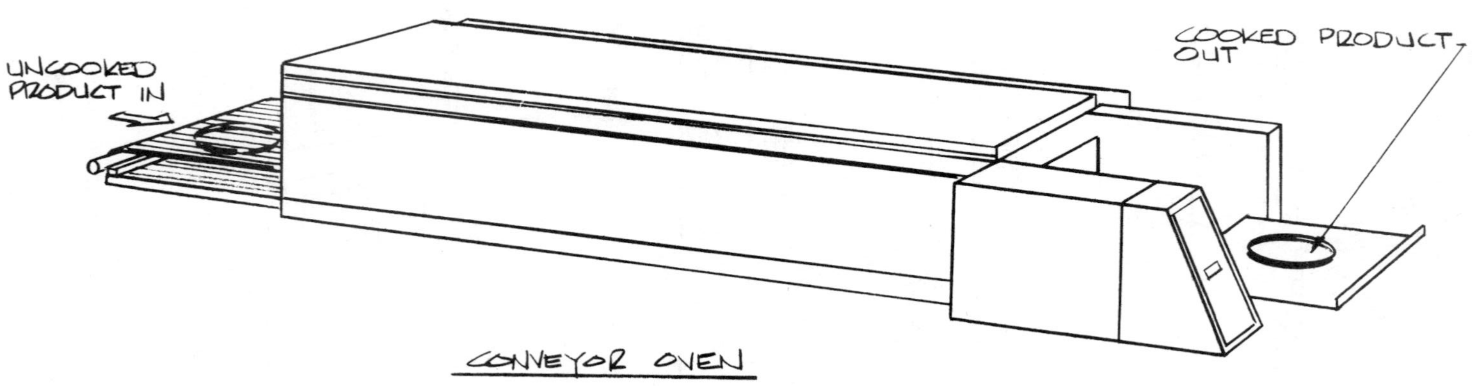

Figure 5-9. Conveyor cooking. Note that specialized ventilation equipment is available for conveyor-style broilers and ovens.

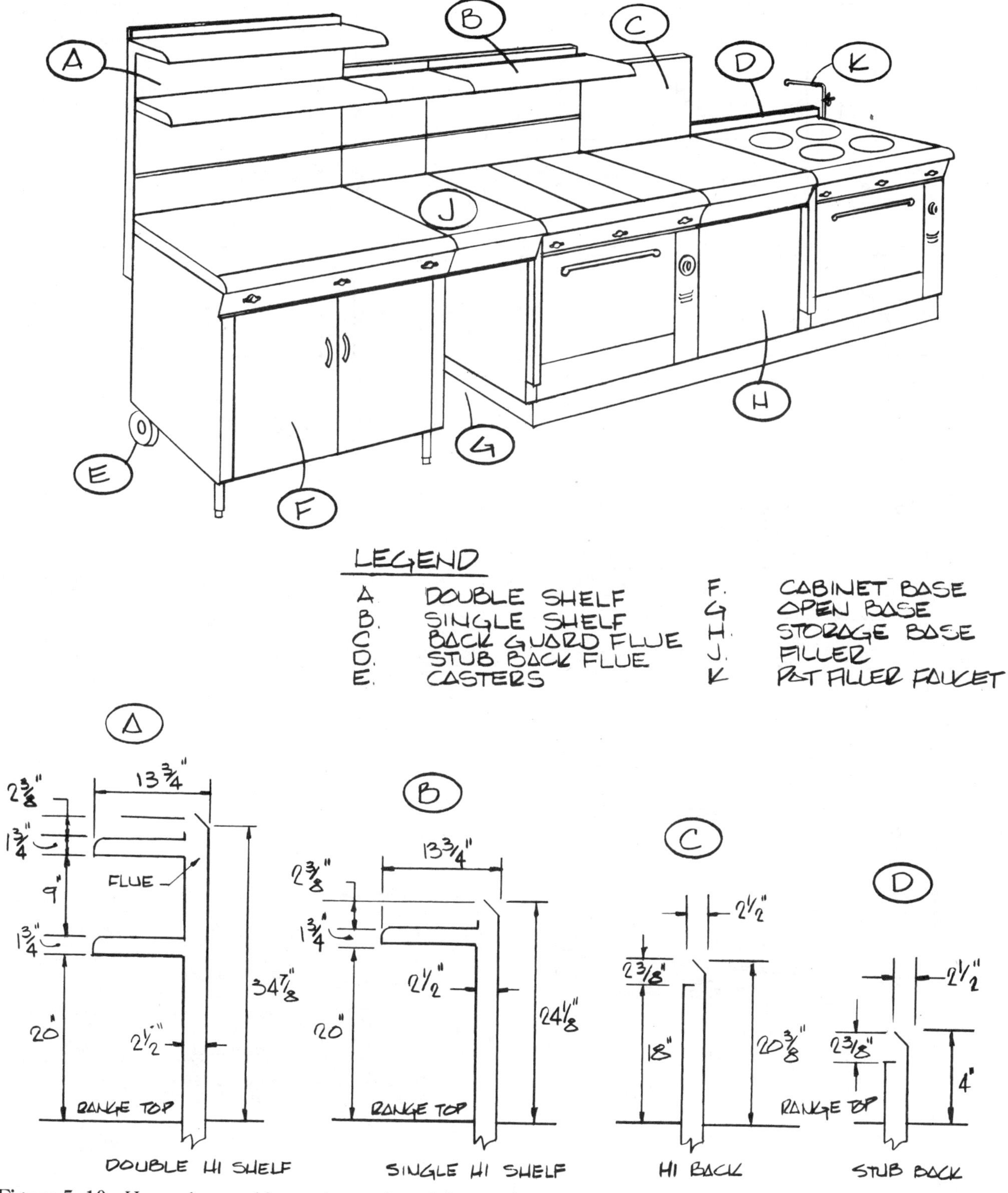

Figure 5-10. Heavy duty cooking options: a few of the popular options, available in gas or electric. There are many sizes and finish styles, which vary by manufacturer. (Courtesy Montague Company)

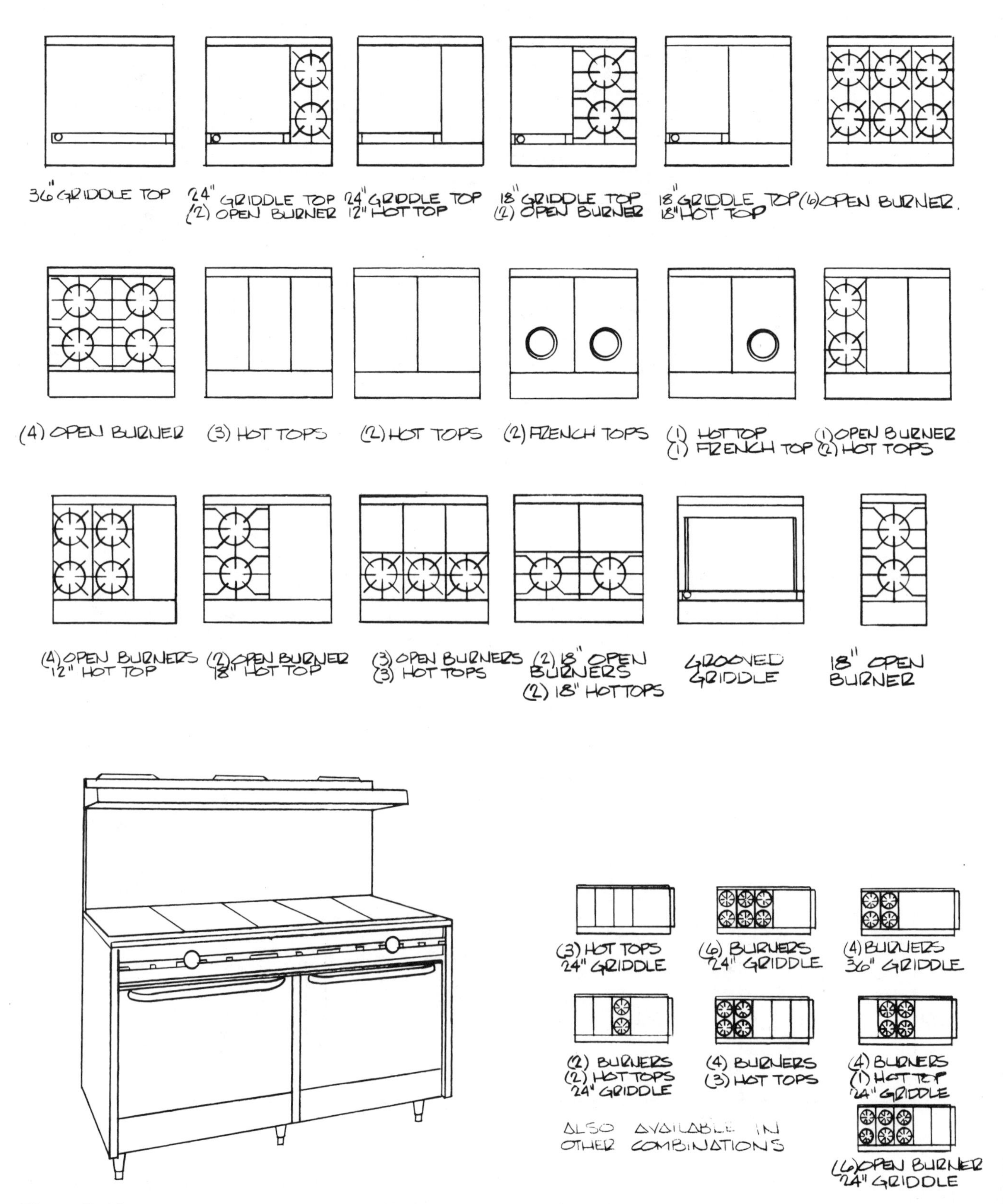

Figure 5-11. Heavy duty range top options. These heavy duty range tops are available in varying widths, from 24 inches to 72 inches, with optional top arrangements as illustrated. Ovens, regular or convection, and back shelf broiler, as seen in Figure 5-6, may be used with these tops.

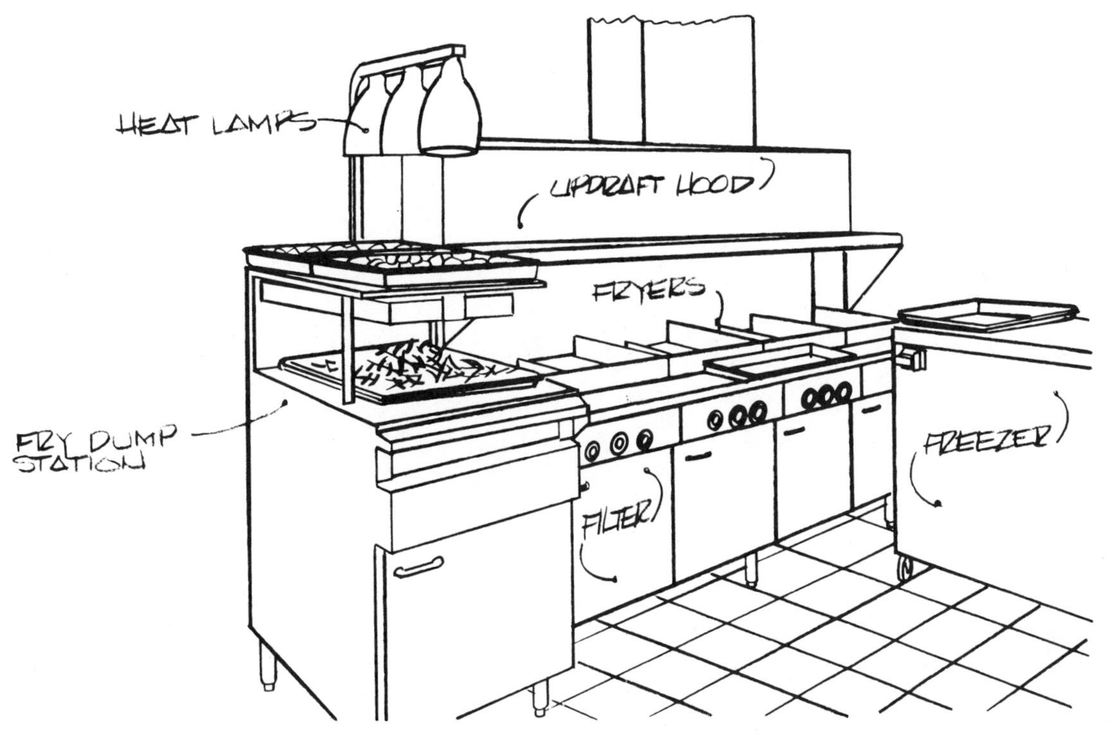

Figure 5-12. Fryer station, showing key options used to complete a fry station. (Courtesy Keating Manufacturing)

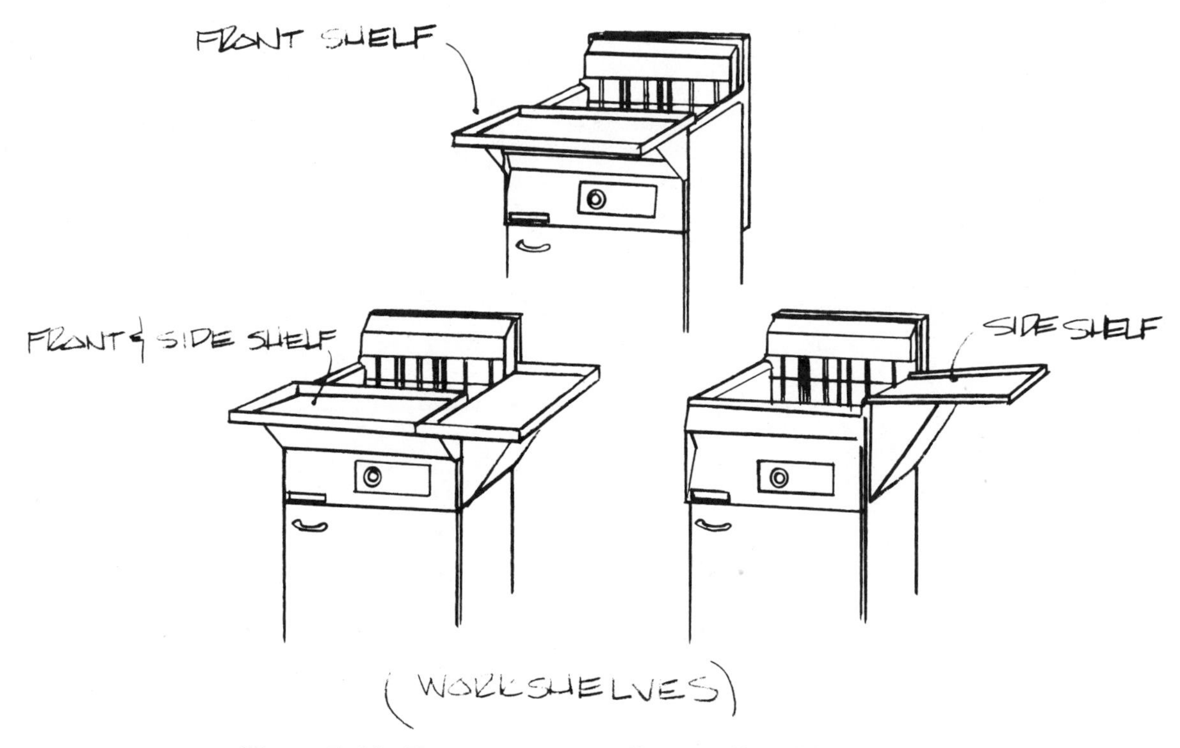

Figure 5-13. Fryer shelf options. (Courtesy Pitco Manufacturing)

6

Commercial Cooking Ventilation

SECTION I: MEANS AND METHODS OF VENTILATION CONTROL

KITCHEN EXHAUST VENTILATION

The Primary Element—the Exhaust Hood

Exhaust hoods are required for three reasons:

1. To create a curtain of air that captures cooking heat and grease particles;
2. To direct the flow of air; and,
3. To protect the surrounding environment from flame, heat, and particulate matter.

The exhaust hood must enhance the air circulation in the kitchen, be easy to clean, be constructed of noncombustible materials and be located where it can do its job, without interfering with the cooking process.

Each hood is designed to match the energy and contaminant loads of the cooking equipment it serves. The hood also needs to accommodate the furnishings and other features of the building in which the kitchen is contained.

The job of the exhaust fan in the hood is to create an air flow that moves gases and grease-laden vapors toward the vent and into the ductwork that will carry the effluent to a discharge point outside of the building.

Make-up air, which is introduced into the kitchen to compensate for the exhaust flow, combines with room air and is then drawn into the hood to cool and stabilize the exhaust gas flow.

Types of Exhaust Hoods

There are two basic types of hoods: the canopy hood and the backshelf, or low side wall, hood.

The canopy hood is an overhead unit installed at a recommended 6 feet, 6 inches A.F.F. (above finished floor) to a maximum of 7 feet, 0 inches A.F.F. The canopy system must incorporate an "overhang" in order to effectively capture the grease-laden vapors. This overhang ranges in size, depending upon the cooking equipment and the building characteristics.

Typically, the canopy length extends at least 6 inches beyond each side of the cooking battery, and 12 inches past the front of the appliance.

The overhang creates a sort of envelope, which holds the hot air and grease close to the cooking appliance so that the exhaust fan can pull the unwanted effluent up and away from the kitchen environment.

The backshelf, or low side wall hood, is a unit designed to exhaust hot air and grease only at the height of the cooking equipment. The unit, sized to the length of the range, fryer, etc., effectively captures the vapors directly from the appliance being used. The

---

Sections I–III of this chapter reprinted courtesy Seco Engineering.

proximity of the hood allows the gases to be pulled in much faster, and, consequently, prohibits the expansion of gas that occurs with a canopy-type unit. Therefore, overhang is not a requirement on this type of unit.

Traditional Filter Hoods

The filter hood utilizes a square or rectangular metal filter to remove the grease from the air stream before it enters the exhaust duct. Filter hoods are referred to as Bulletin 96 Canopies, a reference to NFPA Bulletin 96 that governs construction requirements for commercial kitchen application.

All national codes require that the grease removing filters be classified for this application. Underwriters Laboratories establishes the standards for filters, which are known as "U.L. classified grease extracting filters." All classified filters are designed as a set of interlocking metal baffles that remove grease by centrifugal force. The collected grease drains from the surface by gravity. Filters are installed diagonally, no greater than 45 degrees off the vertical plane.

Prior to the enactment of recent codes, filters were typically furnished with wire mesh that removed grease by impingement. Such filters are now outlawed because of their flammability and the rapid pressure drop associated with grease collection by impingement.

Wash Type Hoods

The wash hood or ventilator, is defined as a "grease extractor" under U.L. Standard #710. The standard states that a listed grease extractor must:

- remove grease without the use of impingement-type filters;
- provide for automatic cleaning of accumulated grease;
- provide for the protection of building ductwork in the event of a fire, and
- be operated by an automatic control system.

Most grease extractors on the market today utilize centrifugal force as the grease extraction method. The ventilator causes the exhaust air to be pulled through a series of tight turns at high velocity, causing the heavier grease particles to be separated from the air stream and collected on the interior hood surface. Through automatic control, a hot water and detergent wash down system is activated (while the exhaust fan is not operating) to remove the grease and other contaminants collected during the operation.

The wash system usually serves the dual purpose of cleaning the hood and preventing fire. It is automatically activated in the event of abnormally high exhaust gas temperatures. High-temperature activation of the system will shut off the exhaust fan and close a fire damper, located either at the duct collar or the entrance to the grease extraction chamber.

The wash ventilator is highly efficient in removing grease. It is best suited for applications where grease loading is high and/or where the cost of cleaning large numbers of filters, interiors and ductwork is excessive.

High Velocity Hoods

High Velocity (HV) hoods combine the designs of a listed grease extractor and filter hood. Their design incorporates the U.L. classified filter as the primary grease extractor, and employs a baffle plate in front of the filter to produce a high velocity slot that directs the exhaust flow.

Air volume selections are the same as for the wash hoods, because the same rules of directional air flow apply. The HV hood produces greater grease extraction efficiency than the standard filter-type hood, but equal to the listed grease extractor. It is used in moderate to heavy grease load applications. The initial cost is slightly higher than the standard filter hood and lower than that of the wash ventilator.

U.L. Hood and Damper Assemblies

Standard filter and high velocity hoods can be constructed as U.L. Hood and Damper Assemblies through the addition of an automatic fire damper, located in the exhaust duct collar. The automatic damper prevents fire from reaching the ductwork; the damper contains the fire and protects other parts of the building.

U.L. listings state the air volumes permitted for specific design situations. In most cases, air volumes remain consistent with Bulletin 96 design, but, in some instances, can be reduced.

Exhaust Extractors—Principles of Operation

Figure 6–1 displays a standard canopy containing a filter. The exhaust fan draws air from the room into the canopy and through the filter. The frying pan on top of the range is the source of contaminants that are working against the air curtain. The air curtain is denoted by the solid arrowed lines from the front edge of the equipment filter. When the air curtain is not strong enough to contain the contaminants, it is very easy for these contaminants, at the velocity they are emanating from the range, to escape into the room. This is why it is important to maintain a 20–60 feet per minute velocity at the front edge, depending upon the type of equipment being ventilated. At 200 to 350 CFM per lineal foot of the canopy, exhaust capture velocity will be 20–60 feet per minute at the front edge of the equipment to the filters. Note that these velocities are obtained without any internal make-up air.

Figure 6–2 displays a U.L. listed grease extractor. The air enters the ventilator through a lineal slot. The forces working against the air curtain are the contaminants from the top of the range. A U.L. listed grease extractor with the high velocity slot creates velocities at the front edge of the cooking equipment of 20–60 feet per minute, depending on the manufacturer's design and the equipment being ventilated. Because a U.L. listed grease extractor uses higher extraction velocities than a filter hood, it can create higher capture velocities at the front edge of the cooking equipment (or lower CFM/lineal foot).

A third functional design combines the filter and grease extractor criteria. It utilizes the high velocity slot of the U.L. grease extractor without the wash system. In place of the centrifugal baffles of the grease extractor are banks of U.L. classified grease filters mounted on a track with removable front baffle for routine cleaning.

Figure 6–3 displays a high velocity style hood which develops capture velocities similar to the grease extractors. The acceleration of the exhaust gases in the slot requires more static pressure to achieve the velocity conversion than a standard filter hood. The HV design operates at lower CFM/FT.

MAKE-UP AIR

Where there is a demand for exhaust there is also a need for make-up air. In the past, the kitchen exhaust system may have ventilated the building. However, energy costs are forcing reconsideration of building codes and designs to minimize such expenses.

Initially, make-up air was not supplied for the kitchen. Windows were opened in the spring, summer and fall while building-heated air was used in winter. Later, air supply "diffuser boxes" were added to the kitchen ceiling, and make-up air units had to heat incoming air to room temperature. With today's energy costs, judgments must be made about how to balance the method of introducing make-up air at the hood against building code ventilation requirements and air conditioning operating expenses.

MAKE-UP AIR CHAMBERS DISTRIBUTION SYSTEMS

Figure 6–4 depicts a standard filter canopy with a make-up air grill in the front panel. Introducing make-up air in this manner forces the air into the kitchen, allowing it to drop and be pulled up into the hood, similar to a hood without make-up air. This results in basically the same capture effect as a standard filter canopy without make-up air. Grills are ideal for dry climates where evaporative cooling is used. However, if the kitchen is air conditioned a drawback results; the temperature of the make-up air in the summertime is

Table 6-1. Table of exhaust hood characteristics.

Hood Style	Per Linial Ft. CFM	Static Pressure	HP	Initial Cost	Operational Cost*
Filter Hood "96" Figure 1	*Greatest* 200–600	Least .4 – .9	Same	*Least*	Highest
Grease Extractor Hood "Wash" Figure 2	*Lowest* 250–350	High 1.3″–1.7″	Same	*Most*	Least
High Velocity Hood "HV 96" Figure 3	*Moderate* 200–350	High .55″–1.7″	Same	*Moderate*	Moderate

*Include cost of energy exhaust, routine daily and periodic maintenance.

higher than that of the conditioned air in the kitchen. The make-up air is pulled into the return air of the HVAC system of the kitchen, causing an increased air conditioning load.

Figure 6–5 shows a standard filter canopy with make-up air being supplied through a linear perimeter slot. The purpose of this type of hood is to have the make-up air travel as short a distance past the top of the range, back into the canopy and through the filter, thus producing a capture velocity curtain. One problem occurs when the heat rising from the range causes this curtain to be pushed upwards, allowing the area below the curtain to have low capture velocity. This permits the contaminants produced by the cooking equipment to move into the kitchen. Another problem is that air delivered from the perimeter slot does not tend to flow in a straight line—it feathers. Any smoke caught in this situation has a tendency to work its way to the outside and, because of the feathering, some of the smoke rolls into the kitchen atmosphere. The make-up air should be heated to 65–70°F to make it comfortable for the chef. Another objection to this system is that the air velocity striking the cooking staff is so strong as to be annoying. It is common to find in practice that the chef has turned off or reduced the make-up air supply to such a low velocity that it defeats the purpose for using this type of system.

Figure 6–6 shows a short-circuit style canopy. Make-up air enters through a lineal slot on the inside of the front of the canopy. The purpose of this system is to bring in untempered air and short-circuit it across the internal position of the canopy to the filter. When short-circuiting of make-up air exceeds 50% of exhaust volume, the capture velocity at the front edge of the cooking equipment will drop to zero. In the range of 30% to 40% short-circuit air, capture velocity will increase to 15 feet per minute. The short circuit hood does an adequate job of forming the air curtain necessary to successfully exhaust when ventilating light-duty cooking equipment.

It is true that a high velocity slot will cause an aspirating effect at the lower edge of the hood, effectively to about 12″–15″. High velocity air enters the hood under the front lower edge, but below 15″ the air movement is virtually zero.

Another difficulty with this design is the velocity at the slot is usually 1,000 to 2,000 FPM. The velocity at the filter is around 300–400 FPM. The make-up air bounces air off of the filter because it cannot accept a velocity that high.

To illustrate, imagine a water hose with a half inch orifice. Now, try to force water through a small hole in the wall 3′ away. Most of the water will simply bounce off the wall, rather than go through the hole. The same effect is true with the air in a canopy.

As the outside temperature drops below 32°F, the air that normally moves straight across the canopy from the front to the filter has a tendency to drop; the colder the outside temperature, the more it will drop, and when this temperature gets into the teens, the air will go all the way to the floor, pulling the contaminants down with it. Cold air does not mix well with hot air being produced at the surface of the cooking equipment. A good analogy of this is a weather front. When a cold front from the north meets warm air from the south, a storm develops. The same thing is true of a short circuit hood. As the cold air enters and falls, it will force the contaminated hot air into the room or down to the floor.

This type of canopy is designed on the principle that hot air will eventually rise. Larger overhangs, such as 12″–24″, will help capture smoke which is lighter than the heavier contaminated particles, but overhangs will not capture the heavier particles that are being forced outward and down to the floor.

Figure 6–7 also depicts a short-circuit style canopy, but instead of a linear slot at the internal front edge, a series of grills are employed. The purpose of the grills is to bring the air in at a lower velocity to avoid causing the air to bounce off the filters as in Figure 6–6. Because it is a short-circuit hood, all of the problems mentioned above will occur, with the exception of the bounce effect.

The difference between Figure 6–8 and Figure 6–7 is that the manufacturer is also introducing make-up air at the rear portion of the range in Figure 6–8. As outside temperature drops toward freezing, it will force the contaminants being produced on the cooking surface outward rather than upward and therefore negate capture. Short circuit designs such as Figures 6–6, 6–7 and 6–8 are very limited by physical conditions. Often manufacturers depend on kitchen personnel to change damper settings for winter or summer use to compensate for changing air volume due to the change in the density of outside air. In reality, it is more likely that the cook will eventually close off the outside air because it interferes with his work or blows on him. Thus, the make-up air supply is eliminated, and the more expensive conditioned air from the building is used in its place.

Lazy-Air systems (Figure 6–9) are low velocity air curtains that create a high pressure area directly in front of the hood. The high pressure area, working in conjunction with the lower pressure developed under the hood from the exhaust, causes a positive air movement through the area between the bottom of the hood and the cooking surface. Using low velocity, the system can utilize make-up air temperatures of 45° to 50°F. In most localities this will reduce the energy consumption of the hood by 50% to 75% over the utilization of room air at 65°–75°F.

It is necessary to temper the air in cold climates (Figure 6–10). The air curtain make-up chamber supplies tempered (50°–55°F min.) or evaporatively

Table 6-2. Table of make-up air characteristics.

	Distribution to	For A/C Kitchen	Discharge Temperature Required	Relief From Radiant Heat	Max. % Of Make-Up Air Recommended	Expansion Volume And/Or Room Air Loss	Personnel Comfort	Comments
Figure 6-4 Front Grill STYLE "G"	Room	No	70°F	Poor	85%	15%	None	Evap. cooled kitchens only.
Figure 6-5 Down Discharge	Chef's Work Area	Yes	70°F	Fair	60%	40%	Poor	Discomfort caused by high velocity supply air.
Figure 6-6 High Velocity Short Circuit	Inside Hood	Yes	35°F	None	50%	50%	None	Requires excessive amount of room air.
Figure 6-7 Low Velocity Short Circuit STYLE WIM	Inside Hood	Yes	35°F	None	60%	40%	None	Requires excessive amount of room air.
Figure 6-8 Multi-point Short Circuit	Inside Hood	Yes	35°F	None	50%	50%	None	Requires greater overhangs and excess room air.
Figure 6-9 LAZY-AIR Curtain Style	Chef's Work Area	Yes	45°–50°	Good	85%	15%	Good-Excellent	Ideal for cold climates with high radiant heat. Ideal for A/C kitchens.
Figure 6-10 Low Velocity Curtain IMD	Chef's Work Area	Yes	50°–55°	Excellent	80%	20%	Excellent	Ideal for mild to hot humid climates or A/C kitchens.
Figure 6-11 Dual Temp DT IMD	½ Air To Inside Hood _+_	Yes	None	Excellent	40% +		Excellent	Ideal for mild to cold climates or A/C kitchens.
Short circuit and air curtain	½ Air To Chef's Area		50°–55°		40%	80%	20%	

cooled air at slightly higher velocities in a curtain in front of the cooking line-up. The chef is cooled by slow moving air.

The curtain effect aids in the capture of gases and particles by enveloping the lighter (less dense) heated air and vapors above the cooking surfaces. Since the make-up air volume is less than the exhaust volume, it will be totally removed in the exhaust process. It is ideal for use in air conditioned kitchens.

The dual tempered make-up air chamber provides two supplies of make-up air (Figure 6–11). The room side supply is tempered as described for Figure 6–10. However, the air supplied to the inside of the hood is untempered and reduces the total heat input while maintaining wintertime employee comfort. Both air supplies are evaporatively cooled during hot weather.

Since the tempered side is the room side of the air curtain delivery, the variable volume of exhaust gases is captured and controlled without seasonal adjustment of supply grills.

Forty percent outside air (ACFM) at 0°F mixed under the hood with 40% tempered air at 55°F, results in an air volume 9.75% greater in terms of standard air (SCFM) at 70°F due to expansion. Further expansion of the gases occurs from the heat of the cooking line-up to develop the full exhaust volume.

On the other hand, 80% 0°F outside make-up air warmed under the hood results in 16% greater volume due to expansion. Therefore, little room remains for the expansion of gas from the line-up on a typical short circuit design.

SECTION II: DESIGN ANALYSIS

DESIGN RULES FOR KITCHEN EXHAUST HOOD SYSTEMS

The overall design analysis in kitchen ventilation requires a review of the cooking equipment to be used, the architectural design, the make-up air design and the budget for the project.

In this evaluation, the following checklist is useful:

Hood Type

( ) 1. Filter-type Extraction: medium to light cooking equipment, grease-laden air is not significant.

( ) 2. Self-cleaning Extraction: medium to heavy duty equipment producing greater amounts of grease-laden vapors.

( ) 3. Canopy-type: for varied equipment heights.

( ) 4. Backshelf-type: for cooking-height equipment only.

( ) 5. Make-up Air Design integrated with exhaust hood.
- ( ) a. Tempered System
- ( ) b. Untempered System
- ( ) c. Dual Tempered/Untempered System

The volume of exhaust air needed to effectively ventilate cooking equipment is derived from local codes, the type of hood preferred, the manufacturer's design criteria and practical experience. With the use of U.L. listed or classified hoods there can be significant savings in fan sizing, ductwork design and operating costs. If U.L. products are used, the CFM (cubic feet per minute) air volumes given in Table 6–3 are usually recommended.

The ranges in the table are given for installations where multiple pieces of equipment may be used under the same hood, with varying degrees of grease-producing capabilities. Light duty equipment includes kettles, steamers, convection ovens and bake ovens. Medium duty equipment includes ranges, fryers, griddles, braising pans and salamander broilers. Heavy duty equipment includes charbroilers, infrared and upright broilers.

With slot-type units (Seco Wash or HV units), as opposed to the filter type, the volume of air can be reduced because of the exhaust velocity of these products. As is the case with backshelf versus canopy units, the proximity or slot velocity units will perform well at the lower volumes and higher velocities. This principle is key to the design of each unit and is the basis for well engineered kitchen ventilation systems.

It is possible to mix and match hood systems to meet cooking equipment requirements, as well as budget limits. In designing such systems, it is important to balance different hood systems to a common static pressure when multiple hoods are to be operated on one exhaust fan. Table 6-4 indicates the static pressure characteristics of the Seco Engineering Systems. This information can aid in the design of the total system.

Table 6-3. Table for exhaust CFM/FT.

	CFM/LINEAR FOOT		
	96 Filter	**Seco Wash**	**HV 96**
Light Duty	(C) 200 (B) N/A	(C) 250 (B) N/A	(C) 200 (B) N/A
Medium	(C) 300 (B) 250–300	(C) 250 (B) 250	(C) 200–250 (B) 200–250
Heavy	(C) 350	(C) 300–350	(C) 300–350
	C = Canopy	B = Backshelf	

SECTION III: SIZING AND APPLICATION DETAILS

Duct Sizing

Exhaust ducts are sized on a constant velocity method. A minimum of 1500 and a maximum of 2200 feet per minute are mandated by building codes. A fully welded 16-gauge black iron or 18-gauge stainless steel is required by NFPA. Most contracting organizations find square ducting better for meeting the code requirements of fully welded construction.

The routing of an exhaust duct is also controlled by code. Most building codes require that the duct leading to the exterior of the building travel the most direct route possible, and that properly designed clean-out ports be provided at specified distances and at each change of direction in the duct run. Exhaust ducts should be installed at least 18 inches away from combustible material. The clearance requirements may be reduced by shielding the combustible materials in various ways. The applicable building codes should be consulted for acceptable means of shielding.

A horizontal exhaust duct should be pitched either toward the hood or toward a clean-out sump located at the low point of the duct system. Usually the sump is located at the point where the horizontal duct turns to the vertical. Clean-out access panels should be located on the sides of the duct with the bottom edge of the opening not less than 1 inch from the bottom of the duct. Some codes have more specific requirements. The panels should be gasketed and fastened with bolts to create a liquid-tight condition not subject to deflection from pressures or temperatures. Some codes do allow joints in ductwork to be made with companion flanges and high temperature sealant. However, most of the country requires all joints to be fully welded.

Most national codes require that exhaust ducts penetrating the roof of a building extend to a point at least

Table 6-4. Characteristic exhaust volume/static pressure relationships at the exhaust collar.

	96 Hoods	Wash Hoods		HV 96	
CFM/FL		**Static**	**Slot**	**Static**	**Slot**
200	96 hoods are balanced	N/A	N/A	.55	3.5″
250	by S.P. of filters.	1.3	3″	.86	3.5″
300	Multiply the filter	1.7	3″	1.25	3.5″
350	pressure drop × 1.15	1.7	4″	1.7	3.5″
400	= Total S.P. of the	1.3	(2) 3″	N/A	N/A
500	hood.	1.3	(2) 3″	N/A	N/A

18 inches above the roof surface. When the horizontal duct runs emanate from the vertical after it passes through the roof, the bottom of the horizontal run also must be 18 inches above the roof surface. Keep in mind that the combustible clearance requirements apply above the roof as well as below the roof and also include the roof curb. For this reason, steel pre-fabricated and insulated roof curbs are recommended.

Exhaust Fans

The following criteria should be used for the selection of exhaust fans operating in conjunction with commercial kitchen hoods.

1. Wheel design should be the non-overloading type, i.e., backward inclined or backward curved design.
2. Adjustable belt-driven fans are recommended because they shield the motor from grease build-up and exhaust air heat. Direct drive fans are not recommended because they may require special high temperature motor insulation and, in some code areas, explosion-proof motors. Direct drive fans prohibit accurate system balancing since volume dampers are not permitted. (See section on dampers.)
3. Fan discharge should be away from building surfaces, normally vertical in direction.
4. Most codes require that the fan discharge be located a minimum of 40 inches above the roof surface. Simultaneous satisfaction of the 18-inch duct height is required as well. Some fans will require the duct to be greater than 18 inches above the roof in order to satisfy the 40-inch discharge height requirement. Other applications may require the discharge to be greater than 40 inches in order to maintain the 18-inch minimum duct height. Many fan manufacturers offer extended wind bands or housings as an option in order to fulfill the requirement.
5. Fans should be easy to clean because grease accumulates on internal surfaces. A drain, with a catch pan or similar device, should be employed.
6. The fan mounting should allow access to the adjacent ductwork. Access panels or hinged fan bases are recommended.

Dampers

1. Exhaust: Generally, building codes state that no damper may be used in a kitchen exhaust duct unless the damper is an integral part of a listed hood (i.e., listed grease extractor or hood and damper assembly). The requirement prohibits the use of back draft dampers. Codes also prohibit the use of volume dampers, smoke and/or fire dampers. Since balancing dampers are not permitted, exact sizing should be used in the design of the ductwork and pressure drop calculating. Only U.L. dampers that are part of the listed hood assembly are permitted.
2. Make-up Air Dampers: Dampers in make-up air ducts for back draft, volume control, smoke and/or fire control are governed by applicable sections of codes referring to supply air ducts. NFPA Bulletin 96 has a mandatory requirement for a fusible link controlled fire damper to be located as part of hoods that introduce any portion of the make-up air into the hood cavity, i.e., short circuit. The use of back draft dampers in cold climates is highly recommended to prevent cold air from entering the building in off hours.

Make-up Air Units

Make-up air units are selected as a percentage of the exhaust air volume—typically, 80–85 percent make-up air, depending upon the method of distribution.

The delivered air temperature is dependent upon the method of introduction. In curtain distribution systems a temperature averaging 50–55°F should be maintained. When make-up air is introduced from the chamber at a low velocity, the unit may operate at 45°F or lower. Where grills distribute the air through the room, the air temperature should be set at 55–65°F. In short circuit applications, a minimum air temperature of 35°F should be maintained. Condensation, spill out and other air density related problems will occur below this point.

Generally, code requirements stipulate that a 10-foot clearance exist between the make-up air intake and the exhaust outlet. It is best to check local code requirements.

In most instances, the solar heat gain on the rooftop machinery is greater than the heat loss. Therefore, insulation is beneficial for exposed duct runs over the roof, for both summer and winter operation.

Make-up Air Considerations

1. Room should always be negative pressure in relation to adjacent public areas.

(*continued* on p. 157)

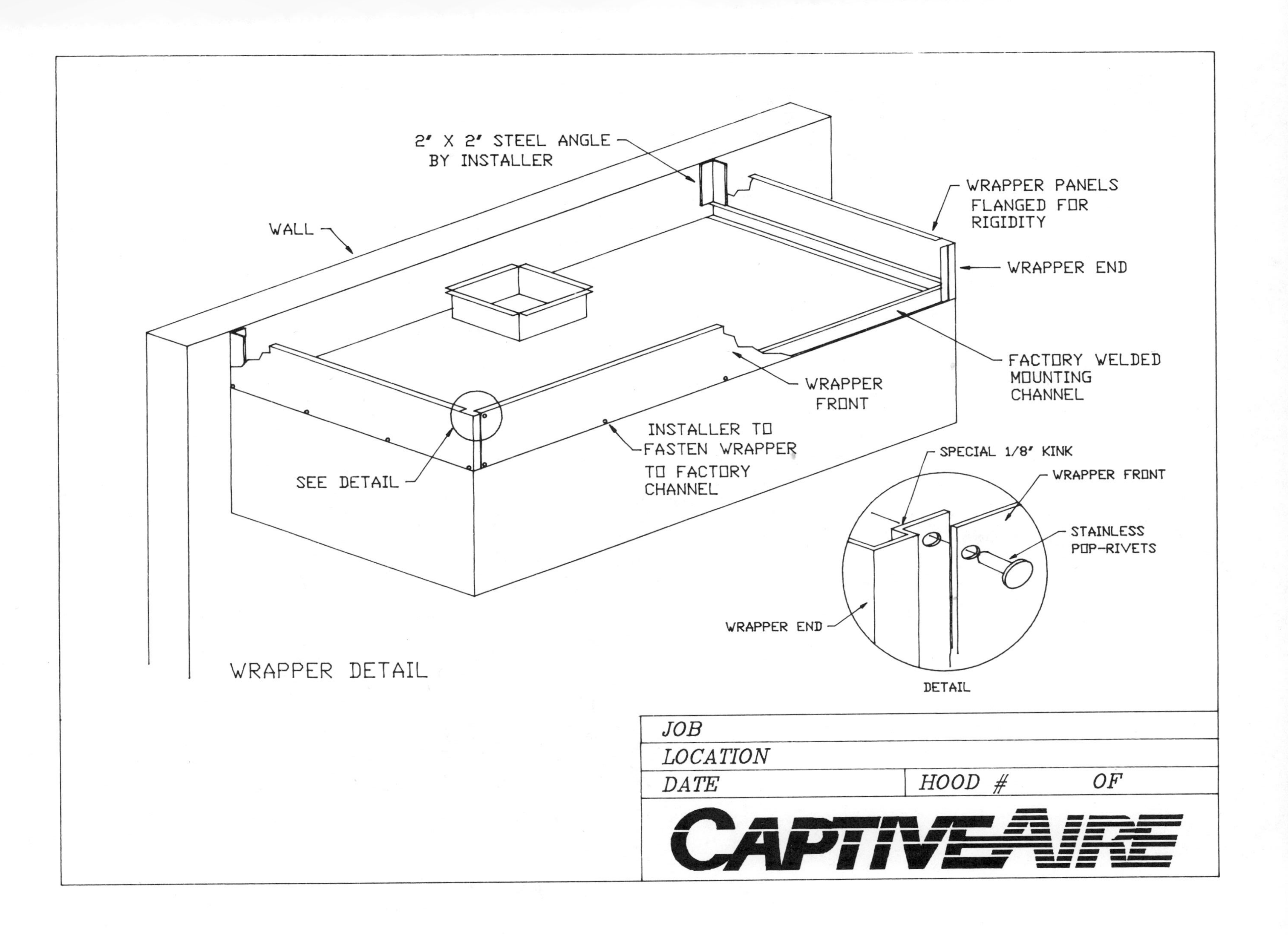
2" X 2" STEEL ANGLE BY INSTALLER
WALL
WRAPPER PANELS FLANGED FOR RIGIDITY
WRAPPER END
FACTORY WELDED MOUNTING CHANNEL
WRAPPER FRONT
INSTALLER TO FASTEN WRAPPER TO FACTORY CHANNEL
SEE DETAIL
SPECIAL 1/8" KINK
WRAPPER FRONT
STAINLESS POP-RIVETS
WRAPPER END
DETAIL
WRAPPER DETAIL
JOB
LOCATION
DATE
HOOD #
OF
CAPTIVEAIRE

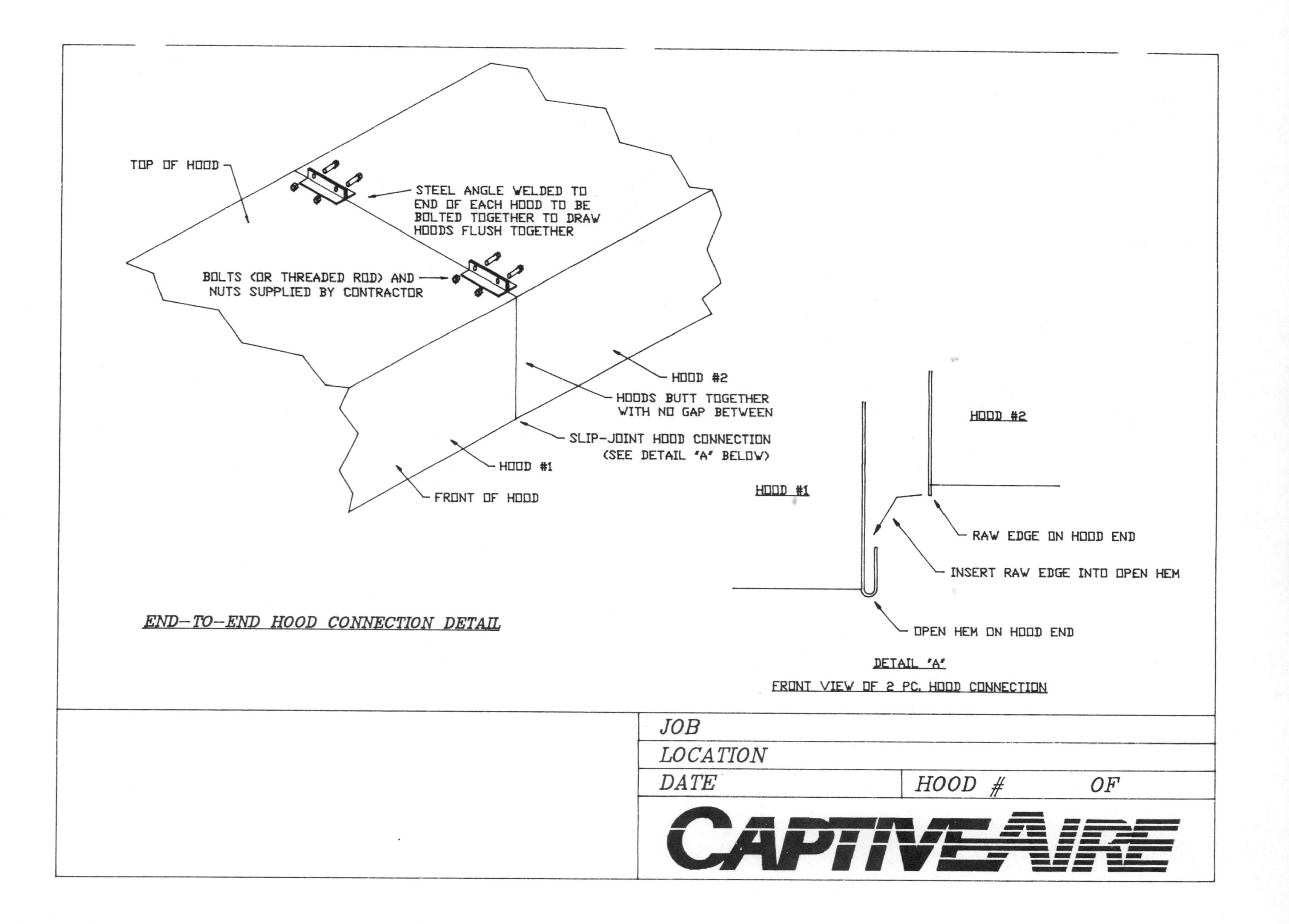
TOP OF HOOD
STEEL ANGLE WELDED TO END OF EACH HOOD TO BE BOLTED TOGETHER TO DRAW HOODS FLUSH TOGETHER
BOLTS (OR THREADED ROD) AND NUTS SUPPLIED BY CONTRACTOR
HOOD #2
HOODS BUTT TOGETHER WITH NO GAP BETWEEN
SLIP-JOINT HOOD CONNECTION (SEE DETAIL "A" BELOW)
HOOD #1
FRONT OF HOOD
END-TO-END HOOD CONNECTION DETAIL
HOOD #2
HOOD #1
RAW EDGE ON HOOD END
INSERT RAW EDGE INTO OPEN HEM
OPEN HEM ON HOOD END
DETAIL "A"
FRONT VIEW OF 2 PC. HOOD CONNECTION
JOB
LOCATION
DATE
HOOD #
OF
CAPTIVEAIRE

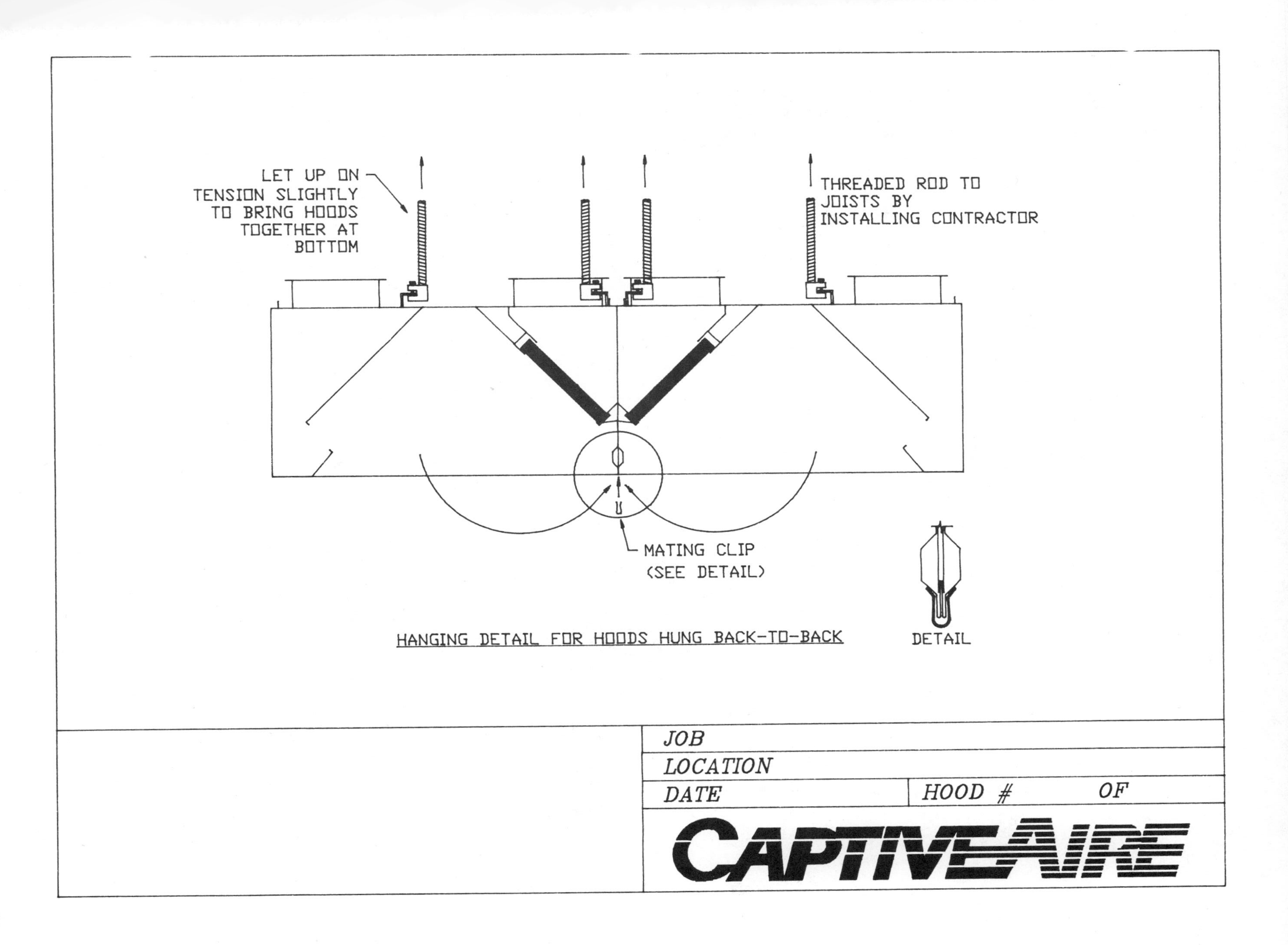
LET UP ON
TENSION SLIGHTLY
TO BRING HOODS
TOGETHER AT
BOTTOM
THREADED ROD TO
JOISTS BY
INSTALLING CONTRACTOR
MATING CLIP
(SEE DETAIL)
DETAIL
HANGING DETAIL FOR HOODS HUNG BACK-TO-BACK
JOB
LOCATION
DATE
HOOD #
OF
CAPTIVEAIRE

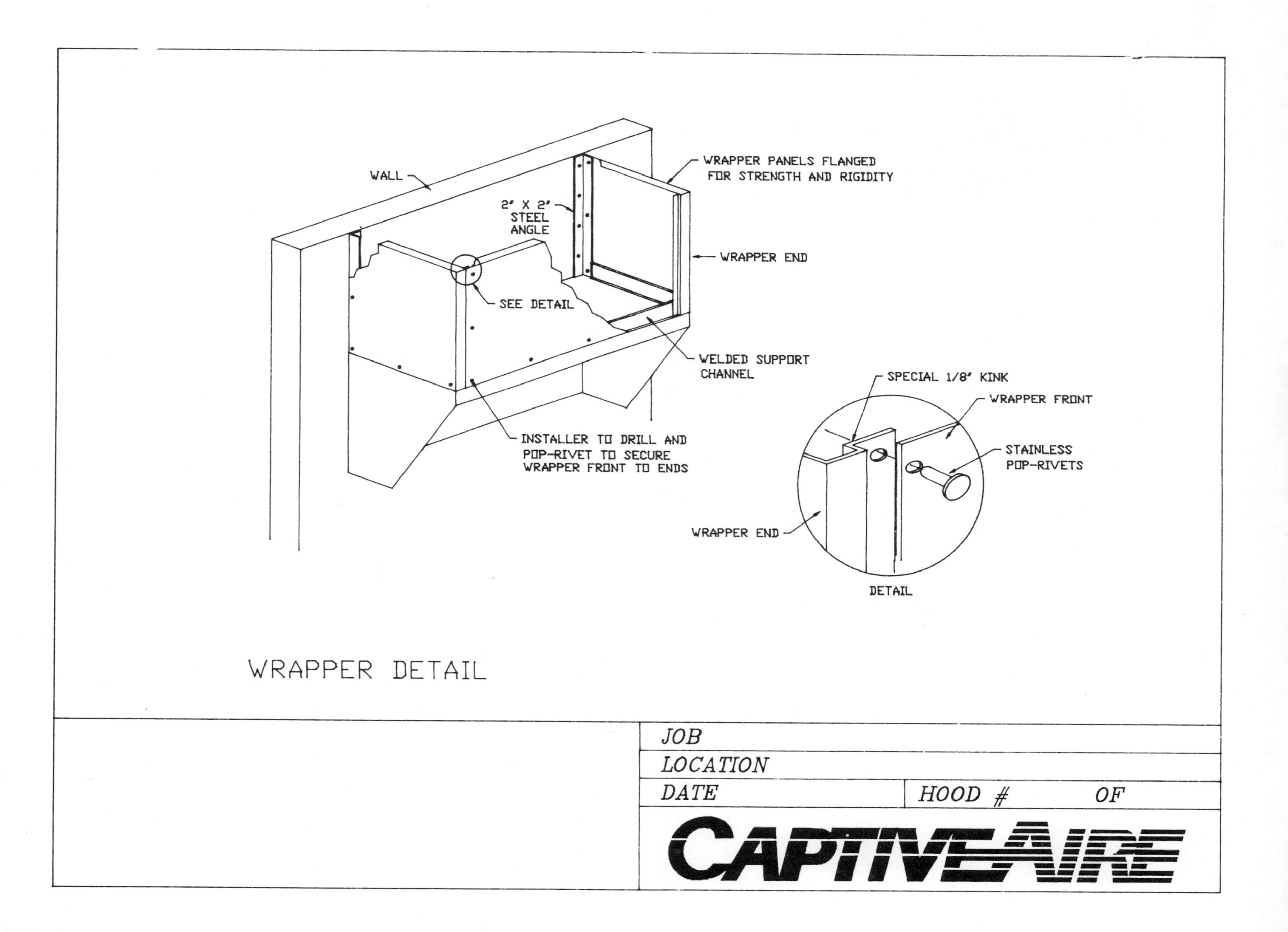
WALL
2" X 2"
STEEL
ANGLE
WRAPPER PANELS FLANGED
FOR STRENGTH AND RIGIDITY
WRAPPER END
SEE DETAIL
WELDED SUPPORT
CHANNEL
INSTALLER TO DRILL AND
POP-RIVET TO SECURE
WRAPPER FRONT TO ENDS
SPECIAL 1/8" KINK
WRAPPER FRONT
STAINLESS
POP-RIVETS
WRAPPER END
DETAIL
WRAPPER DETAIL
JOB
LOCATION
DATE
HOOD #
OF
CAPTIVEAIRE

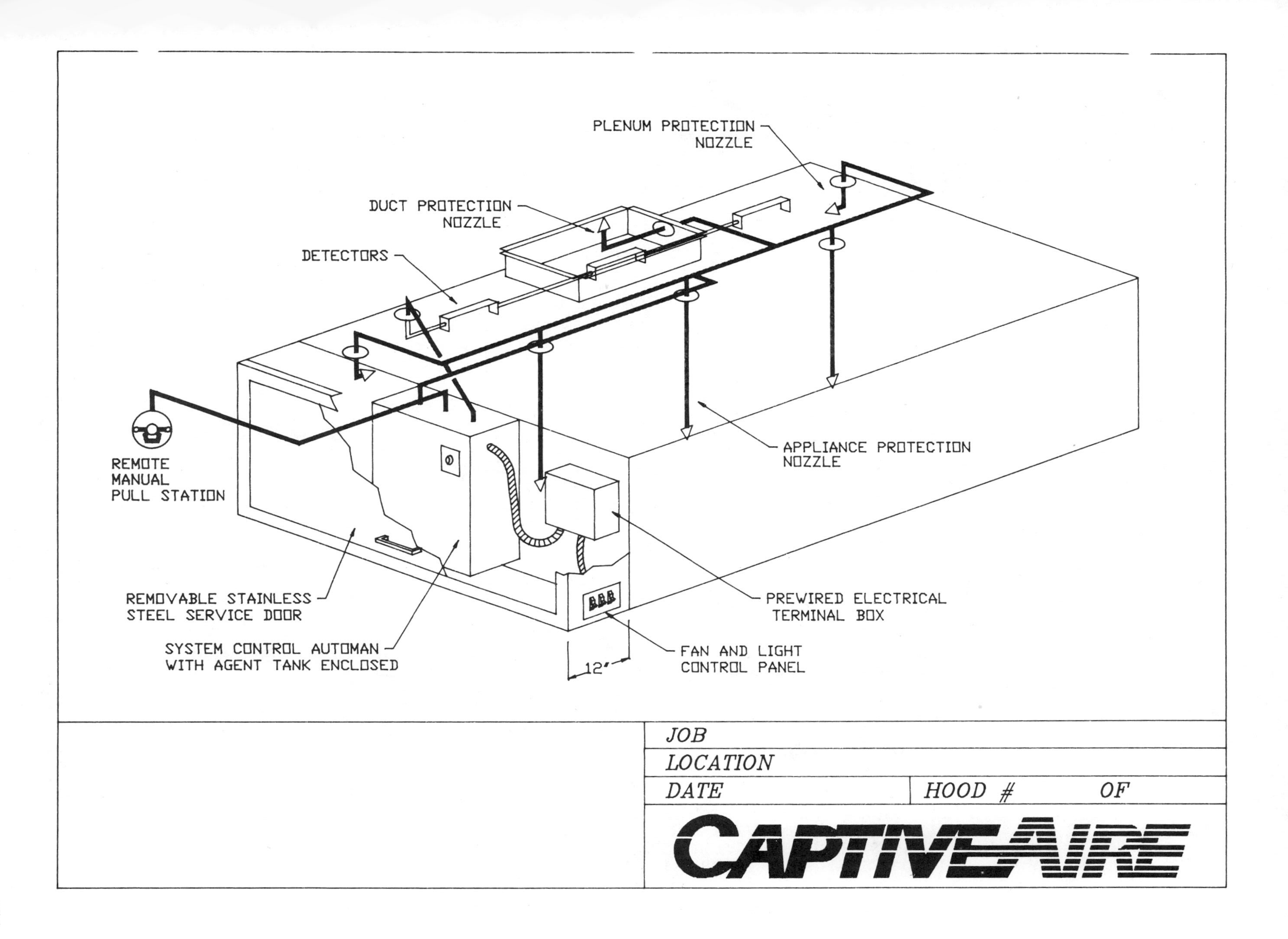
PLENUM PROTECTION NOZZLE
DUCT PROTECTION NOZZLE
DETECTORS
REMOTE MANUAL PULL STATION
APPLIANCE PROTECTION NOZZLE
REMOVABLE STAINLESS STEEL SERVICE DOOR
PREWIRED ELECTRICAL TERMINAL BOX
SYSTEM CONTROL AUTOMAN WITH AGENT TANK ENCLOSED
12"
FAN AND LIGHT CONTROL PANEL
JOB
LOCATION
DATE
HOOD #
OF
CAPTIVEAIRE

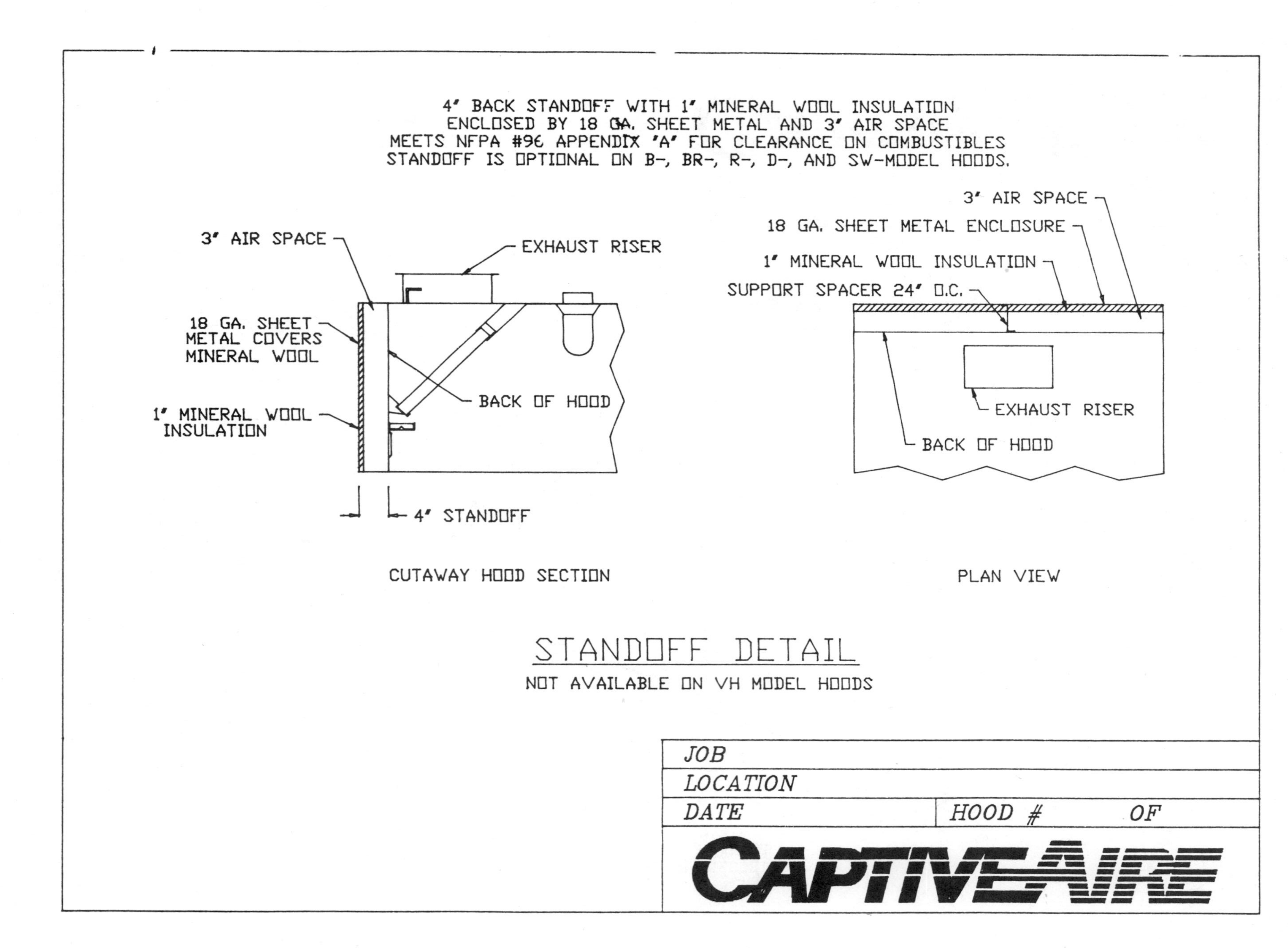

4" BACK STANDOFF WITH 1" MINERAL WOOL INSULATION
ENCLOSED BY 18 GA. SHEET METAL AND 3" AIR SPACE
MEETS NFPA #96 APPENDIX "A" FOR CLEARANCE ON COMBUSTIBLES
STANDOFF IS OPTIONAL ON B-, BR-, R-, D-, AND SW-MODEL HOODS.
3" AIR SPACE
EXHAUST RISER
18 GA. SHEET METAL COVERS MINERAL WOOL
1" MINERAL WOOL INSULATION
BACK OF HOOD
4" STANDOFF
CUTAWAY HOOD SECTION
3" AIR SPACE
18 GA. SHEET METAL ENCLOSURE
1" MINERAL WOOL INSULATION
SUPPORT SPACER 24" O.C.
EXHAUST RISER
BACK OF HOOD
PLAN VIEW
STANDOFF DETAIL
NOT AVAILABLE ON VH MODEL HOODS
JOB
LOCATION
DATE
HOOD #
OF
CAPTIVEAIRE

2. Is hood area air conditioned?
   A. Yes—Use short circuit, Internal Make-up Design or Lazy-Air which comes through the perforated front panel of the hood.
   B. No—Use grills out facing (G) or air through ceiling grills.
3. Room air changes:
   A. A/C Room—5–10 min. air change (6–12 changes/hr.).
   B. Non A/C Room—2–3 min. air change (20–30 changes/hr.).
4. Use IMD or Lazy-Air over high radiant equipment.
5. Use Lazy-Air in areas where heating cost is prime factor. Use IMD in areas where A/C is prime cost factor.
6. Short circuit make-up air should not be more than 50% of exhaust volume.
7. Use IMD chamber—good for up to 80% make-up air to the exhaust quantity. Use Lazy-Air chamber—good for up to 90% make-up air.

Labeling Authorities

Underwriters Laboratories: There are two different U.L. labels and four distinct types of products where the U.L. label might appear on hoods.

Kitchen hoods are labeled either as U.L. listed or U.L. classified. U.L. listed hoods are listed either as grease extractors or hood and damper assemblies. To bear the U.L. listed label, the product must have been tested under actual operating conditions prescribed by the U.L. The procedure tests performance under normal and abnormal conditions. Heavy emphasis is placed upon the product's ability to retain its integrity under fire conditions and to prevent the spread of the fire past the boundaries of the hood. Other tests are run with regard to electrical integrity, employee safety and capture characteristics.

The U.L. classified label might be applied to a hood or a filter as a component of the hood. U.L. classified hoods are reviewed by Underwriters Laboratories to determine if their construction is in compliance with NFPA Bulletin 96. The rigorous performance testing prescribed for U.L. listed products is not required for the classified label. Also, code requirement exemptions granted to listed products do not apply to classified hoods. Hoods used in commercial kitchens today must utilize classified filters.

A U.L. classified filter is tested by Underwriters Laboratories as to fire resistance only. The testing procedure looks for "flammability after exposure to grease laden air" and for maximum flame penetration of the filter under a prescribed condition. Note that nothing in the test procedure relates to the efficiency of grease removal.

Other agencies have various listings or approvals. Most prevalent are the code agencies such as Building Officials and Code Administrators, Int. Inc., International Conference of Building Officials and Southern Building Congress. None of these organizations "approve" hoods. They investigate their compliance. Claims of a product's being BOCA or Southern Building Congress "approved" are misrepresentations. NFPA does not approve or list any product. The only statement regarding NFPA 96 that can be applied to a hood is that it is built in compliance with the suggested norms.

National Codes

The following codes apply to commercial kitchen hood equipment in various localities: NFPA, Bulletin 96; Uniform Mechanical Code Section 312; Southern Building Congress Code; and miscellaneous state and local codes. Special attention should be given to the codes of the following areas: Michigan, Maryland, Chicago, Denver, New York City and Los Angeles. All of these have state and/or city codes that differ greatly from the national codes.

In most localities, the installation and design of commercial kitchen hoods are governed under the mechanical code. However, many areas allow the products to be covered under the Department of Public Health. Sometimes hoods are covered under the jurisdiction of both the mechanical and health inspectors and must meet both sets of codes simultaneously. Areas where extreme caution should be exercised with regard to conflicting health and mechanical codes are Denver, Miami, New York and Chicago.

Lighting

The requirement for certain levels of lighting at the work surface is defined by the local health codes. In almost all instances, some form of lighting device will be required in any canopy-type hoods. The application of these lights is specifically covered under NFPA Bulletin #70, the National Electrical Code. NFPA Bulletin #96 references NFPA #70 as the governing code.

Under a recent change incorporated in the National Electrical Code, all lighting fixtures used in a commercial cooking hood must be listed for the application. To date, the only listing organization that has developed such a standard is Underwriters Laboratories. U.L. has designated that all such fixtures must be installed a minimum of 48 inches above the cooking surface. This provision effectively prohibits the use of lights in shelf-type hoods.

Three types of lights bear the necessary listing for this application. They are: surface-mounted incandescent, recessed-mounted incandescent and recessed-mounted fluorescent fixtures. All lights must be installed in accordance with the terms of their listing.

Provisions of NFPA #70 regulate the installation and wiring for lights. Basically, the National Electric Code considers the inside portion of a hood to be the same as the inside of a contaminated air duct. Thus, the code prohibits the mounting of wiring or conduits inside the hood. The code also requires that certain high-temperature insulation types be used. The only hood shell penetration allowed for lighting is for the mounting of fixtures.

Both OSHA and NSF (National Sanitation Foundation) have requirements regarding the protection of glass globes. Both codes require that kitchens be protected from breaking glass by either a metal guard or by a non-shattering-type globe. Shatter-proof glass and plastic-coated globes are commonly used in kitchens. Also, the glass must be a type that is resistant to high temperatures.

Fire Protection Systems

National codes require that automatic, fixed-type fire protection systems be used for the protection of ducts, plenums and cooking surfaces whenever the cooking process involves the release of grease. U.L. listed grease extractors do not require additional interior protection. The wash system is generally accepted as adequate protection. The types of systems and the general code that covers the application are as follows:

Dry chemical system—NFPA #17
Water foam systems—NFPA #17
Water sprinkler systems—NFPA #13
CO_2 systems—NFPA #12

NFPA #10 also includes requirements for portable, hand-type extinguishers, in addition to fixed systems.

All national codes require the activation of the automatic fire protection system to disconnect the supply of fuel from the cooking line protected by the system. Fire/fuel shut-off is accomplished by the use of shunt trip breakers, contactors and solenoid-activated or mechanically-activated gas valves through a spring and cable linkage. The application of these systems is itself a specialty, and most codes require that the system be designed and installed by certified personnel. Consultation with either the factory or local fire protection equipment dealers is recommended.

Some types of systems and local codes require that exhaust and/or make-up air systems be interlocked with the automatic fire system. Generally, dry chemical, wet foam and water-type systems recommend that the exhaust fan remain operational during system activation. It is desirable, and in some localities mandatory, that activation of the fire protection system shut off the make-up air supply. This shut-off lowers the pressure near the hood and prevents the migration of smoke to other areas.

New York City requires that the exhaust fan be shut off when the fire system is activated.

Controls and Interlock

Simple push-button controls to start exhaust and make-up air systems should be provided for ease of operation by unskilled kitchen personnel. Under normal operation, the exhaust fan should start and operate through an interlock with the make-up air system. Since the make-up air system may require provisions for heat, cooling or vent air, these functions should be provided through a remote control panel. A wash hood must have an additional provision incorporated to complete the mandatory wash cycle at the end of each operation. This is usually accomplished through a control cabinet supplied by the hood manufacturer.

VENTILATION CHECKLIST

Ventilation concerns include:

- Approved construction of hoods
- Adequate lights
- Adequate fireproofing
- Inspection agreement
- Fire control inspection
- Ease of cleaning filters
- Proper fan selection

- Instruction of employees on their responsibilities
- Details of specialized hoods, such as those for broilers and ovens
- Statement on all contracts and drawings that all work shall pass all existing federal, state, and local codes

In addition to the hood details shown in Figures 6–1 through 6–11, general and particular information about hoods, ventilation, hood installation, and fire system details may be found in Figures 6–12 through 6–23.

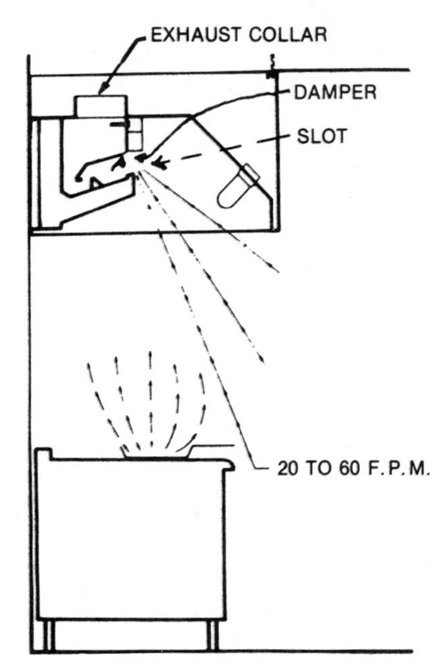

Figure 6-2. Wash hood design. (Courtesy Seco Engineering)

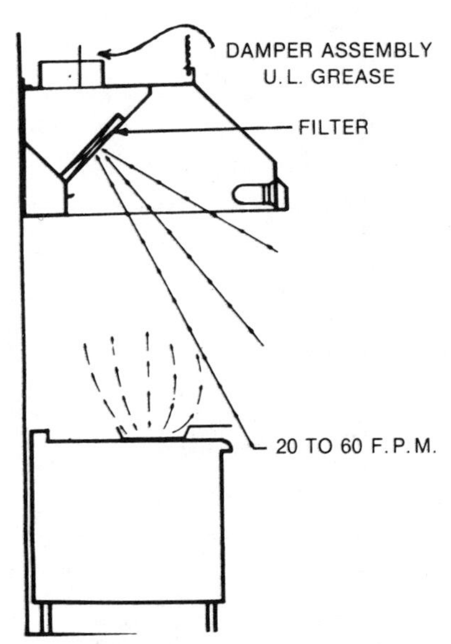

Figure 6-1. Bulletin 96 design or U.L. hood and damper assemblies. (Courtesy Seco Engineering)

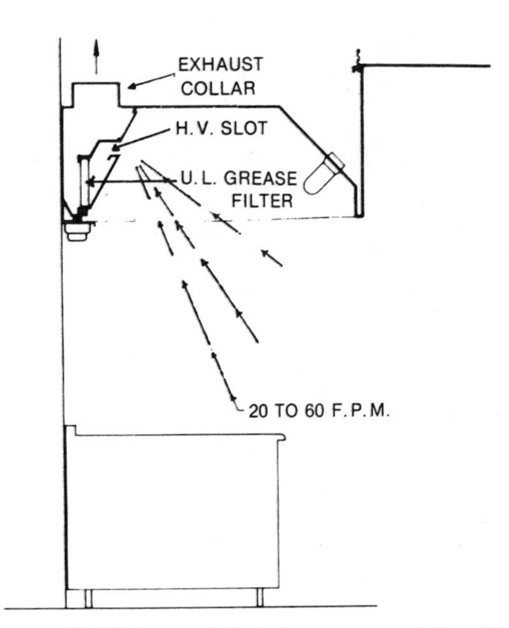

Figure 6-3. U.L. hood and damper assemblies: high velocity 96 design. (Courtesy Seco Engineering)

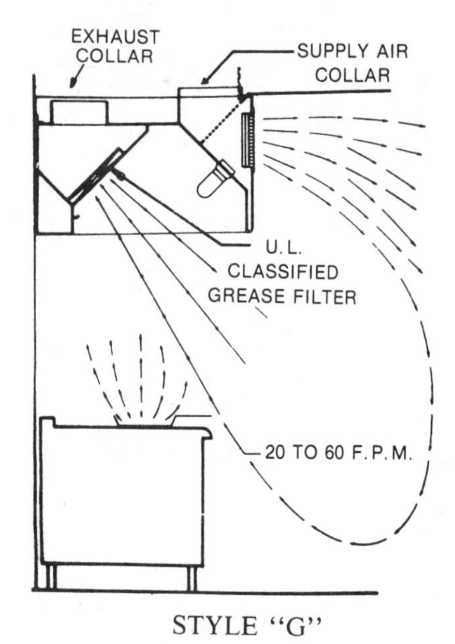

Figure 6-4. Front grill. (Courtesy Seco Engineering)

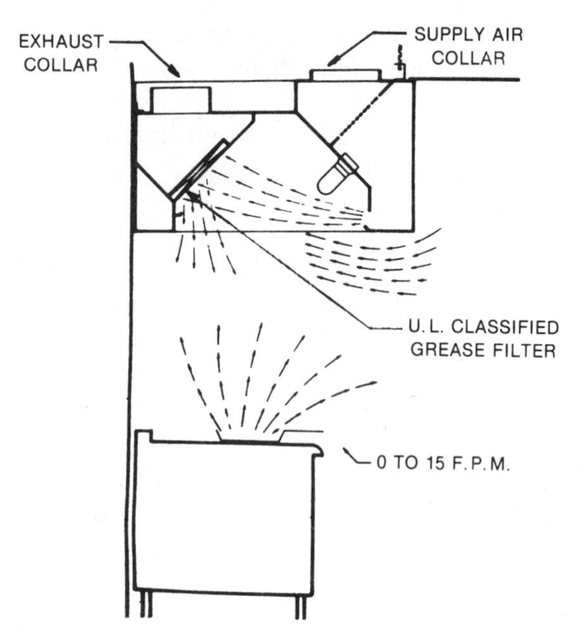

Figure 6-6. High velocity short-circuit make-up air. (Courtesy Seco Engineering)

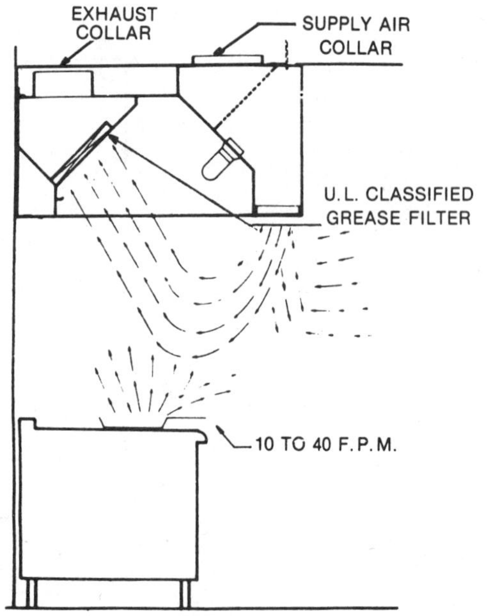

Figure 6-5. Down discharge. (Courtesy Seco Engineering)

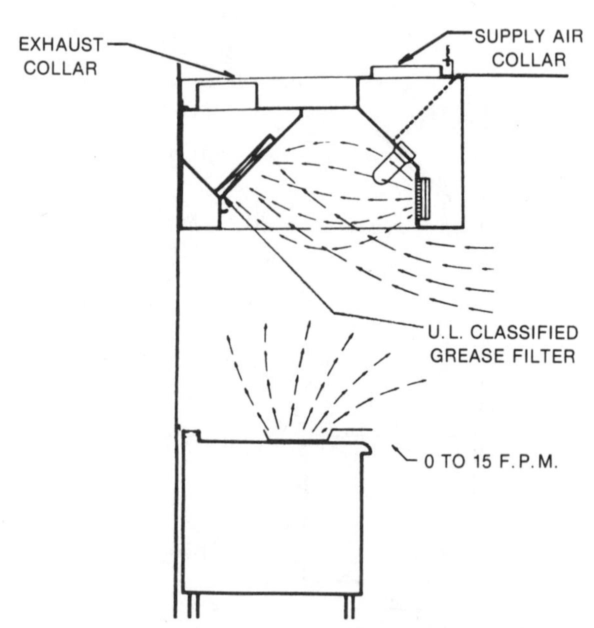

Figure 6-7. Low velocity short-circuit design. (Courtesy Seco Engineering)

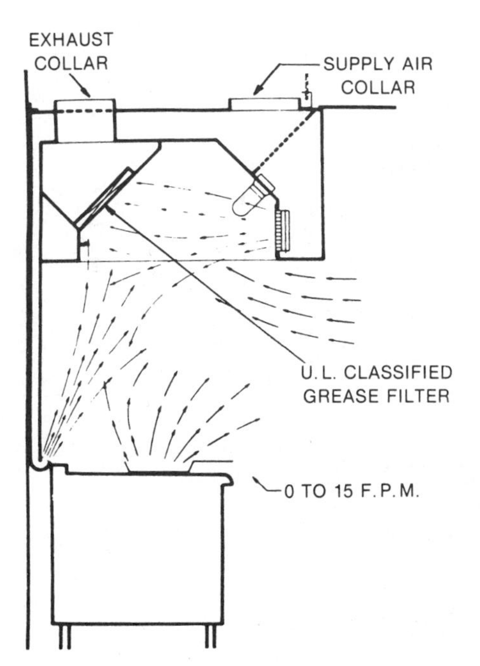

Figure 6-8. Multi-point short-circuit make-up air. (Courtesy Seco Engineering)

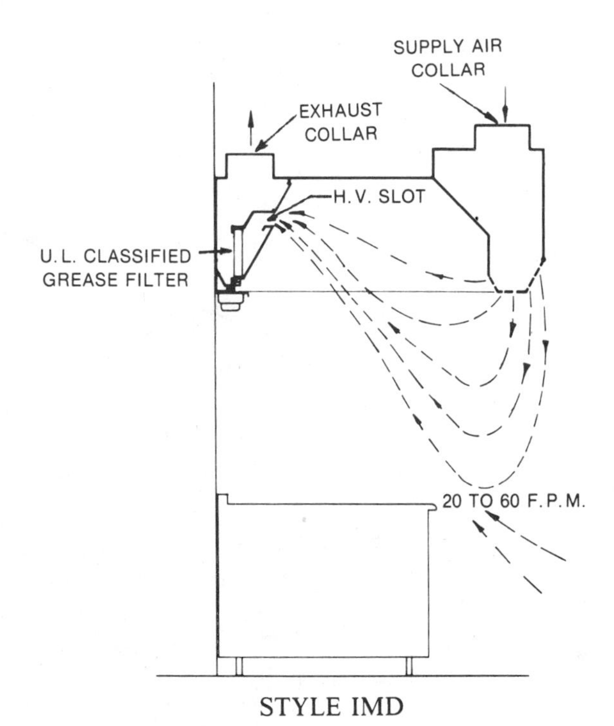

STYLE IMD

Figure 6-10. Low velocity curtain make-up. (Courtesy Seco Engineering)

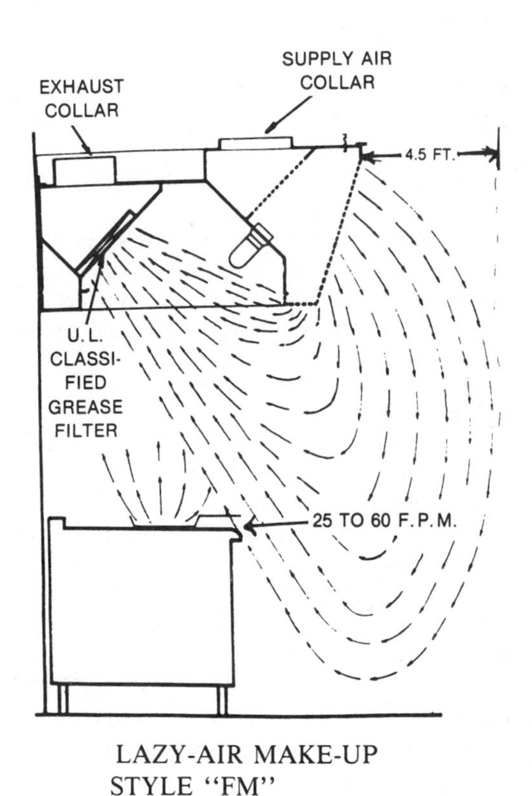

LAZY-AIR MAKE-UP
STYLE "FM"

Figure 6-9. Air curtain/low velocity. (Courtesy Seco Engineering)

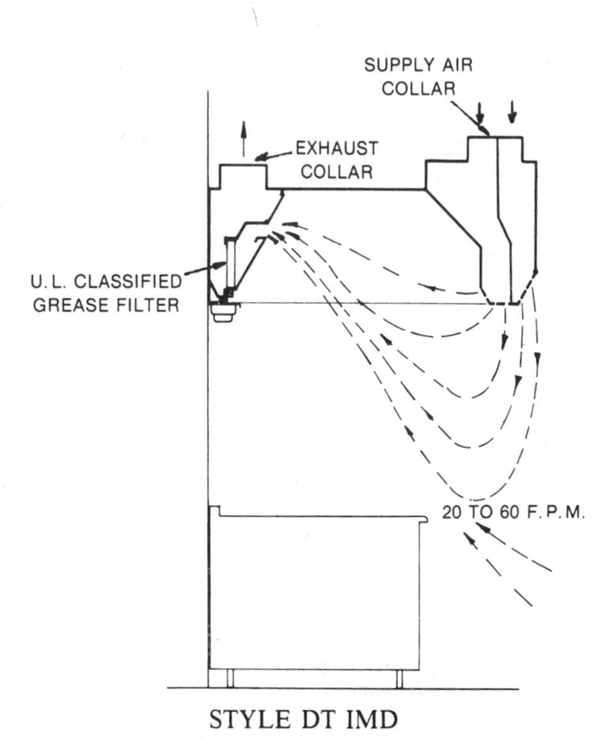

STYLE DT IMD

Figure 6-11. Air curtain using two supplies of make-up air—raw outside air and tempered air. (Courtesy Seco Engineering)

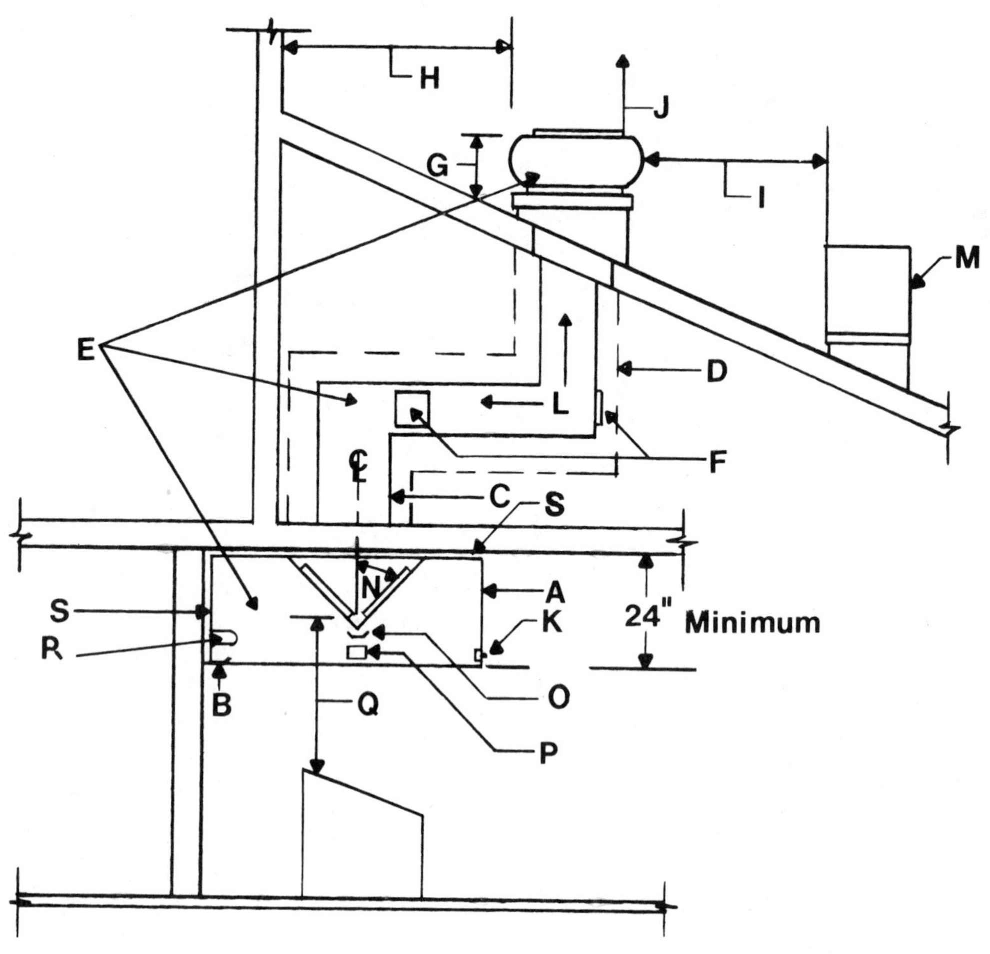

A. Hood body of 18 gauge galv. steel or 20 gauge StSt, all seams and joints liquid tight continuous weld.
B. If grease gutter is necessary, 1-1/2″ width maximum and 1/4″ depth pitched to enclosed metal container with maximum of 1 gallon capacity.
C. Ducts constructed and supported by 16 gauge galv. steel or 18 gauge StSt, all welded construction, liquid tight.
D. Vertical ducts within a building to be located in a continuous enclosure from the ceiling above hood through roof. Enclosure to have 1 hour fire rating for 3 stories or 2 hours for more. Duct to have 6″ clearance (minimum) within enclosure.
E. Each exhaust system to consist of one hood, one duct and one fan. Two hoods cannot be interconnected.
F. Grease tight access panel of duct gauge provided at each change of direction with 1-1/2″ turn-up from bottom vertical to opening.
G. 40″ clearance from exhaust air outlet to roof surface.
H. 10′ 0″ clearance from buildings or grade levels.
I. 10′ 10″ clearance from property lines and air intakes.
J. Vertical flow of exhaust air (up-blast).
K. Indicator light for fan.
L. Duct air velocity a minimum of 1500 feet per minute.
M. Make-up air equal to that exhausted.
N. Filters not to be sloped more than 45° from the vertical.
O. Grease tray to have maximum width of 1-1/2″ and a maximum depth of 1/4″. Pitch to grease container.
P. Grease container to be metal, with lid, and not to exceed one gallon capacity.
Q. 48″ clearance from charcoal broiler and 18″ clearance from fryer.
R. Lighting units mounted on outer surface of hood body with only tight fitting glass enclosure inside the hood proper. Outside covered in steel.
S. Hoods to have 18″ clearance to combustable material, or 1″ of mineral wool bats reinforced with wire mesh and covered with 22 gallon sheet metal, holding hood body 3″ from combustible.

Figures 6-12. Typical hood detail. Typical hood details for a hood system show the various components required to conform to fire regulations. (Commonly called code 96 as adopted by the National Fire Protection Association, the code is subject to periodic change; check your current code.)

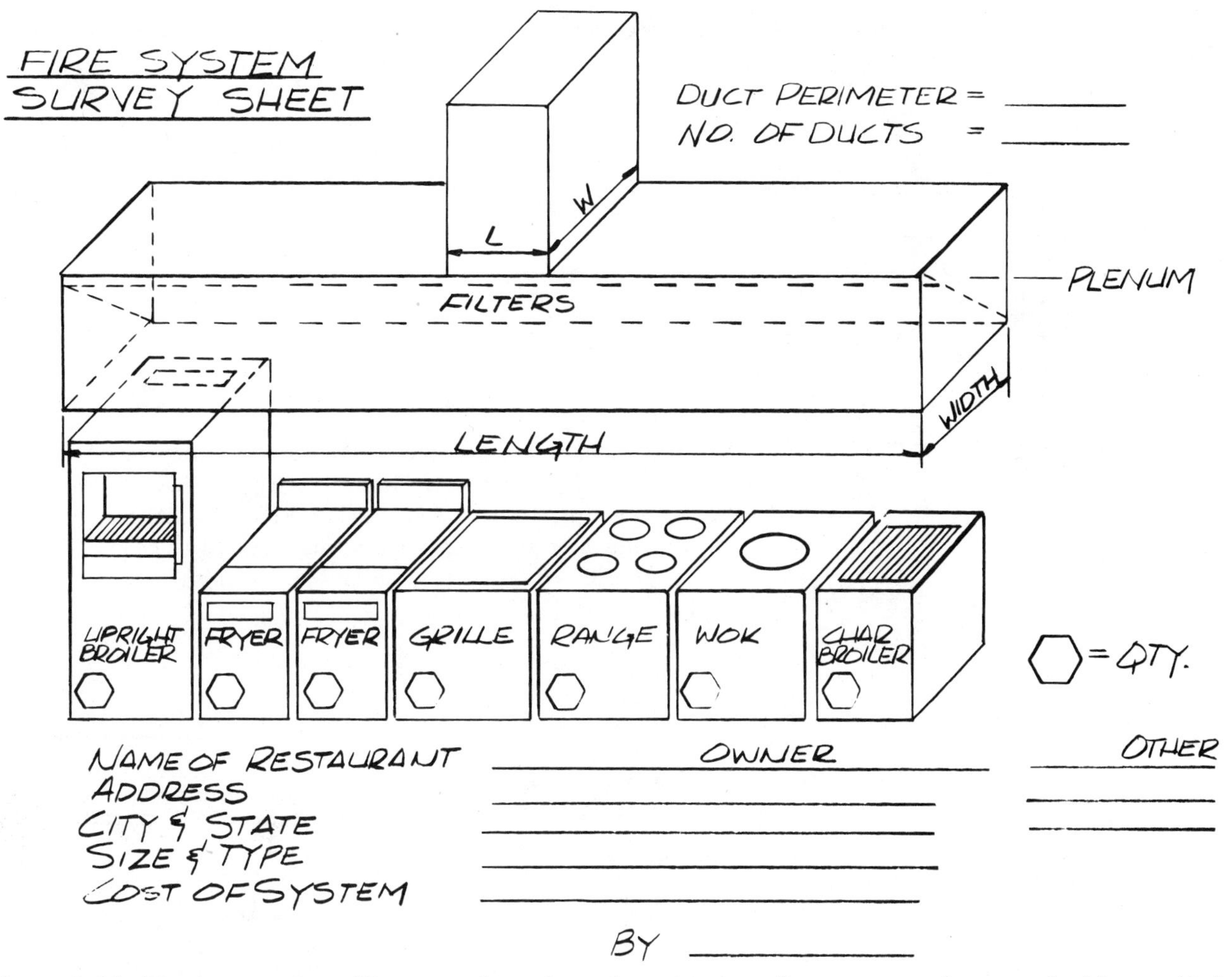

Figure 6-13. Hood survey sheet. The survey form shown for estimating a fire system may be customized for any kitchen to conform to actual conditions. (Courtesy Sturdi-Bilt Manufacturing)

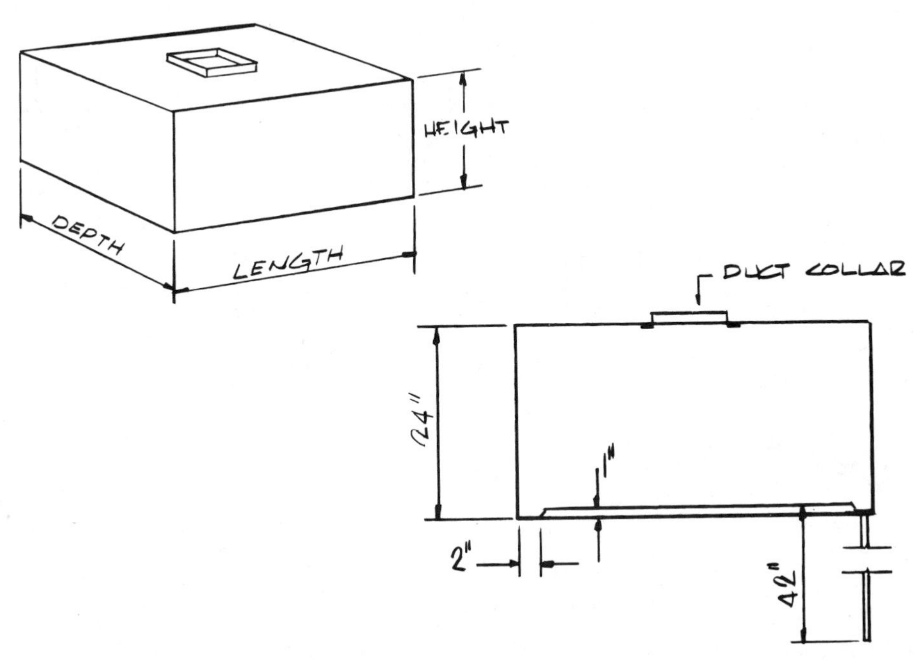

Figure 6-14. Small hood used over small dishwashing machines which should be ducted separately from cooking equipment. (Courtesy Sturdi-Bilt Manufacturing)

Figure 6-15. Pizza oven hood. A special canopy for ovens. Note that area under the filters is available for storage of hot pizzas. This is an excellent ventilator idea that captures heat and odors. Notice that optional makeup air is available. (Courtesy Sturdi-Bilt Manufacturing)

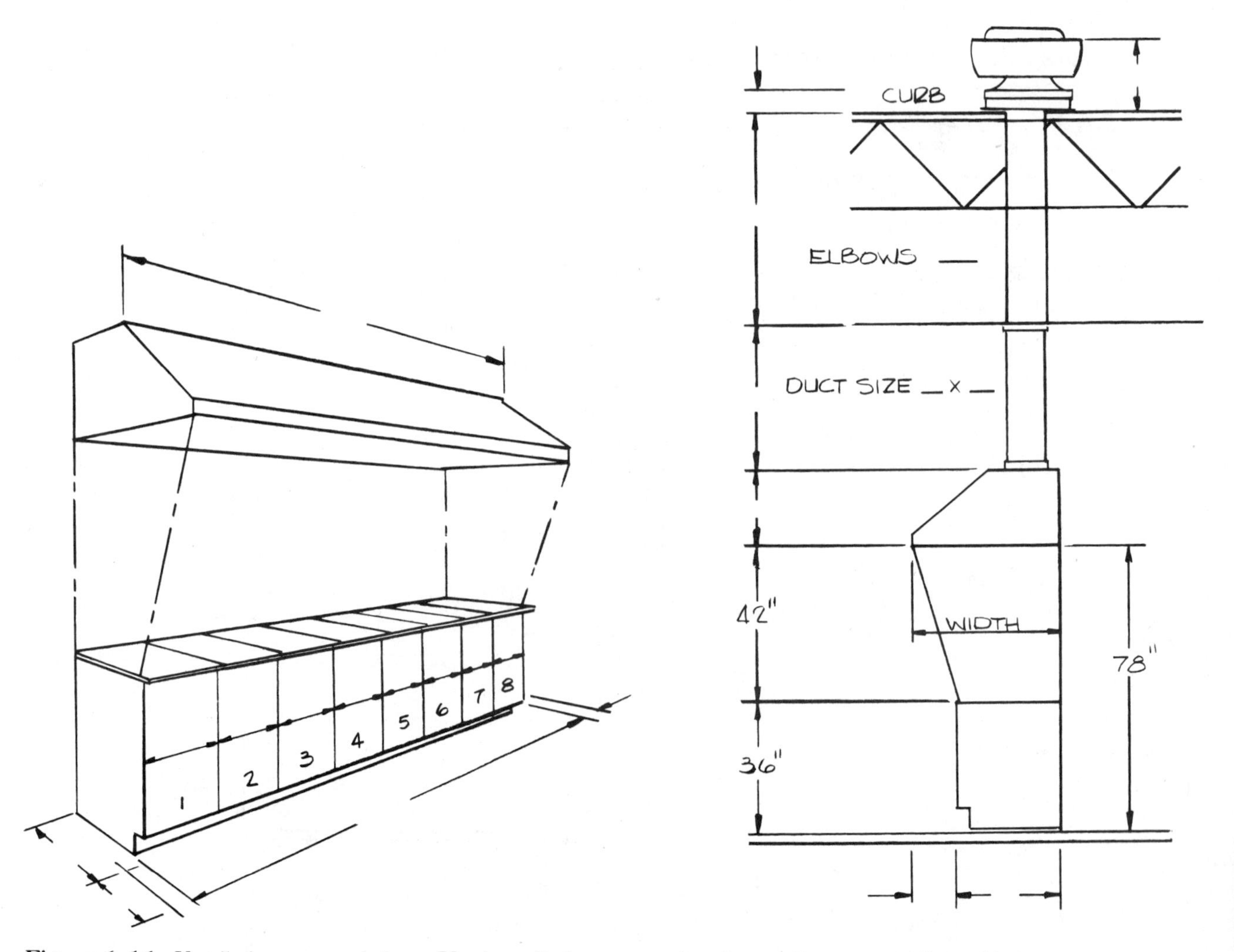

Figure 6-16. Ventilation approval sheet. Used to eliminate any misunderstanding among client, fabricator, installer, and code officials, this form should assist all parties in mutually agreeing on intent of ventilator specifications. (Courtesy Sturdi-Bilt Manufacturing)

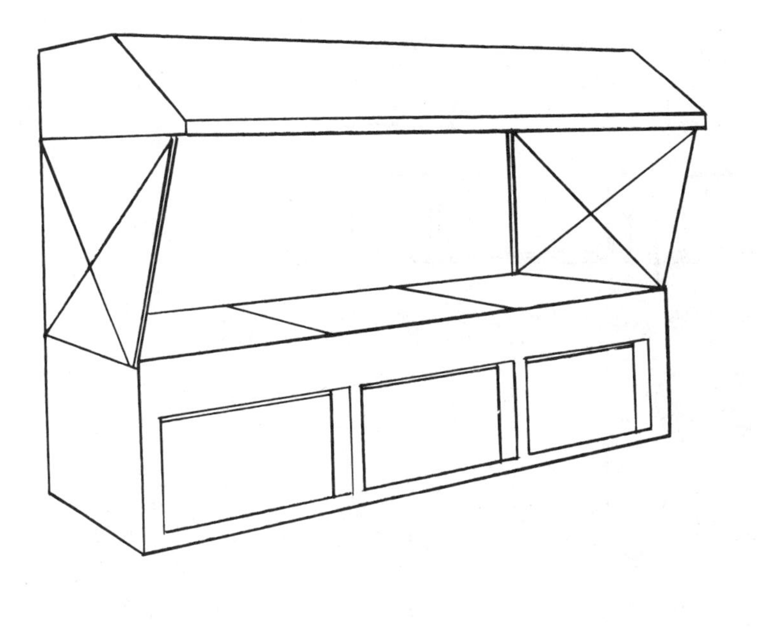

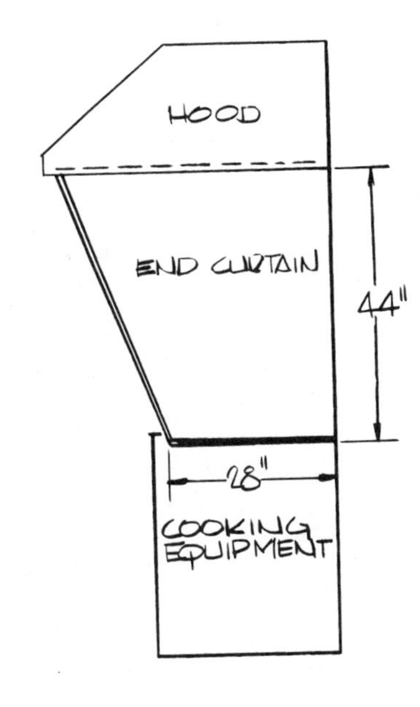

Figure 6-17. Canopy or hood end curtains. Many states recommend this energy-saving feature option. (Courtesy Sturdi-Bilt Manufacturing)

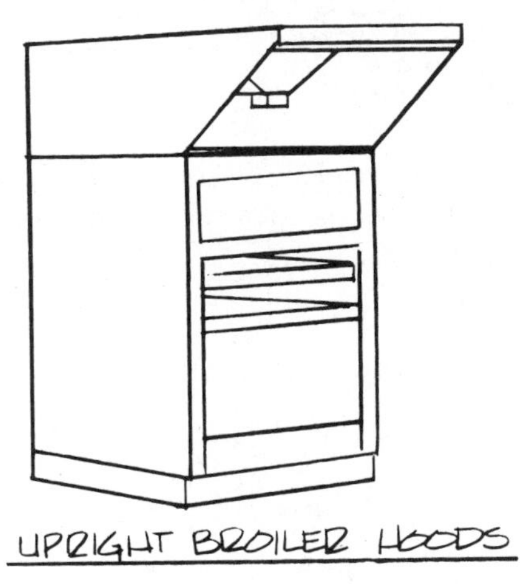

Figure 6-18. Broiler hood. In special conditions, such as an addition to the cooking lineup, this specialized hood may be the answer to a ventilation problem. Often business or menu considerations dictate an equipment change not accommodated by existing ventilators. (Courtesy Sturdi-Bilt Manufacturing)

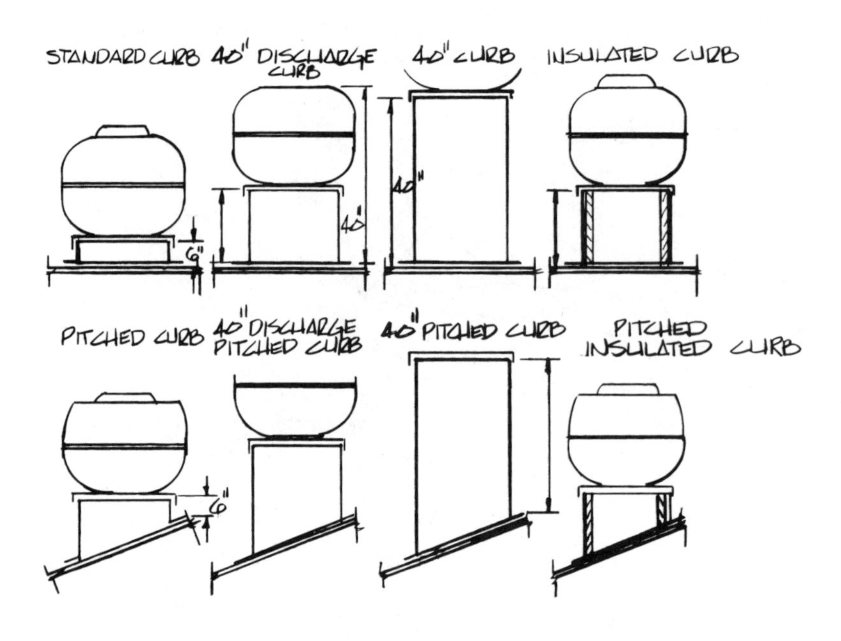

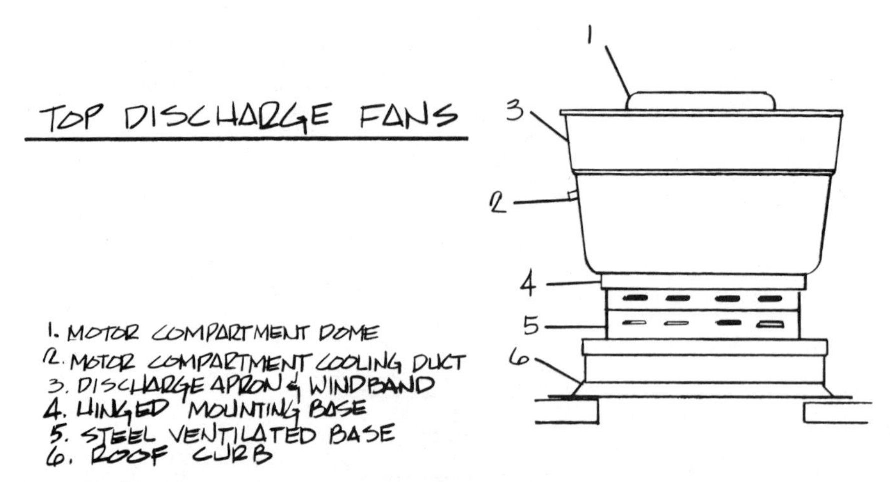

Figure 6-19. Curb details. Top discharge fans and curbing details vary widely. This guide can serve as a helpful introduction to the subject. *Note:* Be sure of who is responsible for roof penetrations and sealing of the roof after installation, especially for bonded roofs. (Courtesy Sturdi-Bilt Manufacturing)

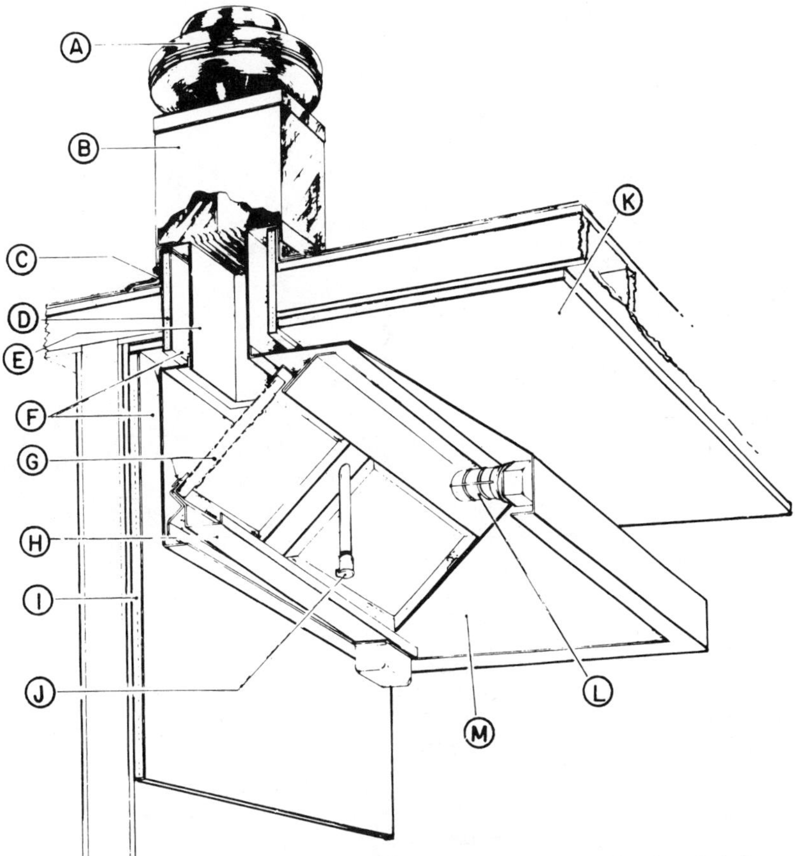

A—Top discharge - centrifugal exhaust fan sized for required C.F.M. exhaust of air.
B—Stack - to extend exhaust to min. of 40" above surface of roof. No. 16 gauge metal, welded seams and back-draft louvers.
C—No. 16 ga. galv. welded roof curb.
D—1" thick rockwool w/wire mesh. Enclosed in 22 ga. galv. iron.
E—16 Ga. all welded - galv. iron duct sized for C.F.M. exhaust req'd.
F—Minimum of 3" air space around duct, behind and above hood.
G—Approved filters. Grease extractors optional.
H—Grease gutter pitched to an approved, removable container.
I—1" thick rockwool w/wire mesh covered w/22 ga. sheetmetal. To be carried down to approved distance below cooking surface of ranges.
J—Typical 'down' nozzle shown - fire protection system to be installed in accordance with all applicable codes.
K—Where top of hood is less than 18" from ceiling insulation, as in 'I'. Shall be applied to ceiling and extend 18" beyond face of hood. A minimum of 3" air space is required between hood and insulation.
L—Vapor-proof, marine type lights.
M—Entire hood to be No. 18 ga. galv. iron or 20 ga. stainless steel with all seams welded.

Figure 6-20. Typical requirements for hood installation in wood frame building. (Reprinted, by permission, from Carl Scriven and James Stevens, *Food Equipment Facts*, © 1988 by Van Nostrand Reinhold)

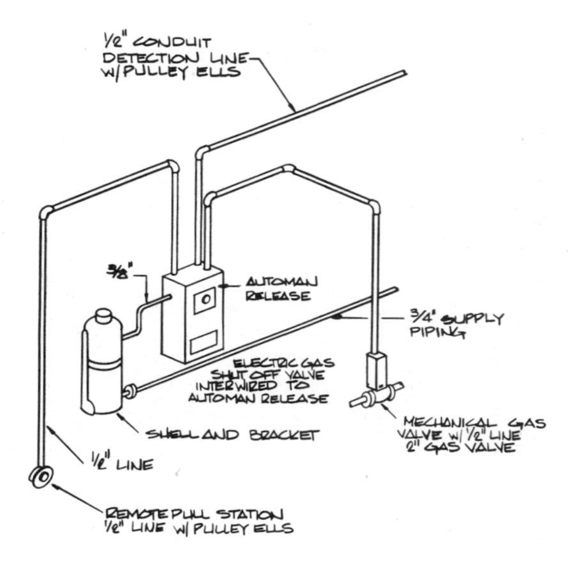

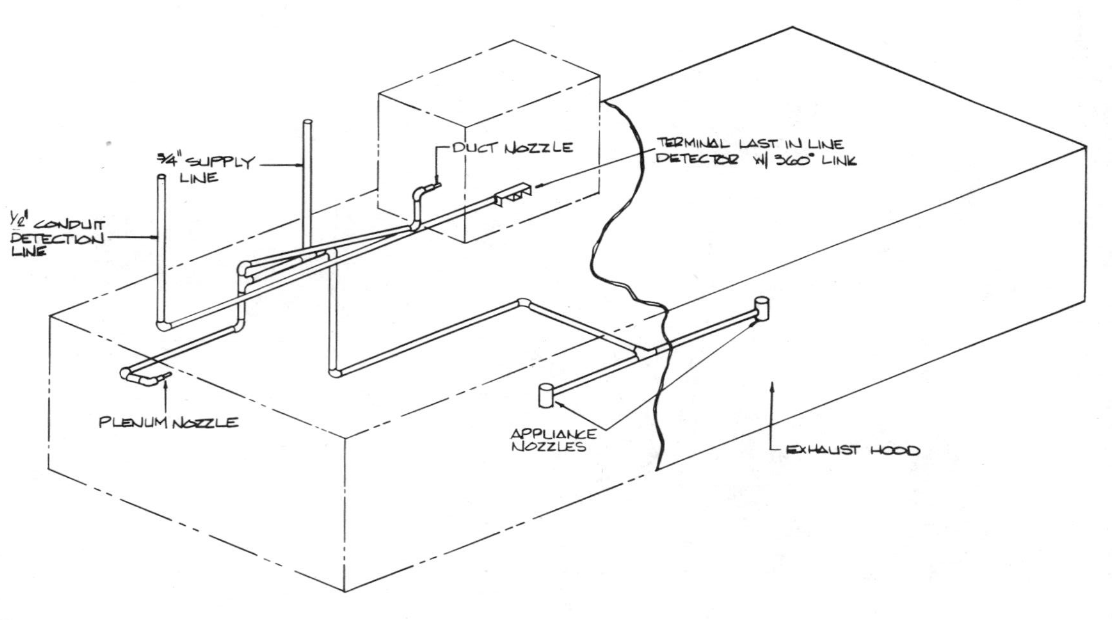

Figure 6-21. Fire system details.

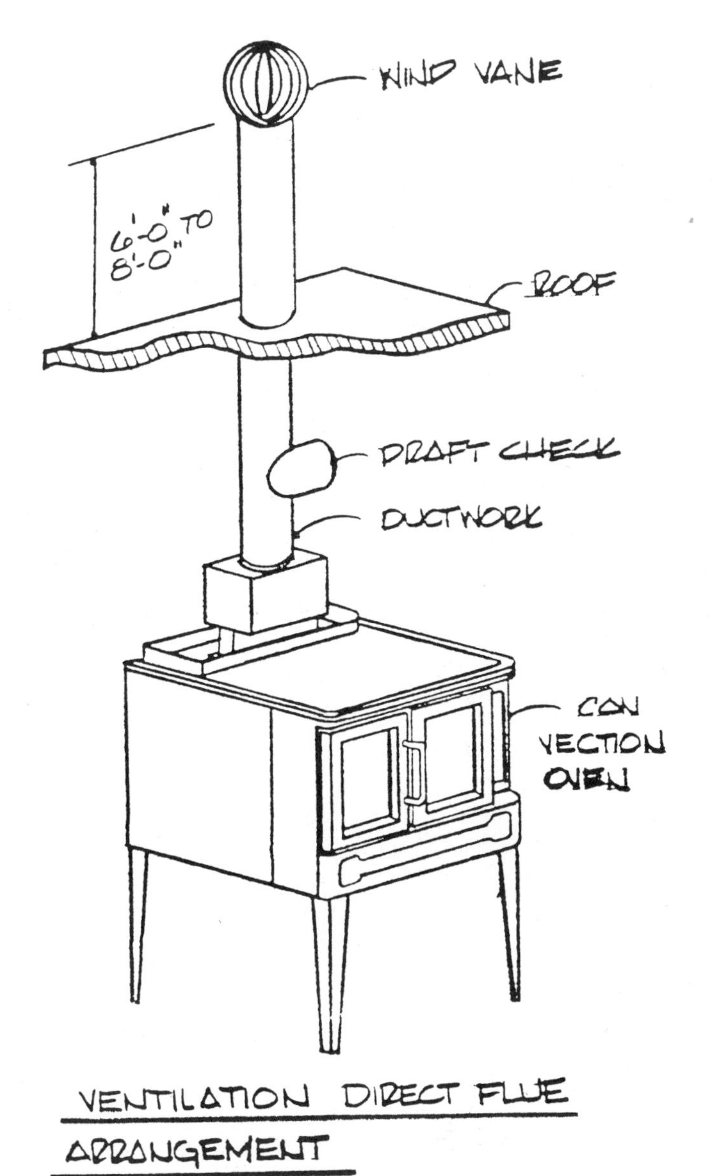

Figure 6-22. Direct oven ventilation. (Courtesy The Blodgett Company)

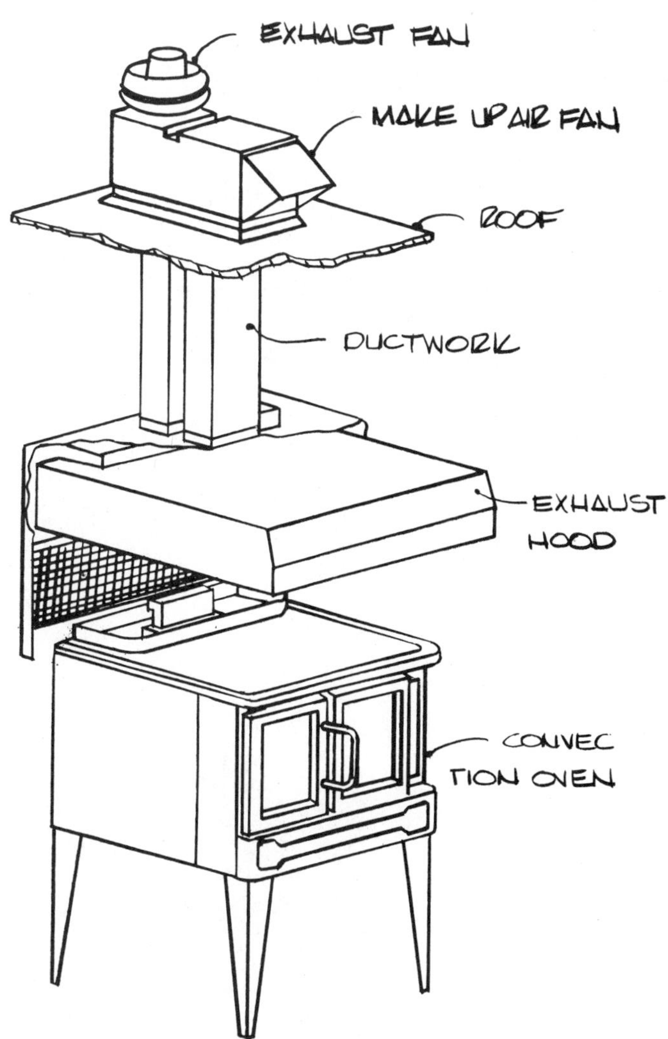

Figure 6-23. Hooded oven ventilation. (Courtesy The Blodgett Company)

7

Serving and Holding

The illustrations of this chapter generally are self-explanatory, depending on the type of operation and the style of service required. The industry abounds with special types of holding equipment.

The most widely used portion pans are based on the 12″ × 20″ foodservice module; both full-size and fractional pans are available in various depths, as shown in Figure 7–1. Users should become familiar with all the possibilities.

Many serving equipment drawings are available, showing options and unique ideas. On custom work one should review the drawings and go over the details closely. Many manufacturers of food equipment are regional, and they can be hard to find. The buyer should consult a full-line equipment dealer for special needs; and if in doubt about whether a certain type of equipment will perform a particular task, the purchaser can ask for a satisfied-user list or visit a recent installation.

Special all-purpose heating devices also are described in this chapter. The authors have tried to show samples of serving areas for all segments of the industry: chef's tables for full-service restaurants; pantry areas and tray systems for institutional settings; and cafeteria and fast-food pickup areas for installations requiring quick meal service.

THE CHEF'S TABLE

The first item after preparation and cooking will be the chef's table, which can vary from a standard steam table unit with a worktable placed beside it to a well-planned and very elaborate factory-constructed unit. Listed below are options to consider when planning it. A chef's table would never require all of them, but careful study of this list will help one to plan for individual requirements.

- Plate storage cabinets (heated or not)
- Lowerators for plates (heated or not)
- Sliding-door cabinets
- Heat lamps
- Overshelves
- Sinks and pipe chase
- Refrigerated base
- Refrigerated top
- Refrigerated drawers
- Freezer base
- Hot food wells
- Hot food bain marie
- Roll warmers
- Soup warmers
- Ice bins
- Call systems
- Order holders
- Tray storage
- Carving boards
- Slicer space
- Pan storage
- Toaster area
- Microwave on or under shelf
- Electrical outlets
- Bread dispenser
- Hot food drawers
- Space for mobile Lowerators
- Factory prewired equipment
- Factory preplumbed equipment with shutoff
- Valves and common drain
- Tile base at site
- Open base (on legs)
- Closed base

Figures 7–2 and 7–3 show customized chef's tables. The chef's table with waitress pickup area of Figure 7–3 was designed for a renovation job where the

STANDARD 12" x 20" MODEL PAN SIZES
(Overall of Flanges)

Full Size	12-3/4" x 20-3/4"
Half Size (short)	12-3/4" x 10-3/8"
Half Size (long)	20-3/4" x 6-3/8"
Two Thirds Size	13-3/4" x 12-3/4"
Third Size	12-3/4" x 6-7/8"
Quarter Size	10-3/8" x 6-3/8"
Sixth Size	6-7/8" x 6-1/4"
Ninth Size	6-3/4" x 4-1/4"

HELPFUL HINTS

When two half size pans are required in one 12" x 20" opening of a serving unit, using the long pans reduces spillage of one item into the other while ladeling the foods to a plate.

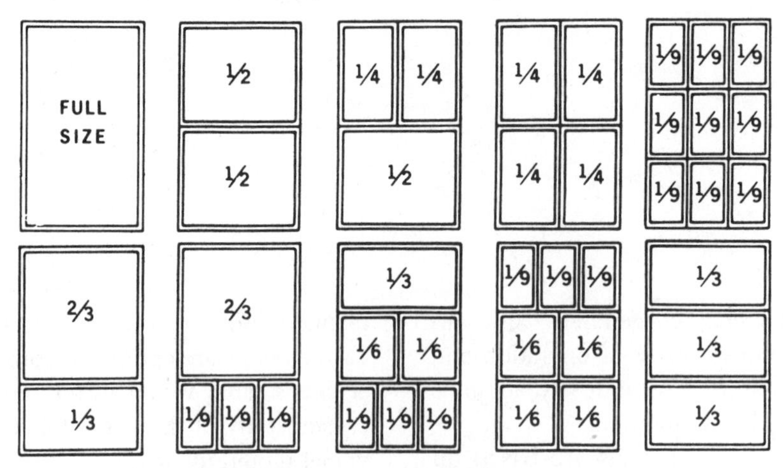

1/2 long pan not shown.

COMMON MULTI-PURPOSE PAN CAPACITIES

FULL SIZE

Depth	Quarts	4 Oz. Portions
2½"	9	72
4"	15	120
6"	22	176
8"	31½	252

HALF SIZE

Depth	Quarts	4 Oz. Portions
2½"	4	32
4"	7	56
6"	10	80
8"	15	120

QUARTER SIZE

Depth	Quarts	4 Oz. Portions
2½"	1-5/8	13
4"	3	24
6"	4¾	38

TWO THIRDS SIZE

Depth	Quarts	4 Oz. Portions
2½"	6	48
4"	10	80
6"	14¼	114

THIRD SIZE

Depth	Quarts	4 Oz. Portions
2½"	2-5/8	21
4"	4½	36
6"	6½	52

SIXTH SIZE

Depth	Quarts	4 Oz. Portions
2½"	1¼	10
4"	2	16
6"	3	24

NINTH SIZE

Depth	Quarts	4 Oz. Portions
2½"	5/8	N.A.
4"	1¼	N.A.

For steam cooking, steam heating or holding of rolls or vegetables in hot food units many of the above pans are available with perforated bottoms and sides. Perforated false bottoms are also available. For use in microwave ovens, serving, holding and freezing Lexan pans are manufactured in all sizes.

kitchen area had very limited space, complicated by building columns. The chef is provided with hot food wells, a cutting board, a sandwich unit, adequate work space, and heated plate elevators. The waitress has a tray storage rack, space to set the trays, and bowl, cup, and plate storage shelves. In a very limited area, she has access to soup, rolls, bread, desserts, and salads.

PANTRY AREA

In hospitals, large hotels, and many institutional foodservice facilities, pantry areas are clearly defined sections of the total operation. Large full-service restaurants will usually have separate sections, set aside from the main cooking area, for the preparation of desserts,

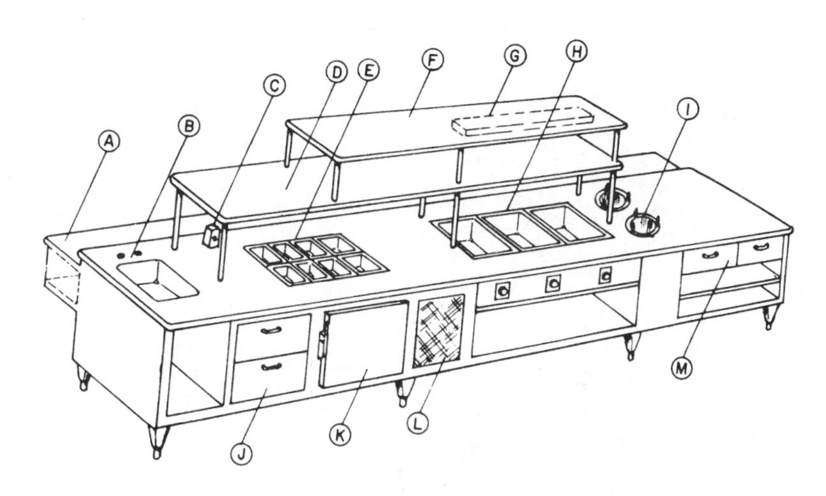

CHEF'S TABLE

A—Tray rest with plate shelf under
B—Sink and faucet holes
C—Electric outlet
D—Space for microwave oven (top shelf cut short)
E—Cold pan or sandwich unit inserts
F—Top shelf
G—Heat lamp
H—Hot food wells
I—Plate elevators
J—Bread drawers
K—Refrigerated base
L—Compressor
M—Tool drawers

Figure 7-2. Chef's table. (Reprinted, by permission, from Carl Scriven and James Stevens, *Food Equipment Facts,* © 1988 by Van Nostrand Reinhold)

Facing page:
Figure 7-1. Standard foodservice pans. Full-size $12\frac{3}{4}'' \times 20\frac{3}{4}''$ pans, of various depths and modular, are available for all major food-cooking and serving equipment in the industry. The fractional pans shown also fit the normal $12'' \times 20''$ opening. These pans will fit mobile trucks, shelving, refrigerators and freezers, ovens, warmers, steam tables, and transport systems, and are available with a variety of flat, domed, hinged, and insulated covers. Proper use of the pan system will also facilitate portion and inventory control. Round pans are adaptable to $12'' \times 20''$ opening using adapter frames. (Reprinted, by permission, from Carl Scriven and James Stevens, *Food Equipment Facts,* © 1988 by Van Nostrand Reinhold)

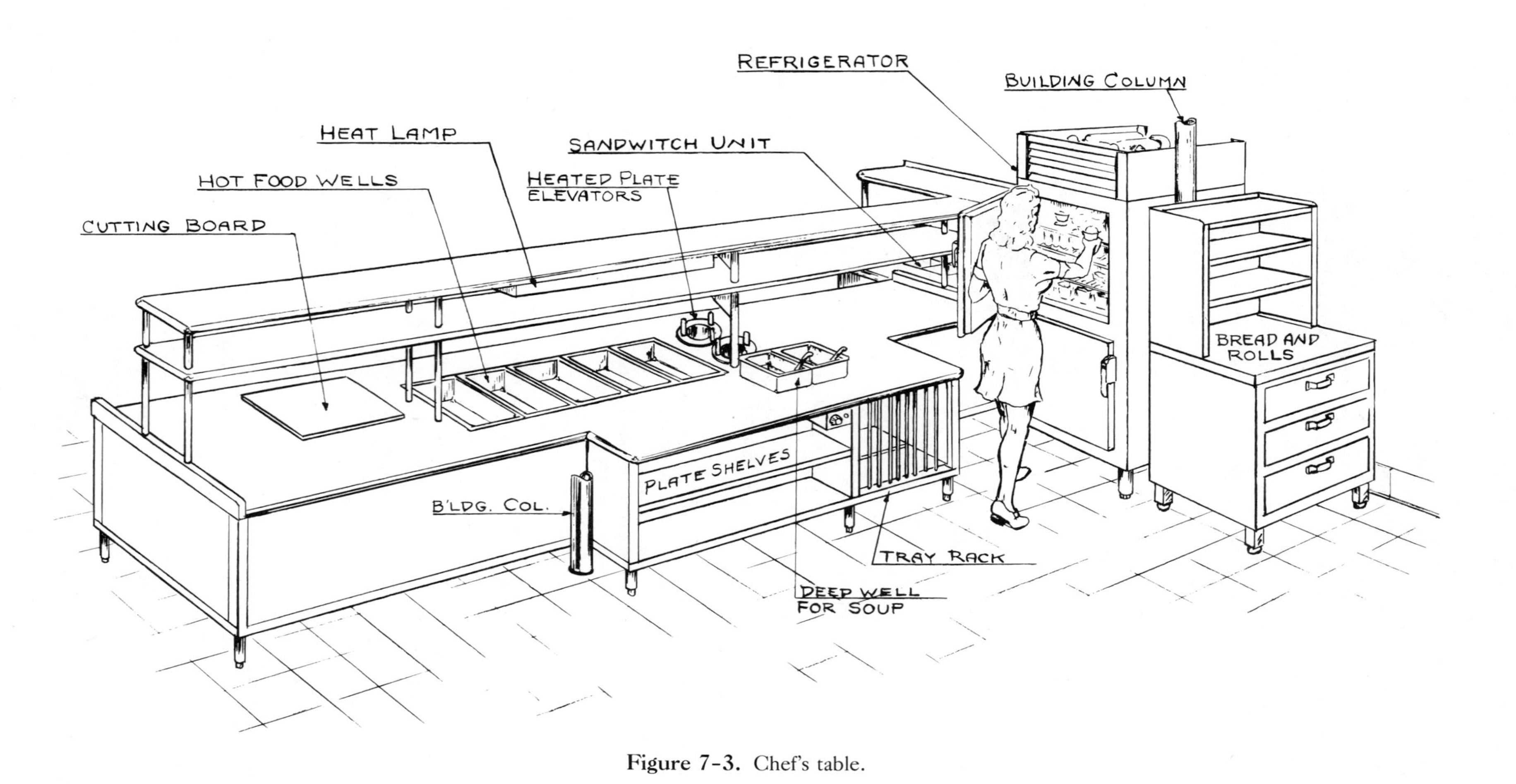

Figure 7-3. Chef's table.

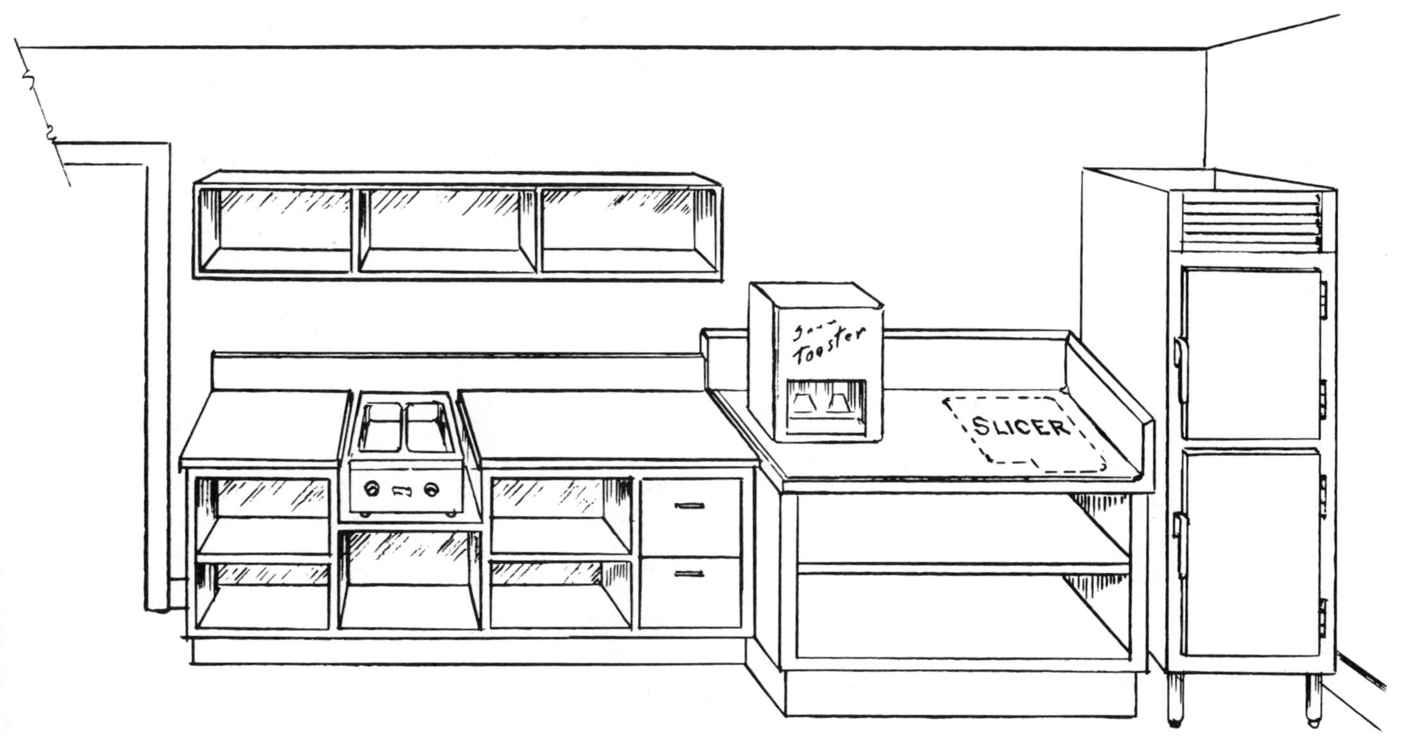

Figure 7-4. Small foodservice pantry area. Shown are a refrigerator for appetizers and desserts, slicer area, toaster, bread drawers, soup warmer, and shelving. Other items to consider would be water fill, microwave, and ice cream. Construction could be stainless steel or a wood laminate combination.

salads, and sometimes complete clam and oyster bars. These separate units are operated by individuals who plate the orders for the serving personnel. The next step down is a separate area housing such items as coffee, beverages, soup, dessert, ice cream, and tea, where the serving personnel prepare and serve the items themselves.

All pantry areas should be carefully designed with the intent of reducing kitchen traffic, relieving the chef of unnecessary work, and improving customer service while still controlling portions and quality.

Listed below are most of the items that should be considered in planning efficient pantry areas. Some of these items are discussed in this chapter; please refer to the index for those described in other chapters, such as ice cream cabinets, sinks, refrigerators, and so on.

- Soup warmers
- Salad prep.
- Desserts
- Refrigerators
- Milk
- Cereal
- Juices
- Dry storage
- Linen basket
- Wastebasket
- Toasters
- Oyster and clam bar
- Egg cookers
- Water and ice
- Microwave ovens
- Ice cream cabinets
- Coffee equipment
- Sinks
- Bread drawers
- Roll warmers
- China and glass storage

Pantry areas often bleed over into waitress stations or combine with them as one unit out in the dining area. When kitchen space limitations make this necessary, serious consideration should be given to shielding the area with partitions or knee walls approximately 5′0″ high. Some of the necessary equipment can be located against the knee wall, with ample aisle space between it and the remaining equipment against the back wall. This design will reduce noise and visual distraction in the dining room and conceal the untidy mess that a pantry area easily can become during rush periods.

Do not forget to provide space for highchair storage.

CAFETERIAS

Equipment styles include mobile, fixed modular, and custom fabrication. Equipment components may include:

- Hot food tables
- Cold food tables
- Cold pans–frost tops
- Sandwich units
- Salad and dessert cases
- Silver trays and cylinders
- Tray trucks
- Cashier's stand
- Refrigerated base
- Hot base
- Sneeze guard
- Tray rails
- Milk dispensers
- Ice cream cabinets
- Grilled food section
- Made-to-order section
- Heat lamps
- Overshelves
- Beverage station
- Toast station
- Cup dispenser
- Plate dispenser
- Saucer dispenser
- Urn section
- Mobile dish units when employees serve
- Bulletin boards
- Product elevators
- Milk carton dispensers
- Ice dispensers

Many of the components for cafeteria counters are illustrated in this chapter. Check the index for others. Power systems in Chapter 9 should be considered. For school installations, the components are largely standardized. Large installations usually require foodservice consultants or the design service of a competent equipment dealer. Space must be carefully allocated. Straight-line, double-sided service units, scatter systems, and checking systems all must be taken into account. Grill and sandwich "made-to-order" sections can cause jam-ups. Beverage sections often require much more space than originally anticipated.

THE REVOLVING CAFETERIA

A relatively new innovation, these units are positioned in the wall between the kitchen and the customer area. The revolving portion is approximately 86 inches in diameter and 75 inches high. The bottom shelf is at counter height. Heat lamps above this shelf keep foods at serving temperatures. Three more shelves are mounted on the superstructure; the top one has an angled mirror to enhance the dessert display, and the two intermediate shelves may display salads, wrapped sandwiches, and so on. Trays are stored in a six-part compartment below the tray rail on the customer side. The unit turns at the rate of one revolution per minute. Selected items are freshly plated and replaced by employees as the shelf segments revolve through the kitchen area. Six to eight patrons may be served simultaneously and proceed to the beverage and cashier station.

The unit is ideally suited for institutional service, in-plant snack bars, and airport and highway cafeterias where items are limited. The basic principle of the unit is that the cafeteria moves past the customer, so the entire line is not forced to move at the pace of the slowest person.

Manufacturers claim that the unit occupies from 35% to 50% less floor space than conventional units, and requires two or more fewer serving personnel to serve 8 to 12 meals per minute.

MOBILE CAFETERIA OR BUFFET UNITS

Such a unit can be prepared from almost any 24-inches-deep, 4- or 5-foot standard component of a cafeteria counter (i.e., flat top section, cold pan unit, four- or five-compartment hot food unit), dressed up with an unlimited choice of decorator panels, with added breath protectors, display shelves, heat lamps, and so on. The addition of casters creates a mobile buffet or cafeteria counter. The buffet units have drop-down plate shelves on each side; the cafeteria units have tray rails on one side and plate shelves or cutting boards on the other. Matching tray and silver stands, cashier stands, special meat carving sections, and 90° interior or exterior corner sections may be obtained. Many styles and variations are available.

Units that accept standard hot food in hand-carried containers, from which the food may be served directly, are available for school feeding and similar institutional service.

Figures 7–5 through 7–22 show many useful features for the foodservice installations discussed in this chapter, and should be consulted as needed.

SERVING AND HOLDING CHECKLIST

Individuals planning serving and holding areas should answer these questions:

- Will we use standard pans (12″ × 20″, 18″ × 26″)?
- Are there adequate drains?
- Are the electrical receptacles adequate?
- Should the equipment be mobile?
- Do hot food wells work wet and dry?
- Are sinks equipped with a lever handle for the drain?
- Are faucet parts available?

- Will we use plate elevators, either drop-in or mobile? Ask to see all options available.
- Will the refrigeration system accept pan glides?
- Can I use deeper pans than shown?
- Does the unit have a cord and plug?
- Can I reach the overshelf?
- Who will attach the heat lamps?
- If needed, where will the order wheels, or check holder, be installed?
- Is a tray lock needed?
- Can we mop around the equipment?
- Are the drawers easily removable and cleanable?
- Do we need a tool pole or tool merry-go-round?
- Will waitress page systems be used?

Item	Weight
___ Steam Table Floor Model, Heavy Duty	
2-12 × 20 Openings	100#
3-12 × 20 Openings	225#
4-12 × 20 Openings	410#
5-12 × 20 Openings	495#
___ Urn Stand	
2′ Long 30″ Deep	
3′ Long 30″ Deep	
4′ Long 30″ Deep	
___ Roll Warmer	
2 Drawer	116#
3 Drawer	229#
___ Heated Holding Cabinet 23 1/4 Wide 32″ Deep 72″ High	200#
___ Table Top Plastic Salad Bar 4′	65#
___ Table Top Plastic Salad Bar 5′	80#
___ Mobile Buffet Line	
30″ Beef Cart	300#
30″ Soup Cart	250#
30″ Solid Top Cart	250#
60″ Solid Top Cart	550#
72″ Solid Top Cart	640#
44″ Frost Top	460#
72″ Frost Top	760#
44″ Ice Pan	360#
72″ Ice Pan	600#
30″ Hot Food	265#
44″ Hot Food	395#
58″ Hot Food	525#
72″ Hot Food	655#
___ Plate Lowerators Mobile, Solid	
2 Hole	100#
3 Hole	132#
4 Hole	160#
___ Ice Cream Cabinets	
30″ × 30″	212#
30″ × 66″	396#
30″ × 90″	460#

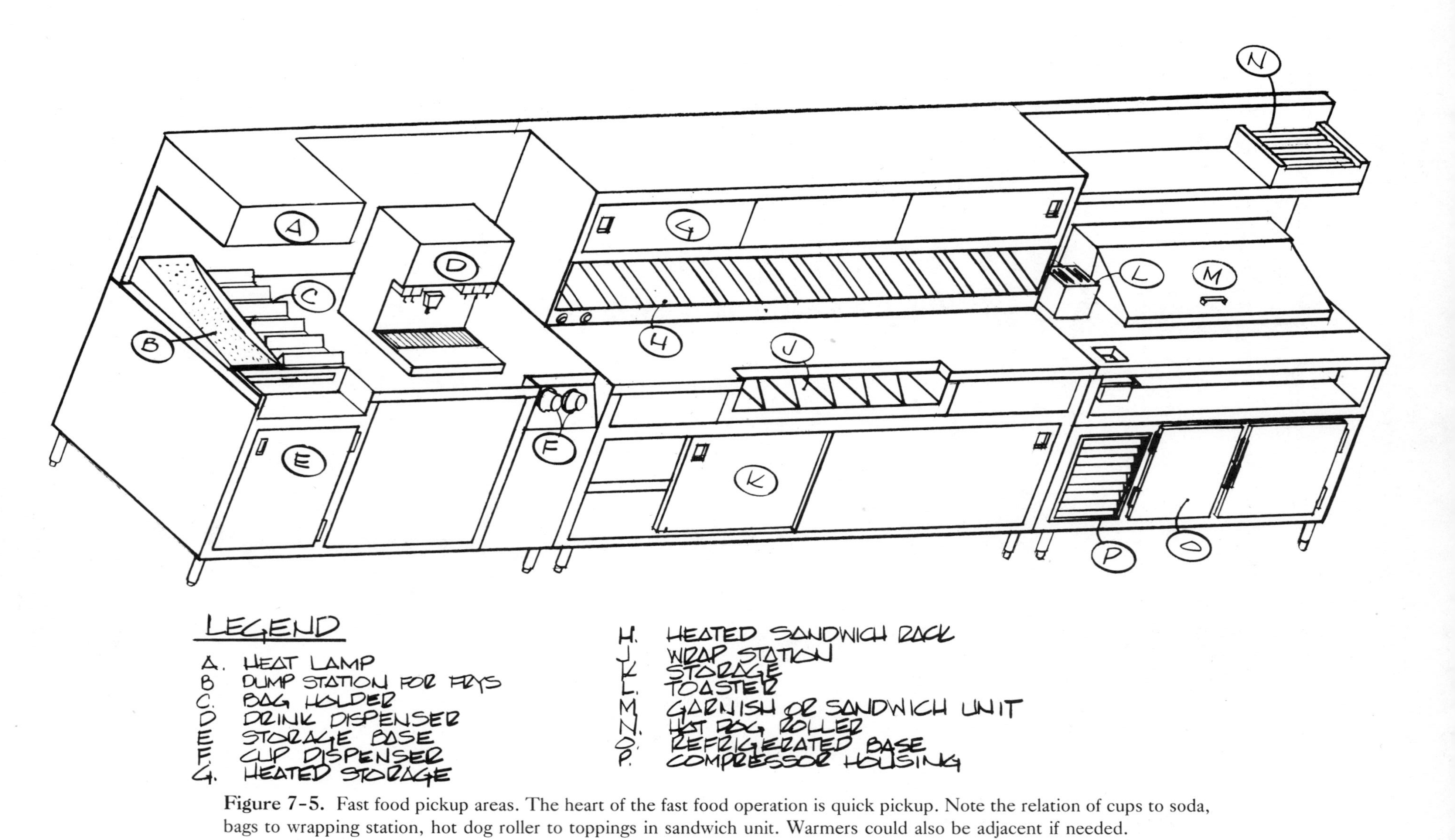

Figure 7-5. Fast food pickup areas. The heart of the fast food operation is quick pickup. Note the relation of cups to soda, bags to wrapping station, hot dog roller to toppings in sandwich unit. Warmers could also be adjacent if needed.

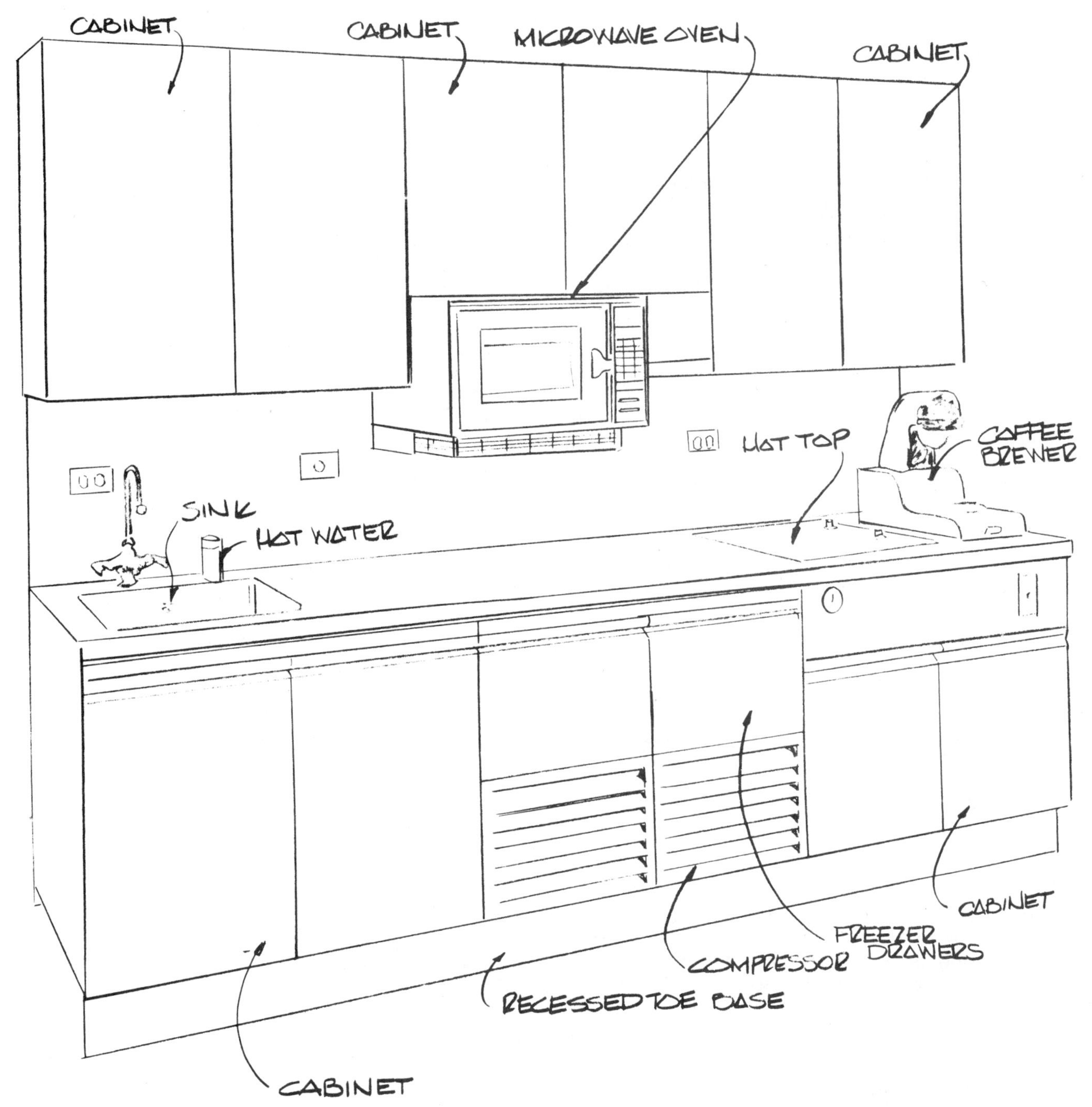

Figure 7-6. Nourishment station. Typical nourishment station found in many health-related facilities is shown in composite form. This self-contained unit is complete, and selecting particular needs from this drawing will assist the planning process. (Courtesy Market Forge)

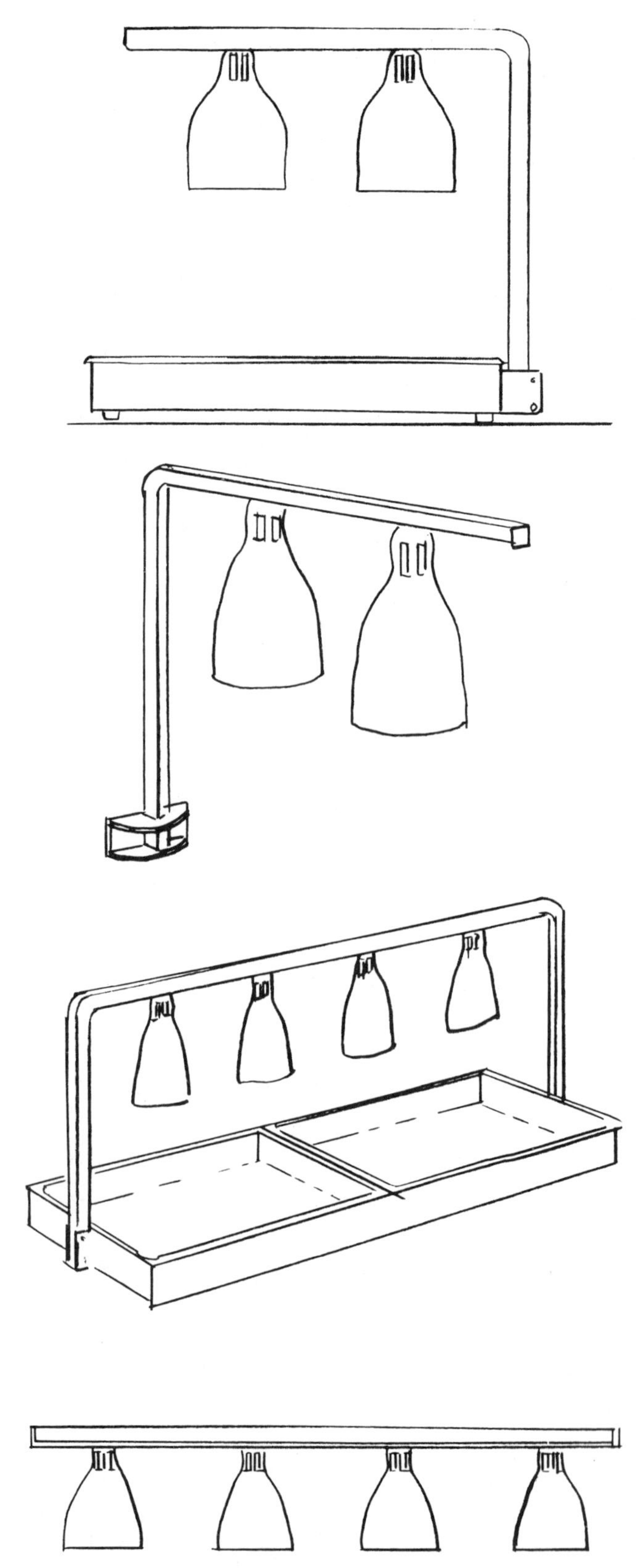

Standard two lamp unit, made of heavy rust-free aluminum throughout, with heavy gauge removable stainless steel pan.

Wall mounted unit, for complete flexibility and where counter space is not available. Available in either fixed position or swivel.

Four lamp unit, ideal for the volume food service operator. Equipped with two removable stainless steel pans.

"Pass-thru" unit, can be manufactured in any length up to twelve feet. It is important to specify accurately the exact length required to fit your pass-thru area when ordering. Allow a minimum of 10¾" from the serving deck to the bottom base of the shade to provide 140 degree heat at the deck.

Figure 7-7. Heat lamps. Heat lamps and various warmers are available for holding a variety of foods at serving temperature. Choosing the right warmers is very critical to quality control. The unique styles shown are engineered to exacting specifications to match menu needs. Consult an equipment representative for proper selection.

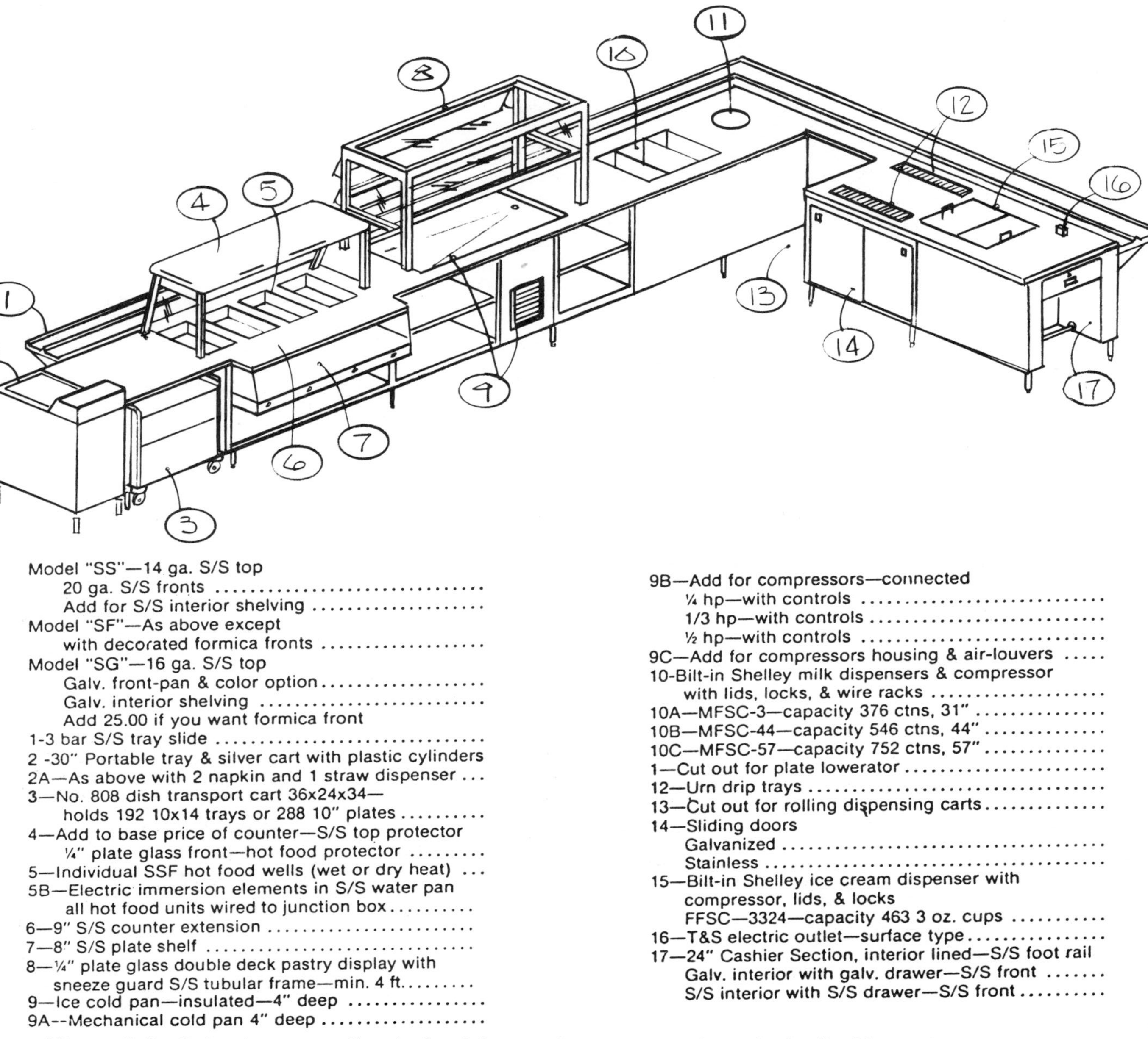

Model "SS"—14 ga. S/S top
20 ga. S/S fronts
Add for S/S interior shelving
Model "SF"—As above except
with decorated formica fronts
Model "SG"—16 ga. S/S top
Galv. front-pan & color option
Galv. interior shelving
Add 25.00 if you want formica front
1-3 bar S/S tray slide
2 -30" Portable tray & silver cart with plastic cylinders
2A—As above with 2 napkin and 1 straw dispenser
3—No. 808 dish transport cart 36x24x34—
holds 192 10x14 trays or 288 10" plates
4—Add to base price of counter—S/S top protector
¼" plate glass front—hot food protector
5—Individual SSF hot food wells (wet or dry heat)
5B—Electric immersion elements in S/S water pan
all hot food units wired to junction box
6—9" S/S counter extension
7—8" S/S plate shelf
8—¼" plate glass double deck pastry display with
sneeze guard S/S tubular frame—min. 4 ft.
9—Ice cold pan—insulated—4" deep
9A--Mechanical cold pan 4" deep
9B—Add for compressors—connected
¼ hp—with controls
1/3 hp—with controls
½ hp—with controls
9C—Add for compressors housing & air-louvers
10-Bilt-in Shelley milk dispensers & compressor
with lids, locks, & wire racks
10A—MFSC-3—capacity 376 ctns, 31"
10B—MFSC-44—capacity 546 ctns, 44"
10C—MFSC-57—capacity 752 ctns, 57"
1—Cut out for plate lowerator
12—Urn drip trays
13—Cut out for rolling dispensing carts
14—Sliding doors
Galvanized
Stainless
15—Bilt-in Shelley ice cream dispenser with
compressor, lids, & locks
FFSC—3324—capacity 463 3 oz. cups
16—T&S electric outlet—surface type
17—24" Cashier Section, interior lined—S/S foot rail
Galv. interior with galv. drawer—S/S front
S/S interior with S/S drawer—S/S front

Figure 7-8. Cafeteria counter. Standard stainless steel counters are shown in detail with popular components.

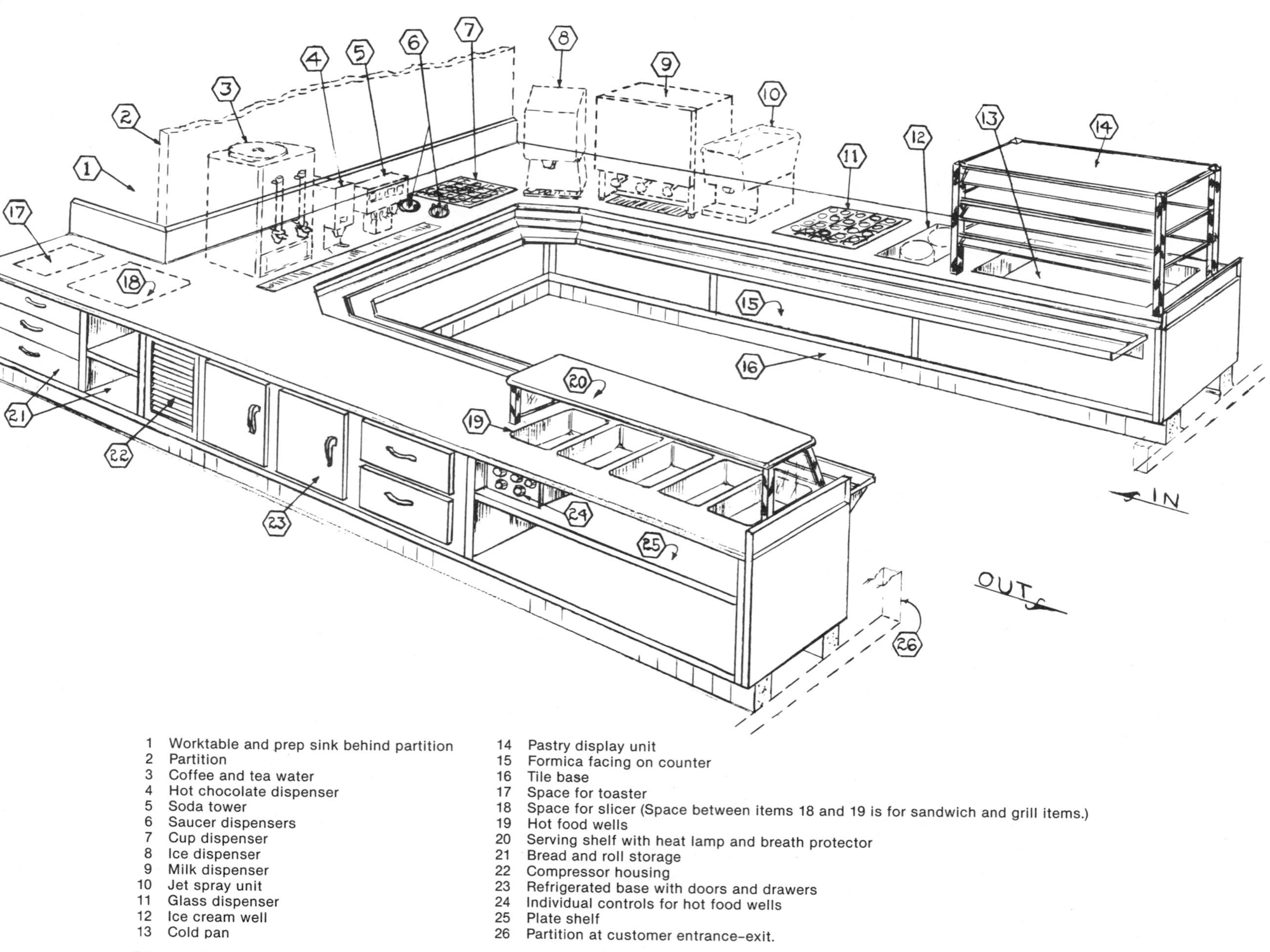

1 Worktable and prep sink behind partition
2 Partition
3 Coffee and tea water
4 Hot chocolate dispenser
5 Soda tower
6 Saucer dispensers
7 Cup dispenser
8 Ice dispenser
9 Milk dispenser
10 Jet spray unit
11 Glass dispenser
12 Ice cream well
13 Cold pan
14 Pastry display unit
15 Formica facing on counter
16 Tile base
17 Space for toaster
18 Space for slicer (Space between items 18 and 19 is for sandwich and grill items.)
19 Hot food wells
20 Serving shelf with heat lamp and breath protector
21 Bread and roll storage
22 Compressor housing
23 Refrigerated base with doors and drawers
24 Individual controls for hot food wells
25 Plate shelf
26 Partition at customer entrance-exit.

Figure 7-9. U-Shaped cafeteria counter, a popular-shaped cafeteria in college feeding. Note the options available.

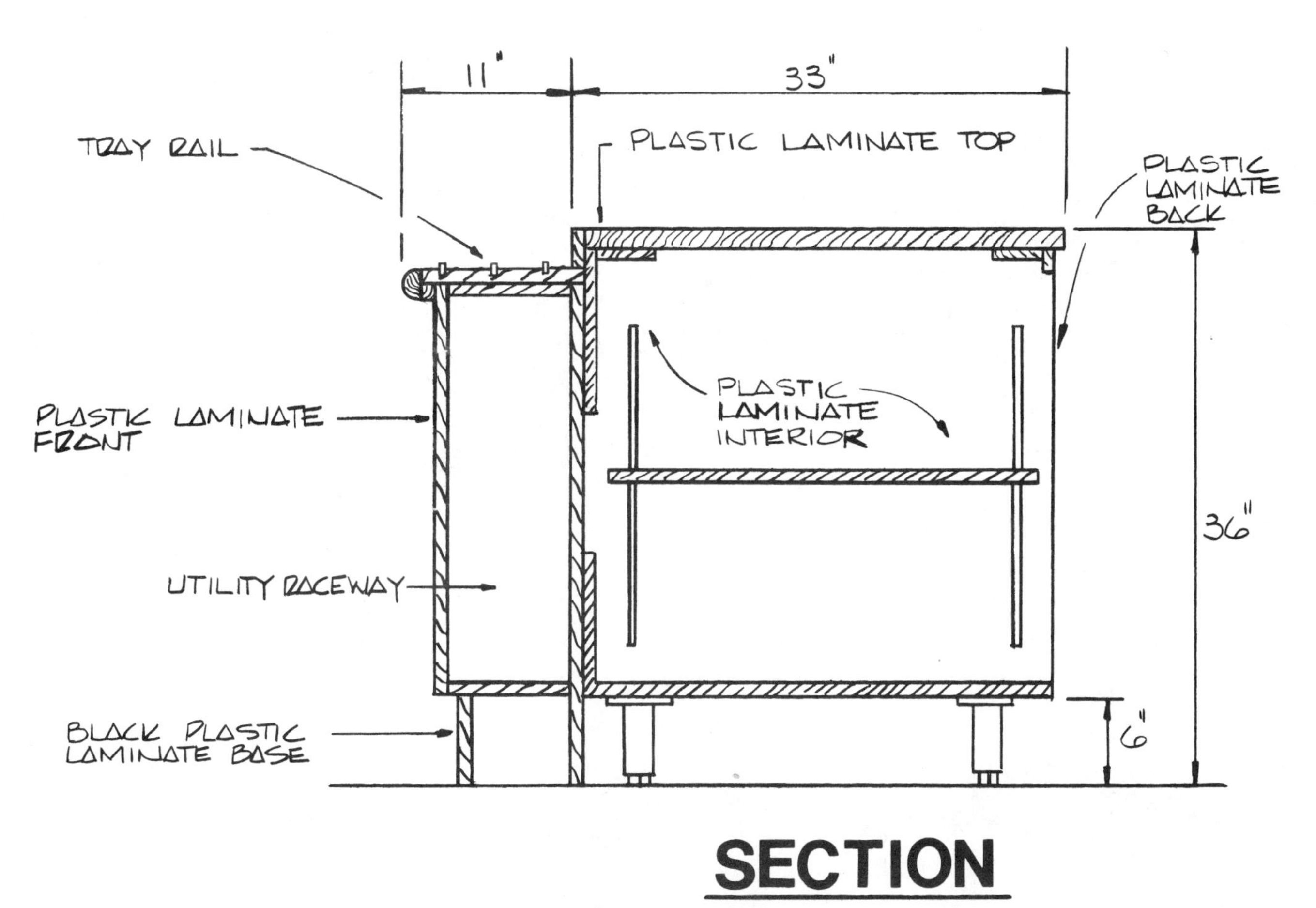

Figure 7-10. Cross view of a custom cafeteria counter, featuring a utility raceway for mechanical connections, adjustable interior shelves, and built-in tray rail. Decorating possibilities with this type of construction include wood, laminate, or stainless steel facing and top construction of plastics, fiberglass, stainless steel, and new materials such as Corian; see equipment representative for details.

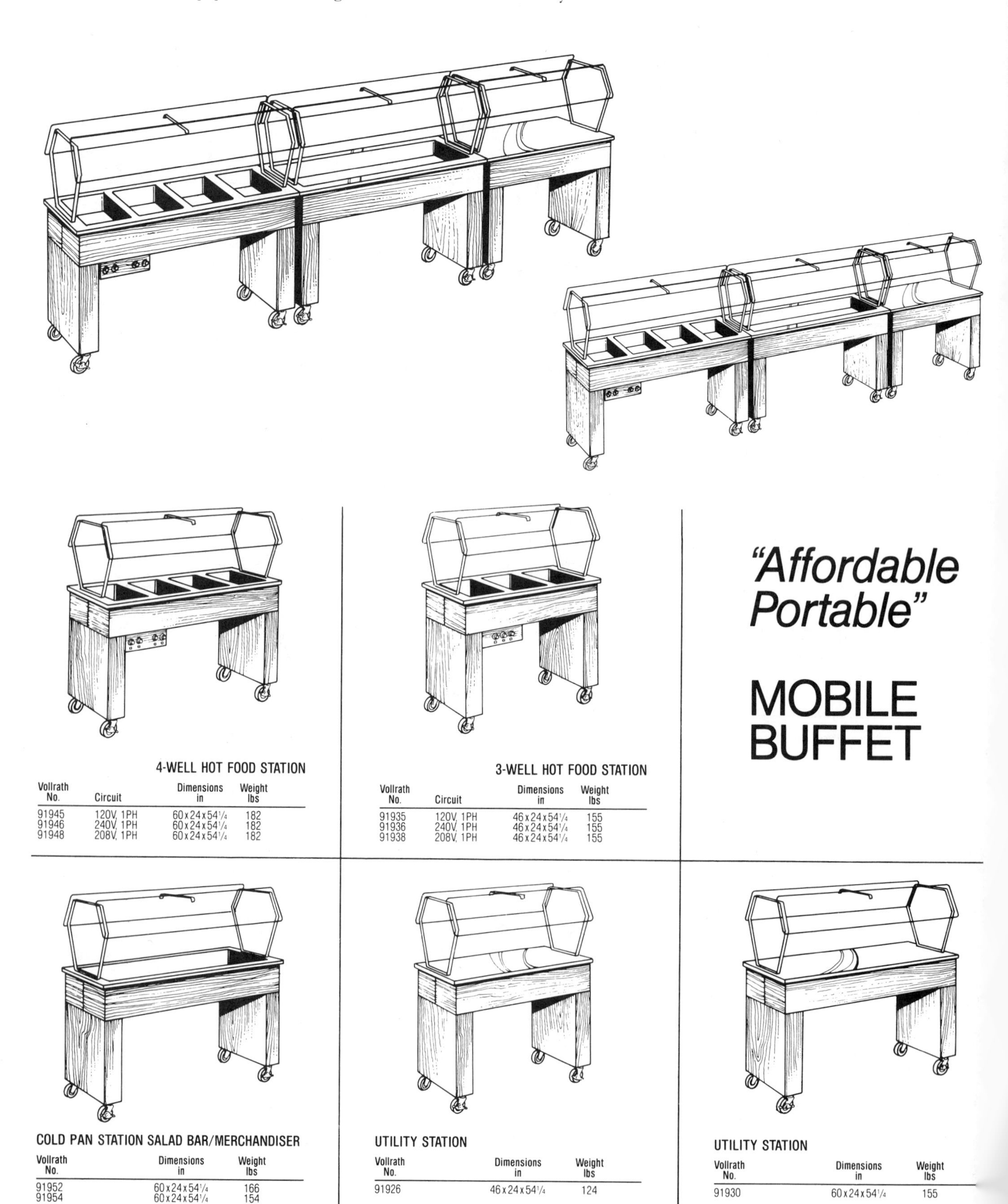

"Affordable Portable"
MOBILE BUFFET
4-WELL HOT FOOD STATION
Vollrath No. Circuit Dimensions in Weight lbs
91945 120V, 1PH 60x24x54¼ 182
91946 240V, 1PH 60x24x54¼ 182
91948 208V, 1PH 60x24x54¼ 182
3-WELL HOT FOOD STATION
Vollrath No. Circuit Dimensions in Weight lbs
91935 120V, 1PH 46x24x54¼ 155
91936 240V, 1PH 46x24x54¼ 155
91938 208V, 1PH 46x24x54¼ 155
COLD PAN STATION SALAD BAR/MERCHANDISER
Vollrath No. Dimensions in Weight lbs
91952 60x24x54¼ 166
91954 60x24x54¼ 154
UTILITY STATION
Vollrath No. Dimensions in Weight lbs
91926 46x24x54¼ 124
UTILITY STATION
Vollrath No. Dimensions in Weight lbs
91930 60x24x54¼ 155

Figures 7-11a,b. Mobile buffet, popular sizes and options. The buffet also can be purchased as shown on legs in lieu of casters. (Courtesy Vollrath Manufacturing)

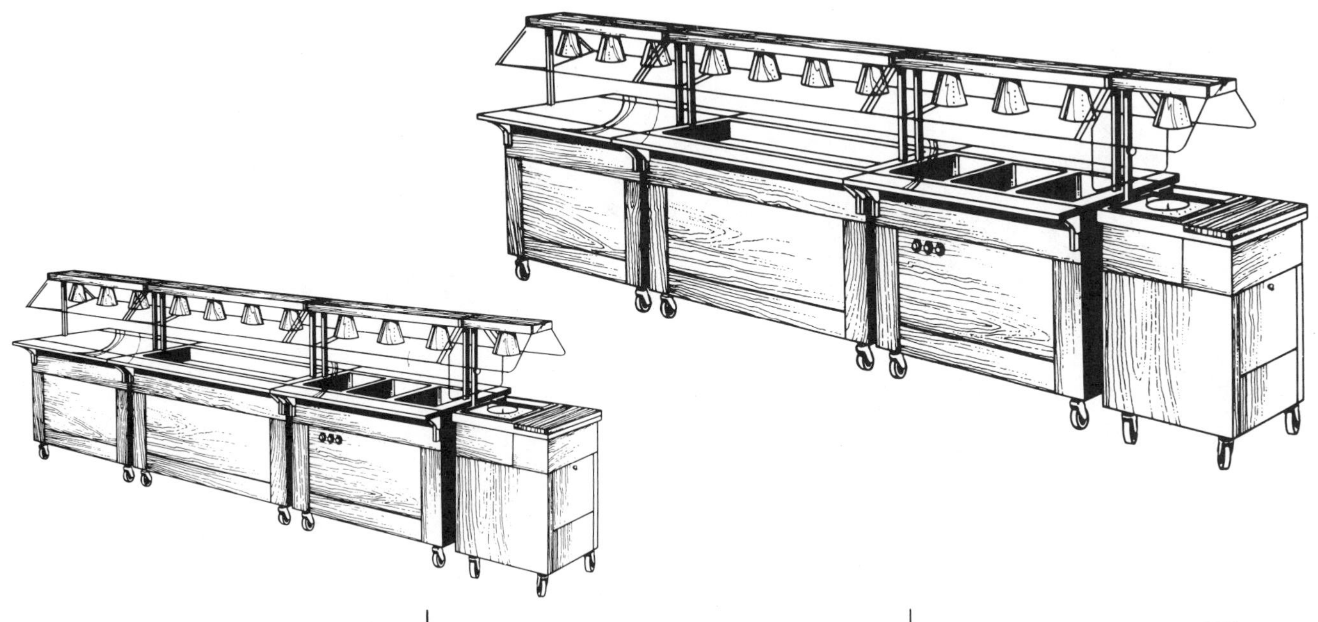

MOBILE BUFFET LINE-UP & UNITS

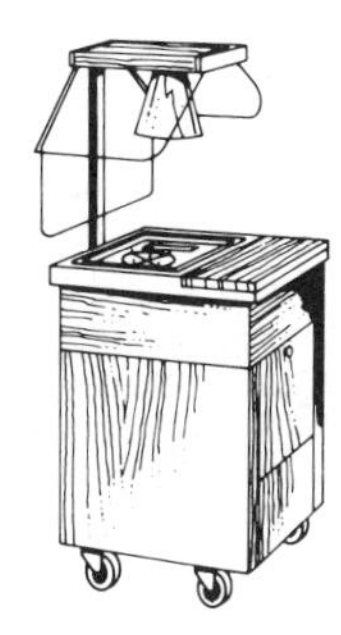

ENTREE CART

Vollrath No.	Circuit	Dimensions in	Weight lbs
91965	120V, 1PH	24x24 to 63	139

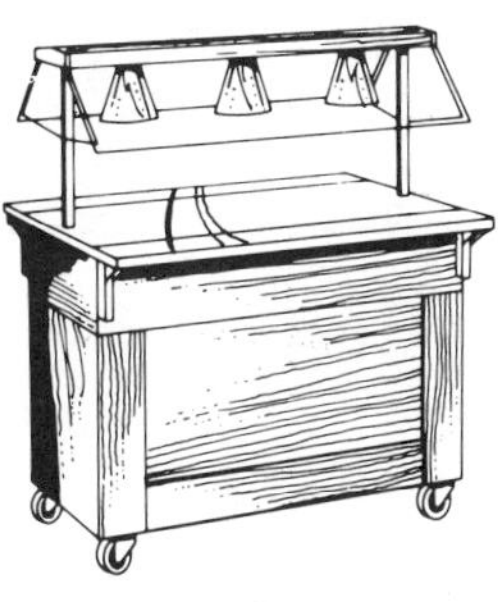

UTILITY STATION

Vollrath No.	Circuit	Dimensions in	Weight lbs
91922	120V, 1PH	46x24x54	294

FOUR-WELL HOT FOOD STATION

Vollrath No.	Circuit	Dimensions in	Weight lbs
99145	120V, 1PH	60x24x54	365
99146	120/240V, 1PH	60x24x54	365
99148	120/208V, 1PH	60x24x54	365

THREE-WELL HOT FOOD STATION

Vollrath No.	Circuit	Dimensions in	Weight lbs
99135	120V, 1PH	46x24x54	327
99136	120/240V, 1PH	46x24x54	327
99138	120/208V, 1PH	46x24x54	327

COLD FOOD STATION/SALAD BAR

Vollrath No.	Circuit	Dimensions in	Weight lbs
91950	120V, 1PH	60x24x54	394
91955 (refrigerated)	120V, 1PH	60x24x54	444

Figure 7-11b

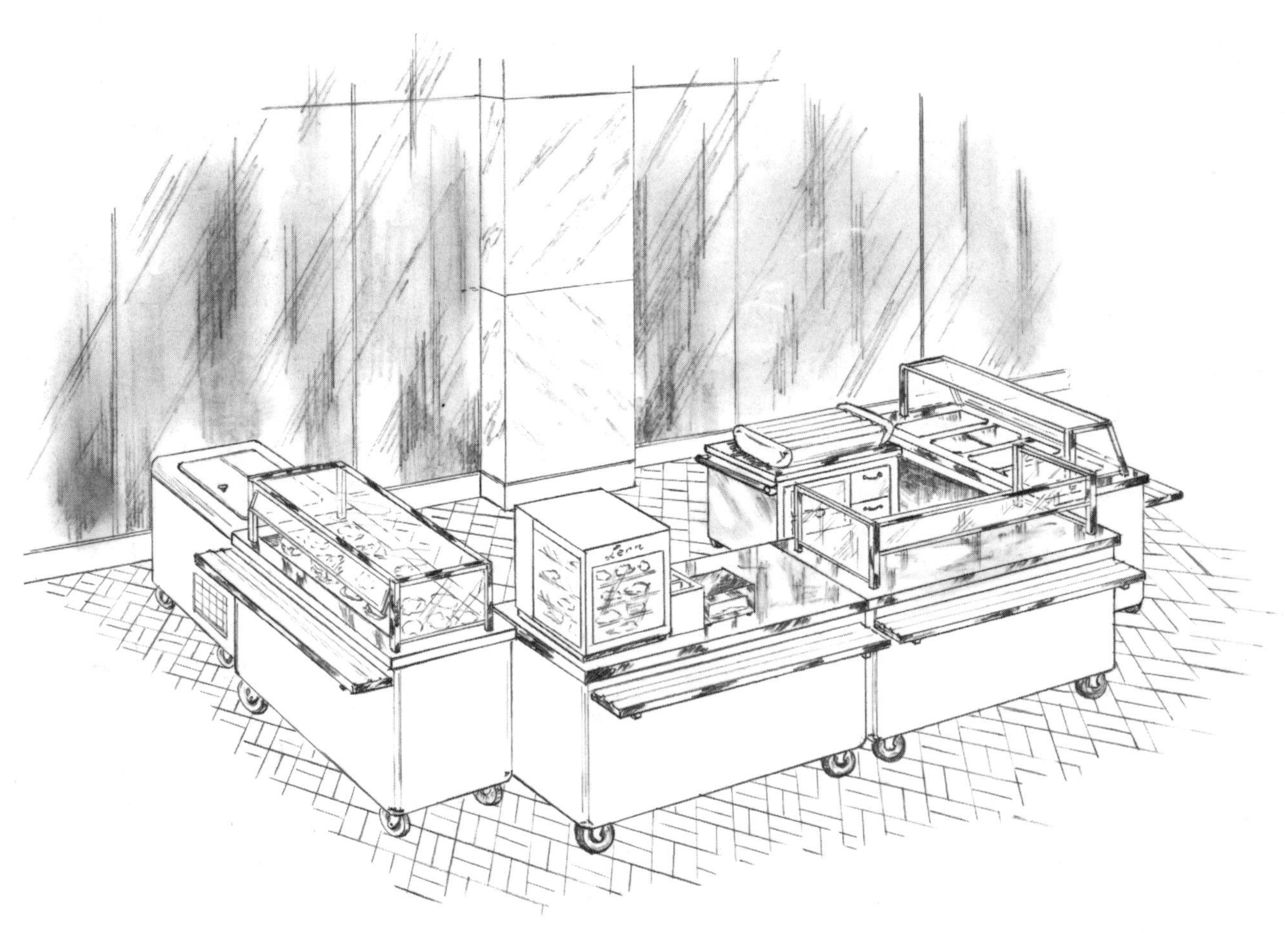

Figure 7-12. Proposed arrangement of equipment without canopy.

INSTRUCTIONS FOR INSTALLATION OF ORDERETTE WHEEL

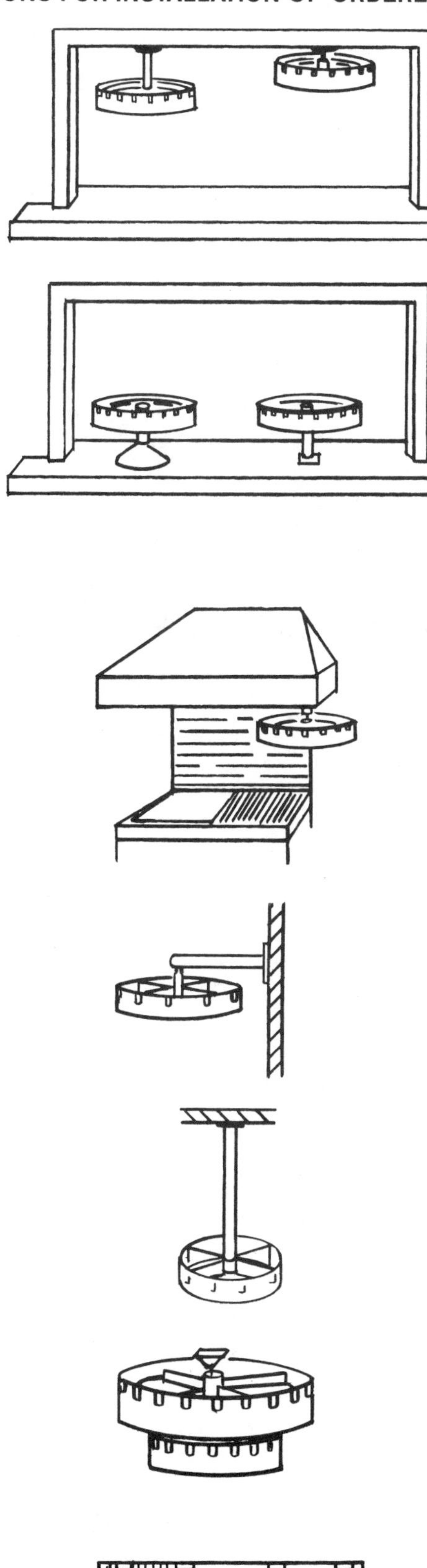

FIGURE 1.

Normal installation. Remove mounting plate and fasten into soffit. Screw axle into plate as far as it will go, then tighten nut firmly against mounting plate.

FIGURE 2.

Where soffit of pass-through window is too high for normal installation, a pedestal is used with the wheel. If the wheel is to be hung with a pedestal, remove and discard the mounting plate. Fasten pedestal to soffit and screw axle into pedestal, tightening nut firmly against pedestal. If counter top installation is desired, follow same procedure as above except fasten pedestal to counter top. Pedestals come in 6″ and 10″ lengths, or 10″ and 14″ movable weighted bases.

FIGURE 3.

For outside cooking area installations, unit may be attached to grease trough around bottom of hood following instructions as in Figure 1, except the use of stove bolts and washers is recommended to close holes and prevent drip. As required, the 6″ or 10″ pedestal may be used to bring the wheel to the proper working height.

FIGURE 4.

Where a wallmount is called for, a wall bracket, as shown, is available. To install wheel on bracket, remove and discard mounting plate, screw axle into bracket and tighten nut firmly against bracket. Wheel can be mounted on top of bracket if desired.

FIGURE 5.

Very high ceiling condition may be overcome with the use of a pedestal bracket made of aluminum rod (1¼″ dia.). Drill holes at bottom and install as in Figure 5.

FIGURE 6.

Where more capacity is required than offered by one wheel, two wheels may be combined as shown by the use of a tread coupler*. This arrangement is also used where it is desireable to keep orders separated, such as salads, hot dishes and sandwiches, or drive-in and restaurant. *Available. No-Charge when ordered with two wheels and requested.

FIGURE 7.

ORDERETTE flat strips with clips are available in any length, 3½″ wide, 3 clips to the foot.

Figure 7-13. Order wheels. Popular styles of ordering wheels are shown with installation ideas. (Courtesy Orderette Manufacturing)

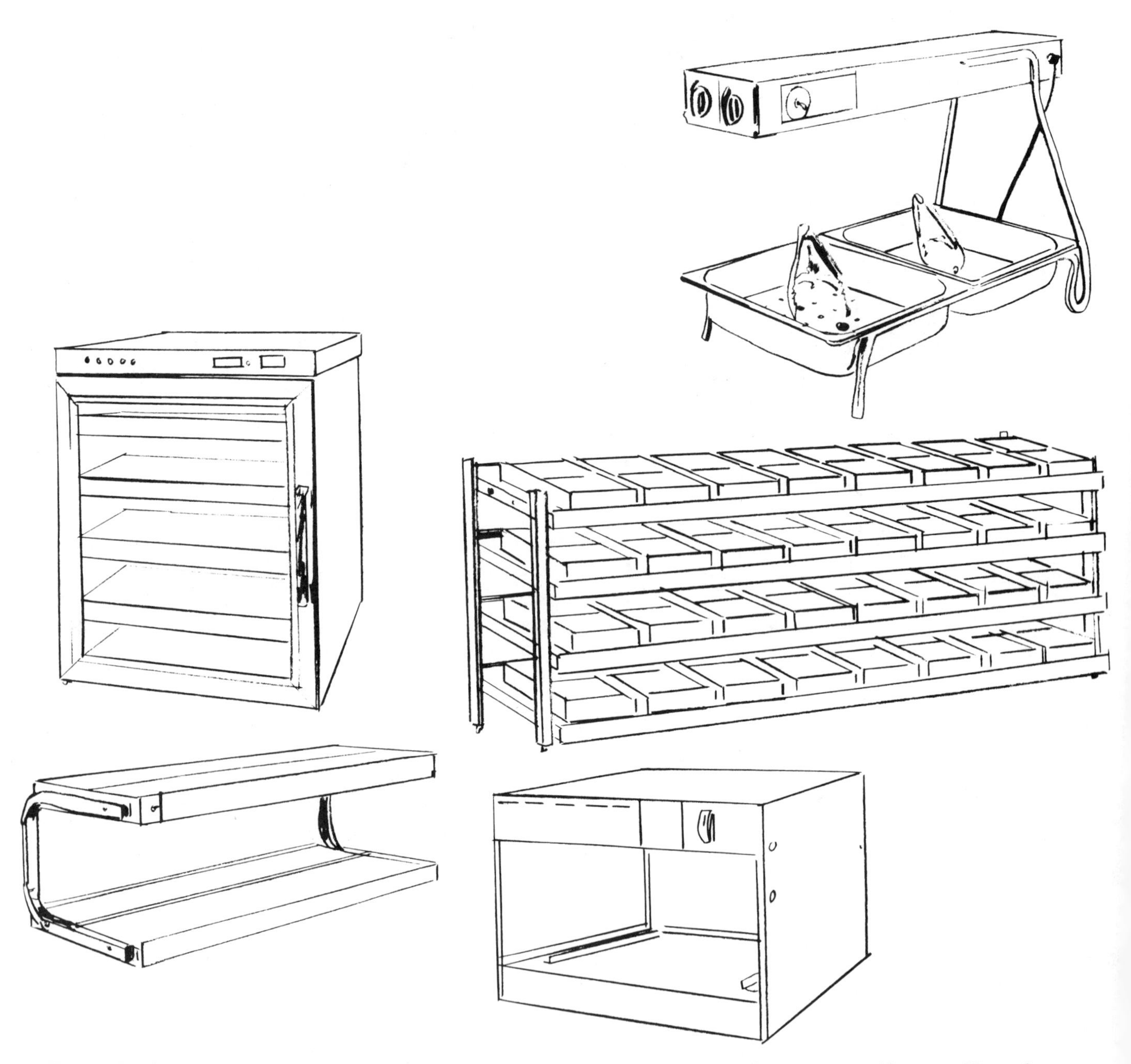

Figure 7-14. Food holding. Creative displays and solutions to maintaining food quality are shown. (Courtesy Hatco Corporation)

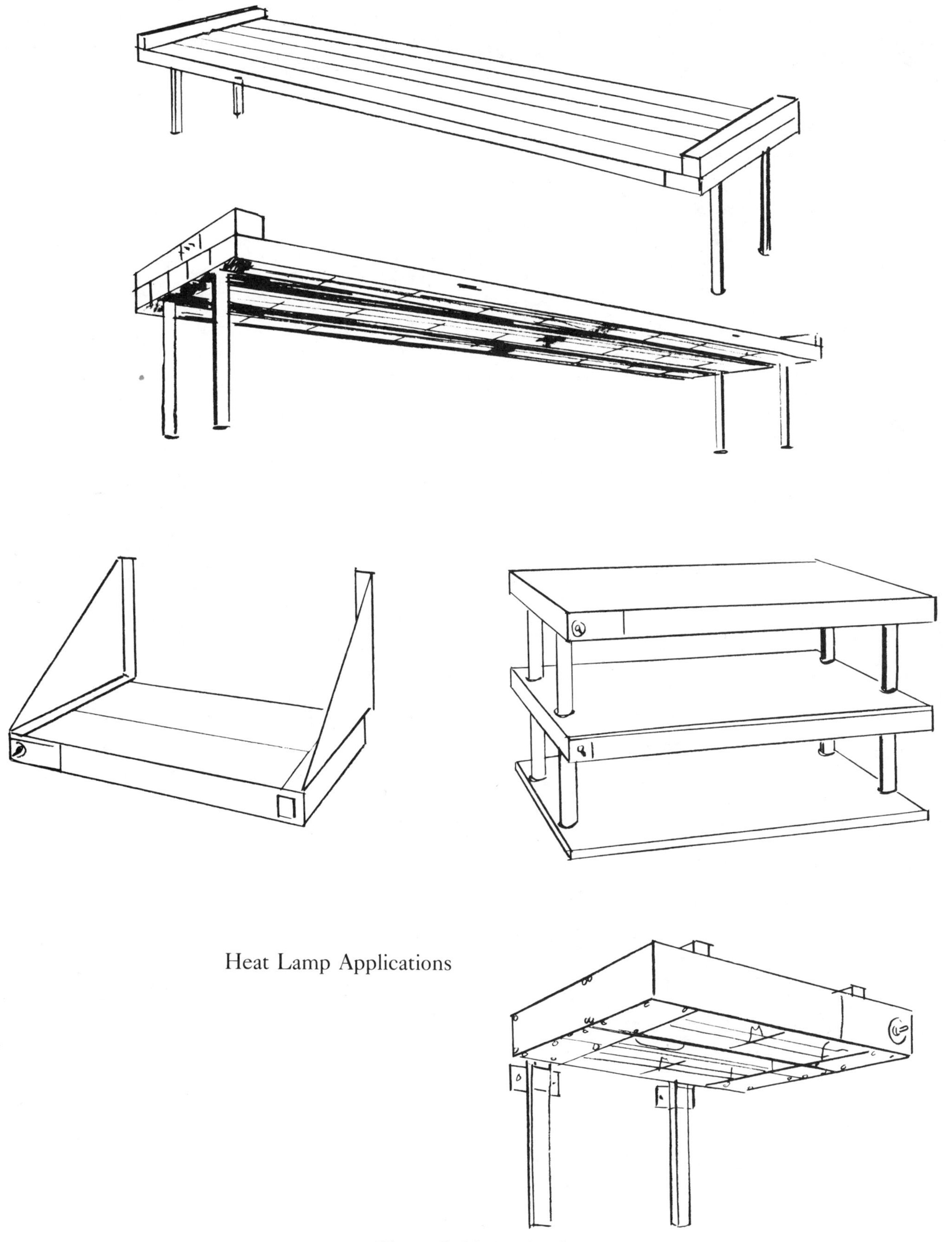

Figure 7-14 *(continued)*

THERMOTAINER IDEAS ON WHERE TO USE FOOD STORAGE UNITS

Installed beneath back counter appliances

Pick-up for hot food in kitchen

Installed under steam table wells

Backing up cafeteria line

Portable units to deliver and store hot food for cafeteria counters or remote feeding areas

Cooks' work table

Built into back counter

Pass-thru installed in wall between kitchen & cafeteria

Hot roll storage mounted on or built into cafeteria counter

Figure 7-15. Insulated warmers. Popular styles of standard foodservice pan warmers are shown built into point-of-service work stations. (Courtesy Franklin Products Corporation)

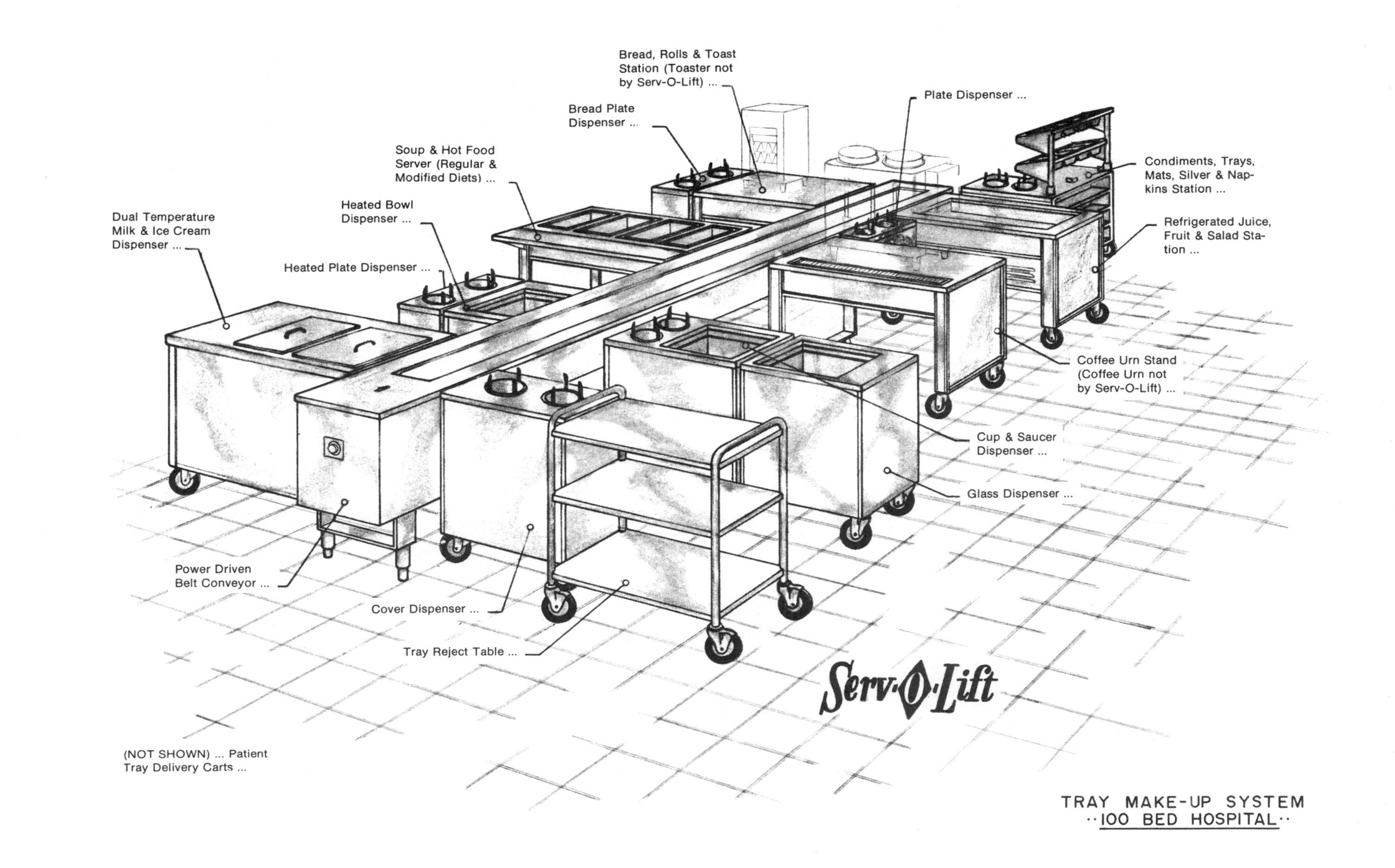

Figure 7-16. Tray makeup system "100 bed hospital." (Courtesy Serv-O-Lift Corporation)

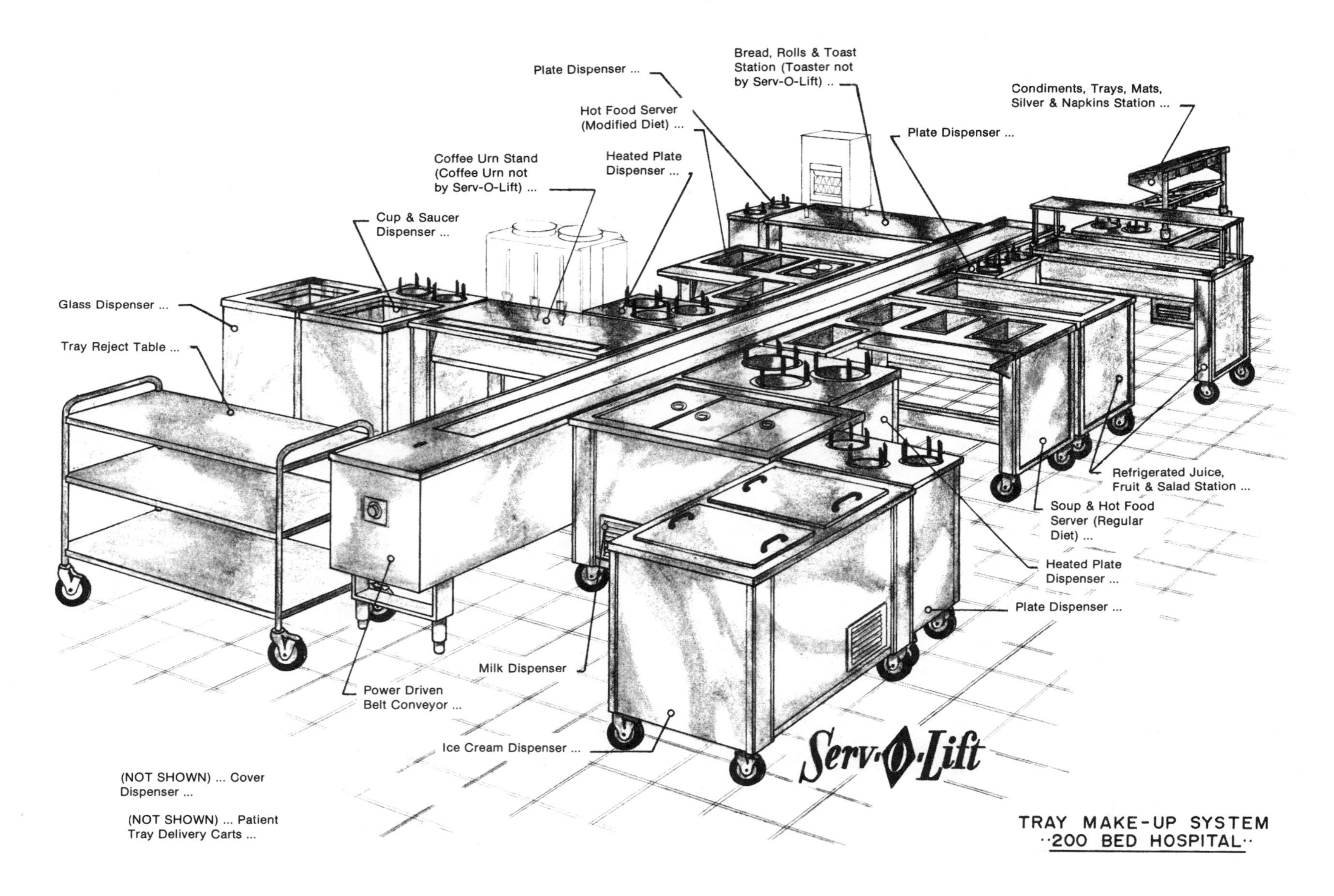

Figure 7-17. Tray makeup system "200 bed hospital." (Courtesy Serv-O-Lift Corporation)

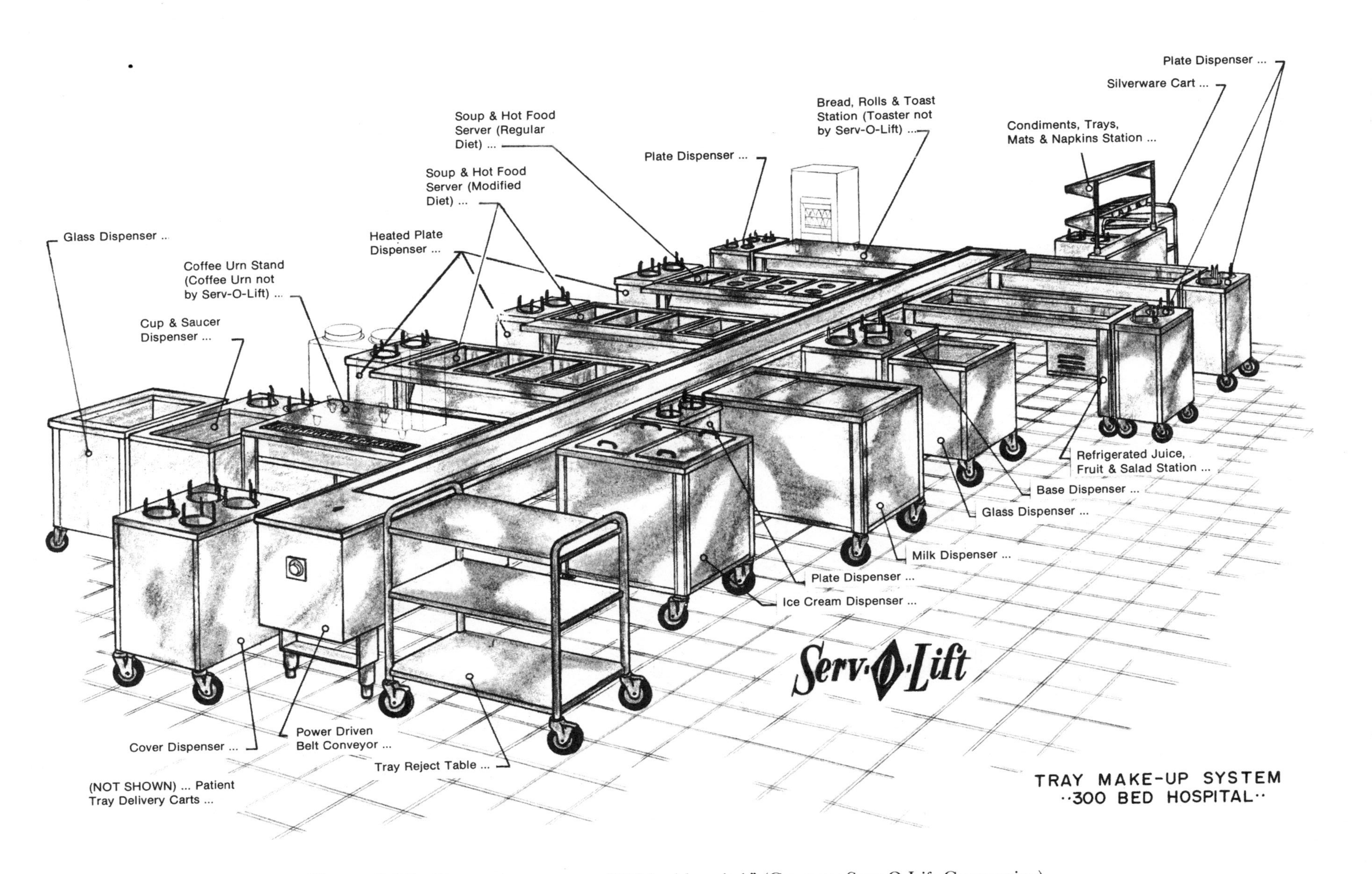

Figure 7-18. Tray makeup system "300 bed hospital." (Courtesy Serv-O-Lift Corporation)

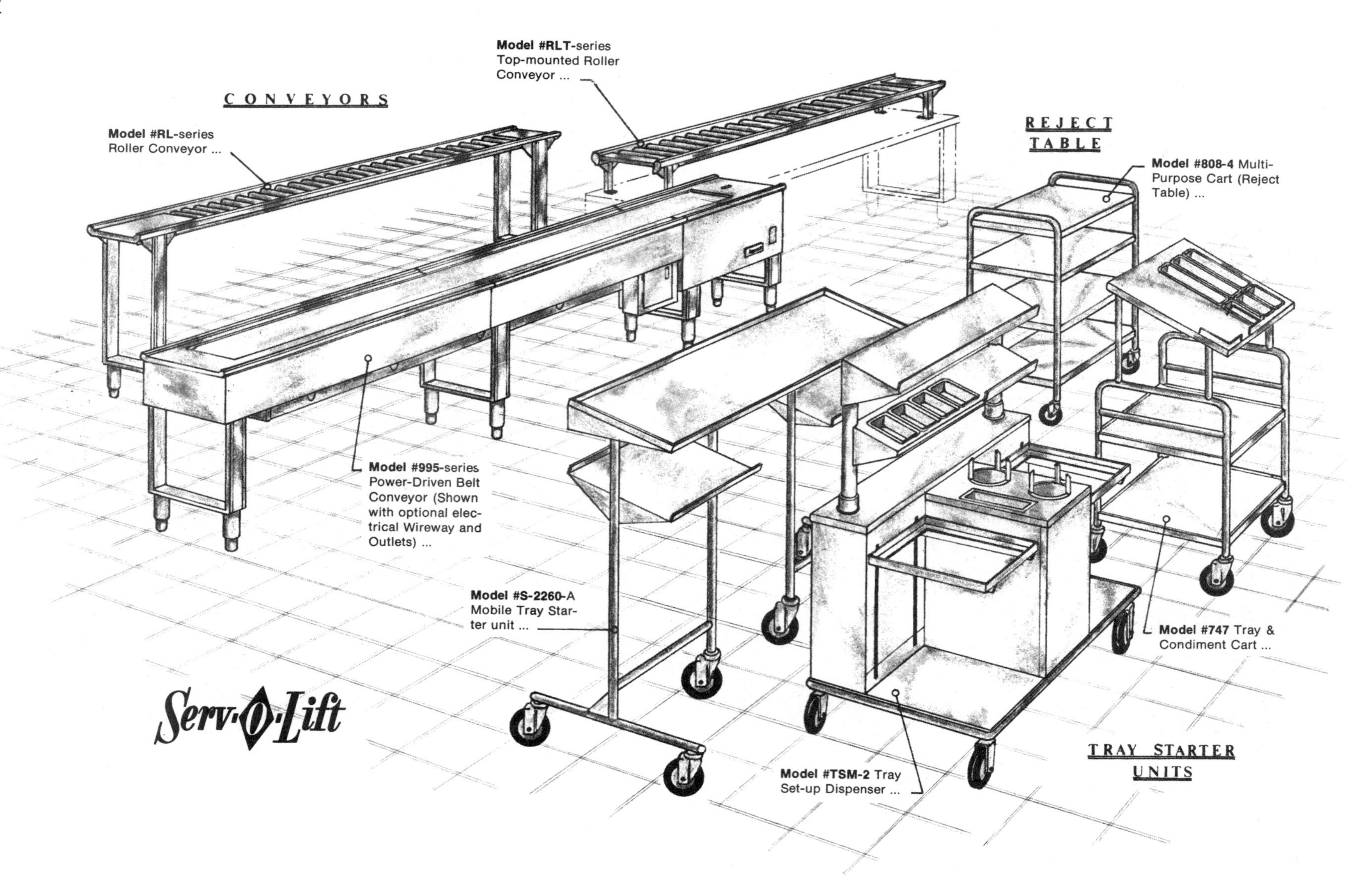

Figure 7-19. Conveyors, reject table, tray starter units. (Courtesy Serv-O-Lift Corporation)

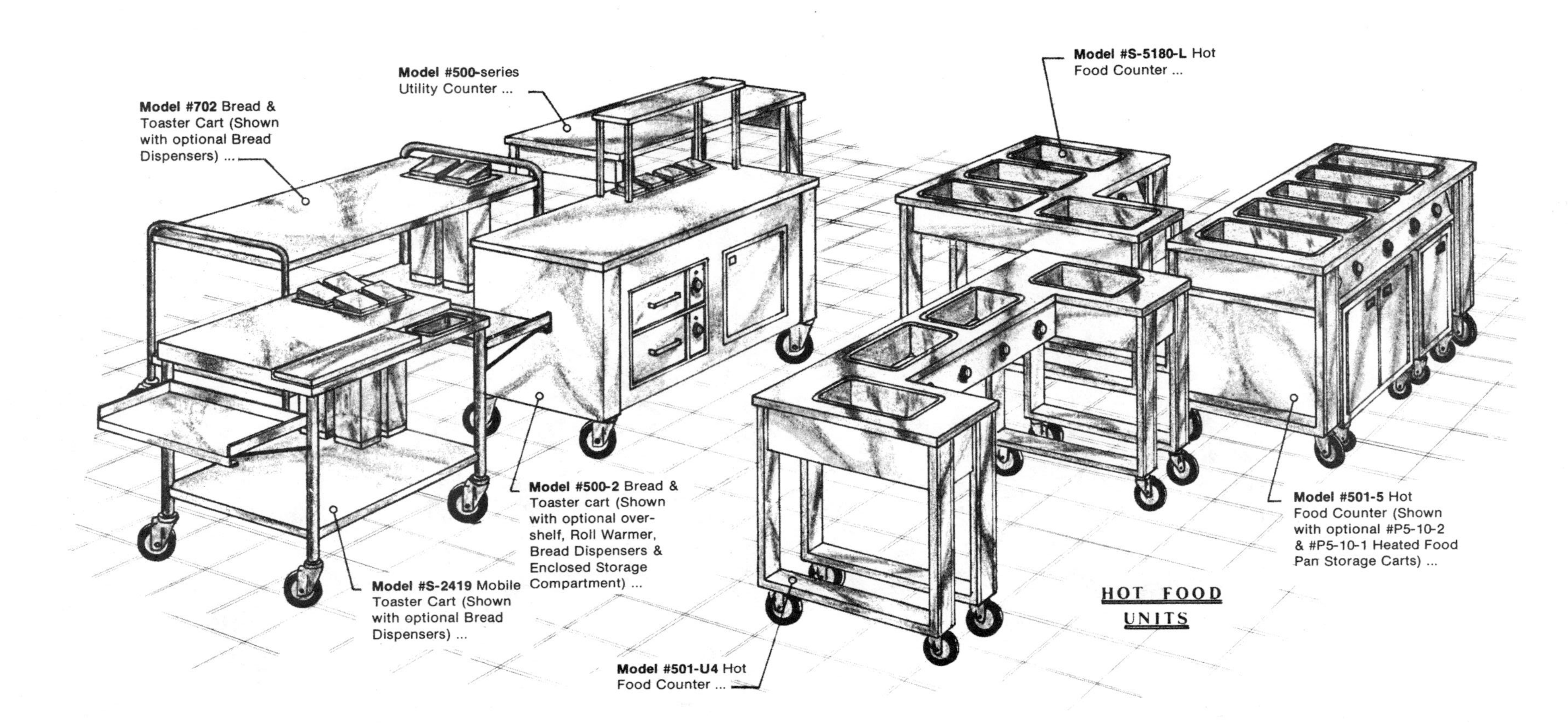

Figure 7-20. Bread, rolls, and toaster stations; hot food units. (Courtesy Serv-O-Lift Corporation)

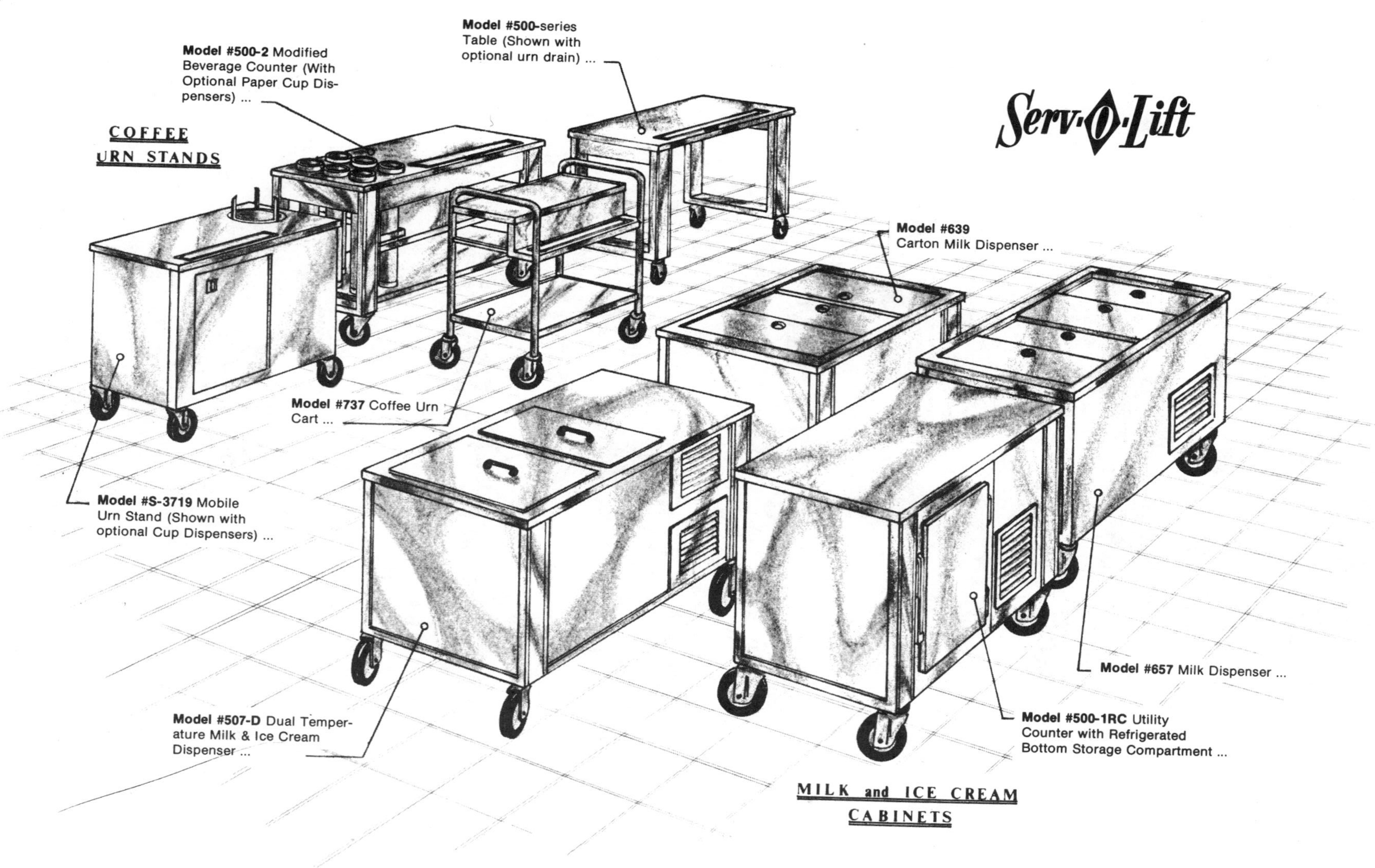

Figure 7-21. Coffee urn stands; milk and ice cream cabinets. (Courtesy Serv-O-Lift Corporation)

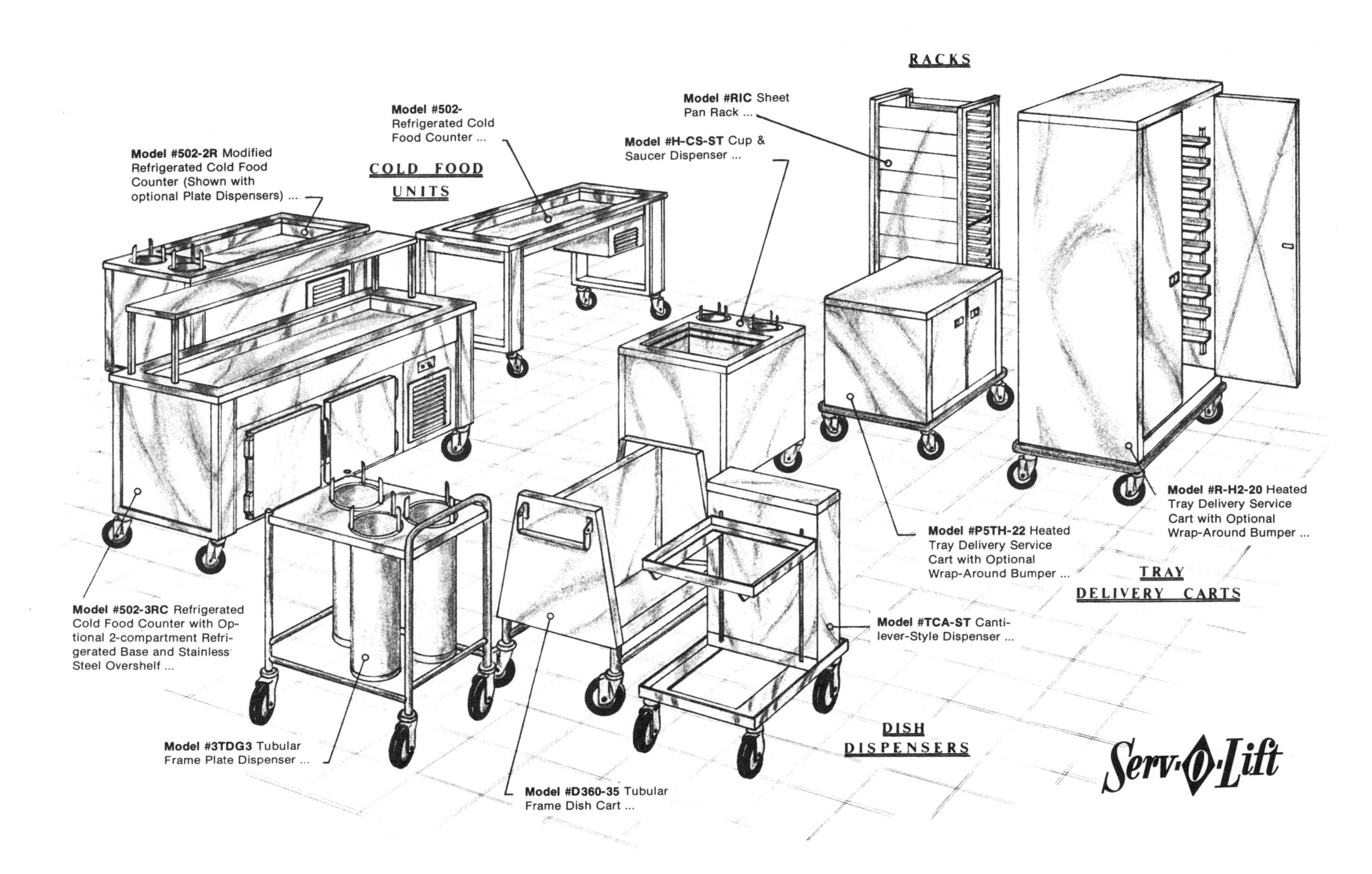

Figure 7-22. Cold food units; racks; tray delivery carts; dish dispensers. (Courtesy Serv-O-Lift Corporation)

8

Warewashing and Sanitation Systems

WAREWASHING

Dish machines are sized by production capability per hour, but the selection of proper warewashing equipment must be carefully analyzed because the variations and possibilities are staggering. (See Figures 8–1 through 8–38.) The variables include space available, type of service, energy considerations, water conditions, local codes, detergent systems, handling systems, and the budget, among others. After much discussion, the authors decided to reduce this chapter to interesting basics, realizing that the user's ultimate choice will be properly laid out, engineered, and installed. The facts presented here will aid user selection.

An expert once formulated this "Basic Law of Dishwashing": There are only two possibilities—either the dish rack moves through a set spray pattern, or the spray pattern moves over the dish rack. Motion of either type is essential to cover all the surfaces of the dishware completely. Understanding this, the user will have mastered the whole concept!

To do an efficient, economical dishwashing job, one must remember five fundamental cost controls:

1. Optimum utilization of the labor of the sanitation personnel.
2. Detergent control through adequate prescraping and prewashing facilities.
3. Machine running time control by timing full loads rather than fractional loads.
4. Wetting agent (rinse dry) control.
5. Reduction of breakage.

The dish machines we present generally require wash water and boosted water at normally accepted temperatures. A consideration of energy-style machines follows (under "Low-Temperature Warewashing Procedures . . .").

Dishwashing, whether manual or mechanical, can be defined as using nothing more than some hot water, detergent, and a lot of motion to clean tableware. In mechanical dishwashing, the three essential ingredients are: (1) hot water at N.S.F.-approved temperatures, (2) detergent, and (3) a sufficient time for water recirculation, and flow pattern.

Water for a commercial dishwasher can be heated by electricity, gas, or steam.

In electric machines the heating units are immersed in the water tank, a process offering the direct-heat advantages found in electric fryers. These units (up to four in some tanks) are usually 5 kw each.

The following warewashing plan sets forth a variety of problem-solving solutions that are in actual operation around the world. It is not the intent of this book to explore the mechanical pros and cons of various manufacturers, or to brainstorm their options. Proper installation and service availability are the rule, and this area of the commercial food operation requires the help of experts. Knowledgeable and able direct factory representatives are available to provide users the assistance they need.

LOW-TEMPERATURE WAREWASHING PROCEDURES AND TROUBLESHOOTING GUIDE

PROCEDURES

1. Always check levels of detergent, sanitizing, and rinse additive prior to operating the machine.
2. Check the upper and lower wash and rinse arms. Clean them as necessary.
3. Inspect and, if necessary, clean the drain screens and scrap trays.
4. Fill the machine with water; the temperature should be 140°F minimum.
5. Rack the dishes, prerinse them thoroughly, load the rack into the machine, and push the start button.
6. Unload the dish machine when the power light goes out. Let the dishes air-dry and place them in storage areas.
7. At the end of each day, drain the machine, clean the arms, scrap the trays, and drain and replace all parts after cleaning.

TROUBLESHOOTING

Condition and Corrective Action

- *Machine won't fill:* Be sure doors are closed. Check to see if power is on. Be sure no valves are shut off on the incoming water line. Be sure drain is in place.
- *Water temperature is low:* Most low-temperature machines do not have heaters. Check the temperature of the incoming water.
- *Machine goes on, but does not pump water:* Be sure the machine is filled to the proper level. Check the wash arms to see that they are not clogged.
- *Audible and visual sanitizer alert is "on":* Check and, if necessary, replenish the sanitizing solution.
- *Poor results:* Check detergent containers. Check temperatures. Check the wash arms. Check the water level in the wash tank. Be sure of good scrapping procedures. Use proper silver, glass, and dishracks, and do not overload.

The above procedures should be utilized to ensure that the machine runs properly and produces clean dishware. The troubleshooting guide represents only some of the problems that you might encounter. As a general rule, if you cannot solve a problem by the above methods and need help, you should contact either your machine representative or your chemical representative.

WAREWASHING AND SANITATION CHECKLIST

The following considerations are important:

- The monthly cost of chemicals.
- Adequacy of water and power supplies.
- Whether the machine needs venting.
- Whether there are enough soil and clean tables.
- Whether to store racks on dollies.
- A shelf for chemicals.
- Adequacy of primary water heat.
- Need for extra racks.
- Need for presoak sink.
- Rack shelves for table, for glasses and cups.
- Adequacy of disposal.
- What options are available for booster.
- Whether a maintenance contract will pay.
- Need for a rack return.
- Need for a curved guide at clean intersection to speed discharge of racks.
- Careful check of shop drawings for gauge of metal, dimensions, and construction of warewash areas. Most dish tables are custom-designed.
- Plate shelf for landing area.

APPROXIMATE SHIPPING WEIGHTS OF SELECTED EQUIPMENT

	Equipment	Weight
___	Undercounter DishWasher	175#
	Single Tank DishWasher	450#
	44″ Conveyor DishWasher	890#
	66″ Conveyor DishWasher	1,250#
	76″ Conveyor DishWasher	1,380#
	86″ Conveyor DishWasher	1,650#

___ Flight Type DishWashers Factory Quoted

___ DishTables Factory Quoted

___ Disposals

1/2 HP	45#
1 HP	50#
3 HP	115#
5 HP	220#

___ Boosters, Compact Electric

9 KW	118#
24 KW	142#
54 KW	142#

ACKNOWLEDGMENTS

Material for the "Warewashing" section was provided by Sam Venezia, District Manager, Hobart Manufacturing. The "Low-Temperature Warewashing Procedures and Troubleshooting Guide" is used courtesy of Economics Lab.

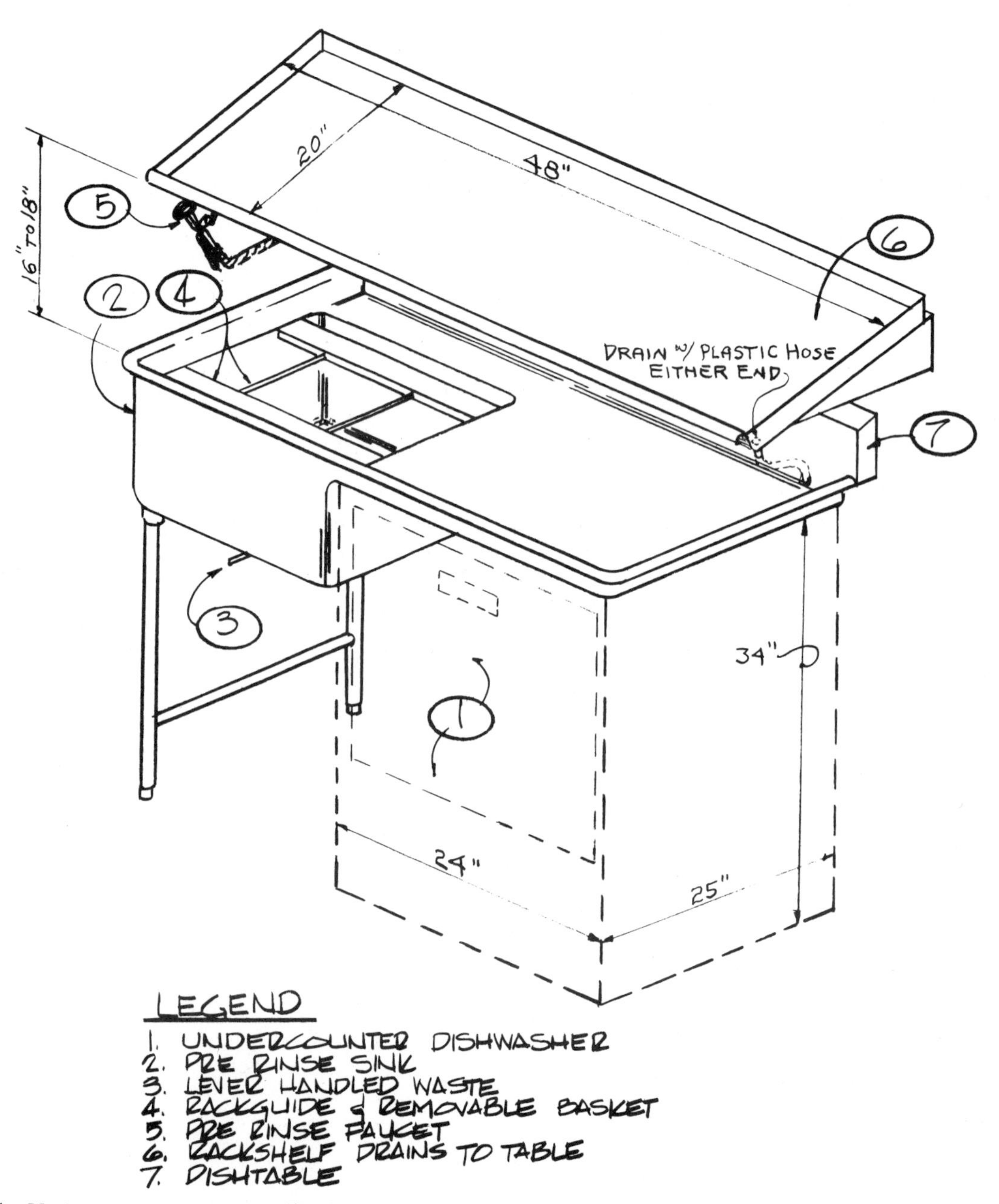

Figure 8-1. Undercounter dishwasher. The small undercounter dishwasher shown with accessories has a 4½-minute cycle with hot water or chemical rinse. Normally the smaller machines will handle china, glass, and silver for about 40 to 45 patrons per hour.

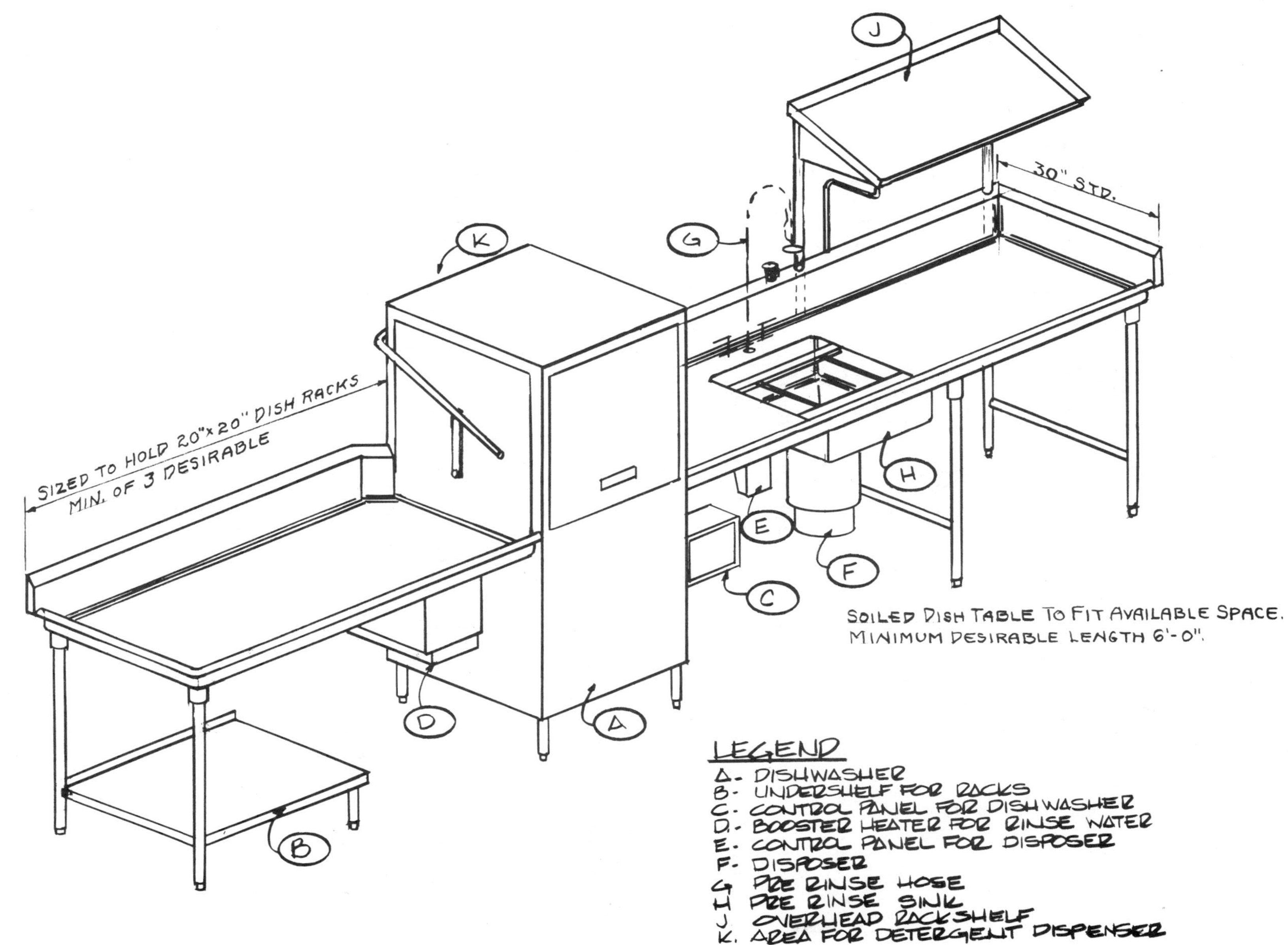

Figure 8-2. Single-tank dishwasher. The dishwasher shown is available for a straight-through operation or a corner installation. All shapes and sizes of tables are available. The rinse can be chemical, or a hot water rinse at 180°F by using a booster. The machines can have left or right operation. This machine is also a door type, as the operator pushes the rack through the door openings. It normally handles the needs of up to 200 persons per hour.

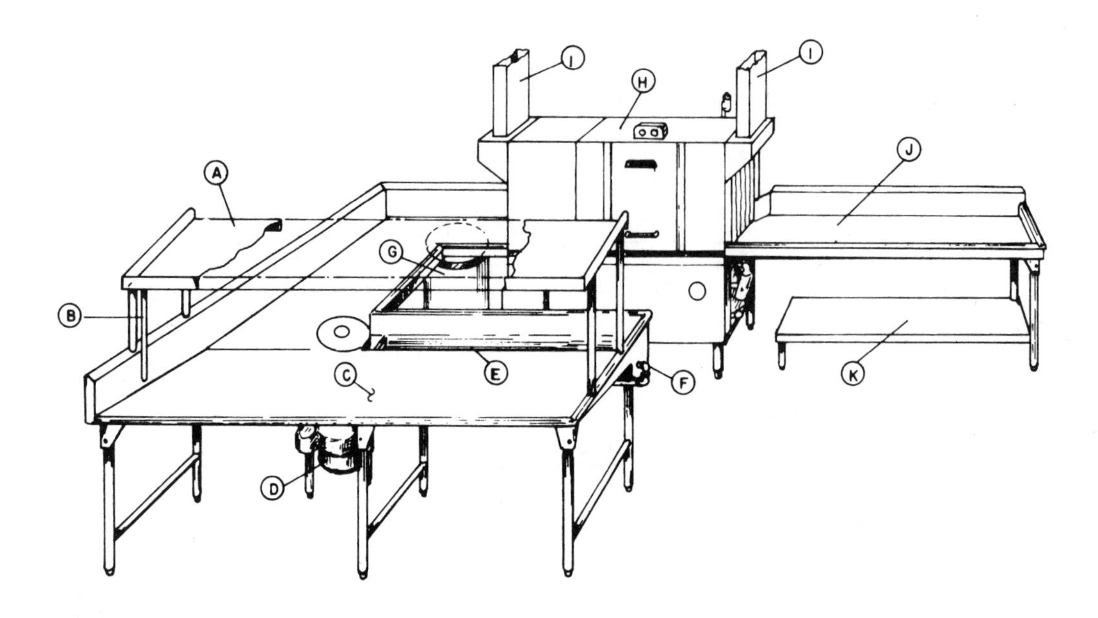

TYPICAL DISHWASHING LAYOUT

A—Rack shelf pitched to waitress' side of soiled dish table
B—Bleeder tube
C—Soiled dish table. Note pitch to trough
D—Garbage disposer. Alternative would be pre-rinse sink
E—Trough to disposer with silver saver stop
F—Water inlet to trough inter-connected with disposer
G—Hot water booster - location optional
H—Dishwashing machine
I—Vent ducts
J—Clean dish table. Suggested minimum length to accommodate 3 dish racks
K—Removable rack storage shelf provides for easy cleaning

Figure 8-3. Conveyor dishwasher. Larger dishwashers such as the 44-inches-long machine in this figure come without a door; the rack is pulled through the machine by conveyor. Much larger systems use pegs; dishes are loaded directly into pegs, and racks are used for glasses, cups, bowls, and silverware. These flight-type machines are for very high-volume operations, such as hospitals, hotels, resorts, and educational institutions. (Reprinted, by permission, from Carl Scriven and James Stevens, *Food Equipment Facts*. © 1988 by Van Nostrand Reinhold.)

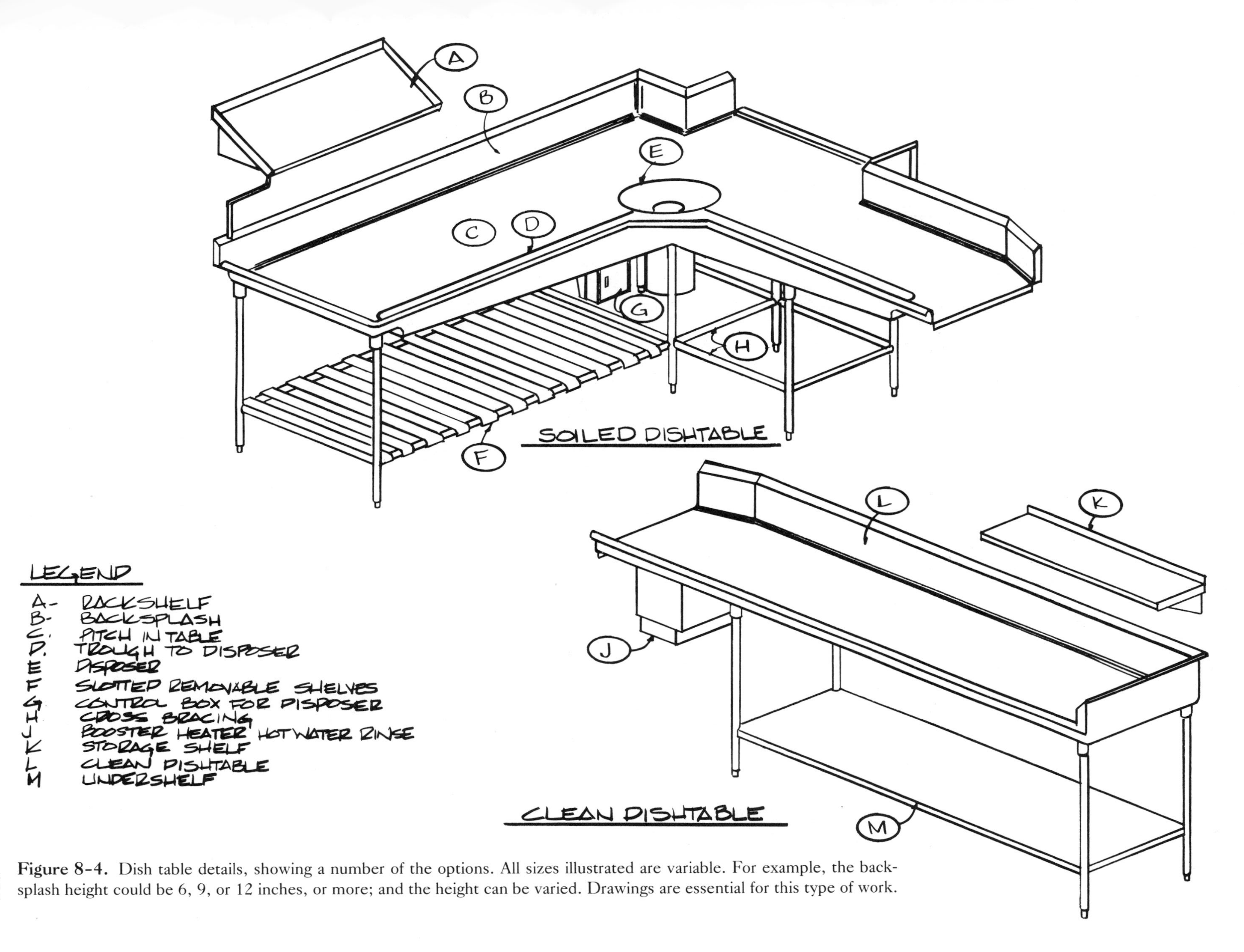

Figure 8-4. Dish table details, showing a number of the options. All sizes illustrated are variable. For example, the backsplash height could be 6, 9, or 12 inches, or more; and the height can be varied. Drawings are essential for this type of work.

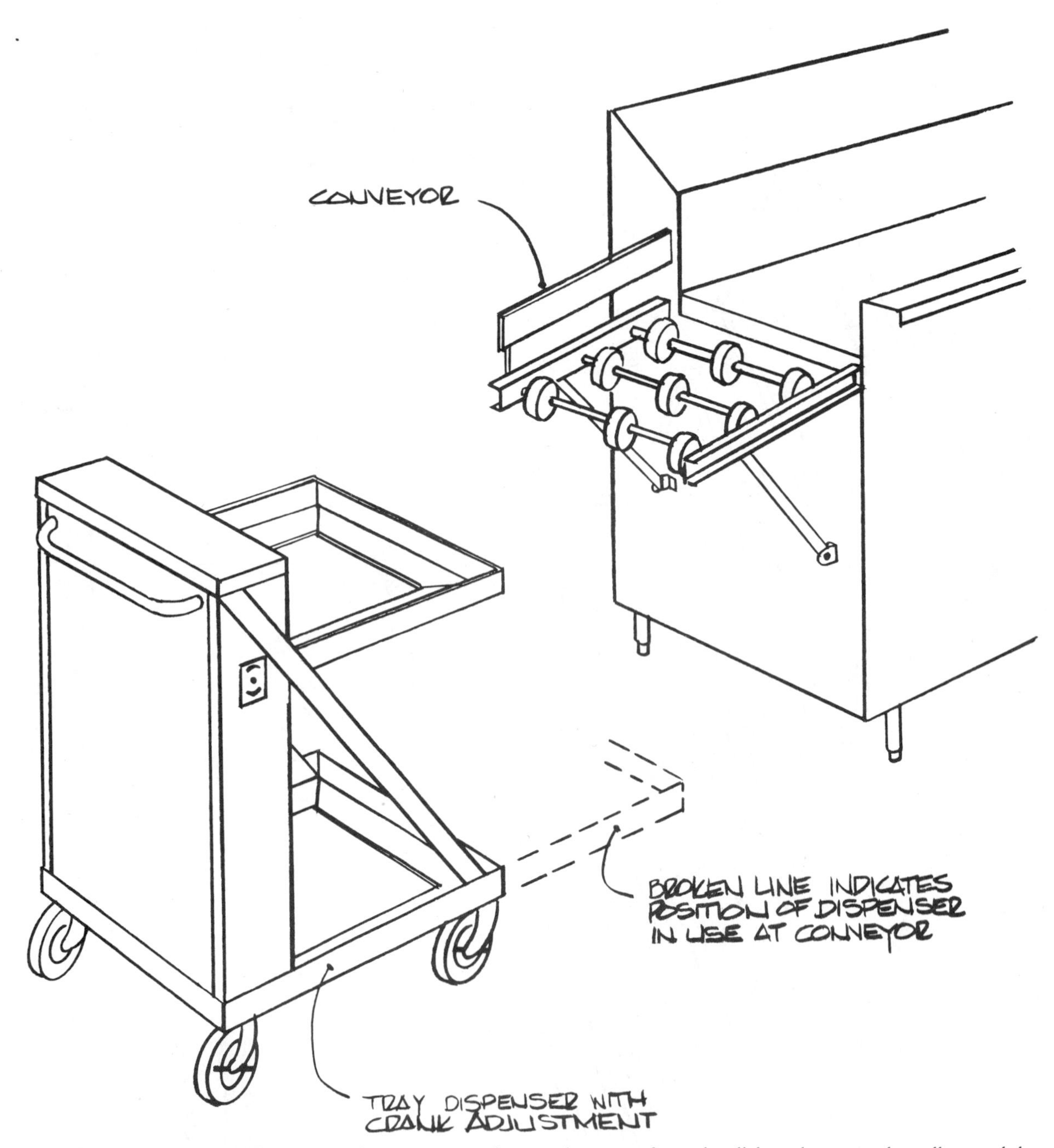

Figure 8-5. Tray dispenser. The automatic tray system shown takes trays from the dishwasher over the rollers and deposits them on a tray dispenser that automatically adjusts to the load. (Courtesy Serv-O-Lift Corporation)

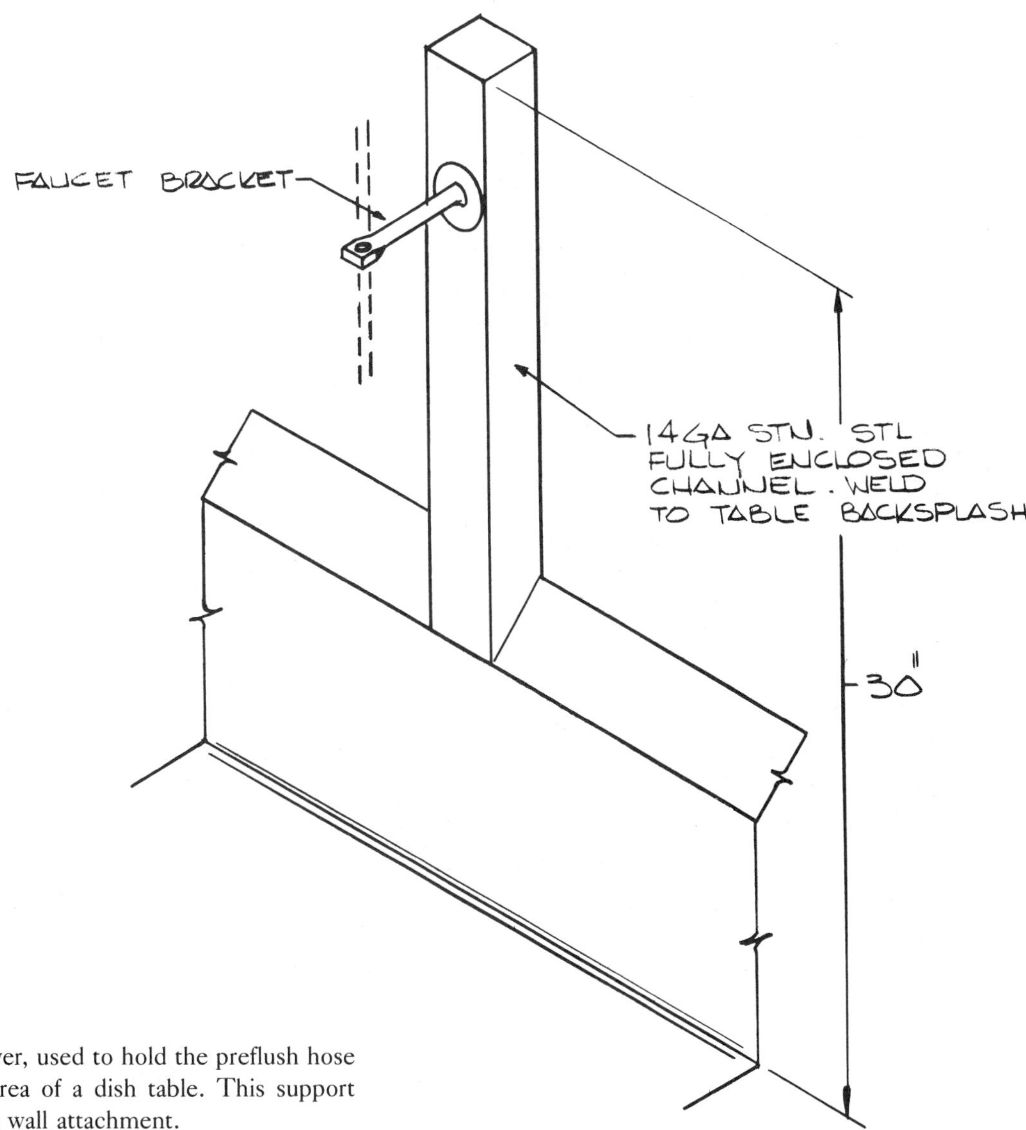

Figure 8-6. Faucet tower, used to hold the preflush hose assembly at the soiled area of a dish table. This support eliminates the need for a wall attachment.

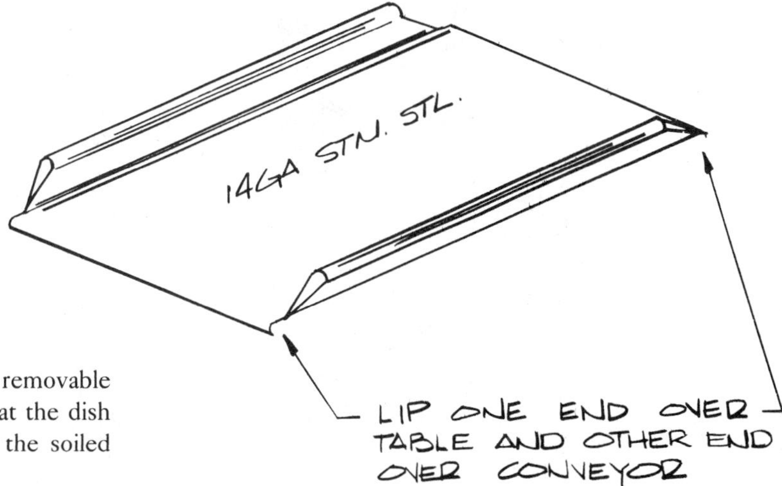

Figure 8-7. Bridge for a dish table. A handy removable bridge allows the operator to bridge two tables at the dish area, or from the conveyor to a table. Sliding the soiled product eliminates lifting.

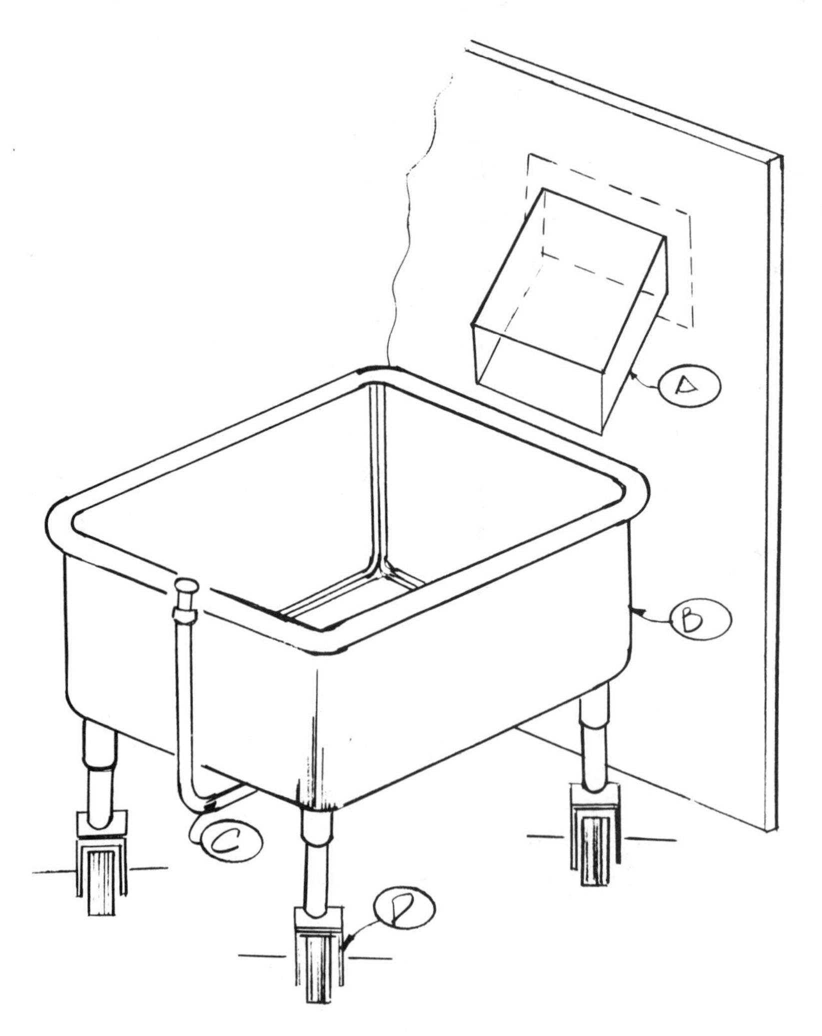

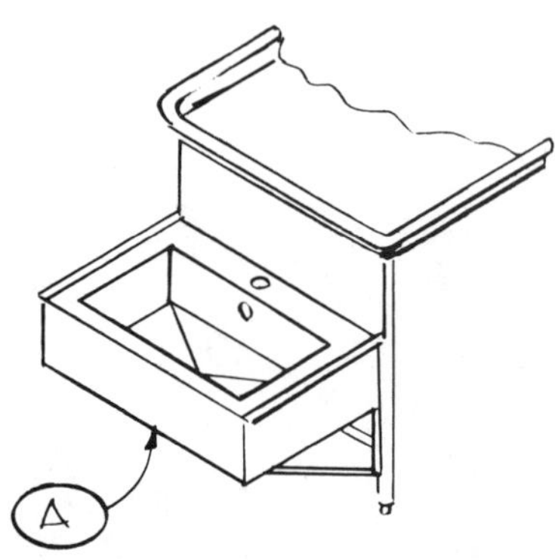

Figure 8-8. Portable soak sink. This sink, as shown, eliminates the loss of a valuable work area on the tabletop and allows self-bussing of silver through a wall or under a table used by the staff. Also shown is a small hand sink that may be attached to the end of a sink drain board or dish table.

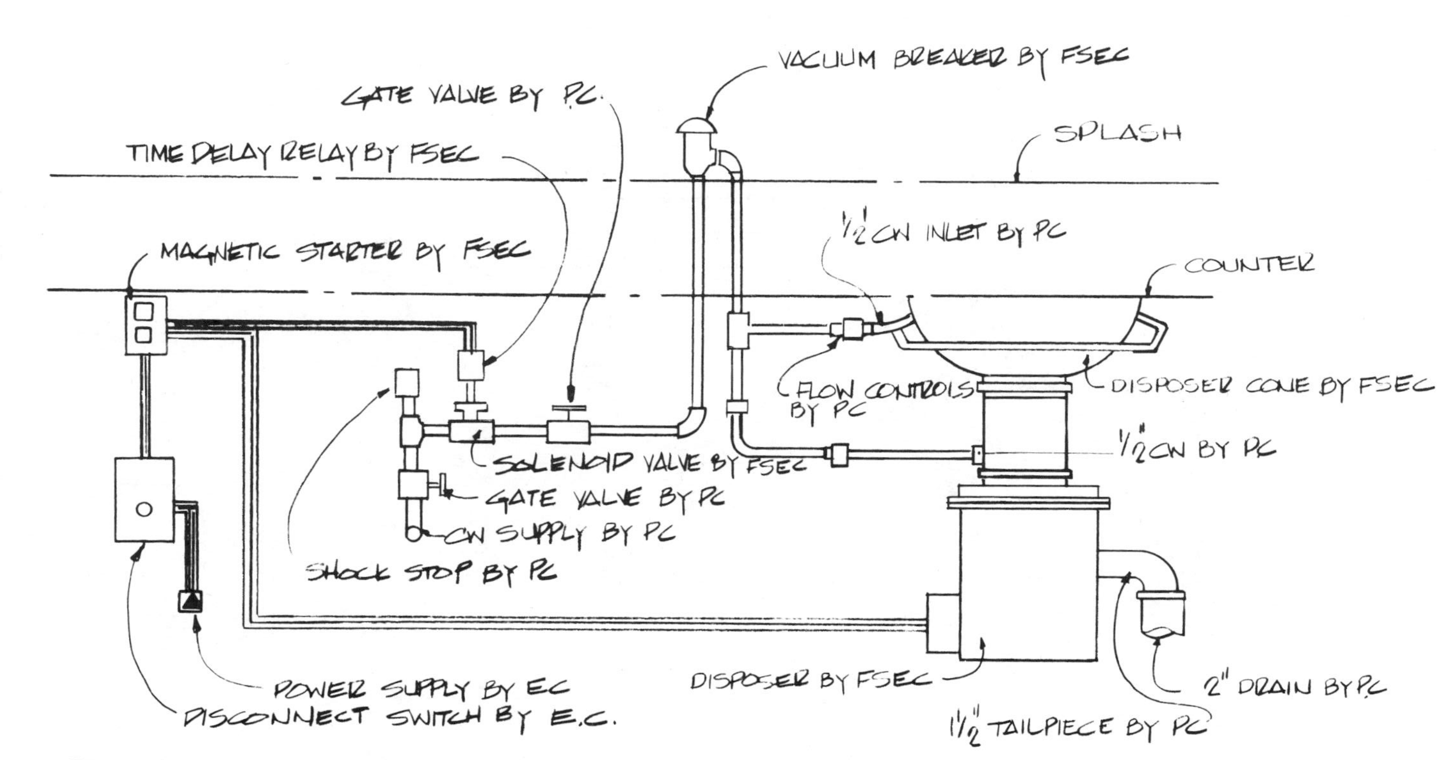

Figure 8-9. Disposal mechanical plan. Showing such a plan to a contractor will clarify a lot of questions about installation. The operator can use this guide to assist his or her own maintenance people in case of a breakdown.

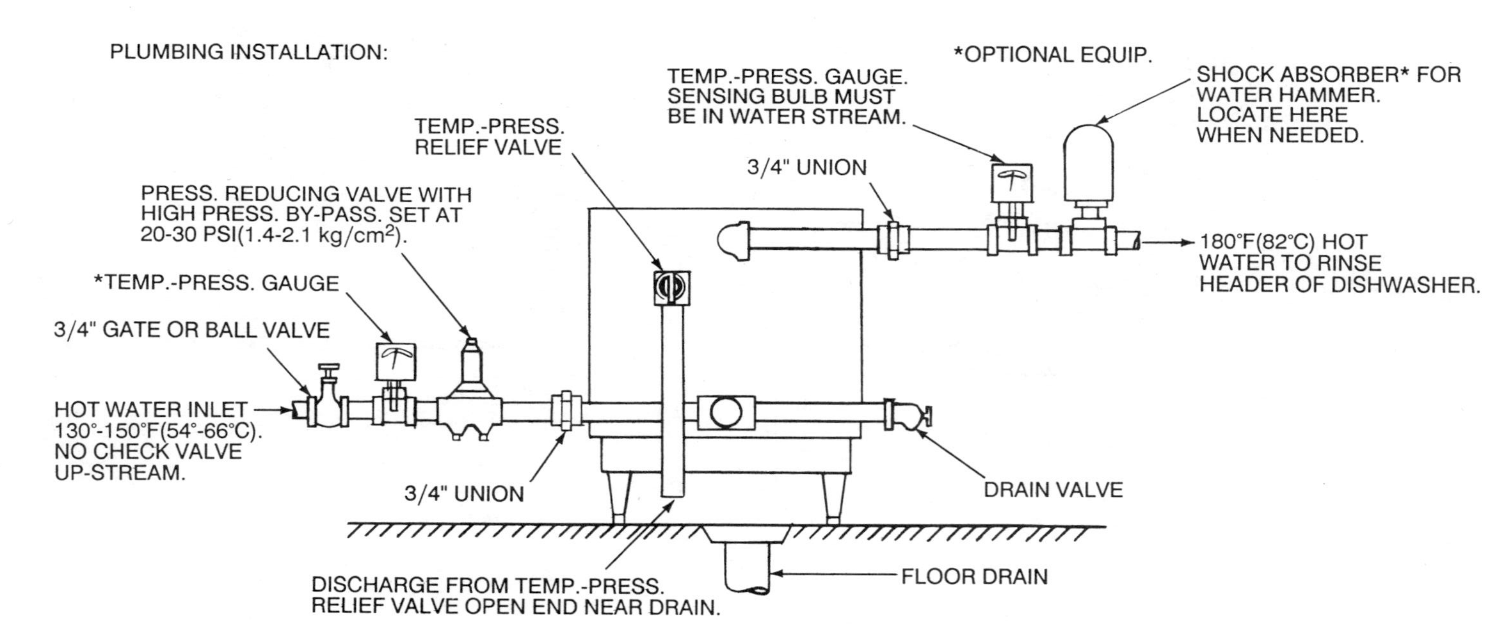

Figure 8-10. Booster guide to installation. This guide has been used for many years to assist in-house maintenance departments, plumbers, and electricians. For installing a new booster, this drawing is an excellent communicator. (Courtesy Hatco Corporation)

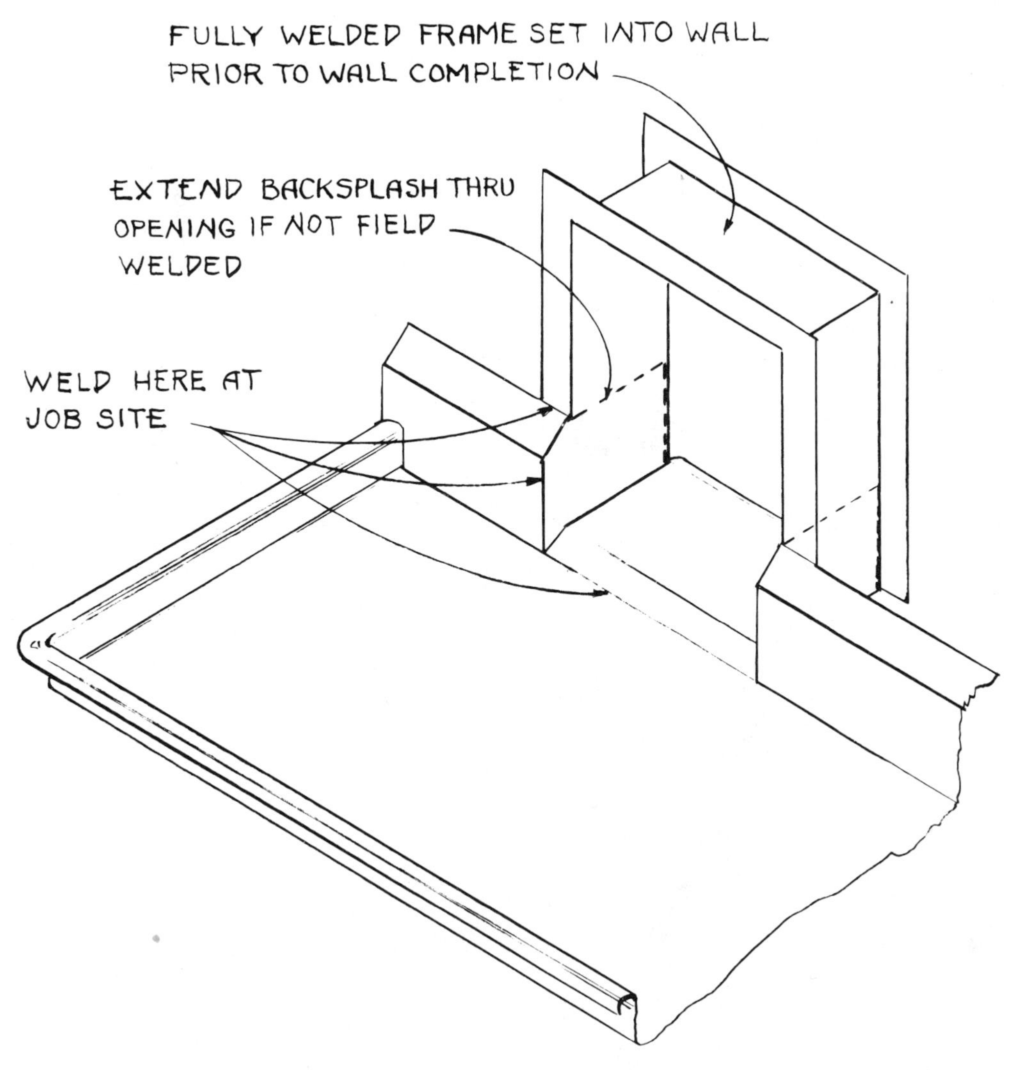

Figure 8-11. Dish pass-through areas with doors are custom-made to fit both new and existing construction. The doors are lockable and must be fire-rated.

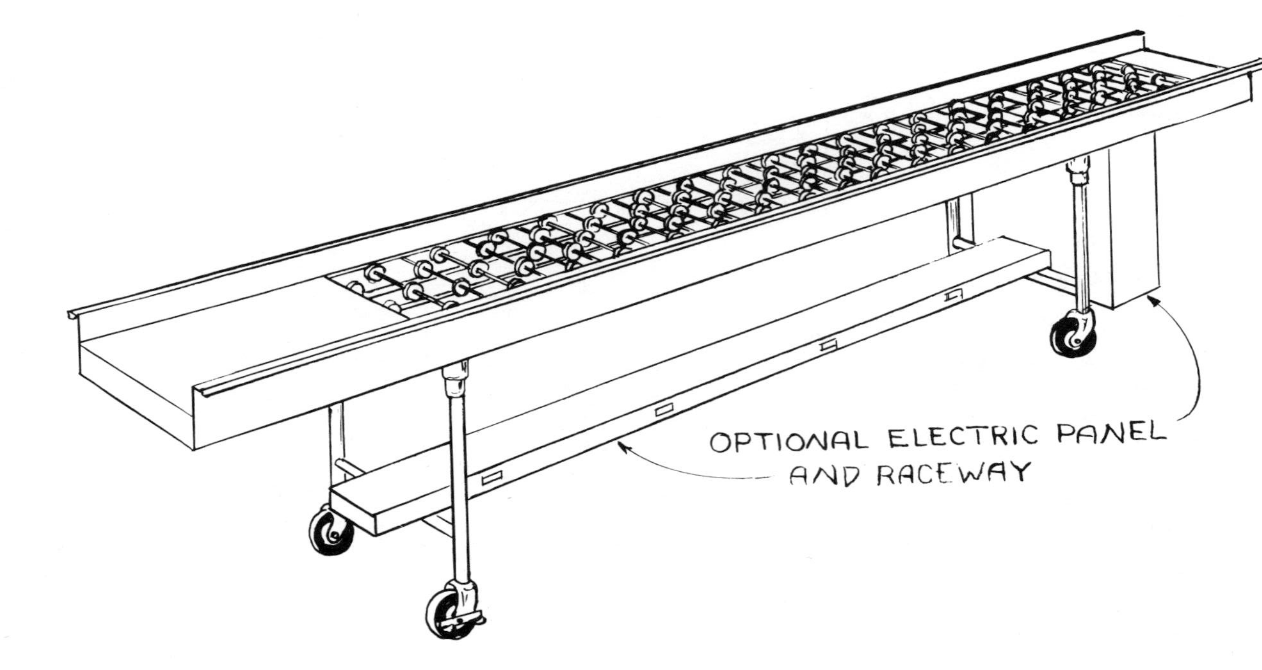

Figure 8-12. Conveyor systems used in dishwashing areas are available in all configurations and custom-built to application. Many are built to mate with the dish machine directly, and are available with numerous options. Shown is a nonelectrical style used in tray makeup systems or for banquet setup. (Courtesy Seco Engineering Systems)

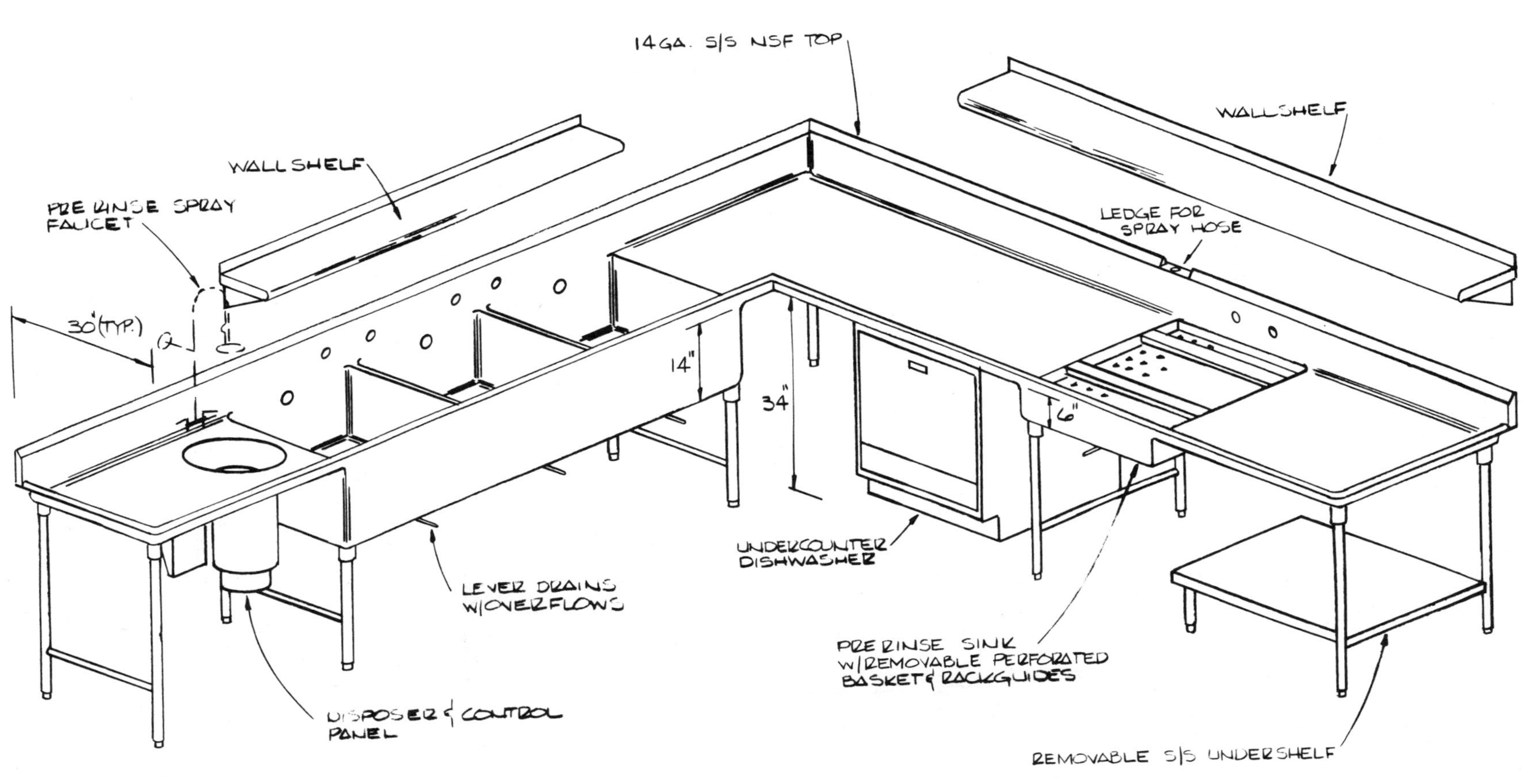

Figure 8-13. L-shaped compartment sink and warewashing sanitation area. (Courtesy Champion Manufacturing)

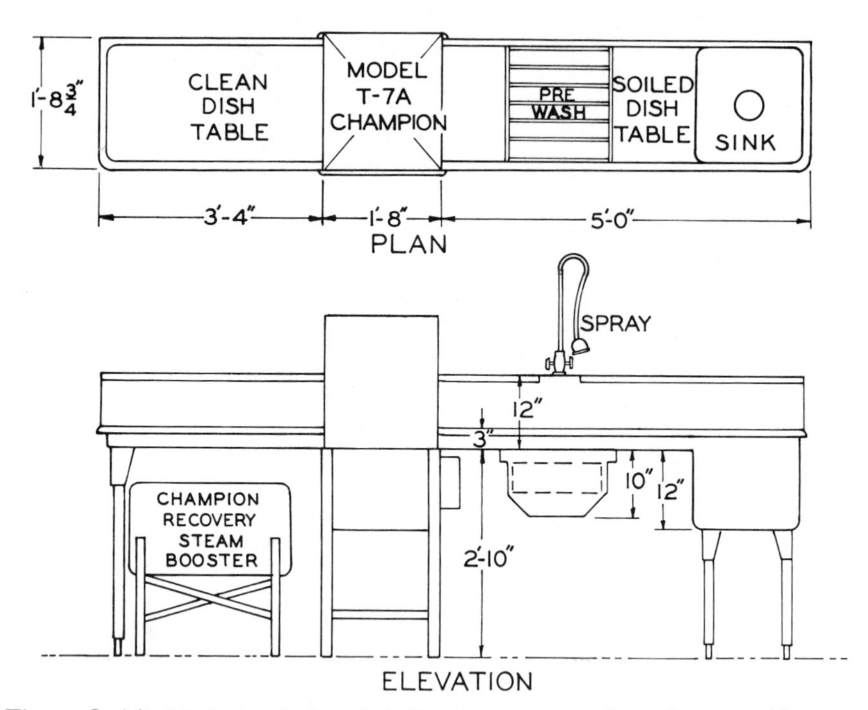

Figure 8-14. Ideal plan for hospital diet kitchen or small ward pantry. (Courtesy Champion Manufacturing)

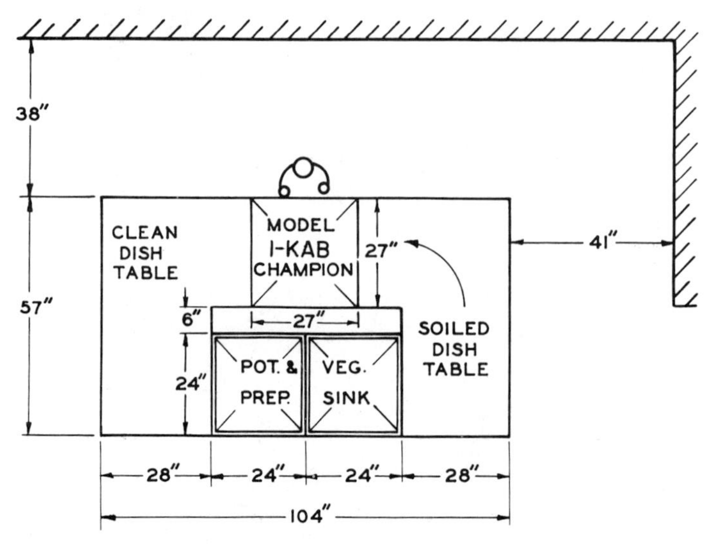

Figure 8-15. Small but workable plan—sinks had to be retained so machine and tables were planned around them. (Courtesy Champion Manufacturing)

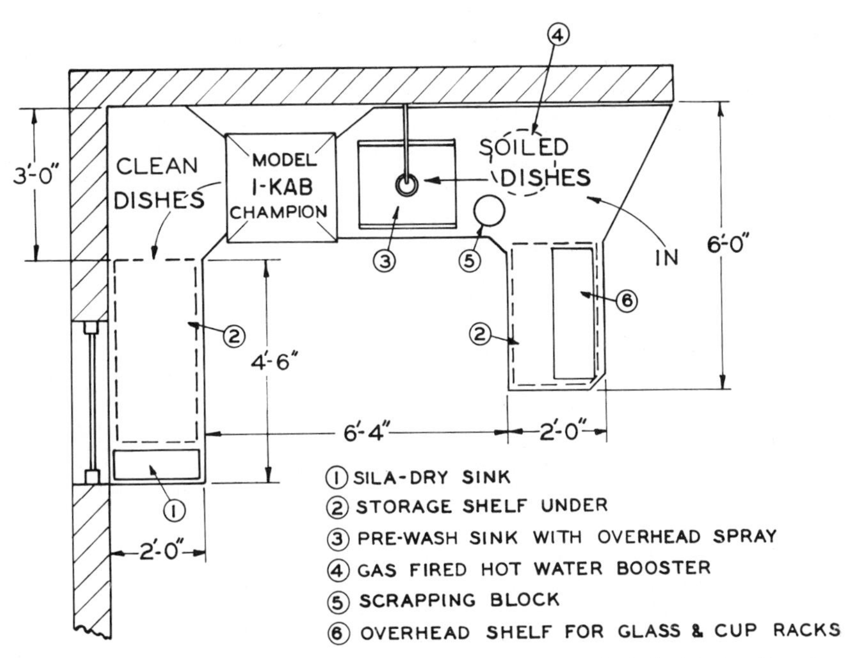

Figure 8-16. Odd-shaped plan to suit limited space. Soiled table is offset from door opening. (Courtesy Champion Manufacturing)

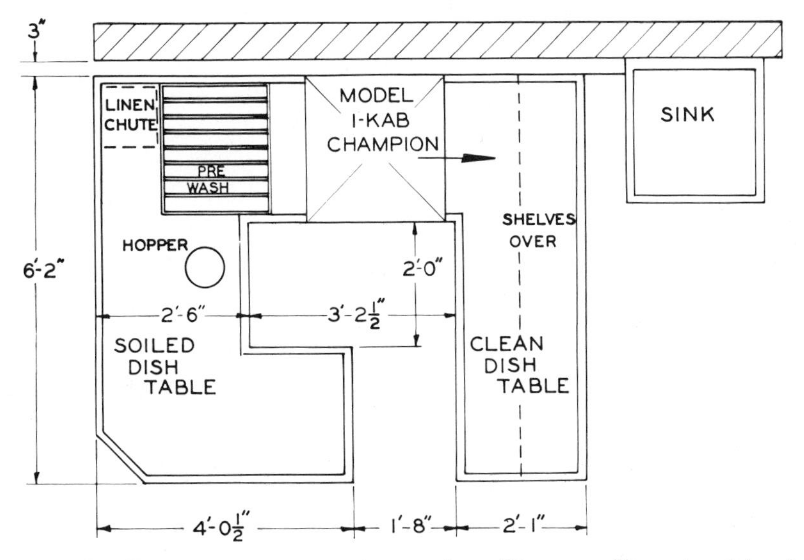

Figure 8-17. Small conventional-type plan. (Courtesy Champion Manufacturing)

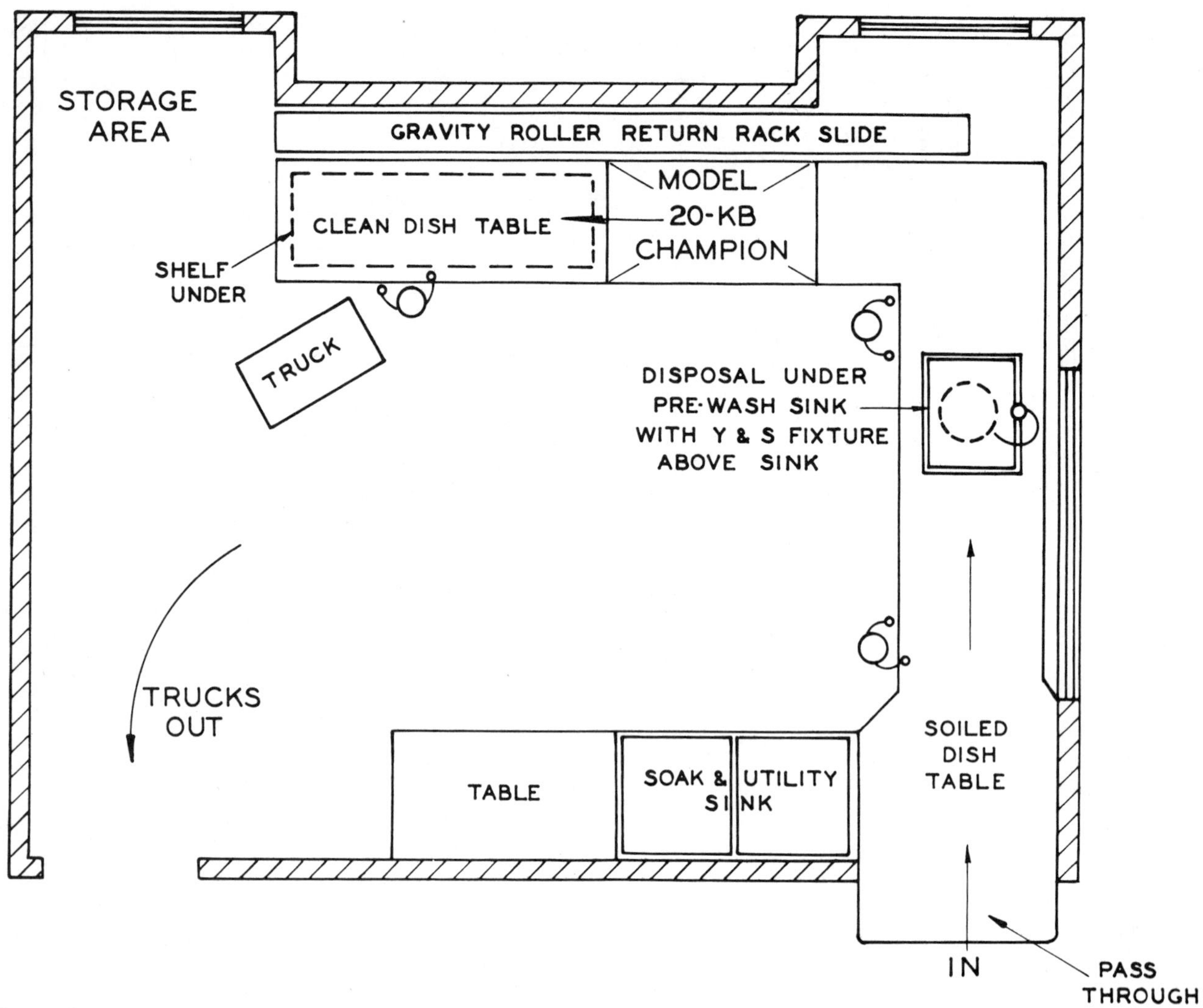

Figure 8-18. Plan devised to satisfy owner's need for just a pass-through into dish pantry. (Courtesy Champion Manufacturing)

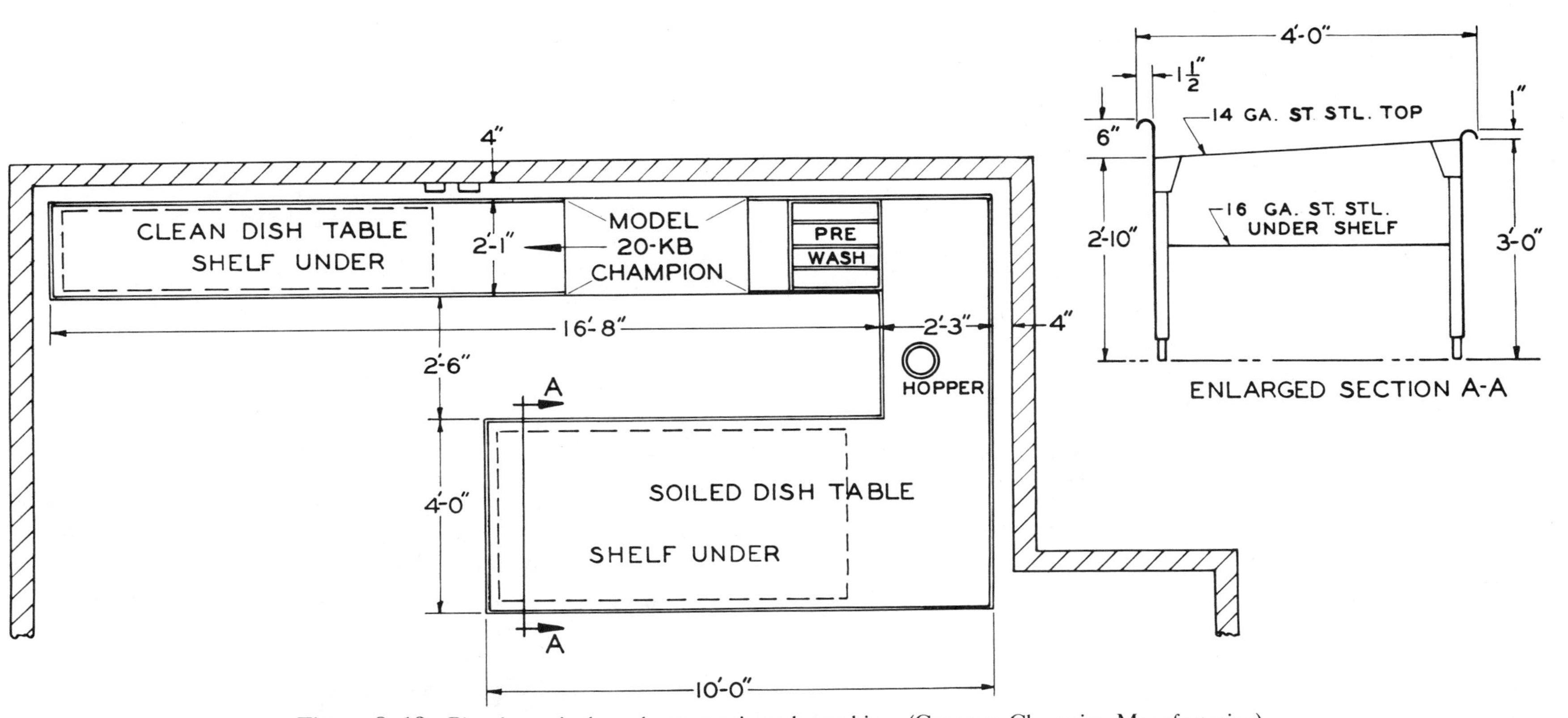

Figure 8-19. Plan for a single-tank automatic rack machine. (Courtesy Champion Manufacturing)

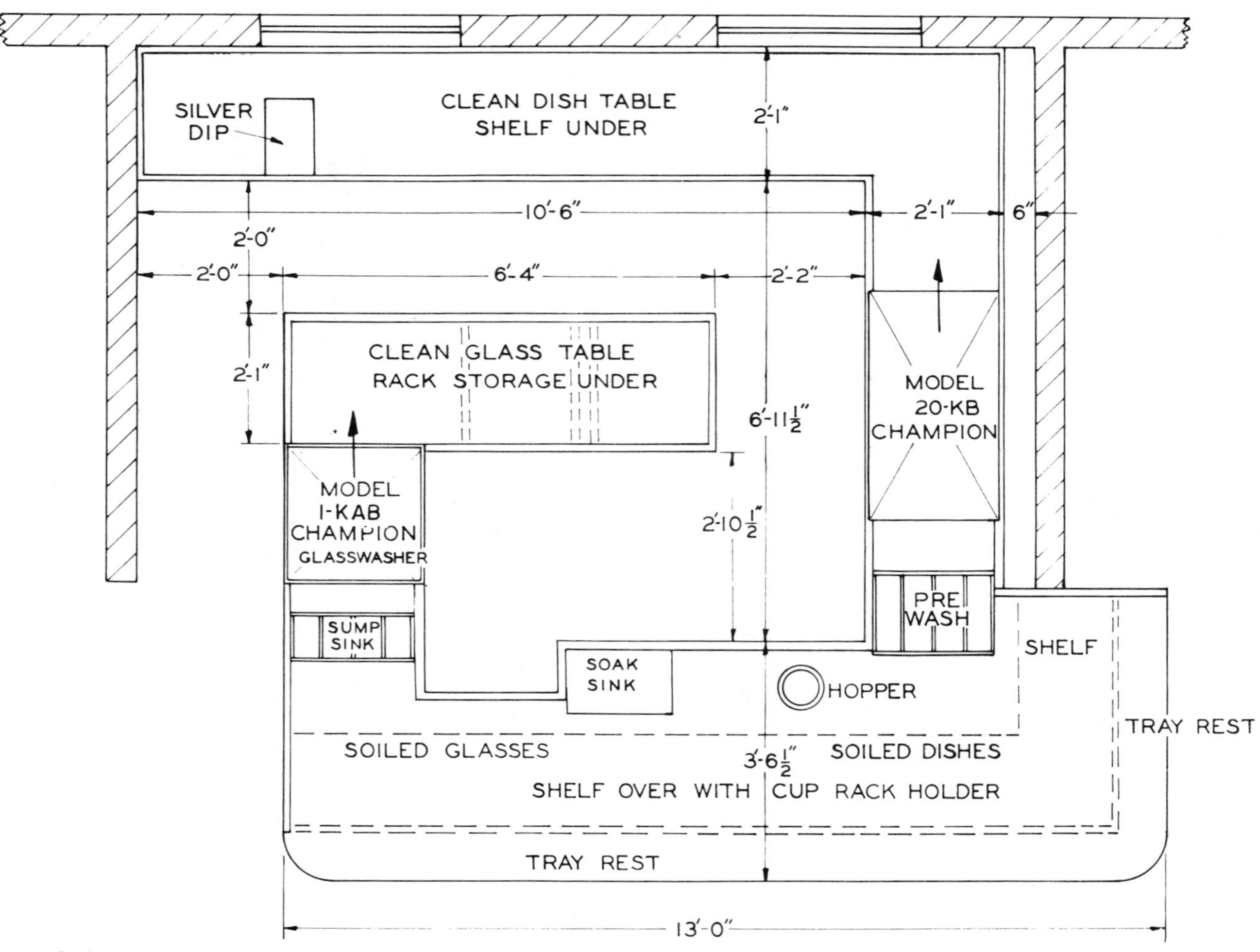

Figure 8-20. Separate machines for dishes and glasses, providing maximum efficiency and good capacity. (Courtesy Champion Manufacturing)

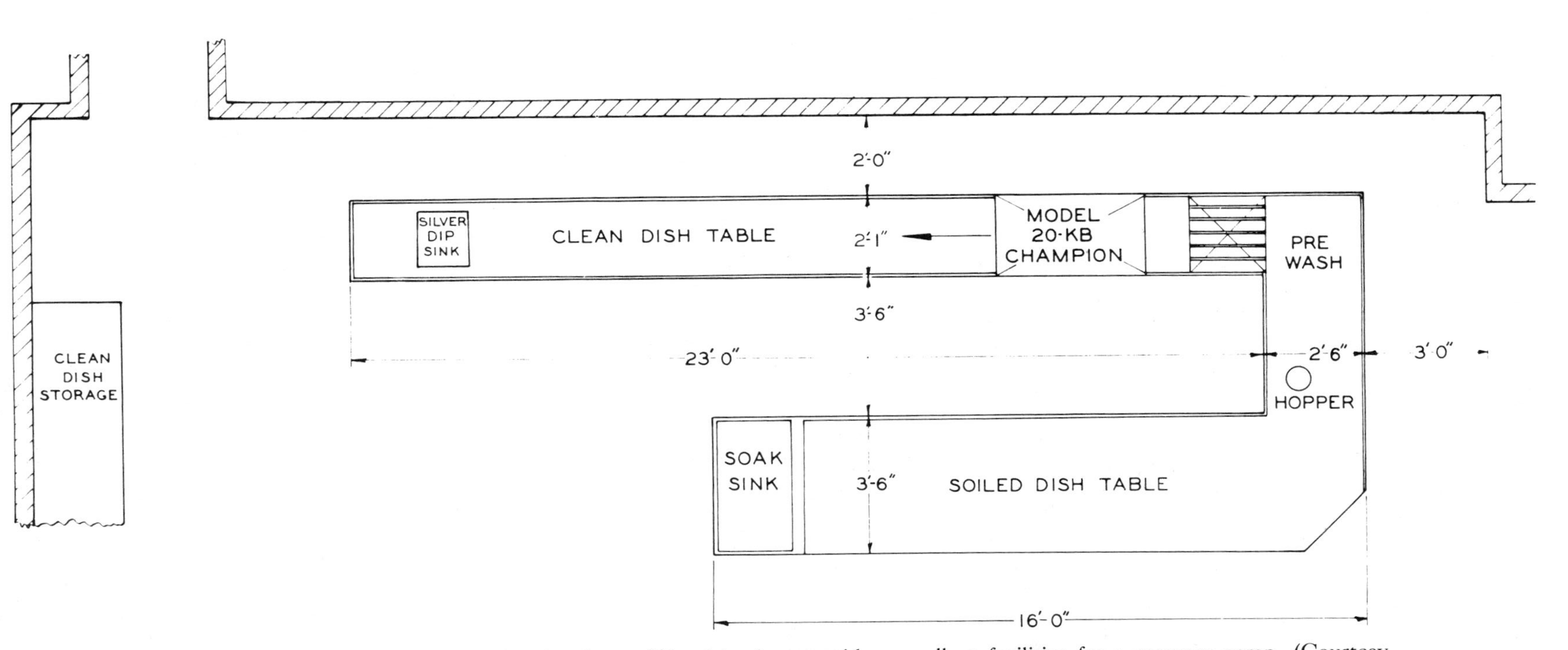

Figure 8-21. Plan that includes rather large dish tables but provides excellent facilities for a summer camp. (Courtesy Champion Manufacturing)

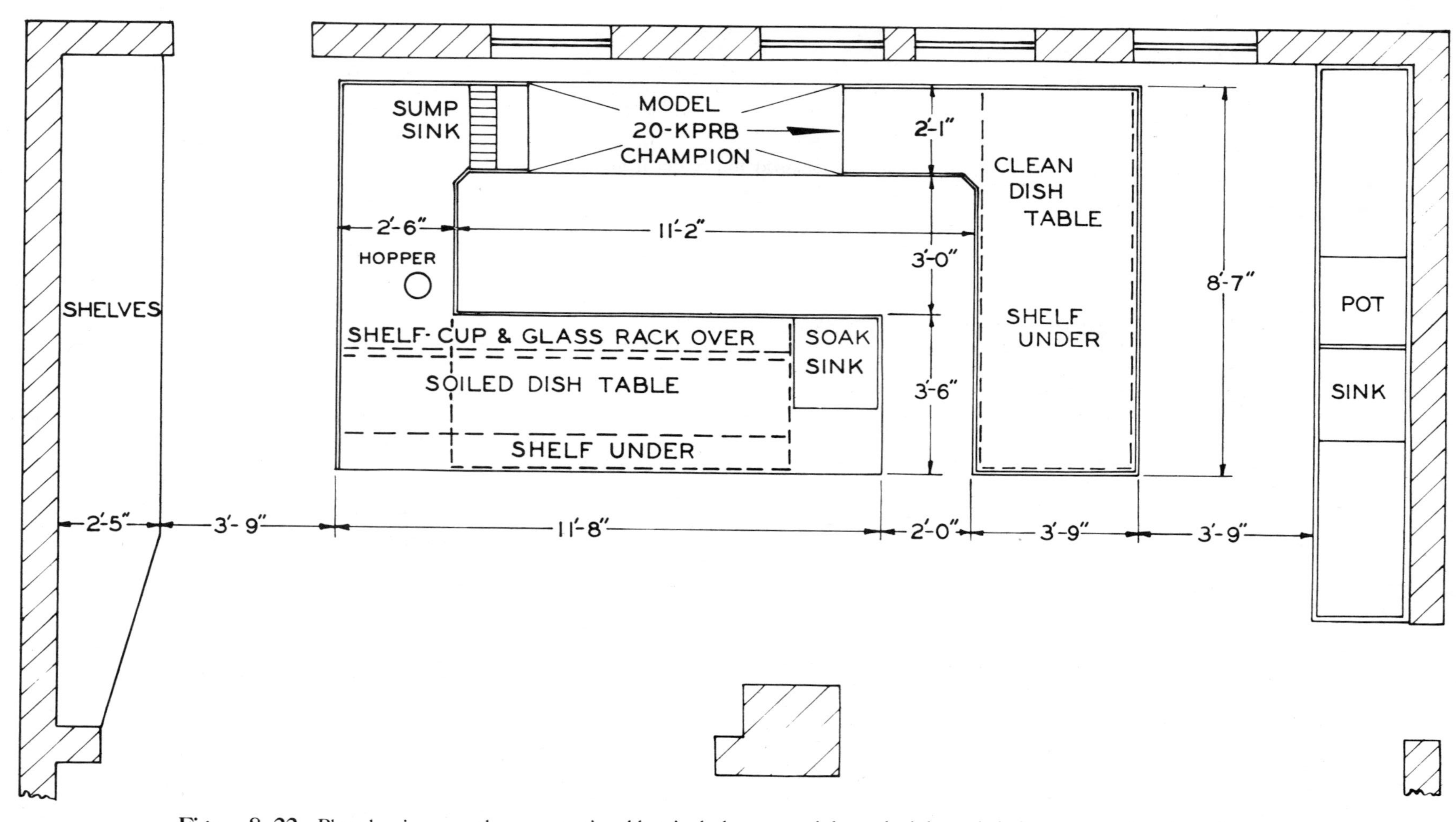

Figure 8-22. Plan that is somewhat conventional but includes sump sink, soak sink, and shelves over and under. (Courtesy Champion Manufacturing)

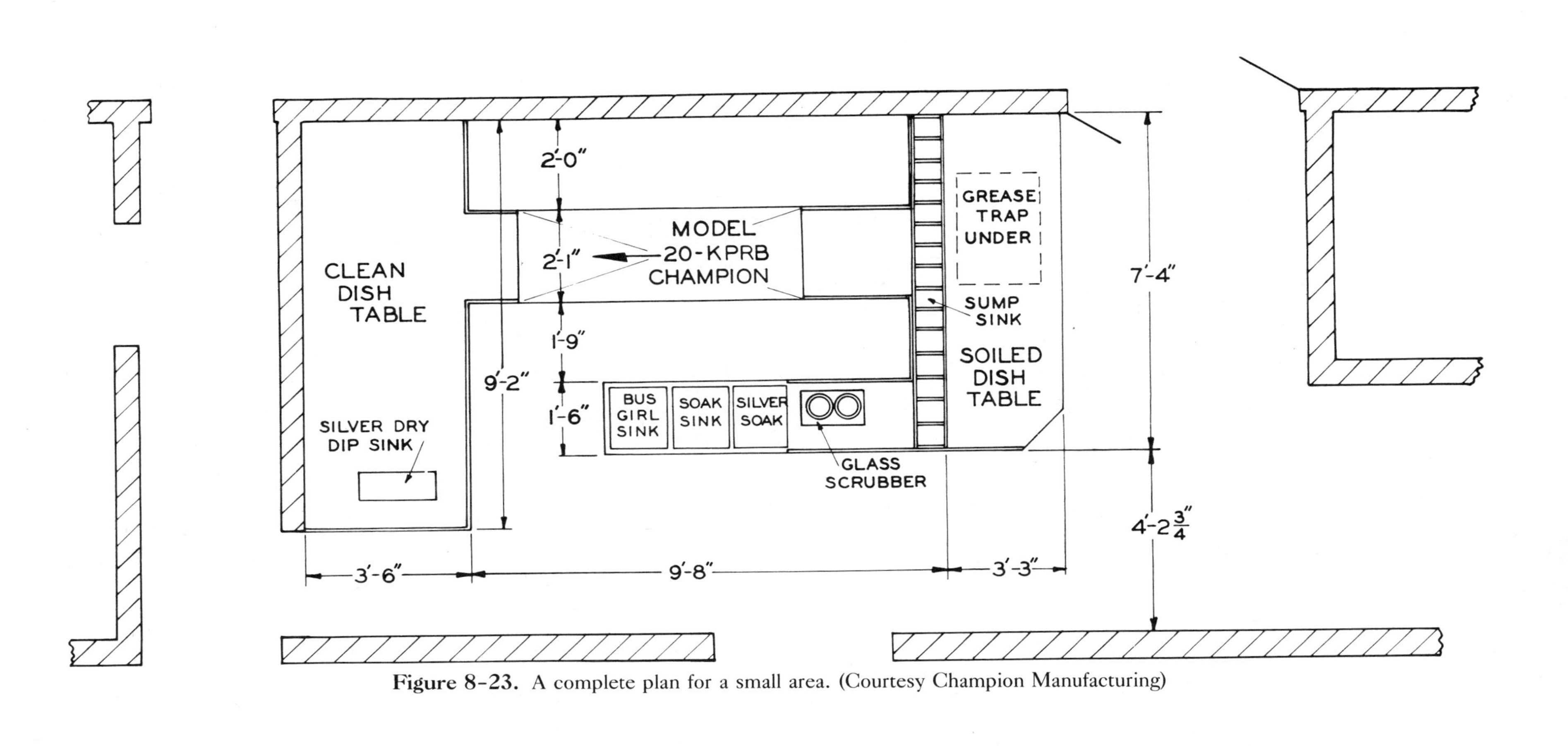

Figure 8-23. A complete plan for a small area. (Courtesy Champion Manufacturing)

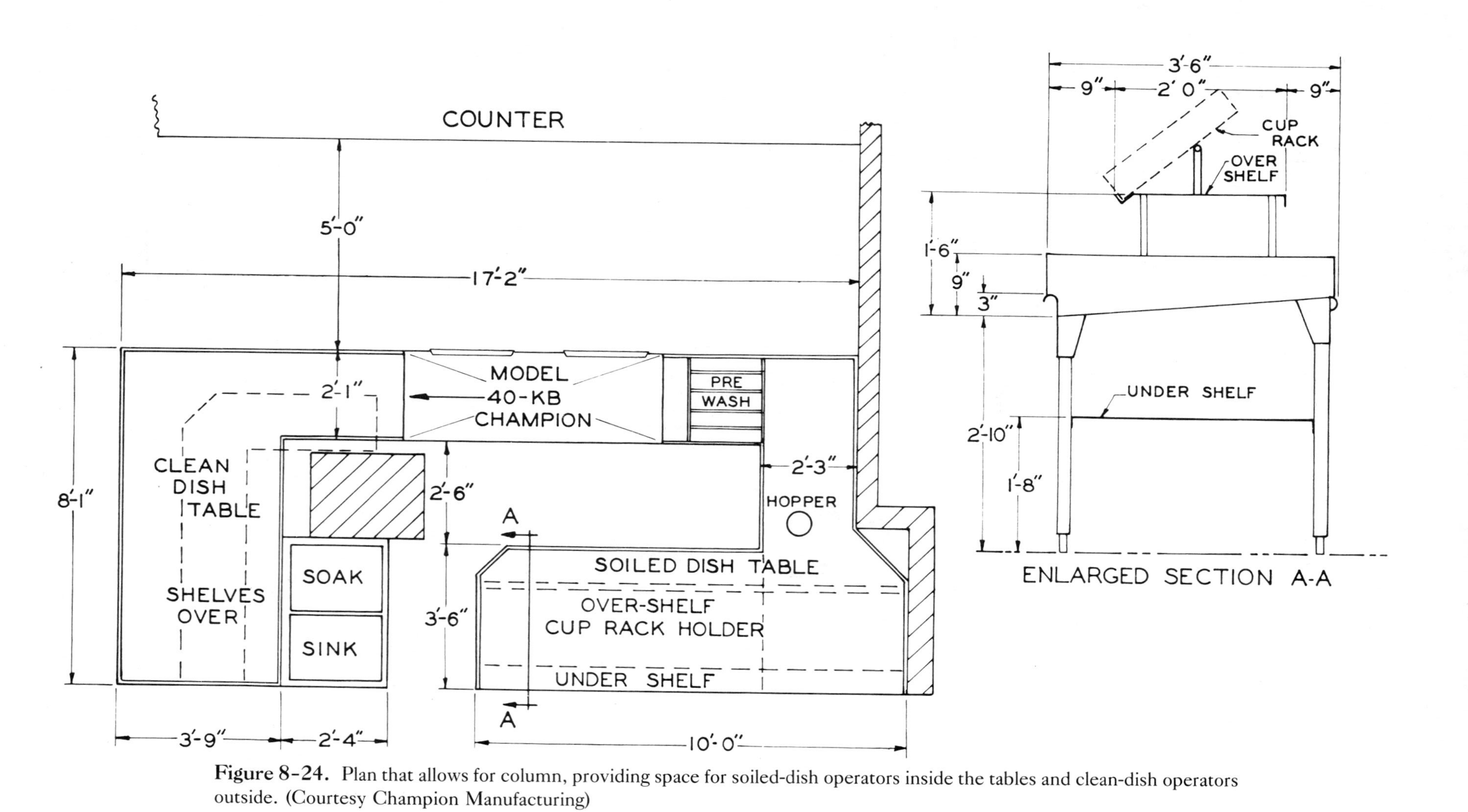

Figure 8-24. Plan that allows for column, providing space for soiled-dish operators inside the tables and clean-dish operators outside. (Courtesy Champion Manufacturing)

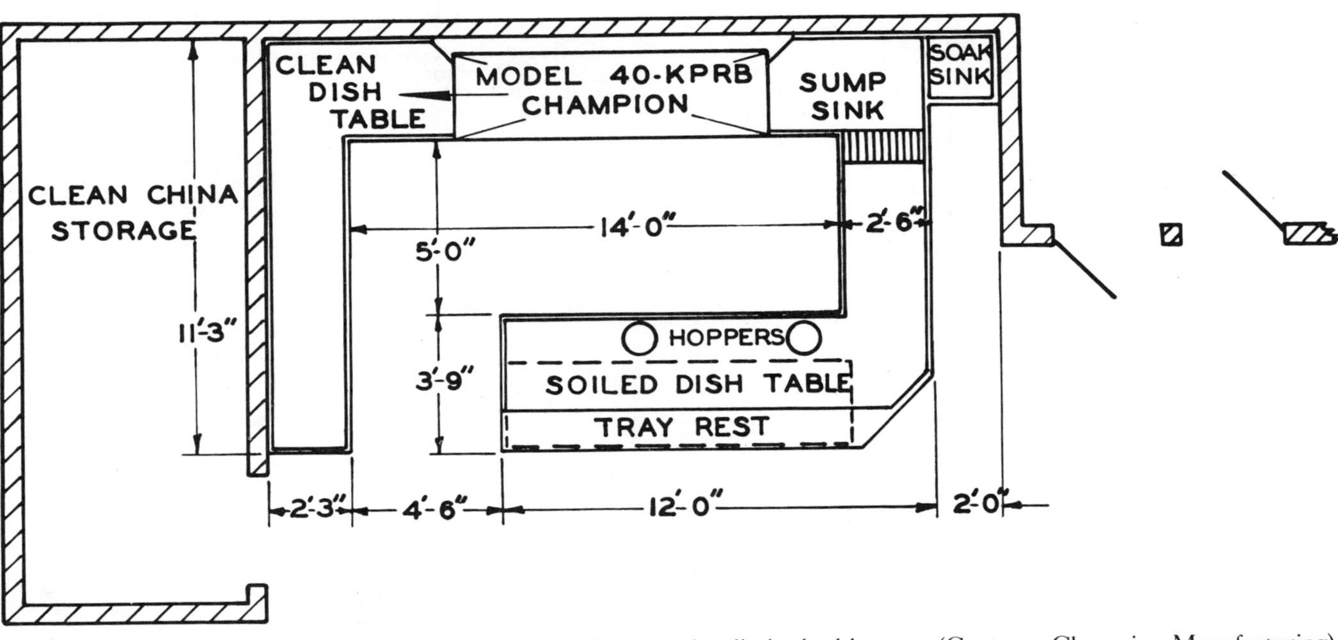

Figure 8-25. Good working plan in small space with somewhat limited table area. (Courtesy Champion Manufacturing)

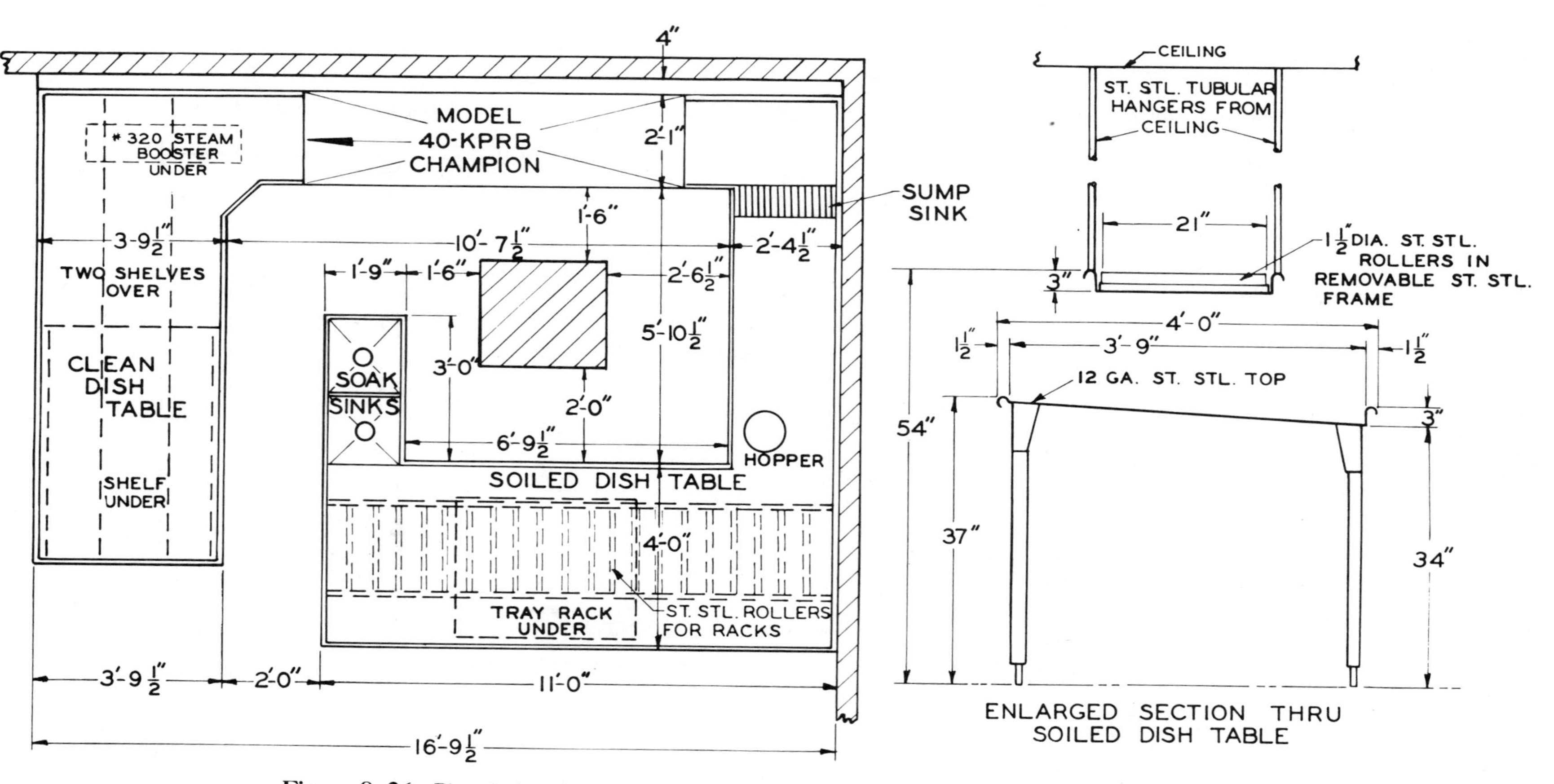

Figure 8-26. Plan designed to accommodate large column. (Courtesy Champion Manufacturing)

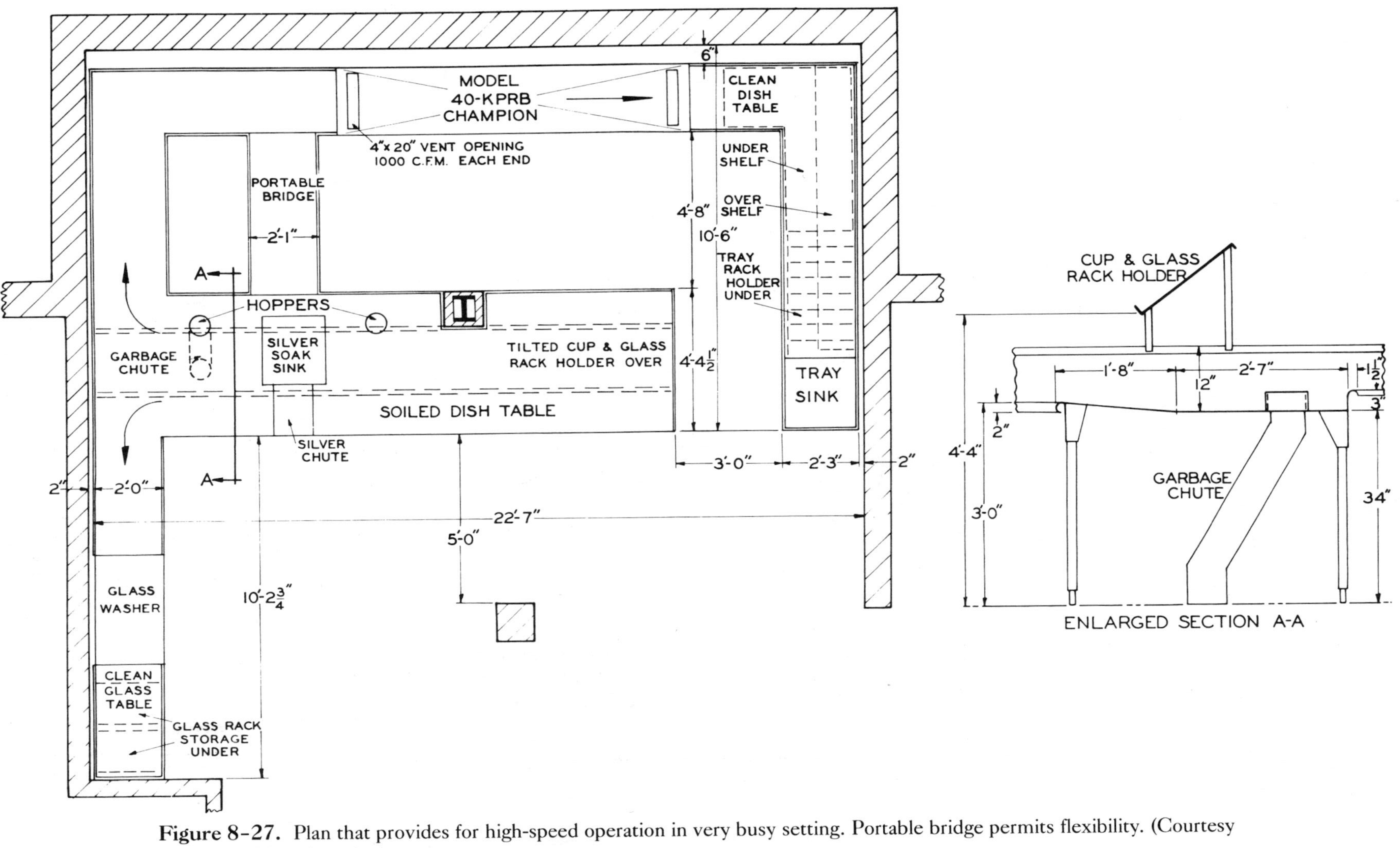

Figure 8-27. Plan that provides for high-speed operation in very busy setting. Portable bridge permits flexibility. (Courtesy Champion Manufacturing)

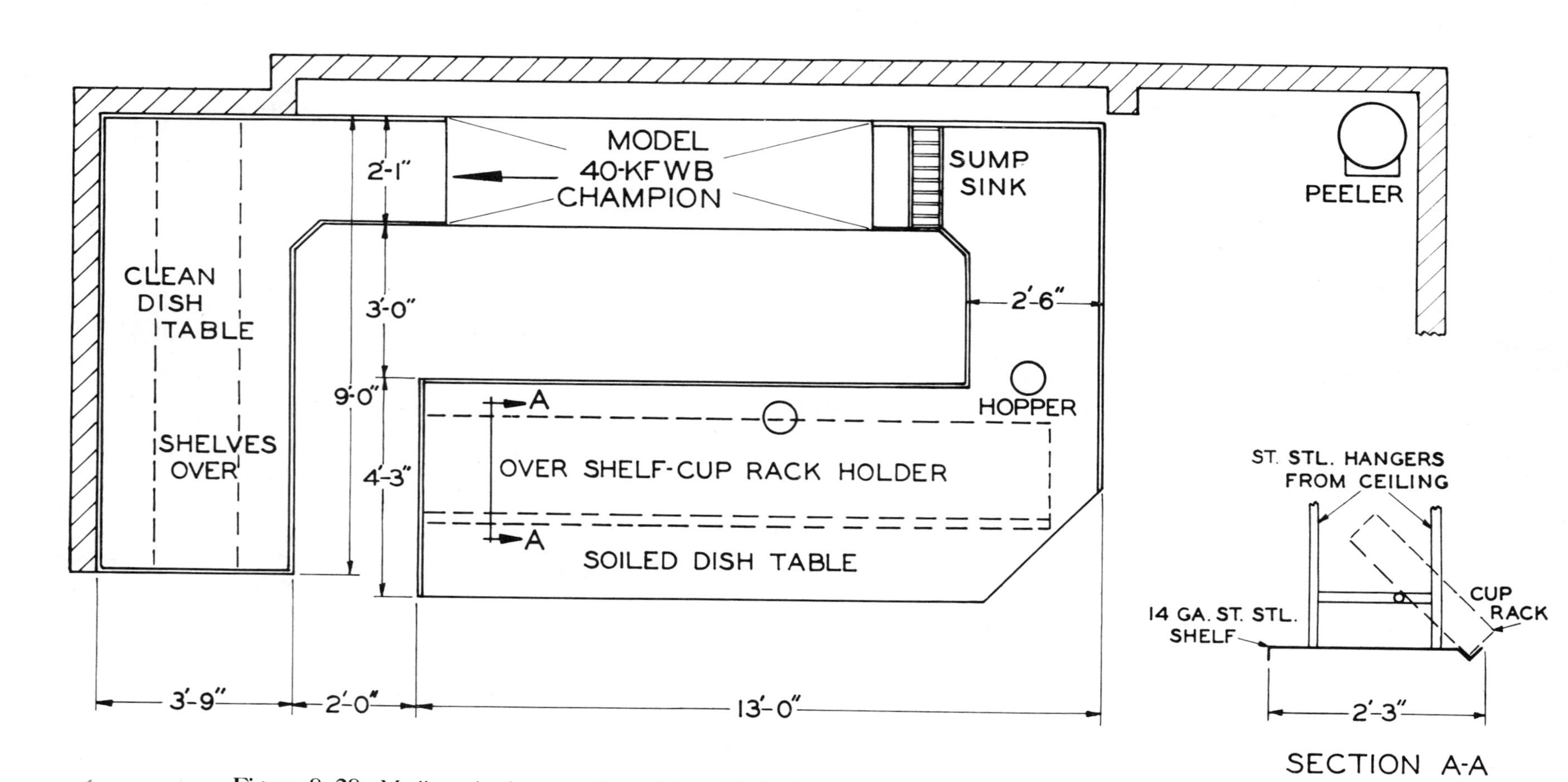

Figure 8-28. Medium-sized automatic machine with fresh water prewash. Note overhanging rack shelf suspended from ceiling. (Courtesy Champion Manufacturing)

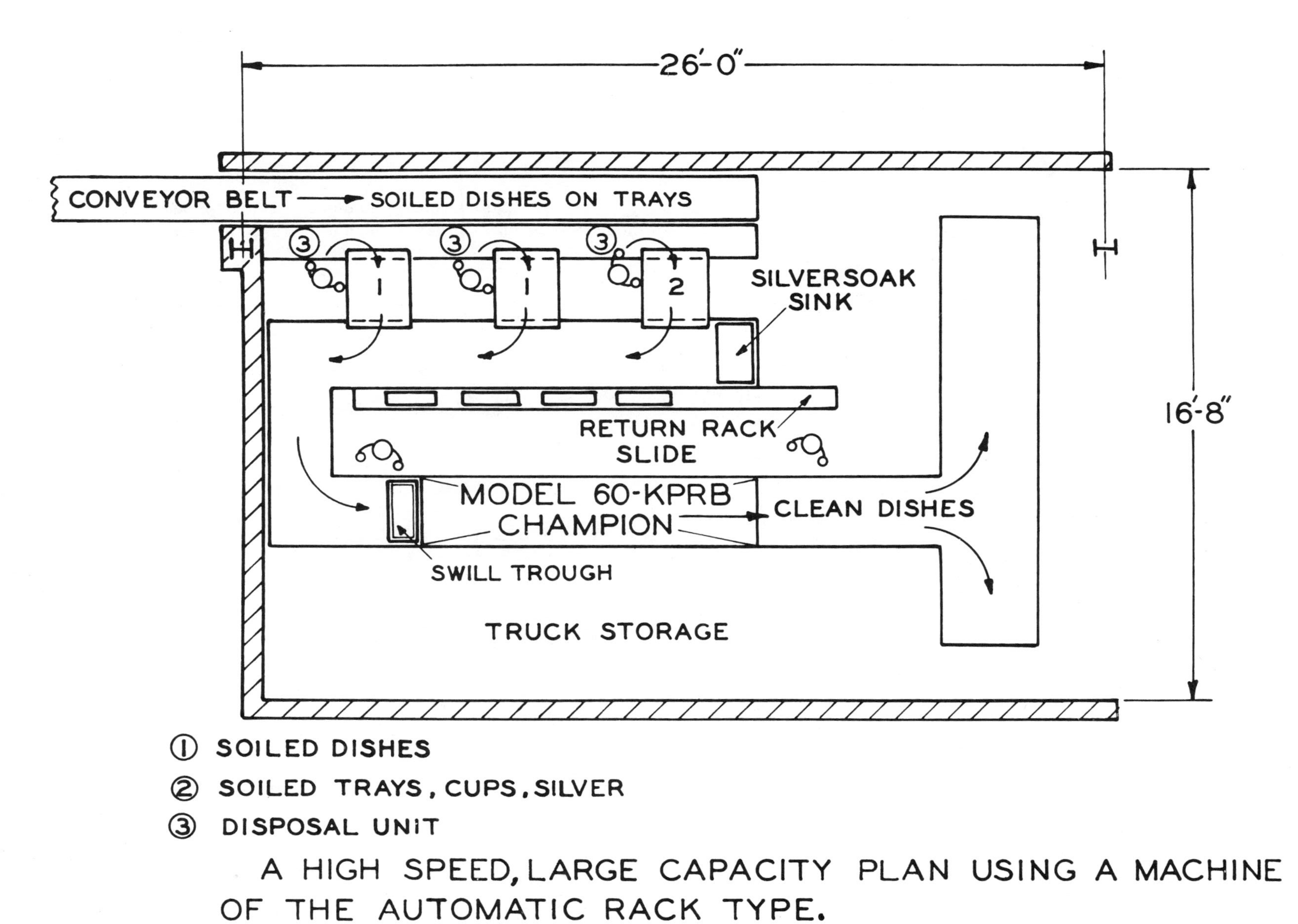

Figure 8-29. High-speed, large-capacity plan using a machine of the automatic rack type. (Courtesy Champion Manufacturing)

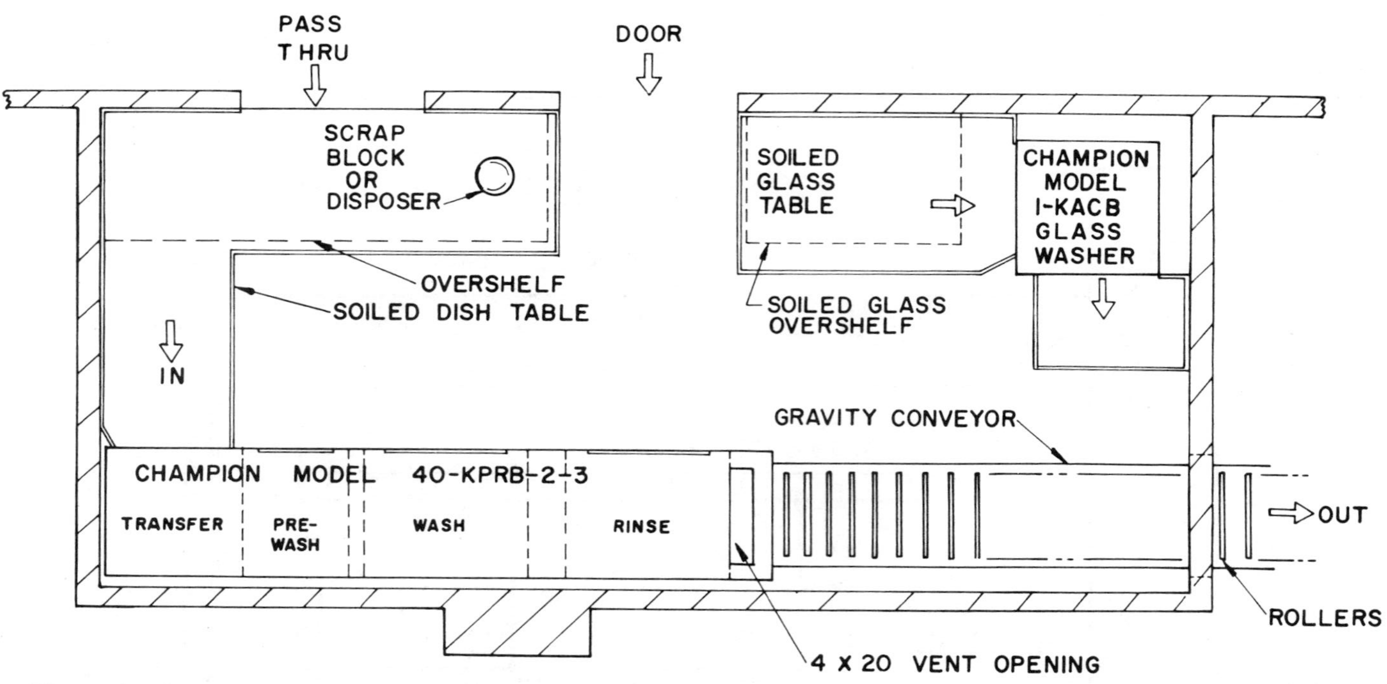

Figure 8-30. Small dish pantry, perfectly suitable for a door-type corner machine and an automatic-rack-type Corner-matic machine. (Courtesy Champion Manufacturing)

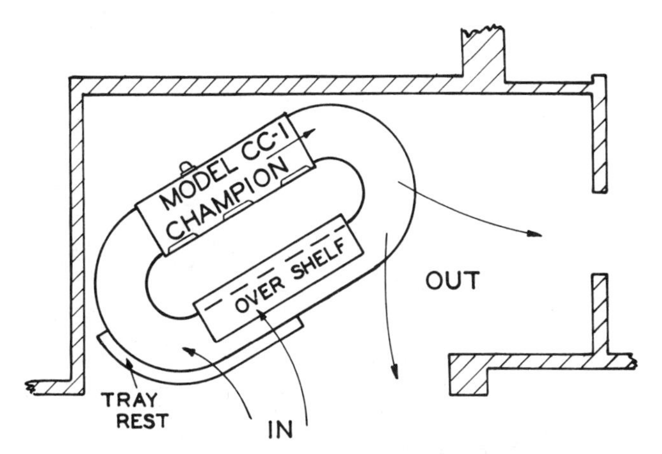

Figure 8-31. Standard model CC-1 Champion "Circ-u-matic" assembly in a small area that required setting the unit at an angle. (Courtesy Champion Manufacturing)

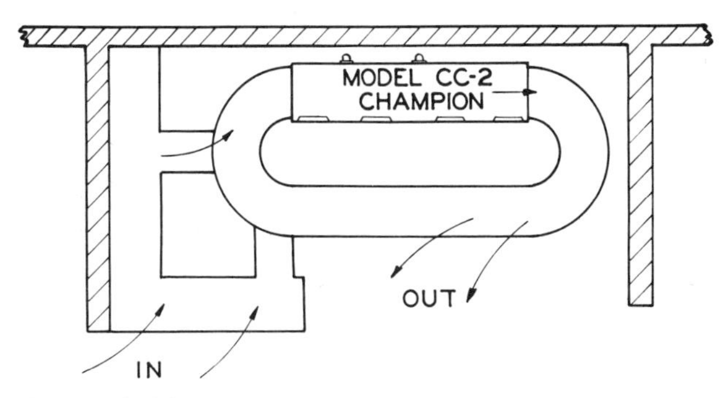

Figure 8-32. Unusual layout necessitated by special requirements. Champion "Circ-u-matic" units can be adapted to a variety of spaces and requirements. (Courtesy Champion Manufacturing)

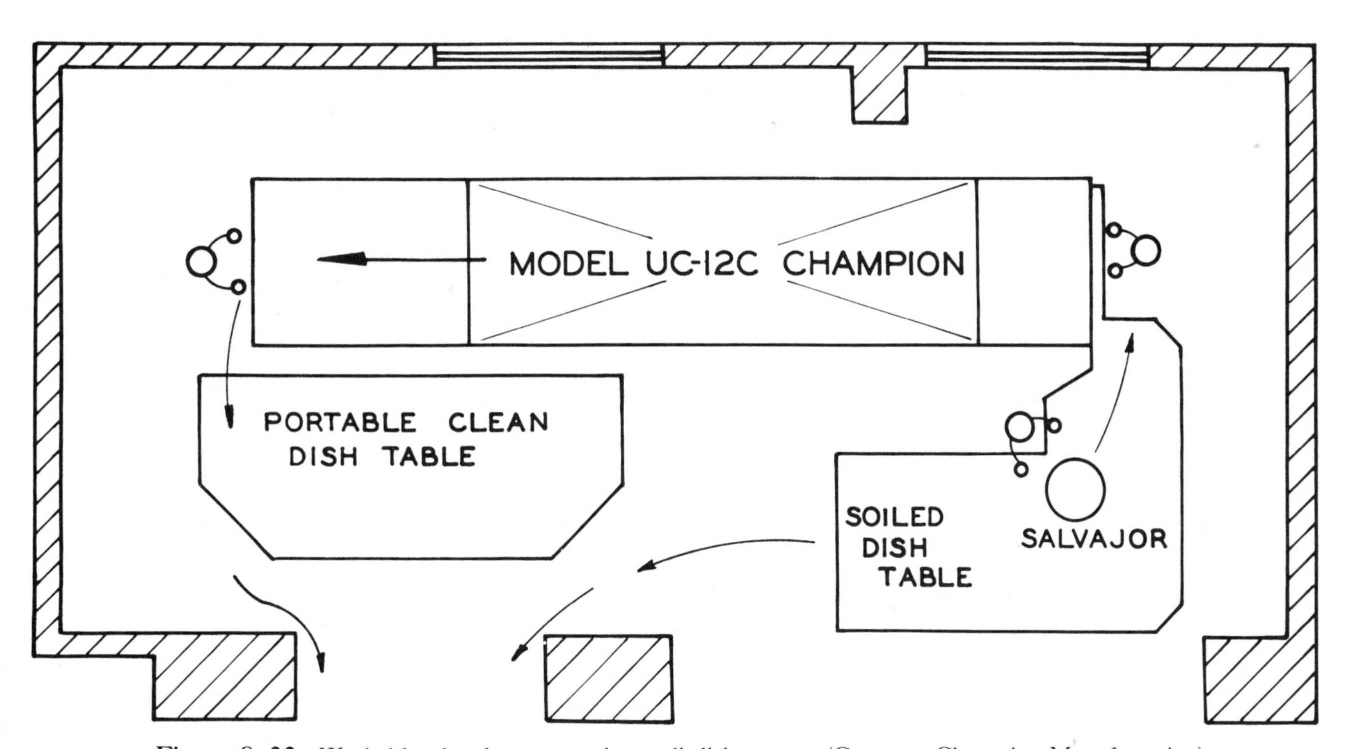

Figure 8-33. Workable plan for extremely small dish pantry. (Courtesy Champion Manufacturing)

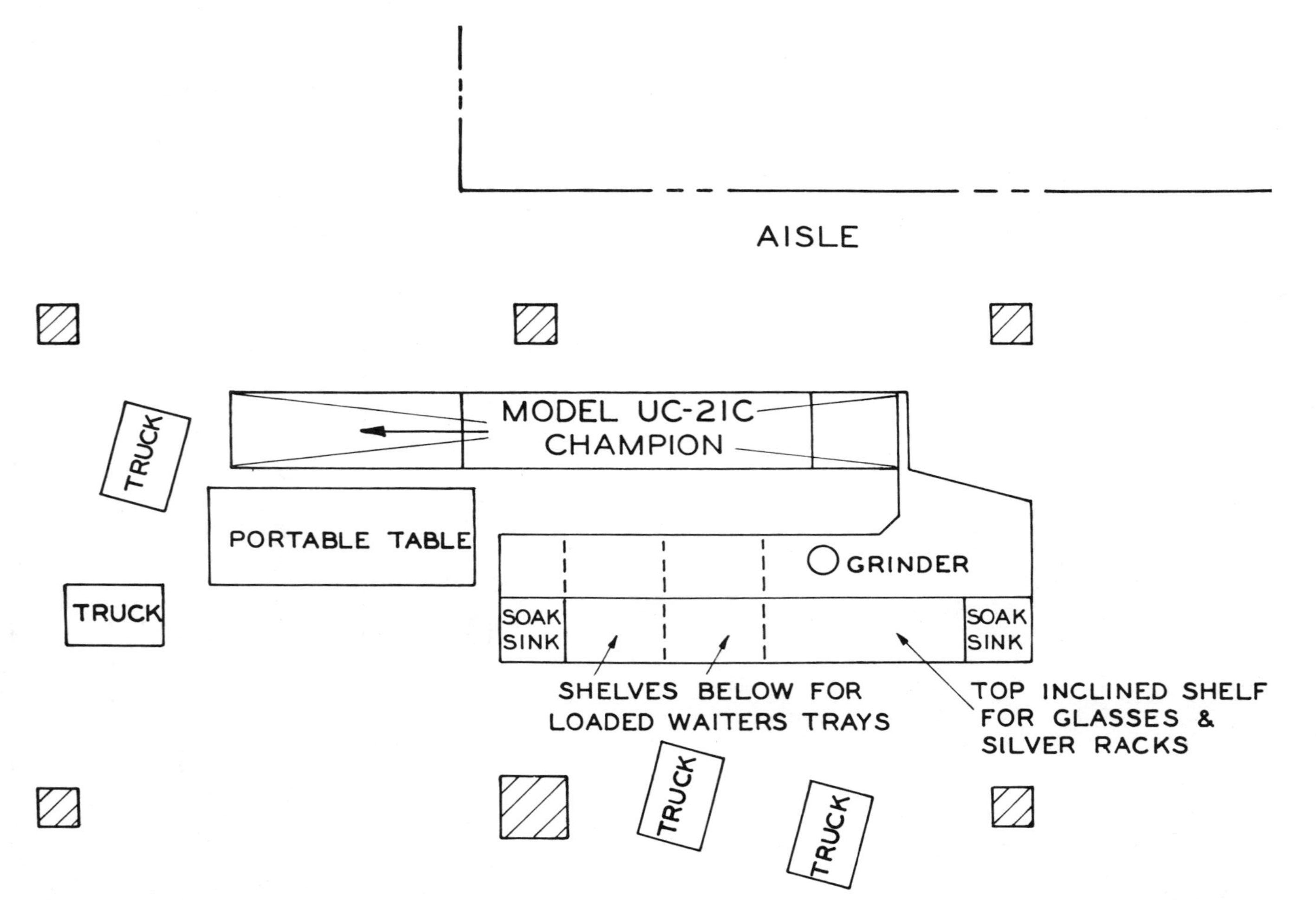

Figure 8-34. Conventional plan for machine of the upright conveyor type, with dish table at soiled end only. (Courtesy Champion Manufacturing)

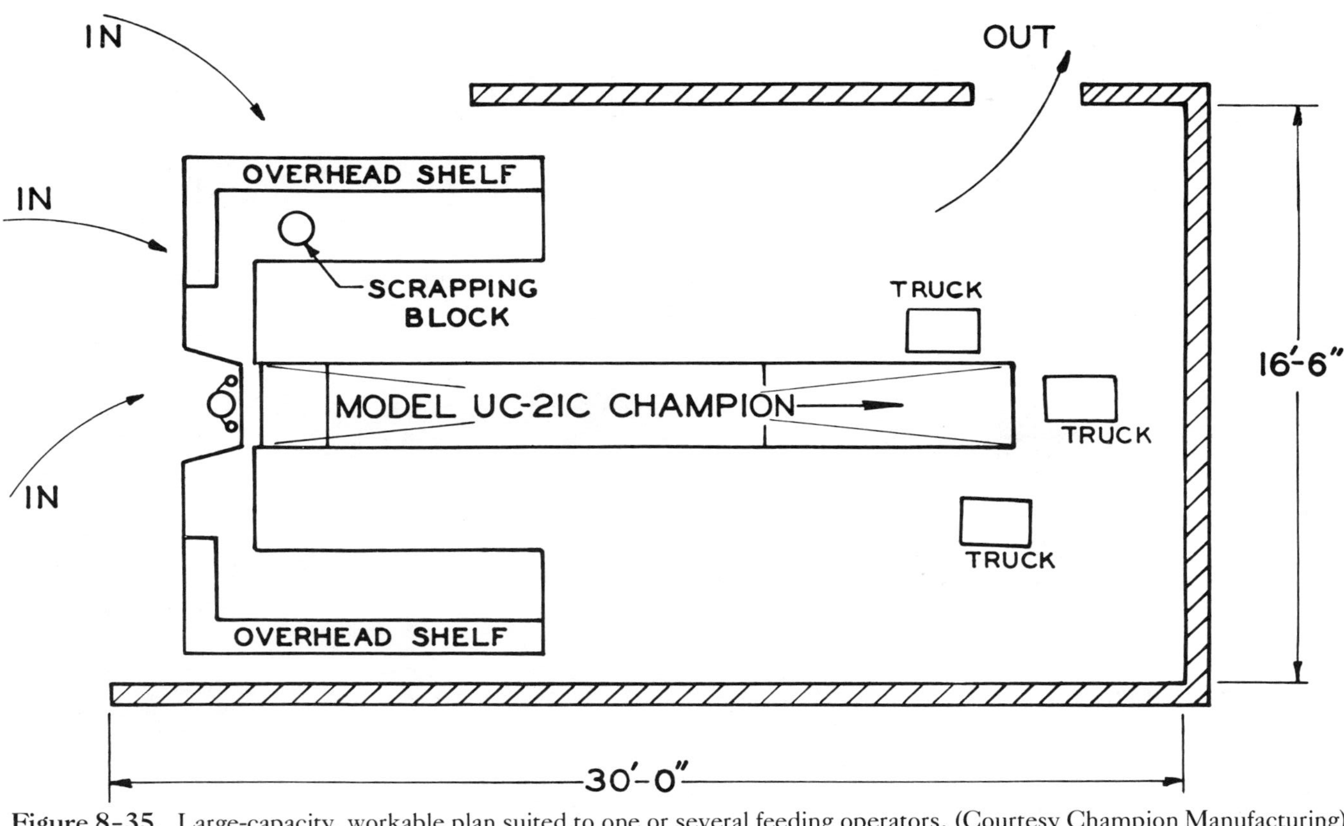

Figure 8-35. Large-capacity, workable plan suited to one or several feeding operators. (Courtesy Champion Manufacturing)

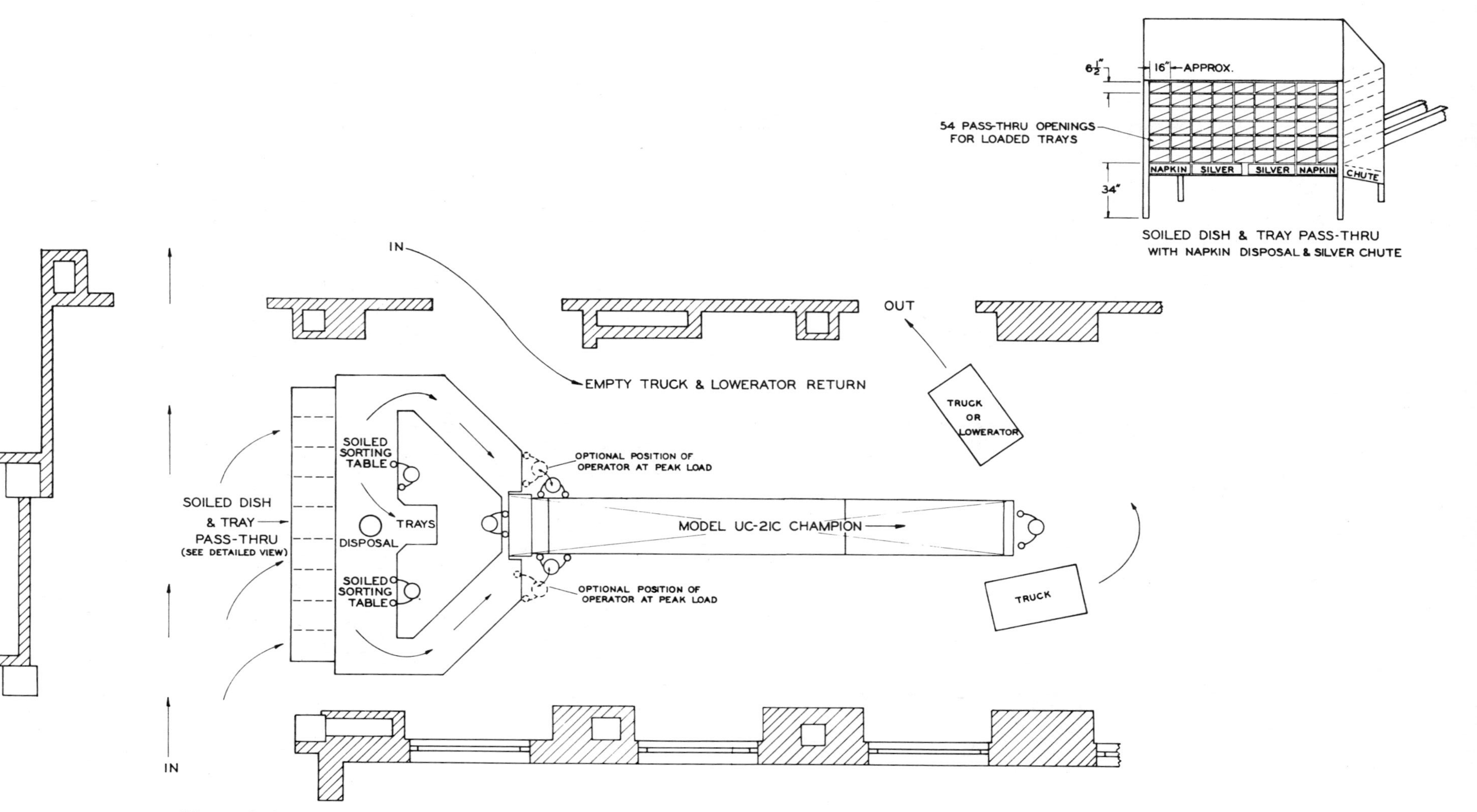

Figure 8-36. Design prepared for large hospital to accommodate work coming in from different areas. (Courtesy Champion Manufacturing)

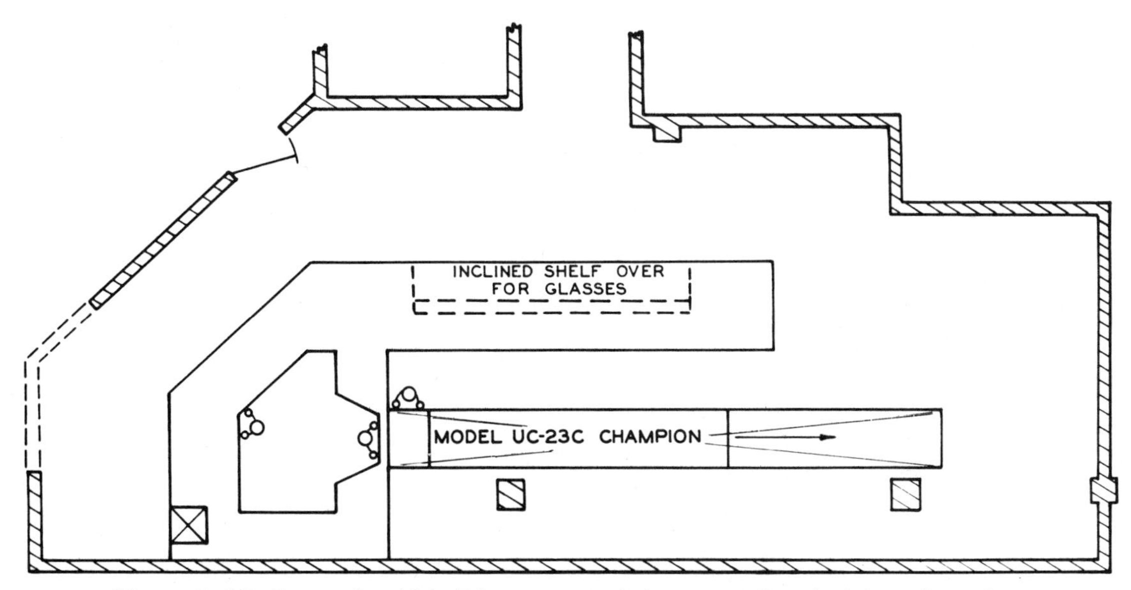

Figure 8-37. Layout in which dishes, cups, and glasses are all washed through one large upright conveyor belt machine. (Courtesy Champion Manufacturing)

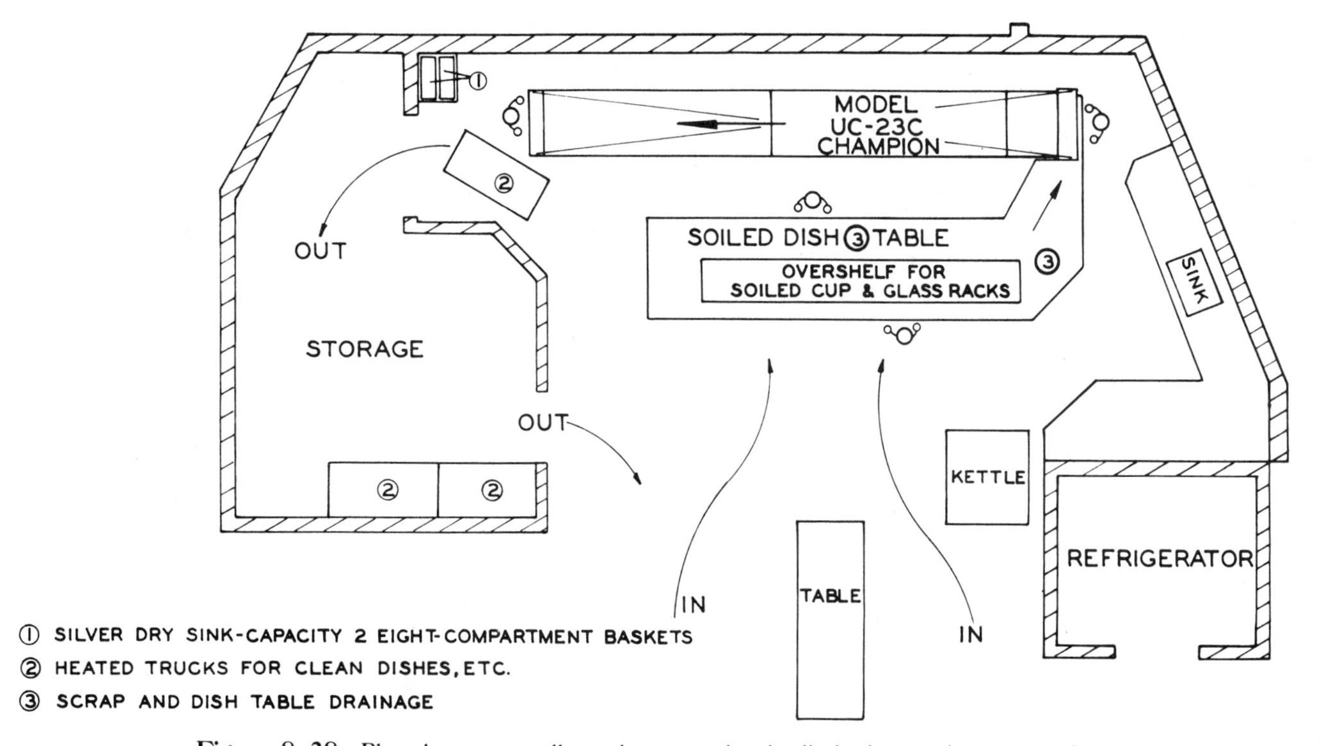

Figure 8-38. Plan that covers all requirements despite limited space in a room of unusual shape. (Courtesy Champion Manufacturing)

9

Utilities and Hardware

This chapter shows many "back of the house" engineering features available for the proper installation of foodservice equipment. Proper installation is critical for required approvals such as those of health and building codes.

A close look at many of the unique devices in the chapter will help end users understand the terminology used, and the drawings show many actual procedures.

Many service calls and much aggravation can be eliminated by proper installation. The proper-size gas line, drain line, and voltage are critical to proper equipment performance. When a piece of equipment is installed, proper start-up is important; so it is best to have the installer and service agency and local representatives on hand at that time.

POWER DISTRIBUTION SYSTEMS

These systems offer numerous features and benefits that should be investigated by anyone planning remodeling or building. They could be extremely advantageous for anyone intending to lease an existing building, particularly if the building has a poured concrete slab floor. (See Figure 9–1, parts a–l.)

In its simplest form, a power distribution system can deliver electricity, gas, steam, and hot and cold water to any point in the building requiring them. The systems' manufacturers claim considerable savings over conventional wiring and plumbing installations. A most important consideration is that the entire power distribution system is an integral part of the equipment, not a part of the building. In the event of relocation, it can be taken out with the rest of the equipment, a factor that qualifies it for tax credits. If energy-saving controls (also available) are incorporated, they may qualify for energy credits.

All or any part of the system may be employed to fill the user's specific needs. Many modules are available.

If it is to be used as a total power distribution system, all supply lines to be incorporated—water, gas, electric, and steam—would be brought to one location and would be distributed to all necessary points of use encased in stainless steel raceways. Any lines not requiring metering or central control could be picked up at individual points of origin. The modular design of the raceways permits lengthening or shortening of the chain. Corner units permit running up over doorways, around pilasters, anywhere. Electric outlets with point-of-use breakers may be counted in the raceways and provide users the flexibility to add or change equipment of varying voltage and amperage.

The raceways, or power chain systems, offer many options and advantages: all amperages up to 100 amps, for voltages from 100 V to 600 V, single- or three-phase. All control wiring is easily connected or disconnected, permitting the addition of fire-fuel shutoff, ground fault protection, and so on. Plumbing and gas quick disconnects may be employed. Steam assemblies include internal insulation. Overhead systems may accommodate any combination of utilities and lighting, signal communication wiring, and customized controls. They may be run along countertops and around corners in backsplash fashion, and house telephone and communications wiring, digital clocks, timers, laboratory fixtures, and plumbing and electrical fixtures. Other options or combinations thereof are available.

Modular, point-of-distribution units to which the power chains or raceways may be connected are as follows:

Power poles: Used for mobile cafeteria and buffet units, point-of-sale displays, telephone, etc., the unit stretches from floor to ceiling and provides power anywhere a ceiling box is installed.

Tray slide unit: The top provides a tray slide for cafeteria counters. Recessed front panels may be stainless steel or Formica to match counters. A power raceway under the tray slide provides any and all utilities for the entire cafeteria counter.

Utility station: This unit houses a digital LED timer for a VCM or mixer, an integral sink, a water meter, and a kettle fill hose. An optional booster heater is available for 190°F water.

Dishwasher energy unit: This unit incorporates a prerinse hose, disposer controls, detergent dispenser, and rinse injector, along with all power and water requirements.

Main cooking battery unit: A power distribution raceway houses all power requirements, disconnects, and any items required for the range battery. This raceway is supported by floor-to-ceiling pylons as required, and is suitable for wall or island installation. An end pylon may house all necessary controls, power, water, and drain line for automatic washdown exhaust hoods. Air makeup controls may be incorporated. A steam energy control unit is available, which eliminates condensate buildup and the necessity to "blow down" every morning. Savings on wasted steam may be substantial. A 7-day, 24-hour timer is included.

Steam control center: This unit contains all necessary valves and traps, a steam purging system, a large-capacity kettle filler, and an electronic digital water meter with automatic shutoff when the number of gallons set on the dial is reached. Electronic steam control ensures perfect cooking; a cantilever supports the kettle, providing ease of cleaning.

Vertical cutter mixer control: This control provides point-of-service disconnect, ground fault protection, internal magnetic overload protection for the motor, a two-minute adjustable LED timer for exact cutting/mixing, and more.

The possibilities and combinations in which the components of a power distribution system may be used are endless.

UTILITIES AND HARDWARE CHECKLIST

The user should answer questions such as these:

- Are floor drains adequate?
- What types of doors are needed for foodservice areas?
- Can we use a power distribution system?
- Will the electrical receptacles, cords, and plugs match?
- Do we have the proper voltage and phase for the equipment?
- Will the equipment seller provide the proper mechanical plan for the installers?
- Will equipment fit through the doors?
- Is the ceiling height adequate?

See Figures 9–2 through 9–11 for a variety of useful ideas for the installation of utilities and hardware in foodservice establishments.

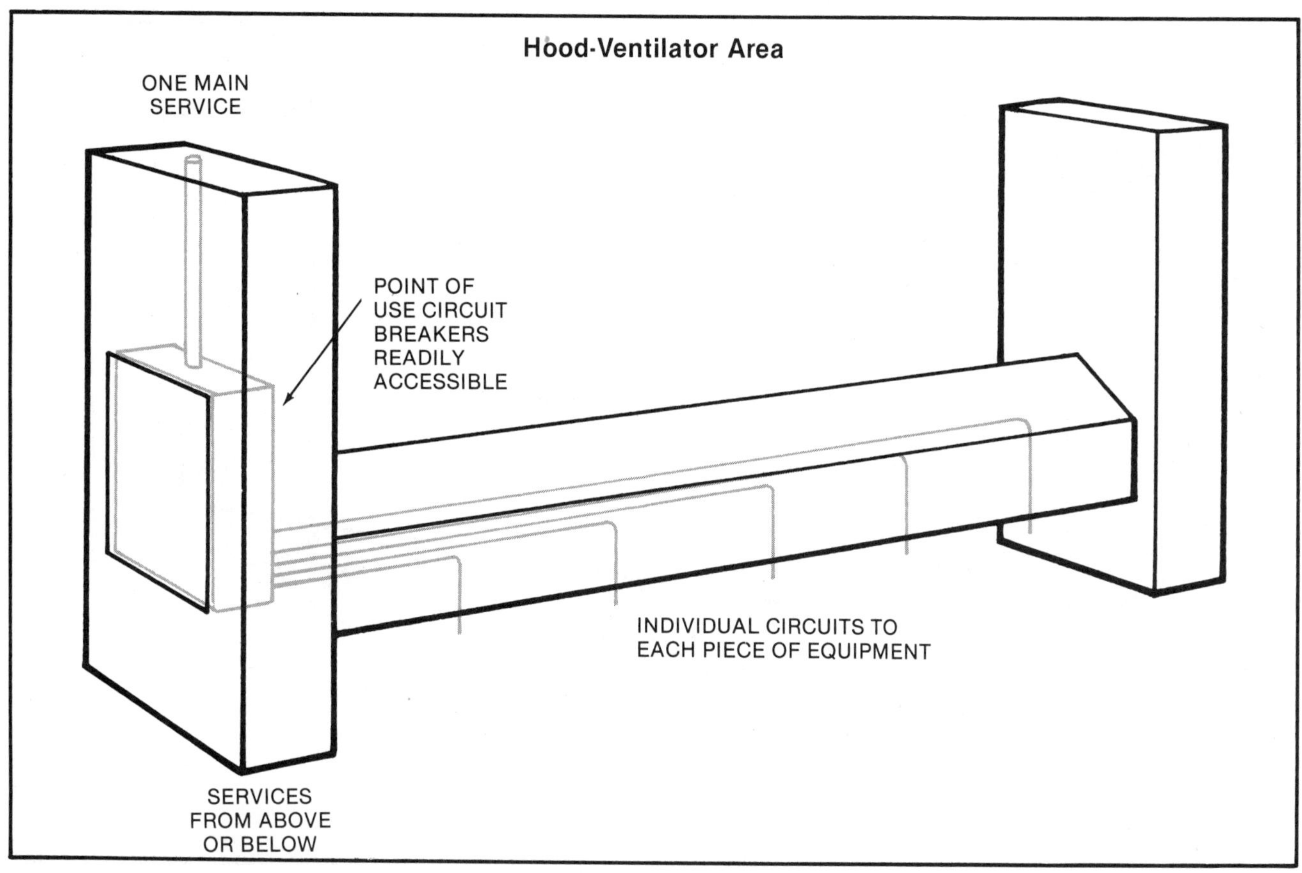

a

THE ELECTRICAL SYSTEM

The electrical system includes a circuit breaker panel box for each main service. Any combination of service voltages can be provided. The system is prewired from branch circuit breakers, through the chase and terminates at receptacles or in sealtite pigtails as specified. Receptacles and sealtite mount to the chase on interchangeable connection plates for relocation flexibility and future expansion.

All electrical conductors are sheathed and insulated for installation, operational and service safety. No dangerous uninsulated buss bars are used in the chase.

Options include: ground fault equipment protection, ground fault personnel protection, automatic fire fuel shut-off, magnetic motor starters, contactors, waterproof receptacle covers and ventilator light switch.

Seco Engineering believes that high quality, time proven components provide the finest product. One-of-a-kind, one-source-only components are never used.

Figure 9-1a-1. Power distribution systems. (Parts 9-1a through 9-1h (pages 237-244) courtesy Seco Engineering Systems; parts 9-1i through 9-1l (pages 245-248) courtesy Avtec Industries)

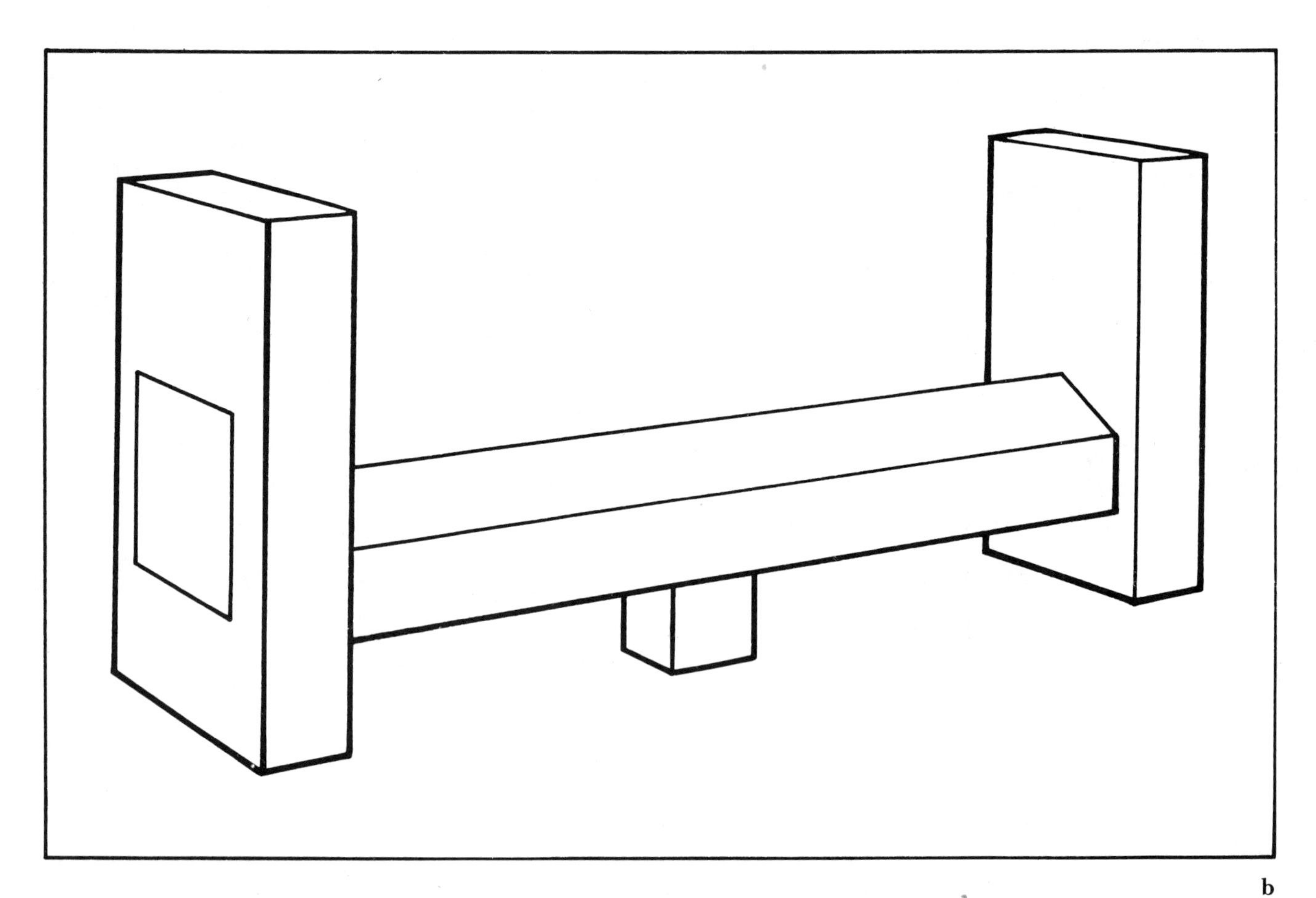

b

THE ENCLOSURE

The enclosure houses the electrical and plumbing components of the system, and is divided into: risers, chase and if required, pedestals.

All exposed sheet metal parts are type 302 stainless steel. Unexposed structural parts are stainless steel or galvanized steel. Stainless steel construction can be used throughout at additional cost. Structural integrity is assured through welded construction. Screws are used only for removable access panels.

Risers extend from the floor and penetrate the ventilator or finished ceiling providing points of entrance for the electric and plumbing services. The electric circuit breaker box, and plumbing shut-off valves and accessories are located in the riser(s). Hinged in-fitting doors with optional key locks provide access to circuit breakers and plumbing shut-off valves. Accessories may be located behind doors or removable panels.

The chase contains individual receptacles and wiring in one compartment, and plumbing connections in the other. The partition between compartments is structural and provides complete separation between plumbing and electrical services.

Pedestals can be provided for incoming services and/or structural support. Generally, chases longer than ten feet require one pedestal, and an additional pedestal for each additional ten feet of chase.

Seco Engineering custom designs Utility Distribution Systems for each application to assure the best performance. Our U.L. listing allows complete design flexibility while assuring local code acceptance.

Figure 9-1b

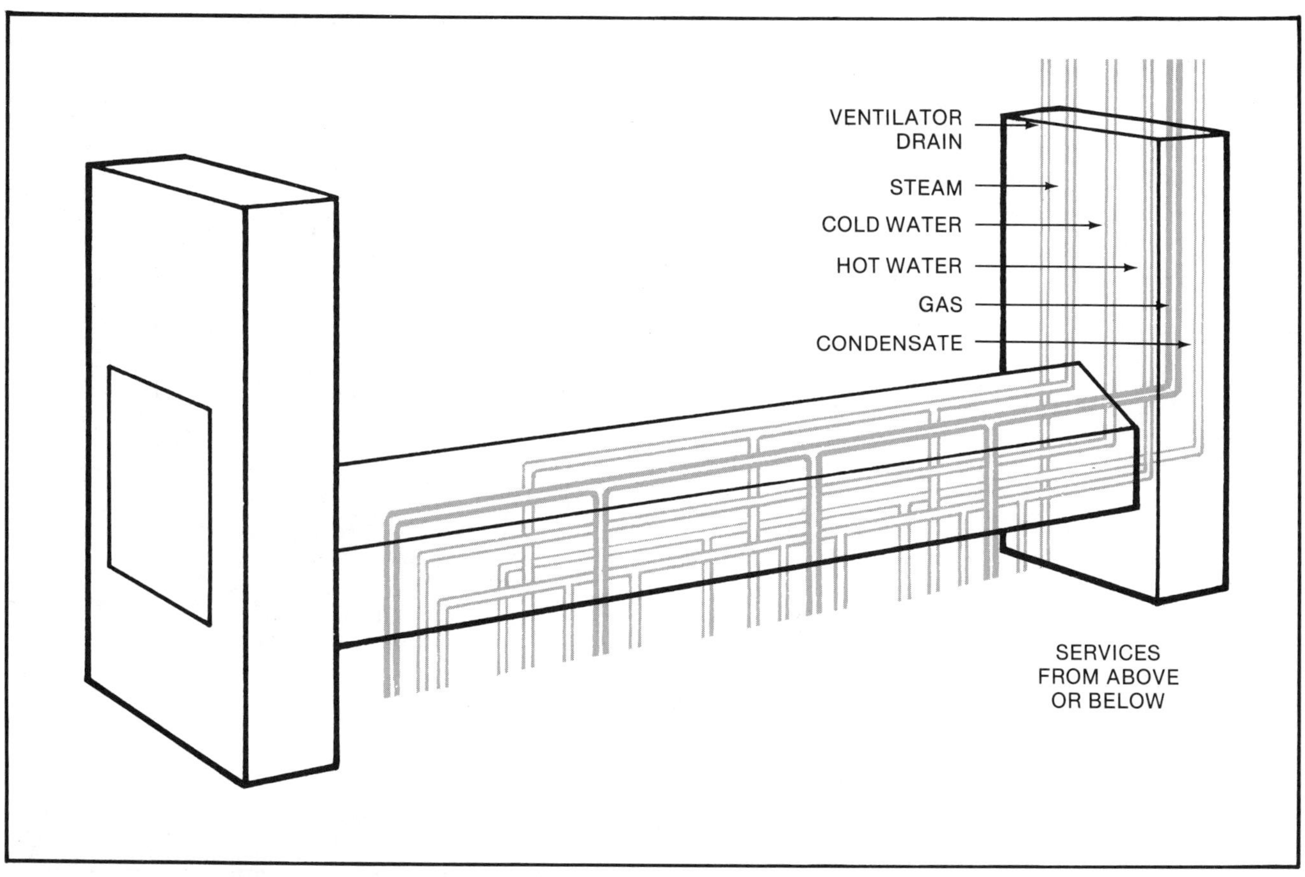

THE PLUMBING SYSTEM

The plumbing system contains one or more of the following: cold water (CW), hot water (HW), gas (G), steam supply (SS), condensate return (CR), drain (D).

The hot and cold water systems are provided with main and branch ball type shut-off valves, Y-strainers, and insulation. Options include: pressure/temperature gauges, quick disconnect hose assemblies, and pressure regulators.

The gas system is provided with main and branch ball type shut-offs and dirt legs, Options include: mechanical or electrical automatic safety shut-off valves, pressure regulators, and quick disconnect hose assemblies.

The steam and condensate systems are provided with main and branch ball type shut-off valves, Y-strainers, insulation and an automatic condensate purging system as standard. (The purging system and proper design of the piping eliminates condensate build up, hammering, and provides instant steam to the equipment.) Options include: pressure/temperature gauges, motorized shut-off valves with time clocks, and quick disconnect hose assemblies.

Seco Engineering has given special attention to the plumbing system. To assure easy installation, the plumbing compartment is exceptionally large and an oversized removable cover allows complete access for future additions.

Figure 9-1c

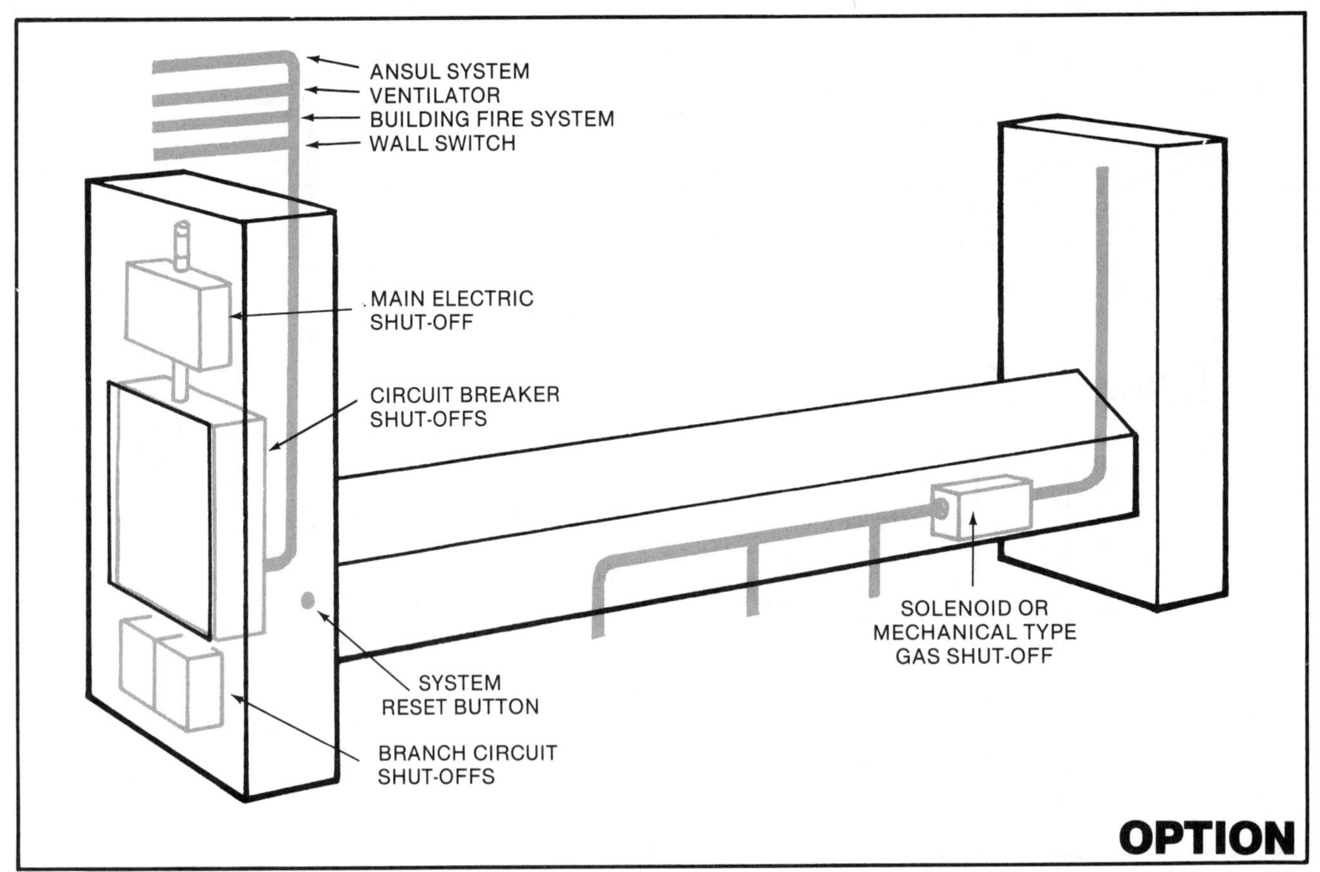

FIRE-FUEL SHUT-OFFS

Automatic fuel shut-off in case of fire is usually required by code and always desirable.

Seco Engineering's U.L. listing provides methods for automatic, fail safe equipment shut down activated by one or more external sources.

The actuation of a wall mounted manual fire switch, the dry chemical system, the ventilator fire system and the buildings fire system can all be connected to the Utility Distribution System causing fuel shut down.

Seco Engineering designs fire-fuel shut-off into the Utility Distribution System after determining the requirements of each item. The signal source requirements are then coordinated with the architect and/or engineer.

Figure 9-1d

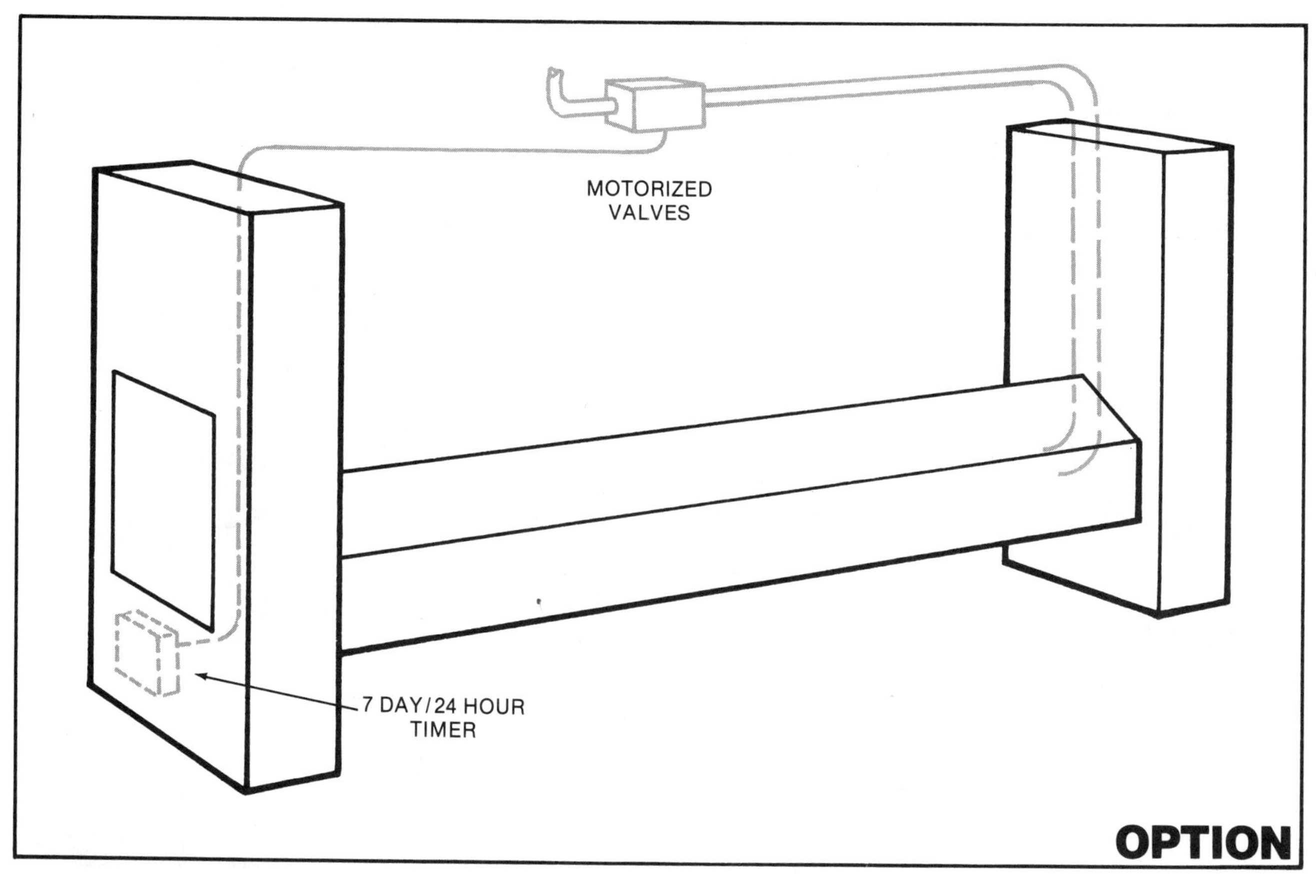

e

MOTORIZED SHUT-OFF VALVES

In any steam system, condensate is formed and must be returned to the boiler or disposed of as waste.

To eliminate wasteful condensate build-up, Seco Engineering offers motorized shut-off valves for steam service. (Solenoid valves could be used but would cause "hammering"). The valve can be operated by a manual switch, 24 hour or 7 day 24 hour timer.

7 DAY 24 HOUR TIMER

Seco Engineering offers 24 hour and 7 day 24 hours timers to control steam valves and electrical equipment.

The timers are field adjustable, self correcting should power be interrupted, and are ideal for use with contactors to automatically pre-heat equipment before personnel arrive to open the kitchen.

Figure 9-1e

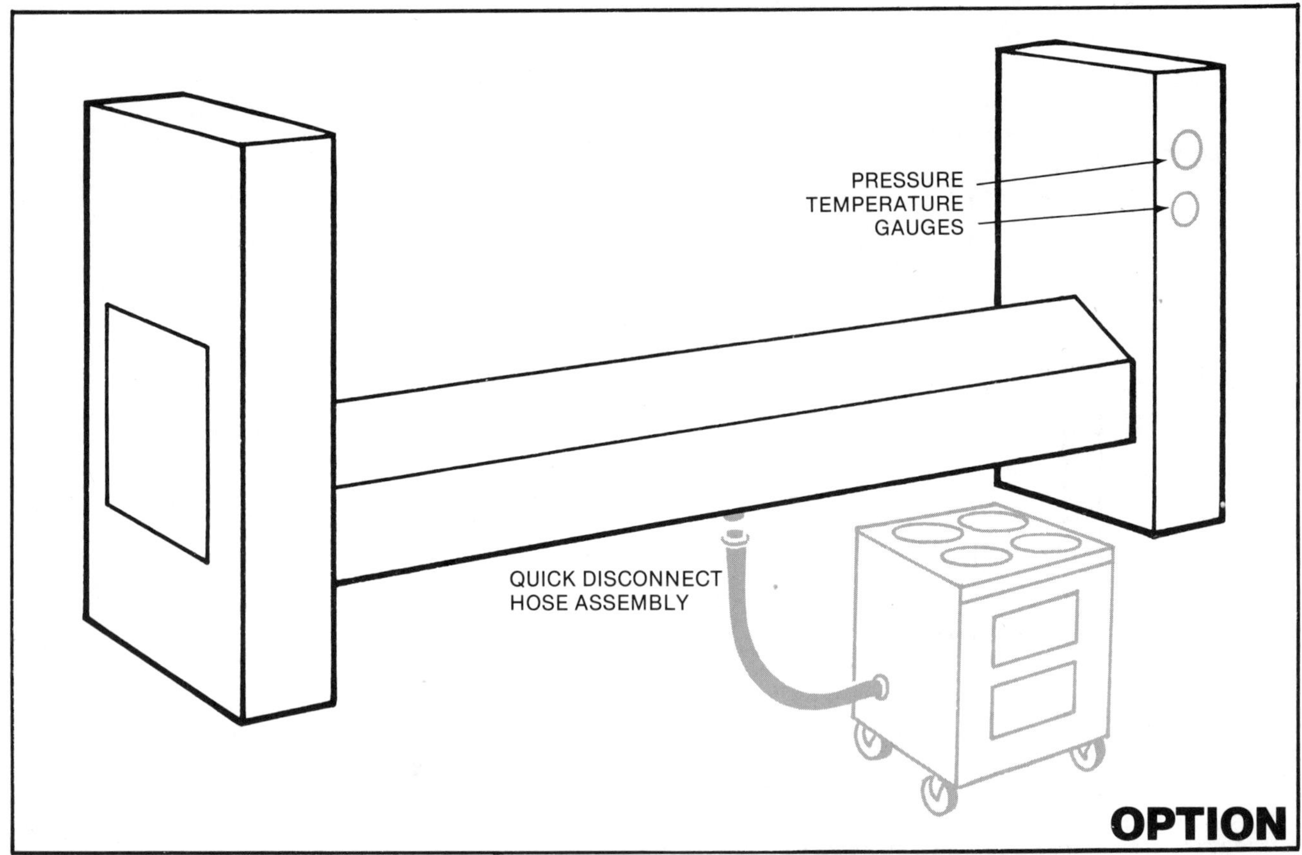

f

QUICK DISCONNECT HOSE ASSEMBLIES

Seco Engineering offers quick disconnect hose assemblies for gas, steam, condensate and water services.

Equipment can be instantly disconnected from the U.D.S. without tools and moved, allowing complete cleaning or service.

These rugged assemblies are constructed of the finest materials. All have braided strain reliefs and are available with easy to clean outer jackets as an option.

TEMPERATURE/PRESSURE GAUGES

When monitoring pressure and/or temperature is required or desired, Seco Engineering offers appropriate gauges.

Gauges can be located behind an access door or surface mounted directly on the riser.

Figure 9-1f

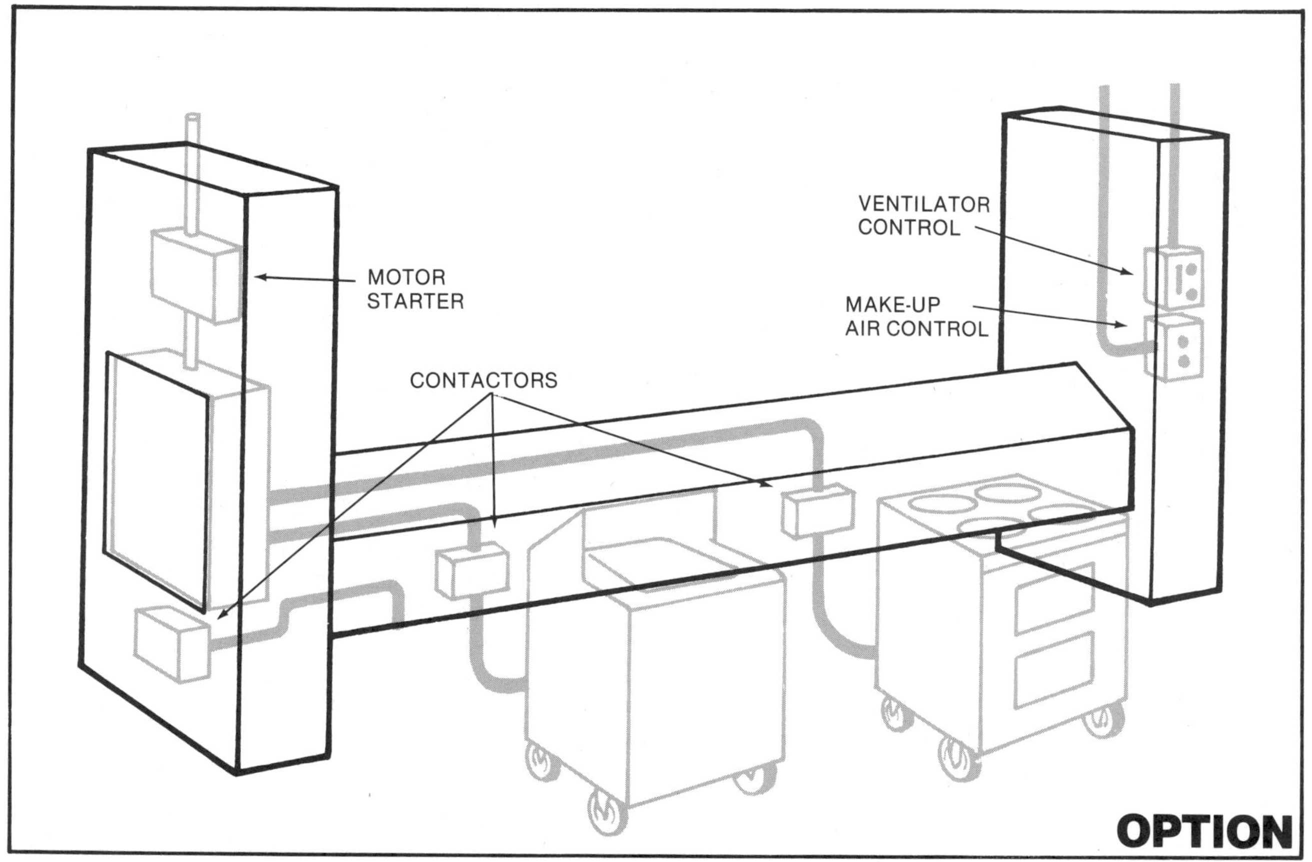

g

MAGNETIC MOTOR AND EQUIPMENT CONTROLLERS

Magnetic motor starters and controllers (contactors) are often required to operate equipment connected to the U.D.S.

Larger exhaust fans require motor starters. Fryers, broilers and other cooking equipment often require contactors for fire-fuel shut-off. Energy management systems require motor starters and contactors to control fans and equipment.

Without a Utility Distribution System, the motor starters and contactors are located on the roof, in the mechanical room, or wherever space is available. The U.D.S. provides a convenient location at the point of use.

VENTILATOR/MAKE-UP AIR INTERFACE

When the Utility Distribution System is used in conjunction with a ventilator and/or make-up air system, the controls can be mounted in the risers providing point of use operation.

Seco Engineering can supply all three systems, designed and built to compliment one another, providing one source coordination.

Note: Controls supplied by others must be U.L. listed.

Figure 9-1g

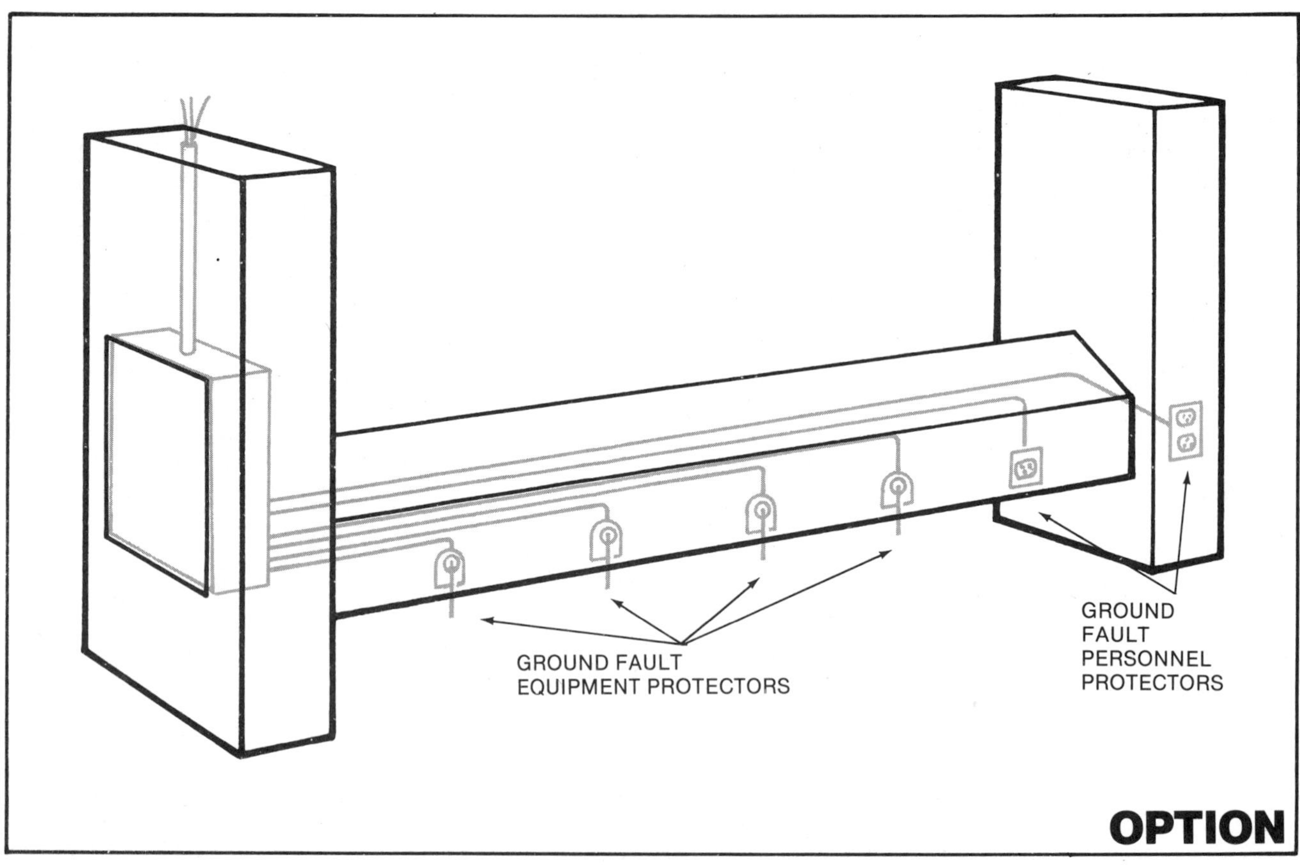

h

GROUND FAULT EQUIPMENT PROTECTION

Cooking and processing equipment, even in the cleanest kitchens, are subject to ground faults (short circuits).

A ground fault can occur when moisture, grease, or other contaminants build up on the electrical components inside the equipment. If this build-up forms a bridge between an electrical component and the equipment enclosure, electrical energy is short circuited to ground, and a ground fault occurs.

Ground faults usually do not trip the equipment circuit breaker until they become severe. Unless ground faults are detected and eliminated, energy is wasted, equipment damage can occur, and a fire hazzard is present.

As an option, Seco Engineering offers U.L. approved ground fault equipment protection incorporated into the Utility Distribution System: individual, automatic, protection for each piece of kitchen equipment. If a ground fault of one half ampere or greater occurs, the power supply to the equipment is automatically turned off indicating that service is required; minor service, not repairs for major failure or fire.

GROUND FAULT PERSONNEL PROTECTION

Underwriters Laboratories Standards 480 and 943 require ground fault personnel protectors to trip at 5 milliampres, plus or minus 1 milliampre.

These extremely sensitive protectors are available for 120 volt, 15 and 20 amp circuits only.

Seco Engineering offers ground fault personnel protectors for use with convenience and single receptacles and will catalogue other models as they become available.

Figure 9-1h

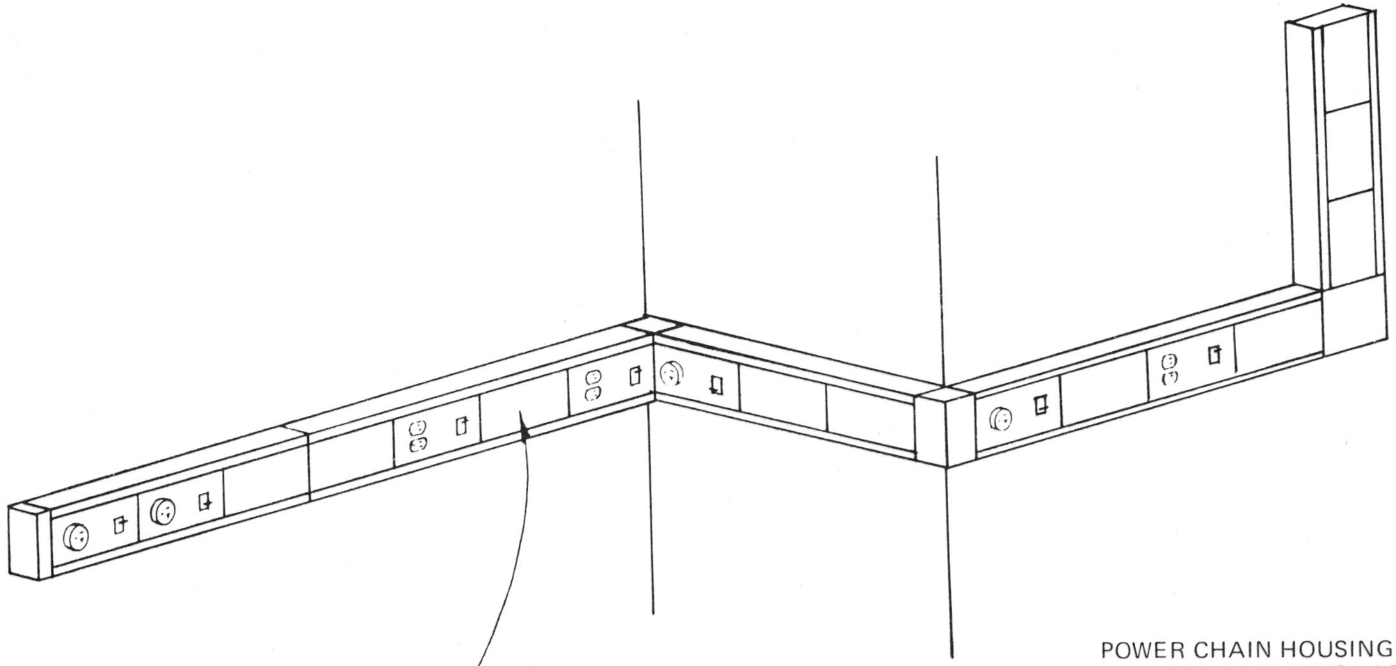

TYPICAL 4″ x 12″ INTERCHANGEABLE LINKS

POWER CHAIN HOUSING IS 2½″ WIDE x 6″ HIGH. INDIVIDUAL "LINKS" ARE 4″ x 12″ AND AVAILABLE IN 1, 2, 3, 4, 5 AND 9 FT. SECTIONS.

END CAPS ARE ONE INCH AND FILLER PIECES ARE AVAILABLE IN ONE INCH INCREMENTS TO MAKE UP ANY REQUIRED LENGTH. INNER AND OUTER CORNER PIECES ARE 2½″ SQUARE; RISOR PIECES ARE 6″ SQUARE.

ALTERNATE WIDTHS ARE 4″ AND 6″.

Figure 9-1i

i

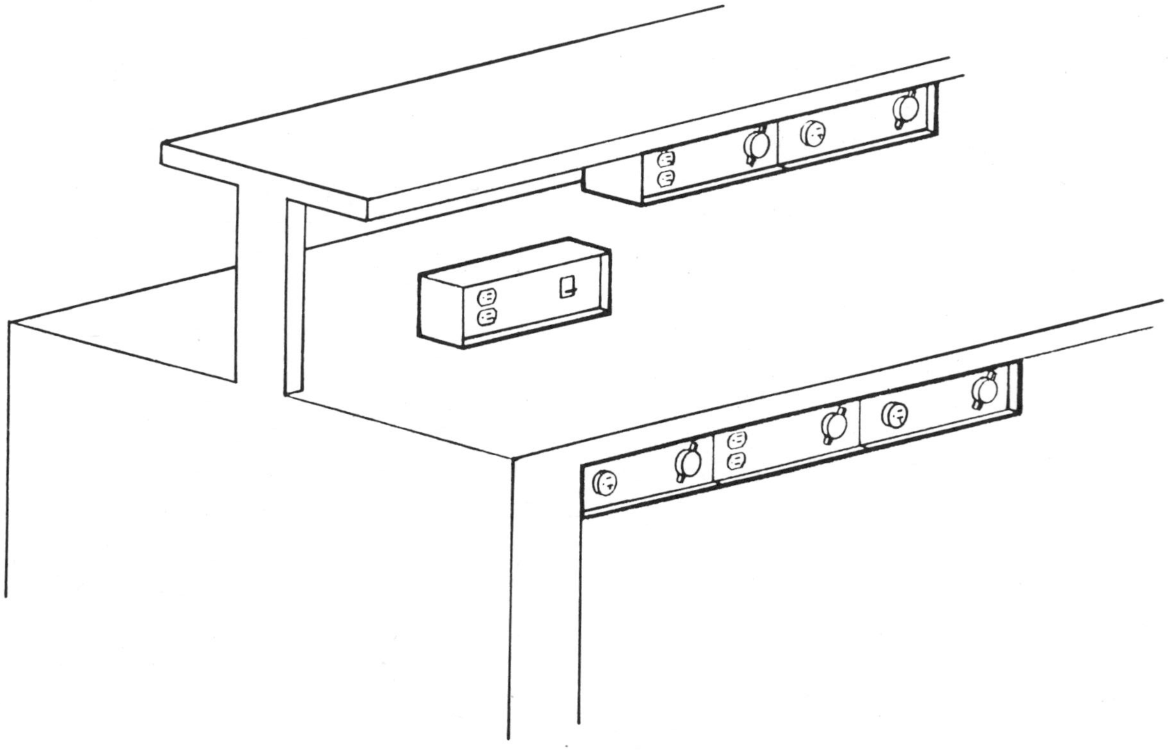

OVERALL HEIGHT IS 4-1/8″

SINGLE HOUSINGS ARE 2½″ DEEP
(BREAKER ACTUATOR REQUIRES 4″ DEPTH)
DOUBLE HOUSINGS ARE 5″ DEEP
(BREAKER ACTUATOR REQUIRES 8″ DEPTH)

Flange adds ¾″ to depth (single) if desired and 1½″ to depth (double).

SINGLE LINK PANEL IS	4-1/8″ x 12-1/8″
DOUBLE LINK PANEL IS	4-1/8″ x 24-1/8″
TRIPLE LINK PANEL IS	4-1/8″ x 36-1/8″

LINKS ARE AVAILABLE WITH SOLID STATE LINEAR TIMER AND DIAL POTENTIOMETER. REQUIRES 5″ DEPTH (SINGLE HOUSING) AND 8″ DEPTH (DOUBLE HOUSING).

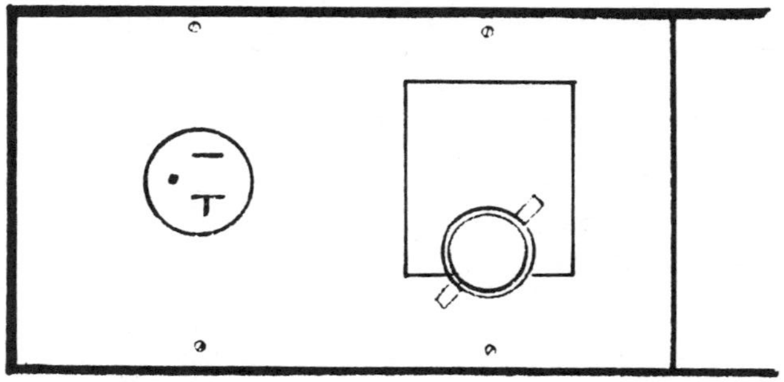

– TYPICAL LINK (4″ x 12″)
(Shown with Optional Breaker Actuator Knob)

Figure 9-1j

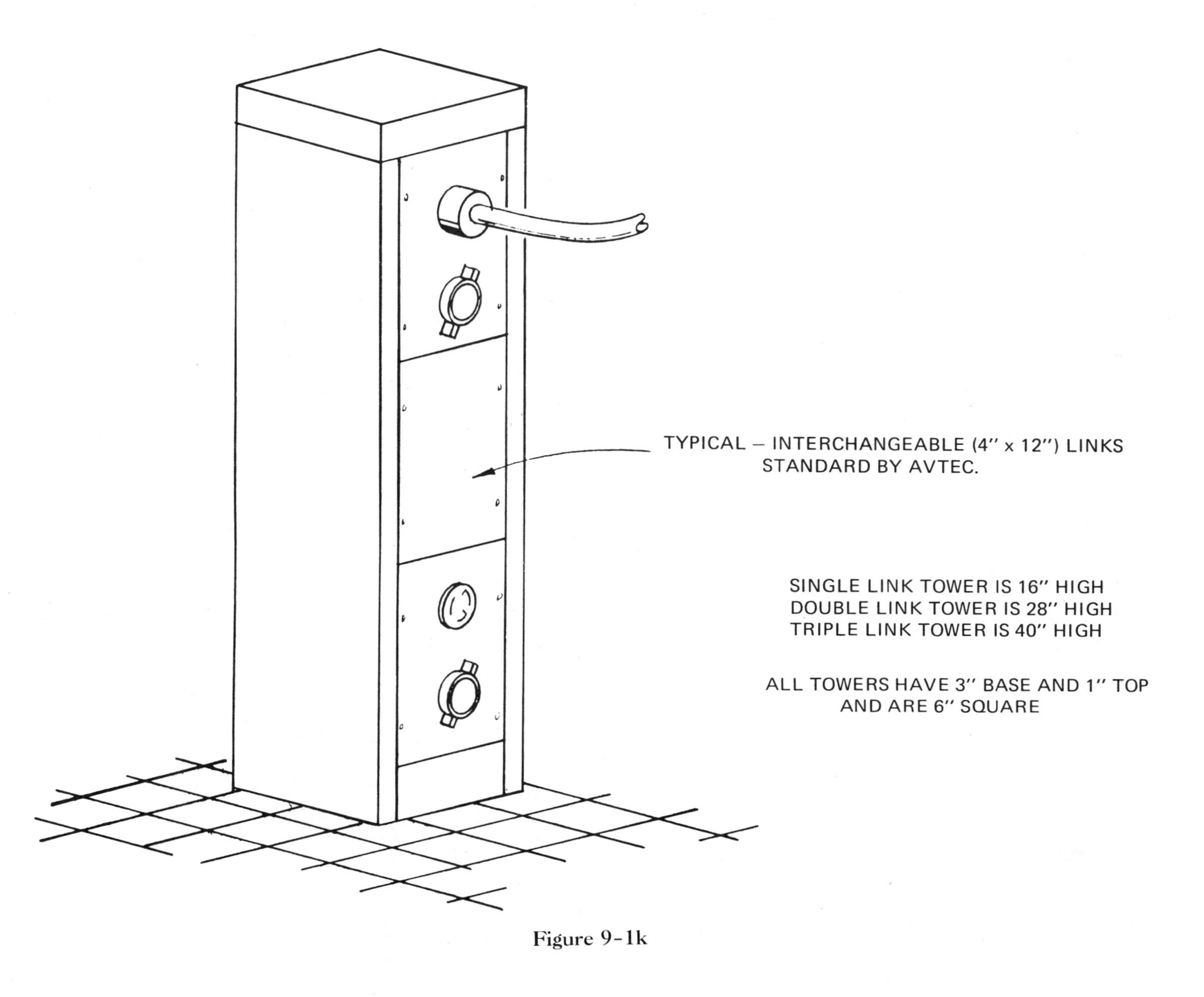
TYPICAL – INTERCHANGEABLE (4" x 12") LINKS
STANDARD BY AVTEC.
SINGLE LINK TOWER IS 16" HIGH
DOUBLE LINK TOWER IS 28" HIGH
TRIPLE LINK TOWER IS 40" HIGH
ALL TOWERS HAVE 3" BASE AND 1" TOP
AND ARE 6" SQUARE

Figure 9-1k

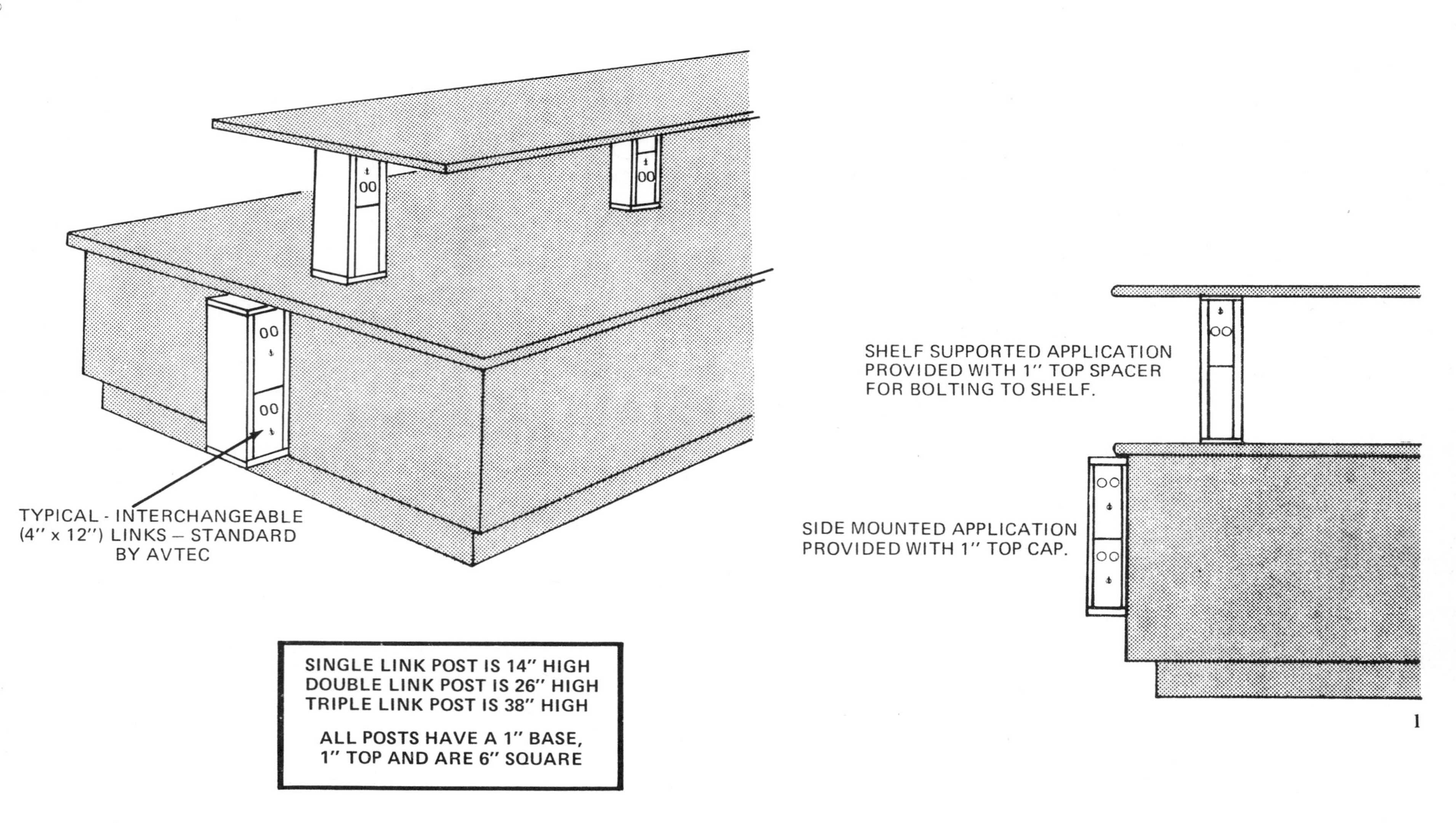

Links are available with solid state linear timer and dial potentiometer. Requires 5" depth (single housing) and 8" depth (double housing).

Figure 9-11

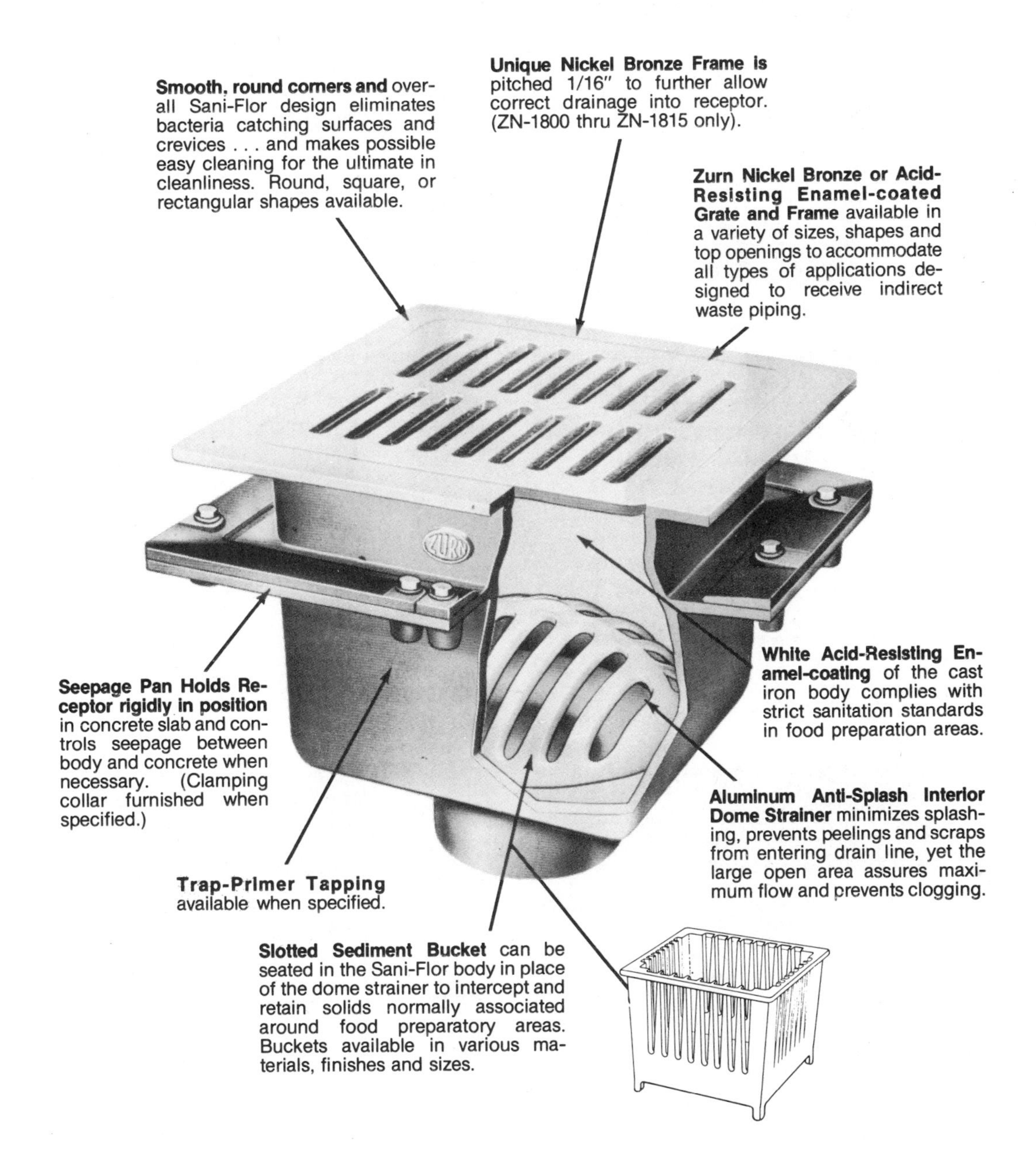

Smooth, round corners and overall Sani-Flor design eliminates bacteria catching surfaces and crevices . . . and makes possible easy cleaning for the ultimate in cleanliness. Round, square, or rectangular shapes available.
Unique Nickel Bronze Frame is pitched 1/16" to further allow correct drainage into receptor. (ZN-1800 thru ZN-1815 only).
Zurn Nickel Bronze or Acid-Resisting Enamel-coated Grate and Frame available in a variety of sizes, shapes and top openings to accommodate all types of applications designed to receive indirect waste piping.
ZURN
White Acid-Resisting Enamel-coating of the cast iron body complies with strict sanitation standards in food preparation areas.
Seepage Pan Holds Receptor rigidly in position in concrete slab and controls seepage between body and concrete when necessary. (Clamping collar furnished when specified.)
Aluminum Anti-Splash Interior Dome Strainer minimizes splashing, prevents peelings and scraps from entering drain line, yet the large open area assures maximum flow and prevents clogging.
Trap-Primer Tapping available when specified.
Slotted Sediment Bucket can be seated in the Sani-Flor body in place of the dome strainer to intercept and retain solids normally associated around food preparatory areas. Buckets available in various materials, finishes and sizes.

Figure 9-2a-c. Foodservice drains: a sampling of drains for foodservice equipment. An architect, consultant, or plumbing contractor can provide the necessary information on available types. See Figure 5-7 for an example of a drain at a steam cooking area. (Courtesy Zurn Manufacturing)

SUFFIX -1 (LESS GRATE)

SUFFIX -2 (1/2 GRATE)

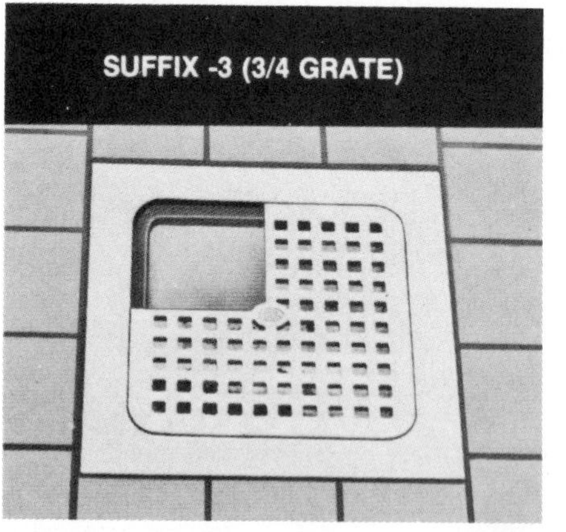
SUFFIX -3 (3/4 GRATE)

SUFFIX -4 (FULL GRATE WITH
CENTER OPENING)

Figure 9-2b

SUFFIX -5 (GRATE WITH 4" DIA. ×
3-3/4" HIGH FUNNEL)
SUFFIX -6 (GRATE WITH 6" DIA. × 6"
HIGH FUNNEL)

SUFFIX -7 (GRATE WITH 6-3/4" × 3" ×
1" HIGH OVAL FUNNEL)
SUFFIX -8 (GRATE WITH 8-7/8" × 3-5/8"
× 3-3/4" HIGH OVAL FUNNEL)

SUFFIX -9 (ANGLE FRAME & GRATE)

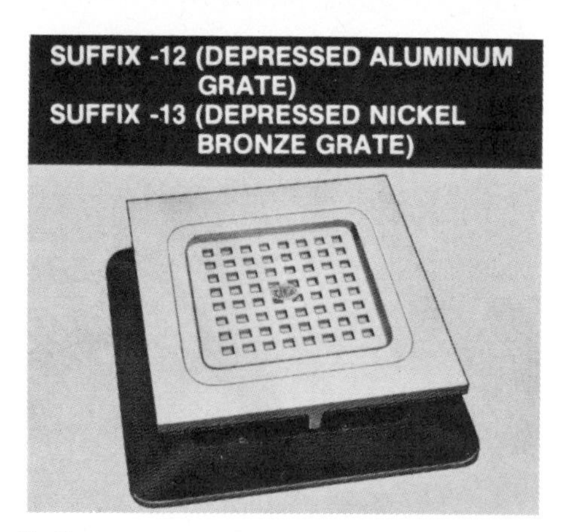
SUFFIX -12 (DEPRESSED ALUMINUM
GRATE)
SUFFIX -13 (DEPRESSED NICKEL
BRONZE GRATE)

Figure 9-2c

SIZING A GREASE TRAP

Single Fixture Installations:

Step No. 1:

Cubic content of a fixture = length × width × depth.

Example: A 3 compartment Scullery Sink overall 56″ × 27″. Each compartment 18″ × 24″ × 12″ = 5,184 cubic inch area; 3 × 5,184 = 15,552 total cubic inch area for 3 compartments.

Step. No. 2:

Content in cubic inches divided by 231 = capacity in U.S. gallons.

Example: $\frac{15{,}552}{231}$ = 67 U.S. gallons

Step No. 3:

Since experience shows that a sink or fixture is seldom filled to the brim and the dishes, pots or pans displace approximately 25% of the water, we suggest 75% of the actual fixture capacity to be used as a basis to establish the drainage load.

Example: 75% of 67 U.S. = approx. 50 U.S.G. drainage load.

Step No. 4:

The most generally accepted drainage period is one minute. Conditions may exist however, (on any given project) whereby a longer drainage period could be considered. Therefore, flow rates for this example would be:—

$$\frac{\text{Drainage Load in Gallons}}{\text{Drainage Load in Minutes}} = \text{Flow rate in GPM}$$

Therefore flow rates for this example would be:—
50 GPM for 1 minute total drainage
25 GPM for 2 minute total drainage (should a longer period be desired)
Caution: This chart is basic information only. Check with local health department codes in your area for proper sizing.

TYPICAL GREASE TRAP CHART

Rating GPM	Lbs. Grease Capacity	Length	Width	Height
4	8	17⅛″	9¾″	10″
7	14	19¼″	12⅛″	11⅛″
10	20	23″	14⅛″	11¾″
15	30	25″	16⅞″	13⅜″
20	40	27⅞″	17⅜″	15″
25	50	29⅞″	20″	17″
35	70	31¾″	22⅝″	18¾″
50	100	33⅝″	24⅝″	21½″

Figure 9-2d

ENGINEERING DATA

INDIRECT CONNECTIONS TO WASTE PIPES

Indirect Wastes. Waste pipes from the following shall not connect directly with any building drain, soil, or waste pipe: a refrigerator, ice box, or other receptacle where food is stored; an appliance, device, or apparatus used in the preparation or processing of food or drink; an appliance, device, or apparatus using water as a cooling or heating medium; a sterilizer, water still, water-treatment device, or water-operated device.

Such waste pipes shall in all cases empty into, and above the flood level or, an open plumbing fixture or shall be connected indirectly to the inlet side of a fixture trap. Indirect waste connections shall not be located in inaccessible or unventilated cellars or other spaces.

Size of Refrigerator Wastes. Refrigerator waste pipes shall not be less than 1¼ inches in diameter for one opening. 1½ inches for 2 or 3 openings, and 2 inches for 4 to 12 openings. Each opening shall have a trap and clean-out so installed as to permit proper flushing and cleaning of the waste pipe.

Overflow Pipes. Overflow pipes from a water-supply tank or exhaust pipes from a water lift shall not be directly connected with any building drain or with any soil or waste pipe, but shall discharge outside the building, or into an open fixture.

INSTALLATION OF PIPING AND TABLE 201-III

Installation of Piping. When a building drain or sewer is installed with a fall of less than 1/16 inch per foot for 10-inch and larger diameters, the minimum permissible velocity should be computed by the formula $h/12l = 0.00008385\ v^2/d$ (for rough pipe), where h is the fall in inches per foot, l the length of pipe in feet, v the velocity in feet per second, and d the diameter in feet. If it is desired to install a building drain or building sewer at a slope that will maintain a velocity above some selected minimum within the specified minimums for the different diameters, the following table 201-III applying to rough pipe may be consulted. In general, the required fall in inches per foot is given approximately by $\sqrt{s/s_1} = v/v_1$ or $s = s_1(v/v_1)^2$, in which s is the fall in inches per foot necessary to give a selected velocity v, and s_1 and v_1 are the fall and resultant velocity for pipe of the same diameter.

Table 201-III.—Approximate velocities for given slopes and diameters

Diameter of pipe	Velocities				
	1/32-inch fall per foot	1/16-inch fall per foot	1/8-inch fall per foot	1/4-inch fall per foot	1/2-inch fall per foot
Inches	*fps*	*fps*	*fps*	*fps*	*fps*
1¼ --	0.57	0.80	1.14	1.61	2.28
1½ --	.62	.88	1.24	1.76	2.45
2 -----	.72	1.02	1.44	**2.03**	2.88
2½ --	.81	1.14	1.61	2.28	3.23
3 -----	.88	1.24	1.76	2.49	3.53
4 -----	1.02	1.44	**2.03**	2.88	4.07
5 -----	1.14	1.61	2.28	3.23	4.56
6 -----	1.24	1.76	2.49	3.53	5.00
8 -----	1.44	**2.03**	2.88	4.07	5.75
10 -----	1.6.	2.28	3.23	4.56	6.44
12 -----	1.76	2.49	3.53	5.00	7.06

Figure 9-3. Indirect connections to waste pipes. Installation of piping. (Courtesy Zurn Manufacturing)

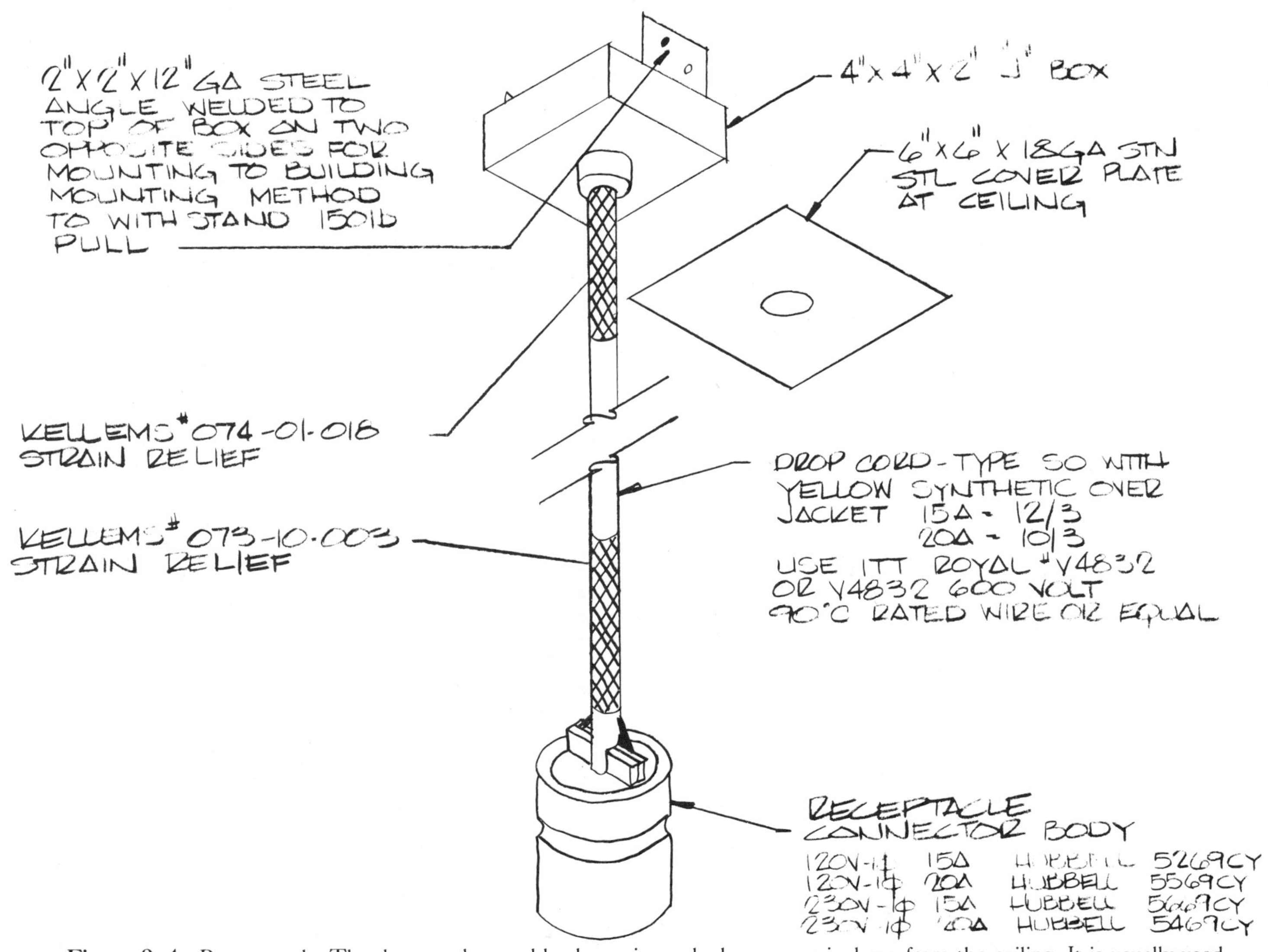

Figure 9-4. Power cords. The drop cord assembly shown is used when power is down from the ceiling. It is usually used when hot and/or cold transport and holding cabinets are used.

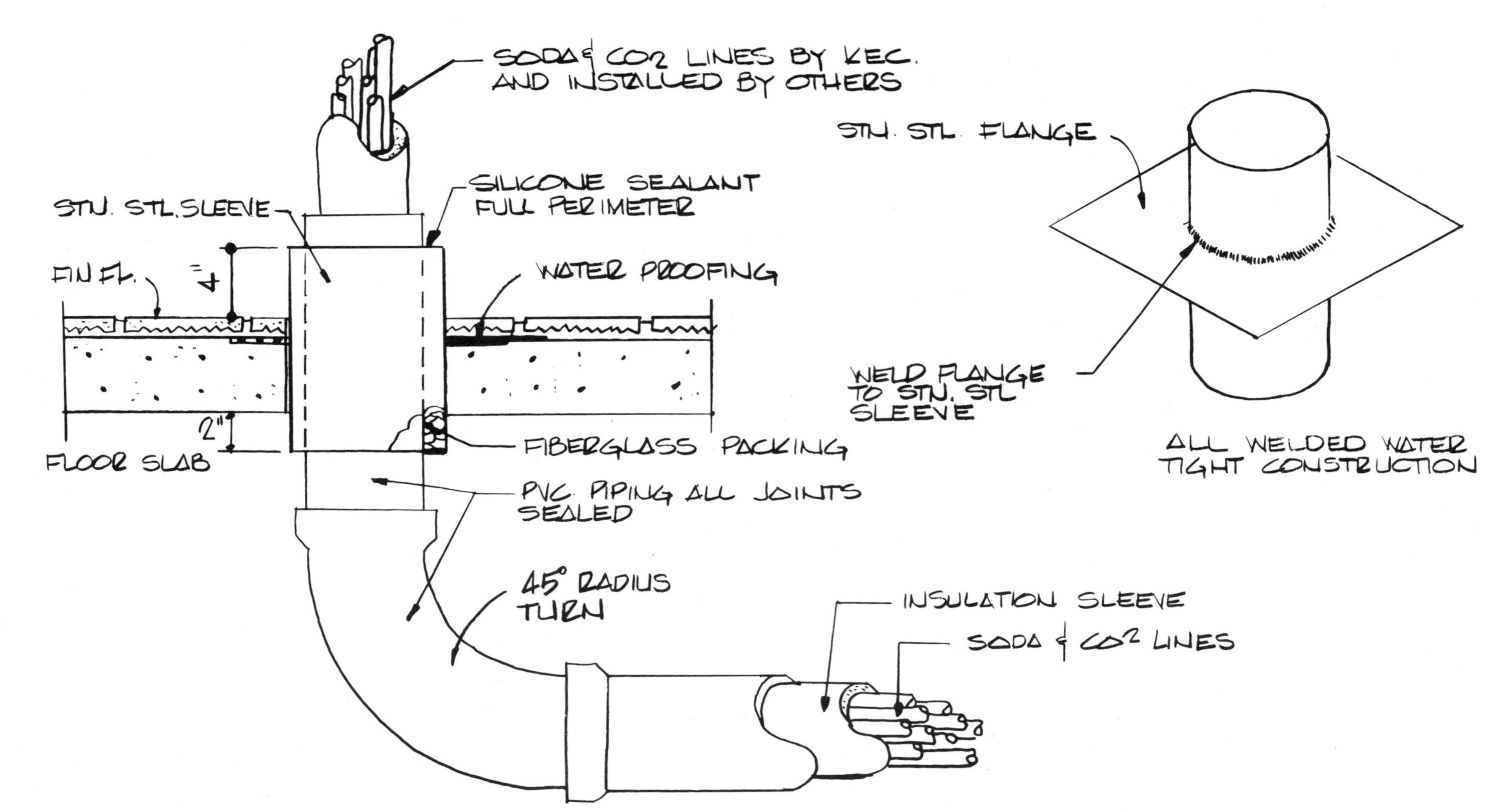

Figure 9-5. Conduit in floor for soda. Floor penetration of conduit for soda lines is shown as a guide only. Actual specifications are supplied by the beverage installer.

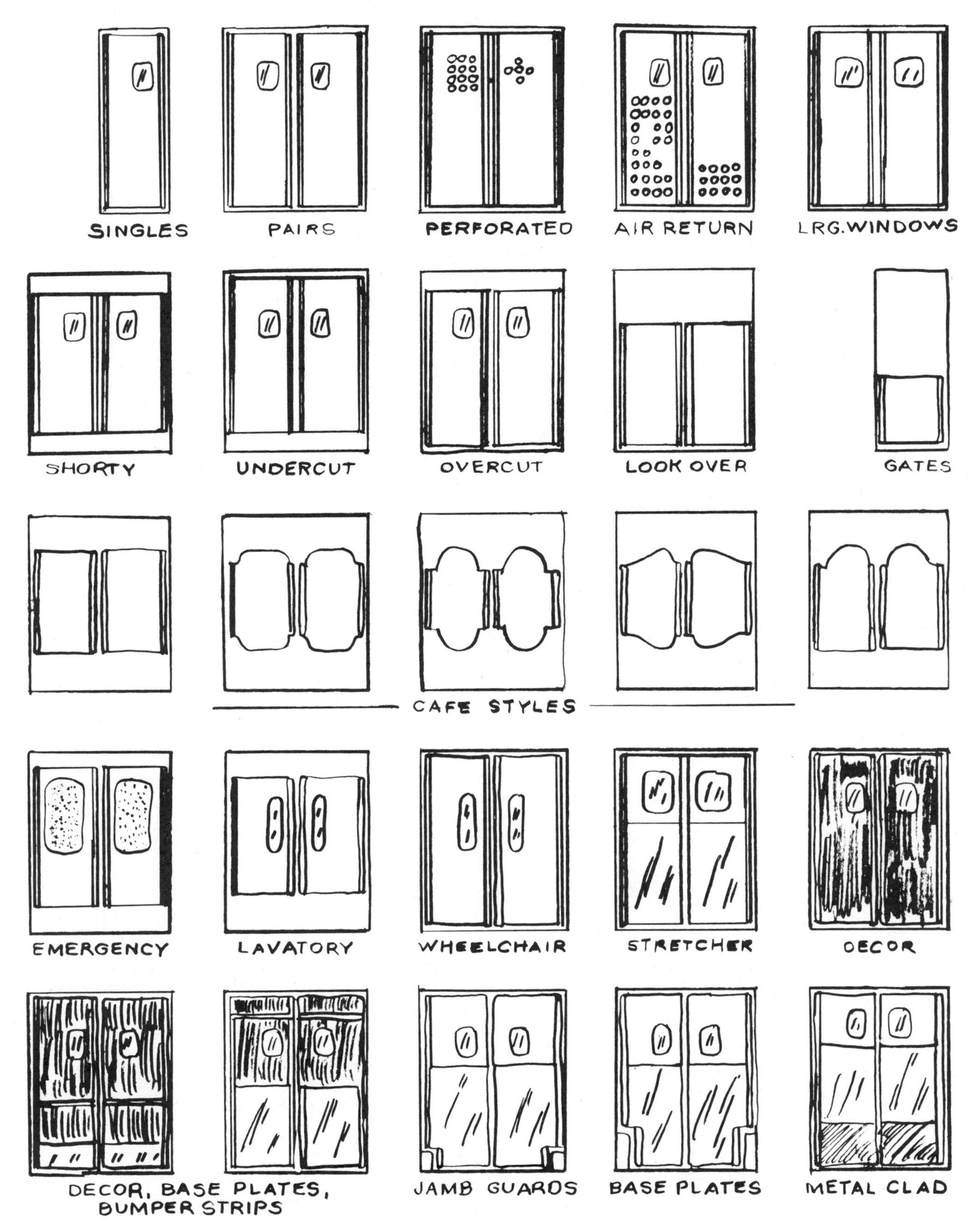

Figure 9-6. Foodservice doors. These doors are available in all shapes and sizes; this selection is shown to stimulate the user's imagination. (Courtesy Eliason Easy Swing Door)

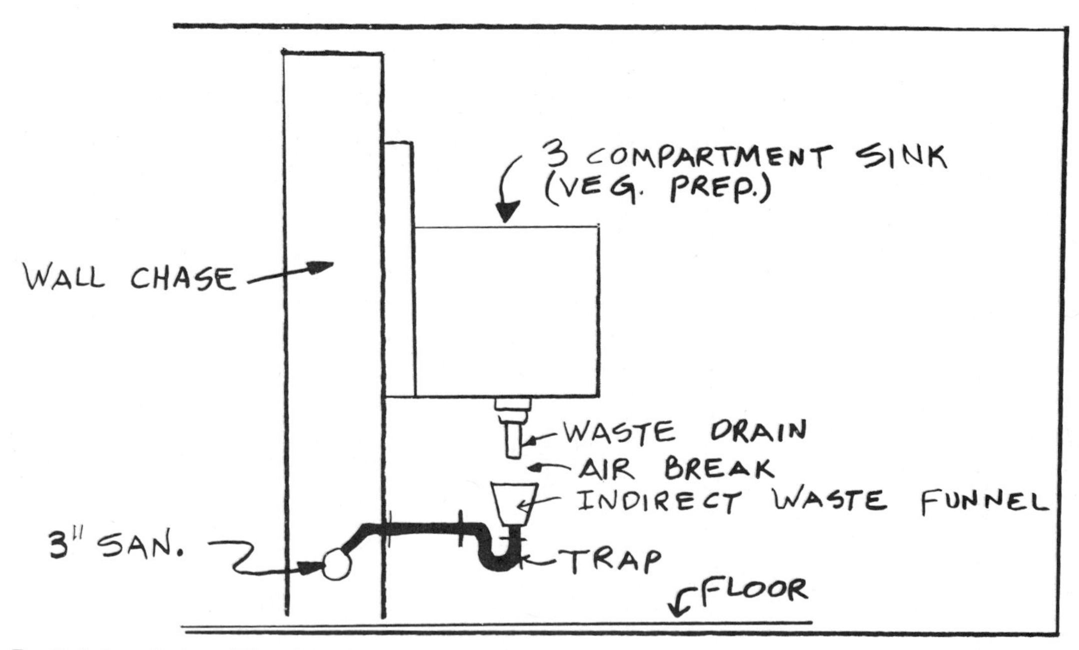

Figure 9-7. Sink installation. The side view of a sink shows an indirect drain. Such drains eliminate backup in case of clogging and are required on many pieces of equipment, such as dishwashers, steam tables, and sinks.

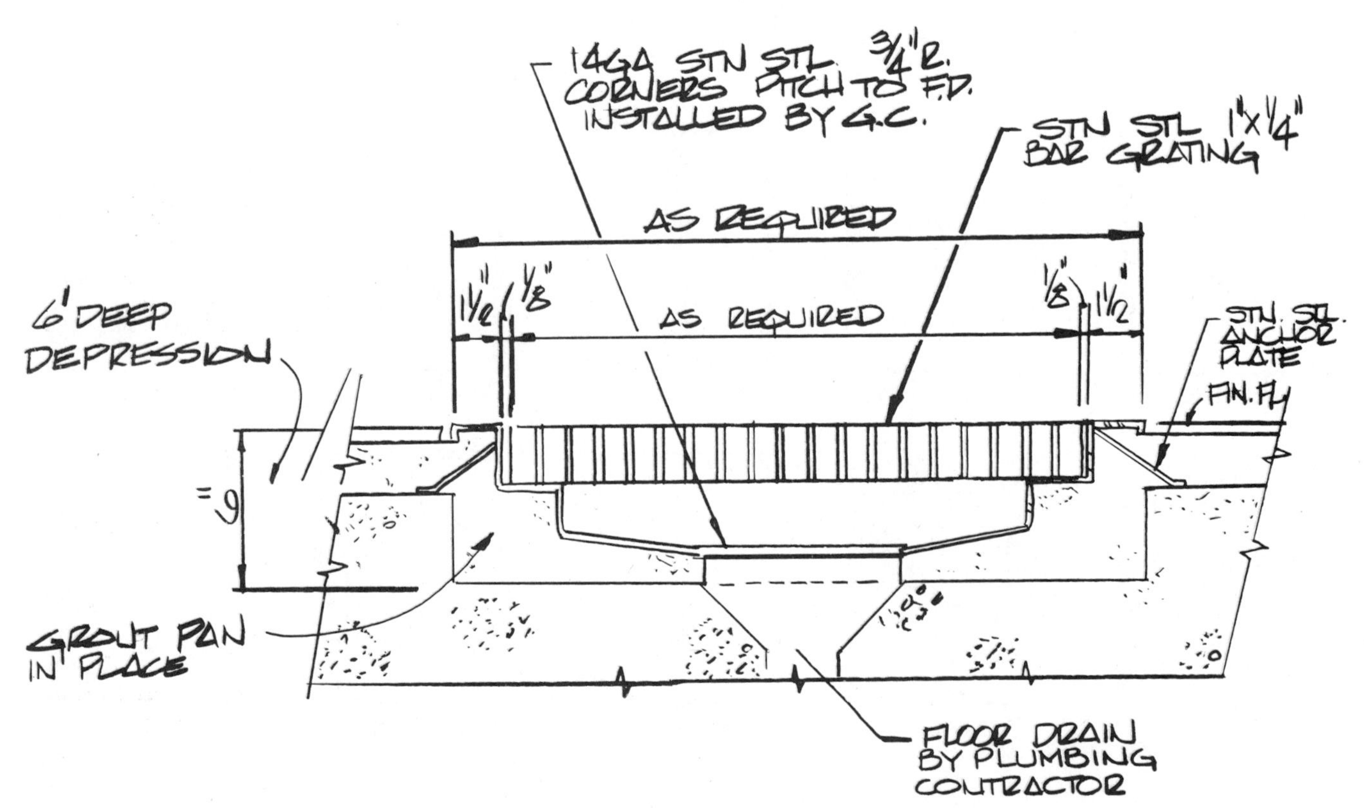

Figure 9-8. Floor drain trough. Typical detail of an installed floor trough for commercial kitchens.

Gas Connectors for Movable Foodservice Appliances

❶ Connect Dormont Supr-Safe Gas Ball Valve to house piping. (An additional steel elbow may be necessary depending on the location of the house piping.)

❷ Connect Dormont Supr-Safe Gas Appliance Connector to Gas Ball Valve. (Note—*Do Not* use pipe dope, teflon tape or any other sealing compound in flare seat of gas connector.)

❸ Join furnished steel elbow to appliance nipple. Elbow should be facing downward.

❹ Attach Supr-Quik quick disconnect (nipple portion) to steel elbow.

❺ Connect both portions of Supr-Quik quick disconnect device (nipple & coupler) to Supr-Safe Gas Connector.

Tighten all connections. Perform leak test with leak test solution. IMPORTANT: Leak test solutions may cause corrosion—water rinse after test, then thoroughly dry.

❻ Restraining Cable:

a. Restraining cable length must be shorter than gas connector.

b. Attach eyelet fasteners to both wall and equipment.

c. Attach spring hooks of restraining cable to eyelet fasteners on wall and equipment.

Note: An alternative installation to that shown above would be to reverse the gas connector so that the quick disconnect is near the house inlet gas pipe (coupler part of quick disconnect attaches to gas ball valve while nipple part attaches to connector). In both installations, the manual gas ball valve must be positioned upstream from the gas connector and the quick disconnect device.

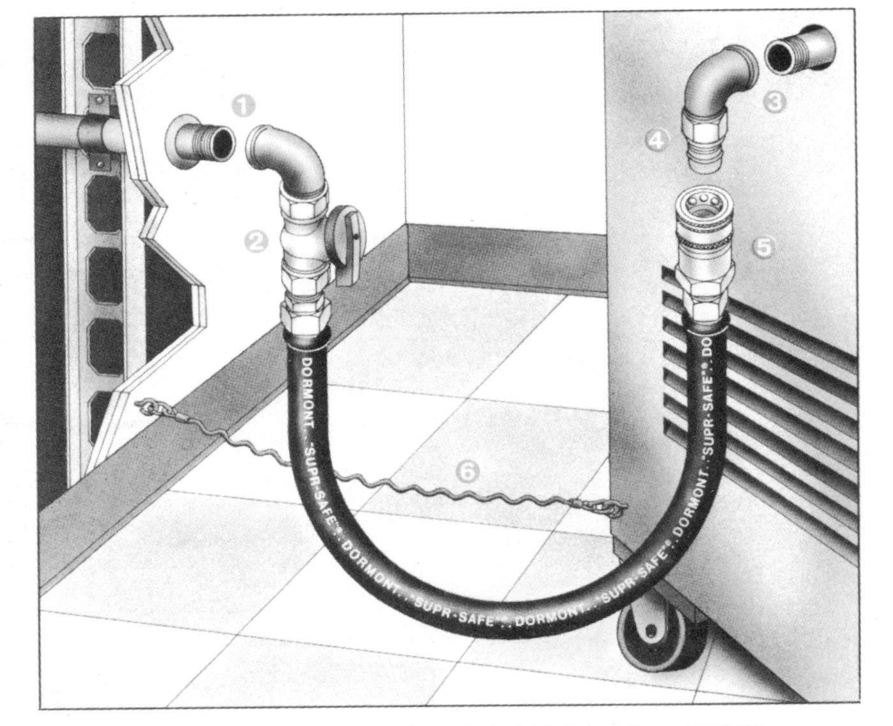

Please refer to installation instructions tag on every connector for detailed information, as specified in ANSI Z21.69

Note: The gas connector must be installed in accordance with the National Fuel Gas Code (ANSI Z223.1) and any State or Local Code requirements.

Dormont Manufacturing Company makes no warranty, representation or condition of any kind, express or implied (including any warranty of merchantability or of fitness) and none shall be implied by law. Dormont shall not be liable for incidental or consequential & damages.

Figure 9–9a,b. Gas appliance installation. Information used by architects, consultants, and the general foodservice trade. (Courtesy Dormont Manufacturing)

Restraining Devices for Movable Appliances

To comply with ANSI Regulation Z21.69, a restraining device is *mandatory* for all types of movable/castered gas appliances. These devices prevent moving a castered appliance too far from the wall before the gas connector has been disconnected, an important safety precaution that prevents damage to the connector and hazardous gas leaks. In all installations, the restraining device must be shorter in length than the gas appliance connector it is protecting.

Dormont supplies two types of restraining devices fabricated from heavy-gauge steel cable and steel fittings. The *coiled* type is available in four fixed lengths and the *adjustable* type in two sizes.

Model Order Numbers

Coiled

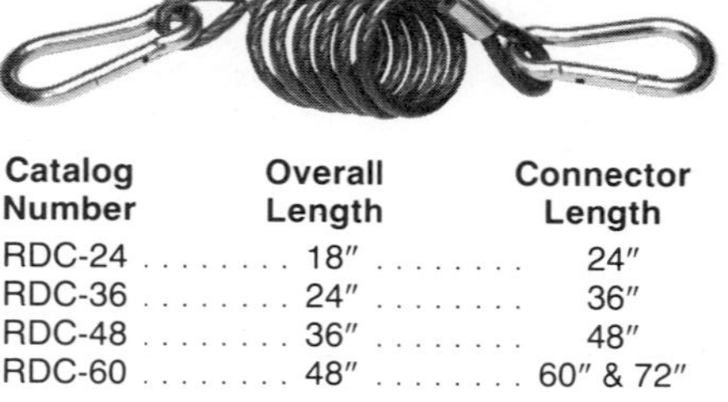

Catalog Number	Overall Length	Connector Length
RDC-24	18″	24″
RDC-36	24″	36″
RDC-48	36″	48″
RDC-60	48″	60″ & 72″

Typical Installation

A typical installation of a *Supr-Safe*® connector with *Supr-Quik*® disconnect and an adjustable restraining device on a castered broiler in its operating position. The restraining device prevents excessive movement of the appliance before the connector has been disconnected.

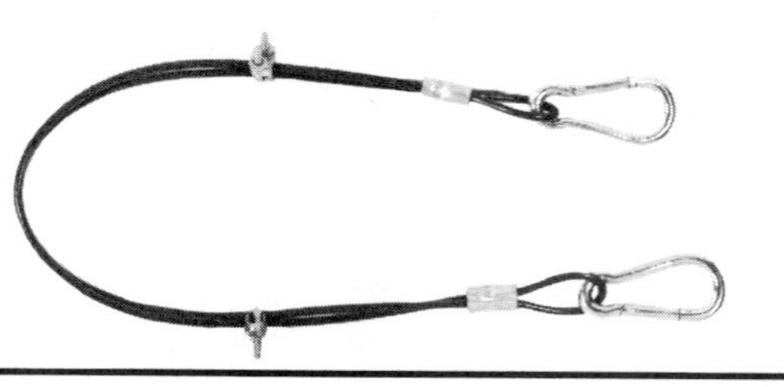

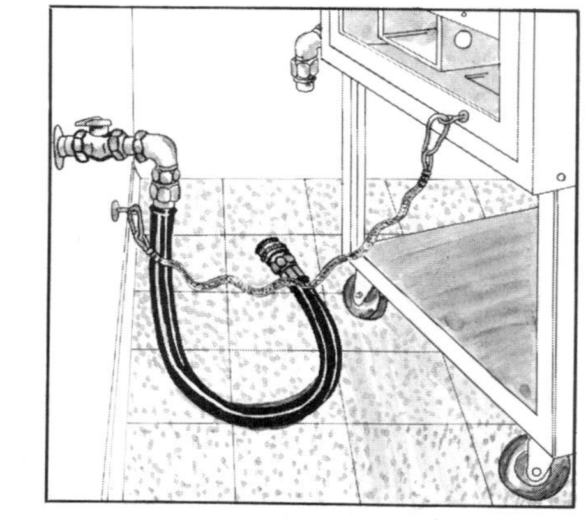

When it's time for cleanup, the broiler is moved far enough from the wall to reach the quick-disconnect and the connector is separated from the appliance. The broiler then can be pulled to the length of the restraining device for quicker and more sanitary area cleaning.

Adjustable

Catalog Number	Adjustment Range
RD-36	Up to 48″
RD-72	Up to 72″

Gas Ball Valves

All gas burning equipment connected to a piping system must have an accessible, approved, manual *shutoff valve* installed upstream of any connector and within 6 feet of the equipment it serves, according to National Fuel Gas Code (ANSI Z223.1) and the American National Standards Institute (ANSI Z21.69). Dormont gas ball valves are design certified by the AGA and CGA as manual shutoff valves for use with all types of fuel gases and with both movable and stationary foodservice equipment.

Figure 9-9b

Model Order Numbers

Straight Valves

Catalog Number	Size/Description
050-FV	½″ FIP x ½″FIP
075-FV	¾″ FIP x ¾″ FIP
100-FV	1″ FIP x 1″ FIP
125-FV	1¼″ FIP x 1¼″ FIP
150-FV	1½″ FIP x 1½″ FIP
200-FV	2″ FIP x 2″ FIP

AMPERAGE SIZING GUIDE-KILOWATTS

KILO-WATTS K.W.'S	*AMPERAGE SINGLE PHASE 1ϕ - (60 HERTZ)*			*AMPERAGE THREE PHASE 3ϕ - (60 HERTZ)*		
	110/1ϕ 125/1ϕ	120/208/1ϕ & 208/1ϕ	120/250/1ϕ & 250/1ϕ	120/208/3ϕ & 208/3ϕ	120/250/3ϕ & 250/3ϕ	440/3ϕ TO 480/3ϕ
.05	.42	.24	.21	.14	.12	.06
.1	.84	.48	.42	.28	.24	.12
.2	1.7	.96	.84	.56	.49	.24
.3	2.5	1.5	1.3	.83	.73	.36
.4	3.4	1.9	1.7	1.1	.97	.48
.5	4.2	2.4	2.1	1.4	1.2	.60
.6	5.0	2.9	2.5	1.7	1.5	.72
.7	5.9	3.4	2.9	2.0	1.7	.84
.8	6.7	3.9	3.4	2.2	2.0	.96
.9	7.5	4.3	3.8	2.5	2.2	1.1
1.0	8.4	4.8	4.2	2.8	2.4	1.2
2.0	16.7	9.6	8.4	5.6	4.9	2.4
3.0	25.0	14.4	12.5	8.3	7.3	3.6
4.0	33.4	19.3	16.7	11.1	9.7	4.8
5.0	41.7	24.1	20.9	13.9	12.1	6.0
6.0	50.0	28.9	25.0	16.7	14.6	7.2
7.0	58.4	33.7	29.2	19.4	17.0	8.5
8.0	66.7	38.5	33.4	22.2	19.4	9.6
9.0	75.0	43.3	37.5	25.0	21.8	10.8
10.0	83.4	48.1	41.7	27.8	24.3	12.0
20.0	166.7	96.2	83.4	55.5	48.5	24.1
30.0	250.0	144.3	125.0	83.3	72.7	36.1
40.0	333.4	192.3	166.7	111.0	96.9	48.1
50.0	416.7	240.4	208.4	138.8	121.2	60.2
60.0	500.0	288.5	250.0	166.6	145.4	72.2
70.0	583.4	336.6	291.7	194.3	169.6	84.2
80.0	666.7	384.6	333.4	222.1	193.9	96.2
90.0	750.0	432.7	375.0	249.8	218.1	108.3
100.0	833.4	480.8	416.7	277.6	242.3	120.3

NOTE: *One kilowatt = 1000 watts. Therefore, to convert watts into kilowatts move decimal point of watts to left three places. (3550. watts = 3.550 K.W.'s) To find amperage, using the above chart a 208/1ϕ - 3.550 K.W. Hot Food Pan is:*

3.00 K.W. = 14.40 AMPS
0.50 K.W. = 2.40 AMPS
0.05 K.W. = .24 AMPS

TOTAL K.W. = 3.55 K.W. or 17.04 AMPS

Figure 9-10. Amperage sizing guide, kilowatts. (Courtesy Avtec Industries)

STANDARD PLUGS AND RECEPTACLES

An industry wide standard has been in effect for a number of years to standardize the configuration of of electrical plugs and receptacles. Cres-Cor and Crown-X equipment is made in accordance with these standards.

Illustrated on this sheet are the standard plugs used on Cres-Cor and Crown-X equipment. Illustrated next to the plugs are the required receptacle configurations. These are shown to serve as a guide.

If you receive Cres-Cor or Crown-X equipment which will not fit into your existing receptacles, then both the receptacle and the supply wiring should be checked by an electrician and changed as required.

VOLTAGE	STD. CORD SIZES	WATTAGE	SINGLE PHASE NON-LOCKING RECEPTACLE	PLUG	SINGLE PHASE LOCKING RECEPTACLE	PLUG
110-120 VOLTS 15 AMPS	18/3 16/3 14/3	USED WITH UNITS OF 1500W OR LESS	5-15R	5-15P	L5-15R	L5-15P
110-120 VOLTS 20 AMPS	12/3	USED WITH UNITS OF 1500-2000 WATTS	5-20R	5-20P	L5-20R	L5-20P
110-120 VOLTS 30 AMPS	10/3	USED WITH UNITS OF 2000-3000 WATTS	5-30R	5-30P	L5-30R	L5-30P
110-120 VOLTS 50 AMPS	6/3	USED WITH UNITS OF 3000-5000 WATTS	5-50R	5-50P	L5-50R	L5-50P
208, 220-240 VOLTS 15 AMPS	18/3 16/3 14/3	USED WITH UNITS OF 3000W OR LESS	6-15R	6-15P	L6-15R	L6-15P
208, 220-240 VOLTS 20 AMPS	12/3	USED WITH UNITS OF 3000-4000 WATTS	6-20R	6-20P	L6-20R	L6-20P
208, 220-240 VOLTS 30 AMPS	10/3	USED WITH UNITS OF 4000-6000 WATTS	6-30R	6-30P	L6-30R	L6-30P
208, 220-240 VOLTS 50 AMPS	6/3	USED WITH UNITS OF 6000-10,000 WATTS	6-50R	6-50P		

Approximate diameter of power supply cords used on Cres-Cor and Crown-X Equipment. Two wire conductors with ground wire. Diameters shown in inches.

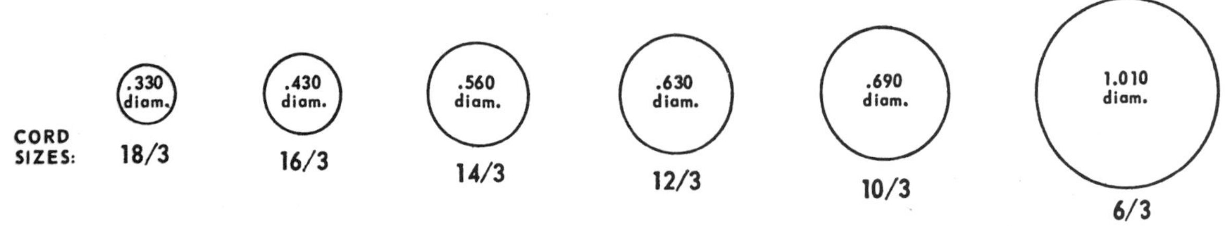

Figure 9-11a-d. Guide to standard electrical installation. (Courtesy Cres-Cor Manufacturing)

ENERGY UNIT MEASURE BTU CONVERSION CHART

Convert energy usage to Btu's (British Thermal Unit) to eliminate differences in unit measurement for types of fuel.

Electricity: kilowatt hours (kwh) x 3413
Natural gas: cubic feet x 1000

Kerosene: gallons x 134,000
Butane: gallons x 103,300

Propane: gallons x 91,600
Steam: pounds x 1000
Coal: pounds x 13,000
Wood: pounds x 8,800

#2 oil: gallons x 138,200
#4 oil: gallons x 144,000
#5 oil: gallons x 150,000
#6 oil: gallons x 152,000

Convert to million Btu's by dividing figures by 1,000,000 OR to therms by dividing figures by 100,000.

ELECTRICAL POWER REQUIREMENT CHART

The following tables are included to aid you in determining the power requirement for your Cres-Cor and Crown-X equipment.

By locating the proper voltage and wattage on the chart, the current consumption of the equipment can be determined. The current consumption shown in the chart is in Amperes.

WATTS

Values shown in chart are Amperes.

VOLTS	500	1000	1500	2000	2500	3000	3500	4000	4500	5000
110-120 Single Phase	4.2	8.3	12.5	16.7	20.8					
208 Single Phase	2.4	4.8	7.2	9.6	12.0	14.4	16.8	19.2	21.6	24.0
220-240 Single Phase	2.1	4.2	6.3	8.3	10.4	12.5	14.6	16.7	18.8	20.8
208 3-Phase	1.4	2.8	4.2	5.6	6.9	8.3	9.7	11.1	12.5	13.9
220-240 3-Phase	1.2	2.4	3.6	4.8	6.0	7.2	8.4	9.6	10.8	12.0
440-480 3-Phase	.6	1.2	1.8	2.4	3.0	3.6	4.2	4.8	5.4	6.0

WATTS

Values shown in chart are Amperes.

VOLTS	5500	6000	6500	7000	7500	8000	8500	9000	9500	10000
110-120 Single Phase										
208 Single Phase	26.4	28.8	31.3	33.7	36.1	38.5	40.9	43.3	45.7	48.1
220-240 Single Phase	22.9	25.0	27.1	29.2	31.3	33.3	35.4	37.5	39.6	41.7
208 3-Phase	15.3	16.7	18.1	19.5	20.8	22.2	23.6	25.0	26.4	27.8
220-240 3-Phase	13.2	14.5	15.7	16.9	18.1	19.3	20.5	21.7	22.9	24.1
440-480 3-Phase	6.6	7.2	7.8	8.4	9.0	9.6	10.2	10.8	11.4	12.0

Figure 9-11b

IMPORTANT ADVICE BEFORE ORDERING AND USING ELECTRICAL EQUIPMENT

Make sure that your order contains all critical information, and is correctly specified.

Every electrical device shipped from the factory carries a nameplate which specifies the voltage and other characteristics of the device. Be suspicious. Always check the nameplate data before connecting the device. Here's what can happen if you fail to follow this simple procedure:

Wires too small will result in improper heating, frequent blowing of fuses, and possible fire hazards.

If you use a 230V device connected to a 115V circuit it will produce only 25 per cent of its rated output.

If you use 230V equipment on 208V lines, you'll lose approximately 20 per cent efficiency, and slow down pre-heat time as well as recovery of temperature.

If you use 208V equipment on 230V lines, you'll boost the wattage by approximately 25 per cent. This overloaded condition will reduce the life of the heating elements. When in doubt, always consult your electric utility specialist and/or electrical contractor before installing new equipment.

Here's a final tip: Always secure a recommendation from your utility specialist for the method of metering to obtain best possible electric rates.

Act on the counsel offered above, and you'll have a top-performing, trouble-free kitchen — and you'll save costs, delays, and loss of efficiency.

UL and CSA have set new standards to protect your personnel and to meet the very latest codes. We have incorporated them in our products.

GLOSSARY OF ELECTRICAL TERMS

Ampere The rate of flow of electricity through a conductor.

BTU British Thermal Units. In terms of heat, 3,413 BTU's equal one kilowatt hour.

Circuit A conductor or a system of conductors through which an electric current flows.

Circuit Breaker or Fuse A load limiting device that automatically interrupts an electric circuit if an overload condition occurs.

Conductor If a material will permit electric current to flow through it, it is known as a "conductor;" if it will not permit current to flow, it is an "insulator."

Cycle Frequency of alternating current expressed in hertz. 60 cycles per second = 60 hertz.

Kilowatt One thousand watts. Most commercial kitchen equipment is rated in kilowatts.

Kilowatt Hours The work done by 1 kw in 1 hour. Kwhrs are recorded by the meter.

Name Plate A metal plate attached to the appliance stating the electrical characteristics of that appliance in volts, watts, amperes, phase, and type of current (AC or DC). It will also usually state the model number and serial number of the appliance.

Single Phase A circuit energized by a single alternating voltage.

Three Phase Three separate sources of alternate current so arranged that the peaks of voltage follow each other in a regular, repeating pattern.

Volt The push that moves electrical current through a conductor.

Watt A unit of electrical power. One watt equals the flow of one amp at a pressure of one volt (Watts = Volts X Amps).

WIRING CAPACITY TABLE

MAXIMUM KW LOAD PER CIRCUIT*				AMPERES CAPACITY			
Single Phase or DC		Three Phase Balanced		Fuse	Switch	Circuit Breaker	Size Type RHW or THW Wire (Awg.)
120V	240V	208V	240V				
2.0	2.8	4.2	4.9	15	30	15	12**
When	3.8	5.7	6.6	20	30	20	12
Appliance	5.7	8.5	9.9	30	30	30	10
Rating	7.6	11.5	13.3	40	60	40	8
Is More	9.6	14.3	16.6	50	60	50	6
Than	11.5	17.2	19.9	60	60	60	6
2.0 KW	13.4	20.1	23.2	70	100	70	4
220-240	15.3	23.0	26.6	80	100	80	4
Volt	17.2	25.9	29.9	90	100	90	2
Equipment	19.2	28.7	33.2	100	100	100	2
Should	21.1	31.6	36.5	110	200	110	2
Be	24.0	35.9	41.5	125	200	125	1
Recommended	28.8	43.1	49.8	150	200	150	0

*KW load is based on 80% of circuit capacity. **For commercial work, wire size should not be smaller than No. 12 Awg. For runs longer than 50 feet, use next larger size wire.

Figure 9-11c

AMPERE FORMULAS

$\frac{W}{V} = A$

Formula for determining Amperes for Single Phase Power Supply:
Watts divided by volts = Amperes:
Example: 200 W ÷ 120 Volts = 1.66 Amperes

Formula for determining Amperes for Three Phase Power Supply:

$\frac{W}{1.73 \times V} = A$ $\frac{\text{Watts}}{1.73 \times \text{Volts}} = \text{Amperes}$ Example: $\frac{8000}{1.73 \times 230} = 20.1$ Amperes

U.S. VOLTAGE / PHASE COMBINATIONS

1. 110-120 Volts - Single Phase :
   A two-wire system consisting of one hot and one neutral wire. The voltage between hot and neutral is 125 volts maximum.

2. 220-240 Volts - Single Phase :
   A two-wire system consisting of two hot wires. The voltage between the two hot wires is 250 Volts maximum.

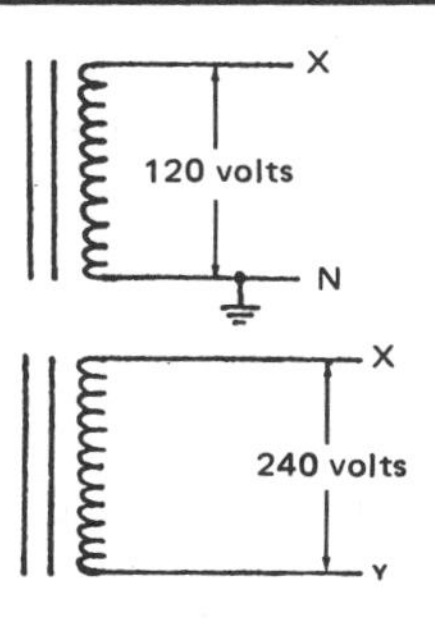

3. 110-120/220-240 Volts - Single Phase :
   (Edison System) A three-wire system consisting of two hot and one neutral wire. The voltage between either hot and neutral is 125 volts maximum and the voltage between the two hot wires is 250 volts maximum.

4. 110-120/208 Volts - Three Phase :
   A four-wire system consisting of three hot and one neutral wire. Used for three phase power circuits and single phase light and power branch circuits. The voltage between any single hot wire and neutral is 125 Volts maximum. Voltage between any two hot wires is 208 volt single phase. Voltage between three hot wires is 208 volt three phase.

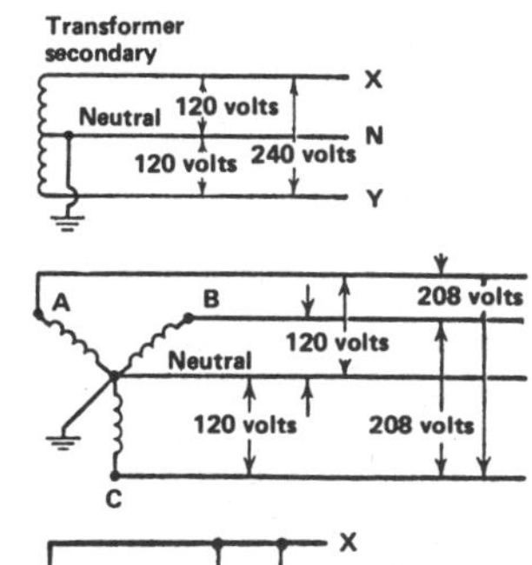

5. 220-240 Volts - Three Phase :
   A three-wire Delta Connected system consisting of three hot wires. The voltage between any two hot wires is 250 Volts maximum.

6. 440-480 Volts - Three Phase :
   A three-wire Delta Connected system consisting of three hot wires. The voltage between any two hot wires is 480 Volts maximum.

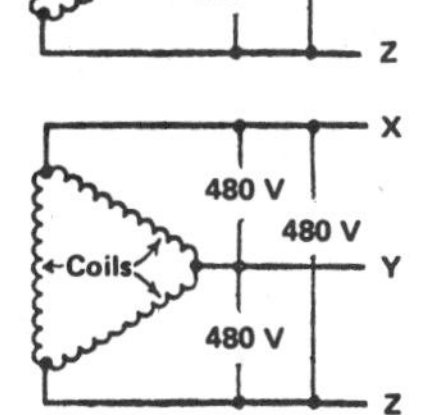

7. 110-120/220-240 Volts - Three Phase :
   A four wire Delta Connected system with Center Tap consisting of three hot wires and one neutral wire. The voltage between either hot line adjacent to the center tap and neutral is 125 Volts maximum. The voltage between any two hot wires is 250 Volts maximum.

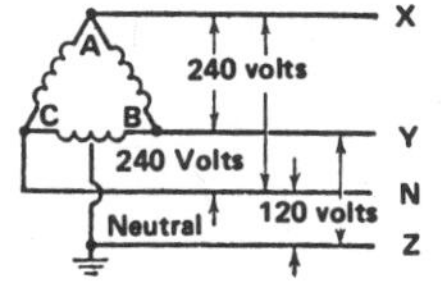

8. 440-480/277 Volts - Three Phase :
   A four-wire system consisting of three hot wires and one neutral wire. Used for 480 Volt three phase power circuits and 277 Volt single phase lighting circuits. The voltage between any hot wire and neutral wire is 277 volts maximum. The voltage between any two hot wires is 480 Volts single phase and between three hot wires is 480 Volts three phase maximum.

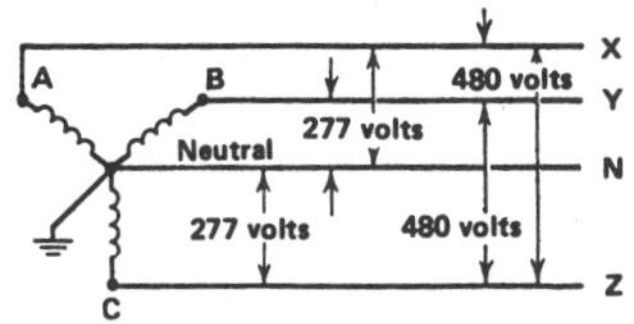

GROUND CONNECTIONS TO ANY OF THE ABOVE SYSTEMS ARE REQUIRED BY CODES.

Figure 9-11d

10

Furniture

This final chapter is intended to give the end user, whether foodservice operator, designer, architect, consultant, or student, an overview of what to look for when putting together the "front of the house" in a restaurant operation. Floor plans and waitress walk-throughs are shown, as are salad bars, chairs, and tables. (See Figures 10–1 through 10–8.) Options for the most popular items used in contract furnishings, such as booths, are studied in detail. Booth construction, type of backs and bases available, tabletop options, and so on, are illustrated. Bars also are shown, as well as fast-food, fun-food, and beverage equipment.

The end user should develop a concept or central theme, with everything in the "front of the house" related to it. A designer can give advice on space planning, construction drawings, color coordination, wall and window treatments, carpet and flooring durability, fire codes, building codes, interior specifications, supervision of construction, and, most important, the lighting and layout plan.

Although the age-old question of value versus price is always a concern with designer services, the money spent here on design is well worth amortizing. The competition in the industry is intense, with every foodservice operation trying to be newer and more distinctive than the others. Without professional advice, an amateur has no chance of creating the desired ambience and environment. Professional associations such as the American Society of Interior Designers (A.S.I.D.) can help end users locate professional designers with the education and training needed to assist them in their ventures. The address of the headquarters of A.S.I.D. is:

A.S.I.D.
National Headquarters
1430 Broadway
New York, N.Y. 10018
(212) 944-9220

COMMERCIAL SEATING

The booth options illustrated vary by manufacturer. Our sample drawings are offered to show the user the variety of work involved in commercial seating and to provide an understanding of the proper value of such purchases. Knowledge of the terminology and materials used will greatly help the buyer. Figure 10–9 shows a few of the back styles available for booths. The tops of backs also can include wood spindles, planters, mirrors, and other decorations. The wall panels shown can be exchanged for walls made by contractors or movable partitions.

Chair styles are shown in Figure 10–6. Figures 10–10 and 10–11 show modular seating and counter stools, both very popular and available in many styles.

BARS

Careful study of bar details is essential for a proper understanding of actual construction. For instance, many types of steps and railings are available. When one is purchasing bar equipment and related furniture, the drawings and submittals for approval made before construction are critical. The buyer must understand the fabric, the finish, the size, the construction, the details of every purchase. All too often the day of delivery is marked by misunderstanding and disappointment because of poor communication. One can avoid this problem by becoming thoroughly familiar with the details of the operation. The questionnaire of Figure 10–12 will help the operator to understand and organize this effort, and Figures 10–13 through 10–18 provide valuable details for the planning stages.

FAST FOODS AND FUN FOODS

The burgeoning fast food/fun food industry is represented by Figures 10–19 through 10–23. The modular seating arrangements of Figure 10–10 also are widely used in such installations.

BEVERAGE SYSTEMS

Beverage systems for beer, wine, and soda are very specialized. Costs of both installation and service afterward are more significant than the original cost of these systems. These highly profitable centers must be skillfully engineered. Figure 10–24 shows the basic components, and local suppliers can provide detailed drawings of the systems for the purchaser's approval.

FURNITURE CHECKLIST

These general questions should be addressed:

- Look at large samples of the material, wood finish, or laminate. Do the seller, manufacturer, and end user all have the same product sample? If an interior designer or architect is used, he or she will handle this.
- Is furniture the right height?
- Can we get parts such as seat pads, brass trim, etc. for the chair, stool, or booth in the future?
- Is the item removable for ease of cleaning?
- Will it fit through the doors?
- Do all materials used pass all federal, state, and local codes?
- Have all utility connections been verified for bar, counter, and service areas?
- Do we have adequate checkout, waiting, coat, and service areas?
- Is water nearby for cleanup?
- Is there enough power for vacuums, smoke eaters, emergency lights, microphones, and televisions?

The following individual areas and items should be considered:

- Tables
- Chairs
- Booths
- Stools
- Water stations
- Coffee stations
- Waitress areas
- Space for beverage equipment
- Coat racks, coat room
- Cash control area
- Adequate lighting
- Safety mats?
- Take-out area?
- Storage area for buffet or catering supplies
- Take-home pickup area
- Glass washing
- Waitress stands
- Public phone area
- Air cleaners
- Vending machines
- Theme
- Menu boards
- Portable dance floor
- Waitress call system
- Emergency lights
- Pedestrial control (ropes, rail)
- Folding chairs, tables

APPROXIMATE SHIPPING WEIGHTS OF SELECTED EQUIPMENT

BAR AREA

___ Glass Froster	24″ Wide	200#
	48″ Wide	285#
___ Direct Draw Beer Dispensers		
	2 Keg	470#
	3 Keg	555#
	4 Keg	740#
___ Deep Well Beverage Coolers		
	50″ Long	264#
	65″ Long	308#
	80″ Long	393#
	95″ Long	453#
___ Bar Sinks		
	5′ 3 Compartment	76#
	8′ 4 Compartment	110#

BAR AREA (Continued)

___ Chairs		
	Metal, Stack	15#
	Metal	20–25#
	Wood	10–20#
___ Booths/42″ Wide Upholstered		
	Single	70#
	Double	125#
___ Table Bases Cast Iron		
	Spread 22″ Square	21#
	30″ Square	25#
	24″ × 30″ Oblong	27#
	5″ × 22″ End Base	18#
___ Table Tops Laminated		
	30″ × 30″	28#
	30″ × 42″	40#
	36″ × 36″	41#
	24″ Round	18#
	36″ Round	32#

floor plan guide

All suggestions given are approximate and minimum. It should be pointed out that no rule of square feet per person can be exact, because too many variables exist. The space consumed by entry and kitchen door aisles, for example, are almost equal in a room of 800 square feet and a room of 1600 square feet, but the percentage of the room used is less in the latter. Seating capacities can only be determined by a final layout, but the approximate capacity of a room can be determined by this rough guide:

Banquet or institutional seating	—	10-12 square ft. per person
Cafeteria or lunchroom seating	—	12-14 square ft. per person
Fine dining	—	14-16 square ft. per person

SUGGESTED TABLE SIZES:

	Banquet Institutional	Lunchroom Cafeteria	Fine Dining
2 persons	24"x24"	24"x30"	24/30"x30/36"
4 persons	30"x30"*	30"x30"*	36"x36" or 42"x42"
4 persons	24"x42"*	24/30"x48"*	30"x48"
6 persons	30"x72"	30"x72"	48" diameter
8 persons	30"x96" to 60" diam.	30"x96"	60/72" diameter
10 persons	72" diameter	30"x120"	96" diameter

***In self-bussed tray service cafeterias, tables should be of adequate size to accommodate the trays.**

SUGGESTED MINIMUM AISLE DIMENSIONS:

	Customer Access Aisles	Service Aisles	Main Aisles
Institutional Banquet	18"	24/30"	48"
Lunchroom Cafeteria	18"	30"	48"
Fine Dining	18"	36"	54"

Allow 18" from edge of table to back of chair in use. For diagonally spaced tables allow 9" more between corners of tables than needed for the type of aisle needed (e.g. for 30" service aisle, allow 39").

As rough rules of thumb, remember that tables laid out diagonally will increase seating capacity, and a smaller quantity of tables with greater seating per table increases seating capacity but reduces flexibility.

TYPICAL SEATING LAYOUTS

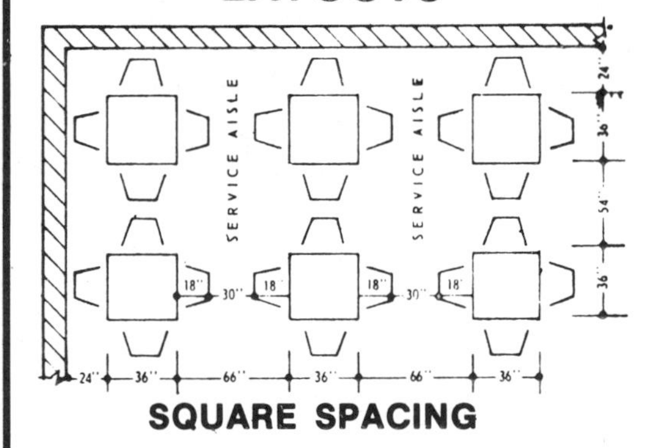

SQUARE SPACING

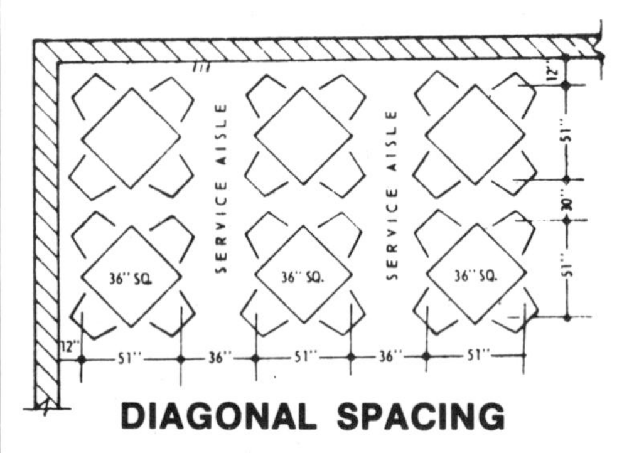

DIAGONAL SPACING

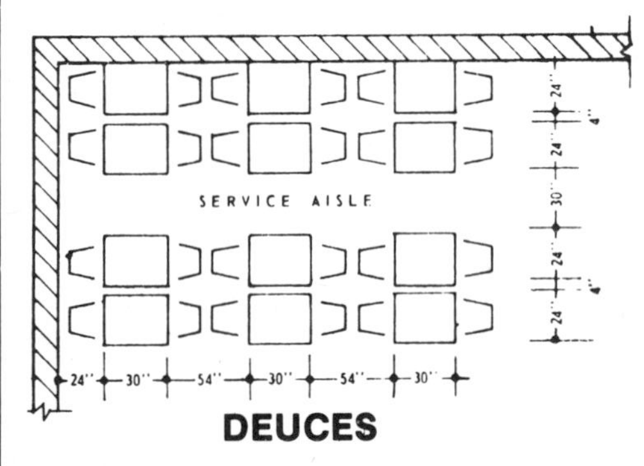

DEUCES

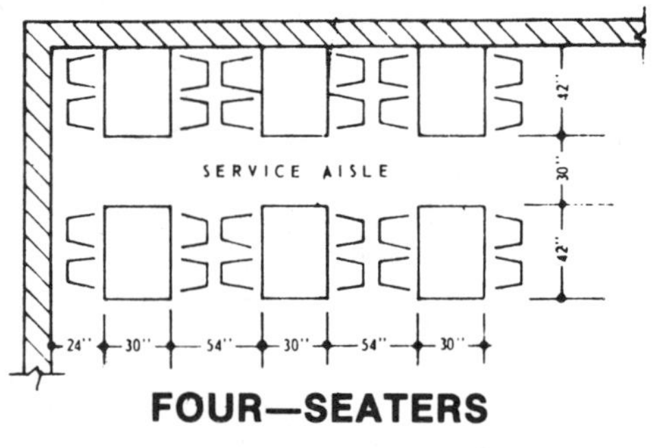

FOUR—SEATERS

Figure 10-1. Floor plan guide. The layout dimensions shown are standard for the foodservice industry. (Courtesy Levey Associates)

SPECIFICATIONS - FLOOR PLANNING - HOW TO ORDER BOOTHS

Units can be adjusted to any desired layout and dimensions applied. Circle and wall booths are constructed to conform to the style of the series selected. All single and double booths install on 5'3" to 5'6" centers with 24" wide top and on 5'9" to 6' center with 30" wide top. Booths can be cut down to fit 62" centers with 24" wide tops when required. **NOTE:** Booths require only 8 sq. ft. of space per person including aisel allowance.

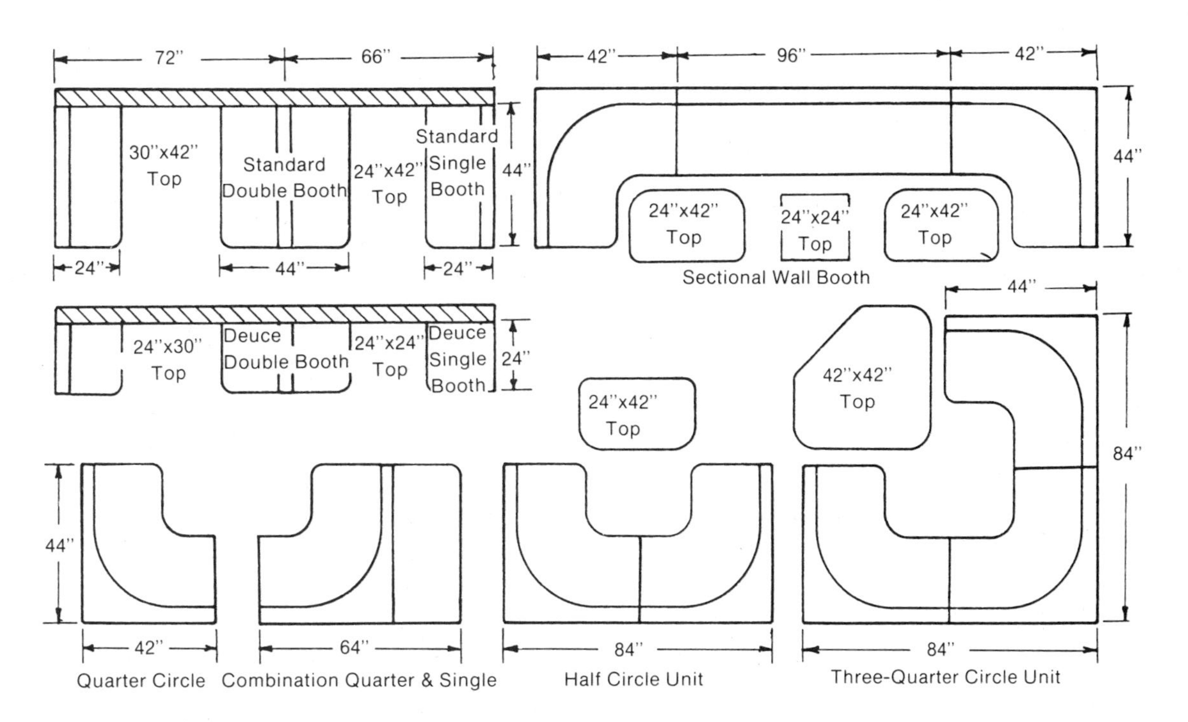

BOOTH COSTUMER

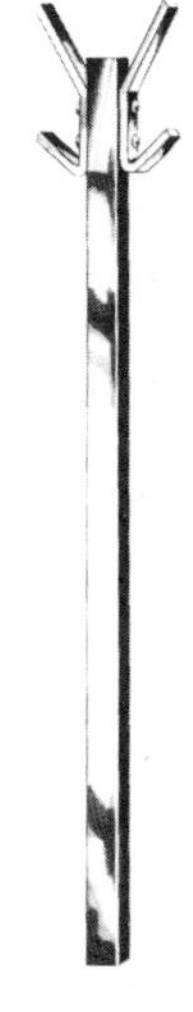

No. 56
60" Long
2 Hook

No. 57
60" Long
3 Hook

SPECIFICATIONS

All booths shipped K.D. to reduce freight costs. All booths have heavy duty wood frames equipped with 15 separately activated LIFETIME NO-SAG springs, insulated with latexed sisal pads and foam rubber, covered with a heavy duty fabric. Backs are wood frame faced with Masonite, padded with 1" foam rubber and upholstered.

TO ORDER

SPECIFY — Serial Number — Height Wanted — Number of single booths — number of double booths — Color, or color combination if different colors are wanted on backs and bottoms.

SPECIFY WALL PANELS if wanted — Length and height, also whether upholstered one side or both sides.

CIRCLE BOOTHS — Are constructed to conform to the style of the series selected.

NOTE: — Single and quarter circle combinations are available at no additional cost, wherever a single unit booth is wanted when a line of booths join with a half or three-quarter circle unit.

NOTE: — The back of the back of circle booths are exposed — specify closing panels, if needed.

WALL BOOTHS—Specify length and whether back of back is to be finished or unfinished.

SPECIAL SIZES — Quarter circle wings are built to extend 42". A "U" or three-quarter circle unit can be enlarged by adding up to 2-1/2 feet to each wing of a quarter circle and figured on the basis of overall lineal wall booth footage.

FOR CORNER SECTIONS — Use a quarter circle and either or both wings can be extended up to 8 ft. Figure price by taking cost of wall booth footage per each wing. (When ordering, a rough sketch on the bottom of the order, showing position of booths and closing panel, helps elimanate errors).

Figure 10-2. Floor seating guide. The illustrations are guides only. The actual layout will be developed on a floor plan, taking into consideration the theme, decor, menu, style of service, relation to serving areas, and other variables. (Courtesy Levey Associates)

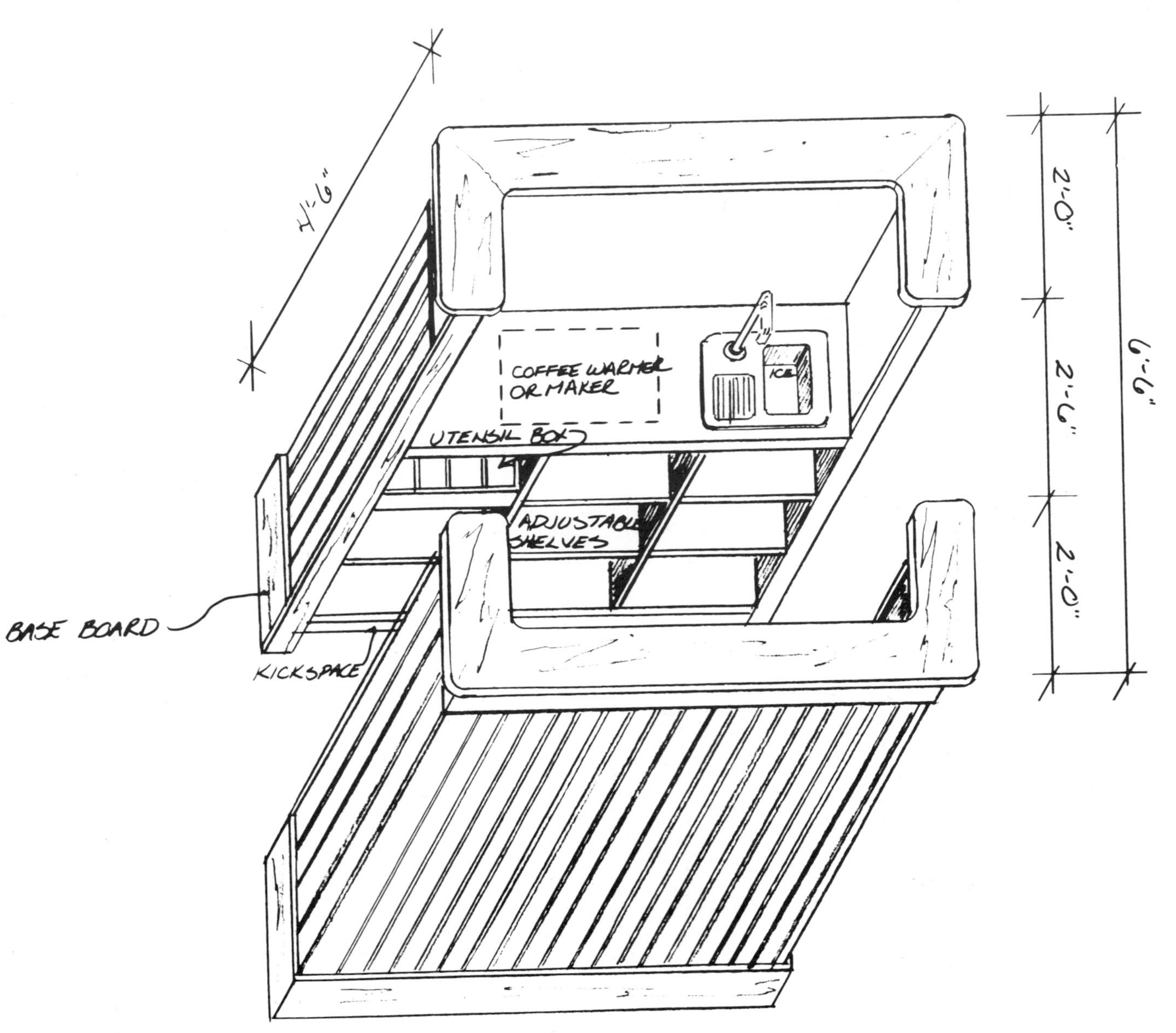

Figure 10-3. Waitress walk-through. The walk-through area shown makes an excellent backdrop for seating, and is very workable as a room divider. Practical interior equipment will vary by need. (Courtesy Erin O'Neill Rollins)

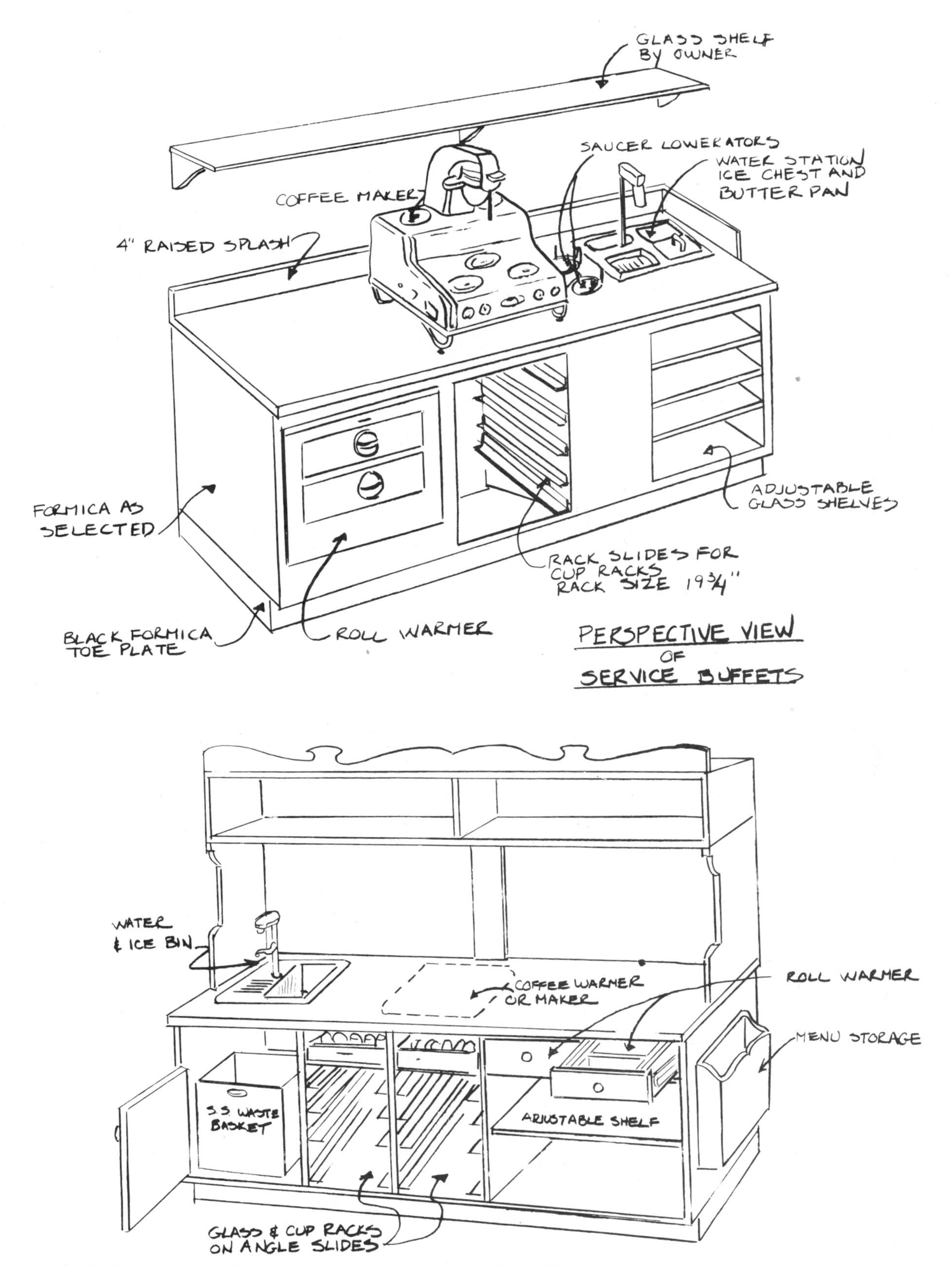

Figure 10-4. Service areas. Two very functional waitress stations. The sizes, construction, equipment, and finish shown are available in custom cabinets. Some manufacturers have stock and modular styles available.

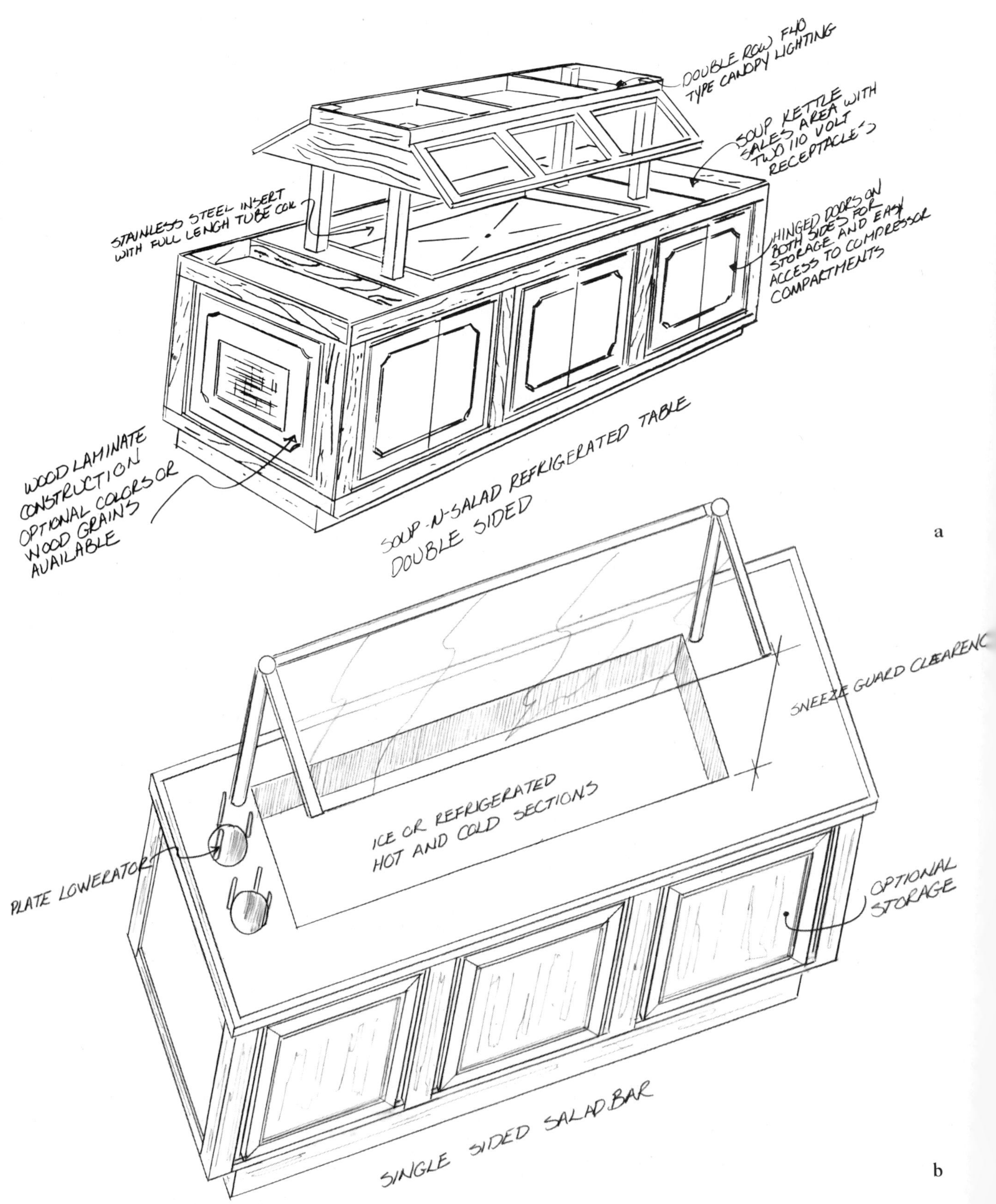

Figure 10-5a,b. Double- and single-sided salad bars. The salad bars shown are double-service designs, with both hot and cold sections available. The cold section can be ice-style or compressor-cooled, or a combination of both. (Courtesy Erin O'Neill Rollins)

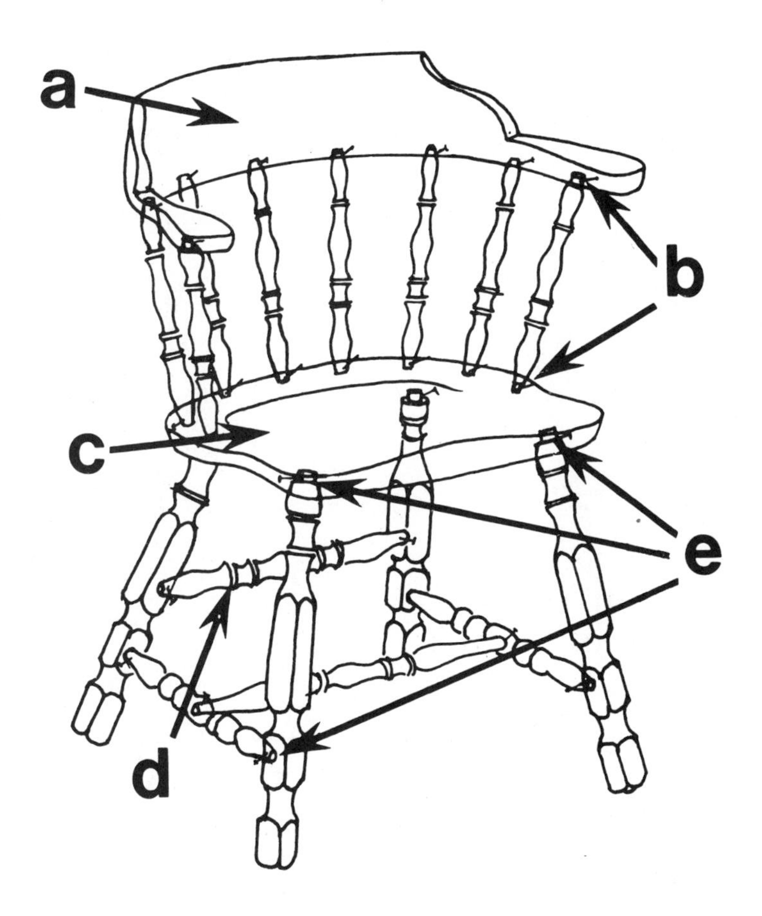

All styles made of fine solid beech hardwood and quality craftsmanship, in the styling of Colonial New England.

Each chair is of the finest construction with EXCLUSIVE features not found in similar chairs.

a. One piece Steam Bent Back for sturdiness.

b. Oversize arm post and spindles are compressed to fit, then secured to seat and back with glue and steel pins.

c. The New "Nevr-Nevr Split" (pat. pending) wood seat construction carries a lifetime guarantee against splitting.

d. Extra back leg stretcher for added stability.

e. Oversize legs and stretchers are compressed to fit securely at all joints when glued and pinned.

Standard Wood Finishes

Maple and Pine. Other finishes available upon request.

Upholstery

All styles of Colonial Chairs are available with upholstered seat and/or back. Plain or Antique Hammered Nail Trim, choice of fabric and color.

Figure 10-6a-c. Chair styles. Hundreds of commercial chairs are available to the consumer in an array of styles, colors, and fabrics. (Courtesy Level Manufacturing)

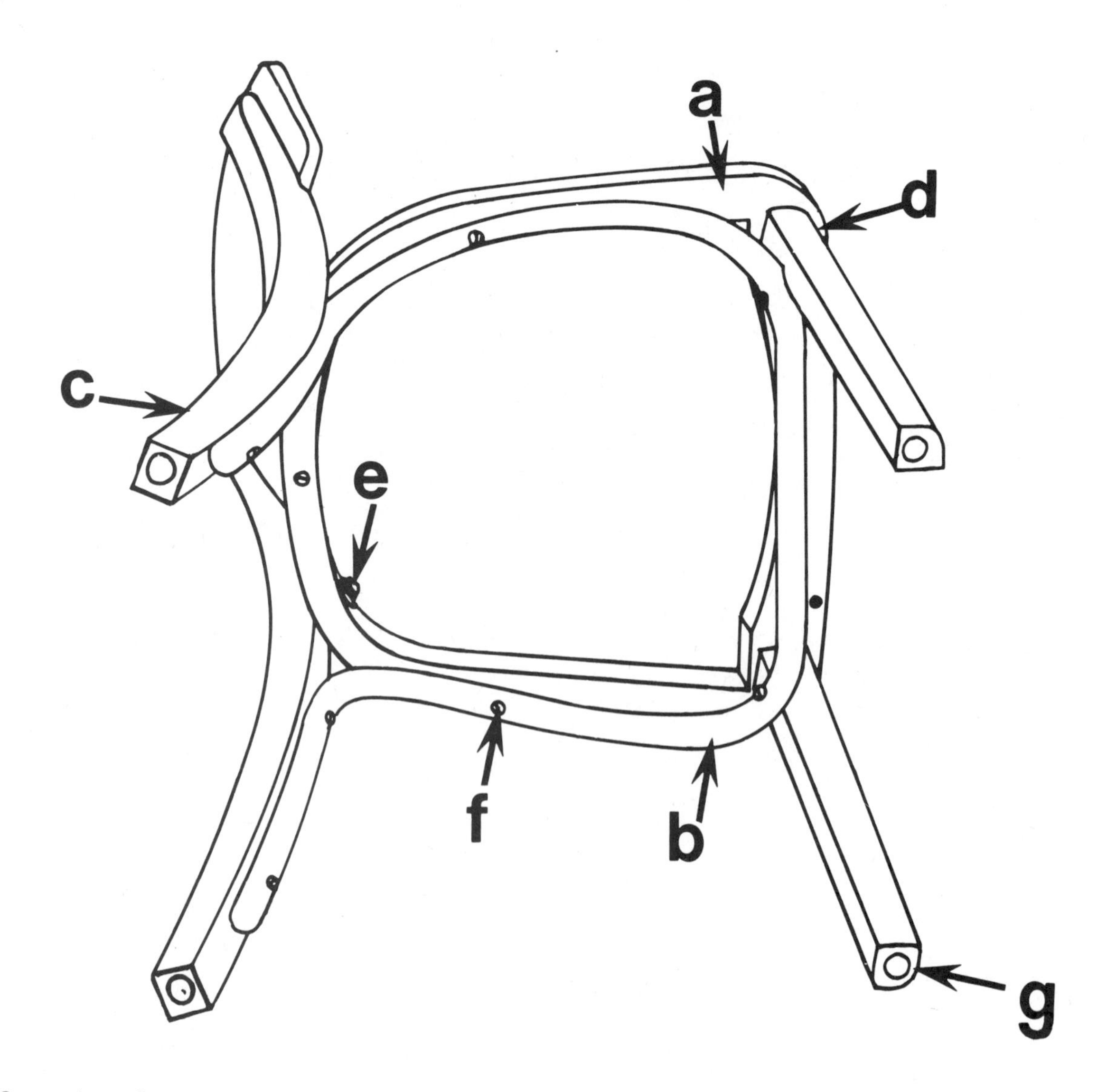

a. Steam bent frame.

b. One piece steam bent bow brace.

c. Steam bent back posts.

d. Front legs mortised and screwed to frame.

e. Heavy bolt which secures back post to frame.

f. Eight screws hold the bow brace securely to back post, frame and front legs.

g. Glides on each leg.

Bentwood Chairs are unconditionally guaranteed against defective workmanship and material.

These chairs demonstrate superior strength attributable to continuously bent solid hardwood framing and heavy duty construction.

Guaranteed to withstand hard everyday usage.

Figure 10-6b

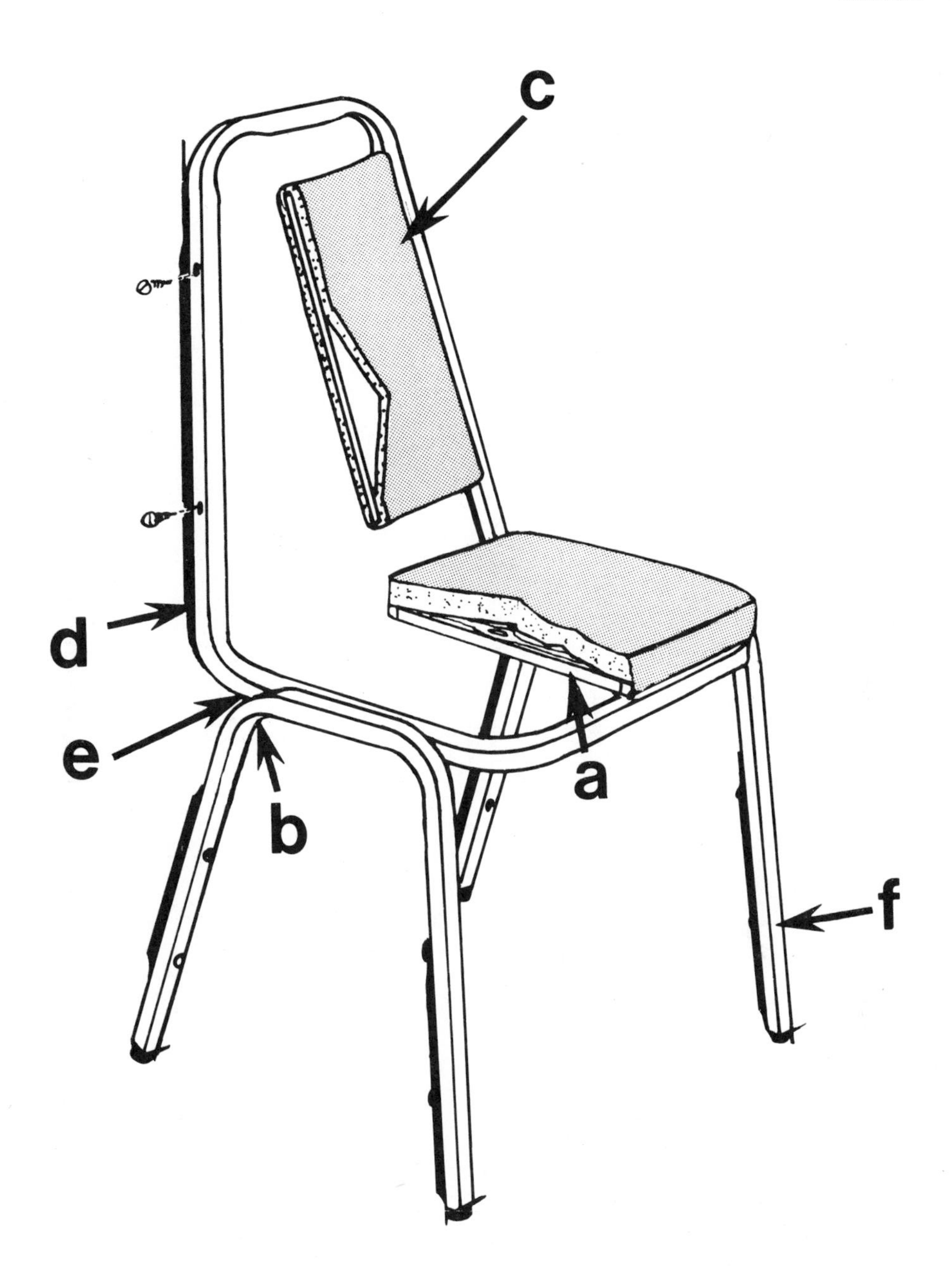

Features:

a. 5/8" - 45# density industrial particleboard.

b. Level's double ribbed compressed bend is structurally superior to other methods.

c. Heavy duty vinyl covered seat and backs are completely sealed.

d. Frames constructed of 16 gauge 13/16" square steel tubing.

e. Frames are welded in 13 separate locations.

f. Level's Fused Epoxy Finish is Electrostatically sprayed and fused at 500°F to all our metal products. This lustrous finish is superior to porcelain being either soft or tough, rigid or flexible without chipping and cracking. This process resists high impact, corrosion, abrasion, and marring, promising lasting beauty to fine furniture.

Figure 10-6c

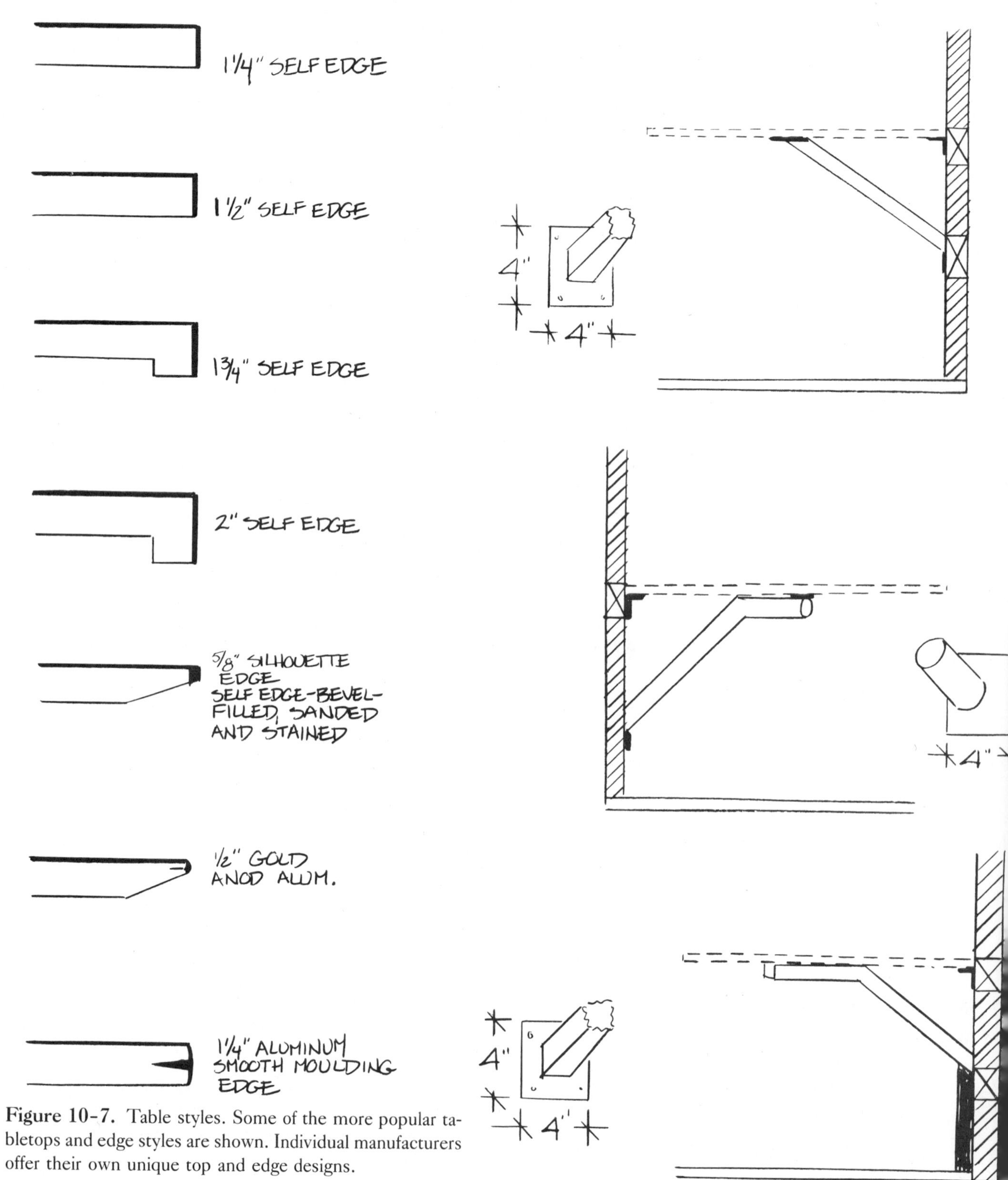

Figure 10-7. Table styles. Some of the more popular tabletops and edge styles are shown. Individual manufacturers offer their own unique top and edge designs.

Figure 10-8. Cantilevered table bases, showing three base styles. *Note:* It is very critical to mount bases directly to wall studs for strength, and preferably return to floor for more support. Other table bases are freestanding and available in many colors and configurations.

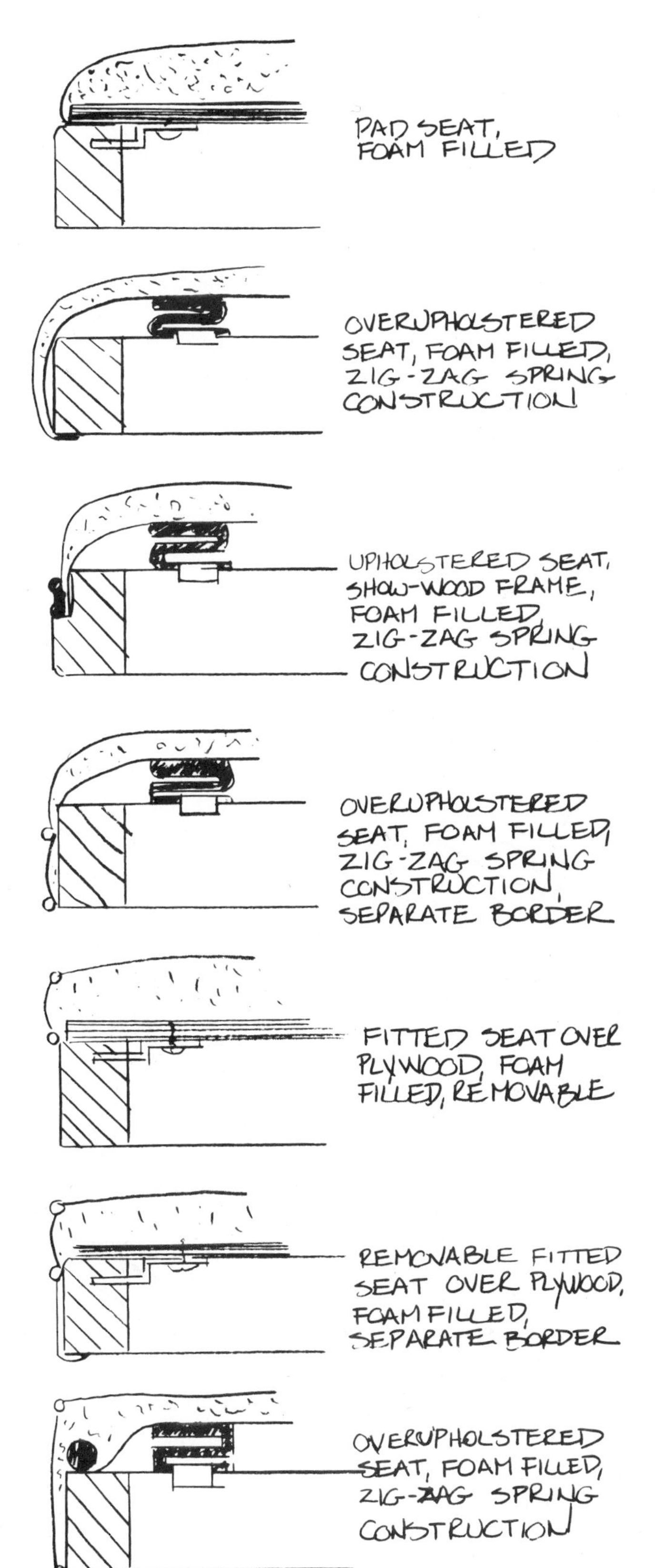

Figure 10-9a–d. Booth construction. In the isometric drawing (Figure 10–9d), two end or single booths are used. All booths are also available as doubles, in one booth with back-to-back seating. Booths can be attached to the floor or freestanding. They are available on a base (shown) or on legs. Against a wall, these same booths can be made into wall lounges. Booths normally range from 24 to 72 inches wide. (Figure 10–9c courtesy L&B Manufacturing)

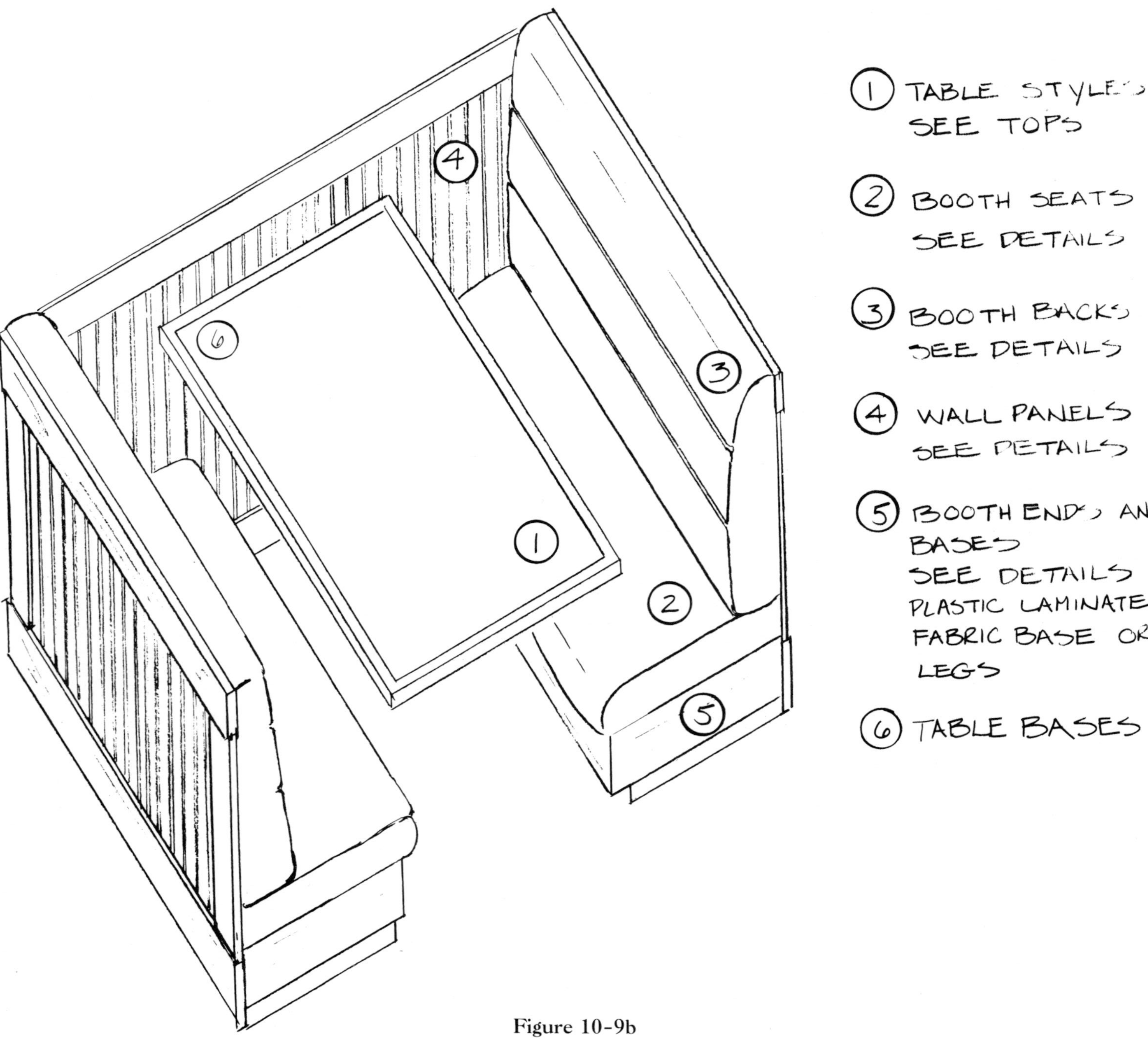

1
2
3
4
5
6
1 TABLE STYLES
SEE TOPS
2 BOOTH SEATS
SEE DETAILS
3 BOOTH BACKS
SEE DETAILS
4 WALL PANELS
SEE DETAILS
5 BOOTH ENDS AND
BASES
SEE DETAILS
PLASTIC LAMINATE OR
FABRIC BASE OR
LEGS
6 TABLE BASES

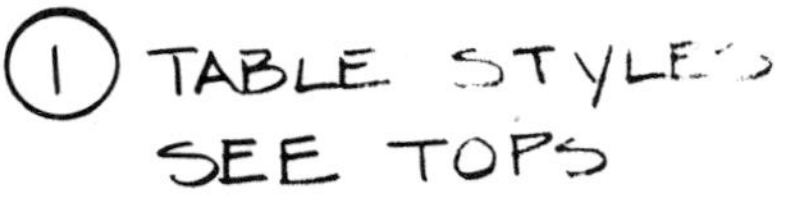

Figure 10-9b

BOOTH BACKS

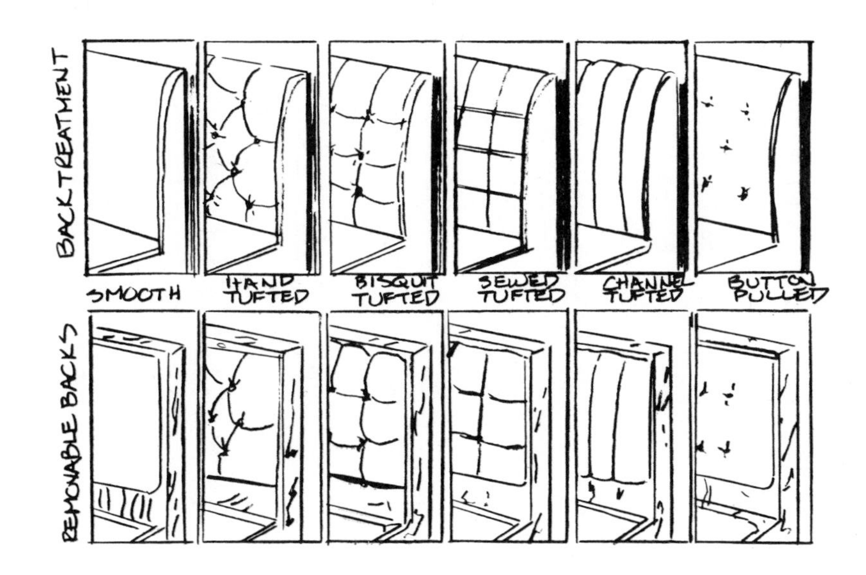

WALL PANELS

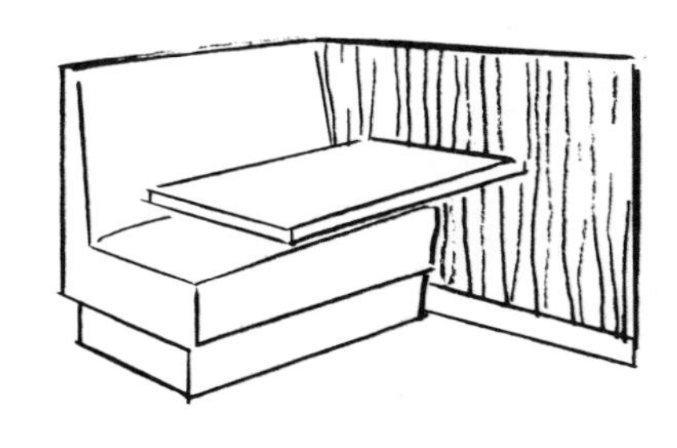

LAMINATE

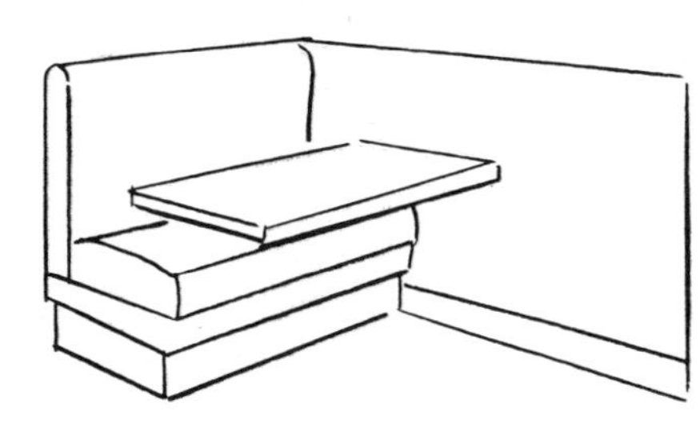

PLAIN

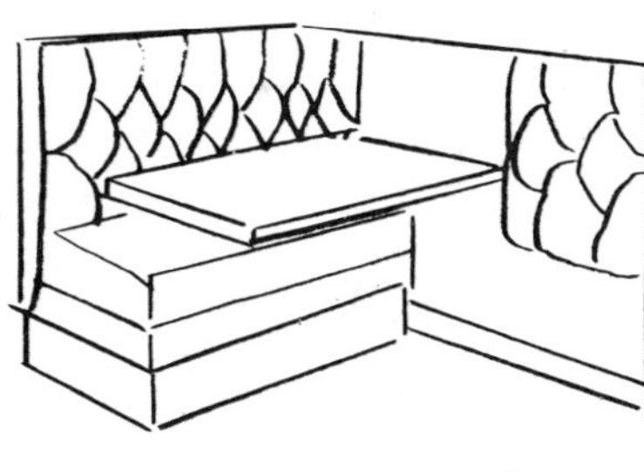

HAND DIAMOND

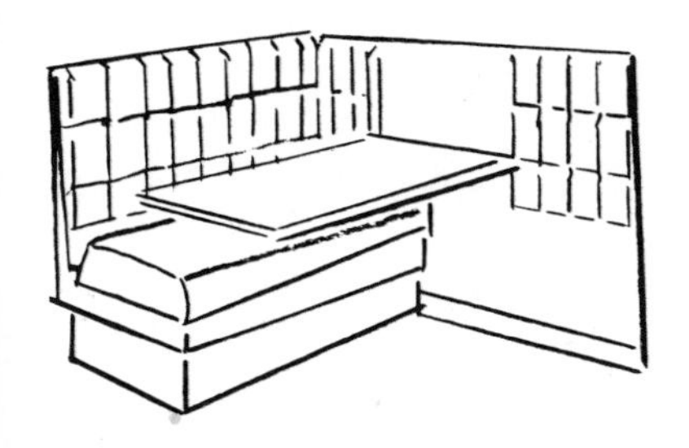

HAND BISCUIT

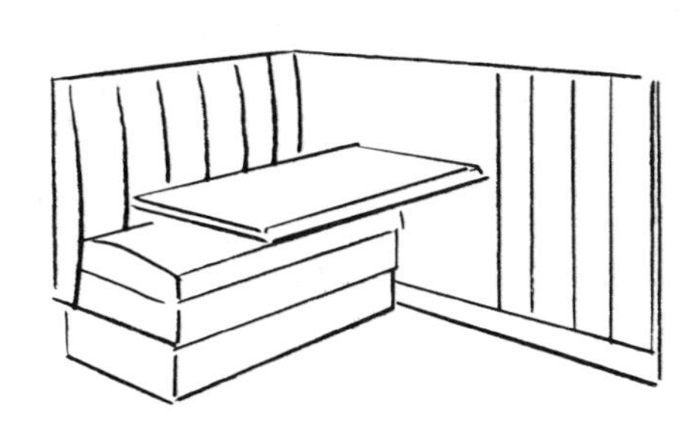

DEEP CHANNEL

LEXINGTON PLAIN

Figure 10-9c

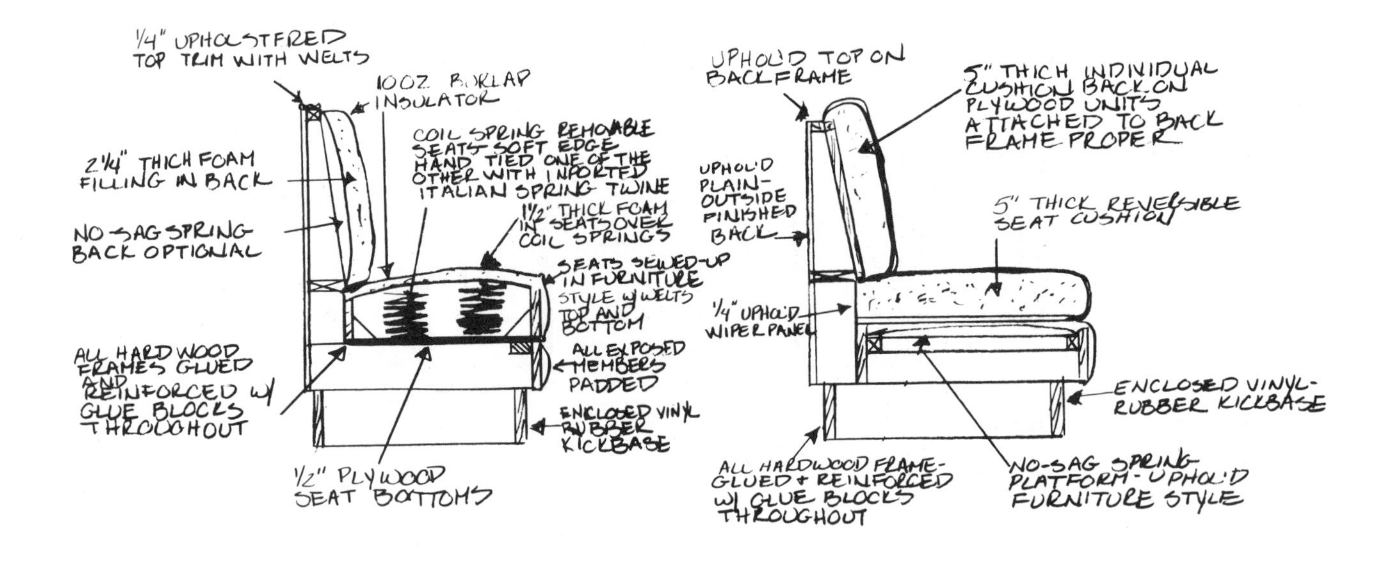
1/4" UPHOLSTERED TOP TRIM WITH WELTS
10 OZ. BURLAP INSULATOR
2 1/4" THICK FOAM FILLING IN BACK
COIL SPRING REMOVABLE SEATS SOFT EDGE HAND TIED ONE OF THE OTHER WITH IMPORTED ITALIAN SPRING TWINE
NO-SAG SPRING BACK OPTIONAL
1 1/2" THICK FOAM IN SEATS OVER COIL SPRINGS
SEATS SEWED-UP IN FURNITURE STYLE W/ WELTS TOP AND BOTTOM
ALL HARDWOOD FRAMES GLUED AND REINFORCED W/ GLUE BLOCKS THROUGHOUT
ALL EXPOSED MEMBERS PADDED
ENCLOSED VINYL RUBBER KICKBASE
1/2" PLYWOOD SEAT BOTTOMS
UPHOL'D TOP ON BACKFRAME
5" THICK INDIVIDUAL CUSHION BACK ON PLYWOOD UNITS ATTACHED TO BACK FRAME PROPER
UPHOL'D PLAIN-OUTSIDE FINISHED BACK
5" THICK REVERSIBLE SEAT CUSHION
1/4" UPHOL'D WIPER PANEL
ENCLOSED VINYL-RUBBER KICKBASE
ALL HARDWOOD FRAME-GLUED & REINFORCED W/ GLUE BLOCKS THROUGHOUT
NO-SAG SPRING PLATFORM-UPHOL'D FURNITURE STYLE

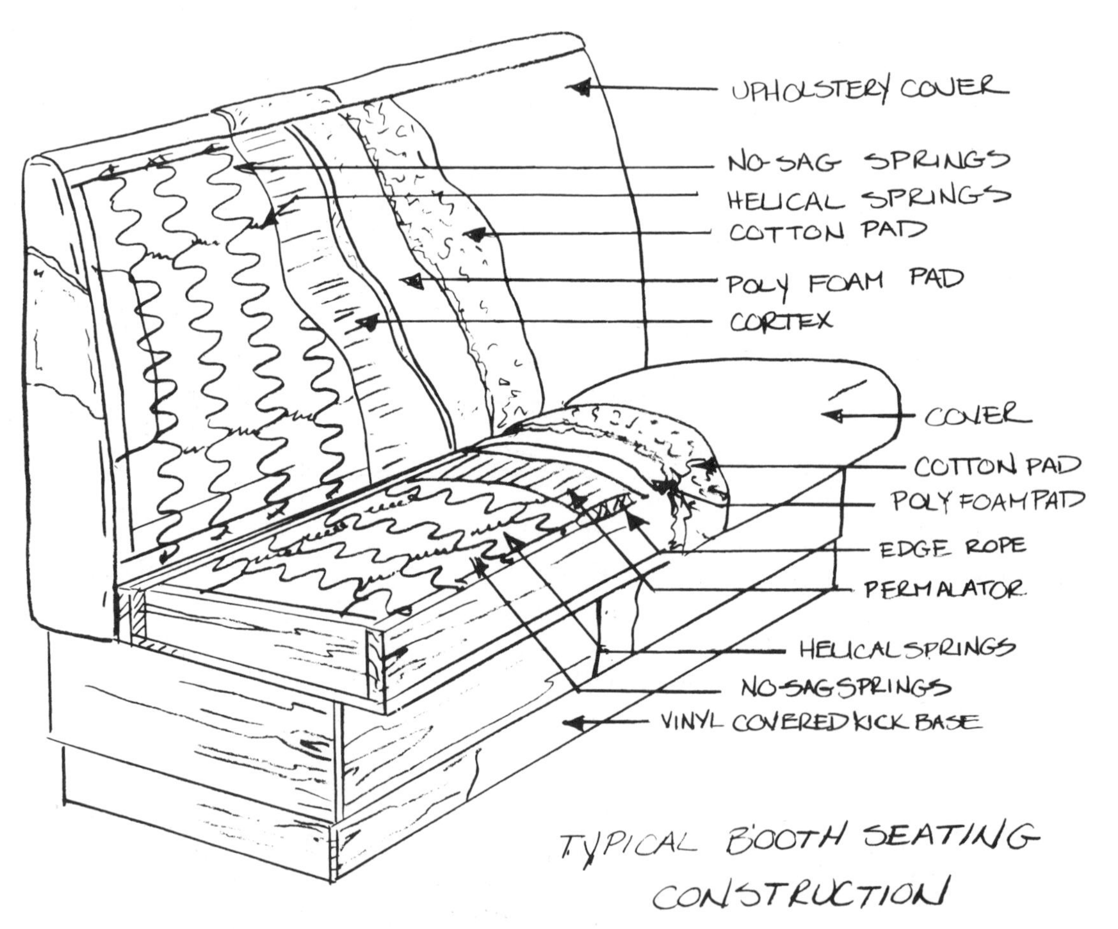
UPHOLSTERY COVER
NO-SAG SPRINGS
HELICAL SPRINGS
COTTON PAD
POLY FOAM PAD
CORTEX
COVER
COTTON PAD
POLY FOAM PAD
EDGE ROPE
PERMALATOR
HELICAL SPRINGS
NO-SAG SPRINGS
VINYL COVERED KICK BASE
TYPICAL BOOTH SEATING CONSTRUCTION

Figure 10-9d

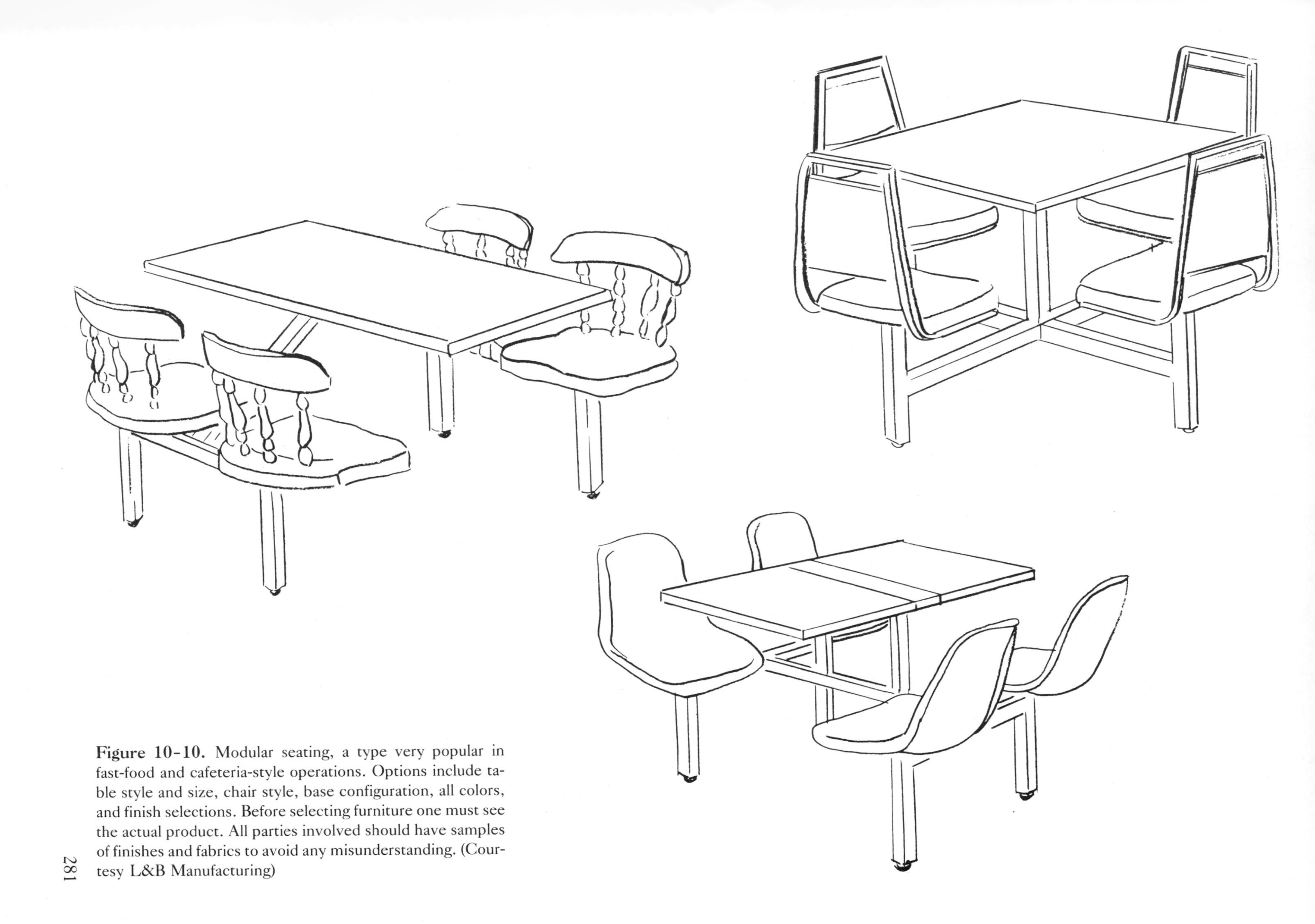

Figure 10-10. Modular seating, a type very popular in fast-food and cafeteria-style operations. Options include table style and size, chair style, base configuration, all colors, and finish selections. Before selecting furniture one must see the actual product. All parties involved should have samples of finishes and fabrics to avoid any misunderstanding. (Courtesy L&B Manufacturing)

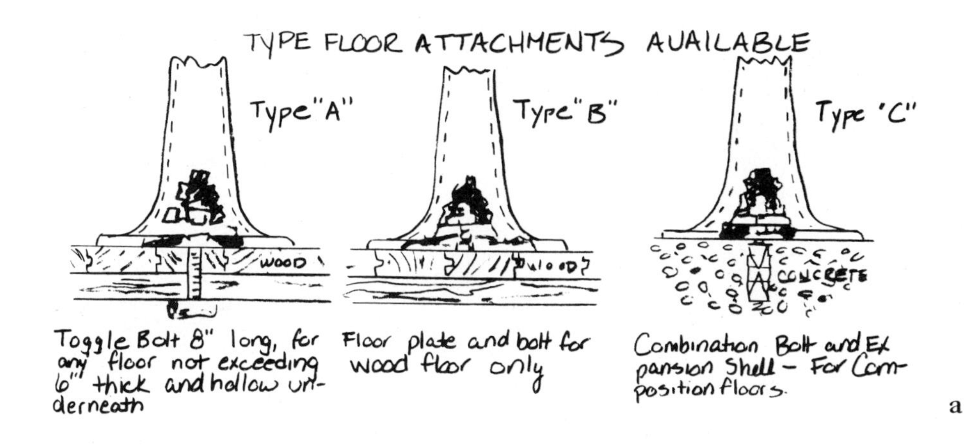

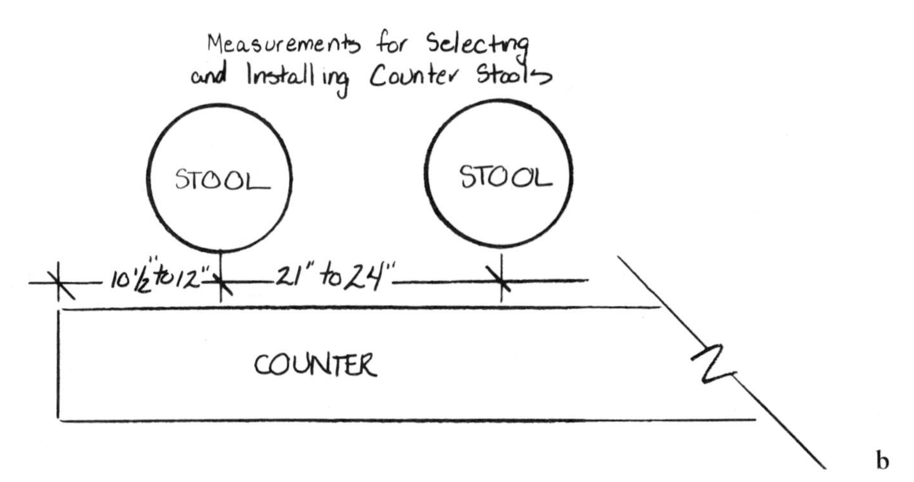

Figure 10-11a,b. Counter stools. Note the types of stool attachments available, and the proper measurements for maximum comfort of patrons.

BAR DESIGN QUESTIONAIRE

A well designed bar requires a good understanding between the bar designer and the client. Please identify your operation by completing this questionaire.

1.0 General

1.1 Theme/Concept

_______ Restaurant and Cocktail lounge

_______ Cocktail Lounge only

_______ Describe decor and/or theme: ______________________________

____

1.2 Space

_______ Size of building lot = ______________________________

_______ Square footage of building = ______________________________

_______ Space allocations

Dining Room(s) = _______% Cocktail Lounge = _______%

Kitchen = _______% Common Area(s) = _______%

Offices = _______% Restrooms = _______%

General Storage= _______% Bar Storage = _______%

Other: _______= _______% Other: _______= _______%

_______ Is a floor plan attached?

_______ Yes _______ No

_______ To be provided on ______________________________

1.3 Sales Analysis

_______ Projected gross sales:

Food=_____% Beverage=_____% Bar Snacks=_____%

_______ Projected beverage sales:

Liquor=____% Beer=____% Wine=____% Non-Alcoholic=_____%

_______ Projected liquor sales:

Highballs and traditional cocktails = _____%

Speciality drinks = ___________%

_______ Projected beer sales:

Bottles/cans=_____% Draft= _______%

_______ Projected wine sales:

Bottle=_____% Glass=_____% Carafe=_____%

Figure 10-12. Bar design questionnaire. (Courtesy Glastender, Inc.)

Bar Design Questionaire
Page 2

________ Projected non-alcoholic sales:

Soft drinks=_____% Bottled water=_____% Other= _____%

1.4 Peak Volume

________ Please complete for the peak hour :

Number of Customers		Drinks consumed Per Hour		Production Requirements
________	x	1	=	________
________	x	2	=	________
________	x	3	=	________
________	x	4	=	________
________	x	_____	=	________
			TOTAL	________ Drinks Per Hour

1.5 Budget

________ What is your budget for:

	$	%
Total Project	$________	________%
General Construction	________	________
Kitchen Equipment	________	________
Bar Equipment	________	________

1.6 Planning

________ This is a single use design? __________

________ This is a prototype for more projects? __________

________ Projected number of units for:

next 12 months=__________ next two to five years=________

2.0 Operations

2.1 Products Served at Bar

Category	Total Number of Brands	Total Number of Bottles in "Par Stock"	Number of Brands: Bottle Poured	Number of Brands: Machine Poured
Liquors	____	________	______	______
Liqueurs, Cordials, Apertifs	____	________	______	______
Bottle & can beer-returnable	____	cases=________		
Bottle & can beer-nonreturnable	____	cases=________		
Draft Beer	____	kegs =________		
Bottle Wine-Room temperature	____	________		

Figure 10-12 *(continued)*

Bar Design Questionaire
Page 3

Category	Total Number of Brands	Total Number of Bottles in "Par Stock"	Number of Brands Bottle Poured	Number of Brands Machine Poured
Bottle Wine - Refrigerated	_____	_____		
Bulk wine-Room temperature	_____	Gal.= _____		
Bulk wine-Refrigerated	_____	Gal.= _____		
Perishables, juices	_____	_____		
Soft drinks	_____	_____	_____	_____
Bottled water-Room temperature	_____	_____	_____	_____
Bottled water-Refrigerated	_____	_____		
Coffee	_____	Check if _____ warmer, or _____ maker		
Hot water	_____			
Iced tea	_____	Check if _____ dispenser		
Cappuccino, Expresso	_____	Check if _____ machine		
Other _____	_____	_____	_____	_____

2.2 Specialty Drinks

_____ Will specialty drinks require _____ soft ice cream or _____ hard ice cream?
_____ Will frozen cocktails be served?
_____ Will specialty drinks require any unusual condiment, garnish, or preparation tool? If so, please list: _____

_____ Attach your drink menu and recipes.

2.3 Condiments

_____ Please list your condiments: _____

_____ _____ _____

_____ _____ _____

_____ _____ _____

2.4 Glassware
Please list your glassware:

Type	Manufacturer	Model No.	Capacity	Model No.	Capacity
Shot Glass	_____	_____	_____	_____	_____
Old Fashion/Rocks	_____	_____	_____	_____	_____
Highball	_____	_____	_____	_____	_____
Chimney/Hurricane	_____	_____	_____	_____	_____
Cordial	_____	_____	_____	_____	_____
Snifter	_____	_____	_____	_____	_____
Cocktail	_____	_____	_____	_____	_____
Champagne	_____	_____	_____	_____	_____
Sour	_____	_____	_____	_____	_____
Port	_____	_____	_____	_____	_____
Wine	_____	_____	_____	_____	_____
Wine Carafe	_____	_____	_____	_____	_____
Beer	_____	_____	_____	_____	_____
Beer Pitcher	_____	_____	_____	_____	_____
Specialty #1	_____	_____	_____	_____	_____
Specialty #2	_____	_____	_____	_____	_____

Figure 10-12 (*continued*)

Bar Design Questionarie
Page 4

2.5 Ice

_______ Please describe your type of ice:
Manufacturer ____________ Cube Size _________________
_______ Is shaved or crushed ice required? ________________
_______ Projected ice capacity required: ______________pounds

2.6 Cash Control

_______ Cash management: (check all that apply)
____ by bartender behind bar
____ by cashier in separate cashier station
____ cocktail servers will carry "banks"
____ hard checks for all sales
____ tabs are allowed
____ pre-check registers for cocktail servers
____ other: ____
_______ List the name of your cash register: _________________
_______ Number of cash drawers: ______________________________
____stacked or ____ side-by-side

2.7 Personnel

_______ Projected number of cocktail stations: ________________
_______ Projected number of bartender shifts: ________________
_______ Projected number of cocktail server shifts: ___________

2.8 Miscellaneous

_______ Do you plan off-sale beer, wine, or liquor?___________
_______ Do you serve bar snacks? _________________
Please identify: _________________________
_______ Are dinner menus kept behind the bar? ________________
_______ Do you promote drinks or food with table tents?________

3.0 Facility

3.1 List name of liquor dispensing equipment: _________________
Number of portion sizes=___________ Number of brands=_________
Number of stations=________________

3.2 Open liquor stock
_______ Is a lighted bottle display required? _______________
_______ Do you use a "We proudly pour" sign or bottle display?
If so, what are the dimensions: ___________________
_______ Should bottle displays have night security covers and
locks? ___________________________

Figure 10-12 *(continued)*

Bar Design Questionaire
Page 5

______ If not, how will you secure open stock? ______________
____

3.3 Bottle and Can Beer

______ Type of refrigeration:
_____Back bar with rear feed walk-in

_____Back bar with ___remote or ___self-contained compressor

_____Top open or ___ door open cooler under the bar

_____List manufacturer: ____________________

______ Does refrigeration require:

_____ Lights? ____________

_____ Locks? ____________

______ Is back up supply under refrigeration? _________

______ Are hanging bottle openers required? ___________

3.4 Draft Beer

______ Where are kegs stored?:

_____ In bar refrigeration

_____ Walk-in behind bar

_____ Remote location

_____ List name of draft beer equipment:__________________

Model number: ______________________

3.5 List name of bulk wine dispensing equipment: ______________________
_____ flexhose, or ____tower

3.6 Type of soft drink equipment:

______ Pre-mix

______ Post-mix

______ Name of manufacturer: __________________________
Model Number: __________________________

______ Is the soda water chilled by _______cold plate, or ________ mechanical system?

______ Is the dispenser a ____flexhose, or ____tower?

______ Are tanks stored ____in bar, or ____ remote?

3.7 Other dispensers or beverage machines:

______ List types and/or names of other dispensers/machines:
_______ Juice - ________________________

_______ Coffee - ________________________

_______ Iced tea - ____________________

_______ Cappuccino, Expresso - _________________

_______ Other __________________________________

Figure 10-12 *(continued)*

Bar Design Questionaire
Page 6

3.8 Specialty Drink Equipment

_______ Name of blenders: #1__________ #2__________
Model Numbers: #1__________ #2 __________

_______ Name of soft service machine or ice cream freezer: __________
Model Number: __________Capacity: __________

_______ Other specialty drink equipment: __________

____

3.9 Condiments

_______ Where are condiments stored over night? __________

_______ Type of condiment containers:

_____ Tray with removable inserts and hinged lid
size = __________
_____ Underbar drawer type
size = __________
_____ Pans built into ice bin sneeze guard
size and number of pans = __________

3.10 Type of mug chiller or froster
_______ Manufacturer: __________

_______ Model Number: __________

3.11 Glassware

_______ Do you require overhead hangers for stemware?__________

_______ Estimated number of glasses in the bar when fully stocked: __________

3.12 Glass Washing

_______ Glass washing will be performed: (please check)

_____ With the kitchen dishwasher
_____ By hand by the bartender with a three or four-compartment sink
_____ By an undercounter, rack-type glasswasher
_____ By an automatic, conveyor glasswasher

_______ The glasswasher will be loaded and unloaded by: (please check)

_____ The bartender only
_____ The bartender and/or the cocktail server
_____ Other: __________

____

3.13 Where is the ice maker located?

_______ In the bar area

_______ In the kitchen

_______ In a separate storage room

_______ Other: __________

_______ How much ice storage is required in the bar?:

__________pounds

Figure 10-12 *(continued)*

Bar Design Questionaire
Page 7

3.14 Cash Register

_____ The dimensions of the cash register= ____________________

_____ The dimensions of the cash drawer= ______________________

3.15 Is a drawer or cabinet required for dry storage?: ____________

_____ Locked

_____ Unlocked

3.16 The following instruments are behind the bar: (Please check all that apply)

_____ Telephone

_____ Light switches and dimmers

_____ Intercom system

_____ Background music controls

_____ Stereo system

_____ Television set

_____ Other- ____

3.17 Seating

_____ Number of seats at bar____Diameter of Cocktail table_______

_____ Number of seats at lounge____Height of Cocktail table______

_____ Square feet per lounge seat ______

3.18 Construction

_____ Bar Height:

_____ Stool seating (42")

_____ Stand Up (44")

_____ Sit Down (30")

_____ Type of bar stool required: (Please check)

_____ With back
_____ Without back
_____ With swivel
_____ Without swivel

_____ Are standup tables required? _______________________

_____ Type of foot rest required: (Please check)
_____ Finished step
_____ Unfinished step
_____ Brass foot rail

_____ Type of arm rest required: (Please check all that apply)
_____ Flush to bar top
_____ Extended from bar top
_____ Padded
_____ Laminated
_____ Wooden rail
_____ Other - _____________________________________

Figure 10-12 (*continued*)

Bar Design Questionaire
Page 8

3.19 Miscellaneous

_______ Is underbar lighting required? _______________

_______ Describe the floor coverings: _______________

____

_______ Is there a facility to wash ashtrays behind the bar? _______________

_______ Where is the timeclock located? _______________

_______ Is there a remote service bar? _______________

_______ What is the most direct, largest opening to get equipment into the building?: _______________

____

____

4.0 Miscellaneous

4.1 Are National Sanitation Foundation (NSF) and Underwriter's Laboratories (UL) regulations strictly enforced in the area? _______________

4.2 Are sealed cold plates required? _______________

4.3 List any other unusual regulations which may affect the bar design: _______________

____

5.0 Personal

This form was completed by:

____
Name

____
Title

____
Company Name

____
Street Address

____
City, State, Zip Code

____
Phone Number

____
Date

Figure 10-12 *(continued)*

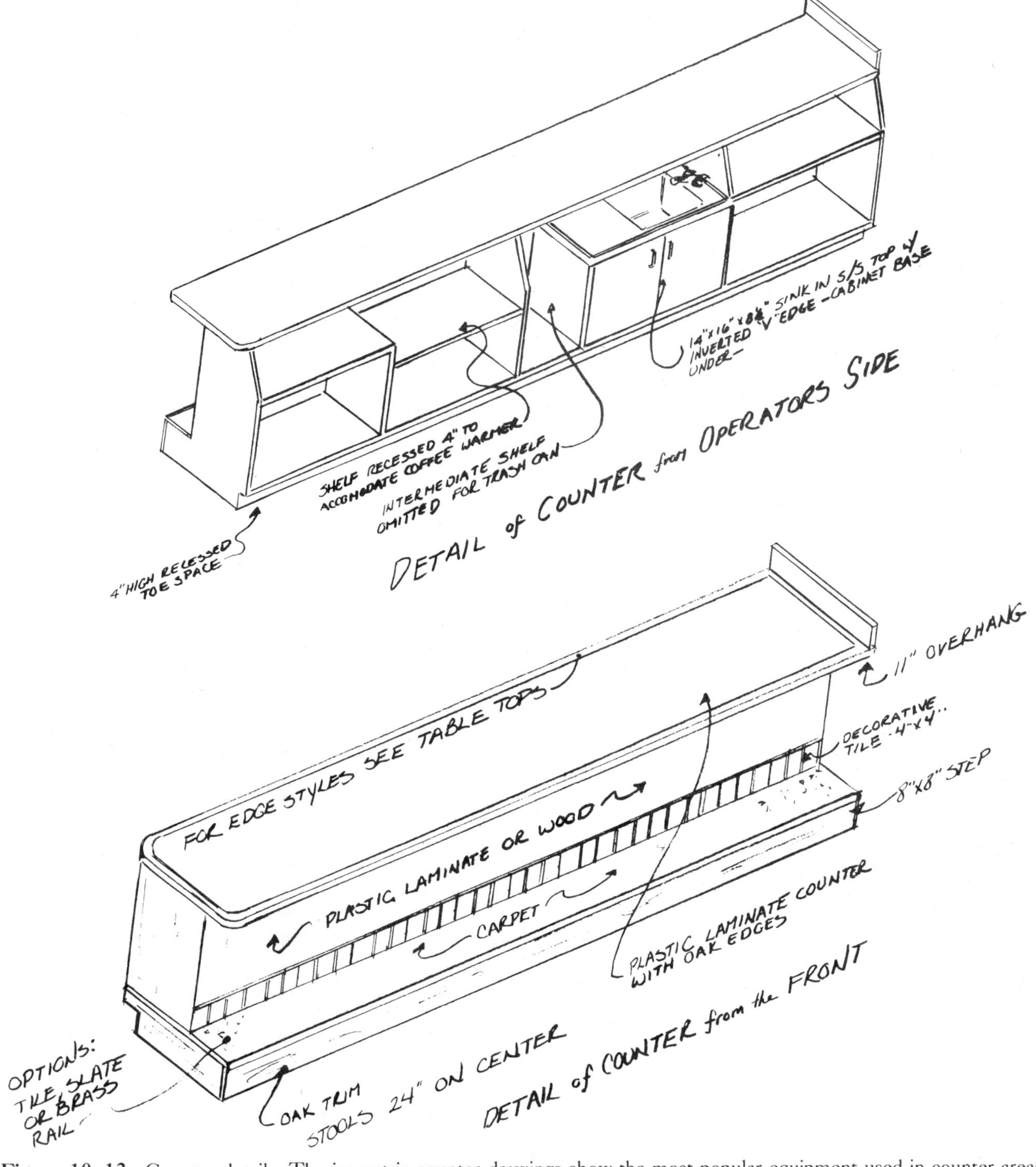

Figure 10-13. Counter details. The isometric counter drawings show the most popular equipment used in counter areas. Here again, the type of service and clientele will determine exact needs. (Courtesy Erin O'Neill Rollins)

HOW TO DETERMINE "LINEAL" FOOTAGE OF
BARS AND COUNTERS

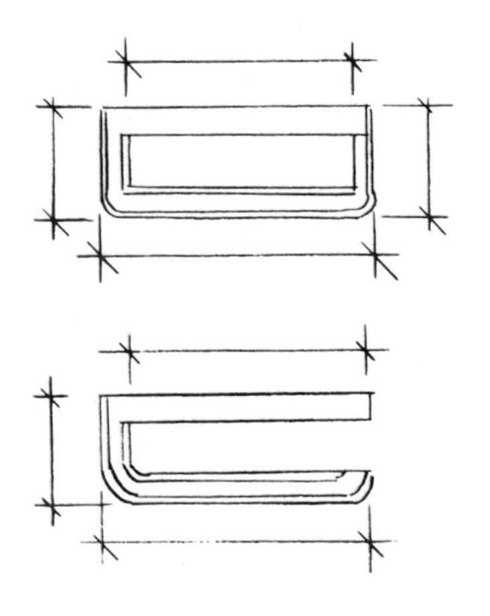

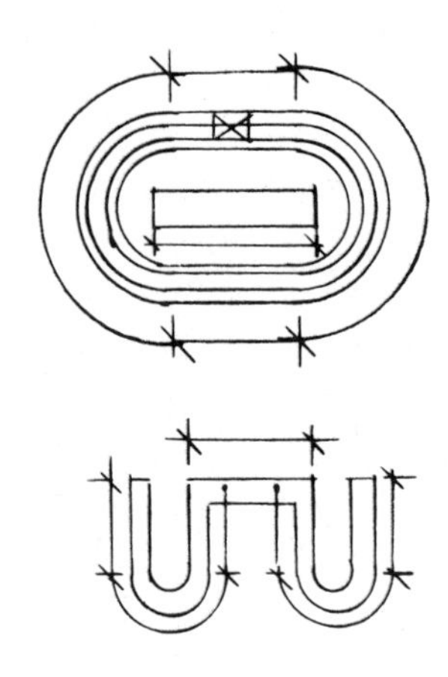

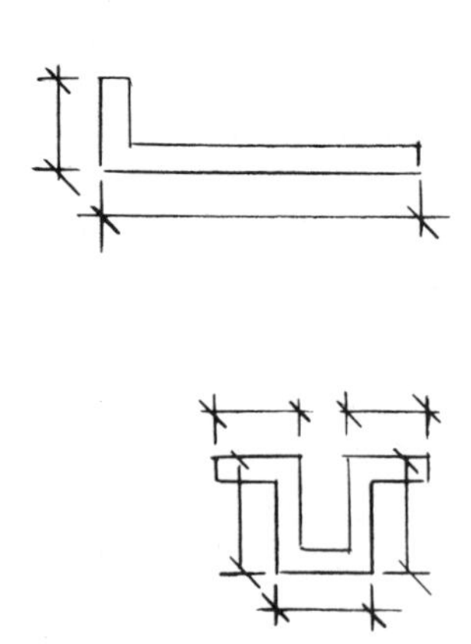

IF TOTAL LENGTH IS NOT EVEN, FIGURE TO NEXT HIGHEST
FOOT. EX: 40'-5" FIGURE 41'-0"

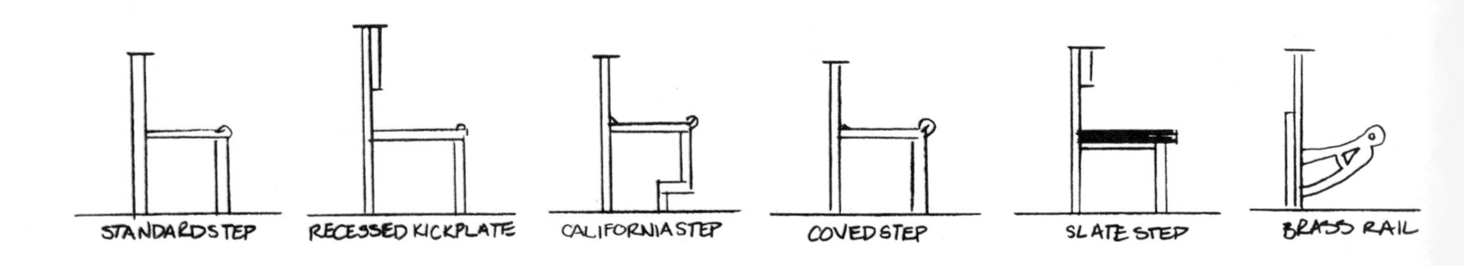

BAR FOOT REST OPTIONS

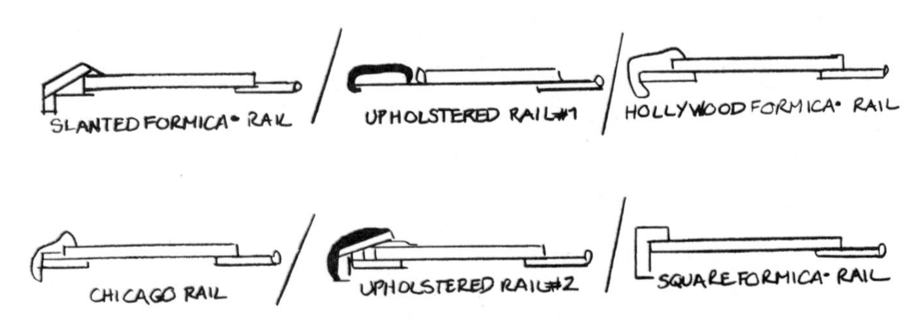

BAR ARM REST OPTIONS

Figure 10-14. Bar options.

SOME TYPICAL BAR CONSTRUCTION DETAILS

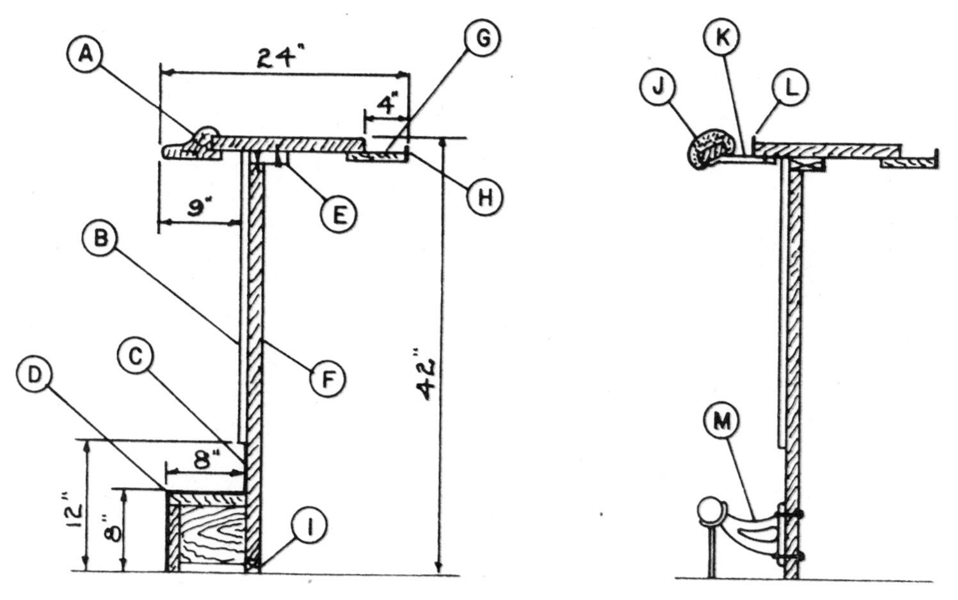

STANDARD BAR DETAILS

A—Arm rest - typical wood shape shown - many styles available including formica finishes

B—Decorative finish - wood panel, tongue and groove board, carpet, upholstery, ceramic tile, you name it, they have it.

C—Kick plate - linoleum, formica, etc.

D—Foot rest - linoleum, slate, hard wood, etc.

E—Cleat - for securing top to die, varies by manufacturer

F—Bar Die - usually ¾" plywood

G—Liquor gutter - usually constructed as shown. May be formed in one piece mahogany bar top.

H—Water stop - ¼" thick black formica or wood. Cut down for cleaning at ends.

I—Shoe - To prevent moisture from separating laminations of the plywood die, a solid wood base strip or metal channel shoe is desirable.

J—Extended arm rest - wood, formica or upholstery. Many styles available.

K—Extension bar - brass or black iron

L—Water stop - same as 'I'

M—Brass foot rest - rail usually 2" dia. swing-away support to floor optional. Check thickness of brass rail your supplier proposes. They are rather expensive.

Figure 10-15. Some typical bar construction details. (Reprinted, by permission, from Carl Scriven and James Stevens, *Food Equipment Facts*, © 1988 by Van Nostrand Reinhold)

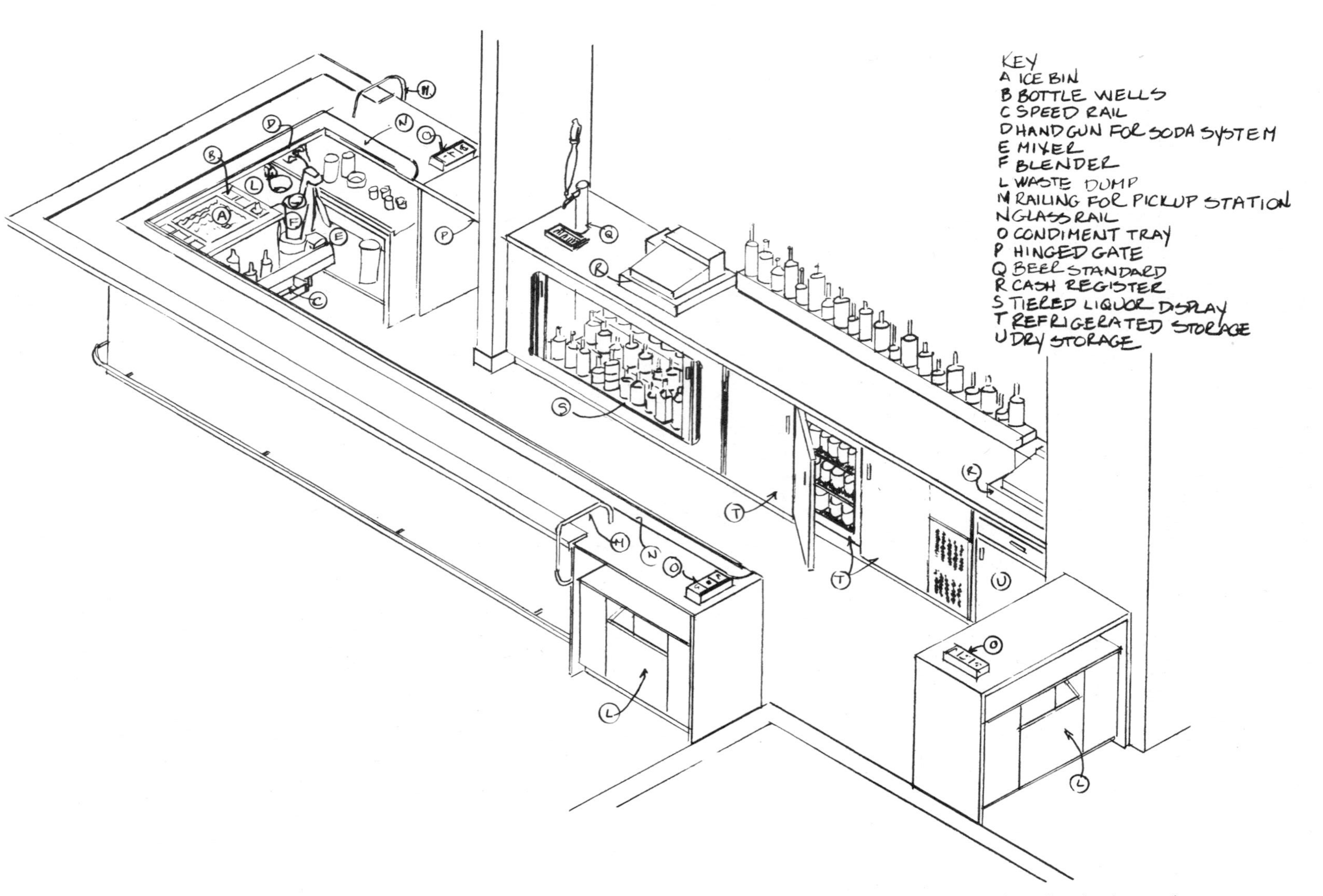

Figure 10-16a–c. Underbar work areas. Custom work stations are shown, with many valuable options for the bartender. This type of drawing should be requested in larger installations before purchase of equipment.

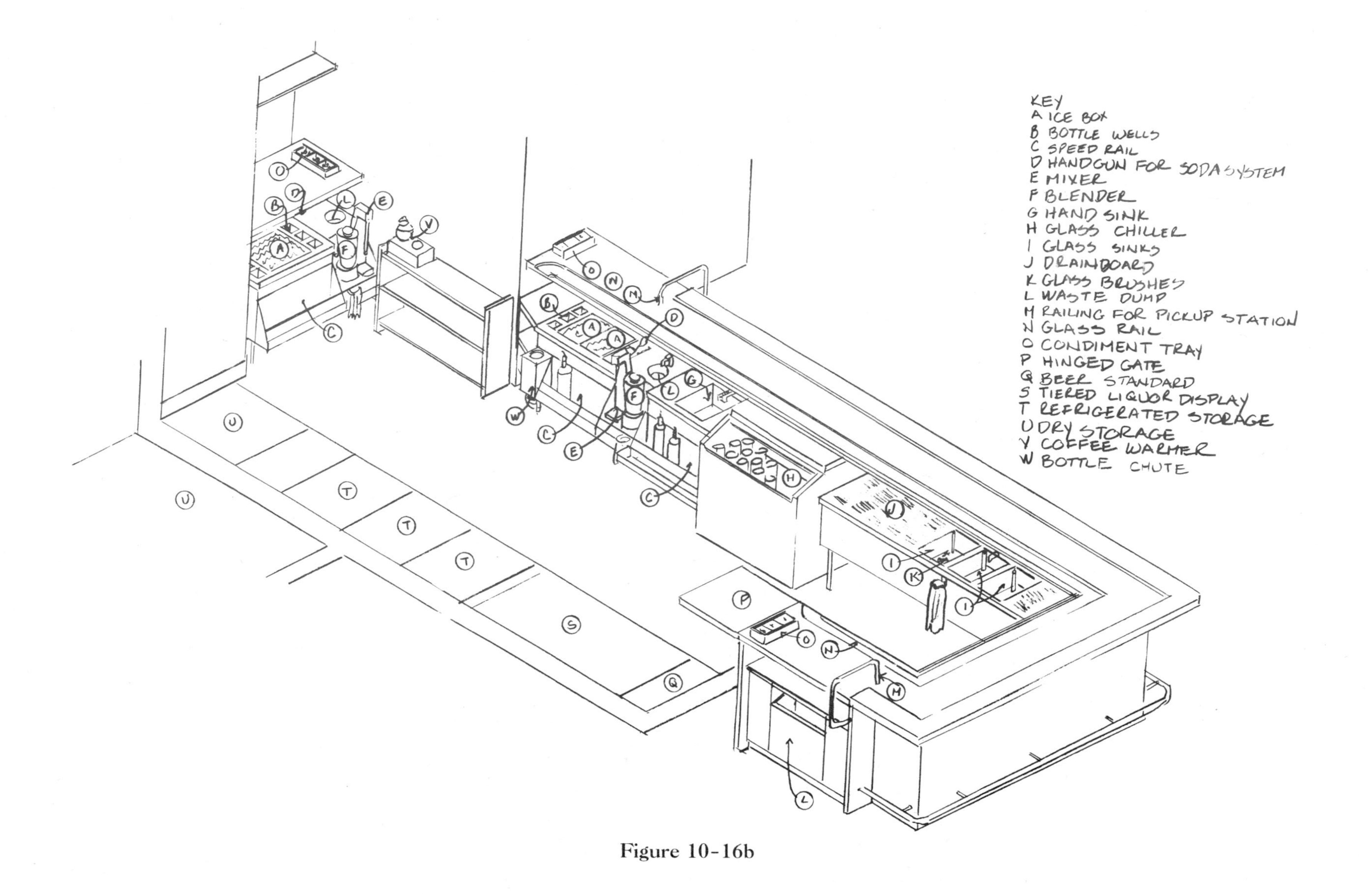
KEY
A ICE BOX
B BOTTLE WELLS
C SPEED RAIL
D HANDGUN FOR SODA SYSTEM
E MIXER
F BLENDER
G HAND SINK
H GLASS CHILLER
I GLASS SINKS
J DRAINBOARD
K GLASS BRUSHES
L WASTE DUMP
M RAILING FOR PICKUP STATION
N GLASS RAIL
O CONDIMENT TRAY
P HINGED GATE
Q BEER STANDARD
S TIERED LIQUOR DISPLAY
T REFRIGERATED STORAGE
U DRY STORAGE
V COFFEE WARMER
W BOTTLE CHUTE

Figure 10-16b

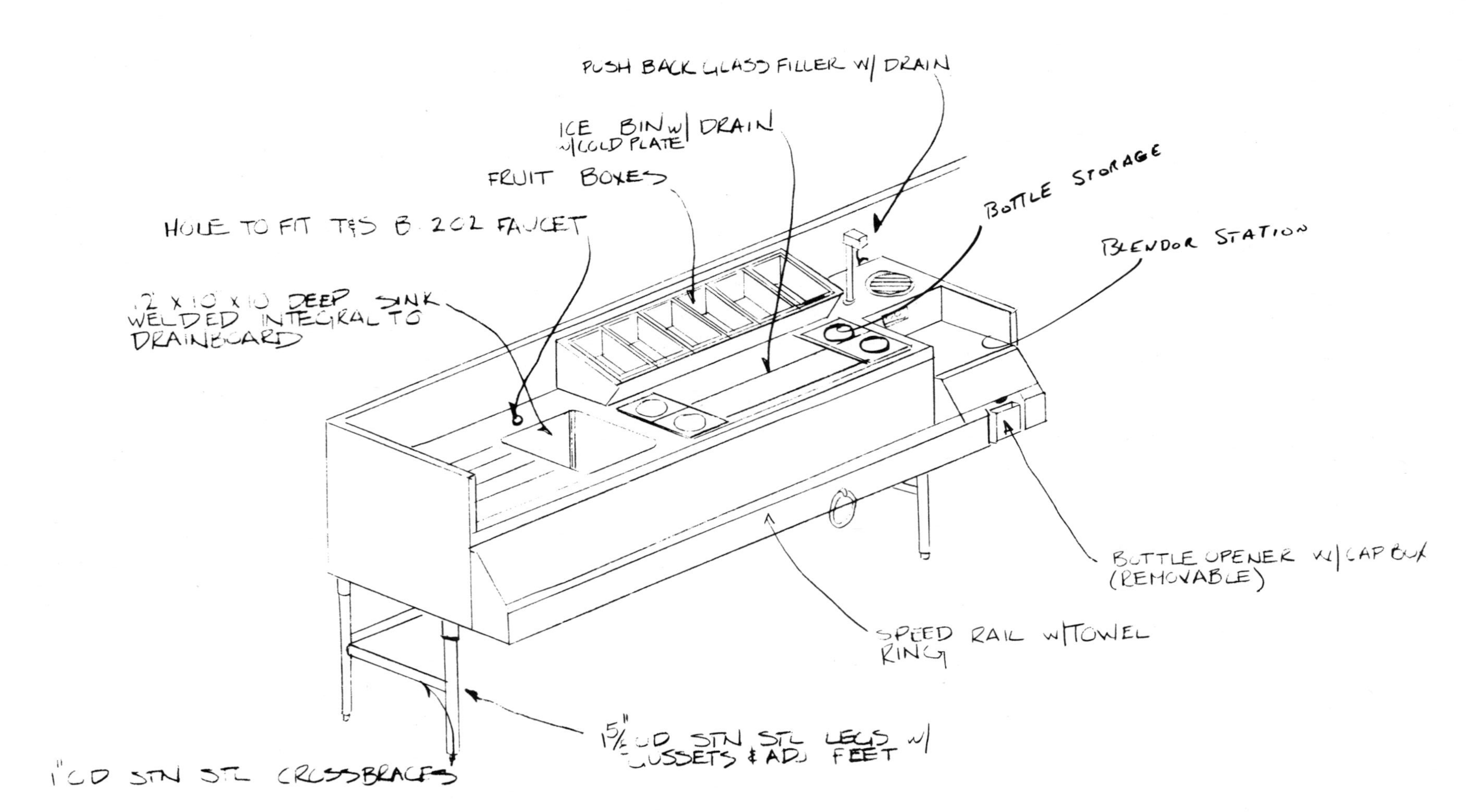
PUSH BACK GLASS FILLER W/ DRAIN
ICE BIN W/ DRAIN
W/COLD PLATE
FRUIT BOXES
BOTTLE STORAGE
HOLE TO FIT T&S B-202 FAUCET
BLENDOR STATION
12 X 10 X 10 DEEP SINK
WELDED INTEGRAL TO
DRAINBOARD
BOTTLE OPENER W/ CAP BOX
(REMOVABLE)
SPEED RAIL W/TOWEL
RING
1 5/8" OD STN STL LEGS W/
GUSSETS & ADJ FEET
1" OD STN STL CROSSBRACES

Figure 10-16c

Figure 10-17. Bar stools–wood and metal styles, showing the features of good construction. Bar stools are normally 30″ high to the seat for use with 42″ bars. Stool frames are constructed of wood or metal, with or without backs and are available fixed seat or swivel. Some swivel stools have an automatic return that will line up the backs in the correct position eliminating constant hand alignment.

If you purchase upholstered bar stools be sure the material is lined with heavy-duty backing. Check the availability of the stools replacement parts such as glides, foot rings, and swivel assemblies from your supplier. Normal bar stool locations are figured 24″ per person, i.e. 24′ = 12 stools.

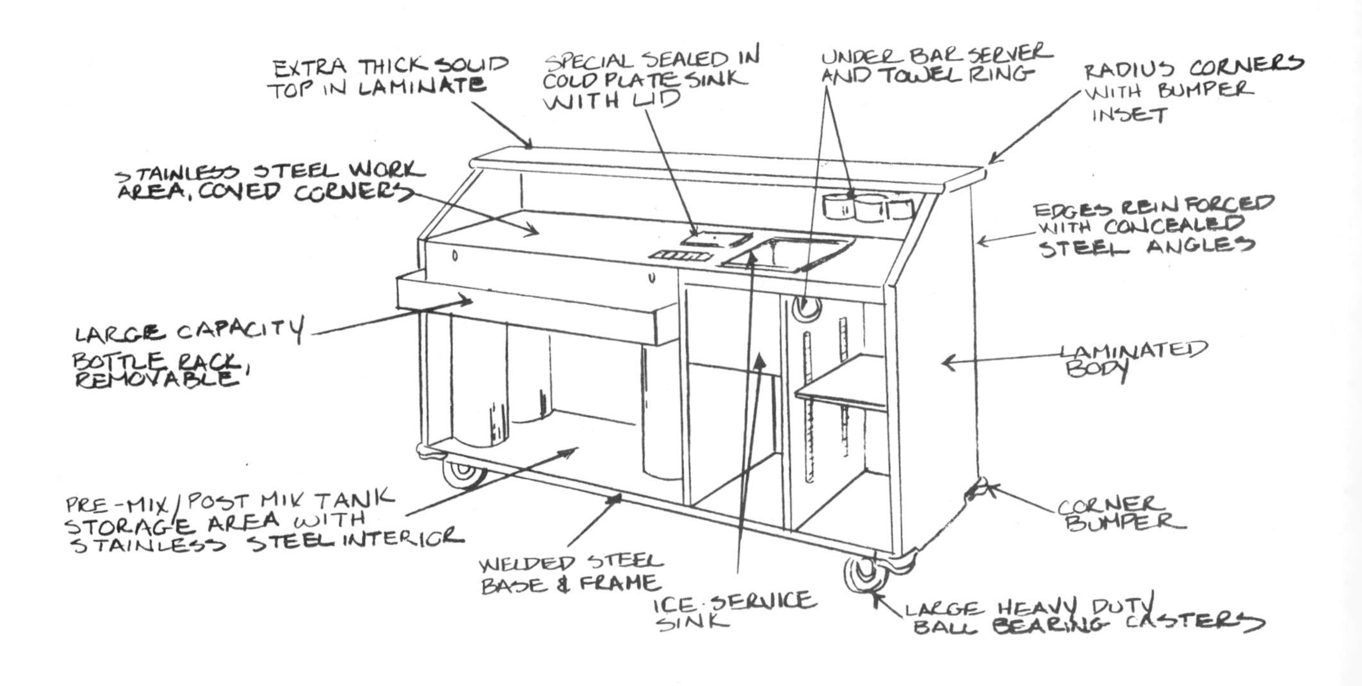

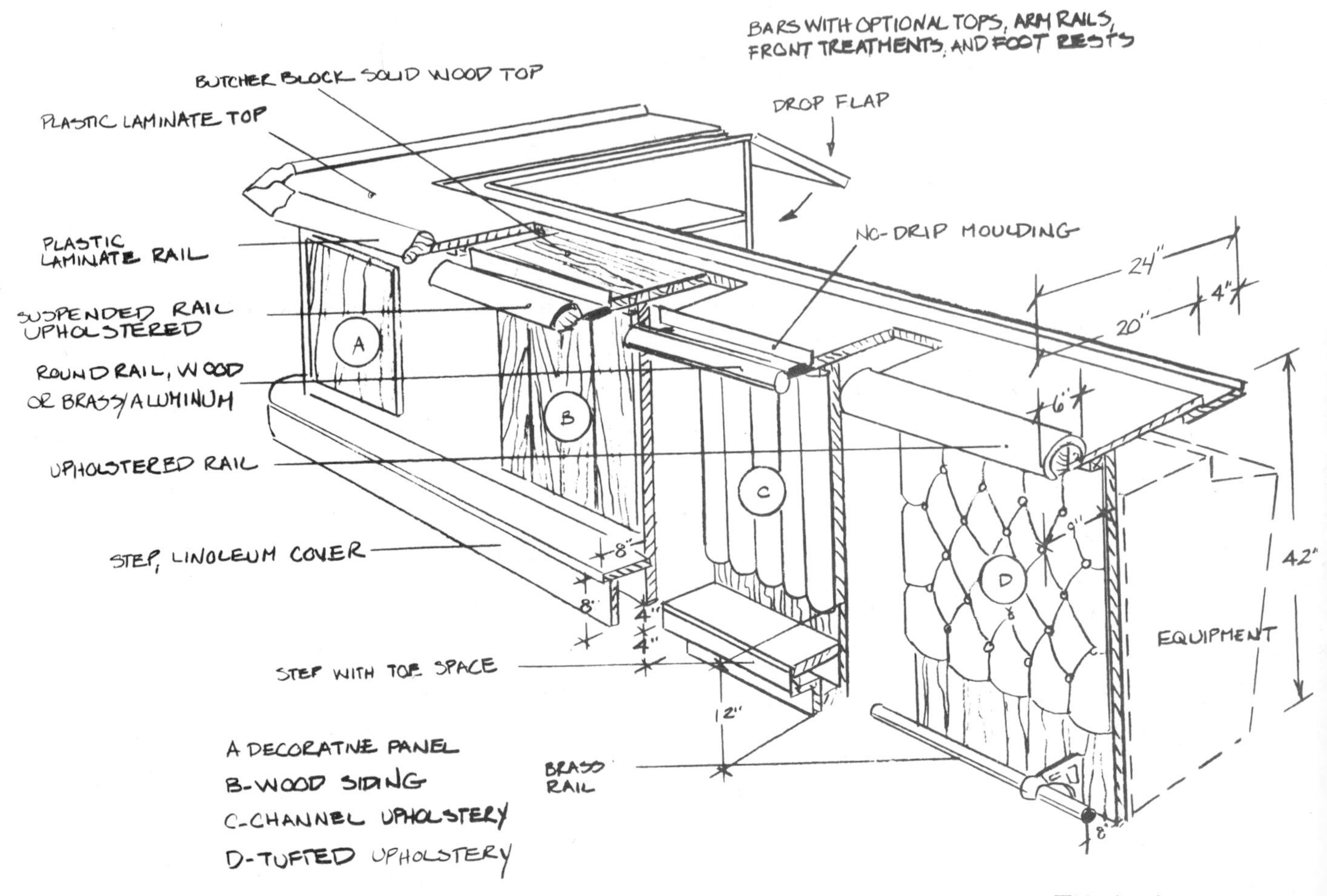

Figure 10-18. Mobile bar. The bar shown is available in many sizes, with a variety of equipment. This drawing can serve to stimulate the user's ideas.

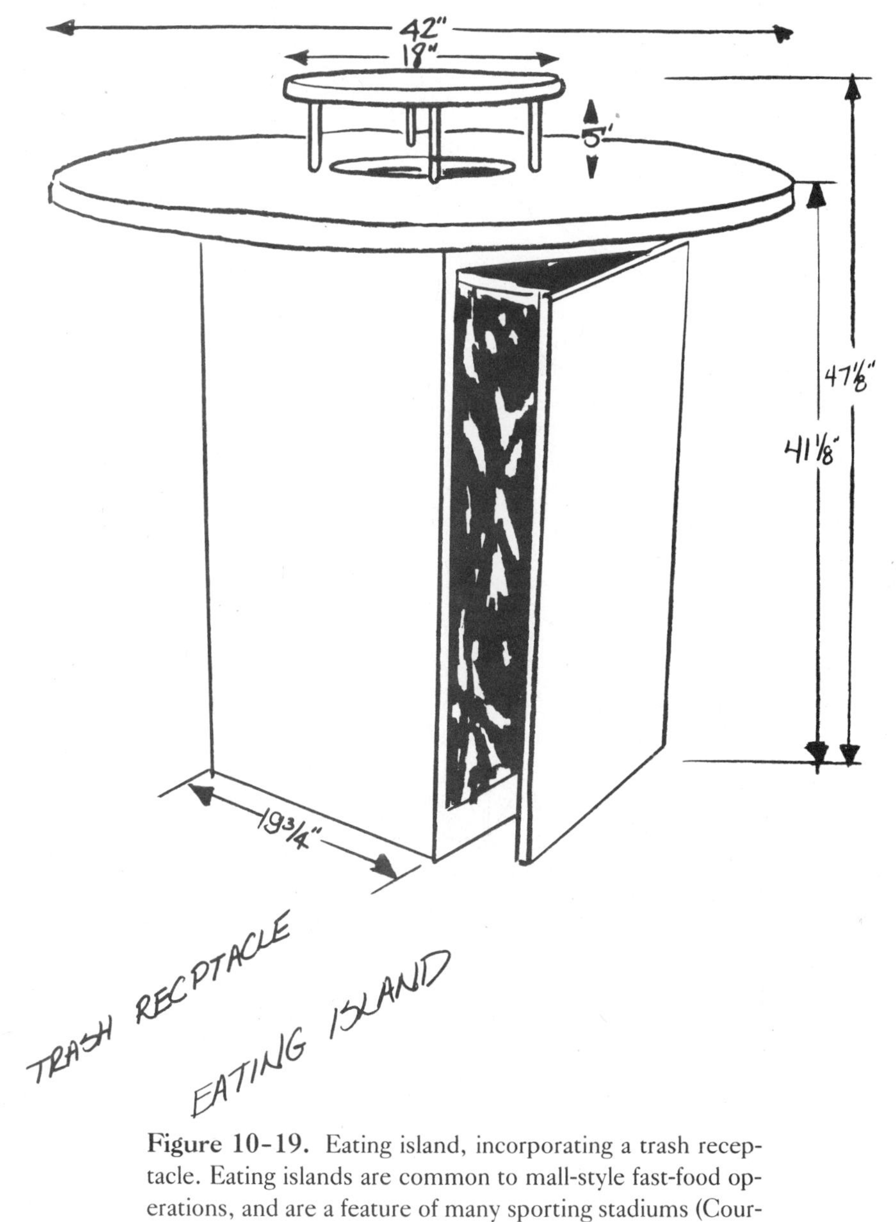

Figure 10-19. Eating island, incorporating a trash receptacle. Eating islands are common to mall-style fast-food operations, and are a feature of many sporting stadiums (Courtesy Eatin' Islands)

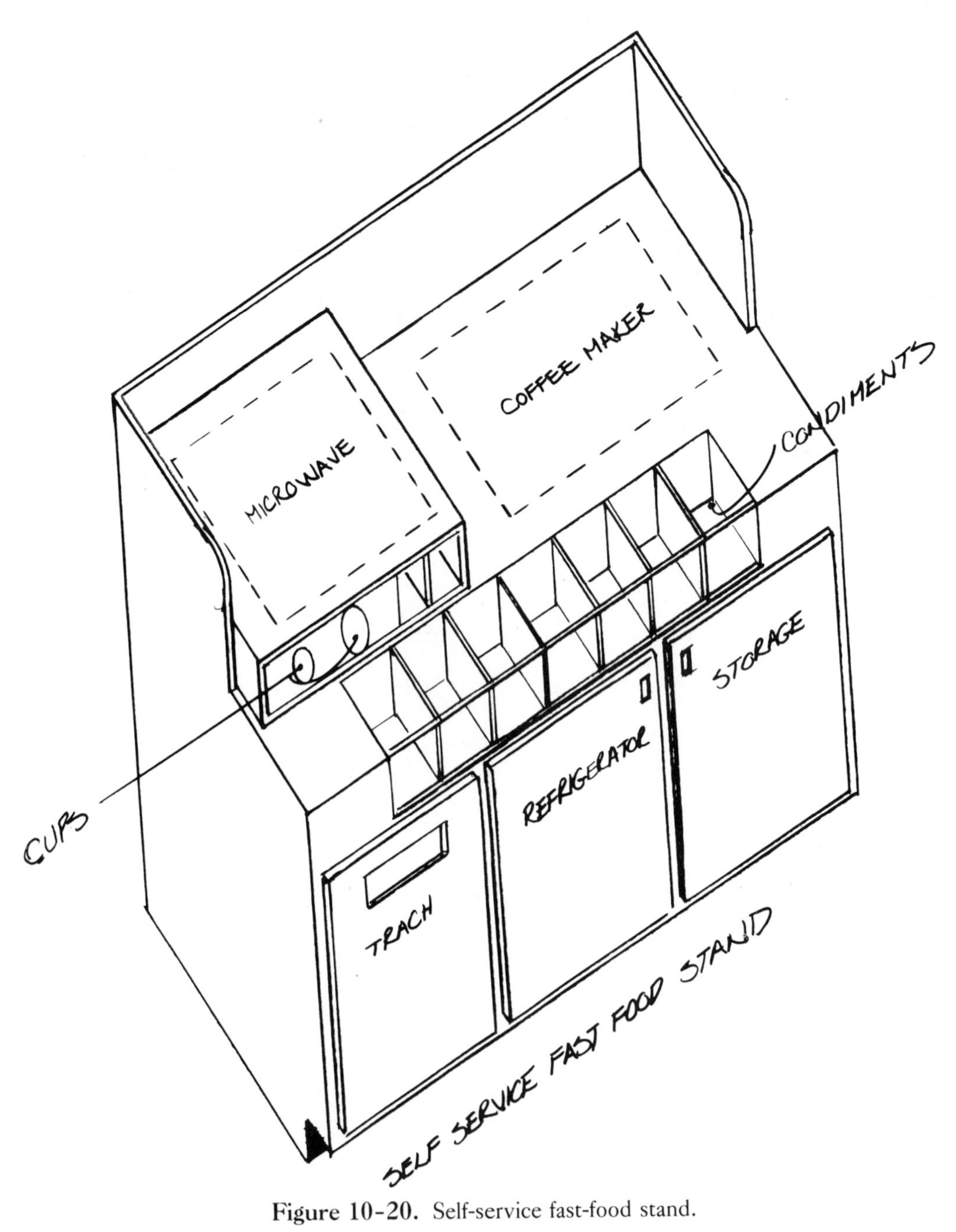

Figure 10-20. Self-service fast-food stand.

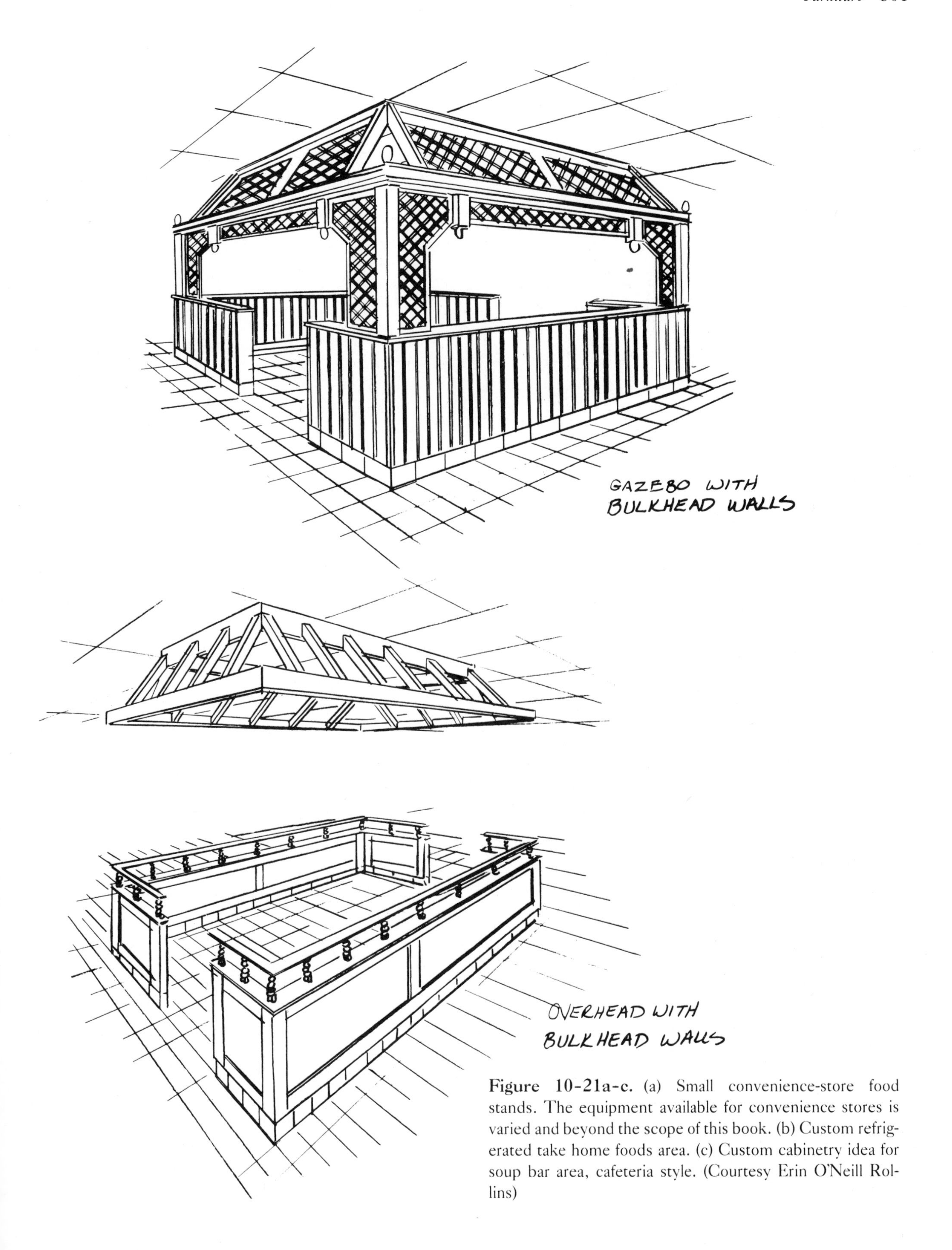

Figure 10-21a-c. (a) Small convenience-store food stands. The equipment available for convenience stores is varied and beyond the scope of this book. (b) Custom refrigerated take home foods area. (c) Custom cabinetry idea for soup bar area, cafeteria style. (Courtesy Erin O'Neill Rollins)

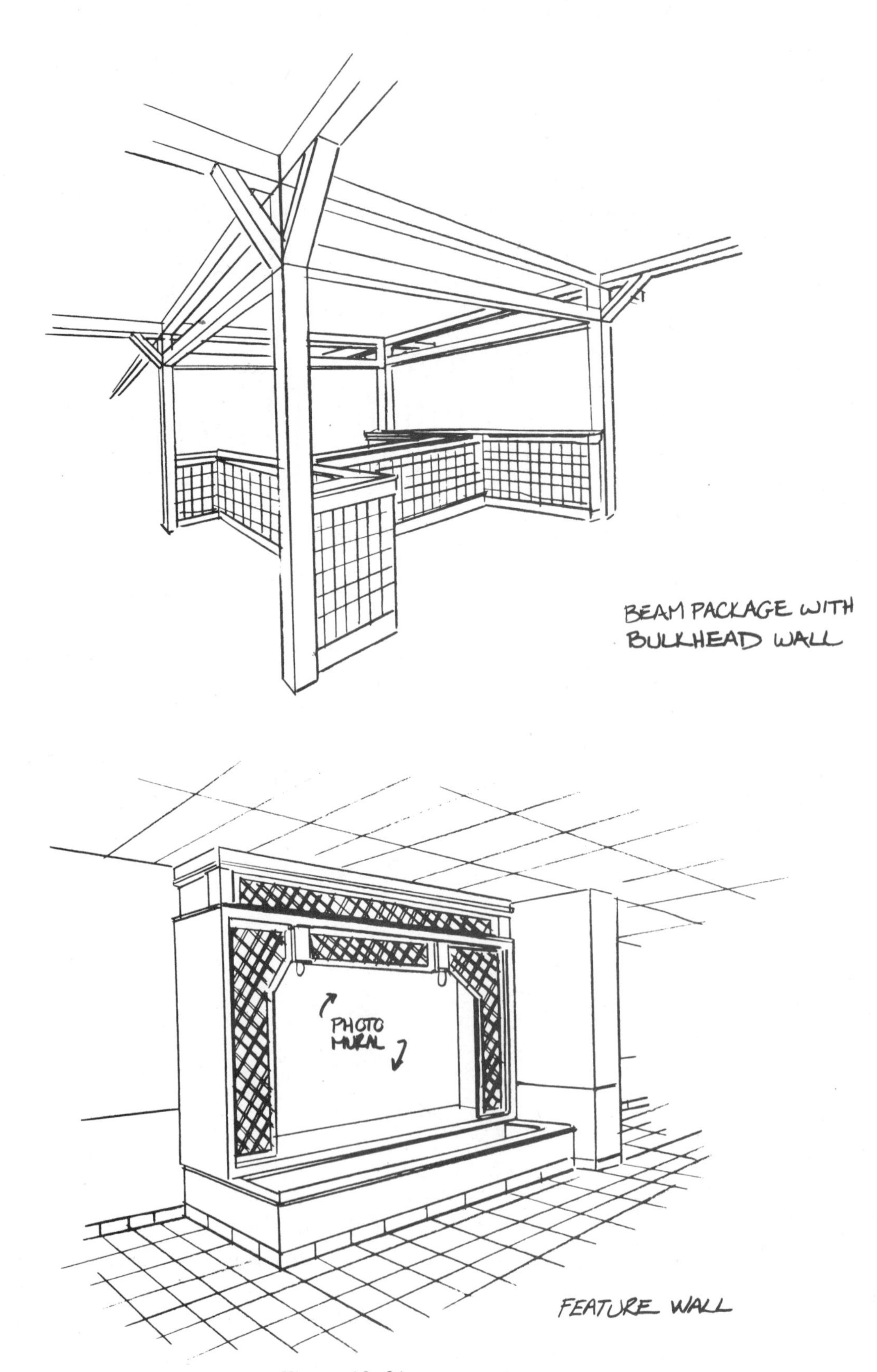

Figure 10-21a (*continued*)

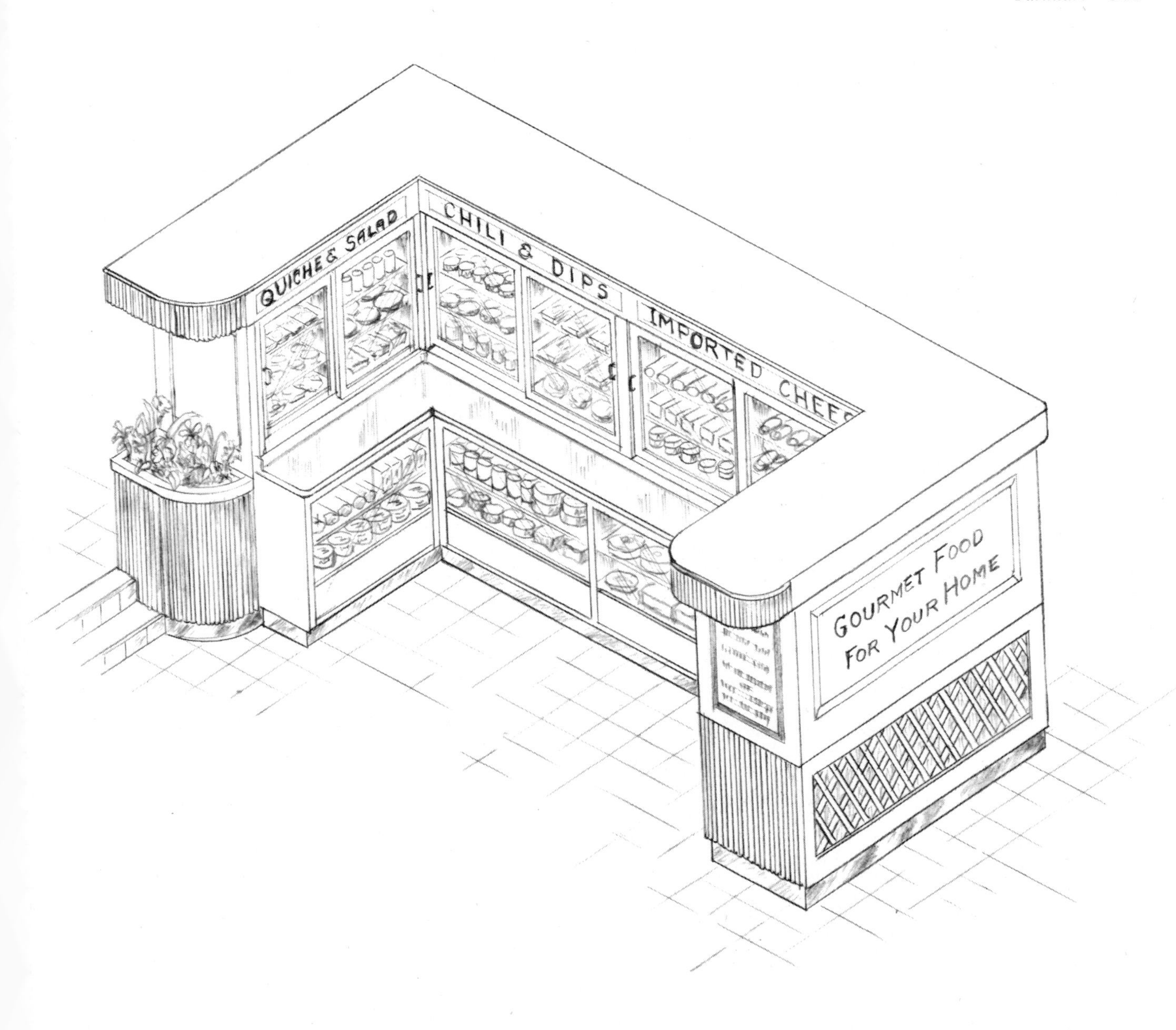

Figure 10-21b

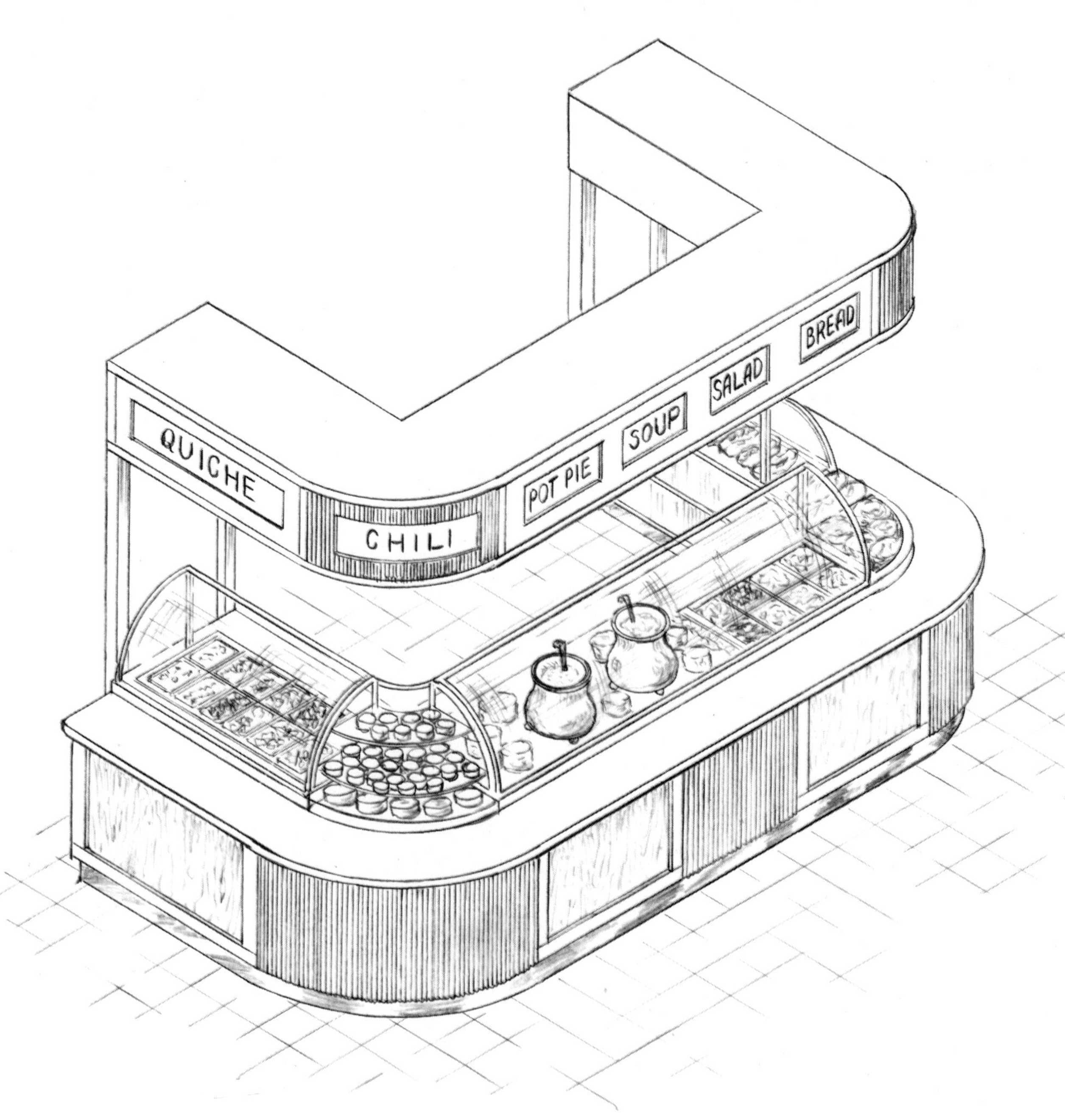

Figure 10-21c

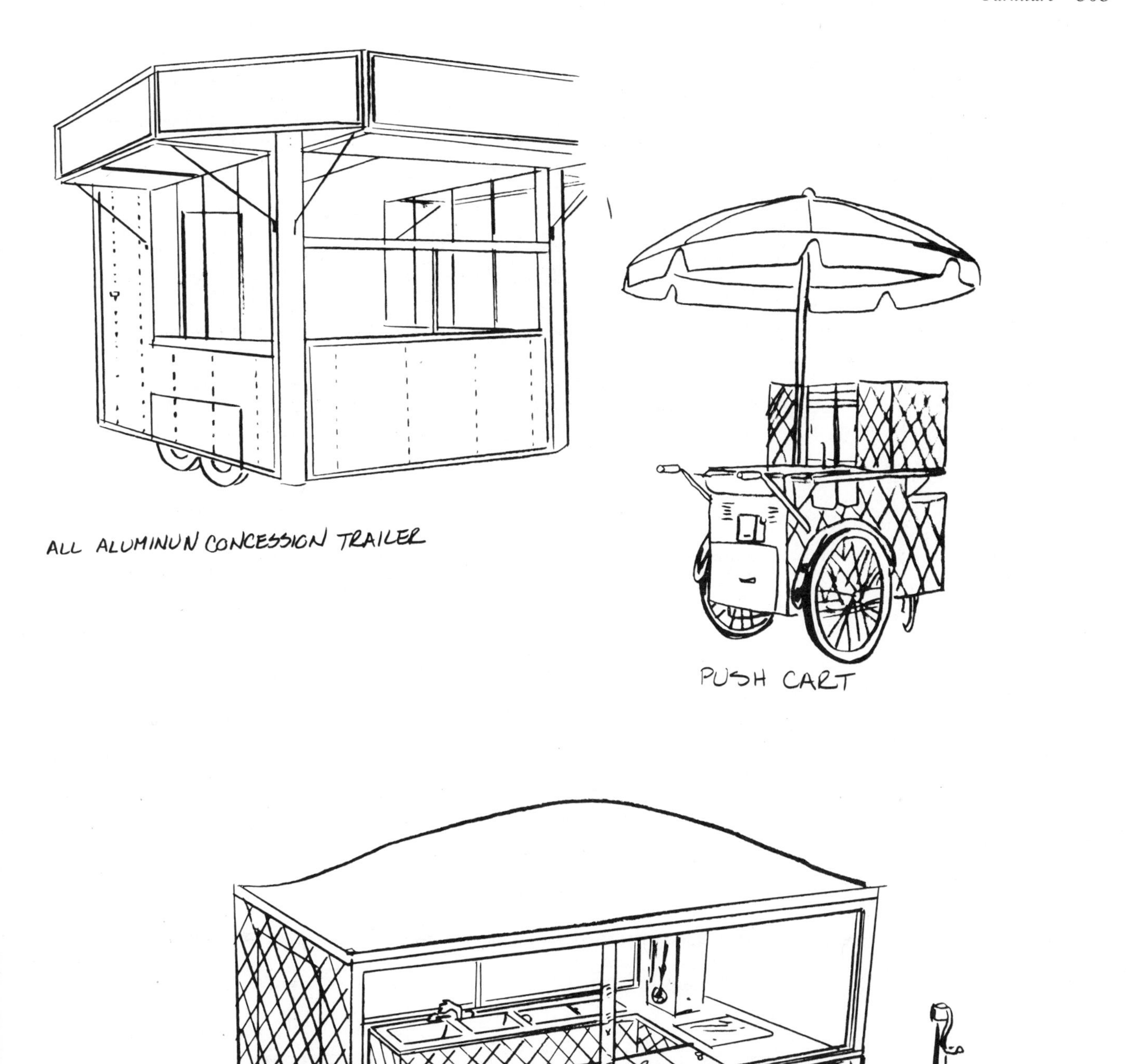

Figure 10-22. Fun foods. Drawings show examples of fun food equipment. Wagons and trailers use both standard and custom equipment; the options are many. Users should be sure any purchase is approved by the health department.

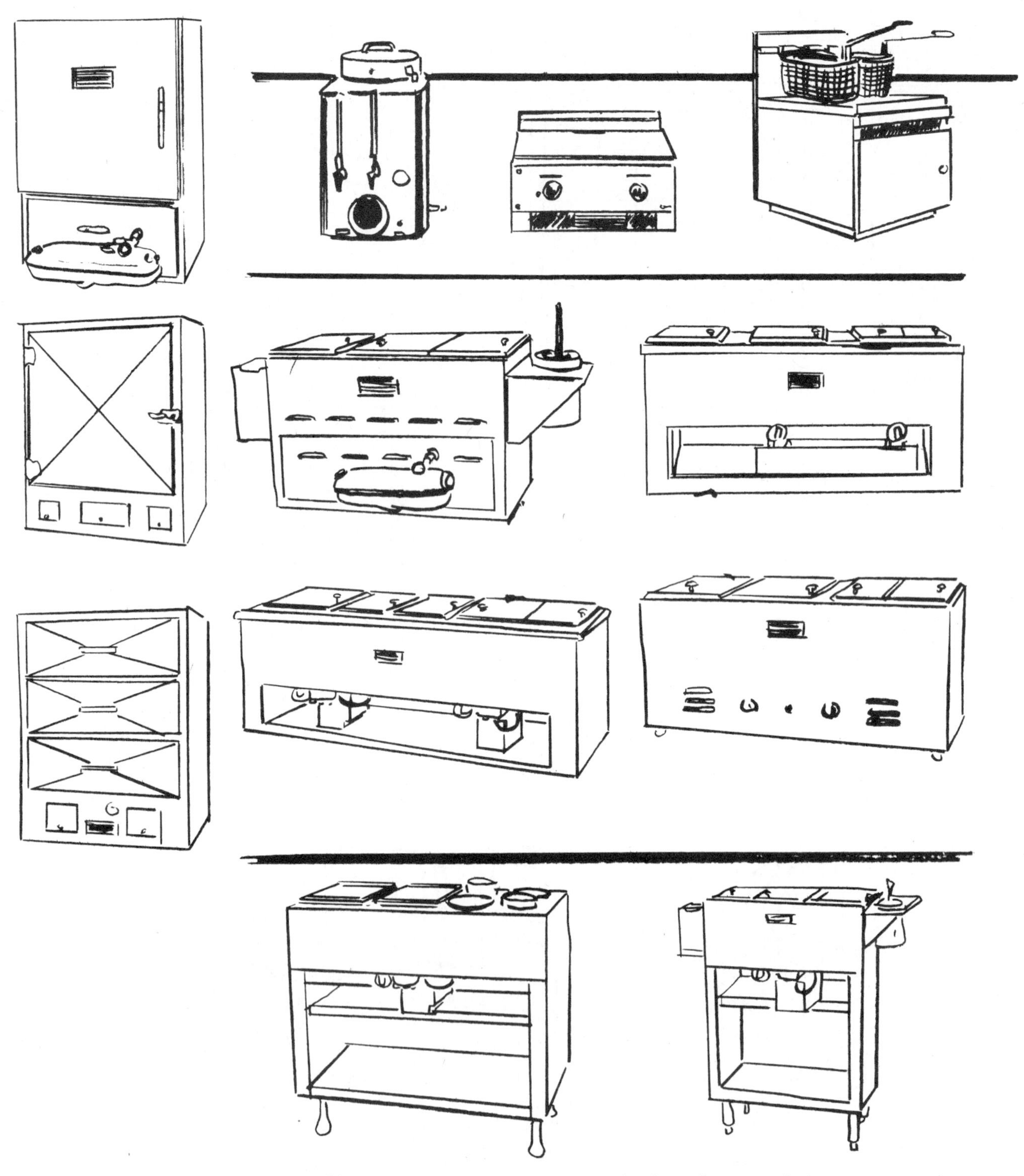

Figure 10-23. Component equipment for fast-food vending operations.

TYPICAL DRINK SYSTEM

1 water filter
2 remote carbonator
3 cooling system
4 CO_2 regulator
5 syrup tank
6 flow-control valves
7 dispensing head
8 CO_2 gas line
9 syrup line
10 carbonated water line

a

TYPICAL DRINK SYSTEM

1 water filter
2 remote carbonator
3 cooling system
4 CO_2 regulator
5 syrup line
7 dispensing head
8 CO_2 gas line
9 syrup line
10 carbonated water line

b

1 soda circuit cooling unit
2 water filter
3 CO_2 cylinder
4 primary CO_2 regulator
5 changeover valve
6 secondary CO_2 regulator
7 manifold
8 syrup tank
9 carbonator
10 trunk/branch line
11 recirculating pump
12 dispenser

c

Figure 10-24a-d. Typical soda and beer systems. (Figure 10–24a–c reprinted, by permission, from Roland E. Greaves, *The Commercial Food Equipment, Repair, and Maintenance Manual*, © 1987 by Van Nostrand Reinhold; Figure 24–d courtesy The Cornelius Company)

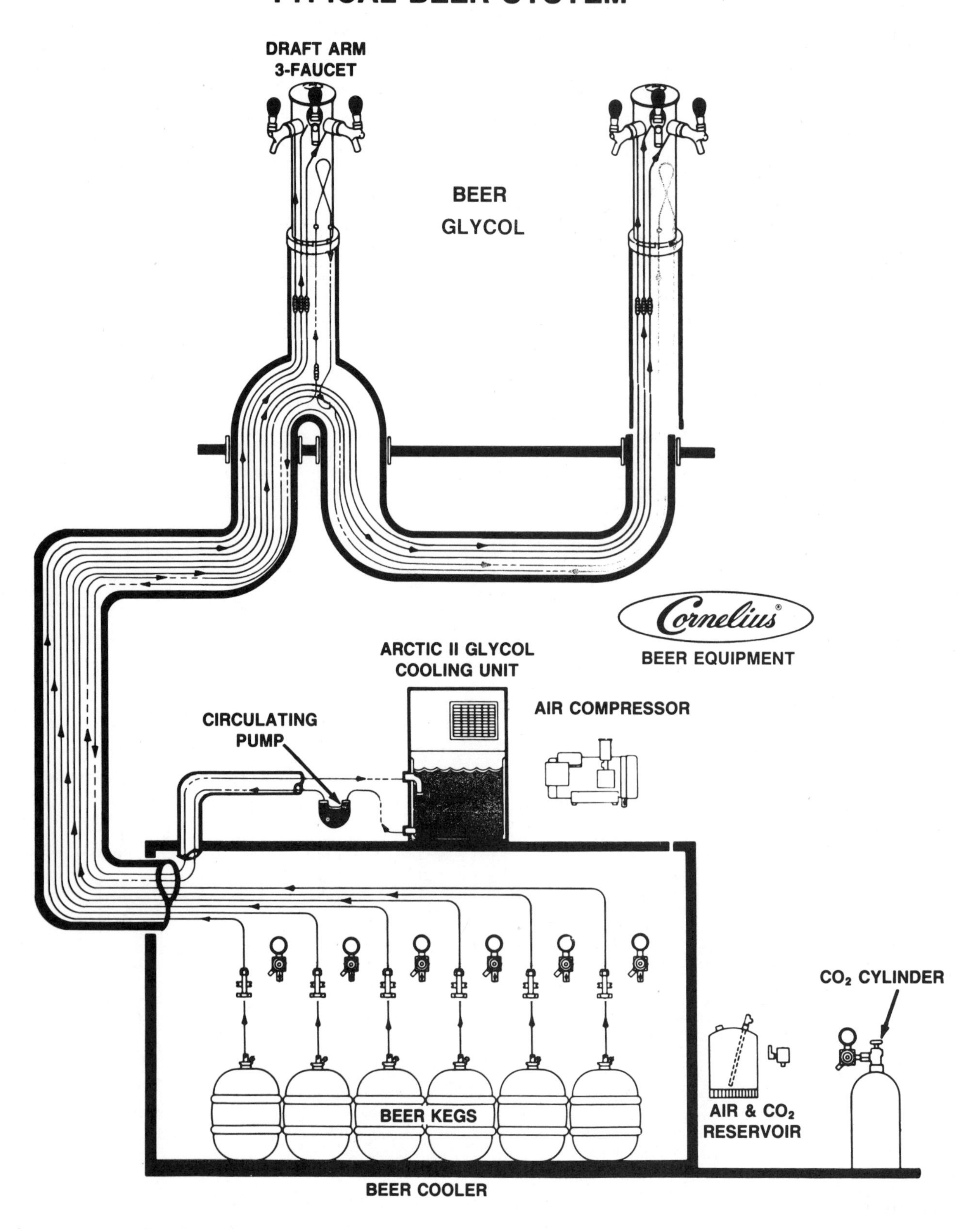
TYPICAL BEER SYSTEM
DRAFT ARM
3-FAUCET
BEER
GLYCOL
Cornelius
BEER EQUIPMENT
ARCTIC II GLYCOL
COOLING UNIT
AIR COMPRESSOR
CIRCULATING
PUMP
CO2 CYLINDER
AIR & CO2
RESERVOIR
BEER KEGS
BEER COOLER

Figure 10-24d

Glossary of Terms

Actual cubic feet per minute (ACFM): cubic feet per minute of air at actual air conditions (as opposed to standard air conditions).

Air, ambient: generally speaking, the air surrounding an object.

Air, dry: air without contained water vapor; air only.

Air, make-up: air required to replace or "make up" air that is exhausted in a building.

Air, outdoor: air taken from outdoors and, therefore, not previously circulated through the system.

Air, outside: external air, atmosphere exterior to refrigerated or conditioned space; ambient (surrounding) air.

Air, recirculated: return air passed through the conditioner before being again supplied to the conditioned space.

Air, reheating of: in an air conditioning system, the final step in treatment, in the event the temperature is too low.

Air, return: air returned from conditioned or refrigerated space.

Air, saturated: moist air in which the partial pressure of the water vapor is equal to the vapor pressure of water at the existing temperature. This occurs when dry air and saturated water vapor coexist at the same dry-bulb temperature.

Air, short circuit: make-up air injected into a canopy, hood, or ventilator to reduce or eliminate the need for tempering.

Air, standard: dry air at a pressure of 760 mm (29.92 in.) Hg at 21°C (69.8°F) temperature and with a specific volume of 0.833 m^3/kg (13.33 ft^3/lb).

Air, tempered: heated or conditioned air.

Air, changes: a method of expressing the amount of air leakage into or out of a building or room in terms of the number of building volumes or room volumes exchanged.

Air curtain: an air stream intended to form a barrier against the mixing of air in one space with that of another.

Air diffuser: a circular, square, or rectangular air distribution outlet, generally located in the ceiling and comprised of defecting members discharging supply air in various directions and planes, and arranged to promote mixing of primary air with secondary room air.

Anemometer: an instrument for measuring the velocity of a fluid.

This glossary is an expansion of Seco Engineering's ventilation glossary. Items marked with an asterisk have been added by the authors from a variety of food equipment industry publications.

Aspiration: production of movement in a fluid by suction created by fluid velocity.

Barometer: instrument for measuring atmospheric pressure.

**Breaker strips:* where it is desired that the temperature of one metal item not transfer to another (i.e., refrigerator doors, cold pans, countertops, etc.), a "breaker strip" consisting of a plastic, usually black, is placed between the two adjoining metal surfaces to break the metal-to-metal contact.

British thermal units (Btu): the heat required to raise the temperature of a pound of water 1°F.

Bulb: temperature-sensing device located in the fluid for which control or indication is provided. The bulb may be liquid-filled, gas-filled, or gas-and-liquid-filled. Changes in temperature produce pressure changes within the bulb that are transmitted to the controller.

Celsius (formerly centigrade): a thermometric scale in which the freezing point of water is denoted 0°C and its boiling point 100°C at normal atmosphere pressure (14.696 psi).

**Channel slides:* term applied to the slides or guides used on the sides of drawers, which are generally constructed with roller bearings, similar to a file drawer. It is always desirable that they be "pitched" in such a manner that the drawers are self-closing; this avoids accidents when drawers are left open by careless employees.

**Chase, pipe:* term commonly used with "cabinet base" and "enclosed fixture," denoting that the shelves or all interior fittings of the cabinet are stopped short of the end enclosure for a distance of approximately 4 inches to permit pipes—water, waste, gas, or electric conduits—to be run up through a fixture from the bottom.

Condensate: the liquid formed by condensation of a vapor. In steam heating, water condensed from steam; in air conditioning, water extracted from air, as by condensation on the cooling coil of a refrigeration machine.

**Conduits:* tubular metal made of varying materials and in various sizes. A conduit is installed in advance, and electrical wires are pulled through it from one point to another, usually from the junction box to the switch and from the switch to the light or other receptacle. It also is used in larger diameters when refrigeration compressors are placed in remote locations. It should be installed, in advance, between the compressor and the location of the fixture to be cooled so that two copper lines, which must be run from the compressor to the fixture, can be installed later.

Control: device for regulation of a system or component in normal operation, manual or automatic. If automatic, the implication is that it is responsive to changes of pressure, temperature, or other property whose magnitude is to be regulated.

Controlled device: one that receives the converted signal from the transmission system and translates it into the appropriate action in the environmental system. For example, a valve opens or closes to regulate fluid flow in the system.

Controller: a instrument that receives the signal from sensing device and translates that signal into the appropriate corrective measure. The correction is then sent to the system-controlled devices through the transmission system.

Convection: transfer of heat by movement of a fluid.

Convection, forced: convection resulting from forced circulation of a fluid, as by a fan, jet, or pump.

Convection, natural: circulation of gas or liquid (usually air or water) due to differences in density resulting from temperature changes.

Cooling, evaporative: process involving the adiabatic exchange of heat between air and a water spray or wetted surface. The water assumes the wet-bulb temperature of the air, which remains constant during its traverse of the exchanger.

**Cove:* term applying to vertical or horizontal corners of fixtures that have turned-up or turned-down edges, simply meaning that these corners are to be rounded and not square so that they can be easily cleaned. The terminology used is usually, "Vertical and horizontal corners are to be covered on a radius of (?) inches" (specify desired radius). The National Sanitation Foundation has established minimum radii for various applications; refer to its "Standards" for this information.

**Curtain wall:* wall that extends down from the ceiling to a designated height, usually just above head level. Such walls are used frequently over the top of serving areas to screen from view as much of the kitchen operation as possible. They also are often used to enclose a canopy or hood, that is, to enclose the metal structure after it has been hung and connected to the vent ducts. This eliminates a very inaccessible area where dirt and debris normally would collect.

Cycle: a complete course of operation of working fluid back to a starting point, measured in thermodynamic terms (functions). Also a general term for any repeated process on any system.

**Disconnect switches or safety cutouts:* Most modern electrical appliances are equipped with operating switches by the manufacturer. It is desirable, however, that a separate disconnect switch or safety cutout be installed on the wall near the fixture by the electrical contractor. Thus, if emergency repair or service of some type is required on the fixture, this switch can be opened and the appliance repaired without endangering the workman.

Draft: a current of air, when referring to the pressure difference that causes air or gases to flow through a flue, chimney, heater, or space; or to a localized effect caused by one or more factors of high air velocity, low ambient temperature, or direction of air flow, whereby more heat is withdrawn from a person's skin than is normally dissipated.

Dry-bulb, room: the dry-bulb (dewpoint, etc.) temperatures of the conditioned room or space.

Duct: a passageway made of sheet metal of other suitable material, not necessarily leaktight, used for conveying air or other gas at low pressures.

**Duo-strainer-type drain:* the type of drain fitting used in the bottom of sinks, also known as a "basket-type" drain. It has a lift-out, perforated, half-spherical basket that serves as both a strainer and a stopper.

Effluent: the outflow of matter produced or given off in the cooking process.

Entropy: ratio of the heat added to a substance to the absolute temperature at which it is added.

Entropy, specific: term sometimes applied to entropy per unit weight.

**Expansion valve:* If element used to admit liquefied gas to the evaporator in the refrigeration cycle (See "Refrigeration," below.) it is not housed within a refrigerated area, a metal box, preferably of stainless steel, of sufficient size to house the valve plus an adequate amount of loose insulating material, is to be provided. The box is to have a removable cover for access when service is necessary. It should be located as close as possible to the point where the refrigerant line enters the fixture.

Face velocity: velocity obtained by dividing the air quantity by the component face area.

Fahrenheit: a thermometric scale in which 32°F denotes freezing and 212°F the boiling point of water under normal pressure at sea level (14.696 psi).

Fan, centrifugal: a fan rotor or wheel located within a scroll-type housing and including driving mechanism supports for either belt drive or direct connection.

Fan performance curve: term that refers to the constant speed performance curve. It is a graphical presentation of static or total pressure and power input over a range of air volume flow rate at a stated inlet density and fan speed. It may include static and mechanical efficiency curves. The range of air volume flow rate covered generally extends from shut-off (zero air volume flow rate) to free delivery (zero fan static pressure). The pressure curves are generally preferred to as the pressure–volume curves.

**Field joints:* joints made "in the field." Some fixtures are too large to be handled through existing corridors or openings in the buildings in which they are to be installed; therefore, it is necessary that some joints be made on site. It is of great importance, however, that the specifications clearly indicate that field joints, particularly on the top of working surfaces, be constructed in such a manner that they can be drawn up tightly.

Flash load: the sudden release of heat energy and contaminants that occurs when food products instantaneously begin the cooking process.

Flow, turbulent: flow fluid in which the fluid moves transversely as well as in the direction of the tube or pipe axis, as opposed to streamline or viscous flow.

Fluid: gas, vapor, or liquid.

Fluid, heat transfer: any gas, vapor, or liquid used to absorb heat from a source at a high-temperature substance.

Free area: total minimum area of the openings in the air outlet or inlet through which air can pass.

Fumes: solid particles commonly formed by the condensation of vapors from normally solid material such as molten metals. Fumes also may be formed by sublimation, distillation, calcination, or chemical reaction wherever such processes create airborne particles predominately below one micron in size. Such solid particles sometimes serve as condensation nuclei for water vapor to form smog.

Gas: usually a highly superheated vapor that, within acceptable limits of accuracy, satisfies the perfect gas laws.

Gravity, specific: density compared to density of standard material; reference usually to water or to air.

Grille: a louvered or perforated covering for an air passage opening which can be located on a wall, ceiling, or floor.

**Gauge:* as applied to metal, an indication of the thickness in decimal parts of an inch. The term confuses many people because of its inverse nature: the lower the number, the thicker the metal. Examples: 14 gauge is a common thickness for tabletops or sinks; 16 gauge is sometimes used for the same purpose, but it is slightly thinner than 14 gauge; 18 gauge is the next lightest gauge in common use, and is usually specified for the bodies of cabinets or enclosed-type bases; 20 gauge is usually specified for narrow shelves; 22 gauge and 24 gauge are lighter gauges, used for wall coverings, etc. (See Tables in "Stainless Steel" section of Chapter 4.) Be sure all gauges of metals required are clearly specified and adhered to by the equipment supplier.

**Gusset:* as used in kitchen equipment, term that applies to a tubular formed socket, approximately 3½ inches high, that is welded or bolted to the underside of a fixture and into which the tubular leg is slipped and then secured in a rigid manner with Allen set screws. These gussets formerly were made "L-shaped"; that is, they only enclosed two sides of the tubular upright. Such gussets, however, are outmoded, and present-day sanitation requirements call for a completely tubular or fully enclosed gusset.

Heat: the form of energy that is transferred by virtue of a temperature difference.

Heat, latent: change of enthalpy during a change of state, usually expressed in Btu/lb. With pure substances, latent heat is absorbed or rejected at constant pressure.

Heat, radiant: the transmission of heat through space by wave motion.

Heat, sensible: heat associated with a change in temperature; specific heat exchange of temperature, in contrast to a heat interchange in which a change of state (latent heat) occurs.

Heat, specific: the ratio of the quantity of heat required to raise the temperature of a given mass of any substance one degree to the quantity required to raise the temperature of an equal mass of a standard substance (usually water at 59°F) one degree.

Heat capacity: the amount of heat necessary to raise the temperature of a given mass one degree. Numerically, the mass multiplied by the specific heat.

Heat conductor: a material capable of readily conducting heat. The opposite of an insulator or insulation.

Heat exchanger: a device specifically designed to transfer heat between two physically separated fluids.

Heat transmission: any time-rate of heat flow; usually refers to conduction, convection, and radiation combined.

Humidity: water vapor within a given space.

Humidity, relative: the ratio of the mol fraction of water vapor present in the air to the mol fraction of water vapor present in saturated air at the same temperature and barometric pressure; approximately it equals the ratio of the partial pressure or density of the water vapor in the air to the saturation pressure or density, respectively, of water vapor at the same temperature.

Impingement: striking, hitting, or dashing upon or against something.

Inch of water (in. W.G.): a unit of pressure equal to the pressure exerted by a column of liquid water 1 inch high at a temperature of 4°C or 39.2°F.

Induction: the capture of part of the ambient air by the jet action of the primary airstream discharging from a controlled device.

Infiltration: air flowing inward as through a wall, crack, etc.

"K" factor: (as used in refrigeration): an engineering term meaning the amount of heat in Btu's that 1 inch

of a given material will transmit per hour per square foot of surface per degree of temperature difference between the inside and outside surfaces. For example, sheet cork board at a density of 5.4 pounds per cubic foot has a "K" factor of 0.25.

**Lever or quick-opening drain:* a type of drain for the sink, or other items of equipment that hold water, that has a fixed perforated strainer on the top and a quick-opening, rotary-type valve on the underside. This valve is actuated by a rod terminating a lever or by a "cross" or "tack" handle that extends out from the position of the drain to be an accessible location near the front of the fixture.

Load: the amount of heat per unit time imposed on a refrigerant system, or the required rate of heat removal.

Outlet velocity: the average velocity of air emerging from an opening, fan, or outlet, measured in the plane of the opening.

Overhang: the distance from the edge of a cooking appliance to the edge of a hood or canopy.

Pressure: the normal force exerted by a homogeneous liquid or gas, per unit of area, on the wall of its container.

Pressure, absolute: pressure referred to that of a perfect vacuum. It is the sum of a gauge pressure and atmospheric pressure.

Pressure, atmospheric: the pressure indicated by a barometer. Standard atmosphere is the pressure equivalent to 14.696 psi or 29.921 in. of mercury at 32°F.

Pressure, high: pressure above atmospheric.

Pressure, hydrostatic: the normal force per unit area that would be exerted by a moving fluid on an infinitesimally small body immersed in it if the body were carried along with the fluid.

Pressure, low: pressure below atmospheric.

Pressure, partial: portion of total gas pressure of a mixture attributable to one component.

Pressure, saturation: for a pure substance at any given temperature, the pressure at which vapor and liquid, or vapor and solid, can coexist in stable equilibrium.

Pressure, static (SP): the normal force per unit area that would be exerted by a moving fluid on a small body immersed in it if the body were carried along with the fluid. Practically, it is the normal force per unit area at a small hole in the wall of the duct through which the fluid flows (piezometer) or on the surface of a stationary tube at a point where the disturbances created by inserting the tube cancel. It is supposed that the thermodynamic properties of a moving fluid depend on static pressure in exactly the same manner that those of the same fluid at rest depend upon its uniform hydrostatic pressure.

Pressure, total (TP): in the theory of the flow of fluids, the sum of the static pressure and the velocity pressure at the point of measurement. Also called dynamic pressure.

Pressure, velocity (VP): in moving fluid, the pressure capable of causing an equivalent velocity, if applied to move the same fluid through an orifice such that all pressure energy expended is converted into kinetic energy.

Pressure, drop: pressure loss in fluid pressure, as from one end of a duct to the other, due to friction, dynamic losses, and changes in velocity pressure.

Primary air: the initial airstream discharged by an air outlet (the air being supplied by a fan or supply duct) prior to any entrainment of the ambient air.

Psychrometer: an instrument for ascertaining the humidity or hygrometric state of the atmosphere.

Psychrometric chart: a graphical representation of the thermodynamic properties of moist air.

**Quick disconnect* (gas, water, steam, air, etc.): devices used for disconnecting appliances for cleaning purposes. It is desirable, from a sanitation point of view, occasionally to move a piece of equipment tightly connected to gas, water, steam, air, or other utilities. There are now available "quick disconnect" spring-type fittings on the end of approved flexible hoses, so that these appliances may be disconnected without tools and moved for cleaning.

**Radial groove:* a design feature used principally for sinks, particularly those made of stainless steel. It is good manufacturing practice to have a series of four radial grooves stamped at the bottom of the sink, in the exact center, radiating out from a drain connection, so that the sink will drain completely when so desired.

**Refrigeration:* a cooling system consisting of four main elements: an evaporator, a compressor, a condenser, and a thermostatic expansion valve. (Additional valves and controls are used in sophisticated systems, but these four are the most important.) The *evaporator* is a coil within the refrigerator that contains liquefied gas at a low temperature; as this liquid picks up and absorbs heat from the surrounding area or products, it vaporizes, returning to a gaseous state. The gas accumulates in the evaporator, building up pressure, until the *compressor* starts up and pumps the gas out of the evaporator while compressing it to a high pressure. This high-pressure gas then flows into the *condenser*, which, by means of air or water cooling, removes the heat and changes it to a liquid. The condenser then stores this liquid until the evaporator, by means of a control actuated by temperature, "calls" for more liquid. The control is a *thermostatic expansion valve*, which has a bulb or sensor, located at a strategic position, that opens the valve when the temperature in the fixture rises, admitting more liquefied gas to the evaporator. Then the cycle repeats itself.

Room dry bulb (dewpoint, etc.): the dry-bulb (dewpoint, etc.) temperature of the conditioned room or space.

Secondary air: the air surrounding an outlet that is captured or entrained by the initial outlet discharge airstream (furnished by a supply duct or fan).

**Solenoid valve:* a valve that electrically controls the flow of a liquid or vice versa; that is, the starting of a motor energizes the solenoid and permits a liquid to flow, or, conversely, the opening of a water valve starts the flow of water, which activates the solenoid and starts a motor.

Standard air density (d): a quantity that has been set at 0.075 lb/ft^3. This corresponds approximately to dry air at 70°F and 29.92 in. Hg. In metric units, the standard air density is 1.2041 kg/m^3 at 20°C and at 101.325kPa.

Standard cubic feet per minute (SCFM): cubic feet per minute of air at standard air conditions (pressure of 29.92 in. Hg at 70°F.)

Standard rating: a rating based on a test performed at standard rating conditions [as determined by industry standards].

**Steam cooking:* The latent heat of a pound of steam at atmospheric pressure is 970 Btu. When steam condenses, as it does when it comes in contact with a cooler surface, the steam gives off its latent heat, which is transferred in cooking to the product being heated or cooked. (Heat always moves from a warm area or mass to a cooler one.) This heat transfer makes cooking with steam, in kettles, steamers, and so forth, highly desirable, particularly where large quantities of food are concerned. Although there is very little difference in the heat content in Btu's of a pound of steam at atmospheric pressure and at 15 pounds pressure (approximately 13 Btu) the temperature of the higher-pressure steam is greater (250°F rather than 212°F), providing a greater differential between the temperature of the steam and that of the product, which results in faster condensation and quicker product heating.

Temperature, dewpoint: the temperature at which the condensation of water vapor in a space begins for a given condition of humidity and pressure as the temperature of the vapor is reduced. The temperature corresponding to saturation (100 percent relative humidity) for a given absolute humidity at constant pressure.

Temperature, dry-bulb: the temperature of a gas or mixture of gases indicated by an accurate thermometer after correction for radiation.

Temperature, effective: an arbitrary index that combines into a single value the effect of temperature, humidity, and air movement on the sensation of warmth or cold felt by the human body. The numerical value is that of the temperature of still, saturated air that would induce an identical situation.

Temperature, wet-bulb: Thermodynamic wet-bulb temperature is the temperature at which liquid or solid water, by evaporating into air, can bring the air to saturation adiabatically at the same temperature. Wet-bulb temperature (without qualification) is the temperature indicated by a wet-bulb psychrometer constructed and used according to specifications.

**Traps:* a device shaped like an inverted, horizontal P, so that water will be accumulated on the bottom of the curved section, thus preventing sewer gases from coming up through the drain. There are several kinds of traps used in food-serving equipment.

**Vacuum breaker:* device that prevents contamination of fresh-water lines by waste water; required by National Sanitation Foundation ordinances. Such contamination could occur with disposals, dishwashers, or any piece of equipment where the overflow line is below the water inlet. To prevent this, a vacuum breaker is mounted in the water line, well below the overflow line, thus eliminating possible back syphoning of waste water into the fresh-water lines.

Velocity: a vector quantity that denotes, at once, the time rate and the direction of a linear motion.

Velocity, outlet: the average discharge velocity of primary air being discharged from the outlet, normally measured in the plane of the opening.

Ventilation: the process of supplying or removing air, by natural or mechanical means, to or from any space. Such air may or may not have been conditioned.

Wet-bulb depression: difference between dry-bulb and wet-bulb temperatures.

ASSOCIATION ADDRESSES

AMERICAN DIETETIC ASSOCIATION 430 N Michigan Av Chicago IL ------------312/280-5000

AMERICAN GAS ASSOCIATION 1515 Wilson Blvd Arlington VA 22209------------703/841-8400

AMERICAN HOTEL & MOTEL ASSOCIATION 888 Seventh Av New York NY 10019 ------------ --------------------------------212/265-4506

AMERICAN RESTAURANT CHINA COUNCIL INC 126 Blue Wing Dr #4 Sonoma CA 95476---- --------------------------------707/938-5909

AMERICAN SCHOOL FOOD SERVICE ASSOCIATION 4101 lliff Av Denver CO 80222-------- --------------------------------303/757-8555

COMMERCIAL FOOD EQUIPMENT SERVICE AGENCIES 60 Revere Drive Suite 500 Northbrook IL 60062 ----------------312/480-9080

FOOD EQUIPMENT MANUFACTURERS ASSOCIATION 111 East Wacker Dr Chicago IL 60611 --------------------------------312/644-6610

FOODSERVICE CONSULTANTS SOCIETY INTERNATIONAL 12345 30th Ave N E Suite H Seattle WA 98125 ------------------206/367-3274

FOODSERVICE EQUIPMENT DISTRIBUTORS ASSOCIATION 332 S Michigan Av Chicago IL 60604---------------------------312/427-9605

INTERNATIONAL FOODSERVICE DISTRIBUTORS ASSOCIATION Division of: North American Wholesale Grocers' Association
201 Park Washington Court Falls Church VA 22046---------------------------703/532-9400

INTERNATIONAL FOODSERVICE MANUFACTURERS ASSOCIATION 321 North Clark St. Chicago IL 60610--------------312/644-8989

MARKETING AGENTS FOR THE FOOD SERVICE INDUSTRY 111 East Wacker Dr Suite 600 Chicago IL 60601--------------312/644-6610

NATIONAL ASSOCIATION OF FOOD EQUIPMENT MANUFACTURERS 111 E Wacker Dr Chicago IL 60601 ----------------------312/644-6610

NATIONAL AUTOMATIC MERCHANDISING ASSOCIATION 7 S Dearborn St Chicago IL 60603 --------------------------------312/346-0370

NATIONAL RESTAURANT ASSOCIATION 150 N Michigan Ave Suite 2000 Chicago IL 60601- --------------------------------312/853-2525

NATIONAL SANITATION FOUNDATION 3475 Plymouth Rd PO Box 1468
Ann Arbor MI 48106 ----------313/769-8010

PERMANENT WARE INSTITUTE 334 S Main St Dayton OH 45402-------------312/263-2070

Index of Figures

Chapter 4
Preparation Equipment

Chapter 5
Cooking Equipment

Chapter 6
Commercial Cooking Ventilation

Chapter 7
Serving and Holding

Chapter 8
Warewashing and Sanitation Systems

Chapter 9
Utilities and Hardware

Chapter 10
Furniture

Subject Index